Nature's Economy is a wide-ranging investigation of ecology's past. It traces the origins of the concept, discusses the thinkers who have shaped it, and shows how it in turn has shaped the modern perception of our place in nature. Our view of the living world is a product of culture, and the development of ecology since the eighteenth century has closely reflected society's changing concerns. Donald Worster focuses on these dramatic shifts in outlook and on the individuals whose work has expressed and influenced society's point of view. The book includes portraits of Linnaeus, Gilbert White, Darwin, Thoreau, and such key twentieth-century ecologists as Rachel Carson, Frederic Clements, Aldo Leopold, James Lovelock, and Eugene Odum. The book concludes with a new Part Six, which looks at the directions ecology has taken most recently.

NATURE'S ECONOMY

STUDIES IN ENVIRONMENT AND HISTORY

Editors

Donald Worster   *University of Kansas*
Alfred Crosby   *University of Texas at Austin*

Advisory Board

Reid Bryson   *Institute for Environmental Studies, University of Wisconsin*
Raymond Dasmann   *College Eight, University of California, Santa Cruz*
E. Le Roy Ladurie   *Collège de France*
William McNeill   *Department of History, University of Chicago*
Carolyn Merchant   *College of Natural Resources, University of California, Berkeley*
Thad Tate   *Institute of Early American History and Culture, College of William and Mary*

Other Books in the Series

Kenneth F. Kiple   *The Caribbean Slave: A Biological History*
Arthur F. McEvoy   *The Fisherman's Problem: Ecology and Law in the California Fisheries, 1850–1980*
Robert Harms   *Games Against Nature: An Eco-Cultural History of the Nunu of Equatorial Africa*
Warren Dean   *Brazil and the Struggle for Rubber: A Study in Environmental History*
Samuel P. Hays   *Beauty, Health, and Permanence: Environmental Politics in the United States, 1955–1985*
Donald Worster   *The Ends of the Earth: Perspectives on Modern Environmental History*
Michael Williams   *Americans and Their Forests: A Historical Geography*
Timothy Silver   *A New Face on the Countryside: Indians, Colonists, and Slaves in South Atlantic Forests, 1500–1800*
Richard H. Grove   *Green Imperialism: Science, Colonial Expansion, and the Emergence of Global Environmentalism, 1660–1860*
Elinor G. K. Melville   *A Plague of Sheep: Environmental Consequences of the Conquest of Mexico*

Donald Worster

University of Kansas

NATURE'S ECONOMY

A History of Ecological Ideas

Second Edition

CAMBRIDGE
UNIVERSITY PRESS

CAMBRIDGE UNIVERSITY PRESS
Cambridge, New York, Melbourne, Madrid, Cape Town,
Singapore, São Paulo, Delhi, Tokyo, Mexico City

Cambridge University Press
32 Avenue of the Americas, New York, NY 10013-2473, USA

www.cambridge.org
Information on this title: www.cambridge.org/9780521468343

First published 1977 by Sierra Club Books
Published by Cambridge University Press 1985
Second edition published 1994
15th printing 2011

A catalog record for this publication is available from the British Library.

ISBN 978-0-521-46834-3 Paperback

To Bev

Contents

Preface

IN RECENT YEARS it has become impossible to talk about man's relation to nature without referring to "ecology." This peculiar field of study has been suddenly called on, in a manner unusual even in our science-impressed age, to play a central intellectual role. Such leading scientists in this area as Rachel Carson, Barry Commoner, Eugene Odum, Paul Ehrlich, and others, have become our new delphic voices, writing best sellers, appearing in the media, shaping government policies, even serving as moral touchstones. So influential has their branch of science become that our time might well be called the "Age of Ecology."

To explain why this call has come in the last half of the twentieth century is not my purpose here, though it is, of course, a matter that should receive serious attention, especially from historians familiar with the dynamics of popular social movements. The aim of this book, however, is not so much to account for the appeal of ecology to our own time as to understand what this field of study has been prior to its recent ascent to oracular power.

There are compelling reasons for seeking such a historical perspective. Like a stranger who has just blown into town, ecology seems a presence without a past. Before committing ourselves too firmly to its tutelage, however, we might do some digging into its previous life—not in the expectation of uncovering grisly deeds, but simply that we may know our teacher better. In that inquiry we might learn more about the kind of science ecology has been, and also more about those aspects of nature which this science has revealed to us. We might see, too, what ecology has *not* told us about nature. How the living world has been perceived through the aid of the science of ecology is thus the main theme of this study in the history of ideas. This perception, I have maintained, has had significant consequences for man's relation to the natural order and will continue to have ever more.

This account will make clear that ecology, even before it had a name, had a history. The term "ecology" did not appear until 1866, and it took almost another hundred years for it to enter the vernacular. But the *idea* of ecology is much older than the name. Its modern history begins in the eighteenth century, when it emerged as a more comprehensive way of looking at the earth's fabric of life: a point of view that sought to describe all of the living organisms of the earth as an interacting whole, often referred to as the "economy of nature." This phrase gave birth to a rich set of ideas out of which emerged the science of today, and I have made it, therefore, the organizing thread of this book.

On close examination, however, the common point of view suggested by an "economy of nature" fragments into *many* views, sometimes leading in thoroughly incompatible directions. "Nature's economy" has been defined by different people for different reasons in different ways, all of which we must sort through as we come to rely more and more on ecology for guidance in our own time. The study of the earth's household of life has opened not one but many doors. My intention here is to ask: Who opened them? Why? What has been seen? Seeking answers to these questions may better prepare us to choose which doors we will want to open in the future.

The reader should not expect in these chapters a traditional treatise on the history of science. By intention as well as training, I approach my theme as an intellectual historian, curious about the origins of our present ecological ideas, their contents, and their practical effects in the past. From this vantage point I have come to believe that the ideas of science are open to much the same kind of treatment as other ideas, such as theological or political thought. Like all of man's intellectual life, scientific ideas grow out of specific cultural conditions and are validated by personal as well as social needs. They are, in short, more closely interwoven with the general fabric of thought than is commonly supposed. Thus, unlike many traditional historians of science who are convinced of the onward and upward march of "truth" and like to keep this chronicle neatly separate from the rest of cultural history, I have blurred the edges a great deal. In fact, my subject is not simply the growth of a narrowly defined field of science but of the larger penumbra of "ecological thought," which is meant to include the literary, economic, and philosophical connections ecology has made.

Unconventional as it may at first seem, this approach works especially well with the history of ecology. While it may be more nearly true to say of mathematics or thermodynamics that it takes its course apart from prevailing intellectual fashions or economic forces, it would be a false assumption to make about the study of ecology. Perhaps because it is a "social" science, dealing with the interrelationships of living creatures, it has never been far removed from the messy, shifting, hurly-burly world of human values. The historian of this interaction must therefore be alert to much more than who contributed what bits of knowledge to the present state of the science; he must range widely over the intellectual landscape of the past. All the same, I have wanted to mark the main achievements of this science, too, and thereby to give historians of science something of value for their own pursuits.

If I am right about the extent to which scientific ideas are rooted in their cultural subsoil, then it must follow that different cultures can produce different scientific traditions. While this is not perhaps an argument one would want to make universal, it does seem to hold true for ecology. There has been a distinctive Anglo-American tradition in this area—never wholly separate from Continental ideas, never wholly a consensus, but withal a single dialogue carried on in a common tongue. In the emergence of ecological ideas the weight of authority lay originally on the British side of this transatlantic tradition, with the Americans content to learn their lessons from such naturalists as William Paley and Charles Darwin. But later that pattern came to be altered, even reversed in some cases; consequently, in the last parts of this book the heavier emphasis is on American leadership.

To be as manageable as possible, this book is organized episodically. I have tried to select and focus on major formative moments in the life history of modern ecology. Each of the book's six parts is about one of those moments, a time when ecological thought underwent a significant transformation. Key figures appear in each part, not as heroic revolutionaries or even as thinkers of great influence in every case, but simply as individuals who participated in those changes and best reveal their meaning to us.

In Part One these representative figures include the parson-naturalist Gilbert White, the great Swedish "man of flowers" Carolus Linnaeus, and a number of others whose ideas helped launch a new science in the eighteenth century. Part Two is devoted to Henry David Thoreau as the chief exponent of what I have called "Romantic ecology"— a cluster of ideas still active today, though perhaps more in the popular understanding of ecology than in the models of most scientists. The mid-nineteenth-century work of Charles Darwin necessarily occupies the pivotal place in the maturing of ecology as a science, and in Part Three I have dwelt at length on both the working out of Darwin's own logic and the philosophical implications of his ecological theories. Part Four brings the narrative into the twentieth century and to America's late frontier regions, where the science of ecology came to have immense public importance. Among the subjects analyzed here are the work of Frederic Clements—his so-called "climax" theory of vegetation—and the major test of that new model in the Dust Bowl disaster of the 1930s. In Part Five, I examine the idea of the ecosystem and its relation to energy physics, along with a rival approach that owed much to the philosopy of Alfred North Whitehead and other modern "organicists"; I also discuss the background of Aldo Leopold's ecology-based land ethic. Finally, in Part Six, the story moves into the post–World War Two period, when ecology became a political movement as well as a sophisticated but extraordinarily diverse science, rocked by many theoretical disputes.

These six episodes might be characterized, according to the jargon of scientific history, as "paradigm shifts," in the course of which an older model of nature is overthrown and a new one takes its place. But it must not be concluded that such shifts wiped out all traces of the old; on the contrary, the present corpus of ecological thought is a conglomeration of all its pasts, like a man who has lived many lives and forgotten none of them. By retracing this intellectual biography we can arrive at a much fuller understanding of how ecology has become what it is, how each of these formative episodes has added to the content—as well as to the ambiguities and contradictions—we find in this science today. Here, then, is what I hope will be the chief contribution of this work: a deeper awareness of the roots of our contemporary perception of nature.

In a work of such broad scope there are bound to be omissions that many readers will regret, both from the perspective of science and that of intellectual history. Though keenly aware of the many blank spots, I can only set forth my long-considered rationale for the shape of this study, its geographical and chronological selectivity, its inclusions and exclusions with respect to specific people discussed, and trust that readers will come to see the appropriateness of my design.

To help readers through the sometimes arcane language of the history of ideas, I have added a glossary of key terms at the end of the book. But philosophical concepts can seldom be neatly pinned down in a paragraph or two; the reader should also be alert to their particular contexts to get their shifting, complicated meanings. The notes and bibliography may serve to guide those who wish to do further reading on a theme or person.

NATURE'S ECONOMY

PART ONE

TWO ROADS DIVERGED: ECOLOGY IN THE EIGHTEENTH CENTURY

THE EIGHTEENTH CENTURY—*the Age of Reason, it is often called—still astonishes us with its fertility of imagination. So much of our modern world began then: in politics, the arts, our industrial apparatus, science, and philosophy. Not least among its innovations was the science of ecology. More than two hundred years ago men were beginning to put together ecological concepts that we have not yet forgotten, such as the "plenitude of nature," food chains, and the notion of equilibrium. In this section I have tried to capture something of that intellectual ferment and what it implied for later generations.*

Two major traditions in ecology emerged in this early period. The first was an "arcadian" stance toward nature, epitomized by Gilbert White, the parson-naturalist of Selborne. This arcadian view advocated a simple, humble life for man with the aim of restoring him to a peaceful coexistence with other organisms. The second, an "imperial" tradition, is best represented in the work of Carolus Linnaeus—the key ecological figure of the age—and of the Linnaeans generally. Their ambition was to establish, through the exercise of reason and by hard work, man's dominion over nature. No such simple dialectical scheme, however, can successfully distill the complexity and tumult of these remarkable formative years. Like the modernity it promoted, the Age of Reason delivered into our hands a most discordant set of ideas.

CHAPTER 1

Science in Arcadia

Less than fifty miles southwest of London, snuggled among the fields and hills of the Hampshire countryside, lies the tranquil village of Selborne. Its red-tiled, malmstone cottages clustered along its narrow, straggling main street seem safely tucked away in innocent seclusion from the chaotic uproar of the capital city and the Machine Age. To be sure, heavy lorries now and then rumble through the village; television antennas sprout starkly from thatched roofs, and high-tension power lines slash across grassy downs. But otherwise Selborne maintains to an astonishing degree its traditional integrity. Each spring the swifts return to their nests in the village, as they have for centuries. Rooks and woodpigeons sing and flutter in the oak forest. In the chalky little stream flowing through the Long Lythe, the valley that falls away to the east of the village, a trout may still be seen feeding in the riffles or a frog kicking its way against the current. From across the pastures a breeze carries the ancient fragrance of clover and meadowsweet. Even now, Selborne persists as a world apart and intact.

So firm is its hold on its past that the Selborne of today might well be taken as the village Washington Irving had in mind one hundred fifty years ago when he wrote of the "moral feeling" that seems to pervade the rural English landscape. It is a scene, he said, that calls up "ideas of order, of quiet, of sober, well-established principles, of heavy usage and reverent custom. [Here] everything seems to be the growth of regular and peaceful existence." And of coexistence, too, one can add; for an apparent mutual tolerance between man and nature is perhaps Selborne's defining characteristic.[1]

Overlooking this green rustic vale and its inhabitants, human and nonhuman, is the church of St. Mary's, a Gothic pile largely built in the reign of Henry VII, though its massive stone font dates back to Saxon times. Its small churchyard is crowded with modest, lichen-dappled gravestones that bear names still represented among the local folk. But casting its shade over yard and church is an even more venerable institution: a massive yew nearly twenty-eight feet in girth and more than twelve hundred years old. Wooden props support its sagging but still verdant branches. This close union of tree and church, rooted together in the same earth, strongly suggests the abiding symbiosis that nature and man enjoy in Selborne. And here, many have ventured to hope, is evidence that mankind everywhere—even in the face of an uprooting technology—can work out a lasting harmony with the natural world.

The most famous citizen in Selborne's long history was its eighteenth-century curate Gilbert White. Like the village itself, he was a quiet, unassuming, unambitious sort, content with his religious duties and his studies of local flora and fauna. He was born in Selborne in 1720, the child of a retired barrister and grandson of the church's vicar. Ten years later the White family took up residence in the Wakes, one of the larger houses on the main avenue, across from the church; later it became Gilbert's own home until he died in 1793. Only the years he spent at Oriel College in Oxford kept him away from Selborne for any extended period. In 1746 he took his M.A. degree, then the following year his deacon's orders, which enabled him to begin his lifelong work in the church. For a short while he was proctor at the university and dean of Oriel; then he began service as a curate in a succession of country livings. In 1751, he returned to Selborne to live and eventually, in the absence of a resident vicar, to perform the parochial offices at St. Mary's. Although not a wealthy man, he lived as a comfortable bachelor on his Oriel fellowship, curacies, and farm properties and investments. His simple life much resembled that of Oliver Goldsmith's pastor in "The Deserted Village": "Remote from towns, he ran his godly race, / Nor e'er had changed, nor wished to change his place."[2]

White's fame came after his death at the age of seventy-three, and it was based entirely on a single book: *The Natural History of Selborne.* It was published in 1789 and has since then become one of the best-loved books in the English language, appearing in over a hundred editions by the mid-twentieth century. The work is a collection of letters on the wildlife, seasons, and antiquities of White's parish, written in a terse, piquant style that reminds one of Izaak Walton or Horace Walpole. Somewhat reluctantly, White revised these letters for publication at the urging of his two correspondents, Thomas Pennant, a famous zoologist of the day, and Daines Barrington, a Welsh barrister and judge. Little of the man's interior self is revealed in his letters. But the reader can at least easily picture him sauntering down the hollow lanes with his pale Malacca walking stick and knee-breeches. For more than two decades he found enough leisure from his religious tasks to travel daily about the parish and to write his friends about what he saw there of nature. Year after year he ambled along the same sheepwalks in quest of new butterflies, or watched the swallows building nests in a neighbor's chimney, or crouched among the ferns to spy on the wild ducks and snipe feeding at Bean's pond. The result was a book that laid the foundations for the natural history essay in England and America. It was also one point of origin, representative if not seminal, for the modern study of ecology.

"The parish I live in," White noted, "is a very abrupt, uneven country, full of hills and woods, and therefore full of birds." The narrow bounds of White's world reached from the Hanger, a wooded escarpment about three hundred feet high and lying just to the west of the Wakes and the village center, to Wolmer Forest, in reality a treeless marsh covering some fifteen or twenty square miles immediately east of the village. On clear afternoons when he took his tea with friends on the beech-covered heights of the Hanger, he could just make out against the horizon the Sussex Downs, little more than ten miles away. Not far to the south lie the coast and the sea, tempering the Selborne climate. A heavy rainfall in the locale has long produced a rich natural flora, and a wide diversity of soils—white and black malm, sand, chalk, clay, freestone—adds more diversity to the naturalist's studies. Perhaps it was these qualities that led a man of considerable sophistication and learning to devote his life to so small a terrain. In any case, in contrast to the general mania among eighteenth-century British scientists for collecting and cataloguing exotic species from the farthest corners of the world, White's attention was remarkably focused on this microcosm, the natural order of his little parish.

As a scientist, White's inquiries were diffuse by later standards, ranging as they did from taxonomy to phenology, the study of seasonal change, and ethology. He has the credit for first distinguishing among the three species of leaf warblers, or "willow wrens," as well as for identifying the harvest mouse and the large noctule bat. In general, however, he was intent on investigating nature as a "philosopher"—that is, on describing "the life and conversation of animals." Throughout his writing, the migrating birds are one of his deepest concerns. In his letters as well as in separate journal notes, he recorded with exhaustive precision the comings and goings of swallows and martins, whose destinies posed so great a puzzle to naturalists of the period, though White himself could never quite escape the common belief that in winter these birds must hibernate under water or in caves rather than cross the sea to remote southern continents. He discovered that swallows, like many insects, propagate on the wing, as well as eat, drink, and bathe in their swooping flight. He also speculated on the effect of a hempseed diet on the color of the bullfinch's plumage and of castration on secondary sexual characteristics. And he followed closely "that wonderful limited faculty" of animal instinct, especially the "maternal affection" that birds, frogs, and house cats show toward their young. Most amusing of all for him was the behavior of his garden tortoise, Timothy, an ancient sluggish creature with "an arbitrary stomach" and a curious practice of tiptoeing about the garden in the early morning, "intent on sexual attachments, which transport him beyond his usual gravity and induce him to forget for a time his ordinary solemn deportment."[3]

But beyond this level of episodic scrutiny and entertainment, White grasped the complex unity in diversity that made of the Selborne environs an ecological whole. Indeed, it can be said that the *Natural History* is one of the most important early contributions to field ecology in English science. To Pennant he wrote in 1768: "All nature is so full that that district produces the greatest variety which is the most examined." This was precisely his own life's program: to see how many creatures the Selborne parish contained and to understand how they were all united in an interrelated system. That White's study was frequently mixed with his religious beliefs was not incidental. He was drawn to an ecological perspective both by an intense attachment to the land and the creatures he had known from childhood and by an equally deep reverence for the divine Providence that had contrived this beautiful living whole. Science and faith had a common issue for White in this integrative point of view.[4]

In order that such a richly varied fauna could live in so small an area, White observed to his friends, the greatest ingenuity was required on the part of the Creator. For example, oxen and cattle, cooling themselves by standing belly-deep in Selborne ponds, were made to provide by their droppings a supply of food for insects, and thereby indirectly for fish. From this marvelous fact, White concluded that "Nature is a great economist," for she "converts the recreation of one animal to the support of another!" With equal skill Providence had fitted out the different species of swallows with peculiar diets, nesting habits, and reproductive patterns and had, as well, "imprinted on their minds" unique migratory impulses. The overall effect of such careful planning was to make each kind of being important to the stable operation of the Selborne microcosm.

The most insignificant insects and reptiles are of much more consequence, and have much more influence in the economy of nature, than the incurious are aware of; and are mighty in their effect, from their minuteness, which renders them less an object of attention; and from their numbers and fecundity. Earthworms, though in appearance a small and despicable link in the chain of nature, yet, if lost would make a lamentable chasm.

The earthworms, White continued, are a food supply for diverse species of birds, which in turn provide fare for foxes and for men. Moreover, by loosening the soil, the lowly worm helps to aerate and manure the farmer's fields—another "extraordinary provision of nature." And as a further proof of "the wisdom of God in the creation," White noted that the essential earthworms are "much addicted to venery, and consequently very prolific." In sum, "Nature is such an economist, that the most incongruous animals can avail themselves of each other!"[5]

These notes of pious admiration for the ecological order apparently did not interfere seriously with another assumption White carried along on his rambles. The productions of nature, he was sure, exist partly, if not chiefly, to provide a benign and profitable environment for mankind. "Providence has been so indulgent to us," he wrote to Pennant, "as to allow but one venomous reptile of the serpent kind in these kingdoms, and that is the viper." As another instance of divine benevolence, he could again turn to the swallows, which

are a most inoffensive, harmless, entertaining, social, and useful tribe of birds; they touch no fruit in our gardens; delight, all except one species, in attaching themselves to our houses; amuse us with their migrations, songs, and marvelous agility; and clear our outlets from the annoyance of gnats and other troublesome insects.

But in the case of those noxious pests that were the troublesome exceptions in an otherwise beneficial natural economy, White decided Providence would need a helping hand from man if its intentions were to be realized. He suggested to Pennant, therefore, a thorough study that would set forth the behavior of the useless and annoying insects as well as "all the known and likely means of destroying them." It would be a contribution from the naturalist that "would be allowed by the public to be a most useful and important work" and a boost to nature's humane purposes.[6]

Along with a sense of Christian devotion, it was this spirit of economic improvement that led White beyond "a mere systematic classification." Although he appreciated the value of taxonomy in bringing intelligible order to the "pathless wilderness" of nature, he insisted that such science should be devoted to the more important end of investigating wildlife and vegetation where they may promise to be "productive of many of the greatest comforts and elegances of life."

Instead of examining the minute distinctions of every various species of each obscure genus, the botanist should endeavor to make himself acquainted with those that are useful. . . . The botanist that could improve the sward of the district where he lived would be a useful member of society: to raise a thick turf on a naked soil would be worth volumes of systematic knowledge; and he would be the best commonwealth's man that could occasion the growth of "two blades of grass where one alone was seen before."

For all that he delighted in nature as affording the possibility for curious and amusing as well as reverent learning, White was at times strongly utilitarian in his science, just as he assumed Providence was in the creation. He was by no means exaggerating when he claimed "never to lose sight of utility" in his walks, always turning to account what he learned about frosts or aphids or earthworms. On the basis of careful ecological study, he believed, the microcosm of Selborne could be managed to better advantage, supporting by human assistance the conclusion that "Nature is a great economist" in providing for man's material needs.[7]

But there was still another important element in White's concept of ecology, one to which later generations particularly would respond with enthusiasm and delight, and that contrasts sharply with his more manipulative purposes. This element was the arcadian harmony with nature he found in his rural life. The Selborne that emerges in the letters is a personal realization of the ancient arcadian dream of reanimating man's loyalties to the earth and its vital energies. Along with other writers of the age, White found in the Greek and Roman pagans, especially in Virgil's *Eclogues* and *Georgics*, a compelling idyll of contentment and peace. And like the poets Cowper, Gray, and Thomson, he believed he had found an exact counterpart to the Virgilian ideal in the English countryside. His poem "The

Naturalist's Summer-Evening Walk" perhaps best conveys White's arcadian perception of Selborne. Setting forth at dusk, the poet-naturalist sees "the Swallow sweep the darkening plain," watches the "timorous hare" come out to feed, and hears the curlew call his mate. The sharply etched world of daylight observation slowly fades behind the obscuring veil of night; and then the economy of nature, which in its finally mysterious operations "mocks man's prying pride," stirs in the poet's breast a "soothing melancholy joy" as he passes through the fields and woods. To be sure, the nature that he encounters and that works so powerfully on his sensibility may seem to an outsider more domesticated than primitive; it is after all a landscape that had been a home for man for centuries.

> Each rural sight, each sound, each smell,
>   combine;
> The tinkling sheep-bell or the breath of
>   kine;
> The new-mown hay scents the swelling
>   breeze,
> Or cottage-chimney smoking through the
>   trees.

But the overwhelming impression in this arcadian writing, as in the letters generally, is of a man eager to accept all nature into his parish sympathies. That desire is what the rediscovery of pagan literature in the eighteenth century was primarily about: a longing to reestablish an inner sense of harmony between man and nature through an outer physical reconciliation.[8]

In another poem, written a few years earlier, White speaks of the villagers' "pastoral dance" on the Plestor (the village green near the church)—a dance that will "bring all Arcady before our eyes." The image of uncomplicated rural felicity, of a simple and natural people living under the watchful care of Providence and their pastor, threads through all of White's letters and emerges for the modern reader almost as the controlling theme of the book. Nature in Selborne is very close to wholly benign: a stable, productive, rational landscape to which human sentiment can easily respond. Its more fearsome aspects have been shut out, and the menace and confusion of urban life are also left at a safe remove. Nevertheless, it is for White still a predominantly natural world, to which man has accommodated himself. And in this pastoral setting, ecological study is the means by which the naturalist establishes communion with nature: it becomes an innocent pursuit of knowledge about one's neighbors, an integral part of the curate's devotional life, excluding in no way a sense of piety, beauty, or humility.[9]

Of course one might contend that the social peace and stability of White's village were misleading; that they concealed the plight of the poor, whose lives began and ended with the monotony of hard labor and skimpy returns, who had no time for tea on hilltops as did the people of "condition," nor leisure to watch cuckoos skimming over a pond. One might argue that the equilibrium between man and nature in Selborne required the remorseless elimination of all creatures deemed unruly, useless, irregular, or hostile. And one might find it hard to believe that a rigorous scientific temperament could lie down alongside piety in such bucolic pastures. There is truth in each of these charges. But to dwell on them is to miss the positive and genuine virtues of Selborne. And in any case, for White himself there seem to have been no contradictions or misgivings. Reverence and science, social distinctions and humane sympathy, utilitarianism and arcadian delight were all mingled in the daily rounds of the parson-naturalist. Only in a more modern consciousness could these reconciliations seem superficial, false, or impossible.

Beyond the little world of Selborne, however, there were forces at work that soon would make almost untenable the assurance of harmony in White's arcadian ecology. During the period when he wrote his letters, from the 1760s to the 1780s, the British nation was rocked by political and economic upheaval. The war for independence waged by the American colonies represented the first major challenge to the mother country's mercantile policy. Then in 1789, the year White's book went to press, the Bastille was captured by Paris revolutionaries and France plunged into political violence that culminated in a reign of terror in

Science in Arcadia • 11

1793, the year White died. At the same time—and perhaps more important in terms of man's relation to nature—England was fast becoming the first society of the world to enter the technological era. It would surely have been impossible for White to have been unaware of these events, but they seem to have been of little consequence to him. Not one of them is even mentioned in the *Natural History*; in his more prosaic daily journal, there are only one or two passing, puzzled references to the French explosion. It would seem that the naturalist of Selborne could appreciate thoroughly the workings of the economy of nature, but almost nothing of the revolution going on in the politics and economy of man.

Less than two hundred miles north of Selborne is the city of Manchester, where in the late eighteenth century the surplus capital accumulated from years of trade with the Orient and the New World financed the development of a new mode of production: the factory system. The organizing skills perfected over two centuries by English merchants, and the rational use of capital to stimulate as well as satisfy demand, were extended with sudden vigor to revolutionize the apparatus of manufacturing. In 1765 James Hargreaves invented the spinning jenny. During the 1770s Richard Arkwright introduced the waterframe for spinning thread. Then in 1785 Edmund Cartwright's power loom completed the transformation of the textile industry to machine production. Along with James Watts' new steam engine, these innovations signaled the end of one long era of human history and the beginning of another. And the driving motive behind this technological development was the pure and simple desire to increase productivity and wealth.

By the time Gilbert White's book appeared, the factory system was spreading over Yorkshire, Lancashire, and Staffordshire. And with the factory came the need for a resident army of workers disciplined to the rhythms of the machine. Hence the population of Lancashire grew by 300 percent in the second half of the century. Manchester doubled in size during the 1790s, becoming a city of 100,000 in a world where most people still lived in small villages like Selborne, population 600. Outside Selborne in the late eighteenth century, movement seemed to be replacing order. As George Trevelyan has described the period, what once had been a slowly moving stream quickly became a thundering cataract plunging over a milldam. During the next century the economic world did not resume its placid pace; on the contrary, its tempo increased. With each decade the bustling cities of northern England grew more rich and productive, albeit more smoke-blackened and fever-ridden as well. Each year farm laborers abandoned villages and hamlets to seek more attractive futures in Manchester, where in fact they found only the most haphazard of living arrangements.[10]

In Gilbert White's lifetime, the expansion in economic expectations that produced the factory system also brought sweeping transformations to English agriculture, especially in the Midlands. In order to feed the growing industrial population, the remnants of a feudal system of communal, subsistence farming had to be destroyed. Thus the soil was commercialized, farmers were taught to produce not for themselves but for urban markets, and much of the rural landscape was made over to produce more food more efficiently. Under the barrage of private enclosure acts passed by Parliament from the 1750s on, the open-field system that had survived in many counties from the Middle Ages was hastily overturned. Extensive heaths, moors, and commons were laid out in small, regular plots and planted to turnips or grazed with sheep. All in all, in the eighteenth and early nineteenth centuries about six and a half million acres of English landscape were transformed into a rationally planned checkerboard of squarish fields enclosed by hedgerows of hawthorn and ash. The landed gentry, who led this revolution at great personal profit to themselves, marched under the new banner of agricultural reformer Arthur Young: "Make two blades of grass grow where one grew before." Thus by 1800 the capitalist aim of increasing personal wealth through progressive, efficient, centralized management had pervaded both agriculture and manufacturing, working from each side to uproot the English laboring classes, redistribute them in the new industrial cities, and discipline them in a new mode of work. From Britain

Science in Arcadia • 13

this economic revolution spread to America and beyond. Never again would it be possible—not even perhaps in Selborne—to take for granted a sense of permanence or stability.[11]

In such a tumult it is no wonder that a book like *The Natural History of Selborne* was ignored for almost half a century. England was much too busy consolidating and adjusting to the processes of modernization, if adjustment is the right word, to read about the crinking of field crickets or the fluting of a plover. But around 1830 the outlines of what Rashleigh Holt-White called "the cult of Gilbert White and Selborne" began to appear. From that time forward, Selborne steadily emerged as a focal point on the map of dream and reverie, the living memory of a world that had been lost. And White himself was suddenly discovered by a new generation that looked back with envy to the graceful, balanced life of the parson-naturalist. Through the next decades there came to Selborne a steady succession of earnest pilgrims—including prominent scientists, poets, and businessmen from both sides of the Atlantic—who were searching for their own psychic roots. Charles Darwin, according to his son, made his "pilgrimage to the shrine of Gilbert White" in the 1850s. The American writer and ambassador to England, James Russell Lowell, visited the Wakes in 1850 and again in 1880, on the first of these occasions describing White's book as "the journal of Adam in Paradise." During his second sojourn, Lowell captured part of the mood that brought the swelling stream of visitors:

> My eye a scene familiar sees,
> And Home! is whispered by the breeze

Within a century after the publication of White's book, Selborne had become a symbol of refuge for the homeless mind of Englishmen and Americans, two peoples joined not only by a common language and heritage but by a shared confusion about where they were going.[12]

A few years after Lowell's second trip, the leading American nature essayist of the late nineteenth century, John Burroughs, came to Selborne to admire "the pastoral quiet and sweetness and harmony of the English landscape." Into White's village, Burroughs wrote, the "disturbing elements of the great hurly-burly outside world do not enter." From the Plestor, it seemed to him, the "great world is far off"; its noise was as faint as "the distant rumble of a wagon heard in the midst of the fields." In the Introduction to an 1895 edition of the *Natural History*, Burroughs wrote that the work offers to the reader "a home air" and that to the traveler Selborne appears "as snug and secluded as a chimney corner." With its aura of peace and domesticity, the Hampshire village was taken by Burroughs and other undiscriminating Americans as representative of England generally, a type of its "island coziness and unity" where all is "one neighborhood" and where one's craving for "the home-like and for the fruits of affectionate occupation of the soil" finally can be satisfied. Several decades later, R. M. Lockley echoed these reactions when he argued that "the essence of Gilbert White" is the "universal love of home and the security of home which is in every man."[13]

The Selborne Society, established to honor White and to promote the study of local natural history, was spreading rapidly when in 1893 the English naturalist W. Warde Fowler wrote a memorial of White's life. On the surface, said Fowler, it seemed ironic that his book should be so much in demand at a time when the world was passing "from a period of poetry and romance into one of stern reality, . . . when the study of economic problems should be driving out of our heads the delights of wild nature or of sport." But in truth it was these very changes, Fowler believed, that made the *Natural History* an attractive antidote, especially for the *anomie* produced by the industrial city.

Surely the spread of the factory system, and the consequent growth of huge towns, has rather strengthened than weakened this love of all things rural. We pine for pure air, for the sight of growing grass, for the foot-path across the meadow, for the stile that invites you to rest before you drop into the deep lane under the hazels. But in the last century there was no need to pine, when there was hardly a town from which a man could not escape into the fields when he would without toiling through the grimy suburbs where the problems of economic science force themselves at every turn on his mind. In those days men loved the country simply as their home, not because they were shut away from it. . . .

For many the mere experience of reading Gilbert White had become a drug to deaden the senses against the landscape of ruin in Manchester, Birmingham, and Pittsburgh, as well as a point of renewed contact with a rural nature shrinking into a vague memory.[14]

The rise of the natural history essay in the latter half of the nineteenth century was an essential legacy of the Selborne cult. It was more than a scientific–literary genre of writing, modeled after White's pioneering achievement. A constant theme of the nature essayists was the search for a lost pastoral haven, for a home in an inhospitable and threatening world. One observer described this new genre as "the literature of rest and delight," from which flowed "streams of healing for the discomforts of civilization." Chief among those unpleasant aspects of modernity was the industrial landscape, and such writers as John Burroughs, John Muir, W. H. Hudson, and Richard Jeffries turned out scores of volumes in which natural history was the vehicle that brought readers to the quiet peace of hay barns, orchards, and mountain valleys. These virtuosi of the nature essay were among the best-selling writers of their age. And it must be emphasized that these writers turned in part to science as a route back to nature.[15]

Industrialism, however, was only one of the "discomforts of civilization." It was soon perceived that science too could become more a threat than an antidote. Many of the nature essayists understood that their bewildered, unhappy readers needed more than the mere temporary escape afforded by reading about nature as encountered in pleasant, woodsy rambles. What was called for, argued one anonymous American writer, was a new "gospel of nature" that would stress the need to recover "a personal relation of every man to the world about him, and through that world to God." Their intention as popular naturalists thus became religious and spiritual as much as scientific. And from this vantage point it was readily apparent that the modern alienation from nature as well as from God was the result of the very science they had embraced. By the late nineteenth century, science as well as economics had gone through a radical set of changes. So in 1889 Burroughs was forced to admit that man had been "fairly turned out into the cold" by the skeptical spirit of the new science; "the cosmic chill" of the purposeless, mechanical universe revealed by Darwin and other scientists had left the human spirit an orphan. The ultimate task therefore for White's successors was to find an alternative to this cold science—not by a retreat into unexamined dogmatism, but by restoring to scientific inquiry some of the warmth, breadth, and piety which had been infused into it by the departed parson-naturalist. Henceforth this became one of the central burdens of the natural history essay.[16]

In this quest, John Burroughs took up late in his life (and evidently with some uncertainty) the philosophy of vitalism propounded by the French neo-Romantic Henri Bergson. Vitalism was the view that plants and animals act according to an indwelling, mysterious power that physics or chemistry cannot analyze. Burroughs saw in it the promise to "transmute and spiritualize science" by replacing the ruling "physico-chemical explanation of life and consciousness" with a creative, unpredictable, organizing energy inherent in all organisms. Nature thereby would become once more "a living joy, something to love," and man would be seen as something more than a mere machine. On a more grandiose scale, Burroughs wanted to expand the theory of vitalism to take in nature as a single entity—"a huge organism pulsing with life, real and potential." Other nature writers also attempted to stake out a vitalistic line of defense against the advancing threat of the physical sciences. W. H. Hudson contended that every organism in nature, and indeed every molecule and atom, not only in some sense possesses a nonmaterial psyche or spirit but also is an interdependent part of the all-inclusive organism of nature, which is animated by one unifying spirit. And John Muir discerned in nature an organic whole held together by "an essential love, overlying, underlying, pervading all things."

The notion of vitalism and its panvitalist or panpsychic extension, as proposed by these leading nature essayists, was a doctrine romantic and religious in tone but was intended to be a scientific axiom to some extent. It was offered as the means to put back into science something of the older arcadian piety and affection. Such a philosophy, moreover, would restore the comprehensive, organic perspective of Gilbert White to a scientific community that had gone far toward dissecting nature into a scattering of unrelated pieces. There emerged repeatedly out of the nature essayists' ponderings an emphasis on such words as "holism" and "organic." The intent of these writers was twofold: first, to endow each creature with a freedom of will and action that would defy analysis by chemistry and physics; and second, to study all nature as a single integrated unity, held together by a rather mysterious organizing force.[17]

This movement was a counterattack against both the new industrial society and the new methods of scientific analysis. Narrow specialization, mathematical abstraction, and extensive reliance on elaborate instruments of measurement were all cited as causes for what was seen as the alienation of scientists—and mankind generally—from nature. The organic doctrine was set with special fervor against the cold, impersonal, urban laboratory; the holistic naturalists commonly proposed a return to direct contact with the living organism in its natural environment. Their insistence on restoring to respectability the label "natural history," associated as it was with images of fields and woods and with broad descriptive intent rather than the irreverent prying and explaining of reductive science, revealed a deep nostalgia for the past. This holistic movement went hand in hand with the rejection of urban technological society, and may be viewed as a search for an arcadian science. Its chief ambitions were to blend science more fully into the whole fabric of human values and to restore the scientist to a more humble, integral role in the human community and the system of nature.

By the twentieth century the "cult of Gilbert White and Selborne" had become strongly identified with the holistic doctrine. It became a regular theme, when offering to the reading public a new edition of *The Natural History of Selborne*, to contrast White with the modern overspecialized scientist. For example, Grant Allen, a leading English nature writer, found in White's book a fascinating glimpse of the man of science at work in the dawning years of the science of biology, and like others in his genre Allen by no means wanted to repudiate this early scientific spirit. The appeal for him of that lost golden age was that a man could make significant contributions to knowledge without surrendering his other roles as parson, citizen, sportsman, or country gentleman. In the new era, on the other hand, the naturalist could not hope to discover important facts or generalizations "without the copious aid of libraries, instruments, collections, cooperation, long specialist training." The part, therefore, had become the whole. Allen believed that submerged in the onrushing tide of modernity was a world that had produced "whole and many-sided men and women" and allowed them to make of themselves "full, evenly-balanced, broad-minded human natures." The modern disintegration of the self, in which the person is nothing more than a fragment, no longer capable of broad sympathies and interests, was traced largely then to the impact on culture of a maturing science.[18]

A second critique of science that emerged out of the Gilbert White cult focused on the isolation of the modern scientist from society and its moral fabric. Cecil Emden, the author of the biographical study *Gilbert White in His Village*, gave this idea special prominence. As the title of his first chapter announced, Emden found White "a very human naturalist," sympathetically involved in the lives of his neighbors, as interested in their affairs as he was in the weather, swallows, or sticklebacks. White's science was not severed from his social affections to become a disinterested, abstract search for facts, with no regard for their consequences or uses. "He was in the fullest sense a member of the village community," Emden wrote; "he fitted easily and happily into its social structure." The yearning for community—a protest against the anonymity of modern urban society—has been, of course, one of the more persistent aspects of the arcadian dream. But Emden directed his readers' attention to the specific case of the scientist, who often seemed to typify best the withdrawal of the specialized individual from full social engagement into enclaves of professional elitism and indifference.[19]

Another editor of White's book, H. J. Massingham, pushed this theme farther to make Selborne "a social organism" and White an "organicist," who studied nature as

Science in Arcadia • 19

an interdependent whole rather than a series of individual parts. As a self-contained community with a deeply rooted sense of identity, Selborne in the eighteenth century was more than the modern urban clustering of "mere particles," Massingham wrote. It was "an interrelated whole" shut away from the "roaring mechanical traffic" and "the noise and unrest of man's external and denatured giddiness." Through his office as resident naturalist, White belonged to the community. And his close social integration with the village helped him toward an understanding of "man's relationship as a whole with his particular environment, in his manifest dealings with the earth considered as a regional whole." Beyond the human order, that is, White glimpsed the larger community of man and nature: "All were parts of one organic whole, which was the countryside, his own but a section of the universal." Open as he was to the vision of interrelatedness, White would have rejected the modern mechanistic theory of "biological automatism," the view that organisms are programmed to behave according to rigid physical laws.[20]

Obviously the Selborne cult had by now entered the realm of mythology. And whether Gilbert White was in fact an organicist or vitalist, as Massingham claimed, is beside the point. What is important is the need felt by these nature essayists to locate a compelling image of an alternative world *and* an alternative science. That, after all, is the principal function of myth: not to establish facts but to create powerful symbols and designs that can explain the inner core of human experience and provide dreams to live by. And it should now be clear that for these writers the vision of the arcadian landscape could not be severed from the ideal of the holistic consciousness. If Selborne could be used as a symbolic contrast to industrial civilization, then its parson-naturalist could serve as a precedent for a different kind of scientist. In place of urban disintegration, the disciples of White dreamed of rural community. Instead of the arrogance of technological civilization toward nature, they called for arcadian humility. In rejecting the dominion of the physico-chemical analysis of the laboratory, they turned back to an older natural history. Rather than a mechanistic reductiveness in science, they advocated an organic synthesis. The fusion of these diverse concerns symbolized by Gilbert White, the pastoral naturalist, is the main cultural significance of the nature essay in England and America.

The idea of holism, in which all nature is approached as a single indivisible unity, like the larger arcadian impulse of which it is a part, has ebbed and flowed with extraordinary persistence throughout the modern period. Biologists and philosophers who may never have read or even heard of Gilbert White have nonetheless added their voices to the holistic movement. Consequently the theory, diffuse from its origins, has assumed many guises, in some cases being still vitalistic while in others it resembles the philosophy of organicism expounded by Alfred North Whitehead. But almost always, whatever its precise definition or level of sophistication, holism has been offered as something more than a critique of science. It has been advocated by those who have an intense distaste for the fragmentation of the industrial culture and its isolation from the natural world. Ludwig von Bertalanffy, a central figure in promoting systems theory in biology, hinted at some of these social complaints when he wrote: "The age of technology is becoming weary of itself—let us hope that an organismic one will follow it to offer new prospects to the future of humanity." The criticism of mechanistic thought implied here is directed at the imagination of technological man as well as at science. Holists have believed that, though an individual scientist may have little directly to do with the machine culture, there is an indirect but essential link between the models science sets up to describe nature and the values and philosophy of the technological society.[21]

In recent years the arcadian reaction as protest against both technology and the ruling scientific paradigms has again been brought to the forefront of attention by a phenomenon known as the "ecology movement." There has emerged from this movement a renewed attack on scientific methodology for its reductive tendencies. Ecologists have insisted that scientists today are in danger of ignoring the complex whole of nature, the quality of organic interrelatedness that defies analysis by the physicist or chemist. Though they are quick to deny a belief in any nonmaterial or vitalist force in the organism or in the ecosystem, ecologists frequently argue that breaking nature down into its atomistic parts cannot result in a true understanding of the whole. Special qualities emerge out of interactions and collectivities; the whole of nature is different from the sum of its parts. These qualities, ecologists maintain, cannot be studied in simplified laboratory models. Nature must be examined in the field, where it is in full possession of its faculties—where it is alive. Barry Commoner, among others, has held up as an ideal the "classical biology" of the eighteenth-century naturalists, who apprehended nature in its living integrity. Commoner has also put up a determined resistance to the claims of the new molecular biologists, who believe that life is to be understood merely as another form of chemistry. Such scientific "blindness," he has argued, has led to a worldwide ecological crisis. Human interventions in nature, including planetary insults by radioactivity and pesticides, have gone unchecked because scientists have failed to understand their effects on the whole as well as on isolated parts.[22]

Technological progress has become an even more popular target of the ecology movement. In fact, many ecologists would agree with William Murdoch and James Connell of the University of California when they contend that it is an essential part of the ecologist's job to dispel modern society's confidence in technology, and more, its faith in unlimited economic growth. In order to protect a finite biosphere, many ecological scientists have planted themselves firmly in the path of an expansionary human economy that has behind it more than two centuries' momentum. Not since the Industrial Revolution have the ambitions of modernization encountered such fierce and widespread resistance.[23]

What is especially surprising in this course of events is that the campaign against technological growth has been led not by poets or artists, as in the past, but by individuals from within the scientific community. So accustomed are we to assume that scientists are generically partisans of the entire ideology of progress, happily adjusted above all others to the machine culture, that the ecology movement has created a vast shock wave of reassessment of the scientist's place in society. Ecologists now find themselves not only marching in the vanguard of anti-technology forces but also serving as teachers for a new generation intent on recovering a sense of the sacred in nature. No wonder, then, that at least one ecologist, Paul Sears, has called his field "a subversive subject." With remarkable suddenness it has mounted a powerful threat to established assumptions in society and in economics, religion, and the humanities, as well as the other sciences and their ways of doing business.[24]

Ecology, however, remains an arcadian as well as a subversive science. Its revolutionary implications are well mixed with reactionary appeals to an earlier time when man's economy worked in harmony with nature's. And there is in Commoner's idealization of the "classical biologists" the same message of thoughtful, deliberate nostalgia that one finds in the Gilbert White cult. Indeed, there is an unmistakable continuity from White's studies of the Selborne countryside to the natural history of Burroughs and Hudson to the science of the contemporary ecologist. To be sure, not every modern ecological scientist would want to be identified with either pastoral dreams or the popular ecology movement. Nevertheless, in our own time ecology has come to represent the arcadian mood that would return man to a garden of natural peace and piety.

This arcadian continuity appears most strikingly in the compassionate figure of the nature writer who more than any other person launched the recent ecology movement, Rachel Carson. Her early writing on the sea and the tidal zone, much of it derived from rambles along the shore of her Maine coastal home, are nature essays squarely in the John Burroughs and Gilbert White tradition. But in her book *Silent Spring* (published in 1962), which marshaled substantial scientific evidence of the threat to life posed by the persistent pesticides, Carson went on to inaugurate the literature of ecological apocalypse. Faced with a society that seemed hellbent to destroy itself and all other forms of life, whether by fission bombs or DDT, she could not maintain the equipoise and complacence of the Selborne parson. Her tone became increasingly one of desperation. But even in the midst of her crusade against dumping the devastating new poisons in the biosphere, she retained some of the arcadian vision and temperament. There was, for example, the same self-effacing humility before the natural world: "We still haven't become mature enough," she said in 1963, "to think of ourselves as only a tiny part of a vast and incredible universe." While some atomic physicists were still boasting of their conquest over matter and promising ever larger bombs, Carson urged scientists and engineers to accept a humbler role and thereby ensure a more secure future for themselves and their fellow species. Eventually the scientific conscience she symbolized became the central creed of the ecology movement: a vision of the unity of life, as taught by science, and a moral ideal of living cooperatively with all members of the natural community. That ethic, one recalls, was also part of the arcadian ideal of Selborne.[25]

But before we settle too securely on the arcadian image in the biography of ecology, it would be wise to inquire further. What else can be said of ecology's ethical implications? Has it always stood in opposition to the technological society, as it so often seems today, or have there been other historical continuities that deny and challenge its arcadian aspect? Were there any ecological ideas that contributed to, rather than opposed, industrialization? And have the profound changes occurring in human society and economy since the late eighteenth century both altered the ways in which scientists approach nature and subtly affected the way men and women today react to the world about them?

We must consider not only the purely internal development of scientific models and methods that have been dominant in different eras; what ecologically oriented naturalists have explicitly said about man's relation to nature, or suggested by their social roles, as well as the environmental consequences that may have been produced by the various models of nature this science has used, must also be taken into account. In short, this inquiry must be alert to *all* the roots of this science of ecology—those that contradict as well as those that affirm the Gilbert White ethos.

To answer some of these questions, we must return to the intellectual milieu of Gilbert White, to the eighteenth century, where modern ecological science and its larger penumbra of ecological philosophy began to take form. Some of the ideas of this age have already been touched on in our discussion of White's letters, but there remains a good deal more to be said about this critical formative time. And for the fuller origins of ecology we must move beyond the perimeters of Selborne to the greater Anglo-American world, indeed to the entire sweep of the Linnaean age in natural history, for a more complete awareness of the tensions, ambiguities, and conflicts that lurk unresolved in this science and the current popular movement it has generated.

CHAPTER 2

The Empire of Reason

THE ARCADIAN VISION has not been the only form of pastoral idyll in our culture. There has been a second important variety that we may call "Christian pastoralism," for it has been a recurrent theme in the western church. It idealizes not man's relationship to nature but the pastor's to his flock of faithful believers. In its origins, the word "pastoral" refers to the care exercised by the shepherd in feeding his sheep and protecting them from harm. Then it also came to mean the spiritual guidance and nourishment given by a minister to his congregation. In contrast to the arcadian ideal, which grew out of pagan culture and carried along in its subsequent revivals the paraphernalia of satyrs, nymphs, and the goat-god Pan piping on his flute, the Christian version focused on the image of the Good Shepherd, as ideally expressed in the life of Jesus Christ. The Good Shepherd of the New Testament was more ascetic and otherworldly than his arcadian counterparts. Probably he was also meant to be more humanitarian, at least toward those fragile human creatures in his sheepfold. In the Christian version of the pastoral dream, the shepherd does not merge with nature through his flock nor is his occupation a protest against urban alienation from the natural world, both of which are key themes in the arcadian version. On the contrary, he is the defender of the flock *against* the hostile forces of nature—wolves, lions, bears—and his profession is to lead his lambs out of this sorry world to greener pastures.

This second variety of pastoralism illustrates nicely what observers have long noticed about Christianity (and its Judaic background): of all the major religions of the world, it has been the most insistently anti-natural. In the mind of the average Christian, argues historian Lynn White, Jr., nature's chief function is to serve man's needs. In extreme cases nature is seen as the source of demonic threats, fleshly appetites, and animal instincts that must be vigorously repressed. No religion, this authority on the medieval period believes, has been more anthropocentric. None has been more rigid in excluding all but man from the realm of divine grace and in denying any moral obligation to the lower species. One thinks, for example, of Pope Pius IX's refusal to allow a society to be organized in Rome to protest against the slaughter of bulls for sport and amusement; an animal, he declared, has no soul and thus has no claim on man's moral sympathies. This general animus against nature in Christianity seems to have been most pronounced in Roman Catholicism and, ironically, in its arch-opponent on so many other matters, the Puritan wing of Protestantism. Christian apologists in recent years have sometimes pointed to one outstanding exception: the man who humbly addressed a canticle to the sun and accepted the birds and beasts as his brethren, St. Francis of Assisi. But such rare exceptions have not disproved the essential truth in the observation that Christianity has maintained a calculated indifference, if not antagonism, toward nature. The good shepherd, the heroic benefactor of man, has almost never been concerned with leading his flock to a broad reverence for life. His pastoral duties have been limited to ensuring the welfare of his human charges, often in the face of a nature that has been seen as corrupt and predatory.[1]

But what about Gilbert White's pastorate in Selborne? Surely here is evidence that the two traditions, pagan and Christian, could lie down amicably in the same rural meadow. That may well be what happened. Unfortunately, we do not have any of the Sunday sermons that White preached to his parishioners at St. Mary's; therefore nothing is known of the place nature occupied in his official teaching. There is today in the church a handsome stained-glass window depicting St. Francis feeding the birds, put up in

White's honor by a later generation; it suggests that at least some recent Christians in the village would not have found it unfitting for a parson to occupy his time with nature as well as with man. As for White himself, it seems most plausible that his Christian inheritance, indelible though it was, had been strongly tempered by his reading of Virgil and other pagan pastoralists. In fact, much of his writing shows hardly a vestige of the Christian clerical mind.

The eighteenth century repeats this pattern of confrontation again and again: faced with powerful competition from a rediscovered paganism, Christianity was forced to mellow considerably its long-standing suspicion of nature. Without altogether giving up its traditional character, it nonetheless acquired a new measure of ecological humility, an awareness that man is only one among a myriad of species. After centuries of psychological isolation, Christians began to show some willingness to draw near to that vast community of being and to merge with it once more. The parson-naturalist as typified by Gilbert White was one outcome of this mood of reconciliation.

Undoubtedly, the advent of science must have been another factor that forced a change in the Christian imagination. James Thomson and Alexander Pope, for instance, owed much of the respect and enthusiasm for nature they expressed in their poetry to this burgeoning influence. And Christianity once again struggled to accommodate itself to the presence of a rival authority. But the relation between science and Christian ideas of morality is much more complicated than this scenario suggests. These two powerful kingdoms of intellectual force were, from another perspective, not rivals at all. On the contrary, western science was from its beginning deeply imbued with the traditional Christian approach to nature. Nicholas Berdyaev, for example, argues that "Christianity alone made possible both positive science and technique." The precise contribution of the Christian faith, he maintains, was that it severed man from nature emotionally. Therein lay the seed for development of the rational objectivity that characterizes modern science, the notion that knowledge requires a strict repression of the viewer's subjective feelings about the object studied. Christianity made this detached, external view of nature possible by overthrowing pagan animism, in which the human mind was submerged in communion with the inner, vital spirit of the natural world. Thanks to this early triumph over the pagan view of nature, western science could proceed to study the earth as a thoroughly profane and analyzable object.[2]

In addition to the gift of objectivity, Christianity may also have contributed to science a technological or mechanistic picture of nature. By denying to nonhuman entities a soul or indwelling spirit, Christianity helped reduce man's perception of nature to the status of a mechanical contrivance. This perspective may have had its first expression in the Genesis account of the creation of the earth and heavens: a detached, divine power contriving out of a vacuum the entire material world. All is fashioned according to a wholly rational, intelligible design that is imposed on chaos. And all will be destroyed when it has ceased to serve the purposes of its Creator. Neither our science nor our technology, it seems likely, would have been possible without the mental preparation afforded by this peculiar myth of origins. The mechanistic view of nature provided the scientist with a world reassuringly predictable because it was devised by a rational mind and made to obey a strict set of laws; it gave the engineer confidence that his own contrivances were part of the divine plan and hence acceptable expressions of piety.

There is, then, this anti-arcadian tradition, ancient in its origins and still highly influential in eighteenth-century ecological writing, that stripped from nature all spiritual qualities and rigidly distanced it from human feelings—promoting a view of creation as a mechanical contrivance. This tradition was historically linked to the good-shepherd version of the pastoral idea; Christianity nurtured it for many centuries, teaching western man that nature was his domain, to be altered and rearranged more or less as he chose.

But this anti-arcadian tradition might be better described as the "imperial" view of nature, for, more explicitly than Christianity ever did, it has made the domination of the earth—often promoted in the name of a purely secular welfare—one of modern man's most important ends. This imperial tradition must receive our attention here, for in the early period of the idea of ecology it was especially militant and popular, so much so that the Gilbert Whites of the age often went unheard. All the Selbornes of the world, it was commonly predicted in expansive rhetoric, were to be torn down and their equilibrium between man and nature replaced by a more aggressively artificial, humanized landscape: a new world in which science would give mankind absolute power over the land and its creatures.

If Gilbert White may be taken as a type, though never pure, of arcadian ecology, then the most appropriate exponent of this imperial ideology must be his countryman Francis Bacon (1561–1626), who served as Lord Chancellor of England a full century before White was born and was an influential philosopher of the scientific method. Not at all attracted to the Virgilian idyll, Bacon promised to the world a manmade paradise, to be rendered astonishingly fertile by science and human management. In that utopia, he predicted, man would recover a place of dignity and honor, as well as the authority over all the other creatures he once enjoyed in the Garden of Eden. Where the arcadian naturalist exemplified a life of quiet reverence before the natural world, Bacon's hero was a man of "Active Science," busy studying how he might remake nature and improve the human estate. Instead of humility, Bacon was all for self-assertiveness: "the enlargement of the bounds of Human Empire, to the effecting of all things possible." Although he was not an especially religious man, he borrowed much of this scientific ideology from his Christian moral training. "The world is made for man," he announced, "not man for the world." Through rigorous objectivity, he would have that belief realized in a practical and earthly, as well as a spiritual, sense. In the Baconian ideology, by a startling and yet clear progression, the good shepherd of the Christian tradition had become a scientist and technocrat. Science offered the means for building a better sheepfold and creating greener pastures.[3]

In the years just before the Industrial Revolution and the rise of a more mature science, these two opposing traditions—arcadian and imperial—were more often than not curiously mixed together. As will become clear, the predominant, sometimes strident, voice in eighteenth-century ecology echoed Bacon's imperialism. But the arcadian ideal was not altogether silent or ignored. Indeed, some naturalists seemed to want to give each ideal its moment of truth. This peculiar ambivalence can be best appreciated by a look at the ideas of the great naturalist Linnaeus, in whose work the ecological thought of the century found its most famous expression.

In the common opinion of the eighteenth century, the outstanding genius in natural history was the Swedish botanist Carl von Linné, popularly known simply as Linnaeus (1707–1778). A businesslike man, ambitious and enterprising, he was an inspiration in science, religion, and personal success for an age that was at once proudly rational, pious, and bourgeois. Through his own indefatigable industry and the patronage of others, he steadily made his way up in life, from his nativity in a lowly rural cottage in the south of Sweden to an honored place in his nation's circle of nobility and in its royal councils. But throughout his climb to worldwide reputation, he never lost the capacity for reverential awe before nature, a piety reminiscent at times of the more retiring Gilbert White. The country around Stenbrohault, where his father located as a rector three months after Linnaeus' birth, was a Scandinavian version of Selborne's pastoral grace: rich, level farmland dotted with pines and firs and flowery meadows. Linnaeus was later to write of days in his youth spent lolling in the grass, listening to the piping and humming of insects. He recalled that in these moments of reverie he could become quite "giddy at the Creator's magnificent arrangement."[4]

Linnaeus had an unusually intense passion for the delights of arrangement. He knew how to put every piece of nature in its precise place, a talent on which he built a formidable scientific reputation with astonishing speed. By 1735, when he was still in his twenties, he had expanded the old notion of the sexuality of plants into a convincing scientific argument, had traveled five thousand miles among the Lapps to botanize the snowy fells of the Arctic Circle, and, most importantly, had devised his own system of plant classification: the *Systema Naturae*. In his later years Linnaeus boasted that he had been "the greatest reformer" ever among students of plants—and it was not a false claim. He might also have added that he was among the most prolific scientists of his day, publishing over a dozen works during a two-and-a-half-year stay in Holland. The "artificial" system of botanical taxonomy that these many writings expounded took all of Europe by storm and was soon being taught both to advanced scholars in universities and to young ladies in their gardens. The system was an accurate reflection of Linnaeus' economical, arranging mind: one simply counted the number of stamens and pistils in a blossom and noted their position to determine where a plant belonged in the divine scheme. A few such calculations, and all living nature could be organized into neat rows of shelves and boxes. After more than a century of taxonomic chaos, during which every scientist seemed to employ his own system, botany finally had been put on an efficient and universal basis.[5]

Two hundred years later, some historians have searched impatiently through Linnaeus' books and concluded that he made no original, important advances. Several have maintained that not even his classifying system and binomial nomenclature were truly novel, both having been anticipated in the work of Ray, Bauhin, and Cesalpino. Such a harsh judgment, however, dismisses too quickly the achievement of Linnaeus. And it underrates the value of elementary order for an era of anarchy in natural history. The task of organizing species into a coherent plan, prosaic as it often seems and erroneous as it turned out to be in its assumptions about the nature of species, was a vital preliminary to the theory of evolution. After all, before anomalies can demand explanation, as in the case of the origin of species problem, someone must first build a structure that makes them visible. Moreover, Linnaeus' simple, cleancut categories made science more attractive and accessible to the public than it has ever been since. His world responded with gratitude and respect; splendid botanical gardens were planted, and the cabinets of poets, curates, and kings were crammed with specimens of nature's creations.[6]

But it is not neat categories or organizational charts alone that make Linnaeus a symbol of the spirit of his time. Throughout western culture, he seemed to demonstrate in his work the reconciliation between love of nature and pursuit of human ambitions, between religious belief and scientific rationalism, for which many were searching. "Without doubt," wrote his biographer Theodor Fries, "the most noteworthy trait of Linné's character was his ardent piety." Sir William Jardine echoed this view in the first volume of *The Naturalist's Library*, when he noted that Linnaeus never lost sight of "the First Great Cause, but looked truly up to Nature's God, as the giver of all his benefits and acquirements." Though a national hero in Sweden, Linnaeus found his greatest following in England and America, especially among parson-naturalists like Gilbert White and the Quaker botanists John and William Bartram of Philadelphia. These men shared his love of the Creator's handiwork as well as his scientific interest in nature. It was a fitting symbol of this Anglo-American adoration that, upon his death in 1778, Linnaeus' books and papers were purchased for a thousand pounds and exported to London. Here the Linnaean Society was formed to carry on his botanical work in the same mingled spirit of Christian reverence, natural piety, and practical enterprise.[7]

In the eighteenth century, one of the most widely admired of Linnaeus' works was his essay "The Oeconomy of Nature." It was written in 1749 as an academic thesis that was then translated into Latin and defended by one of his students at Uppsala. It quickly became the single most important summary of an ecological point of view still in its infancy. It was, moreover, one of a series of tracts on rationalistic religion that were widely read throughout Europe and America. The underlying purpose of this essay, as with other tracts of this sort, was to find the hand of God in nature. Not surprisingly, those who looked most diligently found what they were seeking. As a theological treatise, "The Oeconomy of Nature" does not begin to bear comparison with the writings of a Joseph Butler or a Jonathan Edwards. But as a document in ecological science it is an eloquent and important, if a primitive, first step by a master of the fine arts of organization and arrangement. In presenting the essay to the English public, the translator

Benjamin Stillingfleet praised it as giving "a more comprehensive and distinct view, as it were in a map, of the several parts of nature, their connections and dependencies, than is any where else to be found."[8]

Essentially, "The Oeconomy of Nature" presents a thoroughly static portrait of the geo-biological interactions in nature. All movement takes place in a single confined sphere, planetary in scope. Like the classical Greek naturalists, Linnaeus allows only one kind of change in the natural economic system, a cyclical pattern that keeps returning to its point of departure. At the very foundation of the natural order is the hydrological cycle, the perpetual circulation of water from the "exhalations" of seas and rivers into the form of rainfall and snow, and thence to the sea once more. According to Linnaeus, this model is repeated throughout nature; it is the template or paradigm from which all environmental phenomena take their form: the round of the seasons, the birth and aging of a man, the course of a day, the formation and wearing away of the very rocks. Taking up the different terrestrial kingdoms of "fossils," vegetables, and animals, he demonstrates in each how the same pattern prevails; there is in all three an unending, interlocking process he identifies as "propagation, preservation, and destruction." As the crust of the earth matures, for instance, there begins "a perpetual succession" of plants. Marshes dry up, sphagnum moss gains a foothold, the rushes follow to plant their roots in the porous mold formed by the moss, and so forth, until at last "the whole marsh is changed into a fine and delightful meadow." But someday the meadow must be submerged in water and begin once more its cycle of maturation. Similarly, the "crustaceous liverworts" must await the appearance of bare rocks from a receding sea before they can find a place to grow and so prepare conditions for more advanced species to succeed them. In this rotating wheel of existence all is evolving but nothing is ever changed, because the methods for renewal and preservation contrived by God serve "to perpetuate the established course of nature in a continuous series."

Circulating in the natural economy is a dazzling profusion of species, all made to perform together with symphonic precision. For the purposes of rational order and harmony, Linnaeus explains, the Creator has assigned to each creature its peculiar food, and He also sets firm limits to its geographical range. The horse will not eat the shortleaved water hemlock, but the goat will. The goat in turn leaves the monkshood to the horse, and the cow surrenders the longleaved water hemlock to the sheep. "Hence no plant is absolutely poisonous, but only respectively." Some plants are made to be "impatient of cold" and to live in the tropics, while others thrive in the frigid clime of Siberia. A wise God has endowed each organism with the "cloathing," seeds, roots, or migratory instincts it will need to best perform its role. From the evidence of these special adaptations, Linnaeus concludes that every creature has its "allotted place," which is both its location in space and its function or work in the general economy. No conceivable place stands empty; each has its specialist, equipped to perform its function with skill and dispatch. The scavengers, for instance, labor to keep the earth tidy and clean, and by way of compensation the bursary of nature supplies them with the necessaries of life. By an intricate hierarchical arrangement, each species serves to support others as it earns its own living.

Thus the tree-louse lives upon the plants. The fly called musca aphidovora lives upon the tree-louse. The hornet and wasp fly upon the musca aphidovora. The dragon fly upon the hornet and wasp fly. The spider upon the dragon fly. The small birds on the spider. And lastly the hawk kind on the small birds.

All of animate nature is thus bound together in common interest by the chains of sustenance that link the living to the dead, the predator to its prey, the beetle to the dung on which it feeds.

By assigning to all species their unique kinds of food and by "putting limits to their appetites," Linnaeus maintains, God has set up an enduring community of peaceful coexistence. "An animal of one kind cannot rob those of another kind of its aliment; which, if it happened, would endanger their lives or health." The divine economy guarantees a full abundance to all; there are no scarcities in nature. This happy condition can exist only because the Creator has also established the minimum and maximum rates of reproduction for every plant and animal, expressly forbidding "the bird kind to fall short of the number of eggs allotted to each species." It is the very charge of many species to strive to multiply beyond their present numbers, rather than to hold their population constant. Without such a provision, the predators would soon be out of work. Thus the Creator arranges a system of differential reproduction rates by which the "harmless and esculent animals" will safely reproduce more than the predators, thereby maintaining their own numbers while providing a livelihood for their neighbors. That some creatures are created only to be "miserably butchered by others" is essential to the plan of Providence, in order to keep "a just proportion amongst all the species; and so prevent any one of them increasing too much, to the detriment of men, and other animals."

Man and his ambitions in the natural economy are an integral part of the Linnaean model. Although they are like any other species in living as subordinate parts of the divine order, humans at the same time occupy a special place of dignity and honor.

All these treasures of nature, so artfully contrived, so wonderfully propagated, so providentially supported throughout her three kingdoms, seem intended by the Creator for the sake of man. Every thing may be made subservient to his use; if not immediately, yet mediately, not so to that of other animals. By the help of reason man tames the fiercest animals, pursues and catches the swiftest, nay he is able to reach even those, which lye hidden in the bottom of the sea.

According to Linnaeus, man must vigorously pursue his assigned work of utilizing his fellow species to his own advantage. This responsibility must extend to eliminating the undesirables and multiplying those that are useful to him, an operation "which nature, left to herself, could scarcely effect." Created to praise and emulate the Creator, men fulfill their obligations not by choosing to be "mere idle spectators" but by making nature's productions accrue to the enrichment of the human economy. In a fervent, Bacon-like exhortation to human industry, Linnaeus contends that "the pious consideration of this glorious palace" of nature should suggest an active, imperial kind of religious enthusiasm. From his scientific study of the intricately contrived economic order, he concludes that "all things are made for the sake of man" and that, in the process of "admiring the works of the Creator," man might also be expected to enjoy "all those things, of which he stands in need, in order to pass his life conveniently and pleasantly."

As early as 1530 the word "oeconomy," as employed in the title of Linnaeus' essay, was used to refer to the art of household management. Derived from the Greek word *oikos*, or house, it was eventually extended to mean the political administration of all the resources of a community or state for orderly production. Along another line of development, theologians had long made the Latin *oeconomia* interchangeable with God's "dispensations," and by the seventeenth century "oeconomy" was frequently employed to refer to the divine government of the natural world. God's economy was His extraordinary talent for matching means to ends, for so managing the cosmos that each constituent part performed its work with stunning efficiency. In 1658 Sir Kenelm Digby, who was active in promoting the growth of a natural science compatible with religion, was the first to speak of an "oeconomy of nature." Throughout the eighteenth century, the phrase incorporated portions of all these definitions to denote the grand organization and government of life on earth: the rational ordering of all material resources in an interacting whole. God was seen both as the Supreme Economist who had designed the earth household and as the housekeeper who kept it functioning productively.

Thus the study of "ecology"—a word that appeared in the nineteenth century as a more scientific substitute for the older phrase—was in its very origins imbued with a political and economic as well as Christian view of nature: the earth was perceived as a world that must be somehow managed for maximum output. This tendency to borrow heavily from politics and economics—their values along with their metaphors—is a crucial characteristic in the study of ecology, as we will see here and in other chapters.[9]

"By the Oeconomy of Nature," Linnaeus wrote, "we understand the all-wise disposition of the Creator in relation

The Empire of Reason • 3 7

to natural things, by which they are fitted to produce general ends, and reciprocal uses." In this arrangement, living beings "are so connected, so chained together, that they all aim at the same end, and to this end a vast number of intermediate ends are subservient." The search for "general ends," for an overriding purpose and agency in nature, was the central impetus to the "economical" or ecological approach to natural history.

Besides Linnaeus' pivotal essay, the leading works in this new field ranged from John Ray's *The Wisdom of God Manifested in the Works of Creation* (1691) and William Derham's *Physico-Theology* (1713) to William Paley's *Natural Theology* (1802) and the Bridgewater Treatises (1833-36). All of these were important sources for modern ecological theory; at the same time all were concerned as much with religious as with scientific matters. United by their common repudiation of doctrinal schisms and of claims to private mystical revelations, this school of Linnaeus confidently looked to reason and the testimony of nature to establish their faith on a firm, universally acceptable ground. They also believed that only through science could atheism be confronted without weakness. Thomas Morgan summarized their thesis well:

This perfect Unity, Order, Wisdom, and Design, by which every Individual is necessarily related to, and made a dependent Part of the Whole, necessarily supposes and implies a universal, designing Mind, an all-powerful Agent, who has contrived, adjusted, and disposed the Whole into such Order, Uniformity, concordant Beauty and Harmony, and who continues to support, govern, and direct the Whole.

And according to the evangelist John Wesley, who contributed his own volume on ecology, "the design and will of the Creator is the only physical cause of the general economy of the world."[10]

The Linnaean model of ecology, as echoed in these various writings, rested on three important assumptions about the economic interactions in nature, assumptions firmly grounded in eighteenth-century culture. Each of these had its serious inner tensions and ambiguities, evident in the work of Linnaeus himself, that remained only partially submerged. These difficulties were ignored so long as scientists and theologians were united in the desire to work out a marriage between their fields; however, this union had as many incompatibilities as mutual attractions and was in danger of dissolving from the start. Even after the rift had come, many naturalists refused to acknowledge the failure. Indeed, until 1859—the year Charles Darwin published his *Origin of Species*—a significant proportion of the Anglo-American works touching on ecological themes continued to teach these central principles of the economy of nature worked out by the Linnaeans.

The first of these three ruling axioms in Linnaean ecology was the belief that the Creator had designed an integrated order in nature which functioned like a single, universal, well-oiled machine. In the seventeenth century, modern science had found both a metaphor and a method of analysis that promised to make nature wholly amenable to reason. From the work of Galileo, Descartes, and Newton, in particular, there emerged the figure of a vast celestial contrivance set in operation by an omniscient mechanic-mathematician. The contribution of the old Mosaic account of creation to this new scientific world view has already been suggested. A more immediate influence, however, was the ferment in technological innovation during the very period that modern science was getting its start. It was predictable, then, that scientists should begin to focus on just those aspects of nature that seemed most clearly to resemble the new mechanical artifacts of the workshop. In trying to rationalize natural phenomena on the one hand and the human productive apparatus on the other, scientist and engineer alike were attracted to the mechanistic image of detachable, replaceable parts made to move smoothly together by the external skill of an artisan. Moreover, it was not in the least unusual in the seventeenth or eighteenth century for leading scientists to first explain that nature was simply another machine, and then go on to draw from this larger model mechanical inventions by which man might better his condition. But the more important link between the two professions was intellectual: Both gave a mechanistic answer to the question of what nature is and what it ought to be. Both, moreover, found it necessary to ignore any aspect of nature that could not be made to fit into this mechanical picture.[11]

The mechanization of the modern world view began first in physics and astronomy. On the authority of Isaac Newton, English biologists too were encouraged to take up the mechanical philosophy, and its companion, a utilitarian bias toward nature, followed closely behind. There was an eager rush to see all living organisms as parts of what George Cheyne called "the whole great and complicated Machine of the Universe." Nothing could escape from the mechanical maw. René Descartes declared, for example, that animals are no more than machines, totally incapable of feeling pain or pleasure—a view that had gruesome results in many laboratory experiments in France. In ecology the argument went that, like a planet in its orbit or a gear in its box, each species exists to perform some function in the grand apparatus. The implications of this mechanistic outlook, however, might well have seemed ominous. By reducing plants and animals to insensate matter, mere conglomerates of atomic particles devoid of internal purpose or intelligence, the naturalist was removing the remaining barriers to unrestrained economic exploitation. Man's conjoining species, perhaps himself as well, and the ecological order they formed would be studied as a lifeless, impersonal fabrication, admirable in its cleverness, perhaps, but not suitable for any emotional investment by men and women. The Christian devaluation of nature was thus focused into the even more alienating vision of eighteenth-century mechanism.

But however much they may have been captivated by the precision of the Machine, few of the Linnaean school were prepared to adopt a full-fledged mechanistic materialism that would confine all living nature to the laws of physics. They could not accept the dangerous cosmologies of Descartes and Leibnitz, in which the divine controlling hand was replaced by the fortuitous movement of brute matter. In other words, the mechanical philosophy might become under certain circumstances a first step toward atheism, by denying the Creator's active involvement in nature. Without a constant superintending power to hold the machine together, the pious Linnaeans feared, all the components might fly apart and the entire apparatus collapse. Benjamin Stillingfleet voiced this anxiety in the lines he appended to Linnaeus' essay of 1749:

> Order bereft of thought, uncaus'd effects,
> Fate freely acting, and unerring Chance.
> Where meanless matter to a chaos sinks
> Or something lower still, for without thee
> It crumbles into atoms void of force,
> Void of resistance—it eludes our thought.
> Where laws eternal to the varying code
> Of self-love dwindle. Interest, passion, whim
> Take place of right, and wrong. . . .

Descartes' all-out mechanism threatened to destroy this rational moral order and set up in its stead the chaotic struggle of atom against atom and individual against individual. The problem for the Linnaeans, therefore, was to find a mechanical model that left some room for the influence of a nonmaterial power. Newton, an orthodox Christian, had again pointed the way; for him God was the crucial motive force behind the Cosmic Machine, the unexplainable source of energy that it needed to keep its order perfect and regular. Similarly, Robert Boyle decided after all that a few imperfections in nature were necessary to justify the existence of a God who must intervene now and then to set things right. The Linnaeans too followed this more moderate philosophy of mechanism rather than Descartes'; they tried, in short, to adopt the mechanical metaphor without becoming rigid mechanists in every aspect of their science.[12]

It was a tricky strategy, this attempt to batter down the emotional resistance to science and mechanism without being overrun by the Cartesian extremists in the rear. Some philosophers gave it up as hopeless and turned instead to what would become the major alternative to mechanism: an organismic ecology that made nature analogous, not to a machine, but to the human body—a composite of matter infused with spirit and purpose. The most significant articulation of this thesis came from Henry More, a lecturer at Cambridge who was much taken with the pagan animism of Plato and Plotinus. Like them, More argued for the existence of "a Soul of the World, or Spirit of Nature." He described this force as "a substance incorporeal but without sense and animadversion, pervading the whole matter of the universe, and exercising a plastical power therein ... raising such Phenomena in the world ... as cannot be resolved into mere mechanical powers." On a smaller scale, he posited a vital, organizing power in individual plants and animals which makes these beings more than the "mere motion of matter." This indwelling power is analogous to the "vital congruity" that causes the elements of nature to hold closely together without "gross mechanical" constraint. More replaced the concept of the Supreme Engineer with what he called an *Anima Mundi* as the everyday active force in nature. It would become, especially for the Romantics, the basis for opposition not only to mechanistic science but also to the Baconian outlook and its imperialist ethic toward nature.[13]

For more orthodox persons who would see in this *Anima Mundi* a substitute for God's transcendent relation to nature, More's animism had to be dressed in acceptable garb. The tailor who undertook the fitting was John Ray, a blacksmith's son who graduated from Oxford and later became a close friend of Henry More. Some have also called him the most important naturalist in England before Charles Darwin. After a lifetime of work in taxonomy, Ray, at the age of sixty-four, turned in his work of 1691, *The Wisdom of God Manifested in the Creation*, to "that grand Argument for a God taken from the Phenomenon of the Artificial frame of things." His special targets in this work were Descartes and the "Atomick Theists," who he feared had weakened the case for religious faith by making God an idle spectator while millions of atoms aimlessly collided in the vortices of space. Meanwhile, the true atheists were "laughing in their Sleeves, and not a little triumphing to see the Cause of Theism thus betrayed by its professed Friends and Assertors, and the grand Argument for the same totally slurred by them and so their work done, as it were, to their hands." At first Ray attempted to salvage the mechanical philosophy from the abuses of those who were using it to account for nature "without the intervention and assistance of any superior immaterial agent." After comparing the "vast multitude of different sort of creatures" to such contrivances as "clocks and watches, and pumps and mills, and granadoes and rockets," he suggested that such artificiality in nature must imply the existence of a designing, superintending deity.[14]

But then Ray proceeded to introduce More's "plastical power" into this supposedly finished ecological machine. Living creatures, he maintained, are not mere automatons or lifeless machines, but free agents that operate by "some intelligent Plastick Nature, which may understand and regulate" their growth and movement. This mysterious inner force—a clear anticipation of Henri Bergson's *élan vital*—functions as a power subordinate to the Creator's will; it is derived from his own greater energy. Ray would not go the full distance and make the indwelling regulatory factor identical with God, nor did he fuse its individual manifestations into an *Anima Mundi*, as More proposed. Instead, the ecological system appears as the joint work of a "Wise Superintendent," who lays down the general design, and his intelligent, purposeful agents in nature who furnish the details. The upshot of this compromise between pagan animism and the mechanical metaphor was that Ray could continue to praise the excellent workmanship of God while at the same time explaining any imperfections in nature as the consequence of the "plastick" power at work in the individual organism. Equally important, the compromise maintained nature as a stable, enduring order without denying the obvious realities of change.[15]

Whatever the philosophical difficulties in Ray's middle ground, it could have provided for the Linnaeans an escape of sorts from the entanglements of the simple machine metaphor. By recognizing in living beings the possibility of choice, error, and randomness, Ray in effect admitted that it was impossible to apply rigidly the model of the Newtonian machine to the earth and its species. But the majority of naturalists in the eighteenth century naively persisted in extolling only the precision of the economy of nature, caught up as they were in admiration for the mechanistic design and yet frightened by the Cartesian specter of chaos.

The most popular figure in this school of ecological mechanism, after Linnaeus, was Bishop William Paley, whose *Natural Theology* was an eloquent if largely plagiarized and unsophisticated version of the mechanical theory. The design theorists congratulated themselves—prematurely, as it turned out—on this latest triumph by one of their party. After consorting at length with mechanistic science, however, they eventually found themselves inescapably imprisoned in its camp. While they gloated over their triumphs against the forces of irrationality, pagan heresy, and superstition, plans for their own execution (and by their own weapons) were being laid by a new generation of scientists who were unabashedly nonbelievers. These men would announce that they no longer needed the "hypothesis" of a God; physics would explain it all. Nature would then appear as a self-contrived mechanism that needed no external engineer—or at least none but man.

Besides its mechanical precision, the most widely accepted characteristic of the economy of nature in the Age of Reason was its benevolence. Nature, it was generally agreed, is an order expressive of God's kindness toward his creatures, and especially toward man, for whom the creation primarily exists. Without this divine generosity, argued the Reverend William Derham, a Fellow of the Royal Society, the animals of the earth would have been stuck with organs unsuited to their climate and food.

Consequently all the animal world would have been in a confused, inconvenient, and disorderly commixture. One animal would have wanted food; another habitation, and most of them safety. They would have all flocked to one or a few places, taken up rest in the temperate zones only, and coveted one food, the easiest to come at, and most specious in shew; and so would have poisoned, starved, or greatly incommoded one another. But as the matter is now ordered, the globe is equally bespread, so that no place wanteth proper inhabitants, nor any creature is destitute of a proper place, and all things necessary to its life, health, and pleasure.

Specific examples of the fitness of the environment for its denizens were regularly summoned up to provide what naturalists confidently believed was proof of the goodness of the Creator.[16]

But this optimism was thin ice, easily broken. Fear that it might not support the weight it was given is often apparent in the writings of the Linnaeans. Most threatening of all to the idea of nature's benevolence was the menacing portrayal by the seventeenth-century political philosopher Thomas Hobbes, who was well known, even notorious, for describing nature and the natural condition of mankind as a state of fear, conflict, and violence: "such a war, as is of every man, against every man." Hobbes warned that "without a common power to keep them all in awe," men would live as animals; they would be wholly lacking in virtue and morality as well as in agriculture, arts, and letters. In the absence of external restraint by government, human life would be "solitary, poor, nasty, brutish, and short." The effect of these views was to make of nature again a dangerous chaos, a scene of cruelty and rapine. Once more the Linnaeans had to defend nature's reputation against such slander. But their defense, ironically, accepted much of Hobbes' argument. Nature is no anarchy, they replied, because it already has its laws, laid down by a monarch who rules with absolute control. In other words, what Hobbes wanted for the human estate, an almighty Leviathan, was already in force in nature. Without such a monarch, the naturalists in effect admitted, they would have been left precisely with the Hobbesian jungle—for they, like him, had no confidence in the creatures around them, if left unsupervised and unmanaged. The ecological system of the Linnaeans then became a closely governed state, as well as a well-contrived machine and an orderly household.[17]

One of the most important laws the Creator had established to assure peace in the natural community was what Soame Jenyns described as the "vast and beautiful system of subordination." Each species, it was repeated throughout the century, has been assigned a fixed place in a social hierarchy or scale of being. The Linnaean school counted few leveling democrats. According to *The Spectator* in 1712:

The Creator of the Universe has appointed every thing to a certain Use and Purpose, and determined it to a settled Course and

Sphere of Action, from which, if it in the least deviates, it becomes unfit to answer those Ends for which it was designed. In like Manner is it in the Dispositions of Society, the civil Oeconomy is formed in a Chain as well as the natural; and in either case the Breach but of one Link puts the Whole into some Disorder.

The notion of a chain of being has been analyzed brilliantly by Arthur Lovejoy, but only as a metaphor of organic development in nature that later became influential in evolutionary theory. The infinitude of species ranged on an ascending ladder of nobility was more than a taxonomic system, however; it was also a description of ecological relatedness. The chain of being was a system of economic interdependence and mutual assistance. Even the most exalted creatures must depend upon those lower on the scale for their very existence; man and worm alike live to preserve each other's life. Richard Pulteney spoke of "that perfect order and just subordination of all the several parts of nature, by which they are rendered mutually subservient to the conservation of each other, and of the whole." That the natural economy had its interdependent social ranks and classes appealed to the naturalist as a firm guarantee against Hobbesian violence. But it also, in theory at least, ensured that all creatures in nature, great and small, were accorded some measure of safety and value. Each was granted a right to the resources it needed for survival. Human beings, to be sure, would need more than hedgehogs did for their self-fulfillment, just as lords and ladies required more than peasants did. But all had legitimate claims to make on the earth and on each other.[18]
Even when these rankings had been carefully described, however, there was a residuum of suspicion that perhaps Hobbes was right about nature after all. William Smellie, author of The Philosophy of Natural History, spoke fearfully of "the general system of carnage established by nature" in which "the weaker are uniformly preyed upon by the stronger." And Linnaeus, in his essay "The Polity of Nature," saw a nightmare of animals "not only gorging on the most beautiful flowers, but also mercilessly tearing each other to pieces"; the earth could suddenly appear to be, as he admitted, "a war of all against all." Long before

Alfred Tennyson's lament about a nature "red in tooth and claw," naturalists had to explain the bloodshed and suffering in the world. It was, in fact, the most serious challenge to their assertion of cosmic benevolence and the ascendancy of divine moral principle in nature. William Kirby, in one of the Bridgewater Treatises of the 1830s, summed up the standard rationalization of the presence of conflict and pain in nature—"this mass of seeming evil pervading the whole circuit of the animal creation"; evidently, he decided, it must be God's will that the individual suffer for the benefit of the whole community. And fortunately, "there is an unseen hand directing all to accomplish this great object, and taking care that the destruction shall in no case exceed the necessity." All destruction, it was paradoxically argued, is the means to a continuity of life. Through its dreadful agency comes the possibility for a maximum abundance of species and individuals, and such an abundance or plenitude of being is further proof of God's benevolence.[19]

A more elaborate justification for violence and the predatory system in nature came from John Bruckner, a Lutheran divine of the Linnaean school, in his book *A Philosophical Survey of the Animal Creation* (1768). The task he undertook was to reconcile the "Institution of general Devastation and Carnage" among species with the common assumption of "the felicity of the universe." In the process of finding a persuasive brief for the ways of God in nature, Bruckner developed two sharply contrasting models of animal ecology. In the first he gave a faithful restatement of the machine analogy, so that animals become so many mechanical contraptions moved by tiny springs, all "nicely poized" and interconnected; the larger order of nature too appears as "an assemblage of parts" carefully balanced and spinning in "perpetual motion." In the second model, however, nature is described as "one continued web of life"—a swarming, animated mass of vitality that defies rational ideas of order and economy. Evidently the static Newtonian approach could not begin to express Bruckner's awful sense of the seething exuberance of life, especially as encountered in the tropics, "where the vital substance fermenting as it were into life by the heat of the sun, breaks forth precipitately from its matrix, and spreads with a kind of fury over the whole land." Here the vital juices seem to ooze out of the very soil, and a man can hardly see or breathe as the "moschetos" fly through the air in dense, buzzing clouds.

In every species . . . life may be considered as an impetuous torrent, which is incessantly bearing down, and beating against the banks that oppose its course; and whenever it breaks through this barrier, it spreads into a tremendous ocean.

This life principle—"an inexplicable something . . . which no man can comprehend"—was an inner fire that defied the regular, clockwork precision of the mechanistic model. Nor could it be well appreciated in the tidy northern climate of England, where man had generally managed to domesticate nature. But in the warmer latitudes, this violent energy threatened not only man's hegemony but perhaps even the notion of a Supreme Engineer.[20]

The life force, Bruckner concluded, must be by its very nature a power divided against itself. "One part of life is perpetually at war with the other; one half of this living substance feeds upon another." Like a creature that tries to grow by eating its own members, the principle of life acts as a composite organism that engulfs both prey and predators, hosts and parasites. Even death is turned to advantage by this sovereign torrent that refuses to be defeated or even momentarily abated. By "the wonderful economy of nature," Bruckner marveled, the dead carcass feeds the scavenger and thus does the animating flame, "after it is extinguished in one class of animals, immediately re-kindle itself in another, and burn with fresh lustre and strength." This system of virtual cannibalism is not a failure or weakness in God's design; it is the inescapable natere of life itself, and once brought into existence, its self-propagating capacity leads it to fill up every conceivable nook or cranny. Bruckner was no evolutionist, but in considering the problem of violence he had hit upon an organic power in nature that would not be easily contained in the fixed species and perpetual cycles of matter in Linnaeus' ecological system. The vital energy coursing through nature creates a highly unstable composite; it is

a web of curious contexture, wrought with soft, weak, fragile, delicate materials, forming all together a piece admirable in its construction and destination, and for this very reason subject to ten thousand accidents.

Like John Ray, Bruckner was forced to radically modify the mechanical metaphor in order to cope with an organic world that was alive, aggressive, opportunistic, and thus imperfect. It was also vaguely repulsive in its writhing violence, at times even evil. This was not a nature that could easily be loved.[21]

Yet, for Bruckner, God's purpose in bringing this violent force into being was still grandly benevolent. Providing for the greatest good, he was sure, required the granting of life to the greatest possible number and variety of beings. And this was feasible only by unleashing the organic force. The goal of plenitude, in other words, was the ultimate reason for death and suffering. Only in a world of pure, disembodied intelligence could an infinite variety of beings coexist without preying on one another, and only in such a world could violence be avoided. The earth lives by another principle: to guarantee the "production and conservation" of the fullest possible "abundance of life." From God's benevolence and the exuberance of nature, it is assured that life "has its sweets for all."[22]

One thorny problem, however, was left unresolved by the plenitude principle. The progress of the human species in particular often seriously diminished the number and variety of other species. Bruckner noted that the Americans, for example, in clearing forests to cultivate the land threatened ten species for each one they aided. Was not man then a powerful offender against the order instituted by God? If all beings are joined together by a common inner life force, did a single species have the right to exploit that force to its exclusive benefit? Were human power and selfishness capable of wrecking the plenitude ideal? Bruckner's argument had led him to a kind of ecological ethic that gave to each being a full right to existence and valued each for its unique expression of the vital fire. According to this moral law in nature, the earth cannot exist solely for man but is the common property of all species. Denying that "every thing in the creation has an ultimate reference to man, and that

God exerts his plastic power for man alone," Bruckner went so far as to suggest the "infinite multitude of beings" that must exist on the other planets of the cosmos, far beyond the range of human exploitation. Man clearly was not set up as the proprietor of "the whole plan of providence."[23]

Contradictions in his ecological model, however, held Bruckner back from a full indictment of the disruptive effects of the human species. Neither he nor any other naturalist of his time could believe that a benevolent God would have made it possible for man truly to diminish the abundance of life on earth.

It is, I say, five thousand years at least that one part of the living substance has waged continual war with the other, yet we do not find that this Law of Nature has to this day occasioned the extinction of any one species. Nay, we may add, it is this which has preserved them in that State of perpetual youth and vigor in which we behold them.

Apparently the web of life could withstand anything that a mere human might do, and might, indeed, even benefit from the stimulus of man's aggressions. The paradoxical effect of this notion was to turn Bruckner's criticism into acclaim, insofar as he extolled humankind as "masters and governors" whose special office it is to "watch over all the other species, and maintain the balance betwixt them," even if that duty meant waging all-out warfare against man's natural enemies. To promote his own well-being, Bruckner allowed, man should continue to extend his "empire over the other animals," with the assurance that nature's economy as designed by God will survive all that he does. The ultimate evidence of providential goodness and foresight in nature was that it could endure even man's violence.[24]

The ecological or life ethic implicit in the principle of plenitude was left largely undeveloped by Bruckner and the other Linnaean ecologists. If the order of animate nature was meant to be something more than a mere bauble, they believed, if it has practical value, then it must have been contrived by the divine hand chiefly for the welfare of man, that most noble of species. As God's specially appointed vice-regent on earth, mankind has explicit permission to manage the natural economy for its own profit. Dr. W. S. W. Ruschenberger summed up a theme prominent for almost two centuries in natural history, and indeed all the way back to the Genesis story of creation, when he declared in 1852: "It is among the pleasures of a Christian to believe that God, in his bountiful goodness, created every animate and inanimate thing in nature for the benefit of man." Not everyone would have agreed unreservedly with the brash American, but shadings of the same sentiment were plentiful. William Smellie noted with enthusiastic approval that "the uniform scope of human industry" has been "to diminish the noxious animals, and to augment that of useful vegetables." William Derham saw in the unclothed, unhoused state of primitive man a divinely contrived stimulus to human industry, a perpetual challenge to man from on high to contrive his own environment.[25]

Notwithstanding their regard for nature as prepared by the hand of God, these Linnaeans in England and America were eager to enlist in Lord Bacon's imperialist cause: "the enlargement of the bounds of Human Empire, to the effecting of all things possible." The study of ecology was for them a means to the vigorous conquest of the living world. On the Continent, too, the influence of Bacon was strongly felt in the eighteenth century; in France, for example, Diderot, Condorcet, and Buffon all rushed to herald the coming kingdom of mind over matter and man over nature. Reason was to be the weapon by which this empire would be won—reason defined not merely as the critical faculty of the mind, but as the aggressive power represented in "Active Science."[26]

In contrast to this imperial ethic, John Ray learned from his friend Henry More that it is only the "rusticity" of the human ego that leads men to believe that all nature exists solely for their use. This sense of humility was an integral part of the pagan philosophy revived by More and the Virgilian arcadians. If all creatures, including man, are animated by a universal, indwelling organic spirit, then no one species could conceivably assume that the whole existed for its benefit alone. But even John Ray and Henry More were often less impressed by this argument than by its exact opposite. Like Bacon and other ecological imperialists, Ray maintained that God expects man to establish a rational empire over this earthly abode. Providence, he believed, is well pleased "with the Industry of Man in adorning the Earth with beautiful Cities and Castles, with pleasant Villages and Country Houses, . . . and whatever differenceth a civil and well cultivated Region from a barren and desolate Wilderness." Despite a strong sense of piety toward God as revealed by His creation, the almost universal response of the Linnaeans to the condition of man in his natural state was scorn and disgust. Each species, according to Ray and his colleagues, was put in its place to labor. And for humans, diligence in what Derham liked to call their "business" must bring an elevation in dignity and material condition.[27]

The climate of opinion in the Age of Reason was unblushingly utilitarian, and the Linnaean naturalists did no more than follow the attitude toward nature that dominated in Anglo-American culture. Almost everyone was sure that God intended for all His creation, and for man above all, to be happy on earth; and happiness, in this period, meant material comfort if it meant anything. While scientists busied themselves in collecting and classifying the facts of nature and in aligning their piety with their science, they also managed to create an ecological model that accurately mirrored the popular bourgeois mood. Its fundamental assumption was that the "economy" of nature is designed by Providence to maximize production and efficiency. Hence the principle of plenitude was more often an expression of reverential respect for the useful productiveness of nature than a moral response to the idea of the life force. And for every organism in the system, the naturalist had to discover a utilitarian role. The Reverend Nicholas Collin, for example, asked his fellows at the American Philosophical Society whether it might not be wise to protect "those birds deemed of no value"—at least until it was determined "what part is assigned to them in the oeconomy of nature." Certainly conservation as well as utilization was a part of God's design, and therefore must be a part of man's consciousness too. But usually conservation was conveniently left to Providence. The Linnaean ecological model had much more to say about the human mission to exploit than to preserve.[28]

In its utilitarianism the Linnaean age of ecology strongly echoed the values of the Manchester and Birmingham industrialists and of the English agricultural reformers of the same period. Their view of nature was shared, moreover, by the new students of the human political economy, who were beginning to organize at this time. The relationship was reciprocal and reinforcing. The economist Nehemiah Grew, for example, could move easily from botany to the national economic system; wearing either hat, he could argue untiringly for "augmenting national productive efficiency" by stepping up the exploitation of forests, livestock, and fisheries. Adam Smith, the founding genius of modern economics and a learned disciple of Linnaean natural history, saw nature as no more than a storehouse of raw materials for man's ingenuity. And while the Reverend Thomas Malthus worried more than these others about how many people the land could support, he thoroughly agreed that the natural economy's sole function was to provide for man's ambitions. In such a milieu, it is hardly surprising that naturalists joined the popular chorus, their writings reflecting the ruling managerial and exploitive bias.[29]

The ecology of the Linnaeans, then, dovetailed neatly with the needs of the new factory society. This became starkly clear with the publication in 1855—over a century after Linnaeus' "Oeconomy of Nature,"—of Thomas Ewbank's *The World a Workshop*. It was a kind of culmination of the imperial tradition that had long made nature subservient to man's needs and reason. According to Ewbank, who was a former manufacturer and United States Commissioner of Patents, the earth and its productions have been fitted out expressly "for the cultivation and application of chemical and mechanical science as the basis of human development." The unity of "the general economy of the world" he took as evidence that the planet "was designed for a Factory," furnished by "the Great Engineer" with all the equipment of a complete machine shop, heated

The Empire of Reason • 5 3

by a gigantic furnace at its core, and ready for its chief tenant and manager to go to work.

To meet man's wants through the entire cycle of his destinies, to furnish employment for the varied world of thought within him, to keep pace with his enlarging grasp and power, it was necessary that suitable materials, and objects, and forces, and theatres of action should be provided for him. And so it is, that there is no substance, quality, or condition of matter but what tends to further his operations as a manufacturer; none which does not exhibit the world as a factory, and him in charge of it; and which does not show that such was the grand scope and design of the Creator in preparing it, and placing him on it.

God must be actively emulated in his role of "mechanician" rather than worshipped in spiritual passivity and "the old leaven of mysticism," which tend to retard progress and allow "the earth to grow up a jungle." Man's religious duty is to transform these products of "nature's mills" into new machines for his own use and "to cover the earth with barns, workshops and dwellings, roads and canals." He is, in short, "to become in its widest sense a manufacturer."[30]

At this point some important implications of eighteenth-century ecological theory had come fully into view. Though Linnaeus could not have anticipated all of Ewbank's argument, he nevertheless would have agreed with the manufacturer that the chief characteristic of nature is its productivity, real and potential, and that men must not remain, in his words, "idle spectators" of this useful mechanism. What the hand of God had contrived in the economy of nature must become in turn the incentive for man's contriving genius: that was not only a fair conclusion from the premises of Linnaean ecology, but also its inescapable ethic.

To some extent, Linnaeus and his followers could agree with Gilbert White that the Creator did not plan the order of nature according to "our private principles of economy" nor "always calculate exactly according to our way of reckoning." This admission suggests that the Linnaean model of ecology could serve as a restraint as well as a stimulus to the exploitation of the environment. After all, the handiwork of God was still to be admired as a form of perfection. In their pious approach "through Nature to Nature's God," the Linnaeans were confronted with moral constraints that did not trouble the more thoroughgoing Baconians. Perhaps Mircea Eliade is right when he claims that for a religious man, whatever his creed, nature is always fraught with a sense of the sacred.[31]

Probably the most effective of the moderating influences on the imperialist view of nature, however, came not from Christianity or its theological constraints but from the pagan, arcadian impulse that recurs throughout the period. It was this current of feeling that found expression in the life of the Selborne parson-naturalist and was thence passed on to later generations. In the Age of Reason, this arcadian mood was often swept aside in the rush for man's empire over nature, but it by no means disappeared, in science or in the larger Anglo-American culture. It would surface much later in the writings of naturalists like John Burroughs and ecologists like Rachel Carson, and it was an essential element in the work of Charles Darwin. Most significantly, in terms of the development of ecological values, the arcadian stance gained influence during the first half of the nineteenth century with the rise of the Romantic movement. Arriving on the very heels of the triumph of Baconianism, the Romantics caught up White's relation to nature, carried it far beyond the borders of Selborne parish, and impressed it indelibly on the western consciousness.

PART TWO

THE SUBVERSIVE SCIENCE:

THOREAU'S ROMANTIC ECOLOGY

IF ECOLOGY *is a "subversive subject," as Paul Sears suggests, what is it trying to subvert? Some of the possibilities that come to mind are: the accepted notion of what science does; the values and institutions of expansionary capitalism; the bias against nature in western religion. All of these were targets of the nineteenth-century Romantics; they were the first great subversives of modern times. Understanding their point of view, therefore, will contribute to our understanding of the ecology movement today.*

But the connection between contemporary ecology and Romanticism is even more direct than this sharing of antagonists. The Romantic approach to nature was fundamentally ecological; that is, it was concerned with relation, interdependence, and holism. Nowhere is this similarity of outlook more clearly revealed than in the writings of Henry David Thoreau (1817–1862), the nineteenth-century inheritor of Gilbert White's arcadian legacy. Thoreau was both an active field ecologist and a philosopher of nature whose ideas anticipated much in the mood of our own time. In his life and work we find a key expression of the Romantic stance toward the earth as well as an increasingly complex and sophisticated ecological philosophy. We find in Thoreau, too, a remarkable source of inspiration and guidance for the subversive activism of the recent ecology movement.

CHAPTER 3

A Naturalist in Concord

DESPITE THE TESTIMONY of the newspapers, the contest for the American presidency waged by Franklin Pierce and Winfield Scott was not the only important news of 1852. There were, in fact, a number of more significant events. In that year, for instance, Harriet Beecher Stowe published her *Uncle Tom's Cabin*, which became one of the anti-slavery crusade's most powerful weapons. And in the same year George Sanders set forth in the pages of the *Democratic Review* an eloquent statement of the purposes of the Young America movement, emphasizing aggressive nationalism and manifest destiny. But more pregnant with meaning than any of these, at least for Henry Thoreau, was the arrival of spring in Concord, Massachusetts. A self-styled "inspector of snowstorms" during the winter, he now was on hand to report the vernal revolution for "a journal, of no very wide circulation." Indeed there was but one reader for this news: himself.

According to Thoreau's 1852 dispatches, the ice on Walden Pond began to melt on April 14, though eight inches of snow still covered the ground. Within the space of two more weeks the hylas were peeping in the swamps, the willow catkins and purplish cudweed were blooming, and wild geese were honking their way northward. While most Americans were looking the other way, Thoreau saw the original order of the world's creation recapitulated before his eyes with the coming of that new year. After the March equinox, as the sun seemed to move farther north and the ice began to vanish, the water-loving plants first appeared, and then those growing on bare rocks, on scanty soil, and on land recently bared of frost. Flying insects, waterbugs, and earthworms followed the progress of vegetation, and after them came birds back from their winter havens and rodents from their hibernating burrows, all searching for food and mates. By fits and starts the springing of the seasons had commenced, and so began what the very private reporter Thoreau called his "year of observation."[1]

After several decades of happy, innocent wandering through the local orchards and woods, Thoreau now began at the age of thirty-five to approach nature with more method and precision. He became a self-educated naturalist, a competent field ecologist. Textbooks in hand, he set out to identify each green sprout or returning migrant as it appeared on the Concord scene during the ensuing months. Some fifteen years earlier he had acquired his first botany text, Bigelow's *Plants of Boston and Vicinity*, and as a student at Harvard he had studied William Smellie's eighteenth-century classic of physico-theology, *The Philosophy of Natural History*. Now he began to assemble a more complete naturalist's library and to make trips into Boston to visit the rooms of the Natural History Society. In a battered old hat, his only "botany-box," he fetched home specimens of plants to study: saxifrage and mosses, pennyroyal and dwarf andromeda, the sessile-leaved bellwort and the yellow wood-sorrel. In the mere task of naming them he came to find "a distincter recognition and knowledge of the thing named"—an extension of his circle of acquaintance. "I wanted to know my neighbors," he explained, "to get a little nearer to them." Traveling as many as twenty or thirty miles a day on foot, he might visit the same flower on a half-dozen occasions so that he would know exactly when it blossomed. At the same time, he kept his eyes open for birds, snakes, woodchucks, and "whatever else might offer." Much to his surprise he found that he had not heretofore fully noticed the teeming diversity of his natural surroundings. "I had no idea," he admitted, "that there was so much going on in Heywood's meadow." Where once the bogs and hillsides of Concord had seemed to him a wilderness of "a thousand strange species," they increasingly came to seem the familiar shores of a well-settled land, a world as important to the town as were the shops and houses on the Milldam or Main Street.[2]

The Thoreau of this decade of ramblings, the 1850s, is not nearly so well known today as the man who lived from 1845 to 1847 in a house he built at Walden Pond. His renunciation of society in that famous episode, like the night he spent in the Concord jail for refusing to pay taxes to support the war against Mexico, was certainly more of a shock to the world's comfortable ways. In contrast, relatively little attention has been given to the years after his move back to his parents' house in the center of town; paradoxically, he grew even more intensely intimate with nature than he had been at Walden. Possibly the years spent at the pond were the catalyst needed to free him from the tightly circumscribed sympathies of a Yankee village. In this sense they were only a prelude to his subsequent development; henceforth he could live anywhere and still find ways to remain in close touch with the natural community. Unfortunately, no book like *Walden* emerged from that last decade or so of his short life, and so that continuing and deepening intimacy has been widely ignored. But his journal of some two million words should be sufficient proof that Thoreau himself took those years seriously. It was the time, one might say, of the maturation not only of his science but also of his personal ecological philosophy. Therefore, in interpreting this philosophy here, the principal source of evidence will be the often neglected entries in his journal from the early 1850s until the spring of 1861, when, fatally ill with tuberculosis, he gave up writing altogether. It is not too much to claim that the attitudes toward nature conveyed by Thoreau in these volumes may be his most important legacy to another age. This body of work is also perhaps the best single expression we have of the shift to Romantic ecological thought in England and America.[3]

Like Gilbert White in Selborne, Thoreau found a full and rewarding vocation in studying the workings of animate nature in his native village. From the Sudbury meadows south of Concord to the Carlisle bridge lying to the northwest, the straight-line distance was not much more than seven miles. Winding through the sandy plain of the region were the Assabet and the Sudbury streams, which merged below the town center to form the Concord River, flowing north to the Merrimack and thence to the sea. It was not a grand or expansive world, but it offered abundant promise for the pursuit of natural science. Ringed by low-lying hills, drumlins, and glacial ponds (including Walden, a mile and a half from the village green), the town afforded by means of easy strolls a wide spectrum of habitats to delight the foot-loose naturalist. Although he made and sold pencils to con-tribute to his family's finances as well as taking odd jobs as a lecturer and surveyor, Thoreau was seldom bound to steady, full-time wage employment in the town; thus he could devote at least four hours a day, usually his after-noons, to his principal profession as a walker and reporter of the seasons.

In both his choice of career and his attachment to his home locale, Thoreau seems almost deliberately to have taken Gilbert White's life as a model. In this he was bound to come in conflict with the prejudices of a New England society founded on the Puritan ethic, a society that had never admired the leisured style of the Anglican parson-naturalist nor seen any virtue in sauntering through grassy pastures or pine woods. Thoreau perforce had to find his vocation in an earlier age, and on the other side of the At-lantic to boot. Suitably enough, he kept an edition of White's book on his garret shelf and referred to its contents repeatedly in his journal.[4]

The differences between the two naturalists and their locales, however, were significant. Unlike White, Henry Thoreau was not a respectable gentleman in the eyes of his neighbors, in part because New England had no tolerance for the idleness implied by unemployment, and in part be-cause Thoreau had no regard for affluence or the trappings of respectability. White was an ordained clergyman in his community; Thoreau described the religion of his towns-men as "a rotten squash." Where White cherished the an-cient customs and artifacts of Selborne's medieval past, Thoreau sought the traces of a vanished native people and those pockets of primitive wilderness somehow left un-touched by an expanding society. White had passed his days peacefully unaware of the chaos and tensions begat by economic revolution. But for Thoreau, these changes were hard realities that demanded either accommodation or thoughtful, practical alternatives. In short, America in the 1850s was not the place to find a pastoral idyll or a cozy sinecure. Thoreau lived in a society that was unabashedly new, enterprising, and mobile. Concord itself, only twenty miles west of the Boston seaport and the same distance south of the Lowell factories, was a deceptively rural town. Behind its agrarian façade it was thoroughly permeated by the spirit of economic push. In 1850 it had already been invaded by the Fitchburg Railroad and would never again be a self-sufficient world, independent of national markets and influences.[5]

In addition to these contrasts between the villages of Concord and Selborne there was the intellectual challenge being mounted in Thoreau's day to the assumptions of the eighteenth-century Linnaean ecologists. By the 1850s the synthesis of piety and science represented by Linnaeus, Ray, and White had been reduced to a cracked and dried-out shell; little of its inner vitality remained. Thoreau admired the writings of Linnaeus as well as those of White, and even ranked the Swedish naturalist beside Homer and Chaucer in his pantheon of literary geniuses who had expressed "the purest and deepest love of nature." In his *Fact Book*, a collection of notes from his reading, Thoreau copied out long extracts from Linnaeus' "Oeconomy of Nature" as well as from his other writings and from biographies of his life. "Read Linnaeus at once" was his advice to self in his journal of 1852, "and come down from him as far as you please." But as much as he delighted to linger with the older generation of naturalists, he discovered that he had to "come down" a good distance; their carefully constructed world of intermeshed science and religious values was no longer tenable.[6]

Thoreau's age was rapidly replacing the older static models of the economy of nature with new ones that emphasized ecological change and turbulence. Besides Linnaeus and White, he had also read his Charles Lyell and early Charles Darwin, taking from them a new conception of the earth's geological antiquity and of the power of existing and observable forces to effect vast transformations in nature. From these men and from Geoffroy Saint-Hilaire he also learned of—and was inclined to accept—the theory of the evolutionary development of species. Like these evolutionists, he was less impressed with the planned, mechanical efficiency of nature than with the unsuppressible "greediness and tenacity of life." Every organism, Thoreau noted in the last pages of his journal, is "contending for the possession of the planet," as if "bent on taking entire possession of the globe wherever the climate and soil will permit," and is checked only by equally prolific foes and competitors. The exuberant, explosive power of "the vegetative force" perpetually threatens to overthrow man's dominion and cover the earth once more with a jungle. Such extravagance and prodigality, he early concluded, demonstrate that, contrary to older notions of an exact economic proportioning in all her productions, nature is thrifty only in her simplicity of procedure.

How rich and lavish must be the system which can afford to let so many moons burn all the day as well as the night, though no man stands in need of their light! There is none of that kind of economy in Nature that husbands its stock, but she supplies inexhaustible means to the most frugal methods.

Thoreau not only doubted that nature is as careful and tidy an economist as Linnaeus represented; he was even exhilarated at the prospect of excess and rebelled against the idea of a stingy natural order.[7]

Of course the Linnaean paradigm of ecology would have had lingering attractions for the thrifty Yankee side of Thoreau's mind. He continued to suppose that each toadstool or mud-turtle and every windy day must play a role "indispensable to the economy of nature." Every chink in nature seemed to be occupied by an inhabitant perfectly adapted to its place, so that in the cyclical progress of the year nothing could be declared superfluous. "In our workshops," he wrote,

We pride ourselves on discovering a use for what had previously been regarded as waste, but how partial and accidental our economy compared with Nature's. In Nature nothing is wasted. Every decayed leaf and twig and fibre is only the better fitted to serve in some other department, and all at last are gathered in her compost-heap.

But despite these traditional assertions, Thoreau also found in the economy of plants and animals a disturbing extravagance. The mildewing of the white oak's acorns before they could be eaten by jays or squirrels was a case in point; it loomed like "a glaring imperfection in Nature, that the labor of the oaks for the year should be lost to this extent." Try as he might to explain such anomalies by the Linnaean methods, he could conceive of no important purpose to be served by "this seeming waste."[8]

Throughout the decade of the fifties, the main thrust of Thoreau's scientific studies was ecological. Once he had learned the names of his "neighbors," the appeal of taxonomy gave way to a desire to understand the interrelations among plants, animals, and their habitats. He noted the protective coloring of the pickerel in Concord's brooks, and the "beautiful law of distribution" that gave to each field sparrow its private territory so that "one creature does not too much interfere with another." Evidently from Alexander von Humboldt, the German plant geographer, ecologist, and explorer of South America, he borrowed the idea of classifying plants by their environmental conditions, and thus began to classify local trees and shrubs according to the amount of soil moisture they needed to grow. And following Humboldt's work in the Andes, Thoreau identified the series of vegetation zones on Mt. Monadnock and Mt. Washington in New Hampshire, progressing from lower spruce and fir forests to the lichen-covered rocks of the "cloud zone." In declining an invitation to join the American Association for the Advancement of Science, he wrote in 1853:

. . . the character of my observations, so far as they are scientific, may be inferred from the fact that I am especially attracted by such books of science as White's Selborne and Humboldt's Aspects of Nature.

Both of these writers were scientists of broad, holistic vision; both offered to Thoreau an ecological perspective that he could apply to his own microcosm.[9]

But unlike either White or Humboldt, the most important and most poignant purpose of Thoreau's ecological study was historical: to reconstruct "the actual condition of the place where we dwell, [as it appeared] three centuries ago," before the coming of the white man to America. That purpose, of course, could hardly have occurred to any of the Linnaeans, whose physical surroundings had been for many years as stable as their science was static. In New England, however, Thoreau confronted an ecological system that was being radically remade by the invading species of civilized man. This concrete experience of upheaval could not but reinforce strongly the impact of Lyell and Darwin on his perception of nature. When he looked at the Concord of the mid-nineteenth century, he saw not a flawless Newtonian machine but "a maimed and imperfect nature." It was a symphonic concert from which the more exciting movements had been eliminated, a book that had lost many of its pages.

I take infinite pains to know the phenomena of the spring, for instance, thinking that I have here the entire poem, and then, to my chagrin, I hear that it is but an imperfect copy that I possess and have read, that my ancestors have torn out many of the first leaves and grandest passages, and mutilated it in many places. I should not like to think that some demigod had come before me and picked out some of the best of the stars. I wish to know an entire heaven and an entire earth.

As a naturalist Thoreau labored, as had White before him, to bring together all the natural phenomena of his home environs into a single, interrelated whole, arranged by nature in perpetual balance. But the lesson of American history, the inescapable awareness of violent ecological change caused by economic development, undermined his confidence in the models based on the security and seeming permanence of Old World ecological systems. It was now apparent that man had an enormously greater power to disrupt and exterminate than an earlier, more complacent generation had assumed.[10]

The most profound ecological changes, as Thoreau realized, had occurred in the New England forest cover. When Concord was settled in 1638 its gently rolling terrain was densely shaded by an almost unbroken green canopy. In a few areas, especially along river banks, the Indians had burned temporary clearings to improve their hunting or to plant corn and squash; insects and windstorms left bare spots too, of course. But by and large the primeval forest was a dark, impenetrable jungle. For at least five thousand years the same principal species had sprouted and matured here: white and pitch pines, hemlocks, chestnuts, maples, birches, and oaks. Of these, the largest were the white pines, which in some parts of New England grew to more than 6 feet in diameter and 250 feet in height. This was, in the view of President Timothy Dwight of Yale College, "the noblest forest tree in New England, and probably in the world": tier on tier of bold lateral branches flourishing rich green needles against a soaring black arrow of a trunk. Oaks more than 30 feet in circumference were also found by the earliest English settlers, as well as sugar maples 15 feet around. According to one estimate, a typical forest area of ten square miles supported as many as five black bears, two to three pumas and an equal number of gray wolves, 200 turkeys, 400 white-tailed deer, and up to 20,000 gray squirrels. Some men might have perceived in this splendor of life a generative power to be admired, perhaps even worshipped, but the Puritans who came to lay out Concord and its neighboring towns were a race far removed from such pagan superstitions. They quickly set about to tame this rampant wilderness and make it a decent home for pious Christians.[11]

By 1700, over half a million acres of New England woodlands had been cleared for farming. A century later little remained of the original forest cover in the inhabited areas: where the trees still stood, they were usually second or third growth. And by 1880, only 40 percent of Massachusetts could be classified as wooded land. As the forests vanished, so too went their wild creatures. The predators had as always been the first to go, although Thoreau recorded with astonishment the killing of a last lynx in a nearby town as late as 1860. The hawk, eagle, and turkey had but barely survived the hunters' guns. In the town's rivers the salmon, shad, and alewives had disappeared, likewise almost all the otters. And nowhere in all of

Thoreau's writings, covering a period of more than two decades, does he ever mention seeing a deer in the Massachusetts landscape. On the other hand, Concord of the 1850s was not yet reduced to a biological desert. A trapper could still take as many as 200 muskrats in a year, and mink were there too. Vast flocks of passenger pigeons, ducks, and geese still darkened the sky at seasons. Vulnerable and mutilated though it might be, nature was obviously resilient and tenacious if not pressed too hard. So long as a substantial portion of the forest habitat survived, there was hope that something of the original ecological conditions could be preserved. That possibility, Thoreau came to see, would depend wholly on the will of the human inhabitants of the town.

Other citizens of the state had begun to understand how sweeping were the environmental transformations wrought by civilization, and to regret some of their consequences. The most influential of these people was probably George B. Emerson, a noted Boston educator and president of that city's Society of Natural History from 1837 to 1843. During those years, with support from the legislature, he formed a commission to make a full zoological and botanical survey of Massachusetts. Similar projects were afoot in other states, but more often with the intent of bringing "to light the hidden riches of our country" and discovering "important facts, connected with the agricultural, commercial, and manufacturing interests," as a New York group of scientists promised, than of checking the exploitive onslaught. George Emerson, in contrast, understood that conservation could no longer be left in the hands of the Divine Engineer. For the survey he headed, he himself wrote one of the principal volumes: *A Report on the Trees and Shrubs Growing Naturally in the Forests of Massachusetts* (1846), a nontechnical guide to the state's principal trees. This book is one of the neglected delights of nineteenth-century American natural history and was, in its time, one of the earliest pleas for "a wiser economy" in the use of forests, a pioneering conservation tract. And if only because Thoreau bought the *Report* and relied on it above all other books in his study of the vanishing forest milieu, it merits introducing here in more detail.[12]

"The cunning foresight of the Yankee," George Emerson complained, "seems to desert him when he takes the axe in hand." The wanton destruction of the state's woodlands was endangering not only wildlife and the ecological order, but the very basis of the human economy as well. It is not generally remembered today that until 1870 the United States took the vast part of its energy and materials from the forest. For 250 years, from first settlement to the advent of steel fabrication, America lived in an age of wood. The people of Massachusetts, numbering almost 750,000 when Emerson wrote his book, had to take from the forests almost every product they made: houses, furniture, ships, wagons, sleighs, bridges, brooms, whips, shovels, hoes, casks, boxes, baskets, bootjacks. From the maples they got sugar, from hickories and chestnuts a good supply of nuts. Most basic was their cordwood for winter fuel; according to Emerson, this fuel, costing an average of four dollars a cord, was annually worth five million dollars. The railroads required another 55,000 cords, chiefly pine, for their locomotives. Altogether, then, the state could not have survived without a steady, cheap supply of trees. Even the bark was needed for tanning leather, while sumac and barberry roots supplied valuable dyes to the cloth industry. Yet each year the forests were recklessly cut away, and no provision was made to replant and protect them. By the 1840s Massachusetts was already importing great quantities of both hard- and softwood from Maine and New York; and Emerson warned that "even these foreign resources are fast failing us."[13]

At best, then, the practical art of woodland management existed only at a primitive level in New England. In 1838 Emerson canvassed some of the more knowledgeable people of Massachusetts to gather a fund of folk wisdom for the future. Two chief principles emerged from his survey to guide the woodsman in cutting: for timber, select only the more mature trees, but for fuel, cut the entire woodland "clean and close." In the latter case the consensus of opinion was that the forest would renew itself enough to be profitably cut again every twenty-three years, though the average would vary widely from species to species. "When the trees are principally oak, white, black, and scarlet, the forest may be clean cut three times in a century," Emerson noted. After each cut, some of his correspondents maintained, the old stumps would sprout anew and thus perpetuate the oak woods. But in the experience of others, this seldom happened. Instead, pines would spring up to replace the oak grove, or vice versa. It had long been a vexing problem for the state's farmers to explain why such a succession occurred, and when one's livelihood depended on whether it was oak or pine one had to sell, a reliable answer was vital. According to some countrymen, the cause lay in a magical spontaneous generation that no one could predict. Emerson, though, was sure that by some natural means the older woods must perpetually contain its successor species, either as seeds lying dormant in the soil or as small trees growing unobserved on the forest floor.[14]

It was precisely at this point that Henry Thoreau stepped forward to offer a simple scientific explanation for this perplexing question in woodland management. He had first begun to study the problem in 1856. Then in September of 1857, as he watched a squirrel burying hickory nuts in a stand of hemlocks, he concluded: "This, then, is the way forests are planted." The nuts were often carried far from their parent source, buried at just the right depth for germination, and would begin to sprout if the squirrel was killed or forgot its deposit. The secret of succession, he now understood, was bound up in these little gray and red creatures and their interrelation with the forests. Acorns were buried in a pine woodland, for example, and many would survive to become tiny seedlings growing under the protection of the pines. On the other hand, the wind might carry pine seeds to the base of aged oaks, where they would lodge and take root. The Concord farmers, ignorant of these ecological interdependencies, were in the habit of organizing squirrel hunts to kill as many "vermin" as possible, when it would have been "far more civilized and humane, not to say godlike," to set up a ceremony to honor this brute neighbor for "the great service it performs, in the economy of the universe."[15]

Three years later, Thoreau expanded these observations into a lecture, "The Succession of Forest Trees," delivered at the Middlesex Agricultural Society's annual cattle show in Concord. It has been generally considered the most important contribution to conservation, agriculture, and ecological science he made in his lifetime. Its value to the practical world is documented by the fact that it was later published not only in the Society's *Transactions* for that year but also in the New York *Weekly Tribune*, the *Century*, the *New-England Farmer*, and the Annual Report of the Massachusetts Board of Agriculture. The ecology of the seed was a key theme in the essay, and it continued to be for Thoreau one of the more intriguing of nature's phenomena—so much so that on his death he left about 400 manuscript pages on the subject. But his larger intention was to recommend that his listeners carefully follow nature's methods in their timber economy: "Would it not be well to consult with Nature in the outset? for she is the most extensive and experienced planter of us all." By deliberately planting trees according to the same patterns of succession seen in nature, farmers could provide themselves with a healthy, perpetual woodland crop. Instead, they cut their oaks down, burned the young pines that subsequently appeared, and planted rye for a season or two to earn a little quick cash before letting the land return to trees, invariably the scraggliest of weed species. It was the worst kind of management—"a greediness that defeats its own ends," Thoreau believed—because it vacillated blindly between radical interference and resigned laissez-faire. As a consequence, the land would become barren, supporting only worthless scrub growth rather than a fertile, noble, self-replenishing forest that could provide livelihoods for both squirrels and man.[16]

That Thoreau's major effort as an ecologist should deal with the phenomenon of forest succession is not strange. It was one of the earliest questions raised by American naturalists as they watched the woods around them give way first to this species of trees, then that, and finally to pastures or row crops. To determine what nature would do when let alone, however, was not easy. Lacking the modern knowledge of a pattern of succession that leads to a climax stage, naturalists of Thoreau's time frequently fell back on the model of a farmer's rotation of crops. Along with George Emerson, Thoreau argued that the growth of oaks exhausts the soil for their own acorns so that pines must succeed. Then the pines in turn leave the earth unfit for their seeds, and oaks reclaim the territory. So on and on, it would seem, goes the history of a forest—a perpetual cycle of invasions back and forth. But at the same time, Thoreau was inclined to believe that because the white pine is a more primitive tree than the oak in the "order of development," the process of succession must move from the lower to the higher species. The pines, then, are the "pioneers"; the oak, "the more permanent settler who lays out his improvements." Whichever was the truer model, he was positive about one matter:

In a wood that has been left alone for the longest period the greatest regularity and harmony in the disposition of the trees will be observed, while in our ordinary woods man has often interfered and favored the growth of other kinds than are best fitted to grow there naturally.

The people of Concord would not begin to live in harmony with the land or use it to their greatest advantage until they learned to accept nature as their teacher and to accommodate themselves to its rhythms.[17]

The topic of succession was only a small part of the much more ambitious scheme Thoreau pursued in his last active years as a sauntering naturalist. As he examined the local woodlots he gradually learned how to read the environmental development of the town for a hundred years or more back into its past. A fringe of white pines standing between a stone wall and an open field, for example, could furnish a clue to the evolution of the landscape on the *other* side of the wall, from where the pine seeds had blown many decades earlier. Tree rings on old stumps could tell him what trees grew in Concord, and how many, even before the battle of 1775 with the British redcoats. "Thus you can unroll the rotten papyrus on which the history of the Concord forest is written."

Had he lived longer, perhaps Thoreau would have drawn from these techniques a complete chronicle of man's occupation, use, and misuse of this small New England habitat. It was but one of a number of unfinished projects he left behind, but it would have been the most valuable for students of the American landscape. That such an approach had eluded the historians of his day was for Thoreau a judgment of their capacity simply to see the world before them. Why should the survival of a magnificent forest like the Inches Wood in Boxboro be ignored in history books, he wondered, and the vastly more trivial career of a local politician be included? And how could the scholar justify his insensitivity to man's dependence on nature's order? In an attempt to redress these shortcomings, Thoreau began, through the understanding of succession, to lay hold on the development and fate of the natural environment in his corner of America.[18]

In presenting these ecological studies Thoreau knew how to play the part of a practical economist, but he had something more in mind than how to preserve the resource base of Massachusetts wealth. He hoped that a more scientific approach to forest use would result in the revegetation of a denuded land. "The woods within my recollection have gradually withdrawn further from the village," he complained. Each winter he heard on every side of Concord the ring of axes clearing the forest. (He himself indirectly aided in this deforestation campaign; as a surveyor, he was often hired by local farmers to measure their woodlots so that they could be sold to the highest bidder.) Yet after watching the choppers at Walden Pond and on Fair Haven Hill, he exclaimed with mock relief, "Thank God, men cannot as yet fly, and lay waste the sky as well as the earth! We are safe on that side for the present." In the fall of 1857 he became outraged by the sight of an Irish laborer hired by a farmer to remove a tangle of sumac and grapevines: "If some are prosecuted for abusing children, others deserve to be prosecuted for maltreating the face of nature committed to their care." It was not at all improbable that such people would cut down oaks that had witnessed the transfer of the Concord lands from the Indians to the white man, while inaugurating a local museum with a cartridge-box taken from a British soldier in the Revolutionary War. But were more information available about the lasting damage being worked, it might be possible to reverse this mentality. "We are a young people," Thoreau noted, "and have not learned by experience the consequence of cutting off the forest. One day they will be planted, methinks, and nature reinstated to some extent."[19]

To bring the forest back, even to a limited degree, was Thoreau's chief hope in his ecological writing. The slightest evidence of nature's regenerative power reassured him, as when he spotted young pine seedlings reclaiming a pasture under the farmer's very nose. It convinced him that, do what he might, man could not wholly subdue this stubborn principle of life. In one moment of extravagant reverie, Thoreau went so far as to envision the return of the forest to a total triumph over its human invaders.

At first, perchance, there would be an abundant crop of rank garden weeds and grasses in the cultivated land,—and rankest of all in the cellar-holes,—and of pinweed, hardhack, sumach, blackberry, thimble-berry, raspberry, etc., in the fields and pastures. Elm, ash, maples, etc., would grow vigorously along old garden limits and main streets. Garden weeds and grasses would soon disappear. Huckleberry and blueberry bushes, lambkill, hazel, sweetfern, barberry, elder, also shad-bush, chokeberry, andromeda, and thorns, etc., would rapidly prevail in the deserted pastures. At the same time the wild cherries, birch, poplar, willows, checkerberry would reestablish themselves. Finally the pines, hemlock, spruce, larch, shrub oak, oaks, chestnut, beech, and walnuts would occupy the site of Concord once more. The apple and perhaps all exotic trees and shrubs and a great part of the indigenous ones named above would have disappeared, and the laurel and yew would to some extent be an underwood here, and perchance the red man once more thread his way through the mossy, swamplike, primitive wood.

The process of ecological succession as plotted here in all its profuse energy had nothing to do with a wise timber economy; rather it offered the hope of a resurgent, irrepressible wilderness that man supposedly had vanquished. "I long for wildness," Thoreau wrote, "a nature which I cannot put my foot through . . . , a New Hampshire everlasting and unfallen." The phenomenon of succession reminded him of that wilderness and of the "inextinguishable vitality in Nature."[20]

Of course Thoreau knew that the woodsmen of Massachusetts were not likely to let such an uprising as he describes occur, after having spent so much toil in "redeeming" the land from its savage state. In his journal of 1859, and again in his lecture "Huckleberries," he arrived at a compromise that he believed might satisfy both the demands of civilization and his own need for that whole, unmutilated natural order. Each town, he suggested, should preserve within its borders "a primitive forest" of five hundred or a thousand acres, "where a stick should never be cut for fuel, a common possession, for instruction and recreation." Here men and women might learn how nature's own economy functions. In the 1850s it was still possible to hope for such a preserve, for in spite of all the clearing there yet remained in Concord large plots of land that had been left relatively undisturbed for a few generations: the Easterbrooks country, for example, or portions of Walden Woods. "As some give to Harvard College or another institution, why might not another give a forest or huckleberry field to Concord?" Such an endowment would provide for all an education in environmental humility and restraint. Without a public wilderness tract, on the other hand, the town's learning facilities would be always incomplete, no matter how much was spent on schools. "If we do not look out," Thoreau warned, "we shall find our fine schoolhouse standing in a cowyard at last."[21]

In later decades, expensive private academies continued to appear and prosper throughout the state, and Harvard's endowment continued to grow fatter. The town of Concord at last managed to acquire something of a public forest, though much smaller in extent than Thoreau recommended and repeatedly harvested for wood. But it was only the barest token of restoration. Eventually Concord would increase from 2,000 to 20,000 people, become a commuter suburb, be bisected by a four-lane highway: more civilization, not more wilderness, would be its future. In truth, Thoreau could say that he lived "in the very nick of time." Although over large parts of Massachusetts the trees would return in some force after farming had passed its peak, there would never again be the full richness, diversity, and grandeur of that lost green world. Thoreau watched it yield its final ground.

As a seeker of the primitive forest, Thoreau clearly belongs to the arcadian tradition in ecological thought. The eighteenth-century model of a self-perpetuating natural economy might be overthrown; in its place arose a new awareness of the fragility of that system of relations. Technology might remake Anglo-American society; wilderness then became all the more precious to many. Thus the arcadian impulse that had first emerged in science with Gilbert White grew even more intense with Thoreau. A sense of discontinuity in one area stimulated a tenacious desire for continuity in another. To be sure, the aboriginal forest of America was more appealing to Thoreau than the more tidy garden landscape of rural England. But the arcadian ideal was essentially an ethic, not a specific ecological condition or a single fixed point on a scale of economic development. Thoreau deserves to be included with the other arcadians who followed White because he shared with them a common belief: that man must learn to accommodate himself to the natural order rather than seek to overwhelm and transform it. "Either nature may be changed or man," he noted, and then he went on to ask about the earth: "Does it require to be improved by the hands of man, or is man to live more naturally and so more safely?" His own life was devoted to demonstrating the second alternative. In fact, it was Thoreau who was most responsible for the development of the arcadian ethic into a modern ecological philosophy. Let us then look more closely at that arcadian ideal and how it shaped the life of this most famous of America's naturalists.[22]

CHAPTER 4

Nature Looking into Nature

NINETEENTH-CENTURY Concord was home to many unusual individuals. But only one local citizen was likely to be seen snorting and galloping with glee after a fox on a snowy hillside. Or sitting in the top of a pine tree, swaying with the wind, or crawling about on his hands and knees endeavoring to communicate with a reluctant wood-frog. Reputable burghers were no doubt scandalized to find him wading in a brook with his trousers over his arm on summer afternoons, while Concord's farmers were sweating at their plows. On moonlit nights, while his townsmen slept, he might be out swimming in the nude in the Assabet or lying on Conantum's cliff intoxicated by the music of crickets in the damp grass. Admittedly he was no Walt Whitman in terms of libidinal freedom, but Thoreau did manage to carry into adulthood an openness of instinct, a sensuous attachment to the earth and its vital currents that set aside the typical New Englander's decorum. "My body is all sentient," he exulted. "As I go here or there, I am tickled by this or that I come in contact with, as if I touched the wires of a battery." In his daily excursions over the landscape he was after more than scientific facts. "I keep out of doors," he explained in his journal, "for the sake of the mineral, vegetable, and animal in me." Elsewhere in the town those elements had been repressed and all but forgotten.[1]

In a letter to Lucy Brown written early in his adult life,

Thoreau captured in a sentence the ambition that would ever after define his life's purpose, the motive behind his career as a field ecologist:

I dream of looking abroad summer and winter, with free gaze, from some mountain-side, while my eyes revolve in an Egyptian slime of health,—I to be nature looking into nature with such easy sympathy as the blue-eyed grass looks in the face of the sky.

His scientific excursions of the 1850s continued this search for sensuous contact, for a visceral sense of belonging to the earth and its circle of organisms. To smell or touch a tangible, palpable nature aroused in him a sense of "vast alliances" and universal relatedness. He could then feel himself extended beyond the limits of his individual lump of matter, able to achieve access to the vital energy that is in nature. "We must go out and re-ally ourselves to Nature every day," he wrote in 1856. "We must make root, send out some little fibre at least, even every winter day. I am sensible that I am imbibing health when I open my mouth to the wind." Maturity did not divert Thoreau from his quest for contact with the earth and communion with its ecological processes. "With regard to essentials," he was still saying in 1857, "I have never had occasion to change my mind." To be so closely united with nature that his observations would become profoundly introspective— "nature looking into nature"—was for him from the beginning the essence of being a naturalist.[2]

A day-to-day physical intimacy with nature was the foundation for Thoreau of a new, more intense empiricism. Facts must become experiences for the whole man, not mere abstractions in a disembodied mind. The naturalist must allow himself to be engulfed to his very ears in the odors and textures of sensible reality. He must become, like the muskrat, a limpid eyeball peering out of the sedges of a flooded meadow. By being as fully immersed in his fluid environment as this sleek brown rodent, the naturalist could see his world with all his senses cleansed and alert. And in order to live as a muskrat-naturalist, he must be alert to the value of each day, no matter how inclement. "You wander indefinitely in a beaded coat, wet to the skin of your legs, sit on moss-clad rocks and stumps, and hear the lisping of migrating sparrows flitting amid the shrub oaks, . . . more at home for being abroad, more comfortable for being wet, sinking at each step deep into the thawing earth." Even his bare feet could discover empirical truths not apparent to the well-shod traveler, as when Thoreau one mizzling spring day found the lichens all "swollen and lusty with moisture, your foot sinking into them and pressing the water out as from a sponge." The mere sight of an empty mud-turtle's shell lying under his bedside table could suggest to him that he too was "of the earth earthy." But to wade into "the muddy batter midleg deep," to brush through dense blueberry swamps and through "extensive birch forests all covered with green lice, which cover our clothes and face," was to pursue a fuller awareness of his earthiness than the eyes alone could know.[3]

This intimate knowledge came not only through sinking to the muskrat level of perception but also in putting as much of nature's variety into his stomach as he could. In March 1859 Thoreau wrote: "I felt as if I could eat the very crust of the earth; I never felt so terrene, never sympathized so with the surface of the earth." That sympathy should require much tasting and digesting, real and figurative, was axiomatic to Thoreau's studies. He would not be a "mealy-mouthed" nature lover, approaching the world gingerly—afraid to bite hard, to crack the shell, and so to taste the rich flavor of its nutmeat. Huckleberries, sassafras roots, birch sap, wild apples, acorns—all went into his experimental craw. He would even threaten to devour a woodchuck raw, hoping thus to get some of its wild nature into his own system and to fortify his animal self. No naturalist or ecologist has been more intent on knowing nature by his teeth, tongue, and intestines—on engorging nature into the self as well as merging the self in nature.[4]

"The one life within us and abroad": this phrase of William Wordsworth's well describes Thoreau's vocation as a naturalist and the ideal he sought to realize in his excursions. All natural entities, man and even the rocks included, were joined together for him in a single animated whole. "The earth I tread on is not a dead, inert mass," he maintained in 1851; "it is a body, has a spirit, is organic, and fluid to the influence of its spirit, and to whatever particle of that spirit is in me." In *Walden*, too, he described nature as "not a fossil earth, but a living earth; compared with whose great central life all animal and vegetable life is merely parasitic." Hearing the cawing of a crow in the depths of winter, he felt himself related anew to the universal living organism lying dormant under the crust of ice and snow: "It is not merely crow calling to crow, for it speaks to me too. I am part of one great creature with him; if he has voice, I have ears." And with the coming of spring, he could sense the revitalization of that single, cohering force of life, as it surged and throbbed once more in the land. The eternal mother of life, the generative principle, nature once more brought forth flowers, berries, birch and maple seeds, man and all other living beings. The very granite ledges of the New England pastures seemed to participate in the reanimation of the earth in spring. Health, in a physical and a more than physical sense, was for Thoreau a condition of being in step with these organic rhythms, of nibbling nature's fruits, of merging with the life force. Then at last he could flow through nature's pores.[5]

One of the memorable episodes recorded in Thoreau's journal occurred in early May of 1857. As usual in that time of the year, the rivers were flooding into the Sudbury and Wayland meadows, and the fields and orchards were spotted with puddles of water. Into one such pool Thoreau waded barefoot, pushing his toes down into the cold mud. There appeared around his legs, swarming in a feverish mass, "a hundred toads . . . copulating or preparing to." The amorous scene into which he had wandered was loudly celebrated by the ringing trill of the toads, a sound that seemed to make the very sod tremble: "I was thrilled to my spine and vibrated to it." While on all sides of him the toads swam and leaped on one another in great excitement, the naturalist felt his limbs charged with new force, his singleness overwhelmed by the "one life" of an animate earth. Without that sense of the vital energy in nature, man stands as an alien, severed even from the cold, inert lump of his own body. When Thoreau allowed himself to become too shut in by Concord society, the remedy he needed was to locate once more, so to speak, that pool of toads. Then all life, his own included, would once again become "organized, or a kosmos, which before was inorganic and lumpish." Then all the sympathetic identification with nature which nourished his observations was revived.[6]

In his desire to be a naturalist in the most elemental sense—to be more completely "naturalized"—Thoreau expresses perfectly the arcadian position. As noted earlier, this cluster of ideas and feelings drew its inspiration mainly from the pagan past, especially that of ancient Greece, though undoubtedly the surviving folk traditions of Europe—and, for Thoreau, those of the American Indian—also served as important sources of the arcadian outlook. At the heart of all these varieties of paganism was the belief that nature is a single organic being animated by an indwelling vital principle. In the eighteenth century, Bishop Berkeley noted that the Stoics and Platonists supposed that there is "a life infused throughout all things . . . an inward principle, animal spirit, or natural life, producing and forming within as art doth without, regulating, moderating and reconciling the various notions, qualities, and parts of the mundane system." It is this vital force that governs nature, according to the pagan view, not some Divine Engineer or Leviathan. It is the source of gravity, electricity, magnetism—of all energy. And in ecological terms it is the cohesive power that binds all species of the earth together in a unified organism. For Thoreau, as for the pagans, the world was no mere system of mechanical order but a flux of energy capable of welding all things into an animated *kosmos*.[7]

Beginning with Henry More's *Anima Mundi* and on into the revival of arcadianism, these ancient ideas were revived to counter the mechanistic science developed in the Newtonian era. But the more militant resurgence of the pagan outlook toward nature came in the late eighteenth and early nineteenth centuries with the rise of Romanticism in western culture. Led by such figures as Wordsworth, Schelling, Goethe, and Thoreau, a new generation sought to redefine nature and man's place in the scheme of things. Their inability, or rather, their unwillingness to settle firmly on a single model of nature has been well emphasized, indeed so much so that it is now easy to miss the forest for the trees. For all its diverse permutations, Romanticism found expression in certain common themes, and one of the most recurrent was a fascination with biology and the study of the organic world. Romantics found this field of science a modern approach to the old pagan intuition that all nature is alive and pulsing with energy or spirit. No other single idea was more important to them. And at the very core of this Romantic view of nature was what later generations would come to call an ecological perspective: that is, a search for holistic or integrated perception, an emphasis on interdependence and relatedness in nature, and an intense desire to restore man to a place of intimate intercourse with the vast organism that constitutes the earth. Each of these themes carried the arcadian consciousness to a new level of refinement, assertiveness, and influence.[8]

The Romantics could not say enough about their holistic urge. In the art of Wordsworth, as Newton Stallknecht remarks, the poet's intention was to show nature as a whole, "an intertwined togetherness" and a "community of existence." For Goethe, likewise, the search for a method of perception that would represent nature "at work and alive, manifesting herself in her wholeness in every single part of her being" was paramount. His poem "Epirrhenia" voices a fundamental Romantic argument: "Separateness is the illusion / One and many are the same." This great German poet-naturalist, like his American counterpart, Thoreau, believed that "in organic life nothing is unconnected with the whole." Each part, consequently, may be read as a synopsis of the whole system. The previous age of mechanical deists and physico-theologists, it is true, had also posited a nature joined together in a kind of unity. But their notion of integration was too cold and contrived, too lacking in *essential* coherence, to satisfy the Romantics. What they needed was a sense of inviolable interdependence that no machine analogy could possibly offer. The individual organisms in nature are not like gears and bolts that can be removed and still maintain their identity, nor can the whole be disassembled and then reconstructed like a clock. The Romantics saw nature as a system of necessary relationships that cannot be disturbed in even the most inconspicuous way without changing, perhaps destroying, the equilibrium of the whole. Nor can any creature exist outside the communal organism. In Wordsworthian nature, as

Stallknecht claims, "there is nothing wholly self-sufficient. . . . Each object, although a concrete individual, owes something to the others and, in turn, conditions the others." For such a *gestalt* there can be no tidy structural model. Instead, the Romantic naturalists and artists placed their emphasis on the vital, creative power that flows through the material world like blood through the arteries of the body.[9]

In large measure this Romantic argument for holism and animism was prompted by the growing sense of man's isolation from the natural world, that rather sudden and painful side effect of the progress of industrialization in western nations. On both sides of the Atlantic men and women were being hastily uprooted from their land and their traditions. Tillers of the earth became urban factory hands. And this transformation, which put both physical and psychic distance between man and the rest of nature, brought a gathering protest by many intellectuals against ecological alienation in all its forms. A particular target was western religion, which for centuries had found it necessary to foster a fierce dualism between the human consciousness and the natural world. In the opinion of the German writer Schelling, the *"bête noire"* of the times was "estrangement" of every sort.

Wordsworth would have agreed: he retired to his rural cottage at Grasmere not to escape human society, but because he believed that man must not withdraw into a purely human realm of purely human concerns and thereby shut himself off from the rest of creation. Perhaps most impressive was Thoreau's sojourn at Walden Pond—only a mile from the center of his village but a good deal farther removed in spirit—where he went to recover "a true home in nature, a hearth in the fields and woods, whatever tenement be burned." These men felt passionately that to lose touch with nature's vital current was to invite disease of the body and disintegration of the soul. To be thus disconnected from the ecological community was to be incomplete, sick, fragmented, dying. Thoreau, and the Romantics generally, believed that a renewed, harmonious relation to nature was the only remedy for the spiritual as well as the physical ills that marked their times.[10]

A key word in the Romantic vocabulary was "community." Thoreau, for instance, pursued in his excursions what he called "a community of love," an extended net of natural relationships that he felt could save him from being wholly imprisoned in his private consciousness. Radical individualist though he often appeared in his relations with Concord townsmen, he was at the same time more communal, even in merely human terms, than has been appreciated. After all, to be a nonconformist, as he assuredly was, is not necessarily to be a misanthrope. Probably no man or woman in the village was more closely linked to family, or for that matter to the larger neighborhood; it was inconceivable to him that thousands of Americans should be deserting their homes to go west or to the city.

Think of the consummate folly of attempting to go away from *here*! When the constant endeavor should be to get nearer and nearer *here*. Here are all the friends I ever had or shall have, and as friendly as ever.... A man dwells in his native valley like a corolla in its calyx, like an acorn in its cup. *Here*, of course, is all that you love, all that you expect, all that you are.

Self-seeking ambition, he felt, should not draw one away from loyalty toward one's place of nativity. But unlike those who prate about the individual's duty to social institutions, Thoreau's communal instinct was never compromised by the defense of established authority. Nor was it at all incompatible with a strong sense of personal conscience and moral self-reliance. Most important, it extended to all beings within Concord's borders, not humans exclusively. He continually emphasized that the society of nature is as important to the self's development as is the human variety. Isolated from the natural world, man is like a bird lost from its flock—"fractional, naked, like a single thread or ravelling from the web to which it belongs."[11]

While other Americans of his time extolled in expansive rhetoric the brotherhood of man and the age of democracy, Thoreau's sense of kinship was as wide as all outdoors. "I do not consider the other animals brutes in the common sense," he declared. The muskrat was his brother, the skunk "a lowly human being," the striped bream "my contemporary and my neighbor," the plants of Concord his "co-inhabitants"; even the stars he called his "fellow-creatures." Like St. Francis of Assisi, he embraced the entire animate world on the most tolerant and democratic of terms. Nature was a vast community of equals, and more, a universal, consanguineous family. "The unsympathizing man," he noted, "regards the wildness of some animals . . . as a sin; as if all their virtues consisted in their tamableness." Thoreau's makeup would not allow him to so elevate man above the rest of the earth, or to claim for him any unique rights. He could not accept the idea that man had been given license to reshape the world to suit his own tastes and to seize for his exclusive use the resources provided for all. In this respect, too, Thoreau was a representative voice for an important aspect of Romanticism: in its campaign to restore man to nature, Romanticism was fundamentally biocentric. This doctrine proposes that all nature is alive, and that whatever is alive has a claim on man's moral affections. With the Romantics, a sense of antagonistic dualism gave way to a movement toward fusion, and anthropocentric indifference toward nature yielded to a love for the whole order of being and an acknowledgment of natural kinship.[12]

With this outlook it was inevitable that the Romantics would collide with the humanist moral tradition. The humanist, who typically cherished an elite sense of his own transcendent value—especially in the superiority of his reason to mere animal instinct—was almost by definition an anti-naturalist. He preferred to dwell on the qualities that set man apart, particularly those associated with a rich and full cultural life: libraries, universities, philanthropic institutions. Such assertions of the special importance of man, at times approaching the claim to divinity, could not fail to provoke Thoreau's anger. "There is no place for man-worship," he warned. In the spring of 1852 he wrote:

The poet says the proper study of mankind is man. I say, study to forget all that; take wider views of the universe. That is the egotism of the race. . . . Man is but the place where I stand, and the prospect hence is infinite. It is not a chamber of mirrors which reflect me. Man is a past phenomenon to philosophy. The universe is larger than enough for man's abode.

At night, he pointed out, the proud institutions of the species would disappear like toadstools by the wayside; in the grasses of the western prairies they could all have been submerged out of sight. Thoreau's intention was not to overthrow these achievements but to view them in a less exalted light. He as well as many other Romantics found more in nature to love and respect than humanism had discovered. Western man's long-established confidence that he alone among the earth's creatures stands at the center of the universe was repugnant to a great many Romantics. The aristocratic arrogance of humanism violated the moral sensibilities of these ecological democrats. Man's only valid claim to respect and divinity must come, they believed, through humble, egalitarian participation in the natural community.[13]

A second obstacle to the Romantic intention of recovering a pagan intimacy with nature was the Christian religious dogma. There was in Romanticism a profound capacity for pious devotion, but almost all the leading voices of the new generation refused to accept traditional Christian theology or ethics. Instead, the most common theme in the Romantics' religion was the primacy of nature as a source of inspiration. Nothing was more abhorrent to Goethe or the young Wordsworth than to be shut up in a Christian box of a church, isolated from direct communion with the animating energy of the cosmos. In New England, where the Christian mind had reached new heights of suspicion and invective against the natural order, this Romantic revolt became especially fierce. Thoreau, for example, withdrew from the church at an early age, and late in his life was still hoping that his writings and lectures would help to undermine that institution. Whereas his Puritan predecessors in Concord had brought to the New World, and refined there, an elaborate metaphysics of forest-hating that far exceeded the exigencies of settlement, Thoreau went to the woods deliberately for his spiritual renewal. A few others joined him and became popularly styled as the "Walden Pond Society"; it was commonly understood that this group was one of the three principal religious societies in Concord (after the Unitarians and Congregationalists). As he explained in "Huckleberries," Thoreau had his own sacrament to propose, too: instead of eating and drinking the symbolic body and blood of Jesus Christ, he would pluck and eat wild berries in celebration of nature. His religion was to be a "heath-en" one, drawing its spiritual nourishment from the heaths and woodlands. It could not be contained in the narrow fold of the Good Shepherd, but would leap the fence and "range the surrounding plain."[14]

The effect of the Romantic revolt against Christianity was to diffuse the God-principle throughout nature, often to identify the deity with the "one life" that courses through the ecological system. "If he who makes two blades of grass grow where one grew before is a benefactor," Thoreau wrote, "he who discovers two gods where was only known the one (and such a one!) before is a still greater benefactor." Although he continued to speak of God in the traditional way at times, it was usually in a tone of hesitant ambiguity; now describing God as "a Universal Intelligence," now as "some vast titantic power," and now as "the everlasting Something to which we are allied." To his friend Harrison Blake of Worcester, he wrote in 1850: "I say, God. I am not sure that that is the name. You will know whom I mean." The obscurity in his theology arose from a gnawing doubt about the reality of a controlling Providence. But more important than settling that question was to be alert to all suggestions of a more immanent divine presence in the soughing of the wind or the flowering of a columbine. "It would imply the regeneration of mankind," he believed, "if they were to become elevated enough to truly worship stocks and stones."[15]

Wherever others had looked to nature in similar anticipation, he assumed a spiritual fellowship. He could admire the Druids of ancient Britain, for example, more than the Concord ministry: "There was fine religion in that form of worship and Stonehenge remains as evidence of some vigor in the worshippers." In reading John Evelyn's *Silva: or, A Discourse of Forest-Trees*, published in 1664 and one of the earliest works on forest conservation, Thoreau detected some of that archaic reverence for the sacred oak groves: "Evelyn is as good as several old druids, and his 'Silva' is a new kind of prayerbook, a glorifying of the trees and enjoying them forever, which was the chief end of his life." In such pagan animists, Thoreau encountered a natural piety that had never required an elaborate theology. It was, moreover, a religious ethic that promised a more restrained use of the woodlands. In 1857 he urged that "men tread gently through nature. Let us religiously burn stumps and worship in groves, while Christian vandals lay waste the forest temples to build miles of meeting houses and horsesheds and feed their box stoves." And in his "Huckleberries" lecture, he asked his listeners why New England's Puritan fathers could not have preserved at least some remnants of the primeval forests." At the same time that they built meeting houses why did they not preserve from desecration and destruction far grander temples not made with hands?" More of the Druid and less of the Protestant creed, and America's great forests might have been saved.[16]

Yet another problem for the arcadian naturalist strain in Romanticism was posed by modern science as an approach to nature. But here the issue was a good deal more complicated than in the case of humanism or Christianity. Romantics such as Thoreau and Goethe were strongly attracted to the scientific enterprise. It seemed at first to promise freedom from the prejudices of both the Judeo-Christian and the humanist ethos; it appeared to support their determination to reinvest nature with significance; it emphasized, as they did, the value of sensory experience; it promoted a broader and more detailed acquaintance with one's natural neighbors; and it could offer many intrinsic delights to the inquiring mind. Consequently, Thoreau, quite as much as Goethe, threw himself wholeheartedly into the pursuit of natural history. Even Louis Agassiz, the famous zoologist at Harvard, was not his superior as a field naturalist. So resourceful was he that a twentieth-century scientist could find the limnological studies Thoreau carried out at Walden Pond to be truly "original and genuine," still reliable a hundred years later, despite his makeshift equipment and lack of professional training. But for all this, Thoreau could not relax his vigilance against the influence of science in his own life and times. In the earlier world of Gilbert White, it had been possible to embrace science without much fear that it would undermine natural piety. By the nineteenth century, however, that confidence had been replaced by a suspicion that could quickly turn into hostility, even in such competent naturalists as Thoreau and Goethe. And so the basis for this wariness on the part of the Romantics must be examined.[17]

Objectivity versus Sympathy

According to Eric Heller, the Goethean approach to the study of nature took as its first article of faith that there is a "perfect correspondence between the inner nature of man and the structure of external reality, between the soul and the world." That being so, it made no real difference whether one moved from the soul outward or vice versa; all knowledge of physical nature is ultimately true of the spiritual world too, and what one knows of the self can be applied to the non-self. But, as humans are more familiar with their own lives than with those of other beings, it made the most sense to begin there, with the meaning of one's own experience, and then to extend it by analogy to the entire frame of things. Critics might call this the fallacy of anthropomorphism, but for the Goethean naturalist the label literally had no meaning; that man saw the world as a reflection of his own image could not conceivably be a distortion of nature, for man on the other hand also reflects nature's order—the two are inseparably one. Real knowledge of nature, therefore, is necessarily an introspective process. To look inward is to see the cosmos, to be "nature looking into nature," as Thoreau supposed. At the same time, all knowledge is profoundly ethical: there can be no true understanding that is not founded on "love" or "sympathy," words used repeatedly by Romantics like Thoreau. Love is the recognition of interdependence and that "perfect correspondence" between spirit and matter; sympathy is the capacity to feel intensely the bond of identity or kinship that unites all beings within a single organism. If he does not come to nature by these avenues, the naturalist cannot make any convincing claim to genuine truth. More than that, he violates the moral union of soul and world.[18]

By the middle of the nineteenth century, however, the scientific community appeared to have set its face in another epistemological direction: toward the ideal of detachment and objectivity. The ruling temper of this objectivity has been tersely summed up by the modern historian of science Charles Gillispie: "Science is about nature. It is about things"—and things include only what can be analyzed, measured, and numbered. Asserting that knowledge obtained through sympathetic intuition was idiosyncratic and unverifiable, scientists tended to excise from their sphere of inquiry any hypothesis about nature that bore the taint of personal vision. Such romantic introspection must be subjective, and subjectivism was no longer considered reliable or respectable. The principle of objectivity demanded a cosmos stripped clean of all the emotional and spiritual qualities men and women theretofore had found in the natural world. This demand could only have followed an implicit moral decision on the part of modern science. In effect, the mainstream of scientists refused to accept the Goethean notion of correspondence or its ethic of knowledge. They could see no promise in the doctrine because they were unsure what the Romantics meant by inner spirit, whether it existed in fact, and how spirit might be related to matter. Rather than waste time trying to find out, they tacitly decided to limit "positive knowledge" to a realm in which they had more confidence, the cool hard world of material substance as defined by mathematics. That world was not to be studied through love or sympathy—indeed, could not be, for it was widely subscribed to by scientists that nature had to be cleansed of sentiment and so deliberately made unappealing to human feelings. Such had been the Baconian mission from the first. The quest for objectivity also meant that the outer, physical world was to be kept firmly separated from all religious experience. Science was laying claim to nature, warning the pious to go elsewhere for their inspiration. As Gillispie, himself an ardent apologist for this devaluation of nature, makes clear, the ideal of scientific objectivity involved at least by indirection an ethic and a theology: it was based on the belief that nature is not God, hence is not worthy of man's piety. Even sympathetic response became suspect.[19]

The Romantic rebellion was in large measure a refusal to grant scientific objectivity the authority it demanded as the only guide to truth and nature. Such knowledge as it collects, Thoreau countered, is not worth pursuing; objectivity is spoiled by its insistence on detachment, and is especially repugnant in its rejection of other kinds of inquiry, other visions of truth, as being worthless or untrustworthy. "Our science, so called, is always more barren and mixed up with error than our sympathies are," he argued. According to him, one of the major faults of modern science was its contention that "you should coolly give your chief attention to the phenomenon which excites you as something independent on you, and not as it is related to you. The important fact is its effect on me." His intention here was not to promote an anthropomorphic outlook to the denigration of nature; on the contrary, to see nature from an inner, personal, human perspective was a humble acknowledgment of correspondence and kinship. If a man could *not* study nature as an extension of himself, then it would become an alien world. Hence for Thoreau the manifestations of nature in and by themselves were not the focus of his studies around Concord. "The point of interest is somewhere *between* me and them," he explained. Not a detached, foreign world of objects as "things," not even a system of merely economic relatedness, but a confluence of spirit and matter, must be the vision of the naturalist. Objectivity did not admit that this deeper dimension of relationship could be explored or that it was important to do so. But for the Romantics, knowledge was nothing less than this process of attachment. They sought to reintegrate man's consciousness into the physical world rather than to divide the two spheres. Truth for Goethe or for Thoreau was equivalent to an experience of cosmic commingling.[20]

Partiality versus Total Apprehension

Although he spent much time and money acquiring books, equipment, and data—the tools of science—Thoreau feared being trapped in these partial accounts and so losing sight of the integrated whole of nature. He believed that only by forgetting all that he knew could he truly "know" nature, in the peculiar, deeper sense of the Romantic naturalist. "To conceive of it with *a total apprehension* I must for the thousandth time approach it as something totally strange." Then properties never appreciated before would become apparent, though they might not be discoveries one could write up for the scientific societies. As in natural history, so in every experience: one might learn all there is to be discovered about the typography, color of ink, and number of sentences in a book, but still miss its meaning entirely. "But if you should ever perceive the meaning," he predicted, "you would disregard all the rest." "Meaning" as used above refers of course to the ineffable beauty of the cosmos, but also to the correspondence between self and non-self, inner and outer realms. Possessed by an insatiable hunger for that communion with nature, Thoreau was constantly disappointed by the science on which he fed during the 1850s.

Though science may sometimes compare herself to a child picking up pebbles on the seashore, that is a rare mood with her; ordinarily her practical belief is that it is only a few pebbles which are *not* known, weighed and measured. A new species of fish signifies hardly more than a new name. See what is contributed in the scientific reports. One counts the fin-rays, another measures the intestines, a third daguerreotypes a scale, etc., etc.; otherwise there's nothing to be said. As if all but this were done, and these were very rich and generous contributions to science. Her votaries may be seen wandering along the shore of the ocean of truth, with their backs to the ocean, ready to seize on the shells which are cast up.

Scientists, he feared, had lost through overspecialization and excessive pride in their accomplishments the capacity to see the vast reality out of which they had abstracted their facts. In contrast, Thoreau struggled to hold onto "a living sense of the breadth of the field on whose verge I dwell."[21]

Mechanism versus the Life Force

The Romantic or arcadian naturalist, I have suggested, tried to introduce into the deliberations of science an element of pagan animism. But it was breasting the current of opinion to promote animism, pan-animism, or pan-vitalism as a defensible scientific theory. Sensing this hostility among most scientists of his time, Thoreau, like others of his persuasion, reacted with suspicion and dislike. "Surely the most important part of an animal is its anima, its vital spirit," he wrote in his journal. Yet he found that "most scientific books which treat of animals leave this out altogether, and what they describe are as it were phenomena of dead matter." The whole creature in its living environment seemed to be far less interesting, even to biologists, than a carcass in a museum. In its very language, science failed to convey any sense of the "life that is in nature"; the name *arborvitae*, for instance, was for Thoreau but another dreary label—"it is not a *tree* of *life*." Popular language, and even more the language of the American Indians, reflected the living, organismic world far better than did the jargon of science. For this reason Thoreau preferred to read older, folk naturalists like Gesner and Gerard and to seek out Indian guides in the wilderness. Inaccurate though they often might be by the standards of the scientist, they were nonetheless more truthful in their imaginative grasp of the indwelling energy of nature, the mysterious life force that evaded rational analysis. "The mystery of the life of plants is kindred with that of our lives," Thoreau maintained, "and the physiologist must not presume to explain their growth according to mechanical laws, nor as he might explain some machinery of his own making." But these mysteries were for scientists a wilderness to be penetrated and settled, not left inviolate.[22]

Thoreau too made his excursions into this wilderness, notably to the northern forests of Maine. His purpose, however, was only in part to traverse and map an unknown terrain; it was equally important that in such places one need not fear that everything in nature had been or could be explained by scientific methods. One night in 1857, while camped on the shore of Moosehead Lake, Thoreau came upon a chunk of phosphorescent wood glowing in the darkness.

I let science slide, and rejoiced in that light as if it had been a fellow creature. . . . A scientific *explanation*, as it is called, would have been altogether out of place there. That is for pale daylight. Science with its retorts would have put me to sleep; it was the opportunity to be ignorant that I improved. It suggested to me that there was something to be seen if one had eyes. It made a believer of me more than before. I believed that the woods were not tenantless, but choke-full of honest spirits as good as myself any day,—not an empty chamber in which chemistry was left to work alone, but an inhabited house,—and for a few moments I enjoyed fellowship with them.

This statement seems to indicate that Thoreau had some difficulty, in ordinary moments, in giving credence to his pagan intimations. He was now on vacation in the wilderness, and thus able to suspend his critical faculties long enough to recover "for a few moments" the animistic sensibility; he could be "a believer . . . more than before." But back home in Concord doubt was ever-present, which perhaps is why he hesitated to commit himself to the defense of any particular, detailed philosophy of animism. Mechanistic, reductive science had so deeply invaded his own temperament that he would never be able to adopt a thoroughly pagan outlook, any more than he could realistically expect Concord to be given back to the wilderness. But he had to assume that such passing moments of communication with the spirits of wood and stone, and with the more general life force that gave all nature coherence, were better than none at all. Going Wordsworth one better, he recalled, "I exulted like a 'pagan suckled in a creed' that had never been worn at all, but was bran new, and adequate to the occasion."[23]

Inhumanity versus Reverence for Life

"Every creature," Thoreau wrote in *The Maine Woods*, "is better alive than dead." But apparently one consequence of the devaluation of nature brought about by modern science was a general indifference to natural life on the part of American society. The Massachusetts legislature appropriated large sums of money for the study and extermination of insects or weeds as pests, but they would spend nothing to learn of their value nor to protect other species from abuse. "We do not think first of the good," Thoreau was forced to admit, "but of the harm things will do us." Though God may have pronounced his handiwork good, man asks, "Is it not poisonous?" Even in the matter of birds, the main thrust of popular and scientific opinion was self-centered and calculating.

The legislature will preserve a bird professedly not because it is a beautiful creature, but because it is a good scavenger or the like. This, at least, is the defense set up. It is as if the question were whether some celebrated singer of the human race—some Jenny Lind or another—did more harm or good, should be destroyed, or not, and therefore a committee should be appointed, not to listen to her singing at all, but to examine the contents of her stomach and see if she devoured anything which was injurious to the farmers and gardeners, or which they cannot spare.

This incapacity for reverence toward the many forms of life was apparent even in citizens whose philanthropic and social morality were well developed. It was not unlikely, Thoreau charged, that the tenderhearted president of an anti-slavery society could be found wearing the skins roughly stripped from beavers by Hudson's Bay Company trappers. Closer to home, the wild creatures of the Concord neighborhood were all too often shot at on sight; seeing a strange bird or beast in the woods or along the river seemed to trigger a deadly aggressive response in many of Thoreau's townsmen. In some cases such violence was ironically more a matter of curiosity than hostility. A dead hawk was easier to examine than a live one, however less informing it might be.[24]

What was a casual pastime for the average American male became a consuming passion with most field naturalists. A gun was as essential to their scientific apparatus as a collecting box, and several species were put in danger of extermination by ardent scientists vying for recognition. As a younger man Thoreau accepted, though with misgivings, this insensitivity of science toward living beings; he himself would go even so far, he admitted, as to commit "deliberate murder" if the advancement of science required it. But as he grew older, and more uneasy about the scientific enterprise, he confessed that "The inhumanity of science concerns me, as when I am tempted to kill a rare snake that I may ascertain its species. I feel that this is not the means of acquiring true knowledge." If man is in fact bound together in one great organism with all other creatures, then to kill any of them is to commit suicide. At the very least, Thoreau believed, the life force should not suffer violence merely to satisfy the whims of fashion, the pocketbook of a farmer, or the curiosity of a scientist. But that these things were done repeatedly was evidence that human sympathies had been narrowed by the influence and in the interests of objective science.[25]

Indoor Science versus Indian Wisdom

Thoreau, even more than other Romantics, was an outdoor man. Within the house, mind and body alike are shut away from the vital currents of life and, if long confined, lose all sense of belonging to the natural order. The naturalist above all others must be abroad daily, lest his knowledge lose its spare of life. But even before the age of the elaborate academic research laboratory, it was apparent that science was becoming a housebound, domesticated creature, uneasy in the absence of a roof and a study. The professor sits in his library writing a book about the *Vaccinieae,* Thoreau observed, while someone else actually picks his berries for him and yet another prepares them in a pie. "There will be none of the spirit of the huckleberry" in that book, he feared; "the reading of it will be a weariness to the flesh." In contrast to this distance from his subject matter that the scientist seemed more and more to require, Thoreau pointed to the example of the American Indian. Savage though he was, and doomed to failure in the face of civilization's advance, he had a living experience of nature and a rich store of knowledge. Thoreau marveled how free and unconstrained the Indian stood in the forest, an inhabitant and not a guest: his was "a life within a life." Such direct physical intimacy could not fail to produce a woodslore that had much to offer the scientist. And in his first published essay, "The Natural History of Massachusetts," in which Thoreau reviewed several scientific volumes, he made this primitive outdoor people his own model for acquiring knowledge.

The true man of science will know nature better by his finer organization; he will smell, taste, see, hear, feel, better than other men. His will be a deeper and finer experience. We do not learn by inference and deduction, and the application of mathematics to philosophy, but by direct intercourse and sympathy. . . . The most scientific will still be the healthiest and friendliest man, and possess a more perfect Indian wisdom.

At this point in 1842, Thoreau could still envision a science that would include all the qualities he found lacking in the books he reviewed. He was confident that the scientist could absorb from Indian life a lesson in how best to approach nature.[26]

Ten years later, in the summer of his "year of observation," Thoreau complained to his sister Sophia, "I have become sadly scientific." Throughout the fifties decade, that lament continued to appear in his journal. On one occasion he found that his views were "being narrowed down to the microscope. I see details," he wrote, "not wholes nor the shadow of the whole." On another page he recorded in a painful moment of nostalgia: "Once I was part and parcel of Nature; now I am observant of her." And in 1860, as he was refining his views on ecological succession, he admitted to himself that "all science is only a makeshift, a means to an end which is never attained." Yet, despite these many fears and reservations, Thoreau would not let science go. In this trait, as in so many of his ideas, he resembled Goethe, who doggedly kept on with his experiments in the hope that science, for all its present wrongheadedness, might eventually by his aid be redeemed. Here, in other words, was the type of the arcadian naturalist of this period, who distrusted science as it was practiced but was not willing to give it up completely—a stance that left such men as were capable of maintaining it open to severe inner conflicts and to the scorn of their more orthodox colleagues.[27]

CHAPTER 5

Roots and Branches

THE AMBIVALENCE Thoreau felt toward science was repeated in a number of other areas in his life; indeed, it was the pattern of his entire relation to nature. Much of his daily life was spent trying to come as close as possible to the world around him, to recover a sense of the vital force pumping through himself as it did through nature. All the same, he could not yield wholly and in every moment to this instinct; there were other impulses telling him to hang on to his own identity, stand a bit removed, elevate his thoughts above the mud and slime of earth. "Man cannot afford to be a naturalist," he wrote, "to look at Nature directly, but only with the side of his eye. He must look through and beyond her." It was Thoreau's style to state such moods as though they were absolutes, to be rigidly obeyed at all times. In fact, however, he was a good deal less consistent than his tone here would suggest. As episodic in his manner of living as in his writing, he could not have settled on a single set of responses to nature even had the times been more serene and composed. For him as for other Romantics, truth had to appear in momentary glimpses, though the resulting composite might deny conventional standards of logical coherence. From a single day's experience the most contradictory conclusions would emerge in the journal, conclusions bewildering to a tidier mind and perhaps irreconcilable on a purely intellectual or rational level. But for Thoreau such a pattern was as satisfying an account of existence as he could manage to transcribe. He was content to speak with many voices, confident that the world would ultimately hear them as one.[1]

Besides the pagan animism that dominated his vocation as a naturalist, there was another, radically contrary view of nature that he espoused. It might be called his transcendental side, and was an attitude learned chiefly from the Concord philosopher Ralph Waldo Emerson, who tended to devalue the material world except insofar as it could be put to higher spiritual uses by the human mind. For the most part Thoreau insisted that to be of "the earth earthy" was his chief ambition; at other times, however—though they were rarer—he would strive to defy his instincts and to live "a supernatural life." This mood surfaced most frequently in his early years, before he had taken up scientific study and while he still saw himself as a poet struggling for liberation from a confining world.

I ranged about like a gray moose, looking at the spiring tops of the trees, and fed my imagination on them,—far-away, ideal trees not disturbed by the axe of the wood-cutter, nearer and nearer fringes and eyelashes of my eye. Where was the sap, the fruit, the value of the forest for me, but in that line where it was relieved against the sky? That was my wood-lot; that was my lot in the woods.

Like the white pine that towered far above the surrounding plain, Thoreau too sought to transcend this trivial world, rising above the houses and shops and pasturelands of Concord. It seemed to him at that time that his spiritual needs could never be wholly answered in the material world, even one suffused with vital animating energy. Therefore he must transcend this life; in a more disembodied sphere he would be able to find perfect poetic and moral fulfillment.

In later years this urge diminished somewhat. As the white pines disappeared from the Concord forests, so too did Thoreau's impulse to reach beyond the horizon. Appropriately he turned more and more in the 1850s to the shrub oak, a low, robust, hardy seedling that hugged the earth, for his life's analogy. But, despite this inner ecological succession from pine to oak, he never entirely forgot that earlier soaring ambition. "We soon get through with Nature," he was still saying in 1854. "She excites an expectation which she cannot satisfy. . . . I expected a fauna more infinite and various, birds of more dazzling colors and more celestial song."[2]

In these moments of transcendental longing, Thoreau expressed yet another side of the Romantic mind, one more closely linked to the Christian past. For many Romantics in art, poetry, and religion, the most pressing need of the age was to locate a supersensible reality. Beyond the imperfect, mundane world of nature—especially as revealed by science—they sought a more ideal realm, accessible only to the higher Reason or intuitive imagination. Like the theory of animism, this philosophy of transcendental idealism had its origins in the Neoplatonist movement, with Henry More in the seventeenth century. But for all the overlapping rhetoric of these two sets of ideas, there were also crucial distinctions. Animism wanted to find within nature an immaterial organic principle; transcendentalism preferred to look beyond nature to a grander sphere of ideal forms. As shown in the writings of Blake, Coleridge, Fichte, and Ralph Waldo Emerson, the transcendentalist movement placed little value on nature in and of herself; indeed the transcendentalist was as often repulsed by this slimy, beastly world as any good Christian. The lower order was not coequal with the higher realm of spirit; it was inferior, blemished, incomplete. Rather than looking deeper into nature to find the divine spark, the transcendentalist raised his eyes above this unsatisfying life toward a vision of serene and immortal harmony. In this mood, Thoreau could write: "Our ideal is the only real." Nature as experienced through the body's senses became at these times a distraction, interfering with the possibility of seeing a more genuine and beauteous reality beyond the material veil.[3]

But being a child of New England and its Puritan past strongly conditioned Thoreau's transcendental idealism. He had little taste for any system of metaphysics or theology, but a strong bent toward moralizing. Thus his idea of transcendence was more often expressed as a struggle for moral purity than as a form of mystical communion with the Beyond. Despite the scorn he heaped on Concord's organized religion and its environmental consequences, he was himself unable to wholly escape its tradition of moral earnestness. He therefore identified the ideal with what he called the "higher" or "moral law," a standard or principle toward which he aspired but which always evaded his reach. His entire life as a poet and writer was as much an expression of this moral aspiration as of an aesthetic sensibility. Art that was not uplifting or redeeming was not truly serious; and like one of Concord's ministers preaching to his flock, Thoreau was nothing if not earnest about this subject. This is not at all to say that his moralistic intent resulted in somber, morbid self-flagellation. "Surely joy is the condition of life," he wrote in "The Natural History of Massachusetts." For him, moral purity was a state of sweetness and light, the recovery of a childlike innocence that could attain perfect harmony with the higher law. Such a state would preclude the need for struggle, discipline, or self-transcendence; evil would disappear at last, and morality as a conscious strategy would be unnecessary. Man then would "rise above the necessity of virtue into an unchangeable morning light, in which we have not to choose in a dilemma between right and wrong, but simply to live right on and breathe the circumambient air." In short, Thoreau's transcendental idealism directed human attention away from the present natural order and society's affairs, and toward an Eden-like, perfectionist utopia.[4]

This aspect of Thoreau's life is covered most fully in the chapter "Higher Laws" in *Walden*. Much of that chapter deals with the philosophy of food that he followed while living by the pond, and after. It was "a more innocent and wholesome diet" in which simplicity was the general rule and abstinence from meat the most important specific clause. His refusal to eat meat (not a principle he observed consistently, however) reflected in part a sympathy with his animal kin that forbade his destruction of their lives. But at least as important was an objection to animal food for its "uncleanness." Bread, rice, and vegetables could be consumed with "less trouble and filth," just as water could be substituted for wine and strong drink. In this central ecological experience, then, the nutritional nexus between man and nature, Thoreau was determined to withdraw as far as possible from man's role as predator, a function with biological as well as cultural roots. In so doing he argued that he was participating in the general progress of civilization, and that all men and women would one day leave off eating animals in the pursuit of the perfectionist dream. Like those other New England reformers of the day, Amos Alcott and Charles Lane, who founded the Fruitlands communitarian experiment not far from Concord, Thoreau anticipated that removing meat from the diet would make humans less brutish. Potatoes, on the other hand, were more likely to nourish spiritual growth.[5]

Beyond these dietary principles, Thoreau's life was often unusually fastidious. It was based on a recurrent suspicion of the body and its functions, sexual and excretory as well as digestive, that contrasts sharply with his passionate desire to flow through "the pores of Nature," to feel the vital energy in and around him, and to see the world from the muskrat's level. "We are conscious of an animal in us," he warned, "which awakens in proportion as our higher nature slumbers." This sensual side of man could not be wholly repressed, he acknowledged, but its health and vigor ought not to take precedence over the spiritual law.

He is blessed who is assured that the animal is dying out in him day by day, and the divine being established. Perhaps there is none but has cause for shame on account of the inferior and brutish nature to which he is allied. I fear that we are such gods or demigods only as fauns and satyrs, the divine allied to beasts, the creatures of appetite, and that, to some extent, our very life is our disgrace.

In a more innocent future it might be possible for a man to accept his bodily functions without shame, but not in Concord of the 1850s. There one encountered too many unclean influences, deliberately put in man's way, it seemed, by nature herself. From one of his excursions, Thoreau carried home for further study a strange fungus, the stinkhorn, which unmistakably resembled "a perfect phallus"—"a most disgusting object, yet very suggestive." Such a discovery made him fear that nature was no better than the boys who drew pictures in privies.[6]

In these moods the naturalist exchanged his tone of awe and accommodation for one of defiance: "Nature is hard to overcome, but she must be overcome." Instead of a pagan relaxation, a more strenuous conscience was demanded. "What avails it that you are Christian," he wondered, "if you are not purer than the heathen, if you deny yourself no more, if you are not more religious?" In this line of thought, to worship with the Druids in the sacred groves would be to deify what was base and corrupting. From the seventeenth-century poet John Donne, Thoreau took a motto for his transcendental impulse: "How happy's he who hath due place assigned / To his beasts and disafforested his mind!" The sentiments of this motto make the wilderness side of man's nature an alien presence. The self here is more essentially mind than body; as the dark, threatening woods of the natural man are cut away, the true self emerges more fully: a well-scrubbed, beatific child-adult who has so utterly triumphed over evil as to forget its source. In adopting this motto, Thoreau makes man's alienation from nature not an illness to be cured, but a crucial step toward the liberation of the self. Not health but depravity is the fate of those who let their interior forests and animals run rampant. Spiritual progress, in contrast, requires the steady extermination of the primeval and the expansion of more civilized terrain.[7]

In both his transcendental idealism and the moral urgency he gave it, Thoreau followed rather closely in the footsteps of Ralph Waldo Emerson, a Unitarian minister turned poet and philosopher and a distant cousin to George Emerson, the forest conservationist. Thoreau was one of a great many young men and women in America who read Ralph Waldo Emerson's famous essay "Nature," published in 1836. It suggested a relation of man to his environment that became definitive for perhaps the majority of the new college generation, at least in New England, and might even be described as a manifesto for an important strain of Romantic ecological thought.

Granting that nature has a basic value as a material commodity, Emerson taught that there are other, higher ends that nature might also satisfy, chiefly as a resource for the human imagination. The world of phenomena, he explained, is to be read as a set of outward symbols of spiritual truths. That idea, of course, seems very close to the Goethean doctrine of correspondence, which held that spirit and matter are coequal, integrated realms that reflect one another. Yet there was a subtle but critical distinction: for Emerson the human mind was central to the cosmos, not merely a coordinate sphere with physical nature. The outer world reflects man's spiritual life rather than vice versa, and then only imperfectly. In no way is man assumed to be merely another part of the whole; he *is* the whole— it is summed up in his existence and organized by his imagination.

Of course, Emerson as much as other Romantics perceived nature's marvelous unity, in which nothing can exist apart from the whole. And at times he seems concerned not to mar that interdependence by the elevation of man to a position of centrality. Nevertheless, he firmly believed that the human mind, perhaps with the aid of a more comprehensive or universal mind, is the force that gives coherence and beauty to an imperfect world. "The reason why the world lacks unity, and lies broken in heaps," he claimed, "is because man is disunited with himself." By this he did not mean that man must accept what is already there in perfection, created by God in the beginning, as Jews and Christians would say. Emerson was much more intent on assigning to mankind an essential, ongoing, creative role in the world. He could do this by making reality ideal; the "real" world, the realm of ideas that exists beyond the material illusions, is the continuing, collective creation of the human imagination. This ideal world does not exist merely to be apprehended: it is an organic, growing sphere to which man gives meaning. And only by freeing himself from "the despotism of the senses which binds us to nature as if we were a part of it" can man begin to accept and fulfill this higher role in the order of things. Not the study of a Divine Engineer working alone on brute matter, but of mankind designing a more perfect, ideal nature, was Emerson's encouraging assignment to his young followers. "Build therefore your own world," was his persistent theme. Accept your spiritual lordship over this planet and its creatures.[8]

As with Thoreau, Emerson's program of transcendence had a moralistic, utopian ending. The ideal world to be built would give coherence and meaning to natural chaos, and was also a spiritual standard to which men and women would aspire. It was a system of laws demanding obedience from a still imperfect nature and humanity. And the goal toward which all things moved was a perfectionist one, for Emerson as for Thoreau:

So fast will disagreeable appearances, swine, spiders, snakes, pests, mad-houses, prisons, enemies, vanish; they are temporary and shall be no more seen. The sordor and filths of nature, the sun shall dry up and the wind exhale.

In a more perfect future, spirit will establish its dominion over flesh, the mind over the body, the ideal over the material, humankind over nature. Emerson liked to call this coming millennium "the kingdom of man," meaning thereby a moral victory through imagination and self-discipline. "At present, man applies to nature but half his force," he complained. Man's growing technological power empowers him to reorganize the physical universe, but he has not yet brought to that drive for dominion a higher purpose. The next stage will require an extension of power over the natural man and the physical senses, so that everything morally disagreeable will be exterminated from human consciousness and thus disappear forever. This hopeful-mindedness that Emerson conveyed to the young transcendentalists testified to the continuing influence of Judeo-Christian moralism. Even among the Romantics, rebels against traditional religion though they were, some groups and individuals couched their revolt in terms of apocalypse, regeneration, and millennium.[9]

Francis Bacon, as we suggested earlier, had secularized this moral vision in the early seventeenth century. In his utopian work *The New Atlantis*, the glorious kingdom of man, the new Eden, was to be built by scientists. Now Emerson and other Romantic perfectionists sought to re-spiritualize that dream. In the process, however, they often did not hesitate to embrace the Baconian ideology. Emerson, fresh from a visit to the Comte de Buffon's Jardin des Plantes in Paris, celebrated the work of naturalists in converting the earth to economic use through their contributions to agriculture, manufacturing, and commerce. At home he frequently spoke with expansive pride of the westward march of civilization by means of the steamboat and railroad. He believed that without man's intervention, on the material as well as the spiritual plane, the natural economy would soon fall out of repair and the world would become uninhabitable. Moreover, he shared Bacon's confidence that the earth and its creatures have been given to man to transform. "Nature is thoroughly mediate," he declared. "It is made to serve. It receives the dominion of man as meekly as the ass on which the Saviour rode. It offers all its kingdoms to man as the raw material which he may mold into what is useful." Thus his preferred label for mankind, "the Lords of Life," comprehended much that was also a part of the Baconian strain of scientific utopianism. Now, however, it was time to look toward man's moral estate, and in this higher task, poets and moralists must assume leadership. There was, to be sure, the potential for serious conflict between these two millennial goals, and Emerson in particular was not an uncritical advocate of all technological progress. But the perfectionists and Baconians were allied in being deeply indebted to Christian tradition and in a consequent anthropocentricity. With both groups, nature was understood to be a subordinate world requiring man's reformatory zeal.[10]

This side of the Romantic movement was so strong a force in Henry Thoreau's New England milieu that it is easy enough to understand why its moral earnestness crept into his writing, even when it threatened to contradict his efforts to restore nature in self and out. He too could speak of man as "all in all" and "Nature nothing, but as she draws him out and reflects him." Like Emerson, he could argue that "it is for man the seasons and all their fruits exist." And like the perfectionists he could work for the coming victory over this "slimy, beastly life." But interestingly, Thoreau did not follow Emerson's lead so far as to support the Baconian notion of progress. On the contrary, he rejected the dream of technological dominion over nature as detrimental to man's spiritual growth. This response may be explained in part by his personal asceticism, which caused him to see expanding material wealth as a corrupting influence. A life of voluntary poverty, he maintained, is the only true route to moral redemption. A second explanation lies in his fundamental aversion to the quest for power in any of its forms. Though he might speak of overcoming nature or disafforesting the mind, he nonetheless felt little of Emerson's sharp hunger for power. Compared with his mentor, who must have suffered acutely from a personal sense of helplessness and inferiority which he transferred to modern mankind generally, Thoreau was a relatively secure person. Whereas Emerson labored constantly to improve his fellow man's self-image (and thereby his own), Thoreau was more conscious of the dangers of hubris. He was therefore much more careful than Emerson to limit his transcendentalism to an inner moral realm and to avoid relying heavily on the self-inflating rhetoric of power and dominion.[11]

But to leave Thoreau at this point would be to ignore what may ultimately be most valuable in his ecological philosophy. It has been amply demonstrated that he was a man of contrary moods, especially in his vacillation between pagan naturalism and a transcendental moral vision. What remains is to suggest that these polarities could become complementary views rather than simple opposites. Thoreau, though never one to define himself by neat formulas, recognized in his life an essentially two-sided relation to nature. In 1845, for example, he discerned his psychological makeup "an instinct . . . conducting to a mystic, spiritual life, and also another to a primitive savage life," an observation to which he later added in "Higher Laws": "I reverence them both. I love the wild not less than the good." In 1853 he could stand before an open window, suck in the redolent breeze, and wonder, after all his transcendental striving, "Why have I ever slandered the outward?" In 1856 he was reminded that "both a conscious and an unconscious life are good. Neither is good exclusively, for both have the same source." Each of these self-analyses recognizes that his own peculiar life followed the more universal pattern he summed up in 1859: "Nature works by contraries." Any whole, be it an individual life or the entire ecological order, is a system of paired tensions working against each other, none surmounting its opposite, each in its own existence implying the existence of the other. Nothing was more fundamental to the Romantic mind than this oscillating between extremes—the concept of the dialectic. It suggested at once that all experience is too complex to be captured in a single vision, and at the same time that all apparent contradictions are resolvable at last in a larger organic union. With Ben Jonson, Thoreau might well have argued that "all concord's born of contraries."[12]

In practical terms, Thoreau's dialectical strategy was to learn how to "live the life of a plant or an animal, without living an animal life." He must satisfy a yearning to be ecologically related to foxes and mud-turtles without limiting himself to their level of value and consciousness. He must play his role in the natural economy while standing apart to some degree, as a spectator. Rather than attempt to settle the contending claims to absolute validity made by either of his differing impulses, he took both as necessary and legitimate dimensions of experience and endeavored to give each its due. The result may seem to be a parade of clashing absolutes, but for Thoreau, each instinct was absolute only in the moment of its ascendancy. He would get his feet down to earth, but he would also struggle to free himself from the mud of gross appetite, selfishness, and depravity. Even in his transcendental moments, though, he persisted in using nature as a model for his own reconciliation. Man is very like the trees in the Concord woods, he believed: the individual must be rooted firmly in the earth before it can rise to the heavens. Both its roots and branches are essential to its development.

So the mind develops from the first in two opposite directions: upwards to expand in the light and air; and downwards avoiding the light to form the root. One half is aerial, the other subterranean. The mind is not well balanced and firmly planted, like the oak, which has not as much root as branch, whose roots like those of the white pine are slight and near the surface.

By themselves, Emerson's moral doctrines could not sustain Thoreau for long, for they were aspiring branches that had no roots to support them. They were ideas that were not *soiled* enough. For himself, he would have the roots of a perennial plant: thick, heavy tubers that could support and nourish the most soaring vision of human possibilities.[13]

The test of a philosophy for Thoreau was not in its metaphysical subtlety or formal logic. More important was whether it helped one solve the riddle of everyday living: "How to live. How to get the most life." In a passage that has never been given adequate attention, Thoreau declared: "The real facts of a poet's life would be of more value to us than any work of his art." Extraordinary writer though he was, he undoubtedly assumed that his own chief significance lay not in *belles lettres* but in a practical, living philosophy that had special relevance to man's relation to nature in a time all unsettled and uprooted. His was basically a life founded on material simplicity. He gathered the berries of Concord for his refreshment, collected driftwood from the river for fuel, and cultivated a few beans and potatoes for food. "It is fouler and uglier to have too much than not to have enough," he wrote in his journal. Asceticism is not an adequate label for this pattern of daily existence. In his self-imposed limitation of wants, he found a way to reconcile the apparent contradictions of his instincts, a way to feed both his roots and branches. Simplicity proved to be the perfect means to express his need to be of "the earth earthy" as well as of "the earth spiritual," and more than that, to be a whole person in an age of fragmentation.[14]

Economic simplicity, for example, was crucial to his strain of pagan animism. To internalize a sense of the great, central life in all nature, one must be directly dependent on the earth in as many ways as possible. Therefore, he brought his private economy close to nature's economy. Just the smell of the earth in a January thaw could feed him the vital juices and provide a renewed ecological link:

I derive a real vigor from the scent of the gale wafted over the naked ground, as from strong meats, and realize again how man is the pensioner of Nature. We are always conciliated and cheered when we are fed by [such] an influence, and our needs are felt to be part of the domestic economy of Nature.

At the same time, the ethic of simplicity was essential to Thoreau's other set of impulses, that is, his urge toward transcendence and genuine purification. No spiritual progress could be won, he believed, in the midst of the distracting, corrupting pursuit of material comforts—an observation that has been made, of course, by almost every great

Roots and Branches • 109

moral philosopher in man's history, and almost always to little avail.

Finally, Thoreau would add that a life of simple wants was the only seed that could bring the forest back to New England and so "reinstate nature to some extent." If planted in his townsmen's minds, this seed of simplicity would offer an alternative to the pattern of rising expectations that was denuding the land and transforming it into a manmade world of farms and cities. "Would it not be well," Thoreau wondered, "for us to consider if our deed will warrant the expense of nature?" He was willing to grant that man has as much right as any being to the produce of the earth. But dominion in a physical sense he has never been authorized to grasp; and in Thoreau's mind the quality of kinship and the fear of hubris should make such an ambition repugnant to man's conscience. The doctrine of simplicity, then, was also a philosophy of environmental humility and self-restraint.[15]

In the daily fabric of his life—his personal economy—as well as in his ramblings about Concord, Thoreau came as close as any individual has to embodying the arcadian ideal. That others should follow his version of it precisely and in every detail was not at all his ambition. Each person, he was sure, must find his own salvation, his own reconciliations, his own selfhood. And, as all must do, Thoreau was often forced to compromise his principles when his father, mother, or sisters leaned on him for help. Resent it he sometimes might, but he was never so stiff-necked as to deny his support when it was needed, even if the good deed pulled him away from his communal, familial ties with the larger world of nature. "These things I say, others I do," he confessed.

Imperfect as it may have been, and inconsistent as he was in its execution, Thoreau's subversive ecological philosophy provided later generations with an example by which they might test their own lives. They have found in him not only the reminder that modern man inevitably twists himself into tension with the natural community, but also ideas which suggest how to use that tension creatively: as a single impulse conducting toward a wider range of being—toward a kind of amphibious life, a dwelling at home in two different worlds. It might be impossible for today's millions to pick huckleberries and otherwise pursue Thoreau's style of ecological intimacy. But it was conceivable, even essential, he suggested, that all men and women should strive for a full measure of human dignity without severing their natural roots or forgetting their place on the earth.

PART THREE

THE DISMAL SCIENCE: DARWINIAN ECOLOGY

THE SINGLE MOST IMPORTANT *figure in the history of ecology over the past two or three centuries is Charles Darwin (1809–1882). No one else contributed as much to the development of the idea of ecology into a flourishing field of science, and no other individual has had so much influence generally on western man's perception of nature. We must therefore explore in some detail the life and thought of this remarkable genius, and we must do more than understand Darwin as a scientist; the contours of his ecological ideas were strongly marked both by his personal needs and by the intellectual climate in which he lived.*

Chapter 6 describes an ideological shift away from Thoreau's relation to nature toward a more pessimistic view—the lesson of the Galápagos, I have called it, taken especially to heart by Darwin and Herman Melville. But Darwin learned more than pessimism from his South American travels; he also took away the seeds of his theory of evolution—and of his ecological theory also. Two other scientific travelers, Alexander von Humboldt and Charles Lyell, contributed significantly to Darwin's education, and their influence is examined in Chapter 7.

In Chapter 8 we will analyze the logic or structure of Darwin's revolutionary ecology, a logic shaped in large part by Thomas Malthus and by Darwin's own struggle to be accepted as a scientist in England. The concluding chapter identifies two contradictory moral implications in Darwinism: the mainstream Victorian ethic of domination over nature, and an emerging biocentric attitude that was rooted in arcadian and Romantic values. But whichever ethic one followed, it was apparent that Darwin had made the natural world a far more troubled, unhappy place than before. Ecology after Darwin came to be, as much or more than economics, the dismal science.

CHAPTER 6

A Fallen World

ISLANDS seem always to have occupied a significant place in the environmental imagination of man. Ancient Chinese sailors went east to discover the fabled Isles of the Blest, where immortality was promised to all. Robinson Crusoe, shipwrecked on an island in the New World, found a fictional utopia of absolute self-reliance. And the painter Gauguin escaped from the dreary western life of business-before-pleasure to a Polynesian paradise of natural, indolent, sensual beauty. In each of these cases the apartness of island life offered the promise of a better order of human experience. Here, surrounded by the protective, cleansing sea, men have perceived the chance to begin anew, uncontaminated by past failures. Here, too, many idealists have hoped, nature will treat man more kindly than elsewhere and a reconciliation between the two realms can at last be made secure.

But a few islands seem marked by fate to contradict man's idyllic dreams. These are the Devil's Islands of the world; hard, desert places where the most minimal means of life are lacking or where existence takes on at best a penal depravity. Such has been the persistent image of the group of islands called the Galápagos. Travelers who have touched the shores of these volcanic rocks, which lie some 600 miles west of Ecuador, have found there no breadfruit trees or complaisant maidens. Instead, seen from the deck of a ship, the Galápagos present a cluster of craters and solidified lava flows, supporting a weird and unpromising crop of cacti and low, bushy shrubs. The fierce equatorial sun burns overhead, though the offshore waters are kept cool by a polar current, and penguins live incongruously with lizards on the clinker-strewn beaches. At higher elevations on some of the islands, where moisture is more abundant, mosses and ferns cover the ashes, and sunflowers grow like trees; but these more verdant upper reaches are seldom seen by the transient sailor; hence he leaves with the longing for home all the stronger in his bowels. Yet despite their forbidding prospect, the Galápagos have from the sixteenth century on furnished a haven of sorts to wandering vessels. In that corner of the world, if you were hungry or thirsty and low on supplies, there was no alternative. And so this remote, eerie place came to know a succession of buccaneers, rowdies, and castaways, none of whom stayed for long out of inclination.[1]

In the first half of the nineteenth century, the Galápagos were visited by two more sophisticated travelers who would fix these islands firmly in the Anglo-American consciousness. The first was Charles Darwin, who arrived in September 1835 as ship's naturalist for *H.M.S. Beagle*. Then in the spring of 1841, and again in the winter of 1841–42, Herman Melville, an American seaman aboard the whaler *Acushnet*, scrambled over their hot, blasted terrain. In later years each of these visitors would produce a book of surpassing importance: Darwin, *On the Origin of Species* (1859), and Melville, *Moby Dick* (1851). They would each also leave a record of their visits to the mysterious archipelago. Two very different people they were, with very different purposes at sea and different kinds of fame in store at home. But from their experience of the Galápagos, they were united more than they would ever know by similar visions of nature and its relation to human ideals.

Of the two, the more relevant to the history of ecology, as well as more important to environmental thought generally, was Darwin. He was twenty-six years old when his ship reached the Galápagos; he had been away from his family of father and sisters for almost four years, charting the coastal waters of South America, making scientific expeditions over its interior plains and into the Andean uplands, and collecting rocks, plants, and animals to send back to London and Cambridge. Now he encountered a landscape wholly unlike anything he had seen before. In describing the islands some years later, his first response was geological: each of the fifteen islands in the archipelago, he observed, had surged out of the seabed in a series of recent volcanic upheavals. Precisely how long ago this tumult had occurred he did not attempt to speculate. But its effect on the human eye was still freshly Plutonian: "A broken field of black basaltic lava, thrown into the most rugged waves, and crossed by great fissures, is every where covered by stunted, sunburnt brushwood, which shows little signs of life." But despite appearances, these forlorn lands had acquired a living population of sorts since their late emergence. By some means, there were in residence bats, hawks, great orange centipedes, albatrosses, sea lions, and blue-footed boobies—many of these species to be found nowhere else on earth. Even more than the rocks, these creatures intrigued Darwin. By this point in his travels he had begun to venture more and more beyond his early interest in geology toward the study of biology—especially of the ultimate origin of species and their organization into an economic order. For such investigations the Galápagos supplied essential clues. In these strange islands, he wrote, we are "brought somewhat near to that great fact—that mystery of mysteries—the first appearance of new beings on this earth."[2]

The presence of the sea birds was no puzzle. They could be found all over the Pacific Ocean by virtue of their strong wings and wandering habits. But the land birds, twenty-six kinds in all, were another matter; twenty-five were endemic, including thirteen species of finches that differed not only from their distant mainland relatives but even from one another in appearance, distribution, and eating habits. Some lived on the ground by crushing hard seeds with their heavy nutcracker-like beaks. Others dwelt in trees farther inland, eating insects with their much sharper and slenderer bills, while yet another type resembled a parrot and partook of a fruit diet. According to the long-accepted theory of divine creation, the contriving hand of God was alone responsible for such adaptations. But why should the Creator, in this place only, use a finch to do the work elsewhere done by a parrot? "Seeing this gradation and diversity of structure in one small, intimately related group of birds," Darwin wrote, "one might really fancy that from an original paucity of birds in this archipelago, one species had been taken and modified for different ends." But why should an all-powerful and resourceful Creator have been reduced to such makeshift economies? Turn which way Darwin might, the Galápagos seemed to force common sense into a confrontation with conventional natural theology, and to impel him toward other explanations for the finches' becoming suddenly so adroit and variable. But for the moment at least he was content to be simply "astonished at the amount of creative force, if such an expression may be used, displayed on these small, barren, and rocky islands."³

The dominating presences in the Galápagos, however, were not its finches but its reptiles, especially a giant land tortoise and two fierce-looking iguanas, one terrestrial and the other a most remarkable marine creature. During his month-long stay Darwin came upon the lumbering tortoises everywhere. They were the largest of their kind in the world: the adults each weighed hundreds of pounds and required as many as eight men to lift them from the ground. They could be found munching on the pads of the prickly-pear cactus, and when he came too near they hissed ominously and pulled their heads back into their shells. But in fact they neither feared nor threatened him, living as they did in a world almost entirely free of natural danger and still innocent of the human predator. Though whalers would soon slaughter them to the point of extinction on some islands, they were still the lordly, if sluggish, monarchs of these realms. But more significant for the naturalist was this fact: in the Galápagos they and the lizards seemed to perform the work done elsewhere by herbivorous mammals. Again Darwin was made to wonder why in this place alone the Creator should use reptiles for the same economic function He assigned to deer, antelope, llamas, bison, etc., on the continents. And that a lizard should take to the coastal waters, swim like a seal, and subsist on seaweed exposed at low tide was still another apparent aberration in divine management. Most amazing of all, though, was a phenomenon revealed to him just as he was readying to depart these waters: the tortoises and iguanas were not only unique to this archipelago, but varied from island to island. Surely the "creative force" had here gone berserk in its inventiveness, multiplying forms even where there was no appreciable change in habitat.

Darwin left the Galápagos in mid-October, bound for the more hospitable shores of Tahiti, Australia, and home. He went away with as many questions in his mind as there were specimens in his collecting boxes. How did such unusual creatures first come to live on these islands? Why should they be more closely related to species in the wet tropics of South America than to species on similarly arid islands in other oceans? Why should fully half the species of land birds be finches, of all things? What made this odd jumble of beings into an ecological order that paralleled but was radically distinct from those found in other locales? And, finally, could the natural history of Linnaeus, Ray, and Paley do service any more? Or did the Galápagos demand another kind of explanation, a new kind of science?

Beyond these scientific questions, it would seem as if Darwin also carried away, in his imagination if not his nostrils, the odor of sulphur and brimstone. In the 1845 account of his visit, briefly titled *Journal of Researches*, he recalled the "strange Cyclopean scene" of the islands. Apparently ancient myth seemed especially appropriate to the reality before him. Indeed, to discover here a gang of one-eyed, monstrous blacksmiths toiling at Vulcan's forge could have been little more unlikely than the actual denizens nature had conjured up. Standing on the rim of a crater under the broiling sun, Darwin must have felt himself very far from the Shrewsbury of his youth and the green, happy, natural world he had known there. To be sure, the Galápagos islands had been given reassuring names by earlier visitors: Chatham, James, Albemarle, Culpepper, Abingdon. But the only aspect of England he found echoed in the landscape here were "those parts of Staffordshire, where the great iron-foundries are most numerous." Nature, it was now starkly clear, had its more hideous face, blighted and polluted by its own forces, rivaling the new industrial environment in its desolation. Life in such a world would not be dependably friendly to man's spirit. When Darwin reached the home port of Falmouth in October 1836, he rushed back to a pleasant, rural, humanized environment, a very picture of benevolence and harmony. But in the Galápagos he had seen a side of nature unknown to most of his countrymen, and he would not forget it.[4]

It was precisely on this theme that Darwin's encounter with the Galápagos converged with Herman Melville's. Six years after the departure of the *Beagle*, Melville got his first glimpse of this outlandish creation. Sent ashore by his captain to procure tortoise meat and water, the young seaman from New York entered a world unlike any he had bargained for. He had signed on the *Acushnet* crew back in New Bedford to see the romantic South Seas; but as luck would have it, his first taste of the Pacific islands came in the wrong place for romance. Years later, after deserting his whaling ship in the Marquesas, bumming his way to Honolulu, and enlisting on a merchant vessel, he returned to the United States. Whatever those years had cost him in discomfort and disillusionment, his faraway adventures served him well as raw material for a series of remarkable novels and stories, including "The Encantadas, or Enchanted Isles" (another ancient Spanish name for the Galápagos), which was published in 1856. That isolated archipelago, he confessed, had left him with a recurrent nightmare during the interim between visit and writing. Often, perhaps while sitting in some wooded gorge of the Adirondacks or while dining with friends in the city, he would suddenly find himself thrust back into that other, oddly tragic world where the tortoises wore deep ruts in the rocks endlessly dragging themselves in search of scarce pools of water. "I can hardly resist the feeling," he said of the fateful islands, "that in my time I have indeed slept upon evilly enchanted ground."[5]

While Darwin had somewhat submerged his emotional response to the islands in the more pressing duties of science, Melville gave himself over to the possessing nightmare that the Galápagos had become for him. While on James Island, for example, Darwin had stumbled upon the skull of a captain murdered by his crew, but he did nothing more than record the grisly fact. Melville, however, was haunted by the melancholy stories that gathered around all the islands: episodes of banishment, loneliness, violence, and human desperation. Darwin's briefly Hadean descriptions of the landscape were embellished by Melville, too. One of the smallest of the islands was Rock Rodondo, a kind of natural tower rising 250 feet straight from the sea. Its sheer sides were splashed with long streaks of birdlime, and from its naked top came a "demoniac din" of thousands of sea fowl. This was no place for a robin or canary, Melville declared; it was the home of wild, fierce birds that had never seen a tree, much less warbled a springtime melody from a maple branch. He remembered, too, walking along beaches on some of the larger islands where one could find "decayed bits of sugar-cane, bamboos, and coconuts, washed upon this other and darker world from the charming palm isles to the westward and southward; all the way from Paradise to Tartarus." These rotting fragments of life served only to emphasize for him the "emphatic uninhabitableness" of the entire archipelago. "In no world but a fallen one," he wrote with manifest anguish, "could such lands exist."[6]

That nature here was bleak, depraved, and hostile, at least by human standards, was a shattering revelation for Melville when he came to see its larger meaning. A nature capable of making such landscapes was a force not to be altogether trusted anywhere. He admitted that "the isles are not perhaps unmitigated gloom" and that, like the black-shelled tortoise, there is a bright side if you will turn the creature over.

But after you have done this, and because you have done this, you should not swear that the tortoise has no dark side. Enjoy the bright, keep it turned up perpetually if you can, but be honest, and don't deny the black.

He did not mean to express a total disenchantment with the natural realm. But he warned that even in the quiet beauty of the Adirondacks one could find that "fallen world." The Galápagos followed Melville home, and his mental landscape would never thereafter be free of their memory.[7]

The discovery of the Galápagos, at least as represented and reported by these two men, reintroduced to the Anglo-American mind a potent counterforce to the arcadian vision of Gilbert White's Selborne and Thoreau's Concord. It was not an entirely new point of view, of course; but in the middle and late years of the nineteenth century the anti-arcadian outlook gained renewed energy, and the more hopeful attitude toward nature lost almost all of its intellectual respectability. From a few individual reactions to its distant landscape, the spirit of the Galápagos evolved to characterize an entire culture's sense of its relation to the ecological order of the earth. This trend contrasted sharply with the balanced outlook Thoreau had reached in his life in nature. Thoreau had not been unaware of the darker side; he too heard the "maniacal hooting" of owls and followed them into the swamps. But he preferred to dwell on the brighter possibilities of a sympathetic attachment to the earth. Now, however, in the writings of Melville and Darwin, the pendulum began to swing toward a more pessimistic view of nature. Before long it would be a commonplace that species were the product of blind physical laws, operating without regard for human moral values. The conviction would also spread, with substantial scientific and literary support, that nature could no longer be viewed as a solicitous mother, worthy of her children's love and concern.

The image of the Galápagos certainly was not the sole or sufficient influence that prompted this shift toward a darker vision. For his part, Melville glimpsed the tragic side of man as well as nature in many places he visited and aboard the ships on which he served. And if the opening chapter of *Moby Dick* may be taken in an autobiographical sense—especially when the narrator names himself Ishmael and professedly goes to sea to avoid committing suicide—one can believe that an intense melancholy had blackened Melville's vision before it ever rested on the islands.

Darwin too had been preconditioned by his experience of both man and nature to see and emphasize the gruesome side of the Galápagos; indeed, the entire record of Darwin's travels is replete with atrocity, suffering, and bloodshed. In Brazil he had heard the cries of slaves cruelly beaten by their masters, and had noted along the dusty roads the extraordinary number of wooden crosses set up to mark where blood had been spilled in personal vendettas. On the pampas of Argentina, violence seemed to be the very principle of human life. The gauchos were a colorful but hard and savage lot, gambling wildly, drugging themselves on maté, and slashing at one another with their knives. Even more barbaric were those Indians whom Darwin observed one night swallowing "the steaming blood of the cattle slaughtered for their suppers, and then, being sick from drunkenness, they cast it up again, and were besmeared with filth and gore." And as if all this were not enough, the naturalist found himself in the middle of an all-out war of extermination being waged by General Rosas and the Argentine government's troops against the native inhabitants.[8]

Along with lessons in human malevolence and conflict, his South American experience schooled Darwin in ecological turbulence. Again, the Argentine pampas was his chief teacher. On this great treeless plain, especially along the La Plata River, the arrival of a European population with its domestic stock had worked disaster on the aboriginal order of nature. "The countless herds of horses, cattle, and sheep," he noted, "not only have altered the whole aspect of the vegetation, but they have almost banished the guanaco, deer, and ostrich." Feral dogs and cats now roamed the low hills and riverbanks. Fennel, giant thistles, and the cactus-like cardoon had displaced the vast sweep of native grasses, creating an unproductive and impenetrable wasteland. The new human settlers were wholly unaware of the vital interdependencies of the local natural economy when they set about to reorder it in their own interest. They imported to the New World their familiar cabbage and lettuce, but left behind the associated species of slugs and caterpillars; freed from their natural checks, these plants also overran the countryside. These were the inevitable effects of an invasion of people who not only were ignorant of the natural order but found the pursuit of conquest easier than the principle of cooperation. Darwin did not condemn such ambitions, or the ensuing chaos, but he went away well impressed with the potential for instability in the organic environment, with the fierce competition that can be waged by rivals for space, and with the value of controls over even the most innocuous garden vegetable.[9]

One other set of events may help to demonstrate how thorough and diversified was Darwin's experience of tragedy and upheaval before he ever reached the Galápagos. In Patagonia he went digging for fossils, a recreation that had been popular for at least a half-century and was already filling up museums with strange bones that testified to an unsuspected, alien past. Darwin managed to unearth several well-preserved skeletons of extinct species of Edentates, all of which, he discovered, closely resembled the living sloths, anteaters, and armadillos of the region. But in contrast to the "mere pygmies" that now dwelt here, the creatures that had left their remains in the red Patagonian mud had been "giant monsters." Back in the 1780s the Virginia naturalist Thomas Jefferson had asserted confidently that no links in the economy of nature had been formed "so weak as to be broken." Now in 1834 young Darwin remarked: "It is impossible to reflect on the changed state of the American continent without the deepest astonishment," and wondered, "What, then, has exterminated so many species and whole genera?" It was difficult to believe the modern pygmies could have taken food away from "their numerous gigantic prototypes," as the European cattle were doing to the llamas. Perhaps species, like individuals, die of old age, without the intervention of "some extraordinary agent" or of violence. But whatever their owners' fate, the bones in Darwin's hands gave evidence that the present order of animals was by no means the first to live in this land, that death was as possible for a whole ecological system as it was for any of its members. Such a realization made its contribution to Darwin's awareness of the potent forces arrayed against the living.[10]

Extinction, conflict, depravity, terror—these were far from the qualities of an arcadia. South America generally, as well as the Galápagos Islands, threatened the elemental assumptions about man and nature wrapped up in that hopeful ideal. Instead of White's swallows, Darwin saw great masses of vultures and condors wheeling in the skies; and vampire bats, jaguars, and snakes now infested his mind. Intruding into his consciousness wherever he turned were "the universal signs of violence." But tenderminded as he often was about such gloomy evidences, at the same time he unconsciously sought them out, even relished them, more than he was aware—for they were, ironically, an indispensable part of the glamor of exotic places. The scenes of rugged grandeur afforded a novel sense of exhilaration that made his three and a half years here joyful and thrilling, on balance. He exerted himself heroically to reach those landscapes of "savage magnificence" that made his blood run cold. Volcanoes and earthquakes—where "the earth, the very emblem of solidity, has moved beneath our feet like a thin crust over a fluid"—proved particularly fascinating. Whatever he may have paid in inquietude, at least the failure to find here a cheerful, placid arcadian order had some compensations, perhaps summed up in his bland little phrase about the Chilean earthquake: "the most awful yet interesting spectacle I ever beheld." It was not, consequently, a simple repulsion that he felt when he arrived at the Galápagos and found there a world more forbidding than any he had seen before.[11]

That the Galápagos or the Andes might provide certain pleasures to Darwin precisely because they were savage and terrifying was a consequence of the emotional tutoring he and others of his generation had received. By the 1830s it had become a common impulse on both sides of the Atlantic to seek out especially those natural experiences that left fear in the heart. It was a popular theme among the late Romantics, perhaps their most familiar strategy to achieve a more intense experience, after they had exhausted all the other forms of emotion. While some, like Thoreau, were exploring ways to overcome man's estrangement from nature and giving fresh relevance to arcadian paganism, others came to find that natural joy too tame and to take an increasingly decadent interest in the fearful and demonic forces around them. The contradiction is only partial, for the enthusiasts of fear were in their own peculiar way also seeking a reconciliation between man and nature. But it was a bond of violence they found; to be at one with the world, for them, was to embrace all the tumult, horror, and darkness in it, to commit oneself to struggle and defiance.[12]

But the trick in this quest for dark, fearful adventure was to keep alive an exuberant acceptance of the nature thereby discovered. Nothing was more difficult to sustain for long, as the middle years of the nineteenth century began to show. On every hand, in painting, poetry, and music, a superabundance of terror was presented: roaring lions leaping onto the backs of paralyzed stallions, dreadful torrents plunging over cliffs, thundering volcanoes erupting into lurid skies. How much of such horrors could a healthy attitude toward nature withstand, especially in people historically inclined toward suspicion of nature anyway? At what point would the pleasure of fear suddenly give way to panic? To be sure, many managed to go on indefinitely exulting in the tumult. The young Bostonian Francis Parkman, for example, was delighted to find on the American prairies of the 1840s a world no "soft-hearted philanthropists" could love. "From minnows to men," he announced, "life is an incessant war"; and he celebrated that belief for forty more years in a long series of robust, heroic books. Most, however, could not support the burden of such enthusiasm. War, indeed, was what they clearly saw in nature—the point was inescapable. But their capacity to appreciate that condition soon reached its limit. The late Romantic cultivation of the cold shiver of fear gave way to a more anxious, gloomy mood. Like Melville, many began to see in the shadows of nature a tragic story in which they could simply no longer find pleasure.[13]

One might call this disenchantment the post-Romantic or Victorian outlook toward nature. Either phrase suggests the broad cultural scope of this gathering sentiment and the hold it would maintain over British and American thought for many decades. But the choice of label is less important than the power of what it describes: a vision of an antagonistic, malignant nature, a fearful vision that at moments—as in Melville's haunted Adirondacks—could mount toward paranoia. The very sense of alienation from man's natural milieu that Romanticism had resisted, began to surge back into prominence, to the point of becoming a widely voiced intention or goal. For every Melville, who despite his deep disillusionment recommended that one strive for a balanced outlook, there were many writers who came to see little but the dark side of nature. Alfred Tennyson's "Nature, red in tooth and claw" was practically a cliché even before he uttered it. And this reversal of outlook spawned a crusading ethic that sought not only to set man apart from the fallen world around him, but also to place that world under a strict moral discipline. That impulse became a defining theme among Victorians, much as it had been for their reforming Protestant forebears. While they went on loving their gardens and city parks, where *they* were in control, they were determined to dispel any foolish notions about the innate goodness of natural forces at work on earth.

Charles Darwin in some ways followed this pattern of reaction and ultimately, of course, contributed greatly to it. While in South America and the Galápagos, as already pointed out, he deliberately seasoned his science with the Romantic pursuit of fear. But then followed a series of involuntary and unanticipated encounters with cruelties and suffering that offended his moral sensibilities deeply. Had he not been so well tutored by Romanticism in the omnipresence of terror, perhaps he would have noticed far less of this sort of thing than he did. But notice them he did, and finally his appetite for excitement was sated to the point of nausea. When he returned at last to the safety and order of the British flag in New Zealand, he reacted by joining his captain, Robert Fitzroy, in composing a stout defense of the English missionaries there, and looked forward fervently to "the march of improvement, consequent on the introduction of Christianity throughout the South Sea." As a consequence, he hoped, that part of the world would see much less of cannibalism, murder, licentiousness, and filthy habits, and more of tidy farmyards, regular streets, and decent moral character. Although in the last pages of his *Journal of Researches* he could still praise the "sublimity [of] the primeval forests undefaced by the hand of man," he had begun to congratulate himself on having been born an Englishman, living in an environment made safe for civilization.[14]

The claim here is not that Darwin learned from his southern travels to distrust all nature, including the human species; that would be a distortion of the complicated and ambivalent evolution of his thinking. Along with other Victorians, he continued to maintain a certain degree of faith in natural processes. And he cherished for many years the memory of some of those awful adventures, even flashbacks of the dismal Galápagos. But this much can surely be said: he came home from his travels less a Romantic than he had been when he left. Nature had revealed to him a dimension of her personality that he could not love with unrestrained delight. Back in England, in his scientific notebook of October 1838, he wrote: "It is difficult to believe in the dreadful but quiet war of organic beings going on [in] the peaceful woods & smiling fields." But henceforth it would be his unhappy mission to teach his countrymen to see that hidden, tragic side of nature, the lessons learned in the course of his employment on the *Beagle*.[15]

It was not just to his own generation, however, that Darwin taught the harsh reality behind the often pleasant façade of nature. His influence endured well beyond that of any of his Victorian contemporaries. This was because, unlike Melville or Tennyson, or others who dealt in mere subjective feelings, he gathered and published "facts"— which led to scientific laws, which eventually became, for the great majority, Truth. Buttressed by impersonal, objective support, the pessimistic reaction gained a lasting and virtually unshakable credibility. To dwell on the violence and suffering in nature was, from the mid-nineteenth century on, to be "realistic." This post-Romantic stance toward nature won the imprimatur of science, which increasingly was the authority that mattered most in the world of serious thought, and acquired a persuasive logic that explained exactly why and how it was true. In short, the anti-arcadian outlook—the lesson of the Galápagos—was transformed into an ecological model, and Darwin was incontestably its chief architect.

In handing down this new ecological model, however, science was not an "unmoved mover." No doubt many British and American readers were first introduced to the pessimistic point of view by the works of Darwin, but many more found in his scientific writings confirmation of an attitude they had already begun to form for themselves.

Science thus became as much a validating as an initiating force in the popular environmental thought of the day. This symbiotic relation of science to the larger culture—at least in the area of ecology—has been hinted at here in the career of Charles Darwin; the reactionary spirit began for him outside the limited realm of science and grew to influence his very processes of perception. So more generally in nineteenth-century England and America, science absorbed much from its intellectual milieu. It was indeed a "mover"—a powerful influence for change. But it was itself moved by larger cultural phenomena. How the scientist then went about constructing a validating logic for his anti-arcadian reaction remains to be told.

CHAPTER 7

The Education of a Scientist

IN 1840 THE ENGLISH philosopher and mathematician William Whewell coined the word "scientist." That event, quiet and undramatic though it was, signaled the opening of a new era in the history of man's intellectual relation to the natural world. For one thing, "scientist" suggested a growing professional consciousness. A scientist was something more than an amateur who toyed with Leyden jars or old bones; the label meant that one was a serious member of a new profession, comprised of academically trained minds all devoted to a common enterprise of expertise.[1]

This emerging profession had not only a shared methodology learned in the schools but also, like any other social group, an ethic to guide and justify its work. "Positive knowledge" was the phrase most commonly used to express this ethic. It implied that some kinds of knowledge are more real, concrete, and certain than other kinds, and that only these superior forms—particularly that knowledge founded on empirical study and verifiable by other trained minds—need concern the scientist. His life must be religiously dedicated to augmenting this special fund of knowledge and passing it on to the next generation of his colleagues. If these duties were well performed, mankind would have at its disposal a steadily increasing fund of "reliable" truth. To the extent that a scientist defined himself by his profession, this sense of moral obligation to the ideal of progress in positive knowledge crowded out all competing obligations. Church, state, and family may have been important to the scientist too, but could have no place within the circle of his professional concern. To be sure, science remained a subculture, not a fully independent or sovereign kingdom of ideas. But its moral dedication, success, and discipline soon made it a distinct power to reckon with in Anglo-American culture.

Charles Darwin, at the time of his departure for South America in late 1831, did not belong to this emerging guild of science. He was an outsider, lacking the requisite training and professional commitment. His father, a wealthy provincial physician, hoped his son would either follow in his own steps or, failing that, would get himself a living as a clergyman, and the son dutifully accepted his father's advice. In pursuing these careers at the universities of Edinburgh and Cambridge, he did manage to dabble in the various sciences. He also came to know well some of Britain's leading scientists, especially the botanist John Henslow of Cambridge. But, intent on fulfilling his father's wishes, he seems never to have entertained the notion that he too might seriously pursue a scientific career. When he graduated in 1831, his future course seemed to lead inevitably to a parsonage in some rural village where he might quietly go on with his beetle and shell collecting. That he had read Gilbert White's *Natural History of Selborne* at an early age and been warmly impressed by that man's quaint, unambitious situation suggests pretty much what Darwin wanted from life for himself. Only the sudden, wildly improbable chance to go as ship's naturalist on a voyage round the world upset that long-established aim. Thanks to the very lax standards of the Board of Admiralty and his father's reluctant consent, he got the post and set sail on an expedition for which he had only the most rudimentary preparation and even less understanding of how such an adventure would figure into his future clerical career.[2]

Clearly, such a ready willingness to postpone finding his own little parish testifies to at least some lack of zeal for the Selborne life. In fact, at the time of his graduation Darwin was not altogether sure of what he really wanted to do. One factor contributing to this indecisiveness was yet another book: Alexander von Humboldt's *Personal Narrative* of his travels in Latin America during the years 1799 to 1804. In later recollections Darwin emphasized: "My whole course of life is due to having read and re-read as a youth" this multi-volume work, a sweeping tour de force whose author was widely regarded in the early nineteenth century as the world's premier man of science. Geology, climatology, physics, natural history, and economics were all brought together here in one imposing synthesis. Nothing less than "the whole of the physical aspect of the universe" was Humboldt's range of vision. Too, he gave the reader a stirring, highly colored, romantic account of the sublime landscapes he explored, from the isle of Tenerife to the headwaters of the Orinoco to Mount Chimborazo in Ecuador. After partaking of such a heady brew, Darwin must have found the prospect of a parson-naturalist's life a bit drab. And untrained though he was, he could feel in himself "a burning zeal to add even the most humble contribution to the noble structure of Natural Science." So when the happy opportunity arose for him to follow in Humboldt's footsteps to the exotic New World, he temporarily shelved his sedate future for the more glamorous life of a scientific traveler.[3]

Outsider and amateur he might be, but he was increasingly determined to improve that status and to find for himself a place within the charmed circle. Along with his clinometer and barometer, microscope and geological hammer, he packed aboard ship a small library of key scientific works. The first volume of Charles Lyell's *Principles of Geology*, just recently published in 1830, was among these; it would become, along with Humboldt's work, Darwin's chief guide to the experiences ahead, and Lyell would thus serve as another personal model on which the aspiring Darwin would shape his own career. No better paragon could have been chosen, for Lyell had established himself with that single volume as one of the ruling masters of the English scientific establishment. Darwin's choice of mentor, however, was not based merely on shrewd analysis of where the main chance lay. He found in the *Principles*, as did many others, a fresh and exciting treatment of an old subject. By the time the *Beagle* reached the Cape Verde

Islands, Darwin was convinced of "the wonderful superiority of Lyell's manner of treating geology, compared with that of any other author." Even more than Humboldt, Lyell awakened in the would-be scientist a sense of the satisfactions to be found in professional competence—in expertise and disciplined theory formation.[4]

His reading of Humboldt and Lyell started young Darwin on his way to a different kind of vocation than he had originally planned. They also, where they came together, gave his science an ecological bias from its very beginning. There was as yet no clearly marked subdivision of science known as "ecology," but there did exist in this area a loose cluster of problems and an even looser point of view. To see South America as Darwin saw it, which to some extent was through an ecological prism, it is necessary to understand how these two individuals contributed to his scientific training and outlook.

All of Alexander von Humboldt's writing was marked by an effort to arrive at a holistic view of nature. In a letter to Karl Freiesleben in 1799, written on the eve of his departure for South America, Humboldt explained his program of research:

I shall collect plants and fossils, and with the best of instruments make astronomic observations. Yet this is not the main purpose of my journey. I shall endeavor to find out how nature's forces act upon one another, and in what manner the geographic environment exerts its influence on animals and plants. *In short, I must find out about the harmony of nature.*

No doubt much of the impetus for this resolution came from Humboldt's early acquaintance with Johann von Goethe. For a while they had attended classes together at the university at Jena, and Alexander and his brother Wilhelm had spent many hours talking with Goethe about nature and science. They all shared a dedication to analytical research, providing such research kept in sight larger, more organic relations. For Alexander, this attitude led to the study of geography and of the ecological interactions of plants and animals under the influence of climate.[5]

Among the seven volumes of Alexander von Humboldt's

Personal Narrative was one separately titled *Essay on the Geography of Plants*, which was first published in Paris in 1807. It was written with the help of his traveling companion, Aimé Bonpland, and was dedicated to Goethe. It displayed both the influence of that Romantic philosopher's broad awareness of interdependence and Humboldt's own desire to give this integrative vision some more precise, manageable form. The central concept of the *Geography of Plants* was that the plants of the world must not only be considered in their taxonomic relations but also grouped in relation to the geographic conditions in which they live. Humboldt called these groups "divisions physiognomiques," of which he identified fifteen general categories: there were groups dominated by palms, firs, cacti, grasses, mosses, and so forth. Each major kind of community, in other words, was named after the species most responsible for its composite appearance. The effect of this procedure was to emphasize the visual patterns in vegetation, leading to a basically aesthetic approach to the "ensembles" of nature.[6]

Classifying the aesthetic forms of landscape was only one of Humboldt's purposes, destined to have limited influence on future geographical science. But he and Bonpland also raised the problem of the origin of these plant groups: what factors determined which plants should live in a specific habitat and thereby created these associations? The persistent answer to this question was: climate. One of Humboldt's major contributions was the idea of tracing isothermal lines across the earth, which made graphic the distribution of world climate; these in turn suggested laws about what kinds of plants one might expect to find in any region. And from his expeditions into the Andean *cordillera* he drew another conceptual tool for the plant geographer. Every tropical mountain, he noted, is divided vertically into a series of plant zones, proceeding from the rain forest at the base to mosses and lichens on or near the icy peaks, and these same belts of vegetation can be traced horizontally as one travels from the equator to the poles. There were determinants other than temperature or climate, he added, for these patterns of distribution. Because particular species are joined together in mutual dependence, for example, the presence of one will entail the presence of another. In any case, whether its causes are predominantly climatic or ecological, the plant geographer must deal with distribution as an objective science. He must become a statistician, drawing up tables of temperature statistics and computing the ratios of different species found in different plant communities. The study of physiognomic divisions, he emphasized, was as much a mathematical and scientific as an aesthetic enterprise.

This work by Humboldt, and indeed the sum of his writings, made him a pioneer in ecological biology. Unfortunately, he tried to fence more land than he could plow. But as he wrote in later years: "I like to think that, while I was at fault to tackle from intellectual curiosity too great a variety of scientific interests, I have left on my route some trace of my passing." Indeed he had. Darwin's generation learned from his works not only the excitement of the scientific adventure, the need for a wide integrative view, and the geographical approach to botany; they also discovered some complexities of the natural economy that were not addressed by the eighteenth-century Linnaean school. Humboldt taught them, for instance, to look at nature comparatively: to see each region as a unique ecological assemblage dependent on local or regional conditions, and to study these by placing them side by side—hence an ecology of deserts, of steppes, of tropical jungles, of arctic wastes. In this way he managed to expand the study of ecology from the abstract, worldwide focus of his predecessors to the concrete diversity of the many natural economic orders. A further and highly significant result was to de-emphasize the role of a Creator who controlled from His heavenly perch the earth and its single chain or economy of being. Attention was directed instead to the importance of natural forces such as climate in the creation of peculiar, limited organic systems.[7]

Nonetheless, Humboldt also could fly to the opposite extreme and try to embrace in one grand vision the entire *Kosmos*—which, in fact, became the title of his last book. Especially in his later works, he spoke repeatedly of the "one great whole animated by the breath of life." "General views," he wrote, "lead us habitually to consider each organism as a part of the general creation, and to recognize in the plant or animal not merely an isolated species, but a form linked in the chain of being to other forms either living or extinct." So large and encompassing a synthesis was difficult to reconcile with his analytical science. Although he never surrendered his faith in the value of the scientific approach to nature, he did admit that there are "mooted and perhaps unsolvable problems" that defy such analysis, and that beyond the realm of positive knowledge lies the "harmonious unity" of nature, accessible only to "the vivid and deep emotions."[8]

To blend the particulars of science and an aesthetic sense of the whole of nature into a cohesive enterprise was a fundamental, compelling ambition in Humboldt's work. His trip to Latin America was aimed at developing the new field of plant geography, but he was also eager to experience "the savage beauties of a country guarded by mountains, and shaded by ancient forests." "I was anxious," he revealed in the *Personal Narrative*, "to contemplate nature in all its variety of wild and stupendous scenery." His intention to collect "some facts useful to science" was linked at every point to this aesthetic and spiritual quest. As his English translator pointed out, while Humboldt pursued "the cold research of the understanding" he was nonetheless impressed with nature's sublimity, and "followed her steps with passionate enthusiasm, amidst that solemn and stupendous scenery, those melancholy and sacred solitudes, where she speaks in a voice so well understood by the mysterious sympathy of the feeling heart." This swelling admiration suggests something of the appeal Humboldt's writing had for his readers in the early nineteenth century—an audience that included not only Darwin and Goethe but Charles Lyell, Thomas Jefferson, Louis Agassiz, Ralph Waldo Emerson, and Henry Thoreau as well. By placing reason within a larger framework of feeling and sensibility in his work, Humboldt became one of the most famous figures of his time. It is simply untrue to say, as Erwin Ackerknecht does, that he converted many of his contemporaries from the Romantic religion of nature worship to the more modern religion of science. Rather, his personal career and accomplishments represent a merger of both faiths—made them in fact one, so that science became the principal route to natural piety.[9]

This particular model of the man of science at work was critically important for Darwin when he set sail for South America. In his reconstructed account of his own travels Darwin mentions Humboldt's name more than that of any other scientist. The scientific traveler, he understood from Humboldt's example, must first of all "be a botanist, for in all views plants form the chief embellishment." But the *Journal of Researches* also reflected in the broad scope of its concerns the German's enlarging influence, as Darwin noted the corrupting effects of slavery, the atmospheric electricity in the high Andes, the mining technology of Chile, the habits and appearance of the primitive natives of Tierra del Fuego, and the zoological provinces of the continent. And throughout the voyage—from Tenerife in the Canary Islands to Mauritius in the Indian Ocean—he portrayed with fervor as well as in specific detail the beauty of the landscape. His descriptions of the Brazilian rain forest, for example, when he first went ashore in the New World at Bahia, were thoroughly in the Humboldt manner, at once analytical and passionate. To Professor Henslow, he wrote of Brazil: "Here I first saw a tropical forest in all its sublime grandeur—nothing but the reality can give any idea how wonderful, how magnificent it is. . . . I formerly admired Humboldt, I now almost adore him; he alone gives any notion of the feelings . . . on first entering the tropics."[10]

By and large there is absent from Humboldt's science a theme that would become prominent in Darwin's own ecological thought—the centrality of conflict and violence in nature. The German geographer did observe in Venezuela "the uniform and saddening spectacle of man at variance with man." He also described a particularly gruesome scene of electric eels attacking horses that were swimming in a tropical river. It was more characteristic of him, however, to dwell on the "harmony of nature," not its wars. For the sources for that theme, we must turn to the anti-arcadian, post-Romantic climate of opinion described earlier—a reaction in which Humboldt played no part. We must also consider a more purely scientific influence in this direction,

The Education of a Scientist • 137

one that would surpass even Humboldt in shaping Darwin's professional mind: the *Principles of Geology* by Charles Lyell. From the ideas in this book would come the very marrow of Darwin's science of nature."[11]

The subject of geology had always been essential to discussions of natural economics; plant and animal associations, after all, could hardly be studied without some attention to the ground beneath them. Though he was a geologist and working in another field, Lyell had important things to say about ecological relationships in biology. Most importantly, he revealed in the Linnaean model many serious weaknesses that could not be tolerated by the new scientific mind. That older paradigm, for example, gave no accurate notion of how very old the earth's crust was and how much change had taken place there. To be sure, in "The Oeconomy of Nature," Linnaeus acknowledged time was an active force: the world was committed to a grand, ordained cycle of change that had been followed since the point of genesis. But nothing really new ever appeared in that history; it was like a revolving door in which an immutable ecology was trapped.

Lyell worked from a radically different assumption. Creation, he stated, is perpetually new: it has been in the making since God first began the process eons ago, and it will go on being made and remade forever. The surface of the globe is not simply a one-time, divine contrivance, but the result of a continuing play of observable natural forces—wind, rain, sun—against a pliable crust. Ecology must therefore become historical too; it must emulate geology by understanding the present order of plant–animal interrelationships as the long-accumulated work of nature, not a permanent system installed once and for all by God.[12]

The discovery of a fossil past had much to do with this change of outlook. It had become clear since Linnaeus' time that many fossils were the remnants of now-extinct species, embedded in rock strata of vast antiquity. One way of accounting for these relics which was already well developed on the Continent was the French naturalist Georges Buffon's notion of epochs of the earth. Buffon suggested that the world had been created in a series of discrete periods, each more advanced than the one before and each punctuated by a convulsion or catastrophic upheaval, like Noah's flood. As depicted by the French paleontologist Georges Cuvier, these convulsions took on terrific, awesome splendor. Mountains exploded, seas boiled, and monstrous creatures were buried in rumbling avalanches. These cataclysms occurred between long stretches of tedious calm that were populated by temporary organizations of species, all dest* 'ed one day to die. Finally, with the late appearance of inan, the purposes of the earth were at last realized. The explosions and deluges ceased, and the supremely rational human mind took over the direction of progress, gradually transforming the earth to suit civilized needs.[13]

Unfortunately for this spectacular theory with its comfortable conclusion, it simply did not fit the observed facts, according to Lyell. Some fossils of indisputable antiquity had living representatives still on the earth, which must mean, first, that the cataclysms were not so thorough in their destruction—if they had occurred at all—and second, that the history of the earth and its ecology could not be so neatly periodized. Apart from this, Lyell seems to have preferred a quieter form of transformation and extinction than the catastrophists favored. He felt more comfortable with his own system of gradual evolutionary change than with their history of splendid revolutions.

But it would be wrong to conclude that Lyell's view of nature was more pacific in all ways than that of the Continental naturalists. On the contrary, he introduced into ecological study a theme of violence that had never occurred to any of them, one based on fierce competition between individuals or species for space and food. This motif appeared in the second volume of the *Principles*, published in 1832 and received by the traveler Darwin that same spring in his mail at Montevideo, Uruguay. Unlike the first volume, it raised disturbing questions about how ecological associations are determined and how unstable they might prove to be.

As a historical geologist, indeed the founder of that approach, Lyell studied intensively the rise and fall of mountain chains, the subsidence and reemergence of land bridges between continents, and the wandering routes of rivers and streams. From these studies it was clear to him that modern associations of plants and animals could not always have been maintained in exactly the same spots; they too must shift with the processes of geological change. From Humboldt's plant geography Lyell had already learned to see nature as variety: "one assemblage of species in China, another in the countries bordering the Black Sea and the Caspian, a third in those surrounding the Mediterranean, a fourth in the great platforms of Siberia and Tartary, and so forth." Even a small island might have its unique set of beings. And the oceans too, though less clearly divided, evidently contained different ecological systems. Lyell wished not only to discover the natural forces that determined these specific groupings, but to see them as concomitants of the evolution of the earth's surface. This line of analysis eventually led to an issue completely neglected by the Linnaeans: the continual migrations of organisms over the land and sea, and thus their shifting alignment in nature's economy. In Linnaeus' science, the geographical niches occupied by species were as eternal as the species themselves: God gave each creature its enduring "nature," and with that gift went an assignment of "place" or "station." Even the later discovery of cycles of geological change did not shake the common conviction that elephants *belonged* in Africa and muskrats in America. But the geology of Lyell overturned that confidence, and Lyell set himself to pondering how migration might take place and what ecological effects it would work.[14]

A thorough analysis of the workings of species dispersal was one of Lyell's most important contributions to ecological biology. Animals obviously can walk to new sites, and do—at least until they reach the sea or a river; then other methods come into play, like swimming from the mainland or hitching a ride aboard a floating tree. Birds may be blown off their course by strong winds, sometimes swept far out to sea, and if they are lucky may find new homes on distant, forsaken islands. Seeds too are constantly being carried on journeys to new lands, in the intestines or on the backs of animals or by wind and water currents. Should the migrant find a favorable set of living conditions, it may flourish in its new locale; if not, it soon perishes. Perhaps Lyell's best example of the phenomenon of migration was the Greenland polar bear that forlornly floated out to sea on a chunk of ice. Fortunately, the craft reached Iceland before it melted, and the bear scrambled ashore for a look around. It found no mate, but an untapped abundance of food was waiting: deer, seals, fish, foxes. The ecological effects of this invasion, however, were locally devastating; killing the deer and seals changed the grass and fish populations, which in turn affected the insects and snails. "Thus the numerical proportions of a great number of the inhabitants, both of the land and sea," wrote Lyell, "might be permanently altered by the settling of one new species in the region; and the changes caused indirectly would ramify through all classes of the living creation, and be almost endless."[15]

As Lyell's polar-bear example demonstrated, the Linnaean faith in a perfect, lasting balance of nature was seriously in error. Multiply this one case by thousands of years of migrations and geological alterations, and the economy of nature becomes an exceedingly complex network of interrelations in continual flux. To this must be added still another force for change which Lyell's historical approach to the earth drew attention to: man as a disturber of the natural balance. Over a mere seven or eight centuries of settlement in Great Britain, the human invaders had completely extirpated the bustard, wild horse, boar, beaver, wolf, and bear, as well as greatly decimating the deer, otter, marten, polecat, wildcat, fox, badger, hawk, and raven populations. Even more rapid had been the process of extermination in the Americas, North and South, under European conquest. Everywhere, Lyell observed, man seeks to reduce the natural order to a smaller number of species, mainly those suitable for his economic purposes. "He may succeed perfectly in attaining his object, even though the vegetation be comparatively meager, and the total amount of animal life be greatly lessened."[16]

Henry Thoreau had seen the process of human occupation as a kind of vandalism, like a ruffian tearing pages from a poem. The Scottish poet Robert Burns had even been touched by the plight of a field mouse cast out of its home: "I'm truly sorry man's dominion / Has broken Nature's social union." But Lyell apparently was not at all moved to regret or penitence by the ecological disorder caused by mankind. Violence, he believed, is the universal law of nature and therefore fully acceptable: "The most insignificant and diminutive species, whether in the animal or vegetable kingdom, have each slaughtered their thousands, as they disseminated themselves over the globe." And compared to the environmental changes caused by geological forces, the impact of man on the earth's ecology has been negligible, he maintained. Whatever the source of disruption, a new equilibrium eventually appears, though "it must require ages before such a new adjustment of the relative forces of so many conflicting agents can be definitively established." In their own self-interest, Lyell pointed out, the human race could help this new balance along by assuming the functions that "the inferior beings, extirpated by man, once discharged in the economy of nature."[17]

In drawing attention to the instability of the natural economy, Lyell almost singlehandedly overturned the Linnaean tradition. Or rather, he came very close to doing so—for, oddly enough, he remained a disciple of Linnaeus in many ways. He knew the Swedish naturalist's writings well, and frequently referred in the *Principles* to both "The Polity of Nature" and "The Oeconomy of Nature." And for all his revelations of disturbance and upheaval—or perhaps because of them—he wanted to believe to some degree, like that older providential ecologist, in a system of static order, an essentially conservative nature. At times he would claim that, despite pressures for change, the plant–animal association of any area is virtually impregnable, or he would insist that each province is too well populated with species to admit newcomers. This last he called the principle of "preoccupancy": the invader is almost always solitary, facing a closed, well-knit, long-established community where there are not likely to be any places open for settlement; therefore the migrant can enter only by displacing another creature. Only when the habitat itself is fundamentally altered, its climate or geology transformed, do native species lose their competitive advantage and give way to better-adapted invaders. But however plausible this argument for a stable balance of nature may have seemed, it seriously contradicted Lyell's equally forceful emphasis on the reality of disruption and imbalance.[18]

A parallel problem demonstrates even more sharply Lyell's tendency to cling to eighteenth-century natural history, while simultaneously undermining its main assumptions. Though an evolutionist in matters of rocks and landforms, he remained thoroughly traditional in assuming the fixity of species. He did not challenge the dogma that God had miraculously created every kind of being in the beginning of time and placed each initial pair in some particular corner of the earth. But of course this view had always implied that fixed species meant fixed biological communities too. Could a theory of divine creation leave up to natural forces the maintenance of the vital interdependencies among plants and animals? There was no way out but to make such an argument; the evidence of migrations and invasions, inconsistently handled though it was, pointed to a continual realignment of economic relationships, while religious orthodoxy required that the origin of the earth's creatures must be the work of the divine contriver. Lyell thus had on his hands a drama of ecological variability played by a cast that never changed. To be sure, he did admit some important changes in the cast. There were those fossils of extinct species, for one thing. Here he allowed that the set of organic beings must be constantly diminishing; from an original full creation, their number was always shrinking—given enough time and disturbance from man and geology, it must eventually approach zero. This admission established still another factor for ecological change, since new balances had always to be devised where species became extinct.[19]

There was one idea, however, that was unmistakably foreign to the Linnaeans and about which Lyell was unambiguous. Nature, he declared, is a continuing "struggle for existence." In the earlier view, the only kind of struggle found in nature was that between a predator and its prey. More significant to Lyell, on the other hand, was the competition between two individuals for the same resources. It seems probable that Lyell took this new emphasis in part from the French plant geographer Augustin de Candolle, who had written in 1820: "Toutes les plantes d'un pays, toutes celles d'un lieu donné, sont dans un état de guerre"—everywhere a war for food and space. But Lyell had moved independently toward the same conclusion in his own ecological thought. Once the older model of divine control was abandoned, as he had done in limited areas, the world again became a Hobbesian scene. So long as all species lived in fixed, permanent, eternally assigned stations, there was no reason for violent competition. But introduce natural forces that pushed creatures out of their settled places and sent them in search of new homes in far corners of the earth, and no end of conflict was possible. The English were experiencing this ecological phenomenon firsthand as they continued in the nineteenth century to migrate to new worlds. And Lyell, strongly impressed by such experiences, raised these conditions of transience and struggle to the status of permanent ecological law.[20]

With both Lyell's volumes of the *Principles of Geology* in hand, Charles Darwin learned how to look at—and beneath—the South American landscape. He was equipped to understand the significance of the environmental chaos he found on the Argentine frontier. He could make sense of the rock strata of the Andean mountains and its outwash plains. And he was prepared to see in the Galápagos Islands a story of extraordinary migrations converging there from the American and the other Pacific coasts, creating a unique ecological system on what had been an unpopulated volcanic wasteland. Accident, not God, had brought the tortoises, iguanas, finches, and all the rest to those remote rocks and organized them into an interdependent society. Similar accidents in the future could give that order a totally new structure. Most significantly, the budding naturalist aboard the *Beagle* gained from Lyell an appreciation of the role that conflict must play in the natural economy. He would go on seeking, like Humboldt, that organic unity in nature that made of all beings a single, harmonious, interdependent whole. But he would lay greater stress on the competitive struggle for existence— the inevitable result of a world in the ceaseless throes of creation and destruction.

CHAPTER 8

Scrambling for Place

BY THE TIME he was twenty-six years old,
Darwin had spent almost half a decade circumnavigating
the globe. He had benefited from a scientific education that
surpassed in most ways the training he had missed at home.
While he was still en route, his excellent collections and
reports sent back to England had begun to attract attention.
Adam Sedgwick, Woodwardian professor of geology at
Cambridge, predicted that Darwin would soon win a place
among the leaders of the new scholarly profession: "It was
the best thing in the world for him that he went out on the
voyage of discovery. There was some risk of his turning out
an idle man, but his character will now be fixed, and if God
spares his life, he will have a great name among the
naturalists of Europe."[1]

Darwin himself, however, even after being warmly received by scientists in London on his return, was still not
privately sure of that coveted place in the profession. There
was no question that he could devote his life to science,
should he so choose. From his father he had a sizable income, and his marriage in 1839 to his cousin Emma
Wedgwood of the Staffordshire pottery fortune would make
him even more secure financially. But money could not buy
the drive, self-confidence, acceptance, or achievement that
were essential requirements for lasting professional success. Whatever others may have expected of him, Darwin
was personally far from convinced of his potential to win

fame and recognition as a scientist. Only late in his life, after he had reached the status of undisputed patriarch of British science, did he allow himself a measure of self-satisfaction, and even then it was carefully administered in modest doses mixed with self-denigration. From his child-hood on through his adult career, he continually vacillated between two poles: a desire to make his way vigorously in the face of all competition or hostility, and the yearning to retreat from the arena of such self-assertion. Undoubtedly that ambivalence could be traced to his father's domineer-ing, critical presence, pushing him toward a "productive" life but also undercutting his independence and self-assurance. It led him first toward the Selborne life style, then to South America; it would lead him to London and then again to withdrawal. For half a century his course re-mained erratic and ambivalent.

Immediately on his return home in 1836, Darwin threw himself into the enormous task of sorting through his col-lections, finding scientists who would undertake their clas-sification, and writing up the record of his travels. He was elected secretary of the Geological Society of London and accepted as a Fellow of the Royal Society. He frequently joined the elite company of Lyell, Joseph Hooker, Robert Brown, John Herschel—all scientists—and such leading writers as Thomas Carlyle, Harriet Martineau, and Thomas Macaulay. This active life, however, soon began to tell on his physical stamina. By late 1839 he was forced to give up the strenuous social whirl of an urban intellectual; the energy required to keep pace with parties, conversations, and the struggle for recognition proved to be more than he could afford to spend. A disease contracted in South America was no doubt at least partly responsible for his increasing nervous debilitation. But probably there were also psychological factors, especially a fear of direct com-petitive contact, in what became his persistent need to withdraw now and then into a quieter corner. He sought distraction from the tumult, and above all a refuge to fall back on. It is "intolerable," he wrote in his diary of 1838, "to think of spending one's whole life, like a neuter bee, working, working, and nothing after all." The possibility of marriage was very much on his mind when he made this entry, and not long afterward he turned to that eminently Victorian ideal of retreat: "a nice, soft wife on a sofa with a good fire, and books and music perhaps." In acquiring a wife and family, he hoped to secure a cushion against failure in his drive for place. "Compare this vision," he added, "with the dingy reality of Great Marlborough Street." Thus it was that, like other middle-class London professionals, he came to try to live in two separate worlds: the outer career of striving for place and the inner sanctum of domestic felicity.[2]

But for Darwin this two-lives arrangement did not work for long. In London it was not possible for him, either as a bachelor or married man, to remain sufficiently distant from the scramble for success. The great city around him was variously described in his letters as "filthy," "vile," "odious," and "dirty." But it was not only the polluted air he detested; he found almost every contact there, social or professional, a painful encounter. He needed an environment over which he had more control, where he could screen out these intrusions and the modern competitive life they represented. To Lyell he wrote in 1841:

It has been a bitter mortification for me to digest the conclusion that the "race is for the strong," and that I shall probably do little more but be content to admire the strides others make in science.

That same year he resigned the secretaryship of the Geological Society, and in the following year he purchased a country house at Down, a village in Kent just twenty miles by coach from the metropolis. It was, in his eyes, "a good, very ugly house with 18 acres, situated on a chalk flat, 560 feet above sea. There are peeps of far distant country and the scenery is moderately pretty: its chief merit is its extreme rurality. I think I was never in a more perfectly quiet country.... We are absolutely at the extreme verge of the world." Here, for the next forty years, he would pursue his science in solitude, only entertaining now and then a few of his most intimate friends. At the age of thirty-three he had found a permanent haven "singularly out of the world with nothing to suggest the neighborhood of London," and henceforth he became a prototype of the suburban man —a part of the city's intellectual sphere, but yet not a part.

And as he grew older he ceased altogether to travel to that other world and so became thoroughly isolated, at least physically, from the center of science and affairs.[3]

In 1842, the year that Darwin departed from the city to insulate himself at Down, another man arrived to study "the great towns" that had built British industrial power. Friedrich Engels, the son of a German cotton manufacturer and Karl Marx's future collaborator, found raging in that new urban environment "a war of all against all." The "restless and noisy activity of the streets" was evidence to him of the breakdown of social harmony and cohesion, the emergence of a state of anarchy.

We know well enough that this isolation of the individual—the narrow-minded egotism—is everywhere the fundamental principle of modern society. But nowhere is this selfish egotism so blatantly evident as in the frantic bustle of the great city. The disintegration of society into individuals, each guided by his private principles and each pursuing his own aims, has been pushed to its furthest limits in London. Here indeed human society has been split into its component atoms.

According to Engels, the British people had made the pursuit of self-interest their supreme virtue and had thus sanctioned the merciless exploitation of the poor by rich capitalists. To what extent this critique was true does not matter here; it is important rather for what it suggests of the city's impact on some of its more perceptive visitors. For all its dignified institutions and organizations, London was, for Engels at least, a dismal world of tension, selfishness, and insecurity.[4]

Darwin too had been in truth but a visitor to the city, living there only six years while he ran the race for professional acclaim. It was a short period in his life, but long enough and intense enough to affect his thinking profoundly—or at least to confirm what he had already begun to learn elsewhere. Like Engels, he must have left with a heightened sense of the "war of all against all." But in contrast to the socialist, who explained competition as the peculiar result of new economic forces unleashed in western society, Darwin concluded that he was observing once more the inescapable law of nature at work. Thus the ecological model that emerged in his work during these years in the city emphasized an individualistic conflict between competitors vying for the goods of life. Undoubtedly his London life seemed to confirm what he had seen in South America and the Galápagos. Long after he had moved away to Down, his outlook retained the impress of that urban jungle.

Darwin's years in London, then, represented more than a conventional transition from youthful adventures to sedate marriage. They were among the most decisive episodes in his life, contributing experiences that gave the finishing touches to his science and thought. But of all these intellectual determinants, the best known is still to be mentioned: a book that supported most vividly the analysis of his environment Darwin was beginning to put together. In October 1838 he first read Thomas Malthus' *Essay on Population*. Its immediate effect was stunning; it confirmed for him in a flash all that he had previously felt to be true. In his autobiography of 1876 he wrote:

I happened to read for amusement Malthus on *Population* and, being well prepared to appreciate the struggle for existence which everywhere goes on from long-continued observation of the habits of animals and plants, it at once struck me that under these circumstances favourable variations would tend to be preserved and unfavourable ones to be destroyed. The result of this would be the formation of new species.

Pass over for the moment the argument about species; there was more to Malthus' influence than a clue to evolutionary theory. Ignore too that first clause, for it was surely a bit ingenuous of Darwin to claim that he had been reading Malthus for "amusement": the *Essay on Population* was arguably the least amusing book published in England during the first half of the nineteenth century. (Malthus himself admitted that his work had "a melancholy hue.") It is more likely that Darwin turned to the *Essay* in search of an explanation for the chaotic turbulence, the unfamiliar urban world of push and pull, that he sensed and feared around him. In any case, Darwin's reading of Malthus can make good claim to being the single most important event in the history of Anglo-American ecological thought. Because of its surpassing importance as a formative influence, the Malthusian argument will require some attention here.[5]

It was Malthus who, at the very end of the eighteenth century, gave people reason to call the new study of political economy "the dismal science." Disturbed by the severe famines of that period, by the social displacements due to rapid industrialization, and by the swelling numbers of paupers requiring relief from local rate-payers, the Reverend Malthus formulated his tragic ratios. At best, he claimed, food can increase only in an arithmetic progression (1:2:3:4 and so forth), while population grows at a geometric rate (1:2:4:8:16 and so forth). Obviously, therefore, population must eventually overrun the supply of food, bringing intense competition for wages to meet rising prices, and finally misery and starvation to those "unhappy persons who, in the great lottery of life, have drawn a blank." Writing in 1798, only nine years after the appearance of White's *Natural History of Selborne*, Malthus could not have disagreed more with the providential ecologists. Providence, he cautioned, does not manage the economy of nature with a wholly beneficent hand. The "seeds of life" are scattered profusely over the land, but nature "has been comparatively sparing in the room, and the nourishment necessary to rear them." Nor can man escape "the law which pervades all animated nature." As He did with other species, the Creator made the human capacity for propagation "a power of a superior order" to the capacity of the soil to produce food. This discrepancy must lead to an unending cycle: expansion, then the misery of competition, and finally a forced retrenchment. With this fateful cycle, Malthus introduced a new ecological dimension to Adam Smith's study of human economics, and at the same time offered a gloomy reappraisal of the economy of nature. That balanced order, according to him, must rest on a most unfortunate imbalance, created deliberately by God, between population and resources.[6]

Malthus, as is well known, wrote his *Essay* to refute utopian dreams. But he was just as strongly pessimistic with regard to nostalgic, agrarian idylls. The Industrial Revolution and its dislocations he viewed as not so much a novel, inexplicable turn in economic history as the burden of man's fertility, long in preparing—the inevitable outcome of the curse laid on the species by the Creator Himself. As population increased, the rural landscape had to give way to factories, tenements, and large cities. Should men be returned once more to an Eden where war and contention are unknown, where "unwholesome trades and manufactories do not exist," and where "crowds no longer collect together in great and pestilent cities," they would again destroy their paradise through overpopulation. Malthus did not accept the promises of unlimited material abundance made by the factory owners or utopian reformers, but neither could he find a realistic alternative to the industrial economy in the old rural order. Both ideals overlooked the problem of human sexuality.[7]

But even the pessimist has his comforts. For Malthus they lay in his doggedly cheerful conviction that "evil exists in the world, not to create despair, but activity. We are not patiently to submit to it, but to exert ourselves to avoid it." Only in this way could he explain why God should have designed a world in which the power of the eater to reproduce itself is "of a superior order" to the power of the earth to produce food. The explanation must be simply that, without such a harsh decree, man would long ago have relaxed into the sloth of savagery. Only by the threat of hunger has he been stimulated to exert his full capacities and to advance toward civilization—a goal that for Malthus bore unmistakable divine sanction. Malthus, in other words, had his own version of the gospel of progress. But idylls and utopias not only ignored the inexorable laws of nature, they would also do away with the need for labor and self-discipline, which alone could elevate man to divine grace. Seen rightly, the curse of the species—hard work occasioned by swelling numbers—became a blessing. Without the stimulus and pressure of surplus numbers of people, progress might end and technology stagnate. Ultimately, it was Malthus' fervent belief that man must obey the command of Jehovah to multiply and replenish the land and to achieve mastery over it. All the wild, waste places of the earth must one day be subjected to the plow. Though shadowed at every step by the dreadful consequences of outrunning subsistence, man has this sacred mission to perform: dominion over the earth and all its creatures. To further that end God set in motion the awesome reproductive force.[8]

There was nothing new in the idea that there are strict limits to the population capacity of any area. The Linnaean naturalists, for example, had long been emphatic about the need for restraints to keep each species within its prescribed bounds. What were unprecedented in Malthus' argument were the ironclad ratios and his warnings of impending national apocalypse. And here he could be, and was, criticized for serious logical weaknesses that resulted from a rigidly reductive, mechanical style of reasoning. Take the geometric increase of population, for instance. From North American reports, he concluded that, where unchecked by vice or scarcity, the human population must double every fifteen to twenty-five years. From this hypothetical environment of plenty, and its attendant attitudes toward family size, he abstracted what he took to be the normal reproductive "capacity" of the whole species and applied that rate to the very different environment of England. In so doing, he assumed that the race, like one of the new power looms, must go on producing at the same steady rate; like a breeding machine, the human organism had little power to vary its sexual behavior.

Though more pessimistic in outcome, Malthus' theory of fertility was characterized by the same narrow logic the eighteenth-century naturalists had followed. Like them, he abstracted the individual organism from its place in the natural economy and then discussed its "nature" as a fixed and independent set of qualities instilled by God at the moment of creation. Adaptation to environment was merely the mechanical arrangement by external fiat of essentially atomistic parts within a working unit. The individual organism was a wholly passive part of the process. Similarly, fertility in nature was computed as if it were a mechanical faculty. Malthus discussed, for example, the reproductive rate of the elephant as if it were a function assigned in the beginning, consistent throughout the species, and kept constant under all conditions. Thus only the external checks of predators could prevent elephants—or flies, or people—from overrunning the earth. In other words, the rate of biological reproduction was made the cause rather than the effect of ecological relationships. After the fecundity of a species had been established, outside restraints had to be contrived and applied. No capacity in the organism to adjust to its circumstances, to control its own reproduction, was granted.

In later editions of his work, Malthus tempered his original pessimism somewhat by giving to at least the human organism some measure of control over its fertility. He admitted that educational or cultural changes—especially teaching the lower classes self-control and responsibility—might limit the size of families and reduce the rate of increase. By then, however, the dismal ratios had become part of the folklore of capitalism. Every factory owner could find reassurance in the idea that misery is scientifically inevitable and that charity only makes the problem worse. From Malthus the age had learned the "imperious, all-pervading law of nature"—the unrelenting pressure of population decreed by God.

When Darwin read the *Essay on Population,* he faithfully accepted Malthus' approach to fertility. Every organism, he agreed, has a fixed fertility pattern, established as part of its nature before it ever enters into relations with other species, and thereafter impossible to adjust to different environmental conditions. He thus took fertility to be axiomatic. It was the given on which all his ecological thinking had to be based, the essential determinant of nature's economy. But what determined fertility itself? Unlike Malthus, Darwin did not want to make God responsible for this force. As a scientist he was committed to seeking observable causes for all natural phenomena, be they the evolution of finches, the extinction of ancient Edentates, or the geological history of the earth. But strangely enough, he never applied the same kind of naturalistic analysis to the development of fertility that he applied elsewhere. Fertility was simply *there:* an unvarying, permanent force not subject to modification by the individual's will or by the community's influence. It was a possessing power, never possessed.

Nor did Darwin, when he first read Malthus or at any

Scrambling for Place • 1 5 3

point in his life, have an explanation for the difference between the ratios of population and food increase. What purpose did such an unhappy condition serve? According to Malthus, God alone was responsible for this imbalance; he had created it to make creatures hustle and work. Darwin, on the other hand, simply ignored the challenge of rationalizing this fateful discrepancy. It was enough for him that he had observed in nature a scramble for existence—which must prove the reality of the ratios, whatever their purposes. Yet in other areas he would not be so reticent about teleological questions, though he believed the purposes to be served in nature were those of the individual organism, not of God. Already he had come to see that the characteristics of an organism are not divinely prescribed, but are the results of a long, pragmatic process of selection whereby the species becomes more perfectly attuned to the demands of its environment. It would seem to follow that fertility too is a characteristic upon which natural selection has operated toward the good of the species. All the aspects of reproduction—sex drive, mating season, length of gestation, size of clutch or litter—must also to a large extent reflect ecological circumstances. An organism that persistently overran its food supply would not long survive; therefore the effect of natural selection on fertility would be to harmonize this characteristic with its setting, not put the two at odds. To ensure the welfare and survival of the species, fertility would evolve toward an optimum point—neither too many offspring to feed and care for, nor too few to guarantee a new generation. Such an argument would have been entirely consistent with Darwin's own kind of teleological thinking. It would have revealed the Malthusian ratios to be generally false, except under special conditions of ecological disturbance when old fertility–resource adjustments break down; it also would have drastically diminished the emphasis on violence and conflict in nature. Instead of pursuing it, however, Darwin simply accepted the Malthusian line and seems never to have thought about the problem again.[9]

The Logic of a Reluctant Revolution

With his reading of Malthus, everything fell into place for

Darwin. Since returning to England he had been mulling over the problem of species, sensing that here might lie his chance to make a name as a scientist. Others before him had tried to argue that species are not created, but evolve: his grandfather Erasmus Darwin, Jean Lamarck, and Robert Chambers, to name only the most prominent. But they had all failed, indeed had been laughed at by the scientific establishment. Darwin was determined not to make their mistake; he would wait until he had developed a more plausible, even unshakable, theory of evolution before he aired it to any of his professional colleagues. While still a bachelor living in London, in the summer of 1837, he opened his first notebook on "the transmutation of species." His observations in South America had already convinced him that species can be born by natural means; the concept voiced in the title of his notebook, then, was not an open question for him but an assumed fact that had only to be explained. What, he wondered, has been the means—or, in scientific language, the "mechanism"—by which evolution has been accomplished? By the fall of 1838, only two years after his return, he had found that mechanism: Evolution is the product of natural selection. Those organisms better equipped to deal with their environmental conditions must, under the Malthusian conditions of scarce food or other necessities, drive out their competitors. Any variations among individuals of the same species, a factor the Linnaeans had always ignored, now became crucial determinants of survival and, by accumulation over several generations, the basis for the evolution of new species on the earth. That "mystery of mysteries" Darwin had encountered in the Galápagos had at last been solved.[10]

Twenty-one years later, this theory of evolution by natural selection was put before the public and the scientific community in Darwin's On the Origin of Species. During the intervening two decades he had amassed a staggering body of supporting data for his theory, drawing on the fields of embryology, comparative anatomy, paleontology, and animal breeding. It is clear, however, that Darwin's theory of evolution was grounded in ecology. He knew nothing of modern genetics and had no firm notion of the causes of individual variability. And unlike earlier evolutionists who had been most struck by the physical resemblances among different species, or who had found in the development of the fetus a recapitulation of the history of the race, Darwin came to believe in evolution as a consequence of his observations on geographical distribution and economic struggle in nature. Thus he gave his theory an ecological form in its first working-out, and so he maintained it ever after. This was true in late 1838, when his ideas first coalesced. It was true in 1842, when he dashed off a short sketch for his private use, and in 1844, when he set down a lengthy essay on his hypothesis. And it was still true when the Origin was published in 1859. Because of this remarkable constancy, the finished logic of the Darwinian theory may be reconstructed without retracing in detail those intervening years.[11]

The bedrock idea upon which Darwin built, though he never isolated it as such, was that all survival on earth is socially determined. Nature is "a web of complex relations," he wrote, and no individual organism or species can live independently of that web. A parallel assumption was that even the most insignificant creatures are important to the welfare of their conjoining species; somewhere at least they are "essential members of society, or at some former period may have been so." These "beautiful co-adaptations," as Darwin called them, could be minutely specific. The parasitic mistletoe, for example, must take its nourishment only from certain species of trees; its seeds are dispersed only by certain birds; and its flowers are pollinated only by a particular group of insects. Darwin was especially taken with such cases of relatedness, not only for their ingenuity but for the evidence they provided that nature is "one grand scheme" of cooperative integration. Both the Linnaean "economy of nature" and Humboldt's study of mutually dependent communities were important in shaping Darwin's own view of ecological interdependence.[12]

In the second step of his logic, Darwin again followed the eighteenth-century naturalists very closely. The economy of nature is more than a working composite of organisms, he believed; considered abstractly, it is a system of "places," or what later ecologists would call "niches." Sometimes Darwin preferred to use the more bureaucratic word "office," which he borrowed from Linnaeus' "Polity of Nature." In any case, the word generally meant a feeding role or the sources of an organism's food; for instance, the Galápagos iguana that ate seaweed and thus filled "the same place in Nature" held by coastal herbivores in South America. At other times, Darwin's concept of "place" referred to a more complex and inclusive pattern of behavior. Whales and porpoises, for instance, though warm-blooded mammals, have assumed in modern times the place—the habits and entire manner of living—occupied in the Mesozoic era by the ichthyosaurus, a cold-blooded reptile. As with the providentialists, Darwin's notion of "place" was fully separable from the organism—indeed more so in his case, for he understood that over the long history of the earth a number of very different species might occupy the same place. The earlier process of isolating place from occupant had been thoroughly Platonic in its method: places were ideas that existed in the mind of God before He created inhabitants to fill them. Darwin, on the other hand, substituted the mind of the scientist for the mind of God. It was man who abstracted from the complex economic relations in nature a set of ideal categories to mark off the whole. Like the parallel idea of species, places or offices were meant to be descriptive rather than legislative—rough analytical tools for use by the scientist in contrast to fixed divine commands. But this concept of place suffered the common fate of abstractions, soon becoming as firmly reified in Darwin's mind as in Linnaeus'. Everywhere he looked he saw the same economic places: a hypostatized table of organization into which nature must fit its creations. Hence the giant tortoise of the Galápagos and the bison of North America were seen to perform the same office in nature, though otherwise living in different worlds. [13]

It was in the third step of his logic that Darwin broke most clearly with the traditional ecological view, thanks to help from Lyell and Malthus. He came to realize that no one species can hold a particular place in the economy of nature forever. At every moment each place is up for grabs, and sooner or later a replacement will be found and the old occupant shoved out of the circle to perish alone. In 1859 he wrote: "All organic beings are striving to seize on each place in the economy of nature." Siblings struggle against each other to fill their parent's slot as soon as it is vacated, and even before. Invaders enter a country and seek a place for themselves. The effect of this constant competition is that the entire economy progresses toward an ever greater overall efficiency. On the other hand, Darwin admitted that the natural economy has never been a perfect system. Some office-holders maintain their place with unusual tenacity and survive all challenges from their competitors, but even those who thus endure are only temporarily secure. Others can hold their position only for the briefest moment before more capable species shoulder them aside.[14]

That nature might be imperfect, and hence open to competitive improvement in any of its parts, or in the whole, was a radical departure from the opinion of the eighteenth-century ecologists. Darwin's conviction that the natural economy contains a finite number of slots further increased the likelihood of conflict in nature. Shortly after reading Malthus, he jotted in his notebook: "One might say there is a force like a hundred thousand wedges trying to force every kind of structure into the gaps in the economy of nature, or rather forming gaps by thrusting out the weaker ones." Very simply, the amount of life is too great for the number of available places in the system. There is a chronic labor surplus. New places may be created by drastic environmental change, like a warming of the climate, but the same process probably will eliminate existing slots. Thus Darwin recast Malthus in his own terms: the total number of places in the natural order must remain fairly constant, while new types of organisms must multiply rapidly. As these new forms continue to arise, some old species and most of the new ones must become extinct, for "the number of places in the polity of nature is not indefinitely great." Indeed, Darwin believed that almost all conceivable economic roles are already filled and tenaciously guarded, forcing continual confrontations between life forms, old and new: "We see how full nature [sic]," he wrote, "how finely each holds its place."[15]

In the 1844 essay, Darwin first tried to explain the nature of genetic variation—the fourth step in his ecological model. During periods of geological change, he speculated, plants and animals encounter unfamiliar conditions which mysteriously influence their "germinal vesicles" so that their offspring show marked variation. The same effect might obtain were an animal to migrate to a new environment, where its subsequent offspring would probably show radically new characteristics. In times of scarcity these variations must result in competitive struggles between parent and progeny, which are "not constant but only recurrent in a slight degree at short periods." Nature, it would thus appear, remains peaceful and unvarying over long stretches of time. But as he surveyed the multitude of organisms for which natural selection must account, Darwin began to scale down the degree of variation required to give a competitive edge. At the same time, he extended his estimate of the periods of acute struggle for existence. Rather than the radical, sporadic mutations supposedly induced by major environmental change, the variations needed for the process of natural selection now seemed more likely to be the usually small, even minute, differences in progeny attendant on normal reproduction. "The merest trifle," he wrote in the *Origin*, "would often give the victory to one organic being over another."[16]

At this point in his model, Darwin had constructed a theory of evolution by ecological replacement. As he put it, he had arrived at "the absolute knowledge that species die and others replace them." The economic system always maintained the grand stability of its abstract divisions, and yet due to its changing personnel it was never quite the same. As far as evolution was concerned, according to this theory there were but two ways in which new species could appear and survive. In the first, the new variant organism proves to be more successful in competition and takes someone else's place. In the second, a place in the economy somehow is standing empty, and the variant seizes it. So, Darwin wrote, "if all men were dead, then monkeys make men, men make angels." This latter route involved much less competition, but there was also little opportunity in a crowded world to find unappropriated openings. Now and then, however, one could discover a locale where the table of organization was not yet filled with names. The Galápagos Islands presented just such a situation: so recently emerged and so isolated were they that only a few creatures thus far had come upon their unexploited resources. The absence of competitors contending for a slot allowed the finches to move into many of the available places, to diversify in a way that would have been impossible in large, open continental areas, where constant migration and strong rivals had always kept them caged. So, too, in this underpopulated area could tortoises evolve to fill the role of principal herbivore. Only in such geographically isolated situations—islands or high mountain valleys, for example—could a single taxonomic group fill so many places and do work that elsewhere was done by others. But such situations also create a highly vulnerable ecology: In a world where competition is minimal, each organism's defenses against new immigrants consequently must be weak.[17]

There was, however, a serious fallacy in Darwin's logic as reconstructed here. So far he had been still living in Linnaeus' intellectual world, seeing the "allotted places" in nature as fixed and limited in quantity. But as a historian of the earth, he knew that the shape of the natural economy itself, as well as its personnel, had evolved. It had vastly expanded, diversified, branched out since the first one-celled organism wriggled in its warm, shallow sea. Surely it was wrong, then, to conclude that in most areas all the places were already taken; the great majority could not even have been invented yet. Darwin sensed this fallacy himself and moved to correct it with a final step in his theory's structure, one frequently unmentioned or forgotten—the principle of "divergence." According to his autobiography, the idea first came to him as he was riding in a carriage near his country home. "The modified offspring of all dominant and increasing forms," he would later write, "tend to become adapted to many and highly diversified places in the economy of nature." In other words, rather than competing with one another for the same economic place, offspring may work out wholly new occupations for themselves, diverging from their parents and siblings and exploiting untapped resources and habitats. This process of ecological complication is described in his "Notebooks on Transmutation":

The enormous number of animals in the world depends of [*sic*] their varied structure & complexity. —hence as the forms became complicated, they opened *fresh* means of adding to their complexity.... Without enormous complexity, it is impossible to cover *whole* surface of world with life.

As the degree of divergence widens, more and more living forms can be supported in the same area. This was precisely what the Galápagos finches were doing: not merely filling stereotyped places that had no occupants as yet, but rather creating new places for themselves in a new environment. Similarly, the evolution of a new kind of grass may create a series of new niches for animals still undeveloped, and they in turn may someday serve as prey for new species of predators—all occurring without competition.[18]

Somehow the principle of divergence never got quite enough emphasis in the *Origin of Species*, though it was essential to explaining the history and direction of the ecological system. Nonetheless, Darwin now realized that nature could be said to have a discernible goal: that of a constantly increasing diversity of organic types in any area. In effect, diversity was nature's way of getting round the fiercely competitive struggle for limited resources. So long as all organisms conformed to fixed types, all wanting the same goods, conflict was inevitable. In contrast, deviance from the norm could open a more peaceful route and a well-rewarded one; the organism that was born different and found a way to use its uniqueness might establish itself without the need for competition. One might, that is, create one's own special place that none had ever occupied before—and not at the expense of another's survival. Not all those organisms that avoided the beaten path discovered such a bonanza, but the possibility did exist and had been realized, not by one or two, but by several million enterprising founders of new species and varieties. Eventually, of course, their offspring might exhaust those newfound riches, and then only a fresh initiative could avoid the resurgence of conflict. Still, the principle of divergence ensured that competition was not the only law of nature. Variation, individuality, and deviance were also to be found in the natural economy, as alternatives to confrontation. Above all, nature must now be seen as a creative, innovative force. Within it and in all its organic beings lay the potential to devise new ways of living, an energy and an innate resourcefulness that could make use of resources whose very existence had not been suspected. Only in an uncreative world, locked into rigid patterns of survival, need scarcity and conflict become an inescapable fate.

Darwin never seemed able to focus on these implications of the principle of divergence, however, for they complicated and even contradicted the emphasis he placed on competitive replacement. Sometimes, in fact, a description of divergence was directly followed by the assertion that each new variety must take "the place of" and exterminate "its less well-fitted parent." Understandably, then, Charles Lyell, with whom Darwin continued to correspond after leaving London and to whom he revealed early versions of his theory, was puzzled as to how simple replacement could account for the obvious coexistence of complex and simple beings, if the former were supposed always to eliminate the latter. Did not the Darwinian theory require something like Lamarck's "monads": new simple organisms created continuously and spontaneously at the bottom of nature's ladder? How else were we to get from an ancient economy of one species to the present abundance and diversity of types? Admitting in a letter to Lyell that this problem was "the most serious omission" in the *Origin*, Darwin speculated that members of the primordial parent species of all living and extinct creatures may still be alive on the earth, having kept their own place for millions of years and yet not prevented their children from finding and occupying new places—an impossibility by the strict application of his competitive replacement doctrine. Yet in the same letter, he also predicted that the orangutan must inevitably be "beaten and exterminated" by the genus man. No coexistence here could be possible; nature had decreed but a single place at this advanced level in her economy, and only one of the two species can occupy that place. Competitive replacement, not divergence and tolerance, continued to dominate Darwin's thinking.[19]

To some extent this dodging and confusion can be attributed to Darwin's divided education. Like other biologists of the early nineteenth century, he had been well tutored in a static rationalism based on the model of Linnaeus, for whom nature was a neat mechanical arrangement, perfectly simple, finished, logical. Thus Darwin continued to conceive of the economy as a hypostatized series of fixed places, into which he vainly tried to fit a dynamic, expanding world of organisms. That nature is a growing, creative, unfinished structure—an ongoing elaboration of the life force—was the central theme of Goethe, Humboldt, and the Romantic philosophers of nature from whom Darwin also learned much. The outcome of this mix in his education was indecisiveness. He was never able to reconcile the two outlooks, but muddled along in unresolved ambivalence.

Take for instance the "tree of life" metaphor he introduced in the *Origin* to explain the progress of evolution. Repudiating the straight, linear model of the old chain of being, he suggested that nature is taxonomically more like a tree sending out its branches in many directions, and these in turn put out their own shoots and twigs. The tree does not fill a preordained space; there are no molds into which its branches must be fitted. This metaphor was a typically Romantic concept. It was intended to illustrate that the whole of nature is an organic unity, developing from a single set of roots and diversifying in interconnected branches with no more conflict or competition than that exhibited by the organs of one body. According to this concept, man is related to the great apes but not as their direct descendant; from an earlier common progenitor the two types have diverged along parallel but separate branches. Where was the need, then, for man to "beat" or "exterminate" the orangutan, since both have lived and presumably can go on living together on the earth in their own spheres? As we have seen, the same model of tolerant diversity was reflected in Darwin's ecological thought: it was not always

Scrambling for Place • 163

a system of rigid, abstractly determined places, but at times was described as an innovative, growing organism in which there are as many roles as there are beings evolving to define them. More like a coral colony than a tree, in fact, the animate nature Darwin revealed had no closed life cycle or genetically coded limits of growth. It could continue to diversify its economy toward an open-ended future.[20]

But Darwin would not surrender, even in his tree metaphor, his belief in competitive replacement as the essence of natural selection. To the American botanist Asa Gray in 1857, and to the Linnaean Society in 1858, he presented his tree in a different light: New branches somehow must destroy "the less vigorous" ones, leaving "the dead and lost branches rudely representing extinct genera and families." The biological oddity of a tree that could grow by warfare among its limbs amounted to a tacit admission by Darwin either that his metaphor did not accurately describe animate nature as a taxonomic and ecological whole or that organicism could not be reconciled with his observations of conflict and violence. No organism, of course, matures by simple competition and the replacement of its parts. For nature to be a branching, radiating tree of life, it must have the power to send forth fruits, nuts, flowers, thorns, leaves, and forms yet unheard of in botanical experience, and to maintain all these at once as healthy and mutually beneficial growths.[21]

There remained for Darwin, however, contesting and usually overriding his organismic moods, the brutal, irrefutable fact of individualistic competition. Despite his own examples of the extinct ichthyosaurus and the fossil Edentates of Patagonia—which would seem to be branches that had fallen off without the pressures of competition—he still saw looming in the foreground the somber, tragic specter of Malthusian scarcity and contention. Although he temporized that this "warfare" between closely related species or individuals was only another metaphor and might not always involve actual physical combat or painful death, he also declared in unmistakably warlike language that inferior beings must be "beaten and supplanted" by their superiors in "dreadful" and savage hostility. In his essay of 1844, in the *Origin of Species*, and in *The Descent* of *Man* (1871), he persistently ignored the implications of his principle of ecological divergence and his organismic tree of life. In 1881, near the end of his life, he was as strongly impressed as ever with the universality of violence in man and nature. Noting that "the Caucasian races have beaten the Turkish hollow in the struggle for existence," he added that it seemed to be the law of history and progress that an "endless number of lower races" had to be wiped out by "the higher civilized races." However loosely interpreted it might be, warfare was the abiding reality on earth.[22]

Here, then, in brief outline is the structure of logic that supported Darwin's revolutionary ecological vision. Into its making went all his personal experience of travel and professional anxiety, as well as contributions from Lyell, Humboldt, Malthus, and the entire climate of opinion in Victorian England. Except for the final point on divergence, it was all completed in his head before he moved out of "dirty, odious London" to rural seclusion. But, strange as it seems, it was kept absolutely secret from every scientist and friend in the world, save two or three most intimate and trusted cronies, for over two decades. Altogether this was one of the most astonishing performances in the history of science, indeed of modern thought generally. Clearly Darwin was a most reluctant revolutionary. He simply could not bring himself to storm the barricades or nail his theses on the doors of established authority. Quite possibly, had he not been given a sudden push, he would never have published his theory; and thus the revolution, if it was to occur at all, would have had to find a bolder, more aggressive leader. As it happened, the push came from Alfred Russel Wallace, another academically untrained naturalist, who in 1858 sent Darwin a letter that contained, in essence, the very theory of natural selection over which Darwin had deliberated for so long. Nothing could so quickly have shattered the peace at Down; suddenly the specter of competition had returned in Darwin's own mail. Now he could no longer avoid entering the arena of public scrutiny; if he continued to hang back, someone else might win his place and honor, after all. Within little more than a year his epoch-making *Origin of Species* was in the bookstalls—

done up in a drab green cover but concealing a veritable bombshell.[23]

His incredible reticence and delay were due in part to an extravagant degree of professional caution. Those twenty-one years, however, were not spent merely in piling up more and more data for his case. He was sure all along that he was right, but dreadfully uncertain as to how he would be received if he ever took a public stand. His close friend, the botanist Joseph Hooker, was the first person to whom he dared to reveal his project. In 1844 Darwin sent Hooker a most peculiarly convoluted and apologetic explanation:

At last gleams of light have come and I am almost convinced (quite contrary to the opinion I started with) that species are not (it is like confessing a murder) immutable. . . . I think I have found out (here's presumption!) the simple way by which species become exquisitely adapted to various ends. You will groan and think to yourself, "on what a man have I been wasting my time and writing to." I should five years ago have thought so.

This statement is, first of all, deliberately misleading in its chronology, concealing the fact that Darwin had been firmly convinced of his theory six years earlier. It is also marked throughout by his scarcely contained fear of what other scientists will say about his work and ability, even his long-admiring associate Hooker. Well after his name had become known in the scientific community, Darwin continued to feel keenly that he was an outsider who had yet to prove himself. Indeed, in a sense he was; had he not been, it is unlikely that he would ever have devised his radical theory of natural selection. Scientific revolutions are generally accomplished by those who are not yet fully absorbed into the mainstream of opinion and power. But at the same time he was an outsider who desperately wanted to get in, to be highly regarded and secure in his fame. It was important to him to impress the very people he was challenging. The vision of failure in this delicate enterprise haunted Darwin until 1859 and even beyond, driving him to seclusion, distraction, and procrastination.[24]

Once his own ambition had forced him into the arena, however, all his long-slumbering competitive instincts suddenly awakened. He would not go to London to explain and defend his theory in person, but he would be a most pugnacious spectator from his country seat. Of Hooker, Lyell, and Gray, he inquired whether the *Origin* had "staggered" any scientists—"whether I produce any effect on such a mind." The precise effect he wanted, in fact, was to blast the world of professional expertise with a high charge of intellectual dynamite; nothing less would satisfy his need for impact. Almost immediately after publishing, he donned his combat uniform and sounded the call to arms. To Hooker, in March 1860, he sent a table showing British scientists arranged in columns, some firmly agreeing with him, others going along, still others opposed. Earlier, to Thomas Huxley, he had promised: "If we can once make a compact set of believers, we shall in time conquer." And to Lyell he declared: "I am determined to fight to the last." It was all very Victorian, of course: the thrill of manly combat, the sense of having comrades in arms, the do-or-die spirit of a Rugby football match. That was the side of himself from which Darwin had run away to Down—the strenuous life that, even in abjuring, he could not help but love and enjoy.[25]

Violent encounter, I have been suggesting, was the dominant theme in Darwin's personal makeup: now fear of it, now relish. On balance, he early discovered he was not psychologically or physically equipped to handle much of such strife, or all that he would have liked to taste. But the retreat to rural tranquility did not mean he was through with the problem forever, nor the end of the old back-and-forth pattern of attack and withdrawal. He remained all his life a man nearly obsessed with the ideas of competition, struggle, and conquest—with all the forms of human contact as confrontation. It can be no surprise, then, to find these same themes translated into his science—indeed, made central to his theory. Had he been a chemist or physicist, perhaps this carryover would not have been so obvious, or even possible. But it is difficult even to imagine Darwin in such fields. He wanted to study ecology and evolutionary biology; through them he could see himself and his inner dilemmas mirrored in nature. The degree to which temperament and personal needs determine the choice of field a scientist makes is not always admitted or appreciated. Nor, for that matter, is it always recognized how sharply the private, subjective self may be reflected in supposedly objective data and theory.

Explaining Darwin's ecology by the psychology of the private man need not detract from the brilliantly rational intellectual achievement his science represents. There is no doubt that he was, despite his own self-deflating and grudging appraisal, enormously skilled in close observation and reasoning. At every step of his South American travels he was a mind all alert, unable to let a subject slide by until he had first devised an explanation for it. Whether it was a coral atoll, an agouti hopping in the grass, or a scattering of old bones in a riverbank, he had to know how and why literally everything happened the way it did. The hypotheses of others were never quite so much fun or so satisfying as his own. In short, one finds in Darwin all the model one could want of the inquiring scientist at work, intent on getting as good an explanation as he could for the workings of nature observed around him. He was, it is worth saying again, one of the truly great minds in western history—more than he himself would ever quite believe, but all that he very much wanted to be. If he had lacked such analytical powers, he could never have persuaded so many of his fellow scientists to accept his revolution so quickly. The younger men were as usual the first to rush to his side, but within ten, certainly twenty, years, almost every scientist in the Anglo-American world had come over. On his death in 1882 he was buried in Westminster Abbey, just a few feet from the tomb of Sir Isaac Newton, where his countrymen believed he most appropriately ought to lie. Clearly, then, Darwin's theory of "natural selection through competition" vastly transcended its connections with his personal life to win an entire culture's firm, considered approval.[26]

One can further say that there was truth in the Darwinian ecological model—enduring, permanent, genuine, "positive" truth: valid and important revelations about nature that had never been made before and which could never be ignored thereafter. But there yet remains the simple fact that Darwin's was not *The* Truth; there were other, equally valid dimensions to the natural economy that he ignored or underplayed. The major question raised by his science was not whether savage conflict ever rages in nature, but rather where, when, and how often it occurs. And it is here that nineteenth-century culture, as well as the Darwin *persona*, set a direction for the supposedly inviolable world of science. The emphasis Darwin gave to competitive scrambling for place simply could not have been so credible to people living in another place and time. It is absolutely impossible to conceive such a view of nature coming from, say, a Hopi in the American Southwest. Nor could a Hindu, though living in a land that has known Malthusian conditions of scarcity for a very long time, have devised such a theory, not merely because he lacks the scientific training but because nothing in his religious, social, or personal values could lead him to such an outlook on nature. Even in the limited realm of nineteenth-century western science, it is striking how much of Darwin's work and the social response to his ideas were the products of the Victorian frame of mind in Great Britain and the United States. In the French or German science of the time, a Darwin would not have been possible; nor would a Darwinian controversy have assumed great importance on the Continent, among scientists or the general public. Darwin's culture, as well as his private needs, placed him in a position to see what the human mind previously had missed. But from this vantage point he could not help but get a limited view, in some ways a very distorted view.

CHAPTER 9

The Ascent of Man

CIVILIZATION has never cinched up well on the human frame; now and then it has to be tightened or let out a few notches. The problem is that man, like the rest of nature, is not born civilized, broken to ride and firmly saddled. So it seems ordained that the process of civilizing mankind must go on and on, never getting a secure hold or a perfectly adjusted fit. But in the late Victorian age, from the 1860s to the end of the century, there appeared an unusually fierce determination to make the civilizing process stick good and tight, once and for all. Never before had this ideal seemed so important to attain. In fact, the defining demand of the times may have been the need for an aggressive, resolute, even violent force of Culture to harness and subdue the nature that Darwin, among others, found so menacing. It is, in short, hard to exaggerate the pervasiveness and significance of this impulse toward civilization in the Anglo-American thought of the period.

On the surface, the age seemed one of remarkable confidence and self-assurance. Nowhere was this more true than in the contacts Victorians had with primitive peoples of the world. Darwin, for one, spent several months on the coasts of Tierra del Fuego, among some of the most impoverished savages on the earth (a race now extinct). Absolutely nothing in their manners or way of life appealed to him. They were "the miserable lords of this miserable land"—so benighted as to eat their own grandmothers. As he remembered them, "these poor wretches were stunted in their growth, their hideous faces bedaubed with white paint, their skins filthy and greasy, their hair entangled, their voices discordant, and their gestures violent"; adding that "it was without exception the most curious and interesting spectacle I ever beheld: I could not have believed how wide was the difference between savage and civilized man: it is greater than between a wild and domesticated animal, inasmuch as in man there is a greater power of improvement."[1]

Darwin was not alone in finding a yawning gulf between savagery and civilization. Identified by Victorians generally as the extremes of the human condition, these two archetypes took on immense historical and moral significance. They were seen as totally different worlds, separated by a distance that was all but unbridgeable. There was little doubt in London, Edinburgh, New York, or Chicago that civilization was the nobler state—infinitely, incomparably better in almost every aspect of living—and that savagery was an offense that ought to be crushed out wherever it was found. Hence the deep satisfaction Darwin found in contemplating "the march of improvement" set in motion by Christian missionaries and by the hoisting of the British flag of empire over peoples of the southern hemisphere. The Victorians, believing that they had little to learn from the savage and everything to teach, were grimly willing to assume the burden of acting as mentor. While reminding themselves frequently how arduous and uncertain was the task they undertook, they were nonetheless ready to give it a try, even in those places where their sense of disgust and repulsion was strongest.[2]

Appearances notwithstanding, the Victorians' confidence in the superiority of their own institutions was not quite absolute. Indeed, in the very fervor of their civilizing ambitions, the Victorians revealed not a few misgivings about themselves and their vaunted culture. As economic change picked up momentum around them, they grew more worried than they admitted about their own destiny—all the while endeavoring to share it with the poor savage, without a very clear idea where it was taking any of them. Along with this, the erosion of old religious certitudes, which had

The Ascent of Man • 171

long undergirded their extraordinary self-confidence in confronting other cultures, forced them to seek a new standard of value, a new means of self-validation, a new reason for bringing enlightenment to the backward.

One evidence of this anxious search was the emergence of the science of anthropology in the 1850s, with professional societies appearing soon after in the capital cities. This new science was dedicated, of course, to augmenting man's knowledge about his cultural origins through the study of existing primitive peoples. But in its first few decades of growth, anthropology gave little attention to analyzing the structures and functions of primitive society; all the emphasis was on social dynamics or evolution—the process of change from an archaic condition to civilized modernity. For in a larger sense the motivation behind the scientific study of man was to discover a general direction in the course of human evolution from which fresh social values could be taken, or at least familiar ones receive new credibility. Very quickly anthropologists announced the discovery of just such a pattern, perhaps best summed up by the great student of mythology Sir James Frazer, in a late edition of *The Golden Bough.* The past, he declared, follows "the long march, the slow and toilsome ascent, of humanity from savagery to civilization." The story of the world, in other words, is the story of "the Ascent of Man"—a phrase that would ring through all the late Victorian era and beyond. Here, decked out in the trappings of positivistic science, was a firm law, an inexorable movement toward civilization that humans could not thwart, though they might affect its pace. It was an idea that gave reassuring direction and meaning to a fast-changing milieu, and provided a new rationale for Anglo-American imperial expansion over the earth's surface.[3]

The Victorians' deep interest in contrasting the extremes of savagery and civilization took a great many forms. One finds it in the anthropology of Frazer, E. B. Tylor, and Lewis Henry Morgan; in the historical jurisprudence of Henry Maine and E. W. Burgess; in the social philosophy of Herbert Spencer and John Fiske. It was not least influential in the ecological thought of the period. Indeed, man's relation to the economy of nature was at the very heart of the law of progress from savagery to civilization. According to the American conservationist and geographer George Perkins Marsh, writing in 1860:

It is a marked and most important distinction between the relations of savage and of civilized man to nature, that, while the one is formed and wrought upon in mental as well as in physical characteristics by the peculiarities of his birthplace and other external natural causes, the other is more or less independent of their action, and his development is accordingly, in a corresponding degree, original and self-determined.

Civilization, in this view, is a declaration of independence from the natural world, when man "assumes an aggressive attitude, and thenceforward strives to subdue to his control, and subject to his uses, all her productive and all her motive powers." The savage's cultural inferiority lies in his inability or unwillingness to make that declaration and to take an aggressive stance. So familiar is this distinction today that it generally seems a truism, as it soon became for the Victorians. Their ideal of civilization almost always depended vitally on the vigorous conquest of nature by science and technology.[4]

There were, however, not one but a number of strategies by which that environmental philosophy of domination was presented and defended. In the first place, it was commonly maintained that a policy of ecological conquest was necessary to carry out not only the law of progress but another natural law, announced by Darwin in the *Origin:* the competitive struggle for existence. So Darwin himself would justify the extermination of the orangutan; so in literally thousands of cases would industrialists, politicians, and other public figures rationalize their efforts to turn the natural world to their own account. Charles Lyell, as noted earlier, had pioneered in this philosophy of "might makes right" as applied to man–nature interactions. It had its parallel in the Social Darwinist concept of the responsibility of the rich toward the poor, a view that seemed to remove such relations from the province of morality, but which actually made self-assertion and aggrandizement an ethic that superseded all other values. Between man and nature, too, the law of competition was believed to obtain, and was often seen as the only foundation on which an advanced technological civilization could be built. The logic in this outlook was neatly circular and complete: nature's economy is a world of self-seeking aggression; such a system has produced remarkable evolutionary progress; it must work for the human economy too, since man is a part of nature; man's increasing technological dominion over nature is proof of the survival of the fittest and of the reality of progress in the scheme of things. To call this stance "conservative," as we sometimes do, is highly misleading; on the contrary, it anticipated a radical transformation of the planet, uninhibited by ecological scruples or quietist musings.[5]

But the unequivocal defense of civilization as rule by the strongest, common though it was in popular philosophy, was never wholly persuasive to the Victorian mind. It linked man and nature, civilization and savagery, too closely on a continuum of sheer power, when what the Victorians most desired was to establish a vast moral distance between these poles. A second strategy, which bypassed this objection, was to defend civilization as the necessary, rational management of nature. In this way the law of history dictated a long ascent from chaos and disorder to perfect managerial control. Probably the most important advocate of this view was the American sociologist Lester Ward. A staunch opponent of all efforts to derive from Darwinism a justification of laissez-faire government and rugged individualism, Ward was one of the very earliest proponents of a planned human economy. In contrast to the natural order, he argued, human society should be organized by trained experts as a welfare state, in which all citizens receive equal benefit and the weak are protected from exploitation by the strong. And in his work *The Psychic Factors of Civilization*, published in 1893, he gave these social ideals an ecological counterpart: nature too should be reorganized by scientific intelligence and thereby redeemed, along with society, from its primitive state.[6]

Ward's environmental outlook was thoroughly, even militantly, anti-naturalistic. Unlike the Social Darwinists, he drew a firm line between the "economy of nature" and the "economy of mind." In nature anarchic competition

174 • THE DISMAL SCIENCE

rules, and inefficiency is the result; but in the "economy of mind," human reason—"the collective brain of society"—assumes command, and waste is eliminated. Ward noted that earlier naturalists had "regarded [Nature] as the great economist from whom man was to copy," but he claimed that in truth, "Nature has no economy," no concern for cost or efficiency. Rivers, instead of flowing straight and so delivering their water to the sea with minimum expenditure of energy, lazily meander through plains and valleys. One encounters everywhere in the organic world a "redundant fertility": the herring lays more than 10,000 eggs of which only two will reach maturity, and a large chestnut tree showers the air with as much as a ton of pollen. Elephants are overgrown monstrosities, and redwoods anachronisms. Any good human engineer, in other words, could do a better job of designing the environment than nature has. Rather than leaving it to the haphazard wind to sow his seeds, a sensible planner would clear the ground of all competitors, carefully plant the seeds at proper intervals, and provide all the nutrients where they are lacking. (That Ward grew up on a Midwestern farm is not irrelevant to his ideology; perhaps farmers as a class must see their own labors as more productive than nature's.) Despite his emphasis on collective action for the betterment of mankind, Ward did not find nature to be a collective, interdependent order wherein adaptation and cooperation take precedence over the interests of individual species. Only in a world totally under its own control could any one species pursue its private goals in the rigidly efficient, straight-line fashion Ward admired. That, of course, was precisely the world he wanted to live in, specifically one that was under *man's* absolute and unqualified dominion—much as Francis Bacon had wanted.[7]

But the Baconian ideal of imperialism had a new meaning for Ward: he was also a Victorian, reacting to the new Darwinian ecology. He understood fully what many other Victorians were beginning to accept, that there was no all-wise Contriving Hand designing and managing the natural economy. It was a self-made world, and hence replete with errors, weaknesses, imperfections, and misfits. For Ward, this revelation was easy enough to absorb if he could im-

The Ascent of Man • 175

mediately establish man in the place vacated by God. The collective reason of the human species, as expressed in science and technology, became the only god he needed: a religion of human intelligence that saw the earth as man's subject, available to minister to his needs and, when thoroughly rationalized and made over, to testify to his unique divinity. Civilization in this sense became the surrogate for the outworn, discarded Christian ideal of a heaven to be won. Man must proclaim himself nature's engineer and must then set about creating his own paradise on earth; otherwise, he would go on living depraved and unredeemed in the natural state that Darwin had made to seem so fearful and repulsive. Thus in the exercise of reason over nature, Ward also discovered a path to moral redemption, a means to suppress the savage beast in man, "chaining the competitive egoism that all men have inherited from their animal ancestors."[8]

This last statement suggests a third defense of civilization from an ecological perspective: its role as a necessary moral check against nature. Living in an age of intense moral earnestness, the Victorians were compelled to rest all their arguments ultimately on higher ethical grounds. If nature was indeed Darwin's fallen world, then it must be civilized man's sacred duty to separate himself from that base sphere while at the same time—as he was doing for the barbarians of the world—to rescue as much of it as he controlled. In the English-speaking world, one man above all others made this notion powerfully compelling. This was Thomas Huxley: London professor of anatomy, pugnacious defender of Darwinism, religious agnostic, and high priest of Victorian nature philosophy. Perhaps his preeminence on this issue was due precisely to the fact that he was a renowned scientist who had managed to face the frightening facts of evolution and turn them into moral reassurance. His anatomical studies convinced him that man is biologically linked to the higher apes, a prospect he could not help but find degrading. He declared, "No one is more strongly convinced than I am of the vastness of the gulf between civilized man and the brutes, or is more certain that whether *from* them or not, he is assuredly not *of* them."

"The power of knowledge—the conscience of good and evil—the pitiful tenderness of human affections," he maintained, "raise us out of all real fellowship with the brutes, however closely they may seem to approximate us." Most important among all these distinguishing traits of mankind was "conscience," and upon it Huxley built an ethic of positive alienation from nature and of strenuous endeavor aimed at transforming the lower world into something better.[9]

That morality is a purely human invention was, in essence, Huxley's central point in his famous Romanes lecture of 1893, "Evolution and Ethics." "Social progress," he argued there, "means a checking of the cosmic process at every step, and the substitution for it of another, which may be called the ethical process; the end of which is not the survival of those who may happen to be the fittest, in respect of the whole of the conditions which obtain, but of those who are ethically the best." But how was one to know who the "ethically best" were? If nature more often than not taught murder and rapine, where was man to find a more reliable teacher? Huxley, at least, could not fall back on the church to answer these questions. He had devoted his early career to defending Darwin's ideas against attacks by orthodox religious leaders, and his agnosticism and anti-clericalism had become somewhat notorious. The ultimate origins and authority of morality, therefore, he was forced to leave a mystery; it was simply a phenomenon that was born of nature but owed nothing to her laws. This gap in knowledge, however, did not in the least disturb his confidence. He knew that he knew what was right, and that it was diametrically opposed to the behavior of the ape and tiger. By some highly irregular, inexplicable turn of fate, man alone had been endowed with a moral capacity, which could and must be nurtured by civilization. And yet, while he could not accept the traditional Christian account of the source of a moral ethic, Huxley had no difficulty in summoning up all the sober, determined zeal that western religion had brought to moral issues. He carried on that ancient tradition of moral absolutism, using nature as his dark model for all that was depraved, just as his Puritan predecessors had done. For him as much as for any seventeenth-century divine, "the headquarters of the enemy of ethical virtue" were to be found in nature.[10]

The moral outlook in Huxley's writings and among his contemporaries generally evidenced a strongly ironic twist. On one hand, these Victorians wanted to deny man's participation in the war for survival raging in nature. On the other hand, they could not resist setting up their battle lines someplace else; manly combat still had powerful attractions for them and required only a morally acceptable arena for its pursuit. Huxley's solution was to shift the focus of violence from a man–man to a man–nature confrontation. This was also the recommendation of the American philosopher William James in his 1910 essay "A Moral Equivalent to War." It was seen by both men as wholly legitimate, even honorific, to act aggressively toward nature, so long as that aggression was performed in the name of humanity, decency, virtue, and even health and cleanliness. Competition and struggle, therefore, did not disappear, but rather were limited to a single, all-important front.[11]

The Victorians were concerned of course with the inner dimensions of their war for virtue—the struggle of conscience against the selfish instincts. But they were at least as intent on carrying the crusade against nature to the actual physical surface of the earth, on making the land over to serve as a kind of visible, external evidence of their accession to grace. Huxley's favorite metaphor for this ethic of ecological transformation was the hoary image of the Garden of Eden, implying in this case a civilized landscape surrounded by a wall to guard it from the Darwinian jungle. This garden was to be a place of virtue, but also of material productivity; the two ends were mutually reinforcing. It was, however, to be no limited monastic retreat, but an expanding, dynamic kingdom that one day would embrace the entire world. Already, in Tasmania, Huxley saw the walls moving out to encircle new territory, where a domesticated, "English" flora and fauna were replacing the native wilderness. If humans would restrain their self-seeking ambitions and work for the "corporate whole," they would see this process spread everywhere to create "an earthly paradise, a true Garden of Eden, in which all things should work together towards the well-being of the gardeners." Civilization then, according to this policy, became a process of pacification by concerted force. In its train would come not only a more perfectly moral world but the rich rewards of productivity, wealth, and comfort for the human species.[12]

"Man in the civilized world feels a kind of omnipotence," noted the social critic Edwin P. Hood in 1850. Among the English and Americans especially, the sense of power was strong, buttressed as it was on every side by evidences of the impress of their will. Certainly mastery, strength, pugnacity, toughness, and determination were among the qualities of civilization most admired by Victorians. Walter Houghton speaks of the Victorian "worship of force"—and indeed, this threatened to replace the worship of God, or in some cases served as a substitute for failed religion. Moral doubts and anxieties, fears of inner spiritual weakness could be wiped out in the heat of battle and the thrill of violent physical combat. But a battle for righteousness, in the old Cromwellian style, was much to be preferred over a battle where no moral issue was at stake. One could make civilization itself a holy crusade and set out to conquer nature and the savage world. At least in the case of nature there could be no question, after Darwin, that here was an enemy that fully deserved to be routed and enchained.[13]

In all this rumbling din of manliness, virility, and bellicose moralism, little else was likely to be heard. But a sensitive ear might have detected audible if faint peepings of another attitude toward nature, one that was far less hostile, more conciliatory. As much as Ward, Huxley, or the Social Darwinists, this voice spoke in evolutionary terms, and it echoed their faith in civilization as a redeeming force. But all the same, this voice spoke of recovering a sense of kinship between man and beast, of a moral responsibility to protect the earth from abuse, and of a civilization so secure in its hold that it could afford to loosen the cinchstrap a bit. This voice—or rather voices, for they represented a diverse collection of ideas around a common ethic—may be called the biocentric conscience. Some of its themes had been heard now and then as far back as Gilbert White and the arcadians of the eighteenth century. It had become a much louder force in the Romantic movement, especially among such writers as Thoreau and Goethe. But the biocentric outlook received its most vigorous expression as a consequence of the work of Charles Darwin, who gave it both a personal stamp of approval and a scientific argument. Though it may have been drowned out by the Huxleyan call to battle, it was not to be altogether silenced or unheeded.

In many ways the most important spokesman for the biocentric attitude in ecological thought was Darwin himself. Despite the fact that his own work was in large measure responsible for nature's bad press, he did not follow Huxley or the mainstream of serious Victorian opinion by announcing his secession from the natural world. On the contrary, he managed to hold fairly constant to his youthful enthusiasm for the whole of living nature. But there was a changing tenor to his love. It grew more sober and melancholic, but also more firm and deliberate, as he matured from his juvenile beetle-collecting days. The direction this attachment to the earth and its vital currents would take as he grew older was first suggested in one of the earliest entries in his "Notebooks on Transmutation":

If we choose to let conjecture run wild, then animals, our fellow brethren in pain, diseases, death, suffering and famine—our slaves in the most laborious works, our companions in our amusements—they may partake [of] our origin in one common ancestor—we may be all netted together.

What was a "wild" thought in 1837 grew to become a central theme in Darwin's writings, especially after he had moved to Down and even more after he had gotten *On the Origin of Species* into print. One of the chief lessons of evolution, for him, was that man had not been created with special care in the image of God; therefore, he is one with all other species in a universal brotherhood of living and dying, which he denies only at the risk of cutting himself off from his psychic and biological roots. It was by no means a perfectly happy relationship, nothing like young Wordsworth's leaping, exuberant sense of kinship with nature. But in Darwin's view, a shared experience of suffering as well as of joy could establish a bond between humanity and all other forms of life.[14]

For all the toughmindedness of his natural-selection theory, Darwin could be touched deeply by any evidence of suffering or injustice in the world. He left his medical studies at Edinburgh because he could not stand the sight of blood. For many years after his return to England, he was troubled by the distressing memory of the torturing of black slaves he had witnessed in Brazil. At Down he encouraged the founding of a Friendly Society, a self-help organization for workingmen, and for several years served as its treasurer. "How atrociously unjust are the stamp laws which render it so expensive for the poor man to buy his quarter of an acre," he wrote to his old botany teacher Henslow; "it makes one's blood burn with indignation." All this and more, of course, might be said of other Victorians. But Darwin went farther than most men and women in this respect: he did not place outside the pale of moral concern those species that are inferior in intellect to humans. A friend described him after his death as "a man eminently fond of animals and tender to them. He would not knowingly have inflicted pain on a living creature." In November 1875, before the Royal Commission on Vivisection, he came out of seclusion to testify against the placing of any restraints on medical research—here at least the ethic of knowledge took precedence over other values. But on that occasion he also strongly denounced those who experimented on live animals "for mere damnable curiosity." To a professor of physiology at Uppsala he wrote in 1881: "I have all my life been a strong advocate for humanity to animals, and have done what I could in my writings to enforce this duty." Keenly aware of the "immense amount of pain and suffering in the world," even haunted by its presence, Darwin nonetheless moved in his later years toward an all-embracing reverence for life, not very different from Albert Schweitzer's ethical vision at Lambaréné.[15]

Darwin was not a moral philosopher, any more than Huxley or Lester Ward were. Still, his works had something interesting to say on this theme, and it was not an apology for crude self-assertion. In his *Descent of Man*—the title of which runs so bluntly counter to the contemporary perception of human emergence—he attempted to demonstrate an inner moral as well as outer physical continuity among all species. Shame, wonder, humor, reverence, curiosity, and magnanimity, he suggested, are all qualities that originate in lower species, as do the moral sense and the social instincts. The "brutes," in other words, were not so "brutal" as many assumed. In every respect we are all joined together in a "community of descent." To be sure, Darwin explained all these virtues in utilitarian terms, believing that they must contribute at some point to the survival of the individual and the species. Nonetheless, nature appears as a world essentially held together by lines of "mutual love and sympathy." Though these moral qualities exist in only rudimentary form in the other species compared to their later development in man, they suggest that nature is not simply a theater of violent aggression, or what Huxley described as "the headquarters of the enemy of ethical virtue." This evolution of moral behavior within a natural context had for Darwin its final issue in civilization. As art and music were born of an ancient struggle for survival but have grown beyond that purely utilitarian purpose, so morality evolves toward something more than usefulness or expediency. In its last and highest stage, it becomes a self-transcending sense of mercy, sympathy, and kinship with all of animate existence, including the earth itself. When man has reached that capacity to feel for everything that moves and lives—for being in general, not just one's own family, nation, or even species—then he will have become truly civilized.[16]

This insight seems to have come clearly to Darwin only after he had exorcised the demon of competition in the *Origin*. But it is also most unlikely that he would have arrived at the central thesis of that work, evolution rather than special creation, had he not already embraced a biocentric ethic. After reading the *Origin*, Thomas Huxley exclaimed, "How stupid of me not to have thought of that!" The major obstacle to the idea of evolution, however, was not stupidity; rather it was the traditional assumption of man's uniqueness and divine origin, which made evolution unacceptable and hence a mechanism for the process irrelevant. All the religious controversy that followed the publishing of the *Origin*, the bombastic objections from Bishop Wilberforce and others, did not conceal the fact that the real issue was whether man could admit he was fully a part of nature or not. Adam Sedgwick, for example, who was a religiously orthodox scientist, castigated Darwin for brutalizing mankind and sinking it into degradation. If, he warned, pure maidens were to believe they were born the children of apes—of dark, hairy beasts—they might be led away into unmentionable depravity. But with more confidence in his own species and less mistrust of the lower orders, Darwin declared in 1871 that "it is only our natural prejudice, and that arrogance which made our forefathers declare that they were descended from demi-gods, which leads us to demur" to the evolutionary concept of man's origin. Start as he did, from a more humble, loving attitude toward other creatures, and the most difficult objections to a theory of evolution fell away.[17]

There must have been a number of factors responsible for Darwin's special receptiveness to the idea of evolution, in contrast to other scientists of his time. The strong influence of Humboldt's organicism, and through it the impact of the Romantic philosophy of nature, should be considered prominent among these influences. Perhaps even more important, however, was the fact that Darwin grew up in and gladly returned in his later years to the rural natural-history tradition exemplified by Gilbert White. That tradition possessed a strong, intuitive feeling for the organic unity of man and nature, a sense of respect for and fellowship with other species that became less and less prominent in the new world of professional science. As eager as Darwin was to be accepted by that rising world, he was nonetheless inextricably linked to an older style and ethic. Indeed, he may have been the last and greatest of the broad and pious naturalists, not at all at ease in a laboratory and no good at mathematics. Especially after moving to Down, he sensed at last the rewards of that Gilbert White career he had earlier abandoned for the voyage to South America. Shortly after settling in his "extraordinarily rural and quiet" village, he began drawing up an "Account of Down" which his son Francis suggested might have shown that he intended "to write a natural history diary after the manner of Gilbert White." And fittingly enough, the very last of his writings at Down was *The Formation of Vegetable Mould Through the Action of Earthworms*, suggested to him by White's wry description of the place of worms in the economy of nature. Gavin de Beer has called this last of Darwin's books "a pioneer study in quantitative ecology." But far more than this, it was the work of a man who lovingly and sympathetically embraced the study of even the most lowly creatures in the English rural order. He could not ignore the tooth-and-claw side of things, but neither would he allow that nightmare to alienate him from the natural community of which he was part.[18]

From this angle of vision, it is clear that Darwin, who so effectively shattered the arcadian ideal of nature, nevertheless maintained some ties with·that tradition. He too seems more pagan than Christian in his respect for nonhuman creation, and his theory of evolution returned to western thought an awareness of natural kinship that appears to be universal among pagan cultures, including the so-called primitive peoples of the world. But there was this important difference: Darwin, despite his retreat to a less threatening rural life, still maintained a fervent faith in the reality of progress. Civilization, especially in English hands, was a blessing to the world, not a curse. The savage lives in a woefully inferior state, he believed, a condition scarcely worthy to be called human. Thus, while Darwin was attempting to close the gap between man and other species, he held steadfastly to the distinction between civilization and savagery. A difficult stance it surely was, but it had a certain logic to it, at least for a Victorian. The civilized man, Darwin was saying, cannot sever his ties with his biological past. Nor need he be ashamed to own up to his kinfolk, like some city slicker anxious to forget his uncouth country cousins; the despised relations are worthy of love and respect for what they are, though it may not be much by another's standards. But it is only the fully civilized human who can rise sufficiently far above the struggle for existence as to learn to love all beings and recognize their right to exist in their own way. Ultimately, that is what it means to be civilized and humane: not belligerently chauvinistic about one's own kind, but tolerant, gentle, and sympathetic toward the earth and all that lives. For Darwin those qualities of humaneness would come not from some idyllic, golden past but in further progress toward a more civilized future.

Others in the Anglo-American world were moving toward a similar biocentric outlook. W. H. Hudson, for example, who first read Darwin when he was a boy growing up in Argentina and disliked much of his argument, nonetheless found the message of evolution comforting rather than insulting. "We are no longer isolated," he declared, "standing like starry visitors on a mountain-top, surveying life from the outside; but are on a level with and part and parcel of it." John Muir, the American nature writer, rejected the old Christian notion that the economy of nature had been designed for man's exclusive benefit. "Why," he asked, "should man value himself as more than a small part of the one great unit of creation?" Another American, Edward Evans, attacked "anthropocentric psychology and ethics, which treat man as a being essentially different and inseparably set apart from all other sentient creatures, to which he is bound by no ties of mental affinity or moral obligation." Liberty Hyde Bailey, a biologist at Cornell University, pointed out that "the theme of evolution has overturned our attitude" toward nature. "The living creation is not exclusively man-centered; it is biocentric." And the English novelist Thomas Hardy wrote in 1910:

Few people seem to perceive that the most far-reaching consequence of the establishment of the common origin of species is ethical; that it logically involved a readjustment of altruistic morals, by enlarging, as a necessity of rightness, the application of what has been called "the Golden Rule" from the area of mere mankind to that of the whole animal kingdom.

For each of these men, Darwin seems to have been an important intellectual catalyst. But there were other forces at work too, all converging on a common ethic, including the continuing impact of Romanticism as well as the rise of a popular philanthropic and humanitarian sentiment that promoted legislation to protect animals from abuse and cruelty.[19]

One name in particular became widely identified in the late Victorian era with this movement against an exclusively man-centered moral system: that of Henry Salt. A well-established, properly gowned and top-hatted master at Eton, Salt one day in 1884 rather suddenly decided to chuck the whole business. He forthwith resigned his teaching post and moved with his wife to the Surrey hills to simplify his life, follow a vegetarian diet, advocate socialism, and promote a "broad democratic sentiment of universal sympathy." His academic gown was torn into strips for fastening creepers to the walls, and he raised his own food in his home garden plot. In 1890 he read a paper before the Fabian Society, in which among other things he objected to calling animals "brutes" and insisted that they too be granted the rights of life, liberty, and self-determination. From this beginning came the Humanitarian League, which he founded in 1891 and directed for almost thirty years. Until his death in 1939 Salt continued to lead a quiet but busy life. He was long associated with George Meredith, Algernon Swinburne, George Bernard Shaw, Edward Carpenter, and W. H. Hudson. He wrote excellent biographies of Thoreau and Shelley, popularized the moral philosophy of Schopenhauer and Tolstoy, and was an admired friend of Mahatma Gandhi. On the political front, he waged a tireless campaign against war, capitalism, economic inequality, meat-eating, vivisection, and every other form of cruelty he could discern. In the first decade of the twentieth century, one of his chief causes became protecting the mountains of north Wales from commercial defacement, and preserving their endangered species from vandalism. But the simple, unifying theme that lay behind all these enterprises was expressed best in the title of his last book, *The Creed of Kinship*, published in 1935. "The basis of any real morality," he wrote, "must be the sense of kinship between all living beings." In an earlier work, his autobiography *Seventy Years Among Savages* (1921), that sense of kinship was made the foundation for a new civilization which would bring man and nature back together at last by extending the circle of human ethics to include all sentient beings. And that creed was explicitly linked to Darwinian evolutionary biology.[20]

With Salt as with these other biocentrists, the usual effect of the new ethic was to involve them in conservation advocacy. They were all leaders, for example, in the agitation to protect birdlife from market hunters seeking plumes for milady's hats, which broadened later into other areas of wildlife protection. They supported the establishment of wildlife refuges, public forests, and parks. In all these activities, it must be said, they diverged sharply from the example of Charles Darwin, who despite his work as a biologist and his humanitarian instincts did little to implement politically an ethic of protecting the natural world. Like many other scientists, perhaps, he could never really serve two mistresses; science and its duty of piling up knowledge always made the greater demand on his energies and commitments.

Yet, in the final analysis, the figure of Darwin must remain the most imposing and persuasive force behind the biocentric movement. Conservationist or not, he shared with Salt, Hudson, Hardy, and the rest a quality of feeling about nature that finally may be as important as any of his theories. It survived the shock of the Galápagos, the pessimism of Malthus, and the melancholy reality of competitive selection. It persisted even when his good friends Lyell and Huxley, not to mention the weight of educated British opinion, did not share it, even when they drew from his writings a different moral message than he thought he had put there. For thousands of readers he made ecology the dismal science. But, while he might agree that the natural world is not an altogether pleasant or happy place, he could not for that reason believe that man should repudiate it or feel himself superior to it. He never faltered in his belief that beyond humanity and its affairs lies a living ecological community that has always been man's ultimate home and kin. We are "all netted together"—"fellow brethren" traveling on a single, shared planet.

PART FOUR

O PIONEERS: ECOLOGY ON THE FRONTIER

So far we have been tracing the early shifts in the ecological point of view—the changing integrative visions of nature's economy from the time of White and Linnaeus to Humboldt, Lyell, and Darwin. Like discrete strata of sediments, these visions lie buried deep in the Anglo-American mind.

Now we pass to another stratum, one closer to the surface of our thinking today. In this new layer of ideas, ecology at last acquired a proper name for itself, and we shall examine what this name came to mean in the work of such plant geographers as Eugenius Warming. Ecology also got another model of how the economy of nature works: the concept of succession to a climax state, expressed most authoritatively by a Nebraska scientist, Frederic Clements. This developmental model owed much to the example of human settlement on the prairie frontiers of America, of pioneering in a new land. Finally, the emergent science of ecology was soon thrust boldly into momentous public issues, notably the Dust Bowl episode of the 1930s. Out of that tragedy of a region and its people came a fresh concept of conservation based on ecology. The ecologist, furthermore, had now become a public figure: at once trusted adviser to a nation reassessing its environmental past and reformer with a controversial program to promote.

CHAPTER 10

Words on a Map

"IN THE BEGINNING was the Word"—one of
the most upside-down propositions in western thought.
Find a label for something, it suggests, and you have discovered it. Say the Word, and whole planets, solar systems,
galaxies—light itself—spring forth out of the darkness. Say
something else and they vanish. It is our Genesis illusion:
God spake and the thunder rolled, lightning flashed, matter
was born.

"Ecology" has of late been one of the more important
words to conjure with. Those who discover it often seem to
think they have thereby discovered a new nature, another
world of meaning, a way of salvation. It may come as something of a surprise, then, to find out that the word has been
kicking around for over a century now, that its first articulation had no immediate effect on anybody or anything, and
that long before there was a word there was an evolving
point of view, and the word came well after—not before—
the fact.

This is not to deny the independent power of language.
Words are like empty balloons, inviting us to fill them up
with associations. As they fill they begin to gain intrinsic
force and at last to shape our perceptions and expectations.
So with the word "ecology." At first nothing more than an
unusual coupling of Greek roots, it eventually assumed a
complicated burden of meaning that was a good deal more
flexible and inclusive, perhaps, than its author anticipated.
It became in its own right a potent cultural presence.

First appearing in 1866, *Oecologie* was one of the many neologisms of Ernst Haeckel, the leading German disciple of Darwin and the busiest name-maker of his time. In trying to give a semblance of order to a scientific world that was splitting off into many different lines of inquiry, he suggested that one branch of study might be brought together under the name *Oecologie*. Here might be included all that pertained to "der Wissenshaft von der Oeconomie, von der Lebensweise, von der äusseren Lebensziehungen der organismen zu einander." In the broadest sense it was to be the study of all the environmental conditions of existence, or, as his translator later put it, "the science of the relations of living organisms to the external world, their habitat, customs, energies, parasites, etc."[1]

Haeckel derived the new label from the same root found in the older word "economy": the Greek *oikos*, referring originally to the family household and its daily operations and maintenance. Before the advent of modern political economy, men assumed that national economic affairs could be conceived of as merely extensions of the housekeeper's budget and larder. Likewise in *Oecologie*, Haeckel suggested that the living organisms of the earth constitute a single economic unit resembling a household or family dwelling intimately together, in conflict as well as in mutual aid. In his 1869 inaugural lecture as a professor at Jena, he also put an explicitly Darwinian border around the word: "the body of knowledge concerning the economy of nature [*Naturhaushalt*], . . . the study of all those complex interrelations referred to by Darwin as the condition of the struggle for existence." Though biologists absolutely ignored Haeckel's innovation for several decades in favor of the older phrase "the economy of nature," the new term eventually became popular currency, first as "oecology" and then, after the International Botanical Congress of 1893, in its modern spelling as "ecology." What additional or alternative content beyond these beginnings it was given in the process of diffusion is the major focus of discussion in this chapter.[2]

Putting a new word in the dictionary is much like writing a new name across a blank space on a map: It is still a long way from exploring the wilderness the word signifies, from ranging over its landforms, and from investing the terrain with the associations generated by human familiarity. The geography and character of that land cannot possibly be as vivid or complicated for the original wordsmith as for the explorer in the field. Haeckel it was, then, who inscribed the name *Oecologie* on the map of science; a flourish of his pen and new worlds supposedly leapt into being, albeit worlds he had never really visited. In this act of naming he was like Amerigo Vespucci, who scratched his own name on a map of the New World he had never seen, and so unwittingly begat a hemisphere. But it was the likes of Balboa, Alexander Mackenzie, and Lewis and Clark who located America's true boundaries, its more precise range and substance. They drew the maps that pioneers and homesteaders would later use to find their way into the unknown interior.

Ecology had its indispensable trail-blazers, too, who had been active even before Haeckel. Thus when it was coined, *Oecologie* did not point to some *terra incognita* on the map; it was already familiar country. Charles Darwin had penetrated its borders, as Haeckel noted, and so had Thoreau, White, Linnaeus, and many other explorers already discussed here. But if nothing else, giving it a name focused attention on the terrain and delimited future exploration. New maps began to appear, more systematic, more confined, and more thoroughly detailed over smaller areas. Indeed, an entirely new generation of trail-blazers now entered the field—a vanguard of self-consciously professional "ecologists," as they would eventually call themselves. They, not Haeckel or the earlier group of explorers, would be mainly responsible for identifying the contours of the modern science of ecology. They would give the mere word concrete substance, the name on the map a more precise locus and familiarity. With their exploits a new phase of our subject begins.

The men who drew the map for the freshly christened science of ecology were, appropriately enough, geographers. The prominence of their discipline in the nineteenth century, its contributions to other sciences, and its widespread interest for the general reader are seldom appreciated today. But in its heyday, geography was a powerful cultural force; Humboldt, Lyell, and Darwin are only the most famous of its students. Strictly speaking, however, it was an aberrant group among geographers who first attempted to describe the topography of ecology. In moving beyond the traditional limits of their field, they seized on Haeckel's label to differentiate themselves as an "ecological" party. Throughout most of the nineteenth century, as today, the most familiar school of biogeography was the study of flora and fauna. Essentially this was a matter of compiling statistical data on the distribution of species around the world and then deriving from such data a system for classifying geographic regions. The floristic geographer was bound to be interested in the adaptations of organisms to their environments, a process that Haeckel included in the territory of ecology. But this interest was limited; the controlling purpose of the dominant school was taxonomic more than ecological. To reverse this order of priorities was precisely the intention of the lesser-known, rival school, which was at first known as "physiognomic," then "physiological," and finally as "ecological" geography. This school preferred to talk about the forms of "vegetation" and their determinants rather than about the distribution of the earth's plant species.

All late nineteenth-century geographers were in some measure the heirs of Alexander von Humboldt and so constitute another important link, besides Darwin, between that South American explorer and modern ecology. But the aberrant geographers were the more faithful to the master's own approach and methods. From Humboldt's holistic view they took a lesson in awareness of the interrelated communities formed by the various species of plants growing in an area. Plants, in this system, are social creatures. They gather into societies that may assume composite appearances strikingly different one from another, depending on the life forms that dominate each society. For Humboldt the appeal of this approach to phytogeography was as much aesthetic as scientific: to see and appreciate a forest whole was as important to him as explaining its composition. But Humboldt's disciples, especially August Grisebach at Göttingen, felt a more intense urge to determine as exactly as possible why the physical environment produces a forest rather than a grassland, or a community dominated by palms instead of cacti. In 1838 Grisebach gave the name "formation" to similar assemblages of plants created by similar climates, regardless of variations in constituent species. The tropical rain forests of Africa, South America, and the Indian Archipelago comprise a single type of plant formation, he stated; the deciduous forests and the prairies of all the temperate zones of the world also could be identified as single types of vegetation. All these kinds of formations are responses to peculiar climatic conditions. For Grisebach and other aberrant geographers, the task of categorizing these major kinds of plant societies of the earth and discovering the laws they obey replaced the floristic aim of identifying where the different species of the world are found and how they got there.[3]

From Grisebach on, three principles dominated this new geography: the classification of plants by their adaptive forms or structures rather than taxonomy alone; an emphasis on plants as social beings forming integrated societies; and identification of climate as the crucial determinant of both individual life forms and the communal pattern. The most controversial of these was the last—known at its most simplistic, reductive level as the theory of "temperature summing." Charles Darwin, working more from the perspective of animals than plants, was among those who had persistently discounted the importance of climate as an environmental force shaping the distribution and survival of organisms. Despite his quiet renunciation, this was a popular creed with many, reaching back to Humboldt and even to Buffon in the eighteenth century. Now the ecologically oriented plant geographers, true to the vision of Humboldt's isothermic lines wriggling over the globe, returned the climate factor to the foreground of natural history. And "climate," more often than not, meant broad-gauge, global temperature belts strictly correlated with girdles of latitude. Only as an afterthought were other elements of climate or soil conditions granted a place as factors determining vegetation.

In the United States, the most influential scheme for temperature-dominant biogeography came from C. Hart Merriam, an ornithologist and chief of the federal Division of Economic Ornithology and Mammalogy and later of the Bureau of the Biological Survey. Merriam developed his ideas independently of the aberrant geographers on the Continent. But his work strikingly illustrates the continuing vitality of the Humboldt tradition that soon would acquire the label of scientific ecology.

In the late 1880s Merriam went west to study the fauna of the splendid, glistening San Francisco mountains of northern Arizona. In contrast to the veritable army of explorer–naturalists who had tramped through western valley and desert before him in search of fresh species to report to the world of science, Merriam arrived with but one assistant, a few hundred dollars, and two months' leave to launch his study. Luckily, no site could have been better chosen to dramatize the clustering of North American vegetation into distinct unities. On the low, hot desert plateau to the south he could walk among saguaro cactus, mesquite, and yellow-flowering paloverde, and watch lizards and roadrunners slipping into the shade. But on the peaks themselves he found a vastly different world, one whose residents would be equally at home on the arctic tundra. And in between, on the mountain slopes, lay a clearly demarcated series of plant and animal societies.[4]

Much as Humboldt had done with regard to the Andes, Merriam concluded from this and subsequent trips west that all the mountain zones might be flattened out to correspond to the latitude lines on the map. Estimating each mile of altitude as roughly equivalent to 800 miles of latitude, he derived from this rule two primary life areas in the United States and Canada, both stretching across the entire continent: a southern austral and a northern boreal zone. These two broad bands, extensions as it were from the Arizona deserts and mountains, could be further divided into a total of six more specialized life zones (seven, when one included the tropical zone found only at the extreme tip of Florida). Merriam labeled these subregions the lower austral, upper austral, transition, Canadian, Hudsonian, and arctic–alpine zones; together they represent a system of ecological units precisely scaled to the spectrum of temperature change experienced either in climbing a mountain or traveling north toward the pole. Within the first three of these subregions, he eventually accepted a distinction between the humid eastern part of the United States and the arid west. But otherwise these climatic zones swept across the continent with a bold grandeur.

Later, thousands of Americans absorbed Merriam's notion of life zones from dioramas in natural history museums. And in the process they learned some of the central lessons of ecology: that a piñon jay, for example, belongs in the forest of the upper austral zone, not in the land of Douglas fir or of saguaro; that certain plants and animals keep each other company because, directly or indirectly, they are linked in common dependence on a common climate. But while this popular education flourished, the consensus grew among scientists that simple temperature-summing like Merriam's could not do all the work he assigned it. Other geographers contended that only in mountainous regions, especially in the American Southwest, do the life zones follow the abrupt kind of spatial succession Merriam described. In the American grasslands, on the other hand, geographical succession is much more gradual and proceeds not so much from south to north as from east to west—reflecting a decline in rainfall rather than temperature variations.[5]

Setting aside the question of its strict accuracy as a model, the significance for our inquiry of Merriam's life-zones concept is that it began, not with a floral and faunal catalogue of Arizona, but with the distinctions between habitats from which emerge their respective biological communities. That critical step from one kind of geography to another was also a major element in the transition to modern ecology. It was made possible by a vast body of traditional biogeography amassed by the frontier naturalists and their academic armchair generals, like Professor Asa Gray at Harvard. It was nonetheless a new departure, a reordering of the old data into a distinctly ecological scheme that would stimulate a new kind of research into the structure and dynamics of each of these zones. What distinguishes the daily life of a bird in the Hudsonian life zone from one in the lower austral? scientists subsequently would ask. What common patterns of structure and dependencies may be found in all of these biological associations?

At about the same time that Merriam was mountain-climbing in Arizona, on the continent of Europe Haeckel's label was finally getting attention and beginning to take on substance; the contours of the new map were rapidly being filled in. In this enterprise the chief cartographers were the great European triumvirate of ecological plant-geographers: Oscar Drude, Andreas Schimper, and Eugenius Warming. Their work during the 1890s transformed *Oecologie* from just another neologism to a functioning science with its own peculiar hold on reality. Drude, who was director of the Royal Gardens at Dresden, progressed from floristics to the study of the life histories of particular formations and of "the mutual dependence of the animal and plant kingdoms in their household economy." Schimper, who emigrated from Strasbourg to teach botany at the University of Bonn, had a typically solid German training in experimental physiology, particularly in photosynthesis and the metabolism of plants. But several expeditions to the tropics prompted him to take a new ecological bearing, and he set about applying his laboratory background to the study of the physiological adaptations made by individual plants and whole societies to such external conditions as heat, precipitation, and soil.[6]

The most important of these three pioneers, however, was Eugenius Warming, a Danish professor who produced the key synthesis that forced the scientific world to take note at last of the new field of ecology. His classic work, *Plantesamfund*, was first published in 1895 and then in 1909 was revised and translated into English as *The Oecology of Plants: An Introduction to the Study of Plant Communities*. Described explicitly as a study in "oecological plant geography," the treatise commenced with a thorough review of the impact of habitat factors—light, heat, humidity, soil, terrain, animals—on the growth patterns of plants, focusing especially on the nutritive organs. Warming gave to this process of structural and physiological adjustment to habitat the name "epharmosis." Genetically different plants, he noted, may react to similar environments in similar ways, a phenomenon he called "epharmonic convergence." Both the American cactus and the South African euphorbia, for instance, have responded to their arid homes by developing fleshy, succulent stems and by evolving spines instead of leaves as a means of conserving moisture.[7]

So far, Warming was exploring the subject Schimper had made his special study: the borderland where ecology meets physiology and morphology. But his central theme, which he took sixteen of the seventeen sections in the treatise to develop fully, was that of the communal life of organisms. Ecology, in his view, concerned chiefly "the manifold and complex relations subsisting between the plants and animals that form one community." Each natural assemblage, whether a heath or a hardwood forest, is a society made up of many species, all having similar environmental tolerances. "Like absolute monarchs," a few dominant plants rule the community, determining by their influence which subordinate organisms will be able to coexist. So linked and interwoven "into one common existence" are the lives of all members in the community that "change at one point may bring in its wake far-reaching changes at other points."[8]

As much, of course, had been remarked by naturalists as early as Linnaeus, and even before. But the Copenhagen professor had to his advantage, taken from German scientists for the most part, a more precise vocabulary to discriminate among the degrees and styles of interdependence in the social worlds of plants and animals. The most ubiquitous of these relations is the mode of "commensalism," where several species, as it were, sit down at the same table to eat. Rather than fighting over a common dish, however, commensals complement each other's diet, each feeding on what its tablemates do not want. In some cases several commensals may enjoy benefits from another without reciprocating the favor, as when an oak tree provides nesting sites for squirrels and birds and shade for an anemone blooming at its base. A far less common and more intense kind of interdependence, Warming continued, is the "symbiosis" mode, first named and described in detail by Anton de Bary in 1879. This extreme form of mutualism was stereotypically illustrated by the lichen, a quasi-organism that is really a partnership between an alga and a fungus. Under this heading of "symbiosis" Warming also placed parasitism, where dependence is so intimate it may destroy the generous hosts. Rare though it is, the symbiotic relation might serve as the pure Platonic ideal that all nature imperfectly reflects: an interdependence of life forms that approximates the vital union of organs in an individual body.[9]

The significance for scientists as well as for philosophers of these ecological linkages was that they proved the organic world is not merely a scene of rampant self-reliant individualism. As had Darwin forty years earlier, Warming stressed that almost no species can prosper without aid from others often far removed in the scale of life. But neither did Warming, any more than Darwin, see this as inconsistent with the pursuit of self-interest or with competition for survival. There is such a thing as a war of each against all, fought most hotly among individuals of the same species living together. Particularly in the community considered only as a society of plants—in a stand of pines, for example—

egoism reigns supreme. The plant community has no higher units or personages in the sense employed in connexion with human communities, which have their own organizations and their members cooperating, as prescribed by law, for the common good. . . . There is no thorough or organized division of labour such as is met with in human and animal communities, where certain individuals or groups of individuals work as organs, in the wide sense of the term, for the benefit of the whole community.

Looked at from the exclusive perspective of plants interacting in a habitat, nature becomes only a very loose society in which there is "no cooperation for the common weal"—hardly a real community by man's ideal. But when the view expands to include other, higher organisms living there, the social bonds begin to tighten.[10]

A third feature of Warming's treatise, along with the discussions of epharmosis and communal life, was his system for classifying the major plant formations or communities of the world. In contrast to C. Hart Merriam, he emphasized the role of the water content of soils, which he believed controls more significantly than does temperature the types of biological association. Plants that need a great deal of water to survive he called "hydrophytes," and in congregating with others of like needs they create a hydrophytic formation, like plankton in the sea. Those able to grow in the driest areas are "xerophytes"; those found in habitats of moderate rainfall and soil water, "mesophytes." In all, Warming created—again through that godlike power of the Word—more than a dozen categories, including formations tolerating high salinity, such as the mangrove forest, and plants such as the mosses that grow in the acid soil of the tundra. Within each plant community, the associated species display convergent root structures, transpiration capacity, and techniques of water storage. They are kinfolk by the force of necessity.

The last section of *Plantesamfund* described the processes of ecological succession or dynamics: the transition from one kind of community to another in a given habitat, with its corollaries, the defense of communal territory from invaders and the "peopling of new soil." This, as we will see, was Warming's most influential set of ideas, at least as far as English and American ecologists were concerned: ideas that were to have a far-reaching impact on environmental values and the practice of conservation. Communities, Warming contended, do not remain always the same, forever maintaining a steady state as ordained by some divine power. Old, long-established formations may abruptly disintegrate under external pressures, he observed. The amount of water in the soil can decline or the temperature increase, and societies must change accordingly. Man can destroy a complex biological community by setting fire to a grassland or forest, or by introducing domestic stock or weeds that displace native species. Beavers too, by damming a brook, can drastically alter vegetation. And just as human cultures frequently collapse from within, so an ecological community can bring about its own demise by its own activities. In all these circumstances, there are aggressive opportunists waiting for a chance to invade. These constantly push out against their borders, trying to expand into their neighbor's range or, in some cases, to gain a foothold on bare, unpopulated soil.

In the 1850s, Henry Thoreau had explained the process of forest succession in his Concord environs. Earlier, in the eighteenth century, European naturalists had observed the phenomenon of "development succession" in the Scandinavian bogs. Water-loving hydrophytes would settle a pond and, by trapping mud with their roots, would eventually modify the environment to one more suited to mesophytes, or even xerophytes. The pond or lake would become a bog and then dry land covered by a dense forest. To the far north, in icy, barren habitats more hostile to life, only lichens and mosses could get a foothold as colonists —pioneers, as it were, struggling to prepare a more favorable soil for later tundra settlers. Both Linnaeus and Johannes Steenstrup had observed this pattern. A more spectacular model of this process of succession was the repopulating of the island of Krakatoa near Java, which was nearly obliterated in 1883 by volcanic eruptions. Slowly, as if by some cosmic magician's trick, ferns and lichens appeared on the barren soil, tenaciously carving a homestead for themselves out of the rubble. Someday, Warming and other ecologists anticipated, a richly diverse community of plants and animals would once again make these volcanic rocks their home.

According to Warming, the process of succession has in every habitat a discernible direction: It progresses toward a "climax" formation, or "final community." The ultimate goal of nature, in other words, is nothing less than the most diverse, stable, well-balanced, self-perpetuating society that can be devised to meet the requirements of each habitat. Geographers like Grisebach and Merriam were describing with their "formations" and "life zones" the end products of millions of years of trial-and-error experimentation. And it was this idea of successional development toward a climax equilibrium that Warming made central to the new science of ecology. It was the major legacy of the aberrant geographers to the emerging profession.[11]

Himself a kind of climax to a century of pioneering in plant geography, Warming was also—even more than Haeckel—the transitional figure with whom ecology enters its modern, mature stage. Within a matter of a few years, scientists on both sides of the Atlantic were deep into the study of the very themes he had outlined, including that of the evolution of the climax formation. Many, certainly, continued for some time to be totally mystified by the word "ecology." One Horace White, for instance, wrote to the editor of *Science* in 1902 to demand what was meant by the peculiar new term that had been appearing in the magazine's pages. But, interestingly, a host of readers were ready with replies. Professor Charles Bessey at the University of Nebraska explained that the word had been "in quite general use in th̄ ⌐otanical world for the past eight years." Zoologists, meanwhile, were already complaining of a monopoly on the science by botanists. Several writers referred the questioner to Haeckel's original definition. More curtly, the sociologist Lester Ward told White to use his dictionary. And two years later, Oscar Drude could look back with satisfaction over the near-decade since the publication of Warming's pivotal work and announce that the science was well launched in the field and the laboratory.[12]

There naturally arose ambiguities of intent and program behind the new label. For a number of scientists ecology seemed to promise a refuge from the increasing profusion of recondite specializations. They hoped it would provide a means to put biological studies back together in a grand new synthesis. As Paul Sears has observed: "The rise of the ecologist almost exactly parallels the decline of the naturalist." After Darwin—the last of the great generalists in natural history—ecology came to represent for many a modern substitute for his personal style and the sweeping imagination of an earlier, less fragmented biology, or what the ecologist Charles Elton later called "scientific natural history." For Barrington Moore, editor of the journal *Ecology* in 1915, its promise was even more explicitly philosophical or metabiological: ecology was "a point of view," an integrating outlook rather than a closet specialty. And for still others, ecology meant a chance to avoid the quantitative abstractions of the new Mendelian genetics and cell theory, a chance to return to the fields and woods where nature could be studied in its tangible wholeness.[13]

Yet in other aspects the science of ecology more precisely dovetailed with the highly technical temper of post-Darwinian biology. In particular there arose an entire subdivision soon known as "autecology," which was predominately concerned, as Schimper had been, with the environmental physiology of the individual organism. Many of the new professional ecologists would move into laboratories to investigate such phenomena as phototaxis and phototropism—the control exerted by sunlight over the direction of a zoospore's movement or a plant's growth. Others would develop the concept of "biological clocks," those internal mechanisms that help organisms time their reproductive or migratory cycles. Still others studied the homing stimuli in pigeons; or the effects on plants of a nitrogen or phosphorus deficiency in the soil; or Pavlovian conditioning and the environmental determinants of animal behavior. But generally speaking, these inquiries were not the major thrust, the distinctive impulse that gave ecology its early identity. For this we must return to Warming's emphasis on "the communal life of organisms." Rather than the external approach to physiology, a study of the social relations of the natural world—sometimes called "synecology"—was its *raison d'être*. Victor Shelford, an ecologist at the University of Illinois, was exactly right when in 1919 he defined ecology as "the science of communities." A still more precise definition might be "the science of the *development* of communities"—their progress through succession to the climax stage. Thus Haeckel's vaguely Darwinian description of ecology—his new name on the map of science—acquired a topography, borders, and landmarks through the trail-blazing energy of the geographers. It became both a familiar word on the map and a clearly demarcated terrain. The way was prepared for academic settlers to move in and begin the work of defining and developing even more closely the meanings of the new land.[14]

CHAPTER 11

Clements and the Climax Community

NOT SINCE THE TIME of Linnaeus had the botanists of the English-speaking world found themselves so far in the rear guard of scientific advance. Once again it was the Scandinavians, and even more impressively the Germans, who dominated the indexes of botanical textbooks. Scientists in Great Britain, however, were not slow in learning their lessons from Warming and Schimper, as well as from the new "plant sociologists" working at such schools as Montpellier and Zurich. By 1904 a committee had been formed to study England's vegetation after the manner of these Continental masters. The driving force behind this group was a pair of Scots, William and Robert Smith, who were later described by the Oxford ecologist A. G. Tansley as "the original pioneers of modern ecology in Britain." And one could add the name of a Glasgow biologist, Patrick Geddes, who went on to develop a kind of ecological approach to the city. Tansley himself planned and led the first International Phytogeographical Excursion in 1911, a grandiose field trip with the chief ecological lights from Europe, Britain, and America in its entourage. And in 1913 the British Ecological Society was formed, with Tansley as its first president. The Britons were not to be eclipsed for very long in a field like ecological botany, which had been one of their favorite national pursuits since the days of John Ray.[1]

More surprising perhaps was the ease and vigor with

which the Americans soon jumped into the driver's seat of the accelerating science. According to Drude, writing in 1904, no scientific community had done more than that of the United States to set ecology on its feet as a going concern. When a revised edition of Warming's *Plantesamfund* appeared a few years later, it carried the names of more than a dozen key scientists from the distant and hitherto silent interior of the New World. The secret of this astonishing energy, of course, was that American science had finally come of age, after an infancy that seemed to many patriots abnormally prolonged. By sheer chance, that moment of maturation, in institutions and training, happened to coincide with the launching of a professional, independent ecological science, a circumstance that native opportunism made the best of. Slower than the British to organize, the Americans did not establish their Ecological Society until 1915. But soon after that, A. G. Tansley and others were acknowledging the rise of American intellectual leadership in this field. In particular Tansley singled out two men who, it can safely be said, created a distinctive Anglo-American school of ecological thought that remained dominant until at least the 1940s; they were Henry C. Cowles of the University of Chicago and Frederic Clements of the University of Nebraska. Tansley described Clements' work as a greater influence on British ecology "than any other publication since the foundation works of Warming and Schimper." Although Cowles and Clements worked wholly independently of each other, their thinking flowed in the same channel, one marked and dredged for them by the westward movement of pioneering settlers across the North American continent.[2]

The tradition established by Cowles and Clements came to be known as "dynamic" ecology. It signified an approach that was concerned primarily with the phenomenon of "successional development" in plant communities, described earlier by Warming. Cowles came to the University of Chicago from Oberlin in Ohio, intending to pursue geology and physiography, the study of landforms. Here at the new university—founded in 1891, just a few years before Cowles arrived—a brilliant faculty had been assembled in a remarkably short time by President William Rainey Harper.

Among the natural scientists was John Coulter, one of the nation's leading botanists and a former student of Asa Gray's at Harvard; it was Coulter who persuaded young Cowles to abandon his first love in science for the pursuit of an adolescent ecology. Cowles, with the original German edition of Warming's opus in hand, quickly advanced beyond his graduate teachers. By 1896 he had hit upon the idea of applying the Warming model of succession and climax formation to the vegetation growing along the sandy shores of nearby Lake Michigan. Within another three years he had ready for the science journals a landmark paper; its publication in 1899 immediately placed him in the front ranks of the new field, both in his own country and abroad.[3]

Cowles' discovery in the course of his rambles among the sand dunes by the lake was this: A keen observer, walking inland from the water's edge, could trace a pattern of ecological succession *in space* which paralleled the development of vegetation in time. He discerned, to begin with, several distinct water-tolerant plant societies growing on the different levels of the beaches, all struggling to hold on against the ceaseless lapping and pounding of the waves. Next came a series of humped, rolling dunes, some unstable and wandering, others long-established and anchored by xerophytic formations. Finally, well back from the water, one arrived at an oak woods, a deciduous mesophytic forest that represented the mature, climax type of vegetation in that part of the country. Obviously this location possessed the most favorable conditions for plant life to flourish, and toward this goal of the oak forest nature in that climate generally advanced. But Cowles did not argue that one day the beach too would disappear, transforming the very margin of the lake into a dense woods. To the contrary, so long as water was present in Lake Michigan, the climax formation would be held off by the unique local physiographic character of the beaches and dunes. The plant ecologist could, however, organize the lakeshore into a clear spatial progression, from a watery extreme in which only a limited number of organisms could thrive to a more widely tolerable, mesophytic state that achieved nature's ultimate promise.

On the basis of these crablike backtrackings from the

littoral edge, Cowles concocted a "physiographic" ecology that took into account the effects of all kinds of local land-forms in deflecting or retarding the normal plant succession. Unfortunately he never applied the approach beyond his early dunes work, and almost all his subsequent influence was not as a field researcher but as a popular and forceful teacher of graduate students on the faculty at Chicago. Within a few decades, having failed to publish much beyond his 1899 piece, he had virtually dropped out of sight. The testimony of his students, however—including Victor Shelford, Charles Adams, Paul Sears, and William Copper, who were all to become leaders in the field—is enough to establish Cowles' role as the proverbial solitary and self-reliant pathfinder, America's first professional ecologist. The dunes showed him the process of ecological succession at work, and he in turn imposed that phenomenon vividly on the scientific imaginations of his students.[4]

Concurrent with Cowles' explorations of ecological dynamics in the Great Lakes region—though altogether isolated from them—a strikingly parallel ferment was brewing out on the western prairies at the University of Nebraska in Lincoln. In the 1880s that school was not much more than a name over a door, an ambition newly chiseled in granite to bring practical culture to the pioneer back-country. During that decade, the young scientist Charles Bessey arrived at this outpost of learning. He, like John Coulter, had been trained at Harvard by Asa Gray, and in his baggage were the first college microscopes to cross the Mississippi River. Bessey quickly organized a botanical seminar whose work, in large part, was to record as much of the aboriginal vegetation of the state as possible before it was all plowed under by the hordes of new settlers. Roscoe Pound, one of his first assistants, was sent out with pack-horse, instruments, and collecting boxes to tramp over the sandhills of the northwest corner of the state. Other students fanned out to survey the Nebraska grassland in a race of ecological science against time, homesteaders, and the westward march.[5]

One fall day in 1890 there appeared in Bessey's office a

prim, ascetic, humorless freshman named Frederic Clements. He was sixteen years old, and had been born and reared just down the street from the college—a native son of this rootless frontier world. Bessey immediately put him to work with Pound. Eight years later, Bessey's two protegés published *The Phytogeography of Nebraska*, a work that concerned not only plant distribution in the state but also ecology: "the interrelations of the organic elements of this floral covering." A decade later Pound abandoned botany to study law at Northwestern, eventually becoming dean of the Harvard Law School and a famous advocate of sociological jurisprudence. Frederic Clements, for his part, persisted in ecology, first as a professor at Nebraska up to 1907, then at the University of Minnesota for ten more years, and finally at the Carnegie Institution of Washington until his retirement in 1941. During those four decades, no individual had a more profound impact on the course of American as well as British ecological thought. He was, in the opinion of Tansley, "by far the greatest individual creator of the modern science of vegetation." From Clements' plant studies emerged a coherent and elaborate system of ecological theory that was not only preeminently influential in the new science, but also had important things to say about the pioneers' relation to the American grassland.[6]

Two interrelated themes dominated Clements' writing: the dynamics of ecological succession in the plant community and the organismic character of the plant formation. In *The Development and Structure of Vegetation*, published when he was thirty years old, he declared: "Vegetation is essentially dynamic." Henceforth that would be the central article of his scientific creed. Nature's communities change and develop through time, and the ecologist therefore must become literally a natural historian, chronicling the succession of plant societies that occupy a site for a while and then silently disappear into a fossil past. A more static analysis of a community's presently existing structure never commanded Clements' imagination. Almost from the beginning of his career he was drawn to the cycles of evolution in the landscape, to a Darwinian or perhaps Heraclitian sense of the persistence of flux in botanical formations that cohere only to dissolve again. This was the overarching theme of his chief book, which appeared in 1916: *Plant Succession: An Analysis of the Development of Vegetation.*

Change upon change became the inescapable principle of Clements' science. Yet he also insisted stubbornly and vigorously on the notion that the natural landscape must eventually reach a vaguely final climax stage. Nature's course, he contended, is not an aimless wandering to and fro but a steady flow toward stability that can be exactly plotted by the scientist. In any given habitat there occurs a clear progression through what Clements termed a "sere," a system of developmental stages that begins with a primitive, inherently unbalanced plant assemblage and ends with a complex formation in relatively permanent equilibrium with the surrounding conditions, capable of perpetuating itself forever. Upset or deflect this process, and eventually nature will find a way to get back on the track. What determines the direction and outcome of this unswervable progression is climate. The climax community that evolves in a given area is the product of those complexly intertwined variables of temperature, rainfall, and wind; in some places those forces write their signature as "forest," in others as "grass" or "desert." In the earliest stages of succession, climate is a less potent determinant of vegetation, and the local soil conditions are more influential. But according to Clements, each succeeding community becomes "less controlled by soil or terrain and more by climatic factors until the adult stage or climax is attained." In fact, as the sere unfolds it transforms the very soil itself and thus creates a more benign medium in which the future climax can grow. Each stage thereby readies a home for its successor.[7]

Clements' ecological paradigm is sometimes referred to today as the idea of a "monoclimax" because it allowed only one kind of ultimate formation for each of the broad climatic regions of the world. To be sure, he admitted that subclimaxes may exist as deviant islands in the midst of the great sweeping sea of the mature formation. These local, though almost permanent, pockets of resistance are due to unusual soil conditions and defy the flow of ecological progress like boulders in a stream. Moreover, he went on to devise an incredible array of labels—again the Word!—to identify other exceptions or variations to his system (preclimax, postclimax, eoclimax, panclimax, etc.), thereby adding fuel to the charge that ecology was becoming more a vocation of turning out glossaries than an empirical science. But for all these baroque details, the simple, stark correlation between climate and the climax community remains the essence of Clements' system. He was unshakably confident that in any region of the earth only one kind of community deserves to be called the mature stage: that which conforms most strictly to the macroclimate of the region.

Undoubtedly the explanation for Clements' emphasis on the sere and its climax lies in his underlying, almost metaphysical faith that the development of vegetation must resemble the growth process of an individual plant or animal organism. Further, he asserted that the climax plant formation is in fact a "complex organism"; indeed, one "of a higher order than an individual geranium, robin or chimpanzee. . . . Like them, it is a unified mechanism in which the whole is greater than a sum of its parts and hence it constitutes a new kind of organic being with novel properties." In his major work on succession, Clements made it clear that he was not throwing off half-serious or quaint conceits.

The unit of vegetation, the climax formation, is an organic entity. As an organism, the formation arises, grows, matures, and dies. . . . The climax formation is the adult organism, the fully developed community, of which all initial and medial stages are but stages of development. Succession is the process of the reproduction of a formation, and this reproductive process can no more fail to terminate in the adult form in vegetation than it can in the case of the individual.

The climate determines which "complex organism" among rival formations will survive in the struggle for existence; the losers fall apart and disappear. Once that selection has been made, the internal, irresistible dynamics of organismic growth take over. Just as physical maturation into adulthood is programmed into the genes of the child or seed, so the climax community marches toward an automatic, predetermined fate. Only in occasional freakish instances does the process bog down at a subclimax level of development, a kind of arrested adolescence.[8]

The convergence of modern ecology with organismic philosophy is a phenomenon that will receive more attention in Part Five. For the moment it must be sufficient to suggest the probable source from which Clements took this notion of a "complex organism": the nineteenth-century English philosopher of evolution, Herbert Spencer. Roscoe Pound recalled late in life that he and Clements had read together and frequently discussed Spencer's *Principles of Biology*, "of which we had expected great things in the days when Comtian Spencerian positivism was almost a religion to scientists." Spencer is better-known for the welcome accorded in the United States to his political philosophy, the ideology of social Darwinism, than for the fervent enthusiasm his work evoked among scientists of his day. But in both cases Spencer's audience began to fade away in the early years of the twentieth century; Pound, for instance, soon decided he could get nothing out of the man. In Clements and a few other ecologists, however, the fervor died much more slowly if it died at all. As late as 1929 Clements was still citing Spencer as his chief support for the organismic theory and claiming that the Victorian philosopher had anticipated the principal axioms of his own doctrine of plant succession. This peculiar tenacity of Spencer's influence in the field of ecology justifies a quick flashback over some of his ideas, with the aim of uncovering a few more of the roots of Clements' own science.[9]

As far back as 1860 Spencer had composed for the *Westminster Review* a critique of Plato and Hobbes entitled "The Social Organism." Maintaining that human society is not an article of artifice or manufacture, but a self-evolving organism, he rejected all efforts of reformers and social planners as a form of technological intrusion into nature. But the political issue was quickly put aside as Spencer became engrossed in working out the resemblances between organisms and societies. There were differences too, he admitted, but they weighed little against the "all-important analogies." Profit in commerce, for example, clearly had its counterpart in nutrition and growth in the human body. The House of Commons might be seen as the directing brain of the society, receiving messages from and transmitting them to its constituents and executive "ganglia." And Spencer extended his concept of organismic society to encompass those grand mechanical contrivances that as a former engineer he could not but admire: the railroads and telegraph wires that are the arteries of circulation and the nervous system of the body politic.[10]

Some readers must have found this hybrid organism, a creature half protoplasm and half locomotive, a bit strange. But Spencer himself liked the novelty of it so well he stuck it in his later works on sociology. After all, it merged neatly with his more general philosophy of cosmic evolution, according to which all phenomena show a progression toward greater differentiation and integration, a movement from homogeneity to heterogeneity. For instance, from a primitive past as an undifferentiated tribe much like the African Bushmen, English society had evolved to a higher division of labor as well as to what Victorians saw as a more cooperative, interrelated social whole. In a savage society, Spencer supposed, the loss of a few individual parts means nothing. But in a more advanced organism like a civilized community, "you cannot remove or injure any considerable organ without producing great disturbance or death of the rest." Toward this more perfect state of complex organismic interdependence all human societies must move.[11]

But Spencer would not rest until he had extended his evolutionary organicism from human groups to the ecological realm as well. In the revised 1899 edition of *Principles of Biology*, with the help of the omnipresent A. G. Tansley, he argued that the increasing integration among plants and animals demonstrates the "law of Evolution . . . under its most transcendental form." The fundamental integrating medium in the organic world is the exchange of gases: plants produce oxygen; animals inhale it and give back carbon dioxide. From Darwin's web of life Spencer plucked more such examples of mutual aid, including the dependence of some plants on special insect allies for fertilization. From these and other instances of commensalism and symbiosis, Spencer concluded that the guiding principles in organic nature, as in man's world, are "progressive differentiation" and "progressive integration." This process of ever higher cooperation, he noted, never achieves an absolute goal, but rather continues to advance "towards a moving equilibrium completely adjusted to environing conditions"—or something very close to what Frederic Clements called a climax community.[12]

There was in the Nebraska ecologist's concern for climate and its specific effects on regional vegetation a good deal more empiricism than Spencer could ever show. But otherwise the organismic climax formation may be fairly described as a special ecological dimension of Spencer's thought. And these two men were linked by another theme, this one dealing as much with ethics as with science: the necessity of competition in nature, which played a sometimes dissonant counterpoint to their harmonious chorus of cooperation. For Spencer the social organism was, as suggested earlier, the outcome of the struggle for survival of the fittest. Government or social planners, he warned, must not meddle with this natural process of succession. Clements too declared that competition among plants is "the controlling function in successional development, and is secondary only to the control of climate in the case of climaxes." And like Spencer, as we will see, he was sometimes critical of human interference with the process of sere development and its outcome. It was the paradoxical belief of both of these men that the war of each against all for the essentials of life results in a more harmonious social or ecological organism. Without competition there can be no growth, no progress toward the full communal state, no "moving equilibrium."[13]

The dynamic scheme of ecology had one last stage in its own coming of age. In 1939 Clements joined forces with Victor Shelford, the nation's leading animal ecologist, to produce what they called "bio-ecology." In essence they merged plant and animal communities into a broader "biotic community," or what they also termed the "biome." All living organisms—the "biota"—henceforth would be included whenever they discussed the climax state or the superorganism created through developmental succession. By this collaboration, Clements and Shelford managed at once to bring their ecological theory into closer alignment with Spencerism, which had treated plants and animals together, and to erase a long-standing barrier between two almost independent subfields of ecology. Clements nonetheless maintained his botanical loyalties by continuing to insist that in any biome it is the plants that determine which animals will be included, not vice versa. As in Merriam's life zones, plants are the mediating force between the habitat and its animal population: they are the most immediate and direct translation of the climate into food, as well as an essential buffer against environmental extremes. But, said Clements and Shelford, this special importance of the plant kingdom should not obscure the fact that all living organisms are united in one communal bond. The inorganic conditions of the habitat, in contrast, are outside forces that influence but do not participate in the biotic community's social affairs.[14]

The biome that Clements understood best, and that provided the model for his dynamic ecology, was the North American grassland. This particular plant–animal formation, he believed, must be the climax stage in any region where there is limited rainfall and much exposure to drying winds, where moisture is seasonal and confined to the upper soil layers. All around Clements, as he grew up in a sparsely settled Nebraska, the grassland stretched like a vast inland sea. It covered almost the entire midcontinent: an ancient and abiding legacy of the Rocky Mountains, which had been thrust upward some fifty million years ago. In its most western range, from the foothills east to about the 100th meridian, the grassland was a world dominated by the short buffalo grass, which curled and twisted to a height of four or five inches. Here on the semi-arid High Plains, across much of Montana south to the Texas Panhandle, grew the blue grama grass, too. East of this sprawling land of big skies and dry crackling air, rainfall increased slightly to a total of 20 to 25 inches annually, enough to support the taller mixed prairie—little bluestem, western wheatgrass, needlegrass—that covered most of the Dakotas as well as the central parts of Nebraska, Kansas, and Oklahoma. Still farther east grew the tall bluestem and switchgrass, towering to eight feet high, with roots going down almost as deep in the black humus-rich earth. This tall-grass prairie, which was constantly defending its eastern fringes against encroaching tree species from a more humid region, made perhaps its most impressive stand in the southeast corner of Nebraska where Clements was born and educated.[15]

Here, then, was a virtually unbroken sweep of grass, a single climax community, though grading off into three subregions, extending over hundreds of millions of acres of land. Through its immense history, this formation had been disrupted massively by the Ice Age and more trivially by countless small-scale fluctuations of climate. But according to Clements, what the mountains first created here had endured beyond anything in man's experience of time.

No student of past vegetation entertains a doubt that climaxes have evolved, migrated and disappeared under the compulsion of great climatic changes from the Paleozoic onward, but he is also insistent that they persist through millions of years in the absence of such changes and of destructive disturbances by man. There is good and even conclusive evidence within the limitations of fossil materials that the prairie climax has been in existence for several millions of years at least and with most of the dominant species of today.

The grasses, swaying and rippling in the prairie winds, were the defining life of this grand, expansive biome. But it was also home to pronghorns, rattlers, prairie dogs, meadowlarks, grasshoppers, coyotes, jackrabbits, sandhill cranes. And there were the bison, easily the most visible and important of its animal citizens. Emigrating from Asia over the Bering Strait land bridge early in the Ice Age, these great shaggy beasts passed whole populations of other herbivores migrating in the opposite direction; horses and camels, for example, were abandoning the "New World" for the "Old" in search of greener pastures. So the buffalo came into a world that was theirs for the taking. Eventually they would prosper here and grow to number perhaps 75 million on the North American continent. In their wake, some 40,000 years ago, came human hunters from Asia whose dependence on the bison defined their place in the emerging biotic community. Thus species by species, and over eons of time, there evolved in this wide range of land one of the earth's most distinctive and stable ecological associations. Well into the nineteenth century, this unique community was described as still intact by such American travelers as Stephen Long, Josiah Gregg, and Francis Parkman. "Great American Desert," some of them scrawled on their maps. "Garden of the World," wrote others.[16]

Then abruptly and violently it was destroyed, not by any vast impersonal change in climate but by the invading white man. In a bloody frenzy spanning only a few decades, a small group of market hunters and genteel sportsmen slaughtered all but a few hundred of the bison. The United States Army took care of the Indians. "The year 1876," noted Walter Prescott Webb, "marks practically the end of both." Thereafter homesteaders were free to plow up the grasses, short or tall, and to make the land over to fit their imaginations.[17]

Thus when Clements drew from this grassland his model of a mature biotic community, he was writing about a world that was shortly to vanish. It had been a unique part of what Americans had looked to as the "virgin land"—a phrase suggesting that man's relation with nature is not only economic and utilitarian but also emotional, mythic, and perhaps sexual, in some deep-working sense. When, one wonders, did the land cease to be virginal? When the bison came to wallow and thunder on its sod? When the Indian set up his tipi? When a plow first worked in its humus? Clements avoided that question altogether with his more objective label for the primeval grassland: the climax community. But whether one talked about the virginity of the grassland or about the climax of the biome, it was clear to Clements, as it had been to others, that the white man was not a part of it: he came as a disrupter, an alien, an exploiter.

From the eighteenth century on, biogeographers and ecologists had drawn up their elaborate schemes of classification, usually without ever considering the presence or influence of humans. Man was basically an outsider to their science, and several early ecologists, recognizing this deficiency, had argued that even civilized man belonged with the other animals in the ecological community. Frederic

Clements and the Climax Community • 217

Clements agreed with this aim, at least so far as the Plains Indians were concerned. But the white man was another matter, a complicating presence that overturned or disobeyed natural laws, and it proved far easier to leave him out of the theory of ecological dynamics. He was not really a member of the community, perhaps could not be. Indeed he was responsible for the destruction of the natural pattern of successional development, and gave the idea of a stable climax, even in Clements' time, a certain academic unreality.[18]

Clements apparently never appreciated the considerable irony in this exclusion. Undoubtedly, the coming of the white man into the virgin prairie had suggested some of the main features of his dynamic ecology. In addition to remembering Warming and Spencer, Clements was thinking about the American pioneer when he shaped his ideas of succession and climax. In a 1935 essay, for example, he explicitly compared the development of vegetation with the pattern of settlement on the frontier of the Middle West. The progression of plants in a habitat follows a process of pioneering and settlement, just as man's advance was doing on the prairie. The stages of civilization formed their own kind of sere: first trapper, then hunter, pioneer, homesteader, and finally urbanite. This view of social evolution on the American frontier had been expressed as early as the 1820s by James Fenimore Cooper, and had originally grown out of the notion set forth in the eighteenth century by Condorcet, Buffon, and the French Encyclopedists, that history is a set of stages or epochs progressing from the most primitive society to European civilization. But in North America it was possible to see those stages actually created in the present by westward-moving pioneers. In 1893 the Wisconsin historian Frederick Jackson Turner called this pioneering process decisive in forming the national character of the United States. According to him, it had been an experience that restored life to a decrepit European culture and gave to America and the world a democratic impulse: a regression, as it were, to an earlier stage in the sere, and hence a chance to build toward a new climax community. Now the vanguard of American ecologists, all from the Middle West as was Turner, gravitated almost unconsciously to an ecology of pioneering that exactly paralleled the historian's concern with the evolution of American society on the frontier.[19]

The irony in this convergence of ecology and history was that while the westward-moving frontier contributed a model to a widely influential ecological theory, it also shattered that theory's sanctity. According to the Turner–Cooper view of national development, a mature and complex civilization must emerge out of the pathfinding exploits of a ruder culture; Clements and the mainstream of Anglo-American ecology offered a similar view of the evolution of the biotic community. But the two processes of development were fated to meet, it seemed, in irreconcilable conflict. One would have to give way to the other; it was not possible to have both a climax state of vegetation and a highly developed human culture on the same territory. The first confrontation occurred in the humid forests lying east of the Mississippi River: here the climax growth gave way, if slowly, to the axe and rifle of an invading human society seeking homes, wealth, and empire. By 1850 Thoreau's complaint about the missing members of the Concord biota had become true of by far the better portion of the eastern forest. Then, after leapfrogging to the Pacific coast, the pioneers came finally to the grassland, the last of the American West. Within only a few decades, their conquest of the prairie and plains was complete. But then there occurred something the Cooper–Turner theory of social evolution could not have anticipated. Rather than smoothing the way for a stable, permanent human order, the pioneers and homesteaders unwittingly prepared the soil for a social and ecological disaster: the Dust Bowl of the 1930s.

To that unprecedented experience, tragic both for the land and its people, Clements and other ecologists turned in the "dirty thirties." They tried, as we shall presently see, to find in their science some solutions to land abuse on the prairies and plains. Most ecologists understood by this point that it was no longer possible to leave man out of their textbooks and models. Some reconciliation between the ecological and human patterns of evolution had to be devised, some accommodation reached between faith in nature's ways and sympathy for human ambitions. Thus in the thirties, Clements' climax ecology came under the searching glare of practical experience and encountered its first significant criticism—from farmers, from scientists, from historians. But however this controversy affected the theory of the climax, the Dust Bowl would succeed dramatically in bringing the young science out of academe and into the public consciousness.

CHAPTER 12

Dust Follows the Plow

ON A TYPICAL AFTERNOON the average wind velocity on the Great Plains is about fifteen miles per hour. It is a constant, almost human presence, pressing down with unrelenting force the grasses and row crops, whistling with eerie persistence around the farmer's barn and fences. In the spring of 1934, however, the wind suddenly seemed to become a demon. On April 14 a vast black blizzard of earth came rolling out of the north toward Texas; it whirled and spun in a giant bowl, darkening the sun and covering the land with drifts up to twenty feet high. Less than a month later, on May 10, another great storm moved east toward Chicago, dumping twelve million tons of plains dirt on that city alone. Two days later the storm reached the eastern seaboard. Dust sifted into the White House and fell on ships standing out at sea.[1]

That the wind often carried dust along in its train was a fact familiar enough to settlers in the grassland. There had even been serious dust storms in 1932, in 1913, and farther back, in 1894 and 1886. But none of these was of more than local significance, nor came with such fierce turbulence. The storms of the thirties meant dust was everywhere, blanketing crops and wiping out fence lines, filtering through the cracks around the door—no matter how many wet rags were stuffed in them—and even mixing with the bread dough. And nothing in the past could match the sheer frequency and scale of these most recent storms: There were 22 of regional extent in 1934, 40 in 1935, 68 in 1936, and 72 in 1937, before at last they began to drop off. It was inescapably clear to the entire nation that something was radically, desperately wrong on the western plains.[2]

The most obvious and frequently blamed villain, after the wind, was drought. On the plains, most of the year's rain falls during the spring and summer growing season, from April to July, and it oscillates wildly from year to year around a mean of twenty inches or less—a subhumid climate. In the summer of 1931 the rain did not come at all, or in the following spring, or in the next, and 1934 proved to be the driest year in the history of the region's weather records up till then. Even the more humid prairies suffered; by the end of July the Missouri River area in eastern Nebraska showed no water available for plant growth down to a depth of four feet. These conditions continued through 1940 across the entire grassland, and at times as far east as the Alleghenies. Frequent temperatures of over 100 degrees made this drought even more destructive to the native grasses, but especially to agricultural crops. In Thomas County, Kansas, no wheat at all was harvested in 1933, 1935, 1936, and 1940, and during the intervening years the average yield was at best only a third of pre-drought averages. By 1935 the United States, the vaunted breadbasket of the world, was forced to import wheat from other countries. Farther south, in Hall and Childress counties of Panhandle Texas—the very heart of the Dust Bowl—average cotton ginnings plummeted from 99,000 bales in the late 1920s to 12,500 in 1934 and 26,500 in 1936. "That drought," as one farmer said, "put the fixins to us."[3]

Soon Americans discovered another dramatic symbol of the times to go with blowing dust: the impoverished "Okie" and his wife and children heading out for California. They came in greatest numbers from the "OK state" of Oklahoma, but also from Kansas, Texas, and farther east. Along the highways of the southern plains one saw them at noon camped in the shade of a billboard, carrying on their truckbeds shabby, makeshift tents out of which dangled mattresses and a half-dozen red-brown children: sober, staring faces in faded overalls. Or one passed them chugging west in a battered old Hudson, flat bedsprings tied to the car roof along with odd pieces of lumber and a bucket or two, perhaps with a goat riding in a crate on the running board. And everywhere along the way one heard them telling of their misfortune:

"Come to the end of my row in Rockwell County, Texas."

"Nigh to nothin' as ever I see."

"That year spring came and found us blank."

"Yessir, we're starved, stalled, and stranded."

"Burned out, blowed out, eat out, tractored out."

In the second half of the thirties, they poured into California at the rate of 6,000 a month—a total of 300,000 "Dust Bowl refugees" from 1935 to 1939.[4]

But it was more than drought and dust that threw these people off their land and onto the factory farms of the west coast. Walter Stein has concluded that "most of the Okies came neither from the dust bowl nor from the areas of worst distress in the drought region. That Okies did come from the dust bowl was true; that the average Okie in California was a dust-bowl refugee was false." The typical migrant family had been living in the hills of eastern Oklahoma, on land that was once oak forest, not prairie or plains. Even the Joads of John Steinbeck's *The Grapes of Wrath* hailed from the town of Sallisaw, almost on the Arkansas border and hundreds of miles east of the dust center. Steinbeck, like most other Americans, assumed too simply that people like the Joads were the victims of a natural disaster that gave the banks and landlords an excuse to put them off the land, but in truth, their somber story was only peripherally connected with the drought on the plains. It was largely the outcome of purely social forces that within a decade or two had transformed rich, promising pioneer states into what Carey McWilliams called "a sump-hole of poverty."[5]

In the early 1870s, white families first began to settle in what had been designated the Indian Territory, a "region set aside for the perpetual home for the red man" which was later forcibly annexed as the eastern portion of Oklahoma.

For many years the whites lived here without laws or schools, either as tenants or as defiant intruders. They knew both styles intimately, coming as most of them did from the hill country of the rural South: a restless, violent, often resentful folk who had always lived by hard scrabbling. Few of these families could boast of more than the merest subsistence patch of twenty to forty acres, sometimes leased, sometimes taken from the Indians. A little farther west, during the famous "Sooner runs" of 1889 and 1893, the territory passed into the hands of other white settlers in equally scanty parcels, and soon thereafter into the amalgamating hands of a few wealthy landowners. When Oklahoma became a state in 1907, over half of its farms were small holdings operated by tenants; by 1935, over 60 percent. These tenants and sharecroppers had left behind them in the South a trail of bad farming and soil depletion, and they quickly overworked the land of Oklahoma, too. Their topsoil washed away, and with it any chance they might have had for self-sufficiency. In 1938 it was estimated that 275,000 people, or 28 percent of the farm population of the state, had moved to a new farm during the previous year—an aimless wandering that had begun as far back as the nineteenth century. "The roots of Oklahomans in the land are shallow," admitted Paul Taylor of the University of California, who followed with sympathy their exodus west. The drought and economic depression of the 1930s, it must be understood, only brought renewed desperation to this drifting mass of tenant farmers. Hard as it is to believe, within a single generation their last frontier had already become a rural slum.[6]

On the plains farther west, many of these impoverishing conditions were repeated. As in eastern Oklahoma, there were too many farmers for too few farms, and although in this drier grassland the individual holdings were usually much larger (the 160-acre homestead was typical), they still were not adequate to support a family. But here, where the land is more level, another force for instability came into play: the technological revolution in the form of the tractor. The development after World War One of the small, inexpensive "farmall" machine made it possible for one man to plow and harvest a much larger farm at lower cost per acre.

Given that during the 1920s the total net income from even a 640-acre wheat farm in western Kansas could amount to only $35 a year, the rush to tractors is not hard to understand. But maximum efficiency would never be realized until holdings were consolidated and the surplus population gotten rid of. Luckily for the already wealthy and enterprising few, almost 40 percent of the farmers throughout the entire Great Plains were tenants, and therefore easily sent packing. This process of consolidation was expedited when the Agricultural Adjustment Administration began making crop reduction payments to landowners only (though in fact there was often nothing to reduce); the money generally went not to their tenants but to tractor salesmen. During the first half of the dirty decade, about 150,000 persons emigrated from the plains. Not drought but the machine drove most of these farmers from the land, but perhaps it was easier on their pride to blame their misfortune on nature. In many ways resembling the English peasants uprooted by the eighteenth-century enclosure acts, these surplus tenants were the victims of America's judgment—perhaps justified—that agriculture must be made to pay a higher return. Although they may not have been precisely the Okies Steinbeck knew, these displaced tenants of the plains tumbled west with their more famous eastern cousins.[7]

But whatever "put the fixins" to these various rural folk and sent them fleeing down the road toward the Golden State, that a genuine human tragedy took place during the Dust Bowl years is undeniable. On the southern plains in particular—Texas, New Mexico, Oklahoma, Colorado, and Kansas—the blowing dust often went hand in hand with bankruptcy and welfare. By 1935 in some counties of the region as many as 80 percent of the families were living on relief, and from 1934 to 1936 about 5 million acres of land here were blowing severely. By 1938—the peak year for wind erosion, though not for the most sensational storms—this total had jumped to almost 9 million, scattered over an area of 51 million acres. Soil scientists for the Department of Agriculture estimated in this same year that half of the Great Plains—some 500,000 square miles—had been seriously damaged by erosion, a situation that was bound to produce much economic hardship and misery. As a farmer rightly noted in the *Dallas Farm News* in 1939: "The prairie, once the home of the deer, buffalo and antelope, is now the home of the Dust Bowl and the WPA."[8]

As we have been reviewing here, the causes of the Dust Bowl were complex, more cultural than natural, and certainly not to be summed up in the fact of drought. The root cause of this most destructive episode in America's environmental history was described thus by Archibald MacLeish in the mid-thirties:

The meaning of the dust storms was that grass was dead. The small tornadoes, spectral with earth, which sucked up out of the western wheat fields were the ghosts that said it. Erosion of the soil, whether by wind or water, results not from the sickness of the soil but from the sickness of the vegetation which once held the soil in place. On the Great Plains that vegetation is the grass.

It was man's destruction of the grassland that set the dirt free to blow. Through such ill-advised practices as plowing long straight furrows (often parallel to the wind), leaving large fields bare of all vegetation, replacing a more diverse plant life with a single cash crop, and—most importantly—destroying a native sod that was an indispensable buffer against wind and drought, the farmers themselves unwittingly brought about most of the poverty and discouragement they suffered.[9]

This destruction was not accomplished in a season or two: it was the product of the entire fifty-year period of settlement that preceded the 1934 storms. And in a real sense, the way of life of the Okies, eastern and western, was in large part what destroyed the grass: tenancy, the moving itch, violence toward nature as well as other men, disregard for the land as a permanent home. All of these traits had been long represented, sometimes even celebrated, in the pioneer mentality that still dominated the culture of the region. This mentality and its values were most succinctly wrapped up in the image of the "sodbuster"—an image that had long signified heroic qualities to the American imagination. In that image was also implied, indeed fairly shouted, an environmental ethic of conquest. The advance of the sodbuster across the plains most fundamentally ex-

plains both the blowing dirt and the relief rolls. The sodbuster made the Dust Bowl, and the "Dust Bowl refugees"
were his children.

Sometime in the 1880s the sodbuster came to and began
to conquer the Great Plains. His final victory, as Walter
Prescott Webb has demonstrated, awaited the perfection of
several technological innovations, including the railroad,
plow, windmill, and barbed wire. Surely the most important of these, and invested with an almost sacred meaning
by the homesteader, was the steel plow. This instrument
had been devised to tear apart the dense sod of the tallgrass
prairies of Iowa and Nebraska, to break up root masses that
sometimes weighed four tons to the acre. It was confidently
assumed that fertility would follow the plow; that the
plains remained sterile and useless until cultivated. But beyond the 100th meridian, though the virgin sod here was far
easier to penetrate and thus seemingly more inviting to the
farmer, rainfall begins to drop off to a level that defies all
agriculture. West of that longitude, rain averages less than
twenty inches a year, not enough for intensive, traditional
plowing and cropping. Nevertheless, in 1881 Charles Dana
Wilber, a land speculator in Nebraska, succeeded in mag-
netizing a nation with the gloriously hopeful, go-ahead slogan: "Rain follows the plow." There was no reason for the
sodbuster to hesitate before the Great Plains, he declared.

To those who possess the divine faculty of hope—the optimists of
our times—it will always be a source of pleasure to understand
that the Creator never imposed a perpetual desert upon the earth,
but, on the contrary, has so endowed it that man, by the plow, can
transform it, in any country, into farm areas.

With such reassurance from Wilber and others, the sodbuster rushed out to the plains in unprecedented numbers.
By 1890 there were almost 50,000 people in the westernmost counties of Kansas, four times the 1880 population. And during the same years the number of settlers in
the Texas Panhandle jumped 600 percent.[10]

Then came the disastrous drought of 1894–95, bringing
complete crop failures to thousands and intense dust
storms to many areas. Along with the Panic of 1893, these
conditions led to a vast retreat of the settlement line. In
some plains counties, as many as 90 percent of the home-

steaders abandoned their farms, cursing nature and the banks as they went. And the simple but unsuspected truth in all this was that much of it was unnecessary. According to Edward Higbee, if the Spanish–Mexican system of land grants had been followed, rather than that of the Homestead Act of 1862, these consequences of drought on the plains would not have been nearly so ruinous. As early as 1825 the Mexican government, intent on establishing a grazing rather than a cropping economy in the region, offered 4,000 acres to every settler who agreed to become a rancher. In substantial agreement with this policy were John Wesley Powell and W. D. Johnson, both of the United States Geological Survey, who agreed that livestock ranching—requiring at least one or two thousand acres—was the only safe use of the shortgrass country. The American political establishment, however, would not tolerate such a "feudal," undemocratic policy that supposedly would set up great land-owning barons against the small yeoman homesteader. Not cattle but wheat, they were sure, was God's intention for the plains. But after the disasters of the 1890s they were forced to admit that "there is no god west of Salina."[11]

After 1900 the rains returned in unusual abundance, lasting, except for a few seasons, through World War One. Once again it was boom-time on the plains, stimulated not only by the plentiful moisture but by governmental confidence that new "dry-farming" techniques would yet make the plains blossom like the rose. By 1910 practically all of western Kansas was resettled, as well as eastern Colorado and the Panhandle. Then came the war and an even bigger drive to "plant more wheat for America." President Woodrow Wilson and his Secretary of Agriculture urged Kansas to plant one million more acres to win the war; Oklahoma and Texas had their suggested quotas, too. This pressure of patriotism along with the appeal of good prices took effect in short order: in 1918 the nation harvested 14 million more acres of wheat than in the previous year, a large portion of which was shipped to European allies. Few farmers, however, saved any of the money they made in these years of boom. With wheat selling at over two dollars a bushel and the future looking even rosier, they reinvested their earnings in more land and more machines with which to plant even bigger crops. Then suddenly, with the armistice, came the collapse of the boom markets. But, wrongheaded as it now seems, the conventional wisdom was that to survive the crunch of the postwar decade, investments had to be doubled to achieve greater economies of scale. Soon a truly formidable phalanx of tractors, combines, and trucks were clanking across the fields. By 1925 it was clear, according to Vance Johnson, that "mass production had reached the plains."[12]

In this desperate race against themselves and their creditors, the farmers of the southern plains alone, from 1925 to 1930, plowed up a fragile sod seven times as large as Rhode Island. If surplus was the problem, more surplus would solve it. In the eight principal plains states, the fifty-year record tells clearly the story of the big plow-up. In 1879 about 12 million acres of crops were harvested; in 1899, 54 million acres; in 1919, 88 million; in 1929, 103 million—in wheat and cotton chiefly. As a consequence, fewer and fewer acres were left in native grass and grazed, and these were soon overstocked and their forage value badly damaged. Yet there were also times during the twenties when crops had to be left standing in the fields because market prices were so low: wheat, in some years, dropped to less than a dollar a bushel. Sometimes land was broken only to be left bare and idle, exposed to the eroding wind—a not uncommon practice when the farmer was in fact living far off in a city; there were many such absentee owners, interested in the land only as a fast return on a financial investment. In 1936 the federally appointed Great Plains Committee noted this side of the history of the region's settlement:

A strong speculative urge . . . has been one of the driving forces in the development of the Great Plains. The majority of settlers probably intended to establish homes and farms for themselves, but the purpose of many was speculative gain. This was promoted by public land policy which, under an expansionist settlement, gave little consideration to the long-run stability of the Region.

By the 1930s the western farmers had cut the ground from under their very feet. The committee concluded in the very midst of the Dust Bowl years that at least 15 million acres, extending over 24,000 farms, should be immediately returned to native sod and never plowed again. All in all, 60 million acres of the plains had been badly abused and needed quick attention. After fifty years of being hailed for his heroic exploits, the sodbuster had become a menace to the nation.[13]

During the thirties the Department of Agriculture struggled to reverse within a very few years this half-century's heritage of land abuse. In part this was accomplished by paying farmers to stop producing and to retire their marginal land. It was also achieved by buying at public expense almost 6 million acres of those lands blowing most severely and trying to stabilize them as fast as possible. Eventually these lands were leased back to local residents for forage only. The Taylor Grazing Act of 1934 set aside for leasing to ranchers another 80 million acres in the public domain, all thereby withdrawn from homestead entry. In another part of the effort, chisels and listers were used to turn up heavy clods of earth that would hold the dust. Soils across the region were surveyed and classified according to their safest use. Sudan grass and sorghums were planted in contours and strips and terraces. Billions of trees were set out to provide a system of shelterbelts one mile apart. By 1941 about 75 soil conservation districts had been organized on the plains. No other period in the nation's history saw as much progress toward a full-scale conservation program for agriculture.[14]

One of the most important environmental documents of the decade was the report of the Great Plains Committee, "The Future of the Great Plains," submitted to President Franklin Roosevelt in December 1936. The committee's chairman was Morris Cooke, head of the Rural Electrification Administration, and the other members were Hugh Bennett of the Soil Conservation Service, Harry Hopkins of the Works Progress Administration, Rexford Tugwell of the Resettlement Administration, and Secretary Henry Wallace of the Department of Agriculture. Without a murmur of qualification, the committee concluded that the Dust Bowl was a wholly manmade disaster, produced by a history of misguided efforts to "impose upon the region a system of agriculture to which the Plains are not adapted." The essence of the tragedy, as they understood it, was a failure to heed the lessons of ecology. "Nature," they observed, "has established a balance in the Great Plains by what in human terms would be called the method of trial and error. The white man has disturbed this balance; he must restore it or devise a new one of his own." Unless this were done, Cooke and the others warned, the land would become a desert and the government would have on its hands a perennial, costly problem of relief and salvage.[15]

At the very root of the abuse of the plains lay not only an ignorance of natural science but more importantly a cluster of traditional American attitudes. According to the committee, these included the assumption that the corporate factory farm was more desirable than a smaller family operation, that markets would expand indefinitely, that the pursuit of self-interest and unregulated competition made for social harmony, that humid-land farming practices could be followed on the plains. There was also the pioneering view that America's vast natural resources could never be exhausted. Contrary to early confidence that it would take thousands of years to settle the region, the committee remarked that only a few decades had been required for the plains to become "economically congested." But at the very top of their list of fundamental causes for the Dust Bowl, they placed the misguided notion that man thrives by conquering nature:

It is an inherent characteristic of pioneering settlement to assume that Nature is something of which to take advantage and to exploit; that Nature can be shaped at will to man's convenience. In a superficial sense this is true; felling of trees will clear land for cultivation, planting of seed will yield crops, and applications of water where natural precipitation is low will increase yields. However, in a deeper sense modern science has disclosed that fundamentally Nature is inflexible and demands conformity. . . . We know now, for instance, that it is essential to adjust agricultural economy on the Plains to periods of deficient rather than of abundant rainfall, and to the destructive influence of wind blowing over dry loose soil rather than primarily to a temporary high price for wheat or beef; that it is our ways, not Nature's, which can be changed.

What ultimately was needed for the grasslands, they were saying, was a radically new environmental outlook. The American farmer must learn to walk more humbly on the earth and to conform his economy to nature's, not vice versa. The dogged confidence of the sodbuster that nature can always be bent to human will had been decisively discredited.[16]

Up to this point, the conservation movement in America had been overwhelmingly dominated by a series of uncoordinated resource-management programs, most of them set up around the turn of the century. Forests, water, soils, wildlife were all connected only by the loosest of conceptual threads. The major reason for this single-mindedness was that conservation policies usually had been founded on purely economic grounds; at whatever points resource demand exceeded supply, there sprouted a management program. But in the 1930s, largely as a direct consequence of the Dust Bowl experience, conservation began to move toward a more inclusive, coordinated, ecological perspective. A concern for synthesis and for maintaining the whole community of life in stable equilibrium with its habitat emerged. Undoubtedly this shift of outlook is also partly accounted for by the mood of the nation after the collapse of the Wall Street markets and the entire economic system—a mood that had become more communal and less individualistic. Holistic values everywhere challenged private, atomistic ways of thinking, and the atmosphere of depression also encouraged an unwonted willingness to subordinate economic criteria to broader standards of value, including ecological integrity. One of the unanticipated consequences of the sudden fall of America's economic empire, in other words, was the birth in the public consciousness of a new conservation philosophy, one more responsive to principles of scientific ecology. This new approach was evident in the report of the Great Plains Committee; in the regional planning of the Tennessee Valley Authority headed by David Lilienthal; in the writings of the wildlife expert Aldo Leopold; and in the organismic environmental philosophy of Lewis Mumford. In the space of thirty years, the newly independent science of ecology had moved from the early works of Warming, Cowles, and Clements to a position of considerable influence over government policy and popular values.[17]

A circle of Midwestern scientists led this movement toward ecological conservation, for the grassland in particular. In 1932, for example, Roger Smith, president of the Kansas Academy of Science and entomologist at Kansas State Agricultural College, blamed the devastating outbreaks of insect pests and plant diseases in his state on the plowing of the sod and the concomitant disturbance of the natural community. "Man with his agriculture," Smith wrote, "has upset the age-old balance of nature in the great plains region, and a new balance has not been reached. It probably is a long way off, in fact, since man is constantly changing his agriculture." The result here was that chinch bugs, grasshoppers, and wireworms—all native to the area—had run wild when their natural checks were removed and they were given by unwitting farmers an abundance of attractive new food. By some means, Smith argued, Kansans must establish an artificial system of biological controls to restore order to their land. Then in 1935 the Oklahoma ecologist Paul Sears published a more comprehensive and widely influential critique of land-use practices entitled *Deserts on the March*. Though much of the book dealt with other continents, the consideration that most compelled Sears to produce it was unquestionably the dust storms that seemed to be turning the American West into a desolate, drifting Sahara. First with the destruction of the forests, then of the grasslands, he wrote, "the girdle of green about the inland deserts has been forced to give way and the desert itself literally allowed to expand." Sears advocated the appointment of a resident ecologist to supervise land use in each county with the aim of spreading the view that "all renewable natural resources are linked into a common pattern of relationship."[18]

Both Smith and Sears contended that the pioneers had brought down on their heads this host of Egyptian plagues because they had not appreciated the genius of the climax community of the plains—the unique grass–buffalo biome. Naturally enough, then, they took their lead largely from Frederic Clements, and indeed, Clements' writings on

Dust Follows the Plow • 233

dynamic ecology provided much of the scientific authority for the new ecological conservation movement. From the 1930s on, American environmentalists, lay as well as scientific, relied heavily on Clements' climax theory as a yardstick by which man's intrusions into nature could be measured. Their basic assumption was that the aim of land-use policy should be to leave the climax as undisturbed as possible—not on account of the intrinsic value of virgin wilderness, but more pragmatically because it had proved itself through millennial vicissitudes of climate to be stable, tenacious, and marvelously well adapted to its habitat. Whenever human interference was necessary—and most acknowledged that it was, unless the population dropped abruptly and mankind reverted to a hunting economy—they believed that the best course was to stick as tightly as you could to nature's model.

Two more of Clements' disciples were John Weaver and Evan Flory, both ecologists at the University of Nebraska; they too were among those scientists promoting a grassland conservation program founded on the ideal of the climax community. In 1934 they wrote:

A thorough study of Nature's crops and Nature's way of making the most of a sometimes adverse environment is of scientific importance. It is also fundamental to an understanding of the effect of prairie upon stabilizing such factors as temperature and humidity, and its effect upon stabilizing the soil. It furnishes a basis for measuring the degree of departure of cultural environments from the one approved by Nature as best adapted to the climate and soil.

Man's crops, they believed, are inherently more unstable, more susceptible to disease and extremes of weather, than nature's: this is part of the price civilization must pay for its very existence. But there is no need to pay to the point of bankruptcy or dust bowls. At the very least, they supposed, it would be useful to understand more precisely the penalties for disturbing the ecological balance, and then to question whether Americans were "properly utilizing Nature's prairie garden or exploiting it." Such a comparative study, they warned, "should be made now, before the opportunity with the destruction of the natural vegetation has forever passed."[19]

Clements himself, in his several works on applied ecology written during the thirties, agreed wholeheartedly with these younger colleagues. As early as 1893, when he had been only twenty-three years old, it had been obvious to him that Nebraska homesteaders were committing a serious blunder in destroying the sod covering the sandhills of that state rather than preserving the natural grassland for grazing livestock. He recalled that Charles Bessey too, in the course of botanical surveys during the 1880s and 1890s, had come to understand that there were safer uses for those marginal lands than those he saw practiced. In the *Phytogeography*, published in 1898 by Clements and Pound, "all the essential features of the proper ecological system for the development of the Great Plains had been clearly discerned and set forth." And ignored. Clements and his associates had then been futile voices crying in the wilderness. Now, almost forty years later, he still maintained that the plains were in critical need of a broad regional plan of ecological land management faithful to the climax theory and the nurturing process of succession. It seemed to Clements that only an ecologist could see what special-interest land users such as the engineer, forester, farmer, and subdivider always overlooked: how man's actions in one place can ramify destructively through a whole biota, over thousands of square miles, across an entire nation. Such a program of management might well begin by searching out and protecting those relicts of the pre-settlement formation that still grew free and wild in neglected corners of country cemeteries and along the railroad tracks where farmers could not plow. From these forsaken byways might come regeneration: the healing grass that could cover a multitude of wounds.[20]

In dynamic ecology, it will be recalled, the climax or adult stage is the direct offspring of climate—and weather in the midcontinent is notoriously promiscuous. Ultimately, then, the ecologist must be as much a student of meteorology as of plants and animals. In the final analysis, "there is no basis for assuming either that the earth itself or the life upon it will ever reach final stability," Clements cautioned. But within the narrow span of human time-consciousness, vast periods of relative climatic stasis could be plotted with the aid of fossil records. By the same means, the ecologist might also be able to predict the future climate, knowledge vital to the farmer seeking to achieve a sustainable economy on the plains. The thirties drought, Clements maintained, was neither a freak event nor an omen of abrupt climatic change that would damn the plains to an eternally arid future. At least as far back as 1850, records showed a series of severe droughts in the West. Clements wanted to correlate this pattern with the sunspot cycle: in essence, whenever the sunspots subside to a minimum level, drought occurs. He admitted that this theory rested on a scanty statistical base, and climatologists are debating it still. It does seem clear that a major drought occurs every twenty years or so, whether due to sunspots or other causes. Recurring dry spells are a fact of life in the grassland, Clements warned, and man must explore every avenue of science that might aid in predicting them. Without such knowledge, no permanent settlement was possible.[21]

Clearly, this shift of attention from preserving the biological community in favor of adjusting to the climate, which Clements' writings in the 1930s emphasized, did undercut some of the force of climax conservation. Adaptation to cycles of drought rather than to a mature biome became Clements' dominant theme. This was undoubtedly an easier, more practicable route for farmers to follow, and for all his criticism of them, Clements' sympathies were often on the side of those homesteaders who were still determined to wrest a living from this intractable land. Clements did not altogether abandon the idea of climax preservation; he recommended that the westernmost edge of the shortgrass country be given over to the ranching industry and that millions of the most fragile acres in the Southwest and Great Basin area be set aside wholly for recreation or as wilderness. In these instances the aim would be to maintain the natural climax as much as possible, given the absence of Indians, bison, wolves, and many other elements of the original community. But these were the exceptions in Clements' environmental recommendations. He assumed—indeed had to, in view of the plowman's resolve—

that farming would continue to be the central economic activity in the grasslands, and therefore that man would go on battling against ecological succession. Considered realistically, the function of the ecologist must be to show men how they might manipulate the sere to their advantage, by deflecting or retarding the successional process with greater care and expertise. In forest as well as prairie, Clements noted, "the climax dominants are not necessarily the most valuable to man." Inevitably then, to some extent and in some places, man's economy would always take precedence over nature's.[22]

Despite his more pragmatic admissions, Clements' doctrine of the climax as a natural ideal was by now firmly lodged in the national imagination. And Clements himself could not surrender his admiration for this long-enduring communal order, this complex super-organism nicely adjusted to the vagaries of climate. This feeling created a dilemma for both the man and the nation, not an easy one to resolve. There was that primeval state of nature representing a perfect marvel of adaptation, and yet one belonged to a civilization that, despite the blowing dust, continued to believe it needed the land for its own purposes and could somehow find a way to match nature's ingenuity. The confusion over which direction to turn, so apparent in the sum of Clements' own work, was at the very core of conservationist thought in the 1930s. Not since the coming of the Industrial Revolution to America in the early nineteenth century had there been so keen a debate between the claims of nature and culture. Reinforcing the first of these two sides was a new and profound suspicion of technology in the American mind, a wariness instilled by the collapse of the national economy and its industrial system. The tractor on the plains could become the focus of that suspicion as well as any assembly line in Detroit. Take the tractors and combines, the plows and harrows, out of the grassland and give it back to nature: this was in effect what a number of ecologists and other Americans were saying during the thirties, even those who, like Clements, were also struggling to be responsive to human needs in the region. Moreover, in the theory of the climax community they had a formidable scientific defense for that back-to-nature mood.

But such a pessimistic reaction against technology cut hard against the grain of a society that for the most part retained its confidence in man's managerial skill. This was especially true, of course, among farmers on the High Plains. Substantial numbers of them fitted Archibald Mac-Leish's description of Tom Campbell, who in the twenties signed a lease with the federal government to plow up ten million acres of Indian reservations. "Wheat to him was the occasion, the excuse," wrote MacLeish. "A tractor was the reality, . . . Campbell ran his farm for the machines' sake." He owned no fewer than thirty-three tractors. Such enthusiasm for the machine was not likely to be tempered by a little dust. Another farmer expressed the unrecalcitrant pride and defensive resentment felt by many: "You can say what you want about the way we farm, but those dust storms ain't manmade." And despite the massive mechanization of agriculture, most of the nation still held firmly to the old Jeffersonian faith that the farmer is nature's ally, if not her benefactor. Even in the Dust Bowl era, the mythic ideal of the husbandman living in fruitful marriage with the land would not be obscured by dusty reality: not in the mind of President Roosevelt or in the mind of the suburban middle class or in the mind of the farmer himself. Hence it was most unlikely that the West would be returned to grass and bison. Most of the wheat farmers were there to stay, and to them in particular the climax theory must have seemed at best academic and at worst a threat to their livelihood and hegemony.[23]

There were a number of scientists, too, who found the anti-technology implications in the climax ideal hard to accept. From this objection, as much as from any purely scientific quarrel with Clements, there emerged in the thirties an "anti-climax" party. Earliest to join issue with Clements on this point was Henry Gleason of the University of Michigan. His essay "The Individualistic Concept of the Plant Association," published in 1926, announced by its very title that he did not at all like the organismic notion applied to the plant formation, not even as an occasional metaphor. Plants do form associations, Gleason argued, but these are mere accidental groupings, each the result of unique circumstances and too loosely related to be likened to an organized being. The drift of this reasoning, as it became clear, was toward a repudiation of the carefully orchestrated, precise succession to the climax state. Indeed, Gleason took exactly that step in the next year, warning against a too rigid idea of the sere and its outcome. Clements' weakness had always been his rigidity, and that was the charge Gleason effectively made now by calling for a less formal concept of ecological dynamics. More important, Gleason's "individualistic" view of nature suggested that the climax was a haphazard, imperfect, and shifting organization—one that man need not worry overly much about disturbing.[24]

Not far behind came A. G. Tansley of Oxford, who despite his recognition of the Nebraskan's leadership refused, as he declared, to drink the "pure milk of the Clementsian word." During the period from 1926 to 1935 he delivered a number of sharp rebuttals to the successional-climax school, especially to Clements' young South African disciple, John Phillips, as well as to the old master himself. Tansley was above all insistent that the "monoclimax" ideal would no longer wash. He claimed that in any single climatic region there may be many apparently permanent types of vegetation, all of which deserve to be called climaxes. Special soils may give rise to edaphic climaxes, for example; heavy grazing by animals to a biotic climax; recurrent fires sweeping over an area to a fire climax. But it was the isolation of modern man's activities from the climax ideal that most bothered Tansley—especially the assumption that he is always an intrusive, disruptive force in nature.

It is obvious that modern civilized man upsets the "natural" ecosystems or "biotic communities" on a very large scale. But it would be difficult, not to say impossible, to draw a natural line between the activities of the human tribes which presumably fitted into and formed parts of "biotic communities" and the destructive human activities of the modern world. Is man part of "nature" or not? Can his existence be harmonized with the concept of the "complex organism"? Regarded as an exceptionally powerful biotic factor which increasingly upsets the equilibrium of preexisting ecosystems and eventually destroys them, at the same time forming new ones of very different nature, human activity finds its proper place in ecology.

To these "new ones" Tansley gave the name "anthropogenic" climax, describing a biological system that is artificially created by humans but is as stable and balanced as Clements' primeval climax—a permanent agricultural system, for example. "We cannot confine ourselves to the so-called 'natural' entities," he maintained, "and ignore the processes and expressions of vegetation now so abundantly provided us by the activities of man." Earlier, Tansley had been willing to call this artificial environment a "disturbance climax" or "disclimax." But now he would no longer accept the inferiority implied in those terms; they seemed to reinforce the view that technological man is a corrupting influence.[25]

But the issue Tansley raised here was far more than a mere semantic quibble, a fear of the power of words. Fundamental discords in environmental values were sounding and would not easily be quieted. Basically, Clements' climax ecology looked to primitive nature as a pure state against which the degeneration wrought by civilization could be unfavorably contrasted. By the thirties, however, at the very peak of its popularity, serious weaknesses in this ecological paradigm were becoming apparent. It had to be granted, for instance, that Clements exaggerated the role of climate as the sole, sweeping determinant of the mature formation. It was also convincingly argued that he insisted too strenuously on his inflexible, monolithic system of sere order, a system that nature herself did not always follow. In these respects Clements' critics made a great deal of sense.

The merit of his science, on the other hand, was that it kept in sharp relief the dislocating and mutilating effect civilization has had on the biological community. The charge could indeed be made that Clements segregated modern man from nature and made him an alien in the natural realm, a bull thrashing around in a china shop. But in a more positive light, climax ecology held fresh the memory of a world by which civilization could be measured. As a boy on the frontier, Clements had seen that primeval climax order firsthand, and this experience was surely responsible for his powerful sense of disjunction between man's and nature's worlds. Of course, the distinction between nature and culture had always been emphasized in America. It had been dramatically understood, used over and again in literature and social thought, even made the basis of a national purpose—albeit an ambivalent one, designating nature by turns as a foe to be vanquished and a redeemer to be praised. But in any case, the image of a wild, untrammeled nature was deeply etched on the American consciousness, far more than could be true for Europeans. And the persistent appeal of this image helped make Clements' ecology persuasive and even valid for America.

Tansley, in contrast, could grant that civilization had profoundly altered the course of natural succession, but went on to discount the importance of this. For him, the distinction between nature and civilization had no clear relevance in a long-settled Britain. If nothing else, to insist on it would effectively deprive the ecologist of a subject to study, for virtually none of Clements' climaxes had existed intact on the other side of the Atlantic for several centuries. Tansley's defection from the climax school, however, was not simply aimed at guaranteeing work for himself and his colleagues in their more thoroughly manmade world. Behind his elevation of the anthropogenic climax to equal respectability lay the refusal of the Great Plains farmer to admit that nature's ways are best. Fundamentally, Tansley did not want to accept any climax achieved by purely natural processes as an ideal for man to respect and follow. His concern was not to reestablish man as a part of nature, but to put down the threat to the legitimacy of human empire posed by the natural climax theory. If Tansley was right and there were no meaningful differences between the balance achieved by nature and that contrived by man—if the two systems were at least equals in quality and performance—then what reasonable objection could there be to man's rule over the biological community, or to the further extension of his empire? The effect of Tansley's proposal, in other words, would be to remove ecology as a scientific check on man's aggrandizing growth. The Clements standard of the climatic climax must be replaced, he was saying, by a kind of environmental relativism; there would then be no exterior model against which the artificial environment could be evaluated scientifically. The yardstick would be tossed away, and man would again be free to design his own world.

Some twenty years later, this clash of environmental values was defined more clearly than it had ever been in the thirties. In 1956 James Malin, an agricultural historian at the University of Kansas, made the most comprehensive and revealing argument to date for the "anti-climax" school. He was not a scientist, but his ideas gained a good deal of scientific acceptance. Malin had long been the foremost American scholar on the history of grassland agriculture, especially wheat farming, when he strayed into ecology in the mid-1940s. After a decade of research and writing he published *The Grassland of North America*, a collection of essays that represented the first effort by a historian to incorporate ecology into the study of a region and its culture since Walter Prescott Webb had tried it, though less explicitly, in his classic book *The Great Plains*. But while Webb had emphatically favored livestock ranching over farming as an economy more in harmony with the shortgrass environment, Malin came vigorously to the defense of the pioneering homesteader. The sodbuster, he maintained, had been a hero after all. Unfortunately for his side of the debate, Webb had published his work in 1931, shortly before the advent of the Dust Bowl years; therefore it lacked the most telling evidence against the agrarian empire and its failure to adapt to regional ecology. Malin, in contrast, could not avoid facing and explaining that experience. Indeed, he was truly possessed by it, so much so that it became his central purpose over several decades to justify the role of the farmers in the dust-storm years and to defend their battered reputation not only against Webb but also against the "evangelical conservationists" and ecologists. That revisionist aim required above all, as he soon became aware, a direct refutation of the theory of the climax community. Consequently, not Webb but Frederic Clements became his main target.[26]

Malin's interest in the ecological history of the grassland

peaked from 1952 to 1956, coinciding precisely with the return of drought across the region. Even less rain fell in those years than during the thirties, and once again dust storms blotted out the noonday sun with dark, choking clouds, but now over a larger area. Federal observers attributed the renascent problem in large part to the fact that plains farmers had once again been encouraged by good prices and patriotic appeals during World War Two and the Korean War to go for "all-out production," even on fragile marginal lands. But apparently a *few* lessons had been learned since the dirty thirties; somehow the region narrowly averted a new dust-bowl disaster. From Professor Malin this fortunate turn of events evoked less a sigh of relief than a shout of triumph. This recent history, he claimed, showed that the climax conservationists had wildly exaggerated the tragedy of the 1930s and so had wrongly concluded that farming had no place on the High Plains. In particular he lambasted the documentary film *The Plow That Broke the Plains*, made in 1937 by Pare Lorentz for the Farm Security Administration, as sensationalizing propaganda that had left an indelible slur on the farmer's good name. "No more brazen falsehood was ever perpetrated upon a gullible public," wrote Malin, "than the allegation that the dust storms of the 1930s were caused by the 'plow that broke the Plains.' " On the contrary, he insisted, agricultural enterprise—especially large-scale mechanization—was "a constructive step" forward. The plains had benefited from it rather than being harmed. Nature needed plowing up, and even a little blowing dirt now and then, he argued, to remain vigorous and fertile.[27]

The notion of a superior climax state gave a scientific validation to the conservationist's case against the machine and the farmer; hence, in Malin's view, the influence of Frederic Clements was the ultimate source of this "hysterical" conspiracy against progress. To discredit the climax ideal was Malin's chief aim, expressed thus in 1953:

The conventional or traditional concept of the state of nature must be abandoned—that mythical, idealized condition, in which natural forces, biological and physical, were supposed to exist in a state of virtual equilibrium, undisturbed by man.

Rather than the climatic formation extending unbroken over millions of acres, he believed there were only a handful of small "nuclear areas" that remained relatively stable. All the rest of the grassland had always been in wholesale flux, a chaos of permanent impermanence. When the white man first came upon the prairies, therefore, he discovered not a perfect balance but a world in tumult, awaiting a stabilizing hand. In this view, modern agriculture made possible for the first time a reign of order, peace, and harmony. Only to those primitivistic ecologists who had been blinded by the myth of a perfect, virginal state of nature before civilization corrupted it, was this fact not obvious.[28]

Just as the bison had disturbed the sod with their dusty wallows, and the prairie dogs with their sprawling cities, so the farmer had plowed the land—a civilized version of these other creatures' "natural tillage." In either case, the result was, in Malin's judgment, "the long-term vigor of the vegetation of the grassland." Dust storms too have always been among "the natural phenomena of the Great Plains. They are a part of the economy of nature and are not in themselves necessarily abnormal; at least, not in the sense in which the subject was exploited during the drought decade of the 1930s." As early as 1830, he went on, a missionary-surveyor named Isaac McCoy had reported from north-central Kansas a severe blowing of dust; dozens of other examples could be found in local papers—all before the breaking of the sod. Indeed, it was this very process of wind erosion, Malin claimed, that built a rich and fertile soil. On the plains the soil lacks the distinct layering or profile seen elsewhere; remove a foot or two of the topsoil, and no real damage was done. But sifted by the wind and deposited elsewhere, as in the fertile loess hills of Nebraska, that topsoil could be a useful gift. This incessant process of blowing the dirt to and fro was nature's chief way of improving the land over the million or so years of the Pleistocene epoch.[29]

Like Tansley in England, Malin was unhappy with what seemed in ecology to be a prejudice against civilization: a belief that "only civilized man was evil" and therefore had no moral right to alter the natural order. The preservationist's oft-repeated charge of "rape" for what modern man had done to the grassland especially enraged him, in part because it implied that nature is more than a mere thing, that it has personal character, that it is female and vulnerable. Nor would he accept any distinction between the environmental impact of the Indian and of the white man. Since Folsom Man killed his first bison, humans had been a disruptive force in the grassland ecology, he contended. With the re-introduction of the horse in the sixteenth century and its eventual incorporation into a new plains culture, primitive man became especially destructive, slaughtering the game on every hand. Moreover, from the Berkeley geographer Carl Sauer came support for Malin's belief that the grassland was the result not of low rainfall but of Indians setting fire to the grasses every year to improve hunting. Sauer, who grew up along the heavily forested banks of the Mississippi River, complained that primitive and modern man alike have hated the trees and destroyed them whenever they could. Nothing else, he was sure, could account for such "a great deformation of the vegetation" as the prairie showed: "an impoverished assemblage, not a fully developed organic household or community." Much earlier, Frederic Clements had admitted that fire, whether caused by lightning or Indians, could have been a decisive influence at least in the "ecotone," the narrow no-man's land between forest and grass. But Sauer—and here Malin followed him exactly, though he could not have liked the other's denigration of his homeland grasses—sought to make fire the master over a landscape a thousand miles wide. And, of course, such a man-made origin for the grassland would put the kibosh on all back-to-nature yearnings, all resistance to other kinds of human interference with the "climax order."[30]

This is not the place to answer all of Malin's arguments point by point; each has been refuted more or less successfully in several places, by scientists and others. But at least we can say here that it assuredly was not true, as Sauer and Malin asserted, that the idea of a climax community "assumes the end of change." No one since Darwin, and certainly not Clements, would think seriously that any part of nature is completely or permanently static. A final climax could endure, Clements pointed out, only in the absence of major climatic shifts. But ultimately underlying Malin's objections to the climax theory was a personal motive that really had little to do with issues of fact or fantasy, with the degree of stability or flux in nature. Like the sodbusters he defended, Malin refused to be hedged in by ecological laws. To obey rather than conquer nature was a surrender, in his view, to the chains of determinism. Even if the grass–bison biome was, as Clements said, the mature stage of the sere, one was confronted merely with a fact, not a decree. It is man, not nature, Malin believed, who creates norms and values. If it suits his purposes, he can and should alter the grassland radically and create his own kind of world there. Of course, to urge that civilization, whether for reasons of self-interest or morality, adapt to its biotic environment was not really a deterministic stance. Walter Webb had been accused of a similar crime in writing *The Great Plains*, and he rightly denied the charge. He insisted, to be sure, that American agriculture and institutions must inevitably adapt somewhat to the western environment. More significant, however, was his view that the forage economy of the cowboy was more suited to the climax grassland conditions than that of the farmer, whose technology shattered that harmony and imposed on the land an alien existence. Webb's implied conclusion, like that of the climax conservationists, was that humans can make a choice which route they will follow. To adapt rather than transform need not be deterministic or fatalistic. Rather, it may be the exercise of a highly civilized, mature will and self-discipline.[31]

The ethic of environmental self-restraint had never been taken very seriously by the sodbuster. He generally had bound himself by a different set of chains, those of technological determinism, under the illusion that he was winning freedom from natural forces. Malin too depended on the machine to extricate him from nature. "The contriving brain and skillful hand," he fairly exulted, have refused to be bound by anxieties about a shrinking land heritage, or by propaganda on the Dust Bowl. Conservationists of all sorts, he decided, had become pessimists and critics because they had lost faith in technology. Their fears of the destruction of resources by human mismanagement were totally unfounded, according to Malin:

The potentiality of man to solve problems has not yet been exhausted, and the potentiality of the resources latent in the earth to be brought into the horizon of usefulness is still beyond the power of man to conceive. The key to the situation is not the earth, but the minds of men determined to realize their own potential in act.

Thus Malin preached the familiar homily of cornucopian expansion: that neither nature nor American civilization is a finished product; that change is the law of each; that the machine is wholly legitimate under this law, if not its perfect expression; and that nature is an inexhaustible warehouse of riches for those enterprising enough to dig around.[32]

Hopeful though he was about the promise of technology on the plains, Malin could not preach his transformationist gospel without some qualification. Still a loyal child of the grassland, he resented as much as did Webb or Clements the persistent tendency of Americans from forested, humid areas to regard the prairies as a *deficient* environment, lacking in some element necessary for human welfare. Each region has its unique character, its strengths and weaknesses, he countered, and the newcomer must learn to appreciate that character before setting about to change it. And Malin, on at least one occasion, forgot himself so far as to write: "The degree of success in the occupation by man of any of these land regions could be measured in terms of his ability to fit his culture into conformity with the requirements of maintaining rather than disrupting environmental equilibrium." The grassland biome, he was now arguing, should suggest to its human invaders a set of restraints that would delimit the contours of a distinct regional culture, one that could make a special, unique contribution to the world. It would seem from this comment that nature, not the machine or man, must determine the shape of the region's culture, and that its peculiar and precarious balance must be respected after all.[33]

In such moments of apostasy Malin really gave his case away. For all his scattered pinpricking at the climax model, he could not effectively deflate its credibility, even in his own mind. There did seem to be empirical evidence of something one could call an equilibrium or climax in nature, before the coming of the white man. That order was not perfectly stable; it had its ups and downs, its faults and slippages. Other natural forces were always at work trying to upset it, and sometimes succeeded temporarily. But despite all this, a few million years of evolution had produced on the plains a system that worked extraordinarily well— one that civilized man, for all his ingenuity, would always have trouble matching, and one that he interfered with at the risk of his own well-being. And no amount of quibbling over whether dust might have blown down the streets of Atchison or Amarillo before the 1930s could conceal the simple bleak truth that never in the history of the plains since their discovery by European man had anything approaching the devastation of the Dust Bowl years occurred. But then, never before that point had the natural-growing grass been so quickly and violently ripped apart, and so much of the earth left bare under the wind and sun. Though he might potshot at details, Malin could not really deny these elemental facts, for he himself had lived through them. Indeed, they had been written large enough for the entire nation to see and experience—in lurid skies, in the smell of dust and the taste of grit, in blinding blizzards of dirt, and in the hopeless, defeated faces of migrants on the road, or on relief.

All this is not to say, however, that Malin was easily dismissed. Despite their obvious weaknesses, his arguments presented a formidable challenge to the climax theory of ecology and its environmental message. Nobody before him had marshaled such an effective refutation of Clements and his school—a refutation based primarily on historical research, to be sure, but not without scientific credentials. Consequently, he had a discernible impact on both ecologists and conservationists. To take only one example, his writings were a chief source for the forest ecologist Hugh Raup, manager of the Harvard University forests in Massachusetts and New York. In a 1964 essay, "Ecological Theory and Conservation," Raup applied Malin's view of the primitive grassland to the eastern deciduous forest. His conclusions were pure Malin doctrine: the image of a pre-European virgin forest that was dense, mature, and fully productive is a myth; the stable climax ideal is exaggerated; and traditional environmentalists have been too frightened by scarcity, too cautious in their husbanding of resources. According to Raup:

Ecological and conservation thought at the turn of the century was nearly all in what might be called closed systems of one kind or another. In all of them some kind of balance or near balance was to be achieved. The geologists had their peneplain; the ecologists visualized a self-perpetuating climax; the soil scientists proposed a thoroughly mature soil profile, which eventually would lose all trace of its geological origin and become a sort of balanced organism in itself. It seems to me that social Darwinism, and the entirely competitive models that were constructed for society by the economists of the nineteenth century, were all based upon a slow development towards some kind of social equilibrium. I believe there is evidence in all of these fields that the systems are open, not closed, and that probably there is no consistent trend towards balance. Rather, in the present state of our knowledge and ability to rationalize, we should think in terms of massive uncertainty, flexibility and adjustability.

There was much truth in this analysis, mixed with a great deal of tendentiousness and distortion. Raup was trying to establish that ecological conservationists would place too much restraint on harvesting and transforming the biological community—a policy that was, in his view, timid, unscientific, and even more important, uneconomic.[34]

Other critics besides Malin and Raup contributed to a certain loss of faith in Clements and the climax school, but it nonetheless remains an influential tradition in British and American ecological thought. Indeed, in many science texts of recent years the climax idea has not even been much modified. That observation, of course, does not necessarily make the climax theory true in some conveniently absolute way; there are many who assume too quickly that science can always give them the final, unambiguous word, and they can be satisfied with nothing less. But the succession–climax model, as we have been suggesting all along, is inextricably wrapped up in those muddled, subjective things called human values. Probably there is no final or compelling reply to the question of whether the climax ever existed or not, or at least no answer that science alone can give for all time. The issue of the climax is an enduring conundrum.

Yet its tenacity as a model over so many years, despite stiff and searching criticism, must establish a certain degree of reliability—enough at least to give pause to unrestrained interference with nature. It can be taken as instructive if not conclusive that science keeps returning to some version of the climax. R. H. Whittaker, for instance, in what is basically another revisionist analysis of the theory, nevertheless agreed with Clements that "through succession the community develops from one of scattered pioneers utilizing only a fraction of environmental resources available, to a mature community with maximum utilization of resources on a sustained basis." Then, too, ecologists like Whittaker have not yet been convinced by the anti-climax critics that no practical distinction can be made between a natural prairie and a farmer's cornfield. All discriminations may appear arbitrary in some light, but a distinction need not be valid in every respect in order to be both true and valuable. The old idea that nature's economy is an astonishing success is not yet overthrown. The natural ideal is still there, basically as reliable as ever—for those who seek and are willing to accept guidance from the nonhuman world.[35]

Usually where the climax is ignored or discounted as an ideal, the only criterion left is the marketplace—the very standard that gave America the dirty thirties. But as the veteran grassland ecologist H. L. Shantz pointed out in 1950:

The economic yardstick now used to determine the best use of land is by no means a safe one from an ecological or biological point of view. Economics has given us strip lands over coal beds and stone fields in rich narrow valleys over gold-bearing gravels. Much the same approach gives us barren moss and lichen-covered hills where redwood forests stood; bracken fields where Douglas-fir or cedar and hemlock were produced; great areas of downey chess where bluebunch wheat grass or Idaho fescue produced a dense cover; snakeweed and burrowweed where valuable gramas covered the soil, and nearly bare soil on our mountains once knee-deep in lush vegetation. The sustained high price of wheat has reduced much of the grass cover of the High Plains to nearly bare soil—a potential dust bowl.

At times himself a critic of Clements' dogma, Shantz still remained convinced that nature, in order to make the best possible use of the region's limited rainfall, evolved on the plains a system superior to man's. Though deviance may be unavoidable in some areas, he believed, in others man can protect the natural climax from all intrusion; it can serve as an oracle that speaks truths of which the human contrivers remain ignorant. That course seemed a safe one at least, and may have had the virtue of humility to recommend it too.[36]

There are other explanations for the persistence of the climax ideal in American thought. First, that James Malin himself could slip even momentarily into the Clements persuasion demonstrates its powerful appeal for cultural regionalists. Regionalism, even in Malin's case, has been essentially a rejection of the prospect of a vast homogenized industrial landscape stretching from coast to coast, from which all local and regional uniqueness of ecology and culture have been eliminated. So long as an allegiance to regional peculiarity endures in America, or in Britain for that matter, credence will surely be given to some version of the ecological climax. Regionalism swings on a double hinge: natural geography and cultural heritage. In the theory of the climax, regionalists such as Webb and Malin have a concrete and usable guide to local identity. Though the regionalist must grant more free choice to humans than the ecologist and plant geographer can ascribe to their subjects, both groups want to know how climate and conjoining species have influenced the development of a given community.[37]

The climax theory still appeals, too, because it serves as a model of succession to maturity. It suggests that the receptive student of nature may yet learn how to achieve a man–land harmony, a mature or climax stage in which man thrives, too. With that hope in mind, the North Dakota ecologist Herbert Hanson declared, in his 1939 presidential address to the Ecological Society of America, that it is impossible to secure the adaptation of the plains people to their environment chiefly "by the use of the plow and the wheat plant." Other modes of land use would have to be practiced, including ranching. "Instead of gradual development of the community towards stabilization," he continued, "the pioneers have often been making conditions less favorable, rather than more favorable, as should be the case, for the next generation." What Hanson envisioned was the achievement of an integrated man–nature equilibrium—a cultural as well as biological climax state—for the grassland.

> The United States is passing from its pioneering stage into more advanced stages. . . . The special contribution of ecology is to ferret out relationships with the environment so that man, using this knowledge in conjunction with that obtained from other fields, can strive intelligently to secure balance and stabilization, a goal essential for the "abundant life" and the building of a culture far beyond our present dreams.

On the success of this search for ecological harmony would rest all prospects for a vital, stable Great Plains region.[38]

Long after the black and red and yellow clouds had settled back to earth, and the sunflowers and thistles had begun to reclaim the barren dusty land, the controversy over climax conservation continued. For the grassland, as for any other environment, the issues were not to be easily resolved. Even today it is not unusual to see a dust-devil whirling over the naked dirt of a Panhandle suitcase-farmer who may be too busy totting up his ledgers in a city bank to care where his land is going.

But if all Americans did not learn from the Dust Bowl how to live with even simple prudence on the plains, many nonetheless absorbed from the climax ecologists one perception: that the blanketing, tough-rooted sod that the pioneers found so monotonous and useless knew its business pretty well. And still the larger question remains unanswered in our expanding technological culture: How far can and should man adapt himself to nature? Or how far can and should he go in altering its order for his own ends? Perhaps we are all unredeemably "edge" creatures, never wholly at home either in the dark humid forest or the big open-sky country of the grassland, always struggling to convert both into a Kentucky idyll of shady oak groves dappled across a pastoral meadow. But then we also know that we are animals of remarkable adaptability—when and where we have to be.

The Dust Bowl, the ecologists were arguing in the 1930s, was America's most serious failure to adapt to the natural economy. It was dark proof of a certain truth in Robert Frost's observation that "the land was ours before we were the land's." And they warned that it could happen again someday unless the nation heeded their advice. How much of their argument was true is not finally the main issue here. More germane to our purpose is that as a result of this environmental crisis of the dirty thirties, the most telling in our history, the new profession of ecologists found themselves for the first time serving as land-use advisers to an entire nation. That episode laid the groundwork for a more scientifically fueled conservation movement in America, one that would pick up steam in the decades ahead.

PART FIVE

THE MORALS
OF A SCIENCE:
ETHICS,
ECONOMICS,
AND ECOLOGY

OUR CENTRAL FOCUS *in this history of ecology has been moral: We have been concerned above all with how this science shapes man's view of his place in nature. At every stage in its development, it should now be clear, this peculiar province of thought has come up with conflicting answers to that question—now arcadian, now imperial. In recent years the ethical question has been posed more emphatically and more frequently than ever, and ecologists remain unable to agree on a single, consensual reply.*

The moral ambivalence of ecology has deeply affected the conservation movement. Before 1920, the theory and practice of conservation were dominated by the Progressive ideology of utilitarianism; after 1945, conservation became much more amenable to a preservation policy based on ecology. Between these two points stretched a crucial period of transition: a time of debate, professional introspection, and in a few cases, dramatic personal conversion. Often, contending moral lessons were drawn by scientists from specific environmental issues. Chapter 13 surveys this transitional era and a case in point: the long-running controversy over predator control that led, among other things, to Aldo Leopold's influential idea of an ecological ethic.

During this period, too, the term "nature's economy" gained a fresh meaning. The emergence of what has been called the "New Ecology" brought a model of the environment based on both thermodynamics and modern economics. An analysis of the ecosystem concept, on which the New Ecology relied heavily, reveals that moral values were inherent even in this supposedly mature, objective, neutral description of nature. New techniques for quantifying the flow and use of energy in the ecosystem gave support to the older utilitarian or managerial ethic—a bias that is examined in Chapter 14.

The final chapter points up other connections ecology has made, beyond the limited concerns of science, with various twentieth-century strains in philosophy, sociology, politics, and even religion. The resurgence of organicism, in the writings of Alfred North Whitehead, William Morton Wheeler, the "AEPPS" group, and others, held out hope for a restored community of man with man and man with nature. Yet the split in ecology between this organic, communal ideal and a more pragmatic utilitarianism remains unresolved. In the current "Age of Ecology" the ethical—economic debate continues. Our fundamental task, in this writer's view, is now to choose between these two moral courses, and thus to decide where this science of ecology can and should lead us.

CHAPTER 13

The Value of a Varmint

OUT IN THE American West the howling wilderness still howls, but the timbre and message of its voice have changed. For 300 years of European settlement, the wolf dominated the backcountry. He was a dark, green-eyed demon whose cry sent chills through the American imagination—the symbol of a fierce and powerful nature that defied human rule. Early in the twentieth century, however, that specter of malevolence vanished, and the deep bass song of the wolf was silenced throughout the United States, save in Alaska and an isolated pocket or two in northeastern Minnesota. What remains to us today of this eerie carnivorous world of sound is the voice of that cagey, grinning trickster: *Canis latrans*, El Coyote, the little "prairie wolf." His high tenor wail comes echoing off a moonlit mesquite or sagebrush hillside, answered by the barks and yelps of a scattering of comrades, as though filling the air bereft of his relative's voice. Ancient Indian myth says that "brother coyote" will be the last animal alive on earth, and in fact he has already outlasted many of his primeval associates—the wolf, puma, and grizzly—as well as most of the bison and pronghorns. As long as coyote roams the land, the wilderness will speak. But it will be with the voice of watchful opportunism rather than of fearless brute force.

Ernest Thompson Seton and Vernon Bailey estimated that the original range of the North American wolf covered seven million square miles. Before the coming of the white man there were as many as two million wolves in this area—one for every three and a half square miles. By 1908 the wolf population had shrunk to 200,000, and only 2,000 of these were living in the Transmississippi West, once its stronghold. By 1926 Arizona reported no wolves to be found there, and Wyoming could find but five. Two years later, out of tens of thousands of carnivores killed in western states, only eleven were listed as gray wolves. In 1929 the report of the federal predator control office did not even mention the species. Nor any mountain lions. Nor grizzly bears. The body count showed almost all coyotes, with a sprinkling of badgers, bobcats, foxes, and skunks.

To carry on the message of the wild seems a heavy burden for so small a creature as the coyote, but so far he has managed it fairly well. He has extended his range from the prairie and plains to Point Barrow, Alaska, to northern New England, and to the Hollywood hills. But over the years he has also lost some ground. In vast sections of Texas, Wyoming, Nevada, and Idaho, for example, the nights are deathly still—places where the coyote once romped and sang but now is heard and seen no more. Wit and nerve, it appears, have not always been enough to save him from the wolf's fate. He has been likewise hunted down, but with ever more potent technical weapons: cyanide guns (the "coyote-getter"), airplane sharpshooters with their high-powered rifles, sheep or deer carcasses laced with sodium fluoroacetate—popularly known as Compound 1080 and one of the most lethal poisons ever devised, a single pound of it sufficient to kill a million pounds of animal life. In recent times at least 90,000 coyotes have been killed each year in the United States by such means; from 1915 to 1947 almost two million were exterminated. For all his successes, the coyote clearly has not had an easy time. He has not been feared, as the wolf was—but he has been hated and despised and hounded by the white man perhaps more than any other animal.[1]

The coyote is the quintessential varmint. Unlike his other relative, the fawning house dog, he keeps man at a wary distance, and, as if adding injury to insult, raids the farmer's chickens or the sheepman's lambs. Of course, only

The Value of a Varmint • 259

in a domesticated world could he be thus reduced to the status of marauder; in nature's amoral economy he is simply a predator, who must live at least in part by hunting meat rather than on the more innocent diet of grass. But with the advent of an agrarian economy in the New World, he inevitably became an outcast and an elusive challenge to the controlling, contriving hand of man. More than this, he came to be seen as a moral offender, a sinner, a species of "vermin" that must be eradicated—by any available means. It may be true, as J. Frank Dobie believed, that "sympathy for wild animals, sympathy that is intellectual as much as emotional, has not been a strong element in the traditional American way of life." But we have made distinctions in our national reaction to wildlife, chosen favorites as well as singled out enemies. Here as in other matters, the Anglo-American mind has exhibited a peculiarly intense moralism that, in this case, assigns every species to an absolute ethical category: good or bad. A few wild animals, songbirds chiefly, have been pronounced good; everything else is of use only for target practice. And "varmint" has been the very worst epithet in America's moral lexicon, a label reserved for those species that plumb the depths of depravity. Essentially these are the animals with teeth and claws: the carnivores, including wolves, pumas, bears—and latest in line, coyotes. From the time the Puritans of New England first put a bounty on their heads, the carnivores were most often viewed as implacable, devilish foes who deserved nothing less than total extermination. Hence such laws as the one in Vermont that made it a crime on par with rape or robbery to interfere with the trapping of wolves. Hence this damning description by Theodore Roosevelt of a puma treed and shot on the rim of the Grand Canyon: "the big horse-killing cat, the destroyer of the deer, the lord of stealthy murder, facing his doom with a heart both craven and cruel." As the last of these "outlaws," the coyote has been the object of America's concentrated moralistic fervor, and his tenacious survival represents an outrageous defiance of man's righteous empire over nature.[2]

But in the twentieth century, the coyote, along with other varmints and predators, has come to be viewed in a radically different light by many Americans. Some have seen him not as an outlaw but rather as a useful member of the biological community; indeed, his individual welfare has frequently come to be identified with the well-being of the entire ecological order. The absence of predators means a natural economy badly out of balance; a world without coyotes or wolves or cougars, it has been argued, is a world that is in trouble. From this perspective, the presence of the varmint is reassurance not only of a surviving wilderness but of general environmental health. And a society that insists on total extermination of predators and other unwanted species, and substitutes its own contrivances in their place, has more self-confidence—perhaps more self-righteousness—than it can justify.

This new defense of the varmint, in other words, has been put on an ecological footing. It is at the very center of the shift that has occurred in twentieth-century environmental thought toward a broader, popular ecological consciousness. Like the idea of the climax community, which gained public attention at about the same time—during the 1930s—the defense of the predator was led by a group of professional ecologists. They were, however, as eager to tutor the public in ethical values as in the principles of their science. The story of the varmint's changing reputation is thus the story of the movement in American conservation toward an ecological point of view: an attitude grounded not only in science but in a moral philosophy of interdependence and tolerance.

Much has been written about how the rise of a national conservation movement in the United States brought to an end an era of waste, greed, and over-exploitation on the frontier; how it saved the forests and wildlife for future generations. Conservation has often been hailed as one of America's major contributions to world reform movements, in that its ideas were eventually exported to Great Britain and other nations. All this is true—in a limited sense. What is generally left out of this interpretation is that, for several decades, a major feature of the crusade for resource conservation was a deliberate campaign to destroy wild animals—one of the most efficient, well-organized, and well-financed such efforts in all of man's history. This destruction was not in the least accidental; it was the clearly-stated policy of certain leading conservationists, and a central goal of the government programs they established and ran. It was this policy that finished off the wolf in the early years of the century, and that same conservation ideal has been, and still is, promoting the war against the coyote.

When it first came to national prominence, and fixed its purposes in the public mind, conservation was a major expression of the Progressive political movement. Progressivism was primarily a reformist campaign to clean up politics, regulate large business corporations, and purify the nation's morals. But another important goal of its program was the more efficient management of natural resources in the public domain. One of the chief spokesmen for this effort was Theodore Roosevelt, President of the United States from 1901 to 1909. From his administration—and more broadly, out of the Progressive ideology—there also emerged an official program to rub out the varmint and to make America safe from its depredations. In a sense, not much was new in this Progressive conservation; nature was still valued chiefly as a commodity to be used for man's economic success. But old attitudes were given vastly more effective means for their implementation. For the first time, the resources of the federal government were brought to bear against the predator. Instead of relying on the varmint-blasting frontiersman, the government itself undertook to eliminate the predator once and for all.[3]

The agency appointed to carry out this mission was the Bureau of the Biological Survey in the Department of Agriculture. Founded in 1905, the BBS had a string of predecessors going back to the 1880s, including the old Division of Entomology and the Division of Economic Ornithology and Mammalogy. Throughout this process of bureaucratic molting, the constant element was the man who served as director of each agency: C. Hart Merriam, creator of the "life zones" concept and an authority on the food habits of birds and their threat to crops. For many years Merriam's operation did little more than to assemble a staggering collection of 25,000 stomachs of birds; his real ambition, though, was more purely scientific. Before he resigned, he managed to get the word "economic" dropped from his agency's title and to make it a more disinterested research organ, concerned primarily with the geographical distribution of wildlife. But the BBS, like its counterpart the U.S. Geological Survey, never moved far from a practical bias. In 1901, for example, Merriam turned from the problem of controlling bird pests to the mammal variety, in particular the prairie dog of the Great Plains. The remedy he urged was poison grain. Cattlemen had long used various poisons to kill wolves, but Merriam appears to have been the first federal official to publicly recommend the poisoning of any animal.

After Merriam's departure, the BBS began to concentrate its energies even more on aspects of science with obvious economic value. Congressional pressure to produce results—that familiar nemesis of government-sponsored science—helped push the agency toward a more active concern for the nation's welfare, especially the economic condition of the farmer. By this point, agriculture was a far cry from the world of the simple yeoman farmer tilling the soil to feed his family. It was big business, serving huge international markets, and some in government suspected that it was losing a significant chunk of its profits each year to wild animals. Consequently, in 1906 the BBS began functioning as an information center for the states' bounty systems. It stepped up its work against insect damage to crops. And it began publishing pamphlets on the habits of predators, suggesting the best kinds of scents and poisons to use against each species. In 1907 the Bureau supervised the killing of 1,800 wolves and 23,000 coyotes in the National Forests, a policy that was soon extended to the National Parks as well.[4]

Then in 1915 the BBS began to engage even more directly in what Jenks Cameron calls "the suppressive warfare" against undesirable types. The bounty system, after almost three centuries of trial, had not proved effective enough in cleansing the land of pests and vermin; what was needed, BBS officials decided, was an all-out campaign by a specially trained force of government hunters, trappers, and poisoners. Congress in that year appropriated $125,000 for the killing of wolves on private as well as public land by this professional army: It was the beginning of the end for several species. By 1931, three-fourths of the Bureau's budget went to the predator-control program. By the early 1940s, almost $3 million a year was being spent to eradicate predators and rodents; by 1971, the combined federal–state cooperative program of extermination, headed by the newly renamed Wildlife Services Division of the Bureau of Sport Fisheries and Wildlife in the Department of the Interior, had $8 million to work with. The names changed every few years, as government bureaucracies are wont to do. The budgets increased steadily. And many predators were inexorably pushed toward the void of extinction.[5]

This course of events came about in part because of pressures on government from well-heeled livestock associations, especially those of western sheepmen, many of whom reacted to wolves and coyotes with an almost metaphysical hatred. Their sheep were tragically vulnerable animals, difficult to rear and to protect from a thousand possible mishaps; yet their families' livelihood depended entirely on the safety of those woolly heads. Exacerbating their predicament was the large scale of many ranching enterprises, vastly exceeding the herder's capacity to supervise and guard all the sheep. Instead of enclosing their charges in secure folds, in the ancient tradition of the good shepherd, western ranchers, living in a sparsely vegetated land, began to run them loose over the public range. Then the ranchers asked the government to clear the land of potential hazards. They wanted—needed, from their point of view—to see the West made over into an artificial ecological order, forever free from predators: an idyllic pasture for thousands of bleating flocks. This wish was precisely translated into policy by the federal government's predator program. The West was indeed soon made safe for sheep and profitable for sheepmen, at least until after World War Two, when declining markets—not coyotes—reduced the number of sheep being raised in America to almost half the 1910 total. Reported loss statistics, running as high as $20 million a year, had made it seem in the best interest of the national economy to subsidize the sheep industry with a government trapping force. By the early 1960s, however, it became impossible to show losses high enough to justify continued predator control: in 1962, for instance, the value of sheep lost on National Forest land in California was $3,500, while the control program there cost over $90,000. After a half-century of protection, the stockmen suddenly found themselves on the defensive, forced to accept an end to poisoning on the public lands. In the meantime, though, they had gotten rid of several million varmints on the range.[6]

But the all-out war to exterminate predators was more than the result of the livestock group's economic needs and political leverage. The more important force at work was the attitude toward the land and wildlife espoused by Progressive conservation leaders. These men were motivated by a strong, highly moralistic sense of mission to clean up the world around them, and that ambition encompassed the natural environment along with economic and political corruption. Without their example of moral zeal, the BBS might have gone on collecting stomachs and making maps of life zones. Instead, during the years of Theodore Roosevelt's administration, the Bureau began to reflect this aggressively reformist philosophy. Perhaps the Progressive rhetoric criticizing "predatory capitalism" helped Bureau officials to support a war against animal predators in the West, even to hard-sell the idea to many reluctant westerners. Nature as well as society, it was claimed, harbors ruthless exploiters and criminals who must be banished from the land. Pamphlets began to appear, such as Vernon Bailey's "Destruction of Wolves and Coyotes" in 1908, emphasizing the economic loss caused by these animals and depicting them as diabolical but craven monsters; photographs showed them with legs spread, heads lowered, eyes glowing with cruel cunning. This crusade on the part of conservation leaders in government was not merely to support a powerful ranching industry. Of greater significance was their desire to establish a philosophy of wildlife management in which utility and morality were closely linked goals. On both counts, the predator henceforth would be *persona non grata*. The plan, explains Jenks Cameron, was "first, the repression of undesirable and injurious wild life; second, the protection and encouragement of wild life in its

The Value of a Varmint • 2 6 5

desirable and beneficial forms." These conservationists were dedicated to reorganizing the natural economy in a way that would fulfil their own ideal vision of what nature should be like.[7]

The major architect of the Progressive conservation ideology was Gifford Pinchot, a Pennsylvanian who served as Roosevelt's Chief Forester and in 1905 organized the U.S. Forest Service. In his autobiography, *Breaking New Ground*, Pinchot defined conservation as "the fundamental material policy in human civilization" and again as "the development and use of the earth and all its resources for the enduring good of men." How the nation was to achieve a full, lasting prosperity was the problem that dominated his entire public career. No man in Washington was less selfish than he or more devoted to improving the nation's well-being, moral as well as economic. There was also no doubt about his utilitarian bias toward nature. Prosperity, argued Pinchot, could never be made secure in a society that wasted its natural wealth in the traditional frontier style of grab, gut, and git out. It required instead a program of long-range, careful management that would put resource development on a thoroughly rational and efficient base. The goal of such management would not be private gain or further concentration of wealth, but the greatest economic benefit for all citizens. In 1897 the report of the National Forest Commission, of which Pinchot was a member, concluded that America's remaining and extensive public lands, all in the West, should not be withdrawn completely from future occupation or use. "They must be made to perform their part in the economy of the Nation. Unless the reserved lands of the public domain are made to contribute to the welfare and prosperity of the country, they should be thrown open to settlement and the whole system of reserved lands abandoned." In all of this Pinchot wholly concurred, but especially in the emphasis on the primacy of the "economy of the Nation." Protecting the nation's economy, not nature's, was the central theme of his conservation philosophy. Toward that goal he shaped and directed the Forest Service, marshaling a corps of young men who combined hardheaded business sense with an earnest commitment to their patriotic cause.[8]

Pinchot liked to refer to forest conservation as "tree farming." Instead of mining the woodlands, his corps of rangers would replant cut-over lands, just as a farmer replants his crops each year. "Forestry is handling trees so that one crop follows another," he explained.

The purpose of Forestry, then, is to make the forest produce the largest possible amount of whatever crop or service will be most useful, and keep on producing it for generation after generation of men and trees. . . . A well-handled farm gets more and more productive as the years pass. So does a well-handled forest.

Like Francis Bacon or Lester Ward, Pinchot saw the world as badly in need of managing, and he was convinced that science could teach man to improve on nature, to make its processes more efficient and its crops more abundant. He would not go as far as the Germans toward intensive cultivation, or establish as they did tree farms that resembled factories in their planned orderliness—there was not enough manpower in America to manage nature that intensively over so vast a space. But he would insist that all renewable natural resources, especially forests and wildlife, be approached in the future as crops to be planted, harvested, and cultivated by skilled experts. And like any good American farmer, he could see value in the land chiefly where it could be turned to profit.[9]

Behind Pinchot's conservation philosophy lay an environmental tradition stretching all the way back to the eighteenth century: progressive, scientific agriculture. From the time of "Turnip" Townshend and Arthur Young, who taught England how to make two blades of grass grow where one grew before, progressive agriculture had always promoted a kind of conservation. Its spokesmen had long been a force for closer management of water and woodlands. They had awakened earlier generations to the threat of soil erosion, developed contour plowing, and invented chemical fertilizers to make the earth more productive. In America they had established a number of land grant colleges where students were taught the gospel of wise land use. Thus when Pinchot announced that he was "breaking new ground" in the field of conservation, he ignored two centuries of pioneering. His own contribution, more precisely, was to bring the tradition of progressive agriculture to the management of the *public* lands, especially the forests. Like his predecessors, he made improved "efficiency" and "productivity" the controlling values in conservation. Those words, in fact, became for him sacred symbols, imbued with a potent magic that could turn tree stumps into seats of virtue and beauty. Where the progressive farmer relished the sight of a field plowed in sweeping contours and fences marching briskly over the horizon, Pinchot liked to see his trees well-trimmed, their crowns heading out nicely, their competitors thinned away. No wonder, then, that the Forest Service found its permanent home in the Department of Agriculture, which was dominated by agronomy and productivity experts. In essence, the aim of Progressive conservation was to apply the progressive farmer's techniques to all land in America that fell into the managerial domain of the federal government.

In the history of progessive agriculture, wild creatures had never counted for much. They failed to conform to the farmer's productive purposes and so were seen as useless when not seen as a threat. But there were at least a few agriculturists who had pointed to the beneficial roles birds play in checking insect damage, and even some who had advocated a more ecologically sensitive agrarian economy. In America, for example, there was John Lorain, who in 1825 had published his *Nature and Reason Harmonized in the Practice of Husbandry*. In particular, Lorain criticized the farmer for destroying nature's way of building soil fertility by the accumulation of humus and the work of "animalcula" or bacterial decomposers. Henry Thoreau's 1860 essay on "The Succession of Forest Trees" was a contribution both to ecology and to scientific agriculture. And then in 1864 George Perkins Marsh, a Vermont countryman who became American minister to Italy, brought out his *Man and Nature*, the most extensive work on land management to appear in the English-speaking world up to that date. Marsh spoke both from his own practical experience and close observation of New England farming, and from his extensive reading of Continental naturalists, geographers, foresters, and hydrologists. "The equation of animal and vegetable life," he warned, "is too complicated a problem for human intelligence to solve, and we can never know how wide a circle of disturbance we produce in the harmonies of nature when we throw the smallest pebble in the ocean of organic life." As far as wildlife was concerned, he advised the farmer to err on the side of caution rather than risk eradicating a species that might prove after all to have been a blessing.

But Marsh's approach to land use differed from the one taken by Gifford Pinchot a few decades later. Indeed, the conservation program that emerged under Pinchot's leadership in the early years of the twentieth century paid little attention to ecological complications. It was primarily a program aimed at maximizing the productivity of those major resources in which man had a clear, direct, and immediate interest. If an abundant, lasting supply of trees was wanted, then that became the forester's single-minded goal—not preservation of the more complicated biological matrix in which the trees grew. This strategy, it must be said, had been the major thrust of scientific agriculture all along, and it passed easily into the views of its offspring, conservation.[10]

Pinchot himself seems to have had little interest in wildlife, except as a hunter who liked to bag a trophy now and then with his boss Theodore Roosevelt. But other conservationists found in Pinchot's tree-farming program a challenge to do the same for birds, fish, and mammals; they wanted to create a profession of "game management." It was this group that stepped in to run the BBS and dozens of new state wildlife programs in the early part of the century. Like the primeval forests, shootable species of wild animals had been all but wiped out in many regions of the country by the 1880s. The conservationists' hope was to bring these species back to sustained production so that they could play their part, if not in the nation's economy, at least in its amusement. On deer, in particular, their visions of future plenty fastened. With judicious management, this animal could survive civilization's impact better than any other, and so provide a taste to the hunter of a life of sport on the frontier. It was "big game" in an otherwise diminished world. Game conservation therefore came to mean a flat-

The Value of a Varmint • 269

out effort to increase deer herds across the country by licensing hunters, limiting the take, establishing more stringent seasons, improving habitat, and providing "refuges" and "game preserves" where the seed stock could be maintained in good health. And it had to mean, most emphatically, destroying the predator, who after all was man's competitor for the kill experience and for the meat. He "wasted" a resource that could be turned to account. And his crimes against livestock made him an unacceptable presence in a profit-motivated society. There was, in short, nothing about him worth conserving.[11]

Game management on the public lands began in earnest during the Roosevelt administration. Beginning in 1905, portions of a few National Forests were set aside as refuges, and the predators there were eliminated as fast as possible. Very soon this management policy began to show results. On the northern Arizona plateau, for example, in the Kaibab Forest area designated as the Grand Canyon National Game Preserve, deer numbered only 4,000 in 1906. Eighteen years later their numbers had swollen to nearly 100,000. It appeared as a magnificent curve on the productivity charts, a stunning triumph for Progressive game conservation. But suddenly, in the next year, thousands of deer died from malnutrition; the population explosion had led to overgrazing, overbrowsing, and highlining of trees (eating twigs on branches as high as the deer could reach). According to Irvin Rasmussen, "the range had been so severely damaged that 20,000 was an excessive population." Sixty percent of the total herd was lost in the winters of 1924–25 and 1925–26; by 1939 the Kaibab deer herd, through starvation and hunting, had been brought down to a mere 10,000 animals. Henceforth the Arizona episode became the *cause célèbre* of game management in America. It has stood for a half-century as the classic example of businesslike mismanagement of resources and of ecological ignorance on the part of productivity-minded conservationists. But in 1906 none of this was foreseen among game specialists. Even as late as 1918, when range damage caused by too many deer was first recognized by a few foresters, no official action was taken to modify the policy of single-resource farming of the landscape.[12]

Deer are a species that fits the eighteenth-century model of nature only too well. Unlike some creatures, they seem to have no inherent ability to check their own proliferation and generally require external forces of some kind to keep their numbers in balance with the habitat. There were perhaps many factors at work in the Kaibab explosion, but unquestionably the absence of a predatory check was the most important. From 1906 to 1923 government hunters ranged the area, killing all the predators they could find, and they worked, as usual, with deadly thoroughness. During the period from 1916 to 1931, they trapped or shot 781 mountain lions, 30 wolves, 4,889 coyotes, and 554 bobcats. As late as 1939 they were still going about their mission, despite the ecological disaster it had created earlier. Once instituted, it was reasoned, a management program could not be abruptly discontinued; in their weakened condition, the deer more than ever needed protection from their enemies. On the other hand, it was by that point widely understood that the land could not support an unlimited abundance of "desirable" wildlife resources. The deer, it was now agreed, had to be kept within the carrying capacity of their range. But this was a job that human hunters could perform as well as the vanquished predator, and they were most eager to undertake it. Thus a new manmade ecological order came to exist on the Kaibab Plateau, as elsewhere in America—an ecological order engineered by wildlife managers and requiring their perpetual supervision.[13]

In this early period of wildlife management, the Department of Agriculture had no in-house equivalent to Gifford Pinchot's forestry leadership. The Kaibab episode was more the product of a widely diffused set of assumptions than of one outstanding leader's ideas. But in 1933 a book appeared that soon became the bible of the wildlife profession: Aldo Leopold's *Game Management*. Leopold's work was at once the foundation of this emerging scientific field and the culmination of the entire Progressive environmental philosophy. He had been trained at the Yale Forest School, established with Pinchot family money in 1900 and thereafter recognized as the leading academic center for the productivity outlook on nature. After a period of work in New

Mexico and Arizona, promoting game management more than forestry, Leopold moved in 1924 to Madison, Wisconsin, to serve as associate director of the U.S. Forest Products Laboratory. Again his interest in wildlife proved stronger than his commitment to the Forest Service; and by 1928, with financial aid from the Sporting Arms and Ammunition Manufacturers Institute, he began to study the condition of game in the upper Midwest. In 1933 he assumed the new chair of game management at the University of Wisconsin—teaching his courses, appropriately, in the Department of Agricultural Economics.

Like the foresters, Leopold believed in extending the principles of scientific agriculture to a more comprehensive management of nature. "Effective conservation," he declared, "requires in addition to public sentiment and laws, a deliberate and purposeful manipulation of the environment—the same kind of manipulation as is employed in forestry." Such favorite game species as deer and quail he regarded as "crops" that should be cultivated and harvested in the wild. This agronomic perspective was the essence of his conservation program in 1933, as it had been for Pinchot three decades earlier.[14]

In *Game Management*, Leopold further articulated this view of nature as "resources"—a world to be reorganized and managed to meet social demands. The purpose of management, he explained, is to alter the range "for greater productivity," meaning in this case "the rate at which mature breeding stock produces other mature stock, or mature removable crop." "Like all other agricultural arts," he continued, "game management produces a crop by controlling the environmental factors which hold down the natural increase, or productivity, of the seed stock." Much of his book, therefore, was occupied with identifying those limiting factors with mathematical precision.

Scientists see that before the factors of productivity can be economically manipulated, they must first be discovered and understood; that it is the task of science not only to furnish biological facts, but also to build on them a new technique.

For the wildlife expert, science was a rake to comb more crops out of the field. Leopold, it must be added, did not calculate the value of game animals in dollars and cents alone; they also represented for him a primitive, pioneering past with which he hoped the average citizen, through hunting, could keep faith. For this reason he insisted that the managing hand should touch the natural order lightly—not tear it apart and then put it back together in a too obviously artificial tidiness, but subtly direct its forces to keep the game alive, alert, and evasive. But despite his pursuit of naturalism in manipulating the land, and his ideal of a rough-hewn, low-intensive style of management, Leopold did not wander very far from the well-trod agronomic path. To make the earth more productive was as much his ambition in *Game Management* as it was for any up-to-date Wisconsin farmer. Consequently, his book underscored the economic approach to nature.[15]

Apparently the Kaibab preserve experience did not shake Leopold's confidence in the basic rightness of that progressive environmental stance. He persisted in the campaign against predators, and continued to push control of their numbers as one of the game manager's most effective devices. However, he had considerably tempered his once fierce resentment of the carnivore's presence in nature. In 1920, for instance, he had promised to persevere until "the last wolf or lion in New Mexico" was dead. Five years later he had begun to pipe a slightly different tune; at least he was beginning to wonder whether a policy of total extermination was truly sensible, from an ecological rather than an economic point of view. But his response to that doubt was much delayed; it would be ten years more before it grew to shatter the bedrock of his professional assumptions. In a sense, then, *Game Management* was an anachronism, for Leopold personally and even more so for a number of other conservationists. A few people, more influenced than Leopold by the Kaibab fiasco, were already ahead of him in wondering whether it might not be good to have predators around on occasion. They began to ask whether productivity and efficiency were the only important values in man's relation to nature, and to question the agricultural "crop" bias of conservation and its single-minded, man-centered perspective. They were starting to worry—as was Leopold himself at moments—about the ecological consequences of

The Value of a Varmint • 273

Progressive management. And they were moving to a different set of moral values regarding nature.

For the most part the agronomic mentality held firm, and the war against the coyote and other varmints went on without stint. But midway through the third decade of the century, an ecological stance toward wildlife began to emerge in America. Leopold was rather slow to switch to this new attitude; but when he did, he came over with an eloquence and credibility that quickly made him one of the leaders of the new ecological element. While many students were still absorbing the lessons of Pinchot from *Game Management*, Leopold himself would be attacking most of what that old conservation school had stood for. To fully understand Leopold's conversion and the broader movement it represented, it is necessary to examine those early signs of dissent, to follow those cracks in the wall as they spread across established environmental values.[16]

There were undoubtedly many ordinary people who had always disagreed with the conservation ideology and its policy of exterminating predators. And there were eloquent, highly visible dissenters like John Muir, who founded the Sierra Club and to the time of his death in 1914 opposed the Pinchot philosophy with bitter, sharp-edged passion. But the first noteworthy professional criticism of the BBS and the game specialists on the specific issue of varmints came at the 1923 annual meeting of the American Society of Mammalogists in Philadelphia. A number of scientists, including Joseph Grinnell of the University of California, were alarmed at the disappearance of predatory mammals from America and the methods employed in their elimination. The Bureau, they pointed out, was engaging in "modern poison warfare" with almost no research into its environmental consequences. Possibly the widespread revulsion toward the use of poison gases on the World War One battlefield was at work in this criticism. But the reaction of many mammalogists against poisoning did not fade away along with their ugly memories of the Great War. At the 1923 meeting and for more than a quarter of a century thereafter, the Society would hear at its yearly conferences reports from the critics of predator eradication, along with defenses by the government's and the livestock industry's apologists.[17]

In April 1924, for instance, Charles C. Adams, one of the country's major animal ecologists, spoke on "The Conservation of Predatory Mammals" at the Society's annual meeting. In 1925 the *Journal of Mammalogy* began printing articles, pro and con, on the Bureau's predator program. In 1930 the Society organized a "Symposium on Predatory Animal Control" for its May meeting at the American Museum of Natural History in New York City. Speakers there included W. C. Henderson, associate chief of the BBS, and E. A. Goldman, the Bureau's senior biologist, as well as C. C. Adams, representing the New York State Museum at Albany, E. Raymond Hall and Joseph Dixon of the University of California, and A. Brazier Howell of Johns Hopkins—all critics of the government policy of extermination. During the thirties the Society's Committee on the Problem of Predatory Mammal Control sent scientists into the field with Bureau officials to conduct joint investigations of government hunters and trappers and to report back on the harmful results of poisoning, both for target and nontarget species. And as late as 1950, when it met at Yellowstone National Park, the Mammalogists Society was still voting on, and approving, resolutions critical of the predator policies in Washington. "Our technologies for destruction are adequate," this conference concluded. "We need techniques for living successfully in association with our native fauna and flora." That statement is the essence of the dissenting scientists' position throughout this time of controversy.[18]

During this period from 1925 to 1950, the Society of Mammalogists was the major institutional opponent of the Bureau. But individual scientists, and nonscientists too, joined in the search for a new relation between man and the predator. For that matter, there were scientists in the Society, some of them employed by the BBS, who defended the massive poisoning campaign. So it was not simply a confrontation between science and government that was emerging, but rather a clash between contradictory ethics regarding nature, each claiming science as its validating authority. Much of the debate, to be sure, centered on rival claims to economic prudence, technical disputes over population dynamics, and charges of special-interest politics meddling in scientific areas. But the ultimate point of disagreement was, as usual, on moral values—in particular about man's place in the natural world, and his rights as one species among many. The "ecological point of view" became the rallying cry of the government's critics. By this they meant a scientifically based policy toward wildlife, instead of one founded on economic criteria alone. More important, however, that phrase usually implied a new ethic of coexistence between man and varmint.

The easiest charge to make against the Bureau of Biological Survey and its supporters was that they were excessively zealous in their self-appointed mission to wipe out all predators, rodents, and other "vermin." They had declared total war, regardless of its cost or necessity, while their critics agreed that absolute extermination of any species as a government objective must be opposed. "I do not advocate that predatory mammals be encouraged nor permitted to breed everywhere without restriction," wrote ecologist Lee Dice of the University of Michigan in 1924, "but I am sure that the extermination of any species, predatory or not, in any faunal district, is a serious loss to science." Biology held out too many unsolved questions that the predators might answer for the scientist to be unconcerned about their extinction—on this point there was speedy consensus. Likewise, it was rather easy to find support for the proposal that predators be given a limited sanctuary—analogous to the Indian reservations—in National Parks and other wild areas where no conflict with man could arise. "Only the remote, isolated, or poor lands," wrote C. C. Adams, were suitable for large predator populations. But in every part of the country there were such primitive spaces, supervised by the National Park Service, which had been established in 1916. These areas afforded the best opportunities for bringing Americans safely within the range of predators; in such places all the family could go to see their carnivores without much fear of losing an arm, just like going to the zoo. "We are probably the richest nation on earth," Adams noted:

What would be the cost of maintaining one hundred mountain

lions in North America? Would it stagger American civilization? We have millions of acres in National Forests, in the Public Domain, and in the National Parks. Some of these could be managed in such a fashion that some of these animals could be preserved and eat deer meat!

This idea must have been persuasive, for by 1936 all killing of predators in the National Parks came to an end. That decision was vigorously opposed by the BBS, whose field men began to make secret raids into parklands to get their varmints anyway. And it was not uncommon thereafter to find the borders of a park bristling with cyanide-loaded coyote-getters. But the idea of limited sanctuaries rather than total extermination caught hold.[19]

The Bureau's higher officialdom eventually came to agree with this policy of token preservation, though it was never very successful in conveying that compromise to its hunters in the West. Nor was the Bureau ever quite so energetic in preserving as it had been in destroying the meat-eating animals. Senior biologist Stanley Young, himself once a federal varmint agent who became one of the nation's most respected students of predators, had to agree that in the most remote reaches of the continent, "where these large killers can exist in no direct conflict with man," they might be tolerated. About the National Parks, however, he was less sure. These places were established, he believed, more to protect game species than to give sanctuary to carnivores. And withal he remained obdurate in his assessment of the predator's moral character: the wolf "is one hundred percent criminal, killing for sheer blood lust. . . . All wolves are killers. They are killers either of livestock or of wild game, and this killing is not resorted to just by so-called renegades." Yet Young was not alone among Bureau employees in admiring these villains, for all their depravity. In his now-standard series of studies on the major predators, he repeatedly emphasized that he did not want to see them forever gone from the land. So long as a few could find some godforsaken corner where there would be absolutely no chance of their competing against humans, he was willing to grant them asylum. "In spite of all that is bad about the wolf," he wrote in 1930, "I personally consider this animal our greatest American quadruped and have often wished

The Value of a Varmint • 2 7 7

that it would change its ways just a little so that the hand of man would not be raised so constantly against this predator. In my opinion he is the 'king of predators.'" Impelled by such sentiments, the BBS policy-makers edged away from their goal of all-out eradication, until by the thirties they had firmly substituted the word "control" for "extermination." But though it may have been a more cautious-sounding ideal, controlling predators essentially meant eliminating all of them wherever men wanted to use the land for agriculture or hunting. The large predator, Young continued to insist, "has no place in modern civilization."[20]

To believe that predators should have more than an open-air zoo existence, that they might fill a valuable role in a civilized world, was a more radical proposal, and sure to meet with official resistance. Yet some scientists indeed went this far, drawing from the classic ideal of a "balance of nature" a utilitarian justification for keeping predators on the scene even where economic losses resulted. They maintained that all carnivores, large or small, are an important check not only on the wild herbivores like deer but also on destructive rodents like rats, prairie dogs, mice, and voles. Most rodents are, of course, not popular with man because of the threat they have posed to his health and property. Thus the discovery that coyotes feasted heavily on such vermin could provide this little canine with a useful, even indispensable, social role. Without such an efficient natural enemy, rodents might overrun the world; then poisons would have to be used to solve an imbalance other poisons had created. All in all, nature's system of pest control was safer, more effective, and cheaper than anything the BBS could devise. This line of reasoning was set forth by a number of biologists, beginning in the 1920s, as a counter to government eradication programs, and it would serve as a prototype for an important new kind of conservation: ecological pragmatism. The preservation of natural checks and balances, at least as many of them as possible, would save society the risk and expense of clumsy substitutes. In this way, the predatory varmints came to be seen as valuable stabilizing forces rather than as mere curiosities, to be saved in token numbers only.[21]

But the Bureau was not inclined to grant its critics an

edge in practical economic appeal. Its subsequent self-defense ranged from the cover-up of evidence to a persistent denigration of the coyote's importance as a rodent controller. In 1929 Olaus Murie, one of the Bureau's own wildlife biologists, was asked by the agency head for his thoughts on how the balance of nature was being affected by predator control. Unfortunately, Murie's five-page reply agreed with the critics who claimed that the Bureau was creating chaos in the natural order. The letter was speedily buried in BBS files, and Murie was ordered to stay away from a wildlife conference in St. Louis where he had been scheduled to speak. Around 1936, his paper on the "Food Habits of the Coyote in Jackson Hole, Wyoming" was carefulyl lost in the same obscure file at headquarters into which his letter had disappeared; there was to be no adverse criticism from within the ranks. Meanwhile, the BBS pushed into the public's view every scrap of evidence it could find to demonstrate the negligible effect of coyotes on rodent populations. In a study of some 40,000 items found in coyote stomachs by government trappers from 1918 to 1923, the most frequent contents were rabbit, sheep, or goat meat, bait, beef, carrion, and grass or berries. "The aggregate of domestic livestock, poultry, and game exceeds the rodent item," noted W. C. Henderson. Available food supply and disease, rather than coyotes, must therefore be the most important checks on rodent populations, he concluded.[22]

It might seem that collecting such empirical evidence would be the best way to settle the value of the coyote and other predators to the balance of mature, but, for both sides, the facts were invariably mixed with subjective feelings. If you were a hunting enthusiast, then the predator was a severe check on the population of shootable species, a "race murderer" that had to be eliminated from nature if the game were to survive for sport. If you were a government trapper looking for job security, it was obvious that coyotes and wolves ate only game or livestock, and never touched a rodent. But if you opposed the poisoning policy, there could be no question that predators lived chiefly on crop-damaging rodents, had no effect on game numbers, and seldom bothered to kill sheep or calves. Even today it is far from easy to determine the long-term effects of predators on prey populations, probably because the relationship varies so widely from place to place and species to species. All generalizations on this matter are sure to be found wanting somewhere in nature's economy and the hard data too easily obscured by economic or moral values.[23]

Perhaps because they sensed themselves on treacherous ground here, the Bureau's defenders more often than not chose to throw out the entire balance-of-nature idea, as being at best an unreliable guide to American wildlife policy. E. A. Goldman, for instance, in a 1925 article, "The Predatory Mammal Problem and the Balance of Nature," suggested that "with the occupation of the continent by Europeans bearing firearms, clearing the forests, and settling permanently throughout its extent, the balance of nature has been violently overturned, never to be reestablished." In 1930 the editor of the *New Mexico Conservationist* stated the point bluntly:

It is a sonorous phrase, this Balance of Nature, and we too used to think very highly of it until we discovered that it doesn't mean anything. . . . Nature never has been in balance in any given spot for very long at a time. Something was always occurring to disturb the current regimen. Sometimes it was the invasion by coyotes of a virgin range, sometimes it was a climatic catastrophe which wiped out certain species and left others, and once it was the advent of man upon the continent. . . . The sentimentalist will say that the coyote has as much right to existence as the game animal or bird which he has appropriated for his use, and sentimentally speaking, that logic is without a flaw. Unfortunately, we barbarians of the chase do not want the coyote, and we do want the game animals and birds. And we are willing to risk the effects of jostling Mother Nature's balance a little more in order to satisfy our taste in the matter.

That last sentence is the giveaway. Despite his avowed disenchantment, this individual found it hard to give up wholly the traditional idea of an equilibrium in nature; whether or not it was ever perfectly achieved, it was a useful, perhaps indispensable notion. Like the related idea of a climax stage, the balance of nature, with all its problems, would have to do in lieu of anything better. Defenders of the Bureau seem to have recognized this even while they attacked the idea.[24]

The more pressing issue was whether man should respect and follow natural balancing forces or whether he could safely ignore them. How this question was answered depended on one's confidence in human managerial skills, as well as one's willingness to take risks in order to get the kind of world that was wanted. The anti-predator side believed that man could be happy only in a more thoroughly made-over environment. "Why is it always implied as bad to upset the balance of nature, that is, to alter the natural scheme of things?" asked one pest control agent. "Has not man survived and improved his standard of living in direct proportion to the extent he has gained control of nature and manipulated its balance to his advantage?" E. A. Goldman urged, again in 1925, that since it was impossible to restore the primeval order in America, man might as well face up to the fact that "practical considerations demand that he assume effective control of wild life everywhere." Interference in the past, it would seem, must justify even more interference in the future. To worry unduly about a natural balance was to obstruct progress. In 1948 Ira Gabrielson, then head of the Bureau, insisted that "in any case human interests will dominate the kind of, extent of, and direction of predator control, not the ideal of ecological balance or the rights of predators."[25]

Thus when constructed on purely pragmatic grounds of ecological stability and human self-interest, the defense of predators ran into difficulties. Those who wanted to keep the predator around as a useful check against rodent and herbivore increase had a powerful case, but it could be countered with strong arguments on the financial losses to ranching and hunting. While ecological prudence may have suggested a more cautious control program, man's ambition still was best served by a vigorous effort to purge the land of varmints. Sensing this impasse, some critics began to shift their case for preserving large predators to non-economic grounds: The wolf, coyote, cougar, and grizzly, even where they might get in the way of human purposes, were now said to have a moral right to exist. The purpose of wildlife management, from this view, was to find the best compromise between man and his carnivorous competitors, one that would recognize both as members of the earth's community and seek their reconciliation. Thus there came to be an ethical as well as an economic impetus behind the call for an ecologically determined wildlife policy.

For several decades one of the key spokesmen for this communitarian ideal of management was Olaus Murie. A Minnesotan by birth, he studied wildlife biology at the University of Michigan before joining the Bureau of Biological Survey as a field biologist in 1920, a time when researchers in the agency were outnumbered more than ten to one by hunters and trappers. He spent a number of years roaming the northern wildernesses of the continent, from Labrador and Hudson's Bay to Alaska. In Alaska, Olaus worked alongside his brother Adolph, who in 1939 would begin his landmark study of the timber wolves of Mount McKinley National Park. In the summer of 1927 Olaus and his wife Margaret were sent by the Bureau to Jackson Hole, Wyoming, to study the life history of the elk and the factors affecting its welfare. Olaus worked for the BBS at the National Elk Refuge for almost twenty years, and throughout that time—indeed until his death in 1963—he somehow managed to stand free of the official game-production philosophy, playing the role of a tolerated but unheeded maverick. It could not have been easy for such a peaceable man to be on the outs with so many of his colleagues for so long. He was fierce enough, however, to persist over those two decades in his efforts to convert the Bureau from an anti-predator prejudice to "the ecological view."[26]

At no point in his career did Murie reject all human interference in nature or all efforts to control predators. He accepted the need for management, especially in cases where one or two animals brought severe losses to the small, struggling farmer or rancher trying to make a modest living. What offended Murie's sense of justice was the Bureau's part in stirring up irrational, uncompromising hatred against all predators. In a 1929 memorandum to the agency chief, he noted that while government conservationists were teaching the public restraint in killing migratory birds, they were also sending out "glaring posters, portraying bloody, disagreeable scenes," urging people to eradicate the carnivores. "It seems entirely unnecessary and undesirable," he wrote, "to kill offending creatures in a spirit of hatred." A year later, he recommended to the same person that "sympathy should be felt for wildlife in general and that we should make greater effort to find what *good* there might be in some species which have ill repute." Quite simply, Murie liked varmints. He was partial to the large predators, but admitted that "I also like to see the so-called injurious rodents around." "I dislike no animal because he eats," he explained to Brazier Howell. "If an animal eats to the extent of harming me unduly, I will retaliate, but only to the extent of relieving the situation and without hatred." To Milton Hildebrand of the Sierra Club he declared that it was the injurious predators in particular he wanted to preserve: "They are the ones that are really threatened." Shortly after leaving the Bureau—or rather its successor, the Fish and Wildlife Service—he wrote a letter to its associate director, Clarence Cottam, giving the gist of his criticism:

I know stockmen who are much more tolerant of coyotes than our Service is. I know many hunters who are much more tolerant. I know numerous people who would like to have a tolerant world, a world in which wild creatures may have a share of its products. Many people like to think of the beneficial side, the inspirational and scientific values, of creatures like the coyote, as well as the destructive side. This is the opposite of our official position.

Apparently his two decades of protest had not had much real effect; talk of all-out extermination had ended, at least in higher bureaucratic echelons, but varmints were still varmints. And for the agency man in the field, more often than not, the only good varmint was still a dead one.[27]

After resigning from the Fish and Wildlife Service, Murie became a director and then president of the Wilderness Society during most of the 1950s. His years with the federal government's wildlife agency, from 1920 to 1946, coincided quite closely with the years of agitation by the Society of Mammalogists. And in the larger context, those years witnessed the gradual transition to a new age of popular ecological consciousness. The Dust Bowl experience was one crucial factor in the rise of this new philosophy of conservation; the predator issue was another. By the end of this period, the public was more or less prepared to heed the appeals of Rachel Carson and Barry Commoner, who, like such earlier scientific activists as Clements, Murie, and C. C. Adams, sought in the discipline of ecology the basis for a new relationship between man and nature, and for a new environmental ethic.

Murie and others of his persuasion may not have immediately carried the day, in terms of practical results. But they won over to their side a leading zealot of the Pinchot school, the man widely identified as the father of wildlife management in America: Aldo Leopold. Leopold died in 1948, while fighting a brush fire in Wisconsin, and so belongs essentially to the middle generation of that transition period from a utilitarian to an ecological approach to conservation. Just before his death, however, he finished his now-famous essay "The Land Ethic." More than any other piece of writing, this work signaled the arrival of the Age of Ecology; indeed, it would come to be regarded as the single most concise expression of the new environmental philosophy. It brought together a scientific approach to nature, a high level of ecological sophistication, and a biocentric, communitarian ethic that challenged the dominant economic attitude toward land use.

Leopold's conversion, as noted earlier, was not exactly a sudden awakening on the road to Damascus. Even while breathing out productivity figures and agronomic ardor, he was beginning to edge away from the Progressive frame of mind. During his early years in the Forest Service, for instance, he came around to the very un-Pinchot-like idea that some public lands might be set aside as wilderness or roadless areas, to be protected from all future economic development. In 1924, chiefly through his efforts, more than a half-million acres in New Mexico's Gila National Forest were so designated. When *Game Management* appeared nine years later, it made clear that Leopold had grown more uneasy than ever with his own controlled-environment ideal. He tried to argue there that cropping was only a preliminary to a more advanced relation to the land, a higher stage in man's "moral evolution" that would one day follow.

Twenty years of "progress" have brought the average citizen a vote, a national anthem, a Ford, a bank account, and a high opinion of himself, but not the capacity to live in high density without befouling and denuding his environment, nor a conviction that such capacity, rather than such density, is the true test of whether he is civilized. The practice of game management may be one of the means of developing a culture which will meet this test.

As yet, though, he had not been able to define for himself exactly what that more capable culture or attitude should be. Hence he was forced to speak vaguely of "that new social concept toward which conservation is groping."[28]

In that same year, 1933, Leopold also published an essay entitled "The Conservation Ethic," which gives some notion of where his own gropings were leading. In it he continued to speak of "controlled wild culture or 'management,'" of cropping, and of "industrial forestry." But he also criticized the attitude that land is merely property, to be used in whatever way its owner liked. "The land-relation," he complained, "is still strictly economic, entailing privileges, but not obligations." One of the essay's sub-headings read "Ecology and Economics." Already he had begun to think of the two as not altogether compatible; he was moving away from the view of conservation as resource supply-and-demand toward an attempt "to harmonize our machine civilization with the land whence comes its sustenance"—toward "a universal symbiosis."[29]

According to Leopold's biographer, Susan Flader, this conversion to an ecological basis did not become complete until 1935, when he joined with others to form the Wilderness Society. It was also in that year that he saw firsthand the intensely artificial German methods of management, which he disliked so much that he grew wary even of his own inclination toward regulated landscapes. And during that watershed year, too, he found an old, abandoned shack near Baraboo, Wisconsin, where until his death he would at odd moments live the life of a Gilbert White or Henry Thoreau—a rural naturalist living apart from a technological culture, seeking to intensify his attachment to the earth and its processes. Henceforth Leopold's chief concern was the need to reestablish a personal, coexisting relation with nature, rather than the large-scale, impersonal management of resources by a professional elite.[30]

The Value of a Varmint • 285

The fruit of the Baraboo years was his *Sand County Almanac*, a set of rural natural history sketches published posthumously in 1949. Disenchantment with the modern, overly managed world is the persistent theme of these essays. "Nothing could be more salutary at this stage," he declared, "than a little healthy contempt for a plethora of material blessings. Perhaps such a shift in values can be achieved by reappraising things unnatural, tame, and confined in terms of things natural, wild, and free." His own 120-acre farm, though badly abused by many decades of careless exploitation, was now sprouting scrub oak and pine, a ragged but welcome prophecy of nature's second coming. But elsewhere, and nowhere more so than all around him in the American Midwest, the land was falling into the hands of scientifically-minded farmers trained by the state colleges and extension agents to maximize agricultural output. In place of the prehistoric prairie diversity of plants and wildlife, they standardized the land to corn or wheat or soybeans—"clean farming," they called it—just as Leopold himself had once wanted to raise deer in a perfectly wolfless world. "Have we learned the first principle of conservation: to preserve all the parts of the land mechanism?" he wondered. "No, because even the scientist does not yet recognize all of them." Leopold's disillusionment with the too strictly managed landscape affected even his devotion to science. He had by now come to feel that the typical academic researcher was far too narrow in his perceptions to grasp the wholeness of nature, as would be essential to the practice of a broader kind of conservation. One of the *Sand County* essays was titled "Natural History—The Forgotten Science": It was a plea for a return to outdoor, holistic education, to a style of science open to amateurs and soberminded nature lovers, one more sensitive to "the pleasure to be had in wild things." As it was currently taught in laboratories and universities, he feared, "science serves progress." It was in cahoots with the technological mentality that was regimenting the world in pursuit of mere material advancement. It would have to be changed along with the managerial bias.[31]

The climactic essay in what turned out to be his last book, and thus Leopold's final word on man's place in nature, was "The Land Ethic," written sometime in late 1947 or early 1948. Its theme elaborated ideas put down more briefly elsewhere: essentially, the inadequacy of economic expediency in conservation. In the foreword of *Sand County Almanac*, for example, he had pointed out:

Conservation is getting nowhere because it is incompatible with our Abrahamic concept of land. We abuse land because we regard it as a commodity belonging to us. When we see land as a community to which we belong, we may begin to use it with love and respect.

The "land ethic" he had in mind was precisely this sense of ecological community between man and all other species, replacing "the tedium of the merely economic attitude toward land." Earlier ethical norms had been concerned only with man's duties to others of his own kind; as such they were at least evidence of fellow feeling, of common interest and reciprocal support, "a kind of community instinct in-the-making." Now, he argued, man's own well-being requires that the circle of cooperative, communal relatedness be extended to encompass all beings. Such an ecological ethic would change man's role from master of the earth to "plain member and citizen of it." It was a thoroughly democratic ideal, as utopian in its way as the Progressive desire to make the world over. By this point, Leopold had broken away almost completely from the school of Pinchot-style conservation, on the grounds that it felt "no inhibition against violence; its ideology is agronomic." In contrast, the new conservation "feels the stirrings of an ecological conscience."[32]

Through this long process of personal conversion, Leopold continually came back to the problem of what to do with the predator. In the fate of that order of creatures lay the ultimate practicability of his ecological ethic. It was easy enough to tolerate chickadees, or even garden snakes and field mice; moreover, they were prolific enough to withstand all but the most violent human interference. But the predator, ironically, was a good deal more vulnerable to human power; consequently its future as an integral member of the biotic order hung by the narrow thread of man's willingness to make accommodations. In "Round River," Leopold wrote:

Harmony with land is like harmony with a friend; you cannot cherish his right hand and chop off his left. That is to say, you cannot love game and hate predators; you cannot conserve the waters and waste the ranges; you cannot build the forest and mine the farm. The land is one organism.

To get the varmint accepted as a legitimate part of organic nature, Leopold was not willing to put the case merely on pragmatic or utilitarian grounds. Whether the predator controlled rodents for the farmer or ate only "worthless" species was beside the point. The "more honest" rationale, Leopold believed, was simply "that predators are members of the community, and that no special interest has the right to exterminate them for the sake of a benefit, real or fancied, to itself."[33]

Ecology revealed to Leopold a new dimension in the very old notion of natural rights. This idea, especially strong in Anglo-American culture, had historically been used (as in the Declaration of Independence) to legitimize self-assertion by individuals or nations against a controlling power. By the very order of nature, it was argued, certain inalienable rights belong to all men, but natural rights had never included the rights of nature. The ecological conscience, however, would extend these concepts to all species, even to the earth itself. The rights of life and liberty—perhaps even the pursuit of happiness—must belong to all beings, for all are members in the biotic community. But in contrast to previous appeals for natural rights, this was not a demand made and forced on the ruling class by an excluded minority; rather, it required a moral decision by that powerful elite on behalf of the inarticulate lower orders. To invest the ruling order with the power to determine the justice of its own deeds is always an act of faith, and for that reason alone, the rights of nature must always remain in jeopardy. But in a sense this new doctrine had its own compelling force, apart from human whim. Unless man recognized the rights of the entire earth household, Leopold warned, he might find his own survival threatened by environmental collapse. It had happened before, as recently as the Dust Bowl years.

There was, however, a weakness in Leopold's land ethic that he never really suspected: It was too firmly tied to the science of ecology to escape an economic bias. Among all the sciences, this field undoubtedly came closest to his nostalgic ideal of a natural history wedded to holistic sympathy. But at the very moment he embraced it as the way out of the narrow economic attitude toward nature, ecology was moving in the other direction, toward its own niche in the modern technological society. It was preparing to turn abstract, mathematical, and reductive. Moreover, ecologists were taking up with increasing devotion the very concepts of Progressive, agronomic conservation that Leopold wanted to deemphasize: efficiency, productivity, yield, crop. By the late 1940s, ecology was ready to sweep out all the organismic, communitarian cobwebs that had been accumulating in its corners for so long, and to adopt a new hard-edged mechanism as its dominant stance toward nature. Leopold could not have known all this, of course, but it would soon make his "ecological conscience" a most unstable, perhaps untenable objective.

Yet it must be said that these incompatibilities between science and moral value were already apparent, to some extent, in Leopold's own environmental thought. For all his disenchantment, he never broke away altogether from the economic view of nature. In many ways his land ethic was merely a more enlightened, long-range prudence: a surer means to an infinite expansion of material wealth, as he promised in "Natural History." While he relinquished his ambition to make the land yield only the most desirable crops, he continued to speak in agronomic terms; thus the entire earth became a crop to be harvested, though not one wholly planted or cultivated by man. A concern for "healthy functioning," general productivity, and stability replaced the desire for immediate commercial return. Moreover, while he came to view the land as "a single organism," he persisted in describing it as "an ecological mechanism," in which man functions as one important economic cog. "To keep every cog and wheel," he wrote in an undated essay, "is the first precaution of intelligent tinkering." This vacillation between root metaphors might be construed as casual or superficial, but such a defense ignores the fact that "organism" and "mechanism" had been around for at least three centuries, and during that time had been consistently identified with fundamentally antithetical world views. It might be maintained that Leopold was attempting to reconcile these rivals, at long last, in a new conservation synthesis; his readers will have to assess for themselves how successful this reconciliation was. Nonetheless, he did stop short of examining in detail the tension between these historically opposed sets of values; nor did he address directly and fully the problem of whether a genuine resolution was truly possible. He was, in short, less a philosopher than he might have been for the task he undertook. As a consequence, he may have obscured in the popular consciousness of ecology a fundamental and inescapable source of ambiguity and conflict. People supporting incompatible brands of conservation might all find him an acceptable prophet—until they began to apply the land-ethic idea to concrete situations.[34]

Whether the coyote or wolf might be permitted a place in civilized America seemed, then, to depend on whether economics would continue to dictate environmental values. The varmint's future security lay in the possibility of a shift toward an ecologically based conservation philosophy—so believed Leopold, Murie, and a number of other scientists and wildlife enthusiasts. At this point, however, no one seemed to suspect that ecology was itself evolving toward an economic outlook, that it was absorbing into its theoretical structure the very terms of the old agronomic conservation. The course of that development in scientific theory must now be examined.

CHAPTER 14

Producers and Consumers

"BIO-ECONOMICALLY SPEAKING, it is the duty of the plant world to manufacture the food-stuffs for its complement, the animal world." This principle of organization, claimed an obscure writer in 1910, demonstrates that "the economy of nature" is no idle phrase, but contains a clue to the central animating drive in all beings: to produce, to manufacture, to consume. Nature is nothing more nor less than an economic system. According to this writer, one Hermann Reinheimer, all organisms are "traders" or "economic persons"; they must work to earn their way, either by producing food or by rendering services, and they must enter into commercial relations with one another. In nature's as in man's economy, a community that "ceases to manufacture cannot escape impoverishment." Consequently, Reinheimer wrote,

every day, from sunrise until sunset, myriads of (plant) laboratories, factories, workshops and industries all the world over, on land and in the sea, in the earth and on the surface soil, are incessantly occupied, adding each its little contribution to the general fund of organic wealth....

In order to secure with "ever-increasing efficiency the production and storage of energies that go to sustain and to help advance life, to produce a maximum of organic and social utilities with a minimum of organic cost," nature progressively refines her division of labor. Every organism becomes a specialist, a well-integrated cog in the whole working unit, an operative stationed along the assembly line of the Great Earth Factory.[1]

Reinheimer's fantasy turned out to be more prophetic than he could have imagined. Although quickly lost to history, his book *Evolution by Co-operation: A Study in Bio-Economics* was a striking anticipation of what would come to be a leading motif in ecological theory a half-century later. For example, in 1967 Robert Usinger, a University of California entomologist, portrayed the typical river as an "assembly line" that conveys energy and matter to organisms along the way, to be used in manufacture. "Like any factory," he explained, "the river's productivity is limited by its supply of raw materials and its efficiency in converting these materials into finished products." If biotic capital becomes scarce, the "output of living things will be low." The metaphors used here are more than casual or incidental; they express a common tendency in the scientific ecology of our time. In their theoretical models, ecologists have transformed nature into a reflection of the modern corporate, industrial system. And to a great extent, ecology today has become "bio-economics": a cognate, or perhaps even subordinate, division of economics.[2]

As Reinheimer's title indicates, his little work was one of the many efforts at the turn of the century to refute Darwinian biology, espousing cooperation rather than competition as the truth about nature. The special quality of Reinheimer's vision was that he linked ecological collectivism to the necessities of economic productivity, a correlation that would not have been so apparent to an earlier age of laissez-faire capitalists. Every generation, I have been trying to show, writes its own description of the natural order, which generally reveals as much about human society and its changing concerns as it does about nature. And these descriptions linger on in bits and pieces, often creating incongruous or incompatible juxtapositions. Such was the fate of Darwinism in mid-twentieth-century ecological thought. It was not refuted, really—there were ample expressions of filial piety in the science textbooks, and the struggle for existence remained a persuasive idea. But in many ways the basic ecological outlook shifted to a radically different point of view that made Darwinism not so much wrong as out-moded and boring. The "New Ecology" that had emerged by the middle decades of the twentieth century saw nature through a different set of spectacles: the forms, processes, and values of the modern economic order as shaped by tech-nology.

The characteristics of the modern economic system are familiar to the point of becoming "second nature." We are well aware that ours is an intricate corporate society; self-reliance, it would seem, is a thing of the past. And all the impassioned official rhetoric about the virtues of compe-tition notwithstanding, probably few businessmen in Brit-ain or the United States today really believe that old saw. The restriction of genuine "free enterprise" is a governing ambition of the modern economy, whether one lives under a capitalist or socialist system. Hence the virtues of inter-dependence and cooperation take on new importance, for without them the complex industrial establishment would lurch like some juggernaut into the ditch. But most im-portant here is that interdependence today almost always gets reduced to economic terms. Cooperation is defined, and absorbed, by the functions of production and consump-tion—that is all we mean by social integration, and all we have time for. We will see how thoroughly ecology, too, has become preoccupied with these values.

A second aspect of the modern industrial system is the primacy of efficiency and productivity as human goals. Since the eighteenth century's industrial and agricultural revolutions, these aims have been on the ascendancy in Anglo-American culture, and today are undoubtedly the rul-ing values of our time. With few exceptions, anything that does not meet their test or that challenges their supremacy has little chance of being taken seriously by the public or its leaders. In the preceding chapter it was shown how these ideas dominated conservation during the Progressive period, from the 1890s to World War One. More recently they have become still more pervasive in their social and ecological influence, as well as, increasingly, ends in themselves. This sway coincides with the rise of the professional economist to oracular power. As John Maynard Keynes wrote in 1936:

"The ideas of economists and political philosophers, both when they are right and when they are wrong, are more powerful than is commonly understood. Indeed the world is ruled by little else."[3]

One further characteristic of modern economics will become especially relevant here: the development of a managerial ethos. It has come to be a widespread assumption that neither man nor nature can long survive without direction and control by trained managers. This faith in management is one of the more significant products of technological elaboration: eventually every specialty begins to appear too complex for lay understanding. Moreover, the compulsion to improve output, to reorganize the world for the sake of ever higher economic achievements, creates a corollary reliance on social planning, personnel management, and resource engineering. Letting things alone, it is feared, will lead to stagnation, poverty, idleness, chaos. The technological imperative is that things can always be done better—and must be. That is the only, and the sufficient, rationale for our increasingly managed world.

It was predictable, in view of its history of cultural responsiveness, that the science of ecology would begin to pick up and express in its view of nature these prevailing characteristics of modern society. This process was not effected with a sudden clap of thunder; it was a more imperceptible shift that occurred as the science was growing toward maturity and seeking recognition from older, sister fields. As early as the 1930s, H. G. Wells and Julian Huxley could fairly describe ecology as "the extension of economics to the whole world of life." The direction of that flow of ideas is all-important. Economics took nothing from ecological biology that might have made it more aware of the environmental limits to man's industrial growth. Rather, it was ecology that applied economic thinking to the study of nature. That pattern of one-way influence would remain true for another four decades. It was the essential characteristic of what would come to be known at mid-century as the "New Ecology."[4]

The scientist who laid the foundations for the New Ecology was the Cambridge University zoologist Charles Elton.

In 1927 Elton published his first major work, *Animal Ecology*, which Julian Huxley introduced to the scientific world as a tool of great promise in the more effective management of the plant and animal "industry." Elton himself, describing his subject as "the sociology and economics of animals," claimed that it had greater practical value than any other aspect of zoology. But his more immediate purpose was theoretical: to draw together existing ecological knowledge into a new model of community. Elton was concerned with natural communities—their workings, distribution, and component populations. And although he included a chapter on succession that leaned heavily on Frederic Clements' work, he was much less interested in "dynamics" of this sort than in the structure and functions that exist at any stage of community development. Everywhere on the scholarly scene, an emphasis on such functionalist analysis was replacing the nineteenth century's evolutionary or historical interest. For Elton, as for other social scientists, the form or organization of the community became the central problem, and this has remained true of English and American ecologists up to the present. In Elton's account of the natural community as a simplified economy, twentieth-century ecology found its single most important paradigm.[5]

Elton's work was even more important than Eugenius Warming's in summarizing ecological developments since Darwin. In a sense, he was adding an appendix of these findings to the traditional study of nature, but *Animal Ecology* also set forth fresh concepts that made it more than a mere addendum to Darwinism. On the basis of his own work with the primitive, bare-bones communities of Canada and Scandinavia, Elton suggested four principles that could describe the economy of nature as it operates everywhere on earth.

The first of these he called the "food chain." In every community, plants, through the photosynthetic conversion of sunlight to food, form the first link in a chain of nutrition. Food, one might say, is the essential capital in the natural economic order. The remaining links—usually no more than two or three, and almost never more than four—include the herbivorous animals and their predators. A typical food chain in a North American oak woods might link acorns, quail, and foxes, or acorns, mice, and weasels; with some two hundred species of birds and mammals alone feeding on the oaks, the potential number of food chains is extraordinarily large. Possibly the idea of a food chain had its source in the eighteenth century's favorite metaphor, the "Great Chain of Being." Note, however, that the older notion ranked all species on a single grand staircase, those at the top of the stairs being the most noble and honored. Elton's chains, in contrast, were exclusively economic; they had nothing at all to do with taxonomy. They could be found in nature by the thousands, all showing a common pattern but no two alike in every respect. And the bottom of the chain, rather than the top, is the most important link: The plants make the whole system possible. Elton referred to the sum total of chains in any community as the "food web"—an exceedingly complex design of crisscrossed lines of economic activity. Such webs are easiest to analyze in the relatively unpopulated arctic zones and almost impossible to untangle in the warm, humid tropics, where life forms abound.[6]

In every food chain certain roles must be performed. The plants, for example, are all "producers." Animals can be described as either first- or second-order "consumers," depending on whether they eat plants or other animals. Those animals that feed on the most numerous plants in a habitat, like the bison on prairie grasses, or copepods on diatoms in the sea, are the "key industries" in those economies. In 1926, August Thienemann had introduced the terms "producer," "consumer," and "reducer," or "decomposer," to describe ecological roles in a specific ecological setting; Elton now generalized them for every food chain in nature. These labels emphasized the nutritional interdependence that binds species together—the corporateness of survival— and they became the cues from which ecology would increasingly take an economic direction.[7]

The second and third principles in Elton's synthesis concerned the effects of food size and species populations on the structure of the chains. In general, an animal as large as an elephant cannot survive on food as small and lively as insects; it would need more food than it could catch, and exhaust itself in the chase. A more substantial, stationary, and unresisting kind of food is called for. The giant whale is able to live on tiny crustaceans only because they are so numerous and easy to harvest. The law of nature decrees that each species has an optimum food size, and this law determines the structure of the food chain. "The very existence of food-chains," Elton noted, "is due mainly to the fact that any one animal can only live on food of a certain size. Each stage in an ordinary food-chain has the effect of making a smaller food into a larger one, and so making it available to a larger animal." The chain thus becomes an ascending scale of larger and larger mouths and bellies, except where a predator has the advantage of such special weapons as poison, like the spider, or group tactics, like the wolf pack. Even then, of course, the spider cannot kill and consume an elephant. The only species that ignores these rules is civilized man, with his artificial techniques for more efficient food-gathering. He can kill the largest animals on earth, or he can gather the smallest grain and seeds, and so eat lower on the food chain. But for Elton, modern man is distinctly an outsider, not to be confused with the natural economic system and its workings.

To serve as food for organisms higher up on the food chain, plants and animals near the bottom must be more numerous and reproduce more rapidly. Their fertility is a function of their position in the economic order: The smaller a creature, the more common it is. In contrast, predators at the top of the chain must reproduce more slowly than their prey, or they will end up with nothing to eat. They must also distribute themselves more sparsely across the land; hence every tiger looks for his own hill and defends it against other tigers, or he perishes. The demarcation and defense of private territories for food or breeding insures that each successful individual will have an adequate base for survival. Such territorialism goes on where it must among the birds and mammals, which are constantly required to adjust their density to their food supply. The system of interacting populations resulting from these different behavioral requirements Elton called the "pyramid of numbers." A single plot of ground may provide a home for millions of microscopic soil bacteria, thousands of grass plants and insects, hundreds of trees, a few dozen rabbits, sparrows, and squirrels—and at the apex only a single hawk. As one goes up the chain, the total weight of protoplasm at each level (the "biomass") declines along with the numbers. One lion, for instance, may eat fifty zebras in a year, so that the total physical mass of the predator is but a small fraction of the combined weight of its prey. The plants at the food chain's base constitute by far the greatest part of the mass of living substance on earth.[8]

After the principles of food size and pyramid of numbers, the fourth element in Elton's community structure was the "niche," which, ecologically speaking, is the outcome of the evolutionary process of differentiation and specialization. First given its modern name by the California ornithologist Joseph Grinnell, the niche is essentially Darwin's "place" or "office" in the economy of nature. It was Elton, however, who gave the idea of the niche its prominence in twentieth-century ecology. He defined it as the "status" or "occupation" of an organism in the community: "what it is *doing* and not merely what it looks like." In practice, by emphasizing the economics of the community, he reduced the niche to a matter of food sources, or what an animal is *eating*. All communities, he explained, have similar "ground plans" of niche patterns, as they do of food chains. The arctic fox, for example, which lives on guillemot eggs and on the carrion of seals killed by polar bears, occupies the same niche as the African hyena, which eats the eggs of ostriches and the remains of zebras killed by lions. But within any single community, no two species can occupy the same niche; "competitive exclusion" is the unbreakable rule. The pressure of population increase must generate a fierce competition for food, from which only one species can emerge victorious.[9]

This notion of exclusion, which was also the essence of Darwin's ecological model, was tested in a laboratory by the Russian scientist G. F. Gause, using yeast cells and protozoa in a test-tube environment. Gause published his results confirming competition as the law of nature—a most ironic message from one living in a Marxist state—in his book *The Struggle for Existence* (1934). Elton cited these experiments in support of competitive exclusion in subsequent editions of his own work. But when other biologists began to offer examples of several species coexisting in the same food niche—thus denying the universality of competitive exclusion—the niche concept had to be stretched to include once more all the activities of the organism. For example, all warblers in a spruce woods may eat the same food, but each species builds its nest at a unique, characteristic level in the trees: Thus the niches, considered as patterns of behavior rather than food sources, remained distinctive. But this compromise also made the whole idea so general as to be almost useless, even tautological: The niche is the species, and the species is the niche. Since all species are by definition different, and since behavior as much as bone structure defines a species, it would seem obvious that niches must differ—without necessarily being the outcome of competitive exclusion. Historically, the more important problem with the niche or place idea has been whether to regard niches as preordained, preexisting slots to be filled in nature, or simply as *post hoc* descriptions of what an organism does with its environment. On this matter Elton was silent, as his students have been. Indeed, the niche remains today a favorite principle, especially among competition-minded ecologists.[10]

As he organized nature into an integrated economy, Elton worked within a Darwinian frame to a considerable extent. The prominence of competition theory in his writings was but one vestige of this older science. Another was the emphasis in his fieldwork on invasions of new territory and their ecological consequences—Charles Lyell's interest. Then too, Elton liked to think of his subject as "scientific natural history"; he still wanted to use the old-fashioned, descriptive habits of the field, while at the same time availing himself of experimental laboratory data and mathematical precision. The initial virtue, but also the ultimate liability, of his work was that it relied on many homely, commonplace terms, much as Darwin's had. Take, for instance, the idea of "food" as the currency or basis of exchange in the natural economy. No one could mistake his general meaning, but scientists had to translate his concept into one more susceptible to universal quantification if they were to make any further progress. The future of the science as a set of mathematical formulae required a more radical break with the Darwinian style of natural history than Elton could bring about. The New Ecology, therefore, would go on from Elton's synthesis to build a science more thoroughly bound to physico-chemical processes.

During the mid-forties, Elton began studying the natural history of Wytham Woods, an estate belonging to Oxford University (where he had taken a position in the Department of Zoological Field Studies). Wytham Woods was like an island in its ecological containment: It was surrounded on three sides by a loop in the Thames River. Here he intended to pursue his researches on a micro-scale, much as Gilbert White had done at Selborne, not far to the south. "By understanding thoroughly and over long periods of time the dynamics in such habitats as Wytham Woods we will be able to face conservation problems and understand what goes wrong in our artificially simplified croplands and planted forests," Elton explained in his book *The Pattern of Animal Communities* (1966). Since 1933, in fact, conservation had been an important theme in his writings. Perhaps what touched off this concern was his meeting with Aldo Leopold at the Matamek Conference on Biological Cycles in 1931. That meeting was apparently important for both men; soon thereafter Leopold became a convert to the ecological view of nature, and Elton then began quoting Leopold on the need for a "conservation ethic." Elton maintained from this point forward that, for moral as well as economic reasons, man needs to live more carefully on the earth. As late as 1966 he was worrying that "in giving priority to economic productivity, especially in regard to the production of large cash crops from the land, the human environment itself may gradually become dull, unvaried, charmless, and treated like a factory rather than a place to live in." Wytham Woods fortunately was no factory environment; indeed, for that part of Britain it was still remarkably primitive. But the great paradox in Elton's pleas for a less economically-determined relation to nature was that he continued to describe the ecological community as primarily a system of "producers" and "consumers." And it was his work more than anyone else's that set ecology on the path toward "bio-economics." The distance from his science to society's emphasis on "economic productivity" was in reality not so very great.[11]

A second long step toward the New Ecology was taken by A. G. Tansley, the Oxford botanist. In a 1935 essay, Tansley attempted to rid ecology of all the lingering traces of organismic philosophy, expressed most recently in Clements' description of vegetation as a single living organism. Although Tansley himself had once gone so far as to describe the human community as a "quasi-organism," he now decided that this organismic talk had exceeded the bounds of legitimate scientific inquiry. The often-repeated notion that the plant assemblage is more than the sum of its parts, that it forms a whole which resists reductive analysis, he took to be a fiction worked up by an overexcited imagination. These "wholes," he wrote, "are *in analysis* nothing but the synthesized actions of the components in associations." A mature science, in his view, must isolate "the basic units of nature" and must "split up the story" into its individual parts. It must approach nature as a composite of strictly physical entities organized into a mechanical system. The scientist who knows all the properties of all the parts studied separately can accurately predict their combined result. In addition, Tansley wanted to strike the word "community" from his science's vocabulary because of connotations that he considered misleading and anthropomorphic; some, he feared, might conclude from such language that human associations and those in nature were parallel. Plants and animals in a locale cannot constitute a genuine community, he argued, for no psychic bond can exist between them, and thus they can have no true social order. In short, Tansley hoped to purge from ecology all that was not subject to quantification and analysis, all those obscurities that had been a part of its baggage at least since the Romantic period. He would rescue it from the status of a vaguely mysterious, moralizing "point of view" and make of it instead a hard-edged, mechanistic, nothing-but discipline, marching in closed ranks with the other sciences.[12]

To replace these fuzzy analogies with the organism or the human community, Tansley came up with a new model of organization: the "ecosystem." It was an idea strongly influenced by that masterful science of physics, which early in the twentieth century had begun to talk about energy "fields" and "systems" as a way of getting a more precise handle on natural phenomena than was possible in traditional Newtonian science. Organisms indeed live in closely integrated units, Tansley agreed, but these can best be studied as physical systems, not "organic wholes." Using the ecosystem, all relations among organisms can be described in terms of the purely material exchange of energy and of such chemical substances as water, phosphorus, nitrogen, and other nutrients that are the constituents of "food." These are the real bonds that hold the natural world together; they create a single unit made up of many smaller units—big and little ecosystems. The outmoded concept of an ecological community suggested a sharp disjunction between the living and nonliving substances on earth (part of the Romantic legacy). In contrast, Tansley's ecosystem brought all nature—rocks and gases as well as biota—into a common ordering of material resources. It was more inclusive, paradoxically, because it was first more reductive. Tansley was saying, in fact, that ecologists were stagnating in scientific adolescence precisely because they had not yet succeeded in reducing their subject matter to the laws of physico-chemical activity, which alone could bring about genuine progress toward positive knowledge. As the ecologist David Gates more recently declared: "The dichotomy which existed between biology and physical science retarded the advancement of ecological understanding by several decades. The lack of understanding of biology by the physicist did not retard physics in the least." The discovery of the ecosystem promised to end that dichotomy. It marked ecology's coming of age as an adjunct of physical science. Henceforth it would gradually cease to be set off as a kind of comprehensive biology, and would instead be increasingly absorbed into the physics of energy systems.[13]

The relevance of the ecosystem model to Elton's bioeconomics was not immediately apparent. For the time, all that Tansley's new approach to ecology seemed to indicate was a shift toward an emphasis on energy flow in the ecosystem. And that was enough! All ecological kinships thereafter had to be reworked in terms of energy relations. No energy is created or destroyed by the ecosystem, but only transformed and retransformed before escaping. Most important, the ecologist had to be tutored in the Second Law of Thermodynamics, first formulated by Rudolph Clausius in 1850. According to this law, all energy tends to disperse or become disorganized and unavailable for use, until at last the energy system reaches maximum entropy: a state of total randomness, total equilibrium, death. The ecosystem of the earth, considered from the perspective of energetics, is a way-station on a river of no return. Energy flows through it and disappears eventually into the vast sea of space; there is no way to get back upstream. And unlike water in the hydrological cycle, energy once passed through nature is forever, irretrievably lost. By collecting solar energy for their own use, plants retard this entropic process; they can pass energy on to animals in repackaged or reconcentrated form—some of it at least—and the animals in turn hold it temporarily in organized availability. Put another way, the ecosystem is comparable both to a chain of reservoirs that store running water, and to the dams that make it work before it is released again to rush downstream. But all along the way, some of that flow seeps into the ground and some evaporates into the air, and all that remains must at some point be released. So long as the sun goes on supplying a current of energy, the ecosystem can endure. When that supply runs out, however, the system will collapse.[14]

The idea of energy coursing through nature was not without its own mystical appeal. One can detect, for example, at least a superficial resemblance between this system and those Eastern philosophies of yogic meditation, transcendental energy, and cosmic kinetics that had so appealed to the Romantic poets. But Tansley's mechanistic ecosystem had really nothing in common with the Romantic view of biology—the life-force idea of Goethe and Thoreau. Indeed, it owed nothing to any of its forebears in the history of the science, not even to the crudely mechanistic biology of the eighteenth century. It was born of entirely different parentage: that is, modern thermodynamic physics, not biology. For the first time, mathematicians could see in ecology the opportunity to quantify. Energy flow could be measured at every point in its progress through the ecosystem; for that matter, so could the cycling of geochemical substances such as nitrogen or carbon. But in reducing the living world to ingredients that could be easily measured and graphed, the ecologist was also in danger of removing all the residual emotional impediments to unrestrained manipulation. To describe nature as an organism or community suggested one kind of environmental behavior by man; to speak of it as but "a momentary stay against entropy" suggested a wholly different behavior, and as good as removed it from the ethical realm altogether.

Tansley's ecosystem, unlike the Romantic style of ecology, dovetailed nicely with the agronomic and industrial view of nature as a storehouse of exploitable material resources. That merger between science and economics became still more apparent in the next step toward the New Ecology.

Even before Tansley's ecosystem came on the scene, scientists were learning that energy is the key to the ecological order. Specifically, they were concluding that energy, more accurately than "food," is the medium of exchange in nature, like money in the human economy. In 1926 Edgar Transeau anticipated this new direction in ecological research when he tried to calculate the amount of solar energy accumulated and used to produce a crop in a northern Illinois cornfield during a single growing season. What is the natural energy cost of agriculture, he wondered, and how efficiently is it used in the productive process? To answer these questions, he first studied the net production—the amount of glucose represented in the crop at harvest, counting both stalks and ears—on an area of one hectare. This figure he calculated to be 6,687 kilograms (kg). Since he knew that 3,760 kilocalories (kcal) are needed to produce one kg of glucose, he could estimate that the whole crop required 25.3 million kcal. Another 7.7 million kcal were metabolized in respiration, giving a total or gross production of almost 9,000 kg of glucose, using 33 million kcal. Next he determined that the energy lost in transpiration (the heat escaping into the air from the plants) amounted to 990 million kcal, out of 2,043 million kcal of incident solar radiation. He therefore concluded that the gross production of the cornfield used only 1.6 percent of the total energy available per year, and that the actual corn and silage that was harvested used only 1.2 percent—amazingly low rates of efficiency in energy utilization. The remaining 98-plus percent was going down the river of no return as waste! The farmer was not getting much of the sun's energy into his barn.[15]

For a decade and a half, the promise of Transeau's energy-accounting system was neglected by other ecologists. Then in 1940 Chancey Juday published his findings on the efficiency of "energy capture" in Wisconsin's Lake Mendota. But rather than the energy cost of an agricultural product like corn, he attempted to derive what he called the annual "energy budget" of that natural lake: how much energy was spent and how much was invested in the form of biomass at each level in the system. Among other things, Juday learned that the basic plants in the lake, the phytoplankton and bottom flora, used less than one-half of one percent of the incident solar radiation for their growth, metabolism, and manufacture of food for other organisms. Thus the plants in Lake Mendota proved to be only one-fourth as efficient (to be exact, the respective energy-fixation efficiencies were 0.35 versus 1.6 percent) in capturing solar energy as those in Transeau's cornfield. Obviously there were important implications for agriculture in such an approach. Perhaps, like Transeau, Juday began to explore these ecological energy functions chiefly because he was interested in the efficiency of man's crops compared to nature's. Perhaps he also had an eye to the improvement of both those efficiencies, where possible. In any event, it is significant that he applied to nature the same kind of crop-energetics analysis Transeau had worked out. One cannot help but see in such research the agronomic influence at work: the concern for crops, productivity, yield, and efficiency now being translated into a broader ecological model that could be used to measure natural as well as artificial ecosystems. This school of energetics, with its search for the magnitudes of ecological efficiency in energy capture and utilization, became the third step toward the New Ecology.[16]

What remained was to merge these overlapping ideas of the British scientists, Elton and Tansley, and of the Americans, Juday and Transeau, into a comprehensive account of the energy-based economics of nature. That final step was taken in 1942, when a postgraduate student at Yale, Raymond Lindeman, published a scientific paper entitled "The Trophic–Dynamic Aspect of Ecology." This event may serve to mark the full-blown arrival of the New Ecology. It also coincided roughly with the beginnings of the "Age of Ecology" in postwar Anglo-American culture, the appearance of a wide consciousness of ecological concepts in popular environmental thought. But there was no real connection between the two; indeed, it is safe to say that few in the general public would ever hear of Lindeman or understand what he had accomplished. When his paper was published, he would have been only twenty-seven years old. But shortly before its appearance he died, following a long illness, and the scientific community lost one of its most brilliant new minds. According to his Yale teacher G. Evelyn Hutchinson, Lindeman "came to realize, as others before him had done, that the most profitable method of analysis lay in the reduction of all the interrelated biological events to energetic terms." Hutchinson should have added economics to that reductive breakthrough, for the peculiarity of this new scientific paradigm lay in the fact that energy became economic. "Here for the first time," Hutchinson noted, "we have the interrelated dynamics of a biocoenosis [i.e., an ecological community, or rather, ecosystem] presented in a form that is amenable to a productive abstract analysis."[17]

The specific environment Lindeman studied was Cedar Bog Lake in Minnesota. Such lacustrine systems again and again proved to be the best exemplars of the processes of energy capture and use, chiefly because of the simplified plant populations and the ease of biomass measurement there. But Lindeman's paper was much more than a report on this lake as an isolated example; he wanted to pull together all the major ecological theorizing of the past several decades, including Clements' notion of succession toward climax, into one grand model of "energy-availing" relationships in nature. And he succeeded brilliantly. "Trophic–Dynamic" in the paper's title meant the ecosystem's food or energy cycle, the metabolism of the whole. All resident organisms, he pointed out, may be grouped into a series of more or less discrete "trophic levels": the familiar producers, primary consumers, secondary consumers, decomposers. Other terms might also be used here, such as "autotrophs" for the plants, which generally create their own food by photosynthesis, and "heterotrophs" for animals and bacteria, which must feed on other organic tissues. In the Minnesota lake, the producers were the macrophytic pond weeds and, more important, the microphytic phytoplankton. On these fed the browsers—tadpoles, ducks, certain fishes and insects, tiny copepods and other zooplankton—filling a niche similar to that occupied by terrestrial herbivores. On the browsers in turn depended the second-order consumers, which included other fish, crustaceans, turtles, frogs, and birds. A snapping turtle or an osprey, both carnivorous predators, might represent the third-order consumer. Last came the countless millions of decomposers, bacteria and fungi, which lived in the slimy bottom mud and worked to break down organic substance into recyclable nutrients.

The single most important fact about these trophic levels, in Lindeman's view, was that the energy in use at one level can never be passed on in its entirety to the next higher level. A portion is always lost in the transfer as heat escaping into the atmosphere. The chief goal of Lindeman's ecology was to quantify these losses: to make precise measurements of the shrinkage in available energy as it passes through the ecosystem. He wanted to know, that is, the "productivity" of each level in the food chain and the "efficiency" of energy transfers. Productivity in this case referred not to the numbers of a given species but to the accumulated biomass at any trophic level and the caloric energy required to support that amount of organic matter. Like a farmer figuring his bushels per acre, the ecologist must harvest the "standing crop" or output at each level, weigh it, and compute the energy it took to grow that crop, whether it be plankton, spruce forest, alfalfa, or grasshoppers. But the ecologist must also estimate how much energy/matter in the crop has been already consumed by herbivores (or birds or budworms), as well as the amount used by the crop itself for its own growth and development. This wider value was the "gross production," the sum total of all energy/matter stored or spent at any trophic level. "Net production" was what was left after the energy/matter utilized in respiration was subtracted. Both figures were given in calories (or gram calories). And "productivity" was expressed in terms of the number of calories used, for one purpose or another, on a single square meter or centimeter during a year.

Once the ecologist had these productivity figures in hand for all the trophic levels, he could discover what happens to the captured solar energy as it moves through the ecosystem. He could calculate, that is, the "ecologic efficiencies" of organisms: how much energy they are able to utilize from lower levels and how much of that they in turn pass on, as well as how much they use up in metabolism. At Cedar Bog Lake, Lindeman discovered that the producers on the first level captured only one-tenth of 1 percent of the sun's radiation striking the lake's surface—an even less efficient capture than Juday's Lake Mendota and much less than Transeau's cornfield. The rest of the incident solar radiation was reflected back into space. Of this primary production, over one-fifth was expended in plant respiration, leaving most of the other four-fifths—or the net production—available for the herbivorous consumers. But the herbivores, Lindeman observed, ate only 17 percent of the net production of the plants; the rest went unused or was decomposed. And of what the herbivores did eat, 30 percent was needed for their own metabolism. Then came the carnivores, which consumed only 28.6 percent of their available food energy. To eat more would be to destroy their food base's ability to survive and reproduce effectively; that 28.6 percent was apparently all that they could safely harvest. But the carnivores also used, on the average, 60 percent of their caloric intake in respiration. They had to be more mobile to catch their food, and consequently their metabolism rates were the highest in the food chain.

These efficiency quotients established for Lindeman two main patterns in energy flow. First, organisms become progressively more efficient in their extraction of energy from lower levels as one moves up the food chain. From the 0.10 percent of solar energy captured by the Cedar Bog plants, the efficiency of energy transfer jumped to the 28.6 percent the carnivores harvested from the herbivores' net production (22.3 percent of their gross production). Second, respiration takes an even bigger chunk of the energy as one travels up the chain, rising in Lindeman's sample from 21 percent for plants to 60 percent for carnivores. From these results, it was more than ever clear why Elton's pyramid of numbers had to be so. From a broad base, the natural economy tapered upward toward a progressive diminution of energy. Lawrence Slobodkin has suggested that the average efficiency in energy transfer is about 10 percent. Out of 100 calories of net plant production, only 10 calories could be expected at the herbivore level, and only 1 calorie at the carnivore level. But as Lindeman's and a number of later studies demonstrate, the range about this mean is wide: from 5 to 30 percent, with no consistency in any one ecosystem.[18]

Finally, there was a third pattern in energy flow that Lindeman discovered, one that gave new life and credibility to the Clements theme of plant succession. In the early stages of the successional sere, productivity increases rapidly. This is true equally for the colonization of a bare terrestrial area or for the youthful period of a pond. In the case of the pond, the pioneer stage is oligotrophy, when there is abundant oxygen but few dissolved nutrients in the lake, resulting in that sparklingly clear water often seen in high mountain tarns. Few plants or animals can live in such conditions. Then with the increasing influx of nutrients from the surrounding drainage basin, the condition alters from oligotrophy to mesotrophy to eutrophy to senescence. At first, productivity shoots up dramatically, but in the last stages, the production of organic matter begins to outstrip the rate at which it can be oxidized. The oxygen supply is depleted—and without oxygen, productivity soon falls to zero. Such a process of eutrophication or aging does not come to every pond or lake, only to those in regions well supplied with nutrients. Eventually, as the senescent body of water collects more and more nutrients and detritus, it passes into the rejuvenating, pioneer stages of a terrestrial ecosystem. The dying pond becomes a bog and, eventually, a forest. Once more productivity begins to go up. At the subclimax stage of this second order of vegetation, productivity reaches another peak, then slacks off to some extent during the reign of the climax equilibrium. Lindeman's Cedar Bog Lake had reached the point of senescence, hence its low 0.10 percent photosynthetic efficiency. Lake Mendota, on the other hand, was still in the early stages of eutrophy, and its first level of primary efficiency was a higher 0.35 percent.

More recently, scientists have argued that, in general, land ecosystems show higher productivity and efficiency than aquatic systems, though the exceptions are important. About 80 percent of the earth's surface is ocean and desert, the least productive natural areas. Lack of nutrients in the one case, and lack of moisture in the other, are the limiting factors. The desert ecosystem, the least abundant of all, may produce anywhere from 200 to 600 kilocalories per square meter per year (200–600 $kcal/m^2/yr$), the oceans twice that amount. In an oak or maple forest, as a point of comparison, productivity climbs to 3,600–6,000 $kcal/m^2/yr$; in a spruce woods to 8,400–13,000; in a tropical rain forest to 16,000–24,000. It has long been understood that the most productive natural ecosystems on the earth are in the tropics, where there is both abundant sunshine and rainfall. Among temperate-zone systems, the salt marshes and reed and cattail swamps rank highest. As far as man's own contrived ecosystems are concerned, the American farmer's corn or wheatfield produces on the average 7,500–10,000 $kcal/m^2/yr$—better than a deciduous forest in temperate latitudes, but a poor showing next to a coral reef or a Brazilian jungle. Asian rice paddies do much better; and a Hawaiian sugar plantation, raising a perennial, year-round crop of cane under intense sunlight, may be the world's superproducer—26,500–34,500 $kcal/m^2/yr$. But in all these ecosystems, natural or artificial, the primary efficiency of solar energy capture is typically about 1 percent. Nowhere on earth do plants manage to hold onto more than a minimal sliver of the sun's radiation. And what is not used is immediately lost for all time into the dark heatsink of outer space. It cannot be collected again. Therefore, it pays to make hay while the sun shines. When that great light goes out, all the food factories of the world must stop.[19]

These then are the formative episodes in the development of the New Ecology, an energy–economic model of the environment that began to emerge in the 1920s and was virtually complete by 1950. It is safe to say that this model is still widely followed in Anglo-American ecology. After Lindeman, a new breed of like-minded mathematical ecologists appeared on the academic scene, and they pushed their subject to the front ranks of the "hard sciences." Among the post-war leaders in this surge toward respectability was Lindeman's teacher at Yale, G. Evelyn Hutchinson, as well as Edward Deevey, David Gates, John Phillipson, George Woodwell, Robert MacArthur, and, probably most important of all, Eugene Odum. Not all the older models were abruptly set aside, it is true, but the bioeconomics paradigm ruled. In scientific journals, ecologists reported with an increasingly recondite abstractness and precision on the field-mouse production in an acre of grassland or the "energy budget" of a lizard on a tree trunk. Or they described the newest method for measuring the gain and loss of "nutrient capital" in the soil. Even Thoreau's Walden Pond was measured to determine its "total energy income." In short, ecology at last emerged as a full-blown science of natural economics, fulfilling a vague promise more than two centuries old.[20]

Unrelated as it may have seemed at first, energy turned out to be the key that opened the gate to the economic approach. Without thermodynamics, ecologists might still have been shuffling descriptive labels around and arguing over whether a proclimax precedes or follows a climax and whether a clan is more or less inclusive than a consociation. The "economy of nature" would still be a phrase of loose content. Of course, the study of energy in nature did not necessarily imply an economic framework. But that was the way it was assimilated. Furthermore, by incorporating the idea of energy flow into a larger economic model, the New Ecology established a unique identity among the sciences, rather than becoming subsumed under physics. Without economics, ecologists might have disappeared as an

Producers and Consumers • 311

independent class of researchers; as it is, ecology claimed a clear, safe, and highly prominent place squarely between the two most influential academic disciplines of our time.

To explain this pattern of events simply by the inner dynamics of the scientific world is not very persuasive. It is obvious that the rise of a bioeconomic ecology owed a great deal to its larger cultural milieu. To begin with, there was at work here the still-vigorous influence of Progressive conservation philosophy. In its early years, that program of prudent economic development lacked a practical model for the processes of the natural economy. In 1917 Richard Ely, a professor of political economy at the University of Wisconsin, defined conservation as the division of economics that deals with production. But he did not have then, nor did Gifford Pinchot, a full scientific understanding of how the natural economy in fact works, or any measurements of its productive efficiencies, or in general any mathematical tools for dealing with that system. Without such scientific guidance, neither the economist nor the bureaucrat could go very far toward managing the land for higher production. The scientists of the New Ecology filled these gaps, however belatedly. Indeed, their science was almost perfectly tailored for the needs of a modern-day Ely or Pinchot. Many people wanted to make conservation "applied ecology"; it is less commonly realized that ecology, conversely, became "theoretical conservation." That is, the science came to reflect the agronomic attitude toward nature that Progressive conservationists preached. How else are we to interpret the prominence of "productivity," "efficiency," "yield," and "crop" in the New Ecology's vocabulary? In turn, the New Ecology provided at last the precise guidelines and analytical tools required to farm intensively all the earth's resources. Lacking them, agronomic conservation would have to flounder along in trial-and-error ineptitude.[21]

Other, broader influences were at work on the New Ecology to make it conform so neatly to modern society and its expectation of nature. Darwinism occupied a diminished place in the newest textbooks; the ecosystem, with its interdependent trophic levels, projected a more up-to-date view of the natural order. The weight of interest lay not in hand-to-hand combat for survival, but with integrated circuitry, geochemical cycling, energy transfer. As a modernized economic system, nature now became a corporate state, a chain of factories, an assembly line. Conflict could have little place in such a well-regulated economy. Even strikes were unheard of: The green plants went on producing for the herbivores without shirking, feather-bedding, or complaining. On one of Eugene Odum's flow-charts of an ecosystem, all the energy lines moved smartly along, converging here and shooting off there, looping back to where they began and following the thermodynamic arrows in a mannerly march toward the exit points. A traffic controller or warehouse superintendent could not have asked for a more well programmed world. In this age of computer-run organizations and the carefully arbitrated resolution of all discords, it was probably inevitable that ecology too would come to emphasize the flow of goods and services—or of energy—in a kind of automated, robotized, pacified nature.

Finally, there was the managerial ethos. Here again, ecology kept pace with the times. To an extent that Darwin or John Ray would find incomprehensible, the New Ecologist commonly stepped forward to manage the natural environment. That it had been mismanaged for so long was urged as a sufficient reason for putting scientists and scientifically trained experts in charge now. Entire university science programs appeared under the title "Environmental Management." And indeed, bioeconomics gave the would-be managers plenty to work on; despite its impressive order, nature had all those low productivities and whopping inefficiencies in energy capture to improve. The Baconian sense of mission was not yet dead. N. P. Naumov, probably the leading ecologist in the Soviet Union in his day, admitted that "the goal of studying the factors of productivity is to raise it." This ideal, he suggested, may be realized "by changing organic nature, the species content and ratios, and the means of using and managing the populations." The American forest ecologist Stephen Spurr found in the ecosystem model a more pliable sort of nature. "Beneficial management," he explained, "involves manipulation to maximize the returns to man, while exploitation is management that results in the reduction of the productivity of

Producers and Consumers • 313

the ecosystem over a period of time." And the Canadian-born Kenneth E. F. Watt demonstrated in his book *Ecology and Resource Management* that the new ecological principles lent themselves easily to the agronomic desire to "optimize the harvest of useful tissue,...to obtain maximum production compatible with stability of production."[22]

Not every scientist wanted to be an earth manager, it must be said. And many were strongly critical of the ends toward which society manipulated nature. But it is not fanciful to attribute to the mechanistic, energy-based bioeconomics of the New Ecology a built-in bias toward the management ethos, and even toward a controlled environment serving the best interests of man's economy. In this respect, H. G. Wells and Julian Huxley were again prophetic voices: "Life under Control" was the technocratic vision they announced in a chapter title in 1939. The means to that end were not only to make ecology "an extension of economics to the whole world of life," but also "to make the vital circulation of matter and energy as swift, efficient, and wasteless as it can be made." That, to a large extent, was also the aim of the New Ecology.[23]

If society and its economics shaped the New Ecologists, that influence was a two-way street; we must also ask what cultural impact their account of nature had. Modern man depends heavily on the scientist to explain what kind of world we live in, and now the ecologist's answer was: an economic one. All creatures on the earth are related to one another essentially as producers and consumers; interdependence in such a world must mean sharing a common energy income. And as part of nature, man must be considered primarily as an economic animal—he is at one with all life in a push for greater productivity. Within the scope of bioeconomics, there was little room for that arcadian sense of fellowship found in the science of Gilbert White, Thoreau, or Darwin. Perhaps that spirit of deeper kinship was always an anachronism in a scientific age—a carry-over from a prescientific, pagan frame of mind. And perhaps science is inherently an alienating force, always trying to reduce nature to a mechanistic or physico-chemical system with which only an economic relation is conceivable. In the next chapter these issues, which must be the ultimate questions, will be considered in greater detail.

The New Ecology seemed to suggest a tightly constricted view of nature and of man's place therein. In view of the authority science claims over the interpretation of nature, and which it in fact exercises, it seems reasonable that popular environmental thinking was drawn toward a similarly narrow bioeconomic outlook. From this vantage point, ecology did not seem a very promising counterforce to an economic attitude toward the natural world. The tendency to find in nature a utilitarian, materialistic promise—a set of resources with cash value—was not likely to be overcome, as Aldo Leopold and others had hoped, by following a science that was itself based on an economic model. The best that might be hoped for from the science of ecology, at this turn, was the more careful management of those resources, to preserve the biotic capital while maximizing the income. That of course is a thoroughly sensible strategy in any household, the earth's included. But Leopold had more in mind for his land ethic. He envisioned a "community instinct," by which he meant something close to the arcadian dream of fellow feeling. It was hard, maybe impossible, to derive such a communal sensibility from ecosystem energetics or from trophic—dynamic analysis of the environment. For this reason communalism must find another source of intellectual support than the New Ecology—whether in some other scientific model or beyond science.

CHAPTER 15

Declarations of Interdependence

"ONE-EYED REASON, deficient in its vision of depth." Thus did the Anglo-American philosopher Alfred North Whitehead describe the scientific thought of the eighteenth century. In their approach to nature, he argued, the major thinkers of that age had frozen the mechanical philosophy of Descartes, Galileo, and Newton into a dogmatic reduction of all human experience to "clear-cut definite things, with clear-cut definite relations." And they invariably restricted those relations to the measurable, quantitative impingement of hard material objects, or masses, on one another. Scientific or mechanistic materialism was the name Whitehead gave to this mode of abstraction. It selected from the multitude of experience only those qualities that could be explained by physicochemical laws. Consequently, all nature came via this approach to appear "senseless, valueless, purposeless." Moreover, every plant or animal, every rock crystal or particle of interstellar gas, was held to follow a fixed routine "imposed by external relations which do not spring from the nature of its being." Such thinking, Whitehead maintained, could well boast of its achievements in positive knowledge and of the technological progress it furthered, but as an account of the world he condemned it as willful blindness.[1]

In *Science and the Modern World*, Whitehead claimed that the mechanistic analysis of nature had dominated western thinking, to one degree or another, for three full centuries. But writing in 1925, freshly uprooted from his native England to America, he foresaw the advent of "an age of reconstruction" in science and culture. Reductivism and the unassailable sovereignty of the physical sciences were on the way out; in times to come, biology and the living creature would command much more respect. And as a result, man's perception of nature would recover some of its rich, concrete diversity; its self-determining freedom; its depth, complexity, even mystery, of character; its intrinsic purpose and value. It was to be, in short, an age of organicism. Henceforth scientists would emphasize process, creativity, indefiniteness, the "organic unity of a whole," and "the realisation of events disposed in an interlocked community." Most succinctly, what had been missing from science during those three hundred years, and was now to be revived, was a vision of vital *relatedness*. As in an organism, Whitehead held, the various parts of nature are so closely interdependent, so densely woven into a single web of being, that none may be abstracted without altering its own identity and that of the whole. Everything is hooked to everything else—not superficially, as in a machine, but essentially, as in the human body. Only by rediscovering this depth of relatedness could science be restored to full sight.[2]

To radically restructure the scientific account of nature to accord with the behavior of the organism, so that even the physicist's atom would be seen as a kind of pulsing amoeba pushing its way through space, was no small revolution. It was like picking up a stick and finding in your hand a lively, wriggling snake instead. But Whitehead found encouraging signs that such a reversal was in fact underway, not least in recent developments in the physical sciences themselves. The new theory of relativity, the study of quantum mechanics, and the principle of indeterminacy in matter, all suggested a more complicated, indefinite, unpredictable world than earlier scientists would acknowledge. Among these organismic trends in science, Whitehead might also have included the *gestalt* movement in psychology, which attempted to study the function of the mind as a configuration or pattern of interrelated events rather than a set of independent ideas, sensations, and reflexes. He might have added, too, the emergence of ecology as a mature science, one that was inescapably a relational discipline speaking a relational language. It had been so since its earliest stages, and at the time of Whitehead's writing it was becoming increasingly conscious of its unique ability to see nature as a whole rather than as a series of discrete pieces. True, most of its key scientists would eventually become converts to the physico-chemical doctrine; but for many others, ecology would go on representing the vision of organic relatedness Whitehead articulated. In the public awareness, at least, ecology was on its way to becoming the chief expression of the philosophy of an interdependent nature; this was apparent by the 1930s and even more widely acknowledged by the 1960s. And Whitehead himself can be fairly described as a major prophet of that movement.[3]

Behind the resurgent organicism in ecology and elsewhere, there lay a compelling moral concern, one that Whitehead revealed at a number of points. For example, in discussing the Romantics—his philosophical predecessors—he spoke of the poet Wordsworth's "moral repulsion" toward the mechanistic point of view: "He felt that something had been left out, and that what had been left out comprised everything that was most important." That was Whitehead's complaint, too. Nature had been abruptly exiled by the scientific mechanists from the realms of value, ethics, and beauty. None of these qualities could have an objective existence in the world of matter; they were "secondary" or subjective properties, located only in the mind of the observer and hence irrelevant to the scientific enterprise.[4]

In addition, the sciences had taught men that bodies and minds are "independent individual substances, each existing in its own right apart from any necessary reference to each other." The mechanical philosophy, in other words, functioned as an ontological version of individualism; as a consequence, it gave strong philosophical support to an atomistic social ethic, especially in England and America. This influence was manifested at its worst in the nineteenth century's militantly self-centered *laissez-faire* economy. The materialism of scientific reduction led to materialism of another kind: the singleminded focus on making money, regardless of the social costs.[5]

Whitehead's central theme in *Science and the Modern World* was that the very methods of analysis used by the scientist—not just the technological application of his researches—have moral consequences. After Descartes, ethical and aesthetic values alike had been widely ignored by science, or dismissed as extraneous to the work at hand, be it in the laboratory or factory. Ultimately, therefore, organicism was a movement to restore moral values to the pursuit of science. In particular, by emphasizing the quality of relatedness in the natural world, it would teach mankind a new ethic of interdependence. "Actuality is through and through togetherness," declared Whitehead. That awareness in the theories of science, he predicted, would have sweeping moral consequences for western culture.[6]

Ecology, under its own name, did not appear explicitly in Whitehead's search for relatedness. But in seeking a concrete illustration of what he meant by this quality, he turned to an example that was thoroughly ecological. He compared nature in all its realms to a Brazilian rain forest populated by a wide diversity of tree species, all mutually cooperating.

A single tree by itself is dependent upon all the adverse chances of shifting circumstances. The wind stunts it: the variations in temperature check its foliage: the rains denude its soil: its leaves are blown away and are lost for the purpose of fertilization. You may obtain individual specimens of fine trees either in exceptional circumstances, or where human cultivation has intervened. But in nature the normal way in which trees flourish is by their association in a forest. Each tree may lose something of its individual perfection of growth, but they mutually assist each other in preserving the conditions for survival. The soil is preserved and shaded; and the microbes necessary for its fertility are neither scorched, nor frozen, nor washed away. A forest is the triumph of the organisation of mutually dependent species.

This example represented at once a practical solution to the challenge of environment, a moral ideal of togetherness, and a warning to science not to mistake, in its analytical strategies, the trees for the forest.[7]

The ethic of unrestrained individualism, as well as the mechanistic reductiveness of science, began to encounter a number of other critics around the time that Whitehead came to the United States. There was Lewis Mumford, agitating from the 1920s on for an "organic ideology" that would restore communal values to America—an ideal influenced by the ecological botany of his Scots teacher Patrick Geddes. There was the new communitarian sociology of Robert Park and his students at the University of Chicago, who likewise modeled some of their ideas on the principles of ecology. And many ecologists of the day were not reluctant to draw from their own science a critique of individualism; C. C. Adams, in particular, understood the relevance of Whitehead, Mumford, and Geddes to his work and claimed that, conversely, ecology had much to teach social thinkers about the value of cooperation. In 1935 the Southwestern naturalist Walter Taylor declared that ecology shows "there is little rugged individualism in nature." The biotic community, he went on, acts as a "closely organized cooperative commonwealth of plants and animals . . . [which] is more nearly an individual organism than any of its parts." One year later, in his presidential address before the Ecological Society of America, Taylor added that the key words in his discipline were "integration, *Einheit*, correlation, coordination, synthesis." Among the sciences, ecology was unusually "organicist" or "holistic" in its outlook. As Taylor pointed out, the American Secretary of Agriculture Henry Wallace had recently suggested that "there is as much need today for a Declaration of Interdependence as there was for a Declaration of Independence in 1776."[8]

But the ecologist who spoke most consistently for the organismic philosophy during the early decades of the twentieth century was Whitehead's colleague at Harvard, William Morton Wheeler. Significantly, Wheeler was a lifetime student of the social insects and perhaps the world's leading authority on the ants and termites; from these minuscule creatures he first learned the lesson of self-abnegation and natural interdependence. In a 1910 lecture at Woods Hole, Massachusetts, he depicted the ant colony as a full-fledged "organism"—a comparison he hoped would be taken quite literally by other scientists. An organism, as he put it, may be any "complex, definitely coordinated and therefore individualized system of activities" that carries on all the necessary bodily functions, such as nutrition, reproduction, and self-protection. A nest of ants fitted that definition handily. Most of the ants performed a food-gathering and storing role for the group; a select few were the reproductive organs; and, finally, there was a defensive army. Apparently Wheeler, like Frederic Clements, first came upon this organismic idea through reading Herbert Spencer. And like that polysyllabic genius of Victorian England, Wheeler began stacking up hierarchies of organic wholes. First, at the subcellular level, were "biophores"; then cells; then the individual organism as a whole. At the next level came the various social groups, from the ant colony to the human family to the nation. And finally, embracing all animate existence, was the greater ecological order. The latter societies Wheeler distinguished as "comprehensive" organisms; they were different from other living systems only in their larger scale and consequent looseness of integration. But all exhibited in some measure the quality of organismic interrelatedness he had first observed in the ants.[9]

Through Wheeler's work, the study of ecology incorporated yet another dimension of organic philosophy: the theory of emergent evolution. This notion came to be so thoroughly absorbed into ecological rhetoric that its roots were often forgotten. Emergence was the brainchild of Lloyd Morgan, though its rough outlines had been sketched by the ubiquitous Spencer, and showed, too, the surviving influence of Romantic idealism. In brief, Morgan was trying to locate a middle ground during the prolonged and bitter wrangles between mechanists and vitalists that went on around the turn of the century. The mechanists, led by Harvard physiologist Jacques Loeb among others, had failed to convince Morgan, Wheeler, and other scientists that the essence of life could be replicated in a test tube. The vitalists, who included Henri Bergson and Hans Driesch, had for their part failed to give the scientist something he could work with. Their *élan vital* and "entelechies" seemed to be mystifications, high-sounding labels attached to ignorance, rather than testable hypotheses. The emergentist's way out of this impasse was to argue that nature evolves by sudden leaps. From matter, in a burst of unexpected creativity, emerged the phenomenon of life, and from protoplasm, all improbably, sprang the mind of man. None of these three levels could be studied by the methods used for the others; each required its own special science. As Lloyd Morgan explained it, an emergent was a radically new thing on earth, a being impossible to reduce to a lower level. The most important point about emergence was that it made for unpredictable outcomes in nature. Put substances together under the right circumstances and there was no saying what would happen: life evolving from insensate matter, or mind from the haphazard gropings of protoplasm. When A and B were mixed in the same pot, in other words, the result might be a fresh synthesis rather than a mere mechanical or additive mixture: not AB but C. The theory of emergence thus challenged the entire notion of scientific causality by contending that the consequent just might be fundamentally different from its antecedents. Arthur Lovejoy, in an essay on emergence, speculated: "There may yet emerge out of the latent generative potencies of matter, as they certainly have emerged before in our strange planetary history, new and richer forms of being, such as no prescience of ours could foresee, and no contrivance of ours create."[10]

To Morgan's three levels of emergence—matter, life, and mind—enthusiastic converts began adding others, until the whole doctrine threatened to collapse under the sheer weight of categories. It seemed that everywhere one looked, new synergistic entities were flashing into being from even the most casual intercourse of atomic particles. The outcome of emergence could be a substance as basic as water—an emergent from two gases—or as complexly marvelous as the human brain. And every one of these new levels was an irreducible whole, a synthesis of parts that had left their previous identities behind and become understandable only in their new context. *All* reality, announced J. C. Smuts in 1926, is aggregative, contextual, emergent; "and the progressive development of the resulting wholes at all stages—from the most inchoate, imperfect, inorganic wholes to the most highly developed and organised—is what we call Evolution." Clearly, then, Whitehead was not alone in his search for an alternative to mechanistic materialism. Indeed, the emergentists had made extensive, sometimes extravagant, use of the principle of organicism a decade or two before Whitehead restrained and refined it in the interests of higher philosophy.[11]

It was William Morton Wheeler who gave the theory of emergence a distinctly ecological cast. At the Sixth Congress of Philosophy in 1926 he allowed that some levels of emergence were questionable, or at least appeared less suddenly than had been proposed. The mind, for instance, seemed from a biological, if not a philosophical, vantage point to be simply the final stage of a long accumulation of "minimal emergences." But the most defensible kinds of levels, he believed, were those that had also been the most neglected: the social and ecological groupings in nature, including his organismic ant colony. "Association," he maintained, "may be regarded as the fundamental condition of emergence." These emergent social levels might be comprised of all one species—nature's traditional societies or communities—or they might be heterogeneous aggregates of organisms, organized variously as predator and prey, parasite and host, or as a symbiotic union, paradoxically emerging from one of the less benign levels. And here again, all these sublevels were bound together in the biocoenosis, the ecological community, Darwin's web of life. On this higher level, as on the others, the component species were modified by the process of ecological association, and new qualities appeared in their behavior. The deer came to reflect the presence of the wolf (and vice versa); the bird, the tree; the seaweed, the tidal flow. At every level new patterns of integration formed, so prolific and inclusive that no creature could escape their influence. "There are, in fact, no truly solitary organisms," Wheeler observed; "there is something fundamentally social in living things." Thus ecological emergence led straight back to Whitehead's favorite theme of relatedness as the most conspicuous quality of nature.[12]

In the convergence of all of these different strategies on a common organic creed, there was apparent, if subtly at times, a resurgence of philosophical idealism. Especially important to the idea of emergence, for example, was the nineteenth-century Hegelian notion of nature struggling forward to final perfection, passing en route through a series of metamorphoses. More generally speaking, holism, organicism, and integration could all trace their ancestry to an older idealist tradition: the One incorporating the many in a single, common body. Idealism had never been content with the merely physical world and, since Plato, had fastened its hopes on ultimately achieving an unblemished, immaterial, eternal Idea. This quest for transcendence remained active in the new organicism. Alfred North Whitehead spoke of religion as "the vision of something which stands beyond, behind, and within, the passing flux of immediate things." And certainly, part of the motive behind his organic philosophy was to reconcile science with this ancient faith in an "eternal harmony" and a mystical, unitive force of cosmic "love."[13]

More often, though, the new organicists were less forthright about their idealistic, transcendental underpinnings, or perhaps just less aware of them. They were scientists, after all, or scientifically inclined philosophers, and consequently were uncomfortable with some of the idealist's airy phrases. Above all, they were constrained by their science to stick close to the observable world of matter, imperfect though it might be, rather than fly off in pursuit of immaterial powers and harmonies that defied all analysis whatsoever. In a manner of speaking, they discovered it was possible to adopt the idealist's organicism, while rejecting his explanation—or lack of one—for what holds this world together. The trick in this selective borrowing was to suggest, through empirically verifiable methods, how matter alone manifests the same deep, incommensurable relatedness that idealists had discerned in the organization of nature. This was the principal ambition of Whitehead, Morgan, Wheeler, and a long series of organismic ecologists.

What kept them going, even in the face of failure to impress their colleagues, was more often than not a fervent moral concern. They needed the idealist's organic perspective, whatever its scientific value, as a personal antidote to the fragmented culture around them. Wheeler found in his ant colony a reassuring capacity for "egoistic altruism" in nature: the competitive struggle for existence, "which used to be painted in such lurid colors," was belied by the ability of organisms to inhibit their selfish drives in the interests of their larger welfare and that of other creatures. While he might live, as he believed, in a time of social "disintegration," Wheeler could see in the example of organismic science the promise of "a biologically renovated" morality; he could envision the impending emergence of "greater solidarity and higher ethics." The ecological linking of organicism and emergence made it possible for Wheeler to criticize self-assertion in modern American society and at the same time to predict that further evolution would remedy that fault. Many have noted that organismic idealism has been a constant correlative of the fear of social disorder, *anomie*, and alienation, as with the Romantics a hundred years before Wheeler's time. Man's world is chaotic and divisive; in contrast, nature's is a closely knit community, a universal symbiosis, a single complex organism transcending all petty conflicts. It is a field of matter interfused by vital currents, a life force, an *Anima Mundi*, a Platonic Idea, or what you will. In these variations on the theme of organic relatedness, men and women living in a fragmented age have found a standard of coherence against which to measure their culture.[14]

Anxiety over man's changing relation to nature was another motive, for many, in the renewed quest for an organic science. Since the breakdown of man's preindustrial rural intimacy with the natural world, ecological organicism had been a well-traveled avenue to escape from the debasement of the man–nature community to a bare economic nexus. In this regard Wheeler was again representative. In one of his several defenses of the old-style naturalist against the modern professional, he declared that the former is, like an artist,

more desirous of appreciating and understanding than of explaining the phenomena with which he deals. This may account for the non-mathematical and non-experimental spirit in which he approaches and handles his materials. It may also account for his somewhat unsympathetic attitude towards the bright high school boys now bombinating in the biological laboratories of our universities. He feels that not a few of these neophytes manifest a somewhat gangster attitude towards Nature, so eager are they to assault, scalp or rape her. . . .

Declarations of Interdependence • 325

The vision of organic relatedness clearly fulfilled a fundamental moral need, cautioning in this case against hubris in man's attitude toward nature. Mankind's assertion of supremacy over the natural world was seen as a dangerous form of individualism: one species pursuing its self-interest at the expense of all the others. As Whitehead tied such egoism within human society to the mechanistic philosophy, Wheeler likewise linked environmental exploitation to science's irreverent and reductive analysis of nature. All were consequences, one could say, of "one-eyed reason, deficient in its vision of depth."[15]

After William Morton Wheeler, the leadership among ecological organicists passed into the eminently respectable hands of the "Ecology Group" at the University of Chicago, and their contributions would uplift and sustain the movement for years to come. During the 1930s and -40s this cluster of scientists gathered informally every other Monday evening in the parlor of Professor Warder Allee to share their findings and insights. Allee himself, their guiding spirit, was one of the leading animal ecologists in America and a pious, visionary man who kept the group faithful to its mission: to put ethical idealism on a sound scientific footing. Born in 1885 on a farm near Bloomingdale, Illinois, Allee remained true throughout his life to the influence of his mother, a Quaker. He graduated from a Quaker college, married a Quaker wife, and during the three decades he lived in Chicago was reliably, devoutly attendant at the 57th Street Meeting. From 1921 to 1950, he was a member of the science faculty at the University of Chicago, and in 1929 he was named president of the Ecological Society of America. Around him at Chicago gathered Thomas Park, Alfred Emerson, and Karl Schmidt, as well as Orlando Park from nearby Northwestern University. The offspring of their extended collaboration was the magisterial *Principles of Animal Ecology*, published in 1949 and a classic in its field. (It is now commonly referred to as "AEPPS," after the authors' initials.) The organismic-community concept of modern ecology, the group suggested at one point in that work, "is one of the fruitful ideas contributed by biological science to modern civilization," and certainly it was a chief inspiration in their search for what Emerson called "a scientific basis for ethics." Their earlier, less-known writings stressed this quest even more strongly. There they openly, sometimes dogmatically, strove to extract from nature a set of holistic values to apply to mankind.[16]

Nature, it was their shared conviction, is an other-directed world. The individual counts for little in the ecological order; the social group or the interspecific community is all-important. There are no ecological deviants wandering over the landscape, relishing their sense of apartness; even the "lone wolf" is, in reality, a group-oriented animal. Survival in nature demands participation in the complex network of organisms: a spirit of joining rather than signing off. Allee liked to illustrate this cooperative behavior by citing studies of the effects of toxic reagents on a social organism like a school of fish. When colloidal silver was introduced into their environment, the group as a whole absorbed the poison, so that no one individual got a lethal dose. In other circumstances, the effect of such massing together might be to alter conditions of light intensity, water temperature, or wind velocity toward a more favorable and stable mean. Allee admitted that harmful effects on growth and reproduction could result from too much crowding, but he warned that it was wrong to go to the other extreme—to assume that fewer is always better. In many species, minimal densities are required to successfully cope with environment; therefore, the survival value of forming a crowd is often crucial. These companionable, density-dependent ways could be extended to relations between radically different species: a case in point is the "heterotypical" swarming of many kinds of organisms around a coral reef. In almost all such alliances, cooperation is wholly unconscious—"an automatic mutual interdependence"—which Allee, like Wheeler, took to be "a fundamental trait of living matter."[17]

In September 1941, on the occasion of the fiftieth anniversary of the University of Chicago, the members of the Ecology Group sponsored a symposium on "Levels of Integration in Biological and Social Systems." Other participants included anthropologists Robert Redfield and A. L. Kroeber and sociologist Robert Park. The general consensus of the papers presented was that "the organism and the society are not merely analogues" but virtually the same phenomenon. As Redfield summed up the proceedings, the symposium agreed that "the individual metazoan, the infusorian population, the ant colony, the flock of fowl, the tribe, and the world-economy are all exemplifications of nature's grand strategy": evolution toward greater and greater integration. Even bacteria, even a slime mold, were found to have "synergistic aspects." Confronted with such evidence of nature's overwhelming impulse toward a more tolerant and cooperative unity, mankind had little choice but to submit gracefully. Resist it though they might, men would find themselves compelled to follow Emerson's recommendation and put themselves "in harmony with the forces of progressive evolution which have been directing life since its origin." Apparently that well-used Spencerian–Hegelian maxim could still do service in the quest for a scientific ethic.[18]

Before long, virtually the entire bioscience faculty at Chicago had caught the integrative fever from the AEPPS circle; their colleagues Ralph Lillie, C. M. Child, and Ralph Gerard all eventually brought out their thoughts on the social virtues taught by natural law. Of these three , Gerard was the most earnest; with Allee and Emerson, he must have made Chicago students dizzy, if not claustrophobic, by reciting all the intricate tanglings of ecological interdependence. Gerard's ideas were not really novel, but he did more than anyone else to make plain what had aroused the Chicago organicists to such great moral expectations. In "Higher Levels of Integration," his paper for the anniversary symposium, he concluded that "the ultimate future of human society, however dark it may look to the contemporary sociologist or even to the historian, appears in the eyes of the biologist, sighting down the long perspective of organic evolution, as bright with hope." Those words were uttered in 1941, only a few months before the United States declared war on Hitler, Tojo, and Mussolini. In an age that was charging headlong toward war and totalitarianism, ecological interdependence held a fresh and poignant relevance. On an international level, Gerard admitted, altruism is still a scarce commodity; wars and more wars must occur before "world integration" is finally achieved and "conflicts of the present type become impossible." But until that golden age arrives, he warned, Americans must understand that "isolationism is a biological anachronism." The model of the ecological community, faced with an emergency or outside threat, responds with all shoulders to the common wheel; there are no shirkers or draft evaders in nature. In the biologist's view, the law of life decreed either cooperation for self-preservation, or destruction by one's enemies.[19]

For a more pacific man like Warder Allee, the specter of a suddenly militarizing world must have been a bruising blow to his confidence in the benevolence of natural law. But his response, and that of all the Chicago organicists, was to reaffirm his faith in the overall pattern of increasing worldwide integration based on ecology, regardless of temporary setbacks. Undoubtedly the entire group was whistling in the dark a bit: If they insisted loudly and persistently enough on the inevitability of a harmonious world, they might thereby screw their own courage to the sticking point, and their society's as well. Less than a year after the first atomic bombs were dropped on Japan, Alfred Emerson was still reiterating that "forces are apparent that are guiding us toward an interdependent world unity." Perhaps he had in mind the newly established United Nations as yet another emergent level with organismic promise. That prospect also occurred to Gerard, who earlier had maintained that mankind was moving toward the higher phase of a single world state, or what he called a "human epiorganism."[20]

But the fascist threat represented more than a further stimulus to theories promoting evolutionary progress and international cooperation. Paradoxically, it also taught a harsh lesson on the limits of group conformity. The ideal of social integration, it became starkly clear, could harbor an unexpected danger: the possibility of a totalitarian police state based on the same appeals for self-sacrifice to the whole invoked by the organicists. There was Hitler, calling on pure-blooded Aryans to give their all for the greater glory of the fatherland: Was this where the dream of interdepen-

Declarations of Interdependence • 329

dence led? To tyranny, and to a manipulated, robotized citizenry that had lost all capacity for independent judgment and civil disobedience? Confronted with the example of Nazism, many organicists began to retreat a few paces from the integrative ideal. That kind of state was not at all what they or nature had meant by "relatedness." Their organismic model was, or should have been, intended to be less centralized, less dominated by a single directive power. They understood more fully now the need for a communal system safeguarding diversity, dissent, and individuality— in other words, one in which the traditional Anglo-American personal freedoms could still flourish. For this reason, Wheeler's ant and termite colonies shortly began to disappear from the organicist's pattern book. It was much safer to emphasize the interspecific ecological community, where interdependence existed in a less repressive fashion.

Back in 1920, right after the First World War, William Morton Wheeler had already come to see some of the less innocent aspects of the organismic gospel. He had once celebrated the anthill as a prototype for human society, but the war had shown him quite enough of the ant-like organization man, eager to whip everyone else into a more efficient, well-regulated order. Organisms, Wheeler decided, can become "too integrated" for their own adaptive welfare. His reaction in part was expressed in the desire to see unorganized, primitive wilderness areas set aside on the globe: places where men might go to get away from too much social integration.

As the earth becomes more densely covered with its human populations, it becomes increasingly necessary to retain portions of it in a wild state, i.e., free from the organizing mania of man, as national and city parks or reservations to which we can escape during our holidays from the administrators, organizers, and efficiency experts and everything they stand for; and return to a Nature that really understands the business of organization.

The more spontaneously ordered ecology of the wilderness thus became a means of liberation from the termite-life of technological society, from a world where there was plenty of integration but very little sense of genuine relatedness. Indeed, Wheeler's reaction was thorough enough to make him wonder whether "the optimistic conception of progress as an unceasing movement towards perfection in the human race may be illusory." As civilization advanced, he feared, the individual regressed, until mankind would have descended to the automaton level of the ant—a strict conformist with no sense at all of selfhood.[21]

The Chicago organicists too sounded a note of caution against over-integration now and then. Some reckoned that only the selfish or aggressive aspects of individualism need be transcended; apart from that, the individual should go on preserving its uniqueness. In 1946 Emerson went so far as to allow that even some degree of competition might be tolerable, so long as it did not approach all-out war, and he suggested that a final optimum balance between competitiveness and cooperation might be achieved. Gerard, in response to a critic who had accused him of stoutly supporting Nazi-like repressiveness, maintained that social unification need not lead to coercion or standardization, but rather to "differentiation and free inquiry." But both scientists were certain of one thing: their refusal to abandon the cause of evolution based on organismic law. To retreat from this stand would mean a return to scientific mechanism and all its egoistic moral ills. Somehow the ideal of organic relatedness had to acquire a scientific foundation without libertarian values being endangered in the process.[22]

But before they could fully explore this revised ideal, the Chicago organicists fell silent. After Warder Allee's retirement in 1950, the Ecology Group disbanded, and since then nothing more has been heard from them, singly or collectively. Perhaps the brave new world that followed the war put too great a strain on their optimism and prevented them from persevering further. Or maybe they decided they had succeeded after all in their mission to work out a biology of peace, harmony, and quasi-integration. In any case, their sudden silence left ecological organicism with no important professional voice in the postwar period, and eventually the organismic approach to nature dropped out of the mainstream of the discipline. A few popularizing scientists like Rachel Carson tried to keep the ideal afloat in the 1950s, though without any clear theoretical form, and although the AEPPS textbook continued to be widely used, few paid much attention any longer to its authors' more far-reaching integrative ideals.

By the 1960s, orthodox scientific thought was virtually monopolized by thermodynamics and bioeconomics. The organicists' vision of relatedness was confined to the eco-system model of the New Ecologists, who were quite as reductive in their way as Whitehead's *bêtes noires*, the eighteenth-century *philosophes*. From most professional circles, at least, the metabiological, idealizing tendencies of organicism had been firmly exorcised: Ecology at last had got its head out of the clouds, its feet on solid ground, and its hands on something to measure. After the fading away of the AEPPS group, too, the science was thoroughly disinfected to get rid of every moralizing taint. It was thought that, to qualify as a field of objective knowledge, ecology could have no further dealings with the private, muddled realms of value, philosophy, and ethics. How long the discipline will remain so carefully sterilized is another matter: Organicism has a way of gaining a foothold on even the most unpromising surface.

Although the Chicago school's approach to ecology was not long in being displaced by the hard-nosed positivism of bioeconomics, the urge to explore the interdependence of nature through science did not vanish. On the contrary, what has come to be known in the postwar years as the Age of Ecology is fundamentally the resurgence in popular form of that ambition. Organicism has always had its lay sponsors, and many now have taken up the faith that scientists are increasingly reluctant to acknowledge. Through such widespread nonprofessional enthusiasm, the Age of Ecology has recovered the organic idealist's or mystic's delight in discovering the oneness of life behind the multiplicity of appearance. These latest holists, to be sure, are anxious to claim for their cause the sanction of scientific authority; like Whitehead, Wheeler, and Allee, they argue that science, rightly understood, points the way toward a naturalistic ethic of interdependence. But more often than not, the ecological text they know and cite is either of their own writing or a pastiche from older, superseded models. Few appreciate that the science they are eagerly pursuing took another fork back yonder up the road.

Moreover, the organicism popularly expressed in the Age of Ecology is slightly different in its moral emphasis from its predecessors. Where those earlier seekers after interdependence had taken special interest in working out the salvation of human society, the newer converts are usually more concerned with improving the man–nature relationship. They view ecology as a means to renew the long-lost fellowship and intimacy between man and other living things. A cooperative commonwealth or world brotherhood may be worthy goals, but the task seen as more pressing today is to break down the dualism that isolates man from the rest of nature. There is no precedent in the natural community, say the new organicists, for one species to set itself up as an independent, sovereign kingdom. The idea of man's autarchy can be only a delusion, a kind of schizoid withdrawal into a make-believe world; in truth, there is no escaping the ecological matrix. Once they accept the simple scientific fact of interdependence, men and women can be taught to practice a life-revering ethic such as Aldo Leopold's community citizenship—a close, worldwide relationship between mankind and his biological kin. Whitehead had expressed a similar moral idea, as had many biocentrists, Romantics, and arcadians. But every age believes it has found something new under the sun—and now and then some are right. At the least, one can say that the organicists of the 1960s and -70s go beyond any of their predecessors in promoting what they most often like to call an "ecological ethic": a science-based sense of relatedness between man and nature. Never has it been so widely acknowledged that humanity is not an island unto itself. For many, that realization defines the Age of Ecology.

The Age of Ecology is a still unfolding phenomenon, and we may be too close to it to have a full sense of all its moral ramifications. But one brief reference may serve to sum up how the interdependence ideal has most recently been used and understood. One of the key figures in shaping this new movement was the late Joseph Wood Krutch, who died in 1971 at age seventy-eight. The intellectual conversion that

Krutch underwent may stand for a more general trend in Anglo-American culture. In his earliest work, *The Modern Temper* (published in 1929), Krutch announced that in order to attain full development as a human being he must consciously secede from nature. Man seeks individuality, he contended, but nature does not value the quality, indeed penalizes it in the collective struggle for existence. This was a position perfectly in tune with the alienated mood of 1920s intellectuals. Two decades later, however, he made a dramatic about-face, swinging around to the position that mankind's greater problem was not the stifling of selfhood in group-oriented animal life, but rather the lonely, often desperate isolation of modern man from his only companions on earth—the other species. "We are all in this together," he concluded in 1949, not long after he finished writing a biography of Thoreau. Once a rather melancholic humanist, Krutch now became a kind of pantheist or ethical mystic, caught up in the joy of belonging to "something greater than one's self." Reading Thoreau again and again. was partly responsible for the radical change in his outlook; the other chief stimulus was an education in ecological principles. "Every day," he observed, "the science of ecology is making clearer the factual aspect as it demonstrates those more and more remote interdependencies which, no matter how remote they are, are crucial even for us." Krutch's tutoring in science confirmed him in an organismic sensibility, partly pragmatic but more fundamentally ethical:

We must be a part not only of the human community, but of the whole community; we must acknowledge some sort of oneness not only with our neighbors, our countrymen and our civilization but also some respect for the natural as well as the man-made community. Ours is not only "one world" in the sense usually implied by that term. It is also "one earth." Without some acknowledgement of that fact, men can no more live successfully than they can if they refuse to admit the political and economic interdependency of the various sections of the civilized world. It is not a sentimental but a grimly literal fact that unless we share this terrestrial globe with creatures other than ourselves, we shall not be able to live on it for long.

Science in this case led directly to a moral awakening: a new sense of biological relatedness and communalism.

Krutch was clear-eyed enough to perceive that ecology, "without reverence or love," could become naught but "a shrewder exploitation of what it would be better to admire, to enjoy, and to share in," but his own approach to the science helped turn him from the pursuit of self toward a "sense of the community of living things."[23]

From its impact on Krutch and others, it is clear that ecological biology could still lead to natural piety, no matter how many of its leading scientists had purged themselves of such tendencies. The persistence of this moral undercurrent in an increasingly quantified discipline means, for one thing, that mid-twentieth-century ecology belongs to the lay mind—to the amateur naturalist and the conservationist—as much as to the scientific establishment. Like Thoreau in his time, these people are determined not to wholly surrender this science to academic experts. Ecology has always been unusual among the sciences in its accessibility to the ordinary student of nature; throughout its history it has been shaped by and responsive to the everyday life of all sorts of people: farmers, gamekeepers, foresters, bird watchers, travelers. More than this, it has consistently appealed to many who are otherwise hostile to scientific explanations: It has been a "subversive" or "anti-science" science. Krutch, for one, devoted most of his intellectual life to criticizing reductive and mechanistic science, especially behavioral psychology, before he became more or less reconciled to science via ecology. People such as he, having finally found a science they could trust, were not inclined to give it back to the New Ecologists, with their abstruse calculations of biomass and productivity. As long as ecology was kept in lay hands, it could continue to teach the gospel of organic community, whether or not this was subject to empirical validation.

The hope that nature will show man the way to sound moral values was part of Krutch's faith, and certainly that of the Age of Ecology. But the new organicists are only the latest in a long line of believers who have hitched their wagon to that star: It has been a beacon for Anglo-American culture at least since the eighteenth century. Indeed, few ideas have been recycled as often as the belief that the "Is" of nature must become the "Ought" of man. Ever since Immanuel Kant peremptorily severed the two, men have been trying to stitch them back together, most recently through ecology. Ralph Gerard, among others, contended that a pronounced pattern or observed direction in nature provides man with all the guidance he needs for "should-ness." If nature is found to be a world of interdependence, then man is obliged to consider that characteristic a moral dictum. The evolutionary trend toward closer integration was like a straight path through a dense wood, requiring of the pathfinder that he remain on the track and follow it through. A serious flaw in this argument, of course, is that different men have found different paths, which at times have run at cross-purposes to each other: The social Darwinists were committed to one way, the Chicago organicists to another. The source of much frustration in the search for absolutes is that nature is, above all, protean—far more so than most moral naturalists have been willing to understand. "First follow nature," the sage said. But which road do you take? Whose map do you use? And how can you keep from falling into the ditch?

Over the years, science has probably been the most-used guidebook in this pursuit of moral naturalism. From the divinely contrived balance of Linnaeus and Ray, to Frederic Clements and his climax stage, to Aldo Leopold's ecological ethic, the perennial hope has been that science will show the way. Even those who have been critical of traditional scientific thought, like Krutch and Whitehead, have often found their way back to science, finding its authority indispensable. If mechanistic science produces an every-man-for-himself ethic, then the attempted remedy has been to reform science with organicism, not abandon it altogether.

A little reflection here suggests that "Ought" has been shaping "Is," rather than vice versa. The perceived need for a different ethic demands, as in Whitehead's case, a different perception of nature and a different kind of science. Thus the appeal based on scientific evidence follows rather than precedes the conviction of rightness, and the ultimate source of the moral impulse remains hidden in the human heart. In the case of the ecological ethic, for instance, one might say that its proponents picked out their values first and only afterward came to science for its stamp of approval. It might have been the better part of honesty if they had come out and announced that, for some reason or by some personal standard of value, they were constrained to promote a deeper sense of integration between man and nature, a more-than-economic relatedness—and to let all the appended scientific arguments go. "Ought" might then be its own justification, its own defense, its own persuasion, regardless of what "is."

That more straightforward stance has now and again been adopted by a few intuitionists, mystics, and transcendentalists. Most people, however, have not been so willing to trust their inner voices, perhaps due to lack of self-confidence or out of fear that such wholly individual exercise of choice will lead to the general disintegration of the moral community. Some external and less subjective revelation has been needed and sought through the ages. With the decline of religion and tradition in our own time, science has become the universal standard, and for many, it maintains an aura of absolute sanctity. It is seen as an oracle of objective truth, located well above the shaky ground of moral choice, and therefore a perfectly trustworthy source not only of knowledge but of value. Others, noting how often scientists reflect their cultural milieu, are more skeptical of science's claim to detachment; the quality of trust is strained. But even the somewhat skeptical look to science for the validation of certain truths. If it cannot, by itself, save society, neither can society be saved without it. The moral values inherent in scientific models cannot be accepted without examination, but the guidance such models provide is indispensable.

To judge which of these attitudes is the most valid is not the task at hand. It may be suggested, though, that while "Is" and "Ought" are distinct and unique concepts, any attempt to rigidly separate them is probably misguided. The idea of truth or fact outside the moral context has no meaning for the human mind; it would not be interesting if it did. Whether imperialist, arcadian, organismic, or something else, values have always been woven into the fabric of science. And when the scientist most firmly insists that he has screened out everything but demonstrable fact, he may by that very act, as Whitehead contended, precipitate moral consequences. Of course, some sciences more than others—ecology is perhaps the best example—have an obvious and intimate involvement in social values. But all science, though primarily concerned with the "Is," becomes implicated at some point in the "Ought." Conversely, spinning out moral visions without reference to the material world may ultimately be an empty enterprise; when his moral values depart too far from nature's ways, man will more than likely be frustrated. It may be, too, that in the absence of supernatural guidance, a scientific interpretation of nature is virtually our only remaining source of moral precepts. With all its ambiguities and apparent contradictions, there is really no place to go but nature. It makes sense, then, to keep the difference between "Is" and "Ought" clearly in mind, but not to throw up a wall between them. Scientist and moralist might together explore a potential union of their concerns; might seek a set of empirical facts with ethical meaning, a set of moral truths.

The ecological ethic of interdependence may be the outcome of just such a dialectical relation. It may be, in fact, a moral truth. The intent of these chapters has not been to settle this question with a neat yes or no, but to illuminate the implications of this ethic through an understanding of its roots. In any event, if it is to serve as a ruling value for our time, it must unite a moral sensibility with the testimony of science. Perhaps, too, a quasi-religious conversion, similar to Krutch's, will be needed to open men's eyes to the "oneness" in or beyond nature. Whether this development is likely to come about in our culture the historian is not ready to predict. More to the point here is whether the experience of the past indicates that such an amalgamation of science and moral values is at all feasible. The answer to that question is a cautious yes. Ecological biology, while in general reinforcing certain values more than others, has been and remains intertwined with many of man's ethical principles, social aims, and transcendental ambitions. There is no reason for believing that this science cannot find an appropriate theoretical framework for the ethic of interdependence. If the bioeconomics of the New Ecologists cannot serve, then there are other, more useful, models of nature's economy that await discovery.

PART SIX

THE AGE OF ECOLOGY: SCIENCE AND THE FATE OF THE EARTH

AFTER TWO CENTURIES *of preparation ecology burst onto the international scene during the 1960s. By then scientists of every sort were accustomed to appearing as society's benefactors. They were expected to show nations how to increase their power and citizens how to increase their wealth. But now scientists took on a new role in a more nervous, anxiety-ridden time, for they seemed to hold the secrets of life and death. The physicists, in particular, who created the most terrifying weapon in history, the atomic bomb, were surrounded by an aura like that of the old shamans, manipulating evil spirits. The ecologists, on the other hand, emerged as the guardians of fragile life. The phrase "age of ecology," which came out of the celebration of the first Earth Day in 1970, expressed a grim hopefulness that ecological science would offer nothing less than a blueprint for planetary survival.*

Unfortunately, there were too many contending builders to settle on that blueprint. Ecology achieved intellectual sophistication, academic prominence, and financial security in the postwar years, but also lost much of its coherence. It broke down into a cacophony of subfields, including ecosystematists, populationists, biospherians, theoretical modelers, forest and range managers, agroecologists, toxicologists, limnologists, and biogeographers. Some insisted that human fertility was the greatest threat to the earth, others that industrial pollution was. Nor could

340 • THE AGE OF ECOLOGY

they agree on a basic picture of the world, at least for very long or among a very large group. Some took equilibrium to be the defining quality of nature, others demolished the idea. They had trouble agreeing on how much stability and how much change appeared in nature. They had no end of difficulty in determining what a damaged environment was, or a healthy one. Consequently, ecology could locate no clear, compelling norm in nature for a confused public. Nature was chaos, some even said, and the only order lies in the human mind. Others wondered whether science could ever fully apprehend the intricate complexity of the natural world. An age that began expecting much of science eventually settled for much less: Give us if you can some reliable indication at least of the constraints within which we must live.

CHAPTER 16

Healing the Planet

THE AGE OF ECOLOGY opened on the New Mexican desert, near the town of Alamagordo, on July 16, 1945, with a dazzling fireball of light and a swelling mushroom cloud of radioactive gases. As the world's first atomic bomb went off and the color of the early morning sky changed abruptly from pale blue to blinding white, physicist and project leader J. Robert Oppenheimer felt at first a surge of elated reverence. Then a somber phrase from the *Bhagavad-Gita* flashed into his mind: "I am become Death, the shatterer of worlds." In later years, although Oppenheimer could still describe the making of bombs as "technically sweet," his worry about the consequences of that achievement increased. Other atomic scientists, including Albert Einstein, Hans Bethe, and Leo Szilard, became even more anxiously determined to control that awesome weapon their research had made possible, a determination eventually shared by many ordinary Americans, Japanese, and others. It was increasingly feared that the bomb—however justifiable by the struggle against fascism—had put into humankind's hands a more dreadful power than we might be prepared to handle. For the first time, there existed a technological force that seemed capable of destroying much of the life on the planet. As Oppenheimer warned, humans, through the work of the scientist, now knew sin. The implied question was whether they also knew the way to redemption.[1]

Clearly, Francis Bacon's dream of extending man's empire

over nature, "to the effecting of all things possible," had suddenly taken a macabre, even suicidal, turn. The bomb cast doubt on the entire project of the domination of nature that had been at the heart of modern history. It raised doubts about the moral legitimacy of science, about the tumultuous pace of technology, and about the Enlightenment dream of replacing religious faith with human rationality as the basis of material welfare and virtue. None of those doubts was new, but the development of the atomic bomb gave them an urgency they had never had before. Doubts about the dark side of the Enlightenment legacy spread not only among scientists but also among philosophers, poets, historians, and political leaders.

The fundamental challenge raised by the bomb was whether there was sufficient capacity for restraint in human beings, enough to trust themselves with so much power. Other modern technologies, from the railroad to the airplane, had stirred up controversy, but none of it had significantly slowed their use. There was little precedent, at least in modern Euro-American civilization, for instituting strong collective checks on technological innovations. But the discovery and splitting of the atom was unprecedented too—not at all like laying rails to California, for it involved knowledge of the very structure of matter. The exploitation of that knowledge seemed ultimate, like a divine power. Humans were now playing God. Or were they playing the role of Lucifer, the corrupt angel who rebelled and tried to overthrow the heavenly throne? Theologians might debate the situation, but ultimately the issues must be faced by the new class claiming power, the scientists and technicians, and by the public who had supported them in their uninhibited quest for knowledge. Was either party prepared to exercise restraint over the pursuit of knowledge and its applications? Could either manage to impose effective control over this newest and most deadly military innovation where none had succeeded before? If not, then Bacon's ambition must lead to death and destruction, not only among human beings but among the whole living creation.

The quest for redemption was not slow in finding its voice. Under the threat of the atomic bomb a new moral consciousness called environmentalism began to take form,

Healing the Planet • 343

whose purpose was to use the insights of ecology to restrain the use of modern science-based power over nature. It began, appropriately, in the United States, where the nuclear era was launched, and where, in the summer of 1946, while the afterglow of American victory in the war was still in the air, scientists began to study the environmental effects of manmade radiation. The government planned to test its fourth and fifth bombs (bombs two and three had been dropped on Hiroshima and Nagasaki) in the Marshall Islands, almost three thousand miles south of Hawaii. Here, around a beautiful blue-green lagoon, lay the Bikini Atoll, a necklace of small coral islands that had escaped the ravages of war. The U.S. military chose the site for Operation Crossroads in which they would set off a series of underwater explosions to study the atomic bomb's environmental effects. All the atoll residents were removed, and in their place came 42,000 military personnel, who would watch the experiment. Would the blast open a crack into the subterranean rock, touching off earthquakes all over the world? Would a tidal wave roll from Bikini all the way to Los Angeles? Would the ocean catch on fire? Many worried about the potentially catastrophic environmental effects of this strange new power that had already leveled whole cities, vaporized civilians in their tracks, and left hundreds of thousands of maimed survivors. On July 1 a bomb exploded in the lagoon, lifting millions of tons of water, mud, and ship wreckage into a white column over a mile high, then collapsed back into the ocean, churning up a maelstrom of violence, filling a scoured-out basin with radioactive sludge, while the mushroom cloud of gases and steam continued to mount. A crew in rubber gloves and gas masks shoved a boat into the lagoon to study the impact. They found a live pig blown out of one of the target vessels and floating in the churning water, but there was no tidal wave nor any crack into an abyss. The beaches of Bikini were littered with pieces of rope and canvas, scraps of twisted metal, boards and tires, scums of oil, rusty beer cans, dead fish, and palm fronds, but there were no human casualties. According to relieved officials, the damage was containable and the radioactivity soon dissipated. Nonetheless, the government sent in a team of biologists to study what had happened to the radioactive isotopes. Over the next few years they prowled the sands with Geiger counters, dove into the lagoon waters, and poisoned the fish to study the effects of radiation on them. In what was the first ecological study of the atomic era they wanted to see how the entire food chain had been affected. What they discovered was that, contrary to first impressions, there remained a significant residual radioactivity in the food chain for at least five years after the explosion. Tuna in the surrounding sea carried the residuum in their fatty tissues, and so would anyone who ate them.[2]

The atoll remained a favored site for more weapons testing, including the first American hydrogen fusion bomb, detonated off Namu Island in February 1954. Eighty-five miles away the unsuspecting crew of a Japanese fishing trawler, the *Fukuryu Maru*, was exposed to the H-bomb fallout, and even farther off were a group of Marshall Islanders, who like the fishermen suffered vomiting, burning skin, suppurating lesions, and other radiation-induced sicknesses, some of which lingered for the rest of their lives. Their suffering made them international news, but all were still rather out of American focus.

Less remote and more immediately threatening than the events in the South Pacific was what had begun to take place in the deserts of the American West. Fearful of spies stealing American military secrets (the Russians were now testing their own bombs) and nervous about the high cost of overseas operations, the military moved most of its atomic testing program home to a desolate site north of Las Vegas, the Nevada Proving Grounds, where the first domestic bomb series, code-named Ranger, began in 1951. Here in the southwestern desert, nuclear technology came once more to make grisly progress. The government built a "Doom Town" of suburban-type houses, filled with life-sized mannequins sitting in easy chairs, to determine the potential effects of atomic warfare on its citizens; the fireball from a blast seared not only the dummies and their furniture and automobiles but also the native vegetation of creosote bush and cactus, leaving only bare sand. Hot debris fell repeatedly over the Great Basin throughout the fifties, poisoning flocks of sheep, exposing their herders to damaging radiation, along with other rural residents all over Nevada and Utah, the fallout blowing eastward to Denver, Chicago, and Washington.[3]

The devastation of Bikini Atoll, the poisoning of the domestic and foreign atmosphere with the radioactive isotope strontium 90, and the threat of irreversible genetic damage, along with leukemia, struck the public consciousness with an impact that mere dust storms could never have had. Here was no distant problem or an easily ignored issue; it was a danger to the elemental survival of Americans, a threat coming from their own military defenders against enemy forces. By the mid-fifties the national magazines were filled with stories about bigger and bigger bombs, each of them with the force of millions of tons of TNT, and about their impact on land and air. The National Academy of Sciences released a report on radioactive fallout in 1956, offering only limited reassurance. Atmospheric testing of weapons had so far not raised worldwide radiation to levels significantly greater than those resulting from natural background radioactivity, the report said, and citizens were getting a stronger dose from dental and medical use of X-rays than bombs. On the other hand, even the lowest levels of radiation could have serious effects. And the drive underway to harness the fission process to provide cheap electrical energy was a potentially larger threat still. According to the scientists, the development of peacetime nuclear reactors could produce enough strontium 90 by the end of the century that the dispersal of a mere 1 percent of it would seriously contaminate the entire earth. The disposal of nuclear wastes from those reactors required the most careful monitoring.[4]

That was the picture as it looked a mere decade after the Bikini tests. Not until 1958, however, did the ecological effects of atomic fallout become of more widespread concern to American scientists. In that year scientists organized the Committee for Nuclear Information in St. Louis, whose aim was to strip the secrecy from the government's weapons program and to warn their fellow citizens of the dangers in further nuclear testing and nuclear power. One of its members was the plant physiologist Barry Commoner, who would become a prominent leader in the growing environmental movement.[5] Other scientists began to join this campaign of information and protest, and increasingly they were from the biological disciplines. Their campaign against the radiation threat to the planet set a precedent for scientists taking up political issues, mobilizing public opinion, and, out of guilt as much as responsibility, calling for a new ethic toward nature. The bomb tested at Alamagordo had at last set off a powerful moral reaction.

Rachel Carson was not a prominent leader in that first wave of critical reaction among scientists. For a long while she shunned politics and controversy. But like many other citizens she listened and worried; slowly she joined the reaction. When she made her commitment to speak out, she came armed with facts and eloquence, animated by an intense conviction that the world had entered a more dangerous era than any before and that scientists could no longer pursue their research as usual. Through her writings Carson began to teach people how to think about the new vulnerability of nature, and she became the first to warn the public of a whole new category of toxic substances, organic pesticides made of chlorinated hydrocarbons, that were polluting the earth. Translated into more than two dozen languages, her work inspired a global environmental consciousness.

Carson was born in 1907 and grew up on what was then the rural outskirts of Pittsburgh. With the aid of a scholarship she attended the Pennsylvania College for Women (now Chatham College), then went on to Johns Hopkins University for an M.A. degree in genetics. Her most important scientific training, though, came in summers spent at Woods Hole Marine Biological Laboratory on Cape Cod, where she discovered the ecology of the sea. She felt drawn to it emotionally as well as scientifically and devoted most of her life to its study and enjoyment. What she found in the sea was a vast untouched realm in which living organisms had evolved in an environment quite unlike the land surface. The sea seemed an unspoiled part of nature, whereas the North American continent had, by her lifetime, been explored, settled, and manipulated extensively. Had Carson lived during earlier days, she might have longed to go westward and alone into the wilderness. Instead, this small, shy woman became a marine biologist prowling the wild oceanic world of the East Coast, peering into tide pools, wading at night onto mudflats with bucket and flashlight in hand, diving into deeper waters with a snorkel or pressurized helmet. No one would do more than she to direct American thinking to the vast ocean environment, which comprises three-fourths of the planet's surface.

The decade of the thirties was not a propitious one for a woman seeking a career in the natural sciences. She became her mother's sole financial support and, in 1936, found it necessary to accept a job as junior aquatic biologist with the Bureau of Fisheries, then in the Department of Commerce, later absorbed into the Fish and Wildlife Service of the Department of the Interior. Until 1952 that government agency was her professional home, and she worked her way up to become its chief editor of publications. She resigned when her own writings gave her sufficient income to be independent. Her first book was *Under the Sea Wind* (1941), but it was her second, *The Sea Around Us* (1951), that brought her fame and a small fortune; it was on the bestseller lists for more than eighty weeks and won the National Book Award. A third title, *The Edge of the Sea*, appeared in 1955. By that point Carson had found a new career as a freelance science writer, searching for meaning, beauty, and a mystery still unpenetrated by science in the stories of the sea.

World War Two left an unintended but destructive legacy for nature in many ways other than the atomic bomb. Carson's own government agency had been mobilized to learn more about the marine environment and help devise means to exploit it for food, navigation, and defense. In a second edition of *The Sea Around Us*, published in 1961, Carson acknowledged how much had been changed by the new war-generated technology. Americans and Russians were dumping radioactive wastes in the ocean, and fallout from the testing of bombs was settling over the waters. The effects of those substances on the whole chain of living organisms, from the smallest diatoms to the largest marine mammals, and on man himself, could not be foretold. "Although man's record as a steward of the natural resources of the earth has been a discouraging one," she wrote, "there has been a certain comfort in the belief that the sea, at least, was inviolate, beyond man's ability to change and to despoil. But this belief, unfortunately, has proved to be naive." The fate of Bikini Atoll made that clear.[6]

Carson subsequently turned her attention to other deadly poisons falling from the sky, particularly the persistent pesticides like DDT (dicholoro-diphenyl-trichloroethane) that had also come out of the war years and were spreading through terrestrial food chains and draining into the sea, affecting even penguins at the South Pole. After years of gathering all the scientific data she could find on the ecological consequences of pesticides, she brought out in 1962 a very different book from any she had written heretofore: it bore the ominous title *Silent Spring* and was a measured but severe indictment of modern agriculture, the chemical industry, and applied entomology. The message of the book, still controversial, was that humans were endangering their own lives through an arrogant, manipulative attitude toward other forms of life.

Along with the possibility of the extinction of mankind by nuclear war, the central problem of our age has . . . become the contamination of man's total environment with such substances of incredible potential for harm—substances that accumulate in the tissues of plants and animals and even penetrate the germ cells to shatter or alter the very material of heredity upon which the shape of the future depends.

Carson assembled enough facts to show why the more persistent chemicals must be restricted, but her deeper message was the need for ethical change, away from a spirit of conquest and toward a respect for all forms of life and an acknowledgment of our dependence on them. "The 'control of nature,' " she wrote, "is a phrase conceived in arrogance, born of the Neanderthal age of biology and philosophy, when it was supposed that nature exists for the convenience of man. . . . It is our alarming misfortune that so primitive a science has armed itself with the most modern and terrible weapons, and that in turning them against the insects it has also turned them against the earth."[7]

Recent feminist scholars have argued that Carson's moral critique of the conquest of nature emerged out of a "women's culture" that had long emphasized cooperation and nurturance instead of the pursuit of conquest and wealth.[8] Certainly, Carson drew on many women for support during what became a storm of reaction, much of it belittling to her as a woman. But the acknowledged intellectual influences on her life were men like Albert Schweitzer and Henry Bigelow, and millions of men as well as women looked on her as the prophet of a new ethic toward nature. When she died of cancer at age fifty-six, she had organized no political movement nor had she seen that new environmental ethic become common; however, she had helped make ecology a familiar word and environmentalism a growing international cause.[9]

In the earlier part of this century the word "environment" referred mainly to the external social influences (as opposed to genetic endowment) working on the individual. Environmentalism referred to the belief that the "physical, biological, psychological or cultural environment" was a crucial factor shaping "the structure or behavior of animals, including man."[10] But increasingly as the battle of heredity versus environment lost saliency after World War Two, environment came to mean, particularly and especially, the *natural* influences surrounding people, including flora, fauna, climate, water, and soil; human beings, it was understood, were not passive victims of their surroundings—they were imbedded in them, they interacted with them, and they could have an effect. An environmentalist, consequently, became anyone who was concerned with the preservation of those biophysical surroundings from pollution, depletion, or degradation. For generations technological development had progressed on the premise of transforming, even replacing, the natural world. Environmentalists countered that humans, no matter how impressive their technology, needed to protect that natural world from their own actions in order to survive or live well. Nature is not a realm set apart from humans like another country that one visits from time to time, but instead is a vast, intricate community, a system of connections and interchanges highly vulnerable to disturbance, on which humans must inescapably depend.

The new environmentalism, to be sure, did not appear suddenly on the scene with no precedents or intellectual preparation. Rachel Carson expressed an indebtedness to such nineteenth-century figures as Henry Thoreau and John Muir, who had celebrated nature in a wilder state and sought to reestablish a direct personal relationship with the non-human. Both men devised private strategies for getting outside the cocoon of civilization and into the woods or mountains. But in a nation of over 200 million people, with a far denser web of artifice obscuring the natural order, that kind of private quest had become difficult. Environmentalism was, therefore, not a private relationship, not a kind of retreat, but a decidedly public engagement—a strategy pursued in the courtroom and legislative chamber to defend a relationship found even in the heart of the largest megalopolis.

Other precedents included the conservation movement, which gained momentum in the early twentieth century under the leadership of Gifford Pinchot, Chief Forester during the Theodore Roosevelt administration. But that movement had aimed at preserving national parks and wildlife refuges, setting up a national forest system under sustained-yield management, and protecting the nation's soils and minerals. Typically, conservation had been a movement to put the government in charge of overseeing and even owning the land. Activists like Pinchot argued that American society could not endure without a permanent supply of natural resources, and they feared that a short-sighted consumption might threaten the nation's security. On the other hand, conservationists tended to look on nature as a series of discrete places needing defense—a Yosemite Valley, a pine forest, an eroded farm on the Great Plains. When environmentalism emerged, it maintained some of that same commitment to the program of land conservation; for example, it supported the Wilderness Act of 1964 and a number of endangered species acts. But all the same, the core of the movement was shifting as more and more citizens sensed that the human–nature umbilical itself was under attack and that defending it required a more comprehensive way of thinking.[11]

The emergence of the new viewpoint owed much to a relatively obscure group of thinkers in the two or three decades that preceded the new movement of environmentalism, most of them academics in such fields as ecology and geography. They were the first to see the environment as a set of interactive relationships between humans and the rest of nature. Many of them thought about those relations on a global scale, transcending dramatically the more limited national consciousness of the conservationists. Their ideas often came from abroad: for example, from the Austrian geologist Edward Suess, inventor of the concept of the biosphere; from French and German geographers, who had long debated the question of nature as a limiting factor on human activity; and from a succession of English naturalists, including Charles Darwin, Charles Elton, and Arthur Tansley.[12] A key American figure in this emerging body of thought was Aldo Leopold, who introduced many readers to the science of ecology through his 1949 book of outdoor essays, *A Sand County Almanac*. By the fifties those influences had all come together in a new integrative, interdisciplinary point of view that united the natural and social sciences, a view that might be called human ecology. Avoiding the extremes of environmental determinism, which had tried to reduce cultures to their physical circumstances, and of a technological optimism that was blind to its side-effects, the new view taught that human life must be lived within constraints, both physical and moral.

Examples of that emerging human ecology run all through the late forties and the fifties. Among anthropologists of the period Betty Meggers and Julian Steward, one working in Amazonia, the other in the American Southwest, laid the foundations for "cultural ecology." Among geographers Carl Sauer was the crucial figure—a broad-ranging scholar who produced a number of influential studies of people living in close contact with nature. Two important books published simultaneously in 1948, *Our Plundered Planet,* by Fairfield Osborn, and *Road to Survival*, by William Vogt, both offered a planetary perspective on man's growing effect on his surroundings. Then in 1955 several of those same scholars, and many more from many disciplines and many countries, came together in Princeton, New Jersey, for a symposium on the state of the human–nature relation, dedicated to the memory of the nineteenth-century American conservationist George Perkins Marsh. As much as any event, that Princeton gathering prepared the intellectual ground for the environmental movement.[13]

Take, for example, the contribution by Paul Sears, botanist and chairman of the conservation program at Yale University. Sears reviewed the global impact of human population growth, the intensification of agricultural land-use, water and air pollution in industrial areas, noting along the way that the United States, with less than a tenth of the world's population was consuming more than half of the mineral production. "Man is dependent," he argued, "upon other organisms both for the immediate means of survival and for maintaining habitat conditions under which survival is possible."[14] Neither Sears nor the other 1955 conference-goers called themselves environmentalists, but their focus on the place of humans in the global environment, and their general concern about the state of that environment, all helped give environmentalism a set of defining ideas.

What environmentalism added to those fertile ideas of human ecology was a sense of urgency, bordering at times on apocalyptic fear. The environment was in a state of "crisis." The specter haunting scientists like Carson was death—the death of birds, of ecosystems, of nature itself, and, because of our dependence on nature, the death of humans as well. Though environmentalists sometimes tried to temper their gloom with a more hopeful and politically acceptable emphasis on a "green future" in which cities, economies, and productive technologies would all be reembedded in the tangled web of life, they had trouble convincing themselves that public attitudes were changing fast enough to avert disaster. In his widely admired and influential Reith lectures delivered in 1969 over the BBC, one of Britain's most prominent environmentalists, Frank Fraser Darling, though admitting that Carson's "emotional overtones" made him uncomfortable, also admitted that he could not be an optimist and that he was troubled by the constant necessity, for political reasons, of "expressing faith which at bottom I do not feel."[15]

In 1968, a half-dozen years after *Silent Spring* appeared, the California biologist Paul Ehrlich heard yet another bomb ticking, ready to usher in chaos and mass death: the "population explosion," which had reached over three billion and was increasing at a global average of more than 2 percent a year, and in many poorer countries at a rate of 3 percent or more. Thus, it was not technology alone, but human biology that now had become a factor in the rush to Armageddon. Once more the wraith of Thomas Malthus materialized, warning of approaching limits to human population and human consumption, a prediction echoed in such books as *The Limits to Growth, Blueprint for Survival,* and *Small Is Beautiful,* all of which feared that complex industrial civilization as a whole might be breaking down. In the authors' view, an economy expanding at a geometric ratio, using ever more energy, land, minerals, and water, must eventually run up against the limits of the earth. Looked at as a set of interdependencies rather than as a storehouse of commodities, the environment was not merely a set of things to be used up. Here the environmentalists confronted deeply seated attitudes among traditional economists, business leaders, politicians, and the public about the virtues of economic growth, attitudes underlying the modern economic system and indeed the whole materialistic ethos of modern culture.[16]

Barry Commoner, who had been among the first scientists to move into environmental politics, kept pace with the broadening agenda, though he never became a Malthusian about population or resource scarcity. In 1963 the U.S. Senate ratified a treaty banning the atmospheric testing of nuclear weapons, effectively removing the first great cause from the environmentalist agenda, but Commoner saw that there were plenty of other dangers threatening planetary health. His Committee for Nuclear Information became the Committee for Environmental Information, and publisher of a new magazine called *Environment.* He began studying the damaging effects of nitrate-based chemical fertilizers, seeping from agricultural fields into the public's water supply, on the body's ability to transport oxygen in the blood. He also began alerting the country to what he called "the most blatant example of the environmental crisis in the United States," the galloping eutrophication of 12,000-year-old Lake Erie from phosphates in household detergents. The drive to maximize corporate profit, he maintained, was the force behind the development of those new harmful products, all of which had safer but less lucrative substitutes. In his book, *The Closing Circle,* published in 1971, Commoner argued that the great need was for an awakened public, led by informed scientists, to force the government to restrain the development and marketing of those technologies by corporate America.[17]

By the late sixties that call for regulating the polluters began to have a significant effect on the political process. In 1969 Congress passed the National Environmental Policy Act, which set up a new Environmental Protection Agency and required an "environmental impact statement" for any federally funded project that might cause damage to the earth. Other landmark legislation included clean water acts in 1960, 1965, and 1972 and clean air acts in 1963, 1967, and 1970. In Britain, a Control of Pollution Act passed Parliament in 1974; though it drew on a long history of public health and sanitation reform, it too expressed a rising level of anxiety about the deteriorating environment. By that point the list of pollutants had expanded to include automobile emissions, solid wastes, toxic metals, oil spills, even the heat trapped by the atmospheric buildup of the "greenhouse gas," carbon dioxide.[18]

This discovery of nature's vulnerability came as so great a shock that, for many Britons and Americans, the only appropriate response was talk of revolution. In a trivial vein, new terms were added to the English language like "ecopolitics," "ecocatastrophe," and "ecoawareness." Beyond such Madison Avenue gimmicks, however, more fundamental changes were called for. To cite only one instance, Michael McCloskey, the executive director of the Sierra Club, concluded in 1970 that

a revolution is truly needed—in our values, outlooks and economic organization. For the crisis of our environment stems from a legacy of economic and technical premises which have been pursued in the absence of ecological knowledge. That other revolution, the industrial one that is turning sour, needs to be replaced by a revolution of new attitudes toward growth, goods, space, and living things.

The "oppressor," as perceived here, was more than Commoner's economic class of capitalists who had been the great engine of the Industrial Revolution and of most technological innovation thereafter. Like many other environmentalists, McCloskey was challenging the whole set of *values* associated with the rise of a bourgeois civilization—the *worldview* of the aspiring middle class, with its dedication to technology, unlimited production and consumption, material self-advancement, individualism, and the domination of nature. Similarly, the political scientist William Ophuls insisted that "the basic principles of modern industrial civilization are...incompatible with ecological scarcity and that the whole ideology of modernity growing out of the Enlightenment, especially such central tenets as individualism, may no longer be viable." Time had run out on an entire culture. Nature's economy had been pushed to the breaking point, and "ecology" was to be the rallying cry for a cultural revolution.[19]

If the overthrow of modern bourgeois civilization had become the most radical aim of the ecology movement, it was ironic to find the movement's strongest appeal among the Anglo-American middle class. That fact was well and often noted, with not a little indignation, by the would-be middle classes of the world. Many asked whether the message of ecology was a sermon on the virtues of poverty, to be heeded only by those who were still have-nots. Could middle-class environmentalists, others questioned, bring off a revolution against their own economic self-interest, or did they really mean after all to enact more modest, liberal, pragmatic reforms that would leave the base of the bourgeois culture intact? Was it even conceivable, two hundred years after Watts' steam engine, to abandon the achievements of the Industrial Revolution, or had the chains of history bound us to a self-propelled technology? What would an alternative social order founded on the science of ecology look like—and would the middle class really accept such a world? Perhaps most significant, would the billions of people still living in relative or absolute scarcity want to live there?

The media culmination of those events and gropings for a new order came on April 22, 1970, when citizens around the United States, and many abroad, observed the first Earth Day, a time set aside for sober reflection on environmental conditions. The idea of such a day originated with Senator Gaylord Nelson of Wisconsin, but the main organizer was a twenty-five-year-old antiwar activist, Sam Brown, who held distinctly apocalyptic views about the fate of the earth. He now tried to apply the tactics of student protests against the Vietnam War and race discrimination to the environmental crisis, though some observers thought there was less seriousness in the new cause; burning a credit card somehow did not seem as radical as burning a draft card. A *Newsweek* reporter wrote: "Despite the desperate sickness of the environment, despite the turnout of millions of at least partially awakened Americans, the whole demonstration seemed to lack the necessary passion." Perhaps, if that was so, most Americans had not yet been scared enough. They had not yet absorbed all the fear and pessimism that was driving many scientists. Thus the day became in many communities more of a party than a wake.[20]

There was still plenty of fierce passion in the busiest figure of Earth Day 1970, Barry Commoner, who managed to address audiences on four different campuses in the space of a few hours. Commoner had eminent companions on the day's lecture circuits, including Paul Ehrlich, René Dubos, Ralph Nader, Benjamin Spock, and even the beat poet Allen Ginsberg. At least one prominent figure, however, took a novel approach to the issues agitating students: Secretary of the Interior Walter Hickel traveled to the University of Alaska to speak, where he announced that he would approve the construction of a 800-mile pipeline from the North Slope of that state to supply America's vast fleet of automobiles with gasoline. But most Earth Day speakers called on the public to drive less, conserve more, and to question the automobile—indeed, to question a way of life that was based on maximizing the consumption of oil and other natural resources, on promoting private wealth and national prestige as the highest social goals.

President Richard Nixon, though no environmentalist himself and rebuffed in angling for a campus speaking opportunity, nonetheless called on citizens to make their peace with Mother Nature. Easy words from a man who was still waging a war in Southeast Asia, but the shift in official language was striking. The old imperial slogan that

Carson had protested, "the conquest of nature," had suddenly gone hollow all over the country, even if many of the forces behind the words remained as strong as ever. In a mere quarter of a century the nation had raced from Alamagordo to Earth Day. A period that had begun with the demonstration of an awesome weapon to defend American freedom and empire and the consumer way of life against evil regimes had arrived at the point where that same way of life had itself become the great danger, a danger that lay within, requiring a new kind of defense.

Eventually, environmentalists sought alliances with other groups demanding cultural change—with feminists, some of whom insisted that women were more attuned to grasping ecological interdependencies than men; with ethical radicals who wanted to extend rights to animals, trees, and the rest of nature; and with advocates for poor nations, who demanded protection from environmental damage and toxic dumping done by rich nations. In 1972, when environmentalists, official and nonofficial, assembled in Stockholm, Sweden, from all over the world to survey the global situation, they faced the formidable task of learning to work together, across all the barriers of class, language, ideology, and religion that separated them, in order to meet the now global problems of nuclear proliferation, overpopulation, overconsumption, industrial pollution, and resource exhaustion.

The first Earth Day and the Stockholm event, the first of a series of international environmental conferences, suggested to the American media that the decade of the seventies would become the "Age of Ecology." If the phrase suggested that everyone in the nation or world had accepted the message of ecologists like Carson and the others, then it was surely a joke. Even among the small circle of American and British scientists, there was no consensus on how bad the environmental crisis was, or even whether there was a crisis at all. Nonetheless, a new phase of civilization did seem to be appearing in a fitful, halting, and confused way. The covers of news magazines were now graced by a starkly beautiful image of Earth: a photograph taken from an American spaceship showing a gleaming sphere dappled with green and brown continents, with wide expanses of deep blue water and swirling white clouds, a single unique sphere of life surrounded by unending blackness. That lonely planet, people now understood in a way no previous generation could have done, was actually a small and fragile entity. Though eventually corporations would turn that image into a icon of the global market economy, and the perceptual revolution it had promised would be thwarted by resurgent nationalism, for a while and for many the photograph of earth was a stunning revelation. The planet had come to seem far more singular and yet more fragile than at any other time in human experience. Its thin film of life—humanity's sole means of survival—was far thinner and far more vulnerable than anyone had ever imagined.

The New Physicians

The sudden acceleration of environmental damage after World War Two was largely the consequence of scientific advance. Such was the lesson of Alamogordo; no other explanation could bear as much weight. Human behavior had undergone no radical alterations over the preceding two or three centuries, or, some would say, over the millennia of our species' existence. Nor had the ideology or institution of modern capitalism made any sudden turn or leap, the claims of Barry Commoner to the contrary notwithstanding. Capitalism was still, as it had been for several centuries, the principal underwriter of technological change, and still its largest beneficary, but increasingly it needed science to make change happen. Science obliged, knowledge increased enormously, and societies used that knowledge to create a technological arsenal without precedent. Much of science remained in the service of industrial capitalism, but whatever master it obeyed, the corporation or the nation-state or even its own internal dicta, it was rapidly transforming the earth.

One of the glaring paradoxes of the Age of Ecology was that the public began to follow, even idealize, one small group of scientists in order to fight the ills brought on by science in general. Ecologists, we have seen, were among the first to regret the unrestrained use of that new power and to call for more social control and personal responsibility, a strategy that resembled closing the barn door after the horse had escaped. However belated their response, they deserved much credit for stirring up the new environmental concern. Their task was to educate citizens about the vital world of nature and explain what we were doing to it. In playing that role the ecologist was widely perceived to be the gallant defender of nature's integrity.

That role was reflected in the sudden ubiquity of the word "ecology." Overnight it appeared in the most everyday places and the most astonishing, on day-glo T-shirts, in corporate advertising, and on bridge abutments. It was changing the language of politics and philosophy, as in a number of countries political groups began to identify themselves as "Ecology Parties," though no one had ever proposed forming a political party named after comparative linguistics or advanced paleontology, and as a philosophical movement termed "Deep Ecology" began to appear on several continents, whose goal was to promote "biospherical egalitarianism" among the species, though no one had ever called for a parallel movement of "Deep Entomology" or "Deep Polish Literature."[21] While the man on the street was generally unprepared to say precisely what ecology was, still less to arrange his life according to its teachings, he had granted enough authority to the field to mark off a peculiar era in history.

Behind that popular enthusiasm for the science of ecology lay a hope that it could offer not only a pile of interesting data but also a pathway to moral enlightenment. The hope did not originate wholly with the public but first appeared among eminent ecologists. For instance, back in 1935, Paul Sears had urged Americans to take ecology seriously, promoting it in their universities and making it part of their governing process. "In Great Britain," he pointed out,

the ecologists are being consulted at every step in planning the proper utilization of those parts of the Empire not yet settled, thus... ending the era of haphazard exploitation. There are hopeful, but all too few signs that our own national government realizes the part which ecology must play in a permanent program.[22]

Sears recommended that the United States hire a few thousand ecologists at the county level to advise citizens on land use and environmental degradation; such expertise, he thought, would put the whole nation on a biologically sustainable basis. Later, Sears added that those experts should teach the American people that "body of knowledge, ... that point of view, which peculiarly implies all that is meant by conservation."[23] In other words, the chief responsibility of ecologists should be to indicate "the unbalance which man has produced on this continent" and lead people back to some approximation of nature's original health and stability.[24]

While Americans did not take all of Sears' recommendations to heart—few ecologists were actually put on county payrolls, with an office next door to the tax collector and sheriff—they did take a surprisingly long step in that direction. After the passage of the National Environmental Policy Act, an ecologist could be found at work in every part of the United States (as well as in other countries that had passed similar legislation) writing an environmental impact report or monitoring a human disturbance of the landscape or testifying at a hearing. The ecologist LaMont Cole might complain in 1964 that his colleagues had been "exceedingly timid about becoming involved in public affairs" and complain that "only rarely have they shown signs of genuine outrage as many did over some of the programs of predator control in the West." But after Barry Commoner got his picture on the cover of *Time* magazine in 1970 (as "the Paul Revere of Ecology") and so many ecologists had become politically active at the grassroots level, that complaint lost its force.[25] Even in Britain, where scientists especially disdained the hurly-burly of politics, things were changing. The Oxford ornithologist H. N. Southern, author of an elegant little study on the tawny owl and its prey, in his presidential address to the British Ecological Society, admonished his colleagues to deal with "the crisis that faces our civilization—too many people, too little food and space and a terrifying acceleration of this imbalance within our own life-times." "Who, except an ecologist," he observed, "has any data upon which even to suggest an optimum equilibrium between men and resources in the world.... Our advice is needed at all levels of managing our environment but it is not always asked for. Therefore it is we who must take the initiative." And one of Arthur Tansley's disciples, the Cambridge botanist G. Clifford Evans, in *his* presidential address to the same group, compared the earth to a sack of uncut diamonds; the job of ecologists, he argued, was to persuade people not to throw the whole sack into the stove and burn them up overnight.[26]

But to assume this new leadership ecologists needed not only a more active conscience but also plenty of grants, research facilities, university appointments, and travel opportunities. They must also achieve a unified theory if they were to serve the age. The environmental problems were immense and complicated, ranging from feeding a growing number of African peasants without degrading the soil and groundwater to finding a safe source of electricity for America's cities, from cleansing the industrialized air blowing across continents to saving the Indian tiger and the Alaskan caribou from extinction. Such big problems necessitated a big picture. Ecologists had to educate the public in more than the dynamics of owls eating mice. They had to show how all the pieces of the earth fitted together into a whole and clarify what made that whole healthy or sick.

Two brothers from North Carolina, Eugene and Howard Odum, stepped forth to furnish that unified theory and give ecologists a comprehensive scientific manual for mending the planet. Although neither was ever as popular as Commoner or Carson, they became the intellectual leaders that others needed. It was Eugene in particular who provided direction for the field through a very successful textbook, *Fundamentals of Ecology*, first published with Howard as coauthor in 1953, followed by a second edition in 1959 and a third in 1971, the various editions being translated into twenty languages. According to Robert Burgess, the text was "a huge success, and [its] logic, concepts, integration, and use of mathematics as a universal language have probably done more to influence development in both teaching and research than any other single factor in the last thirty years."[27] Howard's major individual contribution was a book entitled *Environment, Power, and Society*, published in 1971, though, like Eugene, his life-list of publications was long and impressive. Together, they did more than anyone else to define the science in the postwar period.

The Odum boys were the sons of famed regional sociologist Howard W. Odum, director of the Institute for Research in the Social Sciences at the University of North Carolina, and a social reformer. They took from their father a set of intellectual habits and a number of personal values. Like him, they believed in achieving a holistic outlook on the world, not being trapped in overspecialization; and like him, they wanted to see harmony flourish everywhere—harmony in the old divisive South, harmony in the nation, harmony between nations, harmony between humans and nature—instead of bitter, competitive struggle everywhere. Ecology appealed to the boys because it seemed to be a science that dealt with harmony, a harmony found in nature, offering a model for a more organic, cooperative human community.[28] Eugene did his Ph.D. work at the University of Illinois under Victor Shelford, who had been Frederic Clements' associate on the book *Bio-Ecology* (1940) and the main force behind the Ecological Society of America's program to preserve natural areas.[29] The younger Howard, meanwhile, studied at Yale University under G. Evelyn Hutchinson, a brilliant British-born scientist interested in biogeochemistry, the carbon, phosphorous, and nitrogen cycles found in small Connecticut ponds and in the biosphere as a whole, and who had been Raymond Lindeman's teacher also. After finishing their Ph.D.'s the Odums returned south, Eugene to the University of Georgia, where he set up the Institute of Ecology, Howard to the University of Florida. Their careers matured precisely at the time when environmentalism was emerging, and they themselves became ardent environmentalists.

After collaborating on the textbook, the brothers headed in 1954 down to Eniwetok Atoll in the South Pacific, another part of the Marshall Island chain where nuclear bombs were being tested. Howard was recruited for the work by the Atomic Energy Commission because he had done his doctoral dissertation on the biogeochemistry of strontium, which he found had remained at a constant level in the oceans for the past forty million years, though what the bomb was doing to that stability was anybody's guess. In the atoll they analyzed and measured the metabolism of a coral reef, which is a kind of collective organism made up of algae and coelenterate animals evolving together to form a single efficient feeder in waters with very low nutrient content. The reef provided a marvelous example of how such collectivism works, how it spends its energy budget and utilizes its nutrition, and of how "emergent properties," that is, properties that emerge when two or more species work together, appear on the earth. Years later, Eugene identified that field study as a formative experience in his thinking:

The Pacific coral reef, as a kind of oasis in a desert, can stand as an object lesson for man who must now learn that mutualism between autotrophic [green plants] and heterotrophic [organisms that feed on plants, other animals, or detritus] components, and between producers and consumers in the societal realm, coupled with efficient recycling of materials and use of energy, are the keys to maintaining prosperity in a world of limited resources.[30]

They had come to the atoll mainly to help the government understand how nuclear weapons might affect the environment, not to work for world prosperity. But vital support from the Atomic Energy Commission allowed them to do research on broad ecological principles in an ideally isolated laboratory. Support from the same source came when the Savannah River atomic weapons plant was built in Georgia and Eugene was given funds to set up a field laboratory in the neighborhood. What he studied in those Georgian salt-water marshes, tidal estuaries, and abandoned fields, as in the atoll, was the pulsating force of the sun flowing through, animating, and organizing ecosystems.[31]

The Odums believed that ecology must develop a unified theory of the ecosystem, described in precise mathematical and statistical terms, if the field was to be of any practical value. Such a theory must be holistic, not reductive. On one occasion Eugene complained that science and technology had been "so preoccupied with reductionism that supra-individual systems have suffered benign neglect" and scientists had been "unable to respond to the larger-scale problems that now require attention." By focusing on the ecosystem, he believed the field could at once find unity in its diversity and come up with solid recommendations. The ecosystem, he expained, is the basic functional unit in ecology" and refers to "any unit that includes all of the organisms (i.e., the 'community') in a given area interacting with the physical environment so that a flow of energy leads to clearly defined trophic structure, biotic diversity, and material cycles (i.e., exchange of materials between living and nonliving parts) within the system."[32] In other words, the ecosystem, for Odum as for its inventor Tansley, dealt with more than biology; it comprehended both the living and the nonliving. The first and longest section of the Odum textbook dealt predictably with the ecosystem and all its subordinate parts, including energy flows, biogeochemical cycles, communities, and populations of species. All of nature was organized into a hierarchy of levels, the book said, and at the top of the heap was the ecosystem. To understand that highest level was to understand how, in the most comprehensive way, the earth was organized.

When Eugene tried to offer illustrations of what an ecosystem was, however, he revealed how difficult it was going to be to achieve any unified theory—far more difficult, say, than a science focused on the biology of separate species. He identified five examples of ecosystems: a pond, a "watershed unit," a meadow, a laboratory "microecosystem," and a spacecraft. The first was easy enough to see, for the pond had clear boundaries, a fact that had made it an object of integrative science since the nineteenth century.[33] The watershed unit likewise had easily determined boundaries, though calling it an ecosystem seemed to make the flow of water, not solar energy, the organizing principle. The meadow, on the other hand, though an easy enough place to experience, did not have so firm a set of boundaries, especially when one considered the fauna that wandered in and out of the place. In contrast, the laboratory microecosystem could claim more sharply demarcated boundaries, defined by an apparatus of beakers, flasks, and tubing, but it was hardly an entity organized by nature. Similarly, the spacecraft was a human contrivance, not the product of evolution but of engineering. How then could it qualify as one of the fundamental structures of nature? Apparently, what made the spacecraft an ecosystem was that it was a self-contained "life-support system" for an astronaut, in which everything needed for survival had been identified and packed into a single vessel. But then if that was all the notion of an ecosystem meant, a set of gases and nutrients needed by any organism, there must be billions and billions of them—an ecosystem for every single organism on earth. Whose life-support system was the pond or meadow? Whose the Mississippi River watershed? Identifying any of them as the fundamental units of nature was like building a spacecraft, a product of the contriving hand of man. All ecosystems ultimately became, by that logic and definition, nothing more than abstractions in the minds of ecologists.

Odum moved on from his taxonomic difficulties to describe the life histories of ecosystems. What all of them had in common, he maintained, was a "strategy of development," a kind of game plan that gave the whole of nature, as well as its individual components, an overall direction. The word "strategy" suggested, of course, that ecosystems were conscious beings that could set goals for themselves and strive to reach them, though Odum did not really want to push that conclusion; he meant only that ecosystems were self-organizing entities *like organisms*. Their strategy was to achieve "as large and diverse an organic structure as is possible within the limits set by the available energy input and the prevailing physical conditions of existence."[34] Every single ecosystem, he believed, was either moving toward or had already achieved that goal. It was a clear, coherent, and easily observable strategy; and it ended in a healthy state of order, or what he called "homeostasis." That state was not at all like the order that eighteenth-century naturalists had found in nature, which was static and eternal. For Odum, homeostasis was more like the healthy norm of the human body; infections invaded from time to time and disturbed its equilibrium, causing sickness, but then the body rallied its defenses and repelled the invaders. Similarly, the ecosystem was often perturbed, but normally it fluctuated around a single homeostatic point. A state of health involved an endless but successful struggle to maintain that point.[35]

The health of the ecosystem also required a condition of mutualism and cooperation among the many organisms inhabiting an area. From an early stage of intense competition against one another, they moved toward a more symbiotic relationship, like the coral reef. They learned, as it were, to work together to control their surrounding environment, making it more and more suitable as a habitat, until at last they had sufficient influence to protect themselves from stressful cycles of drought and flood, winter and summer, cold and heat; and to extract nutrition in the most efficient manner. In other words, the unifying principle of nature was that organisms learned to work together to manage the physical world around them for maximum efficiency and mutual benefit.

Eugene Odum may have used different terms than his predecessor Frederic Clements, and he may even have had a radically different picture of nature; but he did not depart from Clements' notion that the law of organic nature was to bring order and harmony out of the chaotic materials of existence. In the place of the theory of the "climax" stage he put the notion of a "mature ecosystem," described in a "tabular model of ecological succession." When the ecosystem reached the point of homeostasis, it expended less energy on increasing production and more on securing protection from external vicissitudes: that is, the biomass in an area attained a steady level, neither increasing nor decreasing, and the emphasis in the system lay on keeping it that way—on maintaining a kind of no-growth economy. Then the little, aggressive, weedy organisms common at an early stage in development (the so-called r-selected species that had explosive reproductive potential) gave way to larger, steadier creatures (the K-selected species, with K referring to a state of equilibrium); the latter had less potential for fast growth but also better talents at surviving in dense settlements and keeping the place on an even keel.[36] With the arrival of the K-species came a more diversified community—that is, a greater array of species living together. And there was less loss of nutrients to the outside; such elements as nitrogen, phosphorus, and calcium all stayed in perpetual circulation within the ecosystem rather than leaking out. Those characteristics were all key indicators of environmental maturity, or health, and all of them were supposed to be susceptible to precise measurement and mathematical modeling.

This unified theory of ecology was telling, for the most part, a story without much potential for wild, unpredictable change. Ecosystems did change, and change daily, but over the long term they showed remarkable continuity. Odum acknowledged that far back in geological time the world might have been more tumultuous than today. Drawing from the new subfield of paleoecology, he reviewed how the planet had once gone through profound revolutions, following, for example, the first appearance of photosynthesis, which transformed solar energy into living matter, a process that introduced a radical increase in the level of oxygen in the atmosphere. That was biological evolution at work, and from it had come an explosion of life forms, whole orders of complex multicellular organisms swimming to the surface of the sea and eventually crawling out to colonize the land. By the mid-Paleozoic period, 300 to 400 million years ago, oxygen emanating from those organisms had increased to about 20 percent of the atmosphere. Although it dropped precipitously in the late Paleozoic, eventually it returned to that same level and, over the past 100 million years, remained there in an "oscillating steady state." Odum warned, however, that "man-generated CO_2 and dust pollution might be making this precarious balance more and more 'unsteady.' "[37]

So for the most part nature's wilder days were behind it, and now only humans constituted a deeply disturbing factor. The ecologist did not hesitate to advocate policies to prevent that disturbance. In the final section of his textbook he addressed the subject of "human ecology," by which he meant a set of policies that should govern behavior. They included a tolerance for family planning, birth control, and abortions to reduce human population; comprehensive regional land-use planning; changes in the tax laws to discourage economic growth; development of a "spaceship economy" in which all resources were carefully recycled; and so forth. Such policies were for Odum part of his science—that is, they were regarded as logical deductions from the unified theory of ecology. The scientist had become social planner, seeking to "ecologize" all of society. Obviously, if faithfully followed by any nation, those policies would have revolutionized politics, economics, and culture.

The goal of ecology, then, was to study nature as a model for society. If one interfered too drastically with nature's strategy of development, the effects might be costly: a serious loss of nutrients, a decline in species diversity, an end to biomass stability. The ecosystem would be damaged, and grave human consequences would follow. The most likely source of that damage was no mystery to Odum: it was human beings trying to force up the production of useful commodities and stupidly risking the destruction of their life-support system.

Man has generally been preoccupied with obtaining as much "production" from the landscape as possible, by developing and maintaining early successional types of ecosystems, usually monocultures. But, of course, man does not live by food and fiber alone; he also needs a balanced CO_2–O_2 atmosphere, the climatic buffer provided by oceans and masses of vegetation, and clean (that is, unproductive) water for cultural and industrial uses. Many essential life-cycle resources, not to mention recreational and esthetic needs, are best provided man by the less "productive" landscapes. In other words, the landscape is not just a supply depot but is also the *oikos*—the home—in which we must live.[38]

Odum's view of nature as a series of balanced ecosystems, perfected or incipient, led him to take a strong stand in favor of preserving the landscape in as nearly natural a condition as possible.

On the occasion of the first Earth Day the public's attention was momentarily diverted from the crisis of the environment to the crisis of the spacecraft Apollo 13. On its way home from the moon, the craft had gone awry when an explosion occurred aboard, threatening the life of the crew. After many tense hours, with millions listening in, they had managed to get inside their lunar module and abandon ship. Eugene Odum used the incident years afterward as a model of our environmental situation on "Spaceship Earth." Here too, our life-support system was being destroyed, though in this case we had no handy little module to jump into and rocket away. We had to stay aboard and try to repair the craft. He noted that the earth, unlike Apollo 13, was a "bioregenerative system," that is, it had its own powers of recuperation, unlike a machine. Nonetheless, our predicament was even direr than the astronauts', for we had neither the possibility of escape nor the knowledge adequate to repair the vessel. The Apollo episode furnished a terrific metaphor, one that a Thoreau or Darwin would never have understood but one that spoke vividly to the postwar era. But what did it really say? That we took for granted our earthly life-support system, one that no NASA team could ever duplicate, or pay for? Undoubtedly, that was what the ecologist meant to convey. Yet he also hinted that a species capable of designing an Apollo space-craft-ecosystem, one that could take humans to the moon and get them back, was a species that could also figure out the mechanics of the earth and kept it well tuned.[39]

Just as the ecosystem concept kept blurring the lines between living and nonliving components, so it mixed mechanistic and organic metaphors to a confusing degree. Was the Earth alive or dead? Sick like an organism or malfunctioning like a machine? Did it need a physician or an engineer? Eugene Odum tried to have it both ways. His brother Howard, on the other hand, was unequivocally a spaceship engineer, describing the earth as a set of intricate "electric analogue circuits." Howard had always been intrigued by electricity. When he came to describe a unified theory of the ecosystem, consequently, he converted everything to a system of energy; organisms became mere junction boxes along the circuits. For an age that was also inventing computers and talking the lingo of cybernetics, he furnished an appropriate picture of the earth as a vast electronic apparatus.

Nor was he ambiguous about the practical import of his mechanistic model of nature. He was eager to become what Peter Taylor has called an "eco-technocrat," one who advocates technical solutions to environmental problems.[40] That tendency in ecosystem ecology was described in an earlier chapter on the rise of ecology as bioeconomics. Howard expressed the tendency repeatedly: "The management of nature is ecological engineering," he wrote, one that would mean "a partnership with nature." What he had in mind was "manipulating natural systems into entirely new designs for the good of man and nature." In other words, he would rewire the planet, change the circuits. Like the manager of a push-button factory, with power at his fingertips, he wanted to control the flow of energy through forest and ocean. "Should the auxiliary fossil-fuel and nuclear energy sources fail," he went on, "this control is one of the bright prospects for man." Before the shattering oil embargo of 1973, Howard Odum had became keenly aware of modern society's utter dependence on fossil fuels as a source of energy. He understood the great damage that energy abundance had worked on the earth. In the future, he promised, with better ecological knowledge, mankind could design a world that captured abundant energy from the sun, manipulating all the ecosystems to do so, and live more safely and harmoniously.[41]

Most pupils of the Odums' unified theory probably came away as devoted as Eugene was to preserving large parts of nature in an unmanaged state and, like him, they were probably sure that they had a strong scientific rationale for doing so. We must defend the world's endangered ecosystems, they shouted. We must safeguard the integrity of the Greater Yellowstone ecosystem, the Chesapeake Bay ecosystem, the Serengeti ecosystem. We must protect species diversity, biomass stability, and calcium recycling. We must make the world safe for K-species. Nonetheless, the complicated logic of the Odums' model might easily lead to contradictory policies. Both brothers expressed, along with a reverence for the natural order, a strong admiration for the achievements of technological, Apollo-making man, an admiration so intense that their ecology might end up supporting the old dream of the conquest of earth, now ironically sought in the name of environmentalism. Help the planet produce an endless supply of energy and food. Protect Spaceship Earth from any explosion. Keep it humming forever. Make the world safe for the new race of cosmic adventurers.

The fact that ecosystem ecology secured plenty of funds to carry on its research, and particularly funds from the government, suggests that it was the message of "efficient management" that got heard most loudly in high places. The Atomic Energy Commission, which had been so generous to the Odums, even hiring their students to work at the Oak Ridge National Laboratory and other federal facilities, was hardly interested in promoting fetus abortions or anti-growth tax laws or the rest of those "deductions" from the theory of the ecosystem. Nor was the Office of Naval

Research, which gave money to universities for ecology. Nor was the National Science Foundation, established in 1950 in the early days of the Cold War, an institution that would make American science the best funded in the world, intent on supporting Eugene Odum's political agenda when it began making research grants to the field. All of those sources saw environmental problems as inherently technical, not political or cultural, requiring skilled technocratic steering.

With that understanding dominating the funders' thinking, the dollars and pounds poured into ecosystem research in the 1960s and 1970s like a flooding river onto parched land. In 1961 the International Union of Biological Sciences embraced the idea of an International Biological Program in which many nations would join in an intense, coordinated drive for knowledge. The supporting resolution promised that scientists would soon learn how to modify "the global equilibrium and balance sheet of organic materials and resources, so as to improve the balance sheet by increasing production and reducing losses." Enhancing the world's productivity was to be a prominent goal. Every country must do its part. In Britain, the biologist Barton Worthington, retiring after a long career in Africa, much of it promoting the use of dams and irrigation, was made scientific director of IBP/GB. The Americans were slower to act, partly because of resistance from the powerful molecular biology establishment, jealous of ecology's growing competitiveness for funds. Nevertheless, the ecologists saw the promise before them, and led by Eugene Odum's enthusiastic endorsement, they seized the moment and brought their country formidably into the international effort. Led by W. Frank Blair and Frederick E. Smith, the ecosystem experts dominated IBP/US. They launched ambitious research projects for six critical biomes, or large ecological regions, including the grasslands, deserts, deciduous forests, coniferous forests, tundra, and tropical forests. Not all of those got funded, but those that did were very well funded indeed. The grasslands project, located about thirty miles east of Fort Collins, Colorado, became the biggest and most successful. From 1968 until 1976 it collected over $10 million from the National Science Foundation. The deciduous forest project, located near the Oak Ridge National Laboratory in Tennessee, also did quite well. Altogether, American ecologists got $50 million to study their biomes. Did the public get its money's worth? Opinion was divided, some saying yes and offering the evidence of many new publications, others doubting that we were any closer to a comprehensive knowledge of ecology and wondering what effect, if any, all the research had had on actual use of grasslands or forests. Defenders argued that many graduate students had gotten their start through IBP, and that as a school for training Sears' grassroots professionals the program was a resounding success. According to Blair, though, the main achievement was more theoretical: "the advancement of the concept of the ecosystem as a unit for ecological investigation."[42] The grand design behind IBP was to learn all about ecosystems at the regional level, then spring forward to the entire biosphere and improve global resource management. When the program shut down in 1974, that design was still a long way from completion—indeed, it would never be completed. Nor was the earth in any noticeably better shape from what had been done.

A growing number of ecologists disagreed with the whole approach represented by IBP, with "Big Biology" in general and its munificent funding by government sources, promising more than it could ever deliver. They did not believe that was the way science progressed and looked with suspicion on any grand synthesizing design, the bigger the worse. Instead of trying to describe the whole "system," the critics maintained, whether the grassland biome system or the pond ecosystem or the Planet Earth system, science ought to be looking at very small parts and getting positive knowledge about what was going on there. Theory must be discrete and detailed. Above all, it must venture predictions that could be tested and proved or disproved. Ecology was still a weak science, not because it lacked sustained funding, but because it lacked solid theory; it dealt too much in large, untestable abstractions and insoluble questions. Good theories simplify and abstract, the critics said, which the Odums' notion of unified theory at the global level failed to do; their work was more metabiology than science.

The leading figure in that dissenting party was Robert

MacArthur, an ecologist who had the kind of "superbrain" charisma commonly enjoyed by celebrities in physics. He showed little interest in the Odums' grand flow of energy and matter through air, seas, and coral reefs alike; instead, he wanted to find detailed patterns in the populations of animals. Ecology must be primarily the study of one species reacting upon another, he felt, a study focused on demography, fluctuating numbers, competition, predation, dispersal, geographical distribution. The fewer the number of species studied the more fruitful the research. A closely detailed study of the interrelations of warblers in a hardwood forest would reveal more reliable truth about ecological dynamics than all the eastern deciduous biome models could ever do. The scientist should be engaged in forming hypotheses about how those warblers divided up the habitat and testing those hypotheses on other species in other places. "Predict, predict, predict" was MacArthur's credo. An ecology that makes no testable predictions is not yet a science. He would seek a theoretical ecology based on narrower research, more mathematics, and stronger predictability.

MacArthur was another of G. Evelyn Hutchinson's graduate students at Yale, completing his work in 1957 with a dissertation on the regulation of warbler numbers in the Maine woods. He then taught at the University of Pennsylvania and Princeton University, where he established a strong ecology program that remains to this day. Hutchinson introduced him to a very different set of questions than he did Howard Odum, who had been in his seminars earlier. Odum learned about the global linkage between biology and chemistry in the grand "biospheric" tradition of the Russian scientist Vladimir Vernadsky. MacArthur, on the other hand, gravitated to another school, that of the experimental populationists like Vito Volterra (Italian), Alfred Lotka (American), Raymond Pearl (American), Georgii Gause (Russian), and A. J. Nicholson (Australian). Most important were the famous "Lotka–Volterra equations" describing predator–prey interactions in a simplified laboratory setting. All of those predecessors had tried to show mathematically how two or more interacting species reached a state of equilibrium, either between a predator and its prey, a parasite and its host, or competitors for the same food. Also important was the British ornithologist David Lack, who published his influential study of natural regulation, replete with many graphs on the rise and fall of species numbers, on the variance of clutch sizes as birds adjust their egg laying to environmental conditions, while MacArthur was still a graduate student, studying birds of his own. The mystery of those demographic relations, so vital to the balance of nature, intrigued the young scientist, and he joined the effort to reveal some of them.[43]

MacArthur was convinced that the structure of any ecological community, the fauna and flora living together in a place, was determined by the interaction of organisms, not by fortuitous external factors like climate. If he was right, then the interactions could be plotted and predicted, and the community structure described likewise. Nature would appear as a machine, and true science, he argued, is always "machinery oriented."[44] If he was wrong, then ecological communities were merely the accidents of time, resisting any scientific explanation. Eventually, he found the means to test his ideas. Most land and sea communities were complexly intertwined with others, resisting mechanistic analysis. Science needed laboratory experiments where conditions could be controlled, as Gause had done with his test-tube predators going after their prey. But the test-tube results were too far removed from reality to convey complete confidence. MacArthur needed a more natural laboratory. In the mid-1960s he, along with his research partner Edward O. Wilson of Harvard University, found an ideal one among the islands of the Caribbean. There were islands aplenty, some large, some small, some close to land masses, others far away. Approaching them comparatively, the ecologist could find reliable answers to questions about the relation of population growth to density, the diversity of species found in an area, the competition for place, the conditions of equilibrium. What the Galápagos were for Darwin, the Caribbean was for MacArthur and Wilson, a microcosm of evolution and biogeography. They may have produced fewer pathbreaking hypotheses than did Darwin, observing and thinking all alone with little support other than a free hammock aboard a ship, but their work set ecology going in a different direction.

Among other things, MacArthur and Wilson discovered that the number of species represented on an island depends on its size—big islands like Cuba supported more species than small islands—and it depends on location, with remote islands having a smaller number of species than ones close to large land masses. More interesting, the number of species always reached an equilibrium point. If an island was denuded, colonists began to arrive and repopulate the habitat, just as the case of Krakatoa, covered with volcanic ash in 1883, had demonstrated. But the number of species would eventually reach a point of stability; species did not keep on increasing forever, adding indefinitely to the diversity, but reached a point where any new colonization must be matched by an extinction. The diversity of insects, birds, lizards, and the like might look very different after repopulation than before, because exact community composition was contingent on changing circumstances, but the degree of diversity always ended up the same. The number of species able to settle was a function of a stabilized carrying capacity and therefore that number was regular, predictable, and susceptible to mathematical equations. Ignore the taxonomy then, which was trivial; focus instead on the consistent pattern of community structure.

Here was the long-awaited fruit of a more sophisticated, theoretical ecology, but many wondered whether better science only meant more work expended on proving smaller ideas. How would all the elaborate mathematics help to preserve the earth from degradation? Indeed, the quest for predictable hypotheses seemed to bring its own kind of environmental degradation. MacArthur and Wilson called at the end of their monograph for radical manipulation of those island laboratories:

There are many places in the world where islands are both very small and numerous: for example, the red mangrove islets of many tropical countries, the sand islets of the Caribbean, the Indian Ocean, the forested islets of the Canadian lakes, the lakes themselves, the hardwood "hammocks" of tropical grassland, the coniferous enclaves in tundra and on mountain tops. In these little places it is possible to remove elements of a biota or the entire biota, manually or by poisoning, or to add elements. Miniature "Krakataus" [Krakatoas] can be generated at will and in sufficient replication to yield statistically sound results.[45]

Chilling thoughts emanating from warm places. We murder to dissect, Wordsworth had complained, but he had no idea that whole biota might be killed to test a few interesting equations.

The speculation became deed when, in 1966–67, Wilson and Daniel Simberloff undertook to "defaunate" a total of seven "experimental islands" in the Florida Keys, averaging fifteen meters across, all red mangrove islets, in order to study the colonization process. They had to kill the existing fauna, consisting mainly of insects and spiders, to track the rate of resettlement by colonists from other islands. Hand-held sprays failed to get all the creatures, so they draped tents over the target islands and pumped in the fumigant methyl bromide which left some of the vegetation brown but did no lasting damage. During the following year they monitored the appearance of new colonists until they had hard evidence for the MacArthur–Wilson theory that an equilibrium stage, when no new invaders could get a foothold, was the regular outcome.[46]

So ecology progressed from asking impossibly large, insoluable questions about the global ecosystem to making precise experiments about faunal relations and keeping a precise body count. Meanwhile, the popular young enthusiasts painting "ecology now" on the side of buildings hardly had a clue that that was the way segments of the science were going. They wanted to heal the earth, and heal it fast. They were not interested in the minute details of the populationists, in logistic curves, competitive exclusion, the response of fertility to density, or techniques for defaunation. Among hard-nosed ecologists, the name MacArthur may have thrilled and challenged, but it was not a name that the public recognized or turned to for advice on how to deal with the global crisis. "MacArthur contributed almost nothing to the area of ecologic management," writes one of his ardent admirers. "I believe he rather disapproved of using ecology theory for management, impact statements, and the like. He seemed to feel that nature enriched the naturalist, and hence the world, in spiritual ways, so that there was a greater harvest of peace and truth than of lumber in a forest."[47] Perhaps so, though MacArthur was as silent about that "greater harvest" as he was about lumber.

Of course, the mathematical theory school argued that they were dishing up "real science," not peddling mere metaphors and worldviews for which the public had an unfortunate appetite. That was a false distinction. MacArthur thought in metaphorical terms too; he was simply less aware of them than he was those of others. To be "machinery-oriented," as he proclaimed he was, was to think of nature as a metaphorical machine. The significance of that fact did not escape other scientists, including the Finnish zoologist Yrjö Haila, who argued that "science is bound to language," which is to say, it cannot help thinking in terms of metaphors. And metaphors imply worldviews. Haila specifically showed how the MacArthur–Wilson work on island biogeography, though striving for neutral, quantitative, analytic models in ecology, was based on "a worldview of mechanistic determinism, incorporating a corpuscular view of matter and a mechanical view of causality," going back all the way to Descartes and Newton. That worldview had long tried, in the name of intellectual progress, to reduce nature's complexity to "a network of mechanistic, one-to-one causal chains." The only novelty in MacArthur's case was the brilliance with which he applied it to population ecology and his effectiveness in recruiting other scientists to follow his lead, winning many in the profession away from the Odums' holistic ecosystem as a unified theory.[48]

Beyond the campuses, however, ecology continued to suggest a very different worldview, a more holistic, organismic picture of the world associated with environmentalism and the Odums. But there too the Odums were eventually eclipsed by an even grander vision that came, as it were, from outer space. It had all the breathtaking impact of the newest technology, the most up-to-date science, yet paradoxically resonated with the oldest pagan beliefs. All the organisms of the earth, the public began to hear, were joined together into a single common living entity whose name was Gaia. She was ancient, she was female, she was the Earth Mother, and she held our destiny in her hands. Humans were only a minute part of Gaia, a hurtful part perhaps, but a part that was both incapable of living without her or of doing any ultimate damage. For many scientists the notion of Gaia was profoundly wrongheaded, but its creator was emphatically a distinguished scientist who was proposing a hypothesis supported by considerable evidence. Thus, Gaia became eventually the most widely discussed scientific metaphor of the Age of Ecology, overshadowing Eugene Odum's Spaceship Earth and Howard's electrical circuit board, and, at least with some scientists and many lay people, overshadowing Robert MacArthur's reductive search for the "machinery."

Gaia was born as an idea at the Jet Propulsion Laboratory in Pasadena, California, where in the late 1960s the staff was trying to detect through space probes whether there might be any life on Mars or Venus. Did anyone know how to define life, let alone find it through remote sensing? That was a fundamental embarrassment, solved by ignoring it. Visiting the group was a small, elfish Briton, James Lovelock, born in 1919, now nearly fifty years old, with doctorates from Manchester and London universities in chemistry and medicine, and a roving bent. For twenty years he had worked as staff scientist at the National Institute for Medical Research, then traveled to America where he taught engineering, physiology, and cybernetics briefly at Harvard, Yale, and Baylor Universities. Along the way he became an inventor of many devices, including an instrument for detecting trace elements in the atmosphere, a valuable tool for a polluted planet. The income from his inventions allowed him to leave academe behind and live as an independent scientist in the rural Wiltshire countryside, venturing out from time to time as a consultant. Now, he proposed a creative solution to the JPL's problem.

What Lovelock knew exceptionally well was the subject of atmospheric gases. Why, he wondered, was the atmosphere of Earth so radically different from that of Mars or Venus? Their atmospheres were almost wholly composed of carbon dioxide, 95 to 98 percent, while CO_2 was only a fraction of 1 percent of the earth's atmosphere. On the other hand, our air was 79 percent nitrogen, the other planets' a mere 2 or 3 percent, while we enjoyed a high oxygen level and theirs was a tiny trace. Other anomalies existed: the earth's average surface temperature, for example, was far below what it ought to have been in view of its position in the solar system; it ought to have been boiling hot, yet it averaged a comfortable thirteen degrees centigrade, wonderfully fit for life. In fact, the earth was in a great number of ways peculiarly suited for supporting living organisms, a fact noted earlier by Lawrence Henderson.[49] If the oxygen level suddenly fell, life as we know it would die; if it increased, then fires would burn uncontrollably and, again, life would disappear. The explanations offered by physical scientists for this happy median condition were thin and unpersuasive—the living planet, according to them, was an improbable accident. Something had upset the laws of thermodynamics and chemistry, it would seem, something not present on either Mars or Venus. That something, Lovelock concluded, was life itself. Life was not simply the beneficiary of improbable physical conditions; it was the active force making them improbable. He could no more define life than the biologists could, but he argued that life would be found wherever a planet's atmosphere showed its shaping presence. Life had first appeared on earth three and a half billion years ago, and since then the air had changed its composition while the temperature had remained virtually constant. Life was not, therefore, an insignificant passenger riding on a massive rock through space, but an extraordinary agency that had turned that rock into a commodious home—the only such home around.

The notion that life and the atmosphere had coevolved was not so very hard for scientists to take, though Lovelock pushed it farther than anyone else. Skepticism arose when he tried to give a name to the phenomenon. He might have used some "high-tech" acronym that no one would have objected to; instead, after consulting with his fellow Wiltshire villager, author William Golding, he chose Gaia, the name of the Greek goddess of gē, or earth, whose root appears in the words geology and geography. Gaia suggested that life collectively had the attributes of a person. Of course, that was not exactly what Lovelock meant to say, but he was fond of describing Gaia as a single being, of using the pronoun "she," and referring to "her" ability to "learn" how to manage things. What he meant to say, when he was being less poetic, was that the thirty million or so species worked together to control the chemistry of the planet to their mutual advantage. They had no conscious purpose in doing so, only a shared instinct for survival. Was Gaia then a fancy term for the combined effect of their independent actions? Or was she rather a new kind of entity, a great super-organism, the largest living creature on earth? Lovelock wobbled toward the latter notion, with much equivocating, and the scientific community held its nose in disgust.

When Lovelock first introduced his hypothesis at a Princeton scientific meeting in 1969, only two members of his audience found it appealing: a Swedish chemist, Gunnar Sillen, and an American microbiologist, Lynn Margulis, the latter known for her maverick views on the evolution of cooperation (she demonstrated that cells with nuclei, the eukaryotes, had evolved from communities of bacteria). Margulis became his chief ally at later meetings. Together, they marshaled evidence from laboratory research, computer models, and field studies of microorganisms floating along the seashore, the most important species in atmospheric chemistry. Their message, in simplest terms, was that "the biota and its environment constitute a single homeostatic system that opposes changes unfavorable for life." Not surprisingly, the message appealed to Eugene Odum, who incorporated the Gaian language into his later writings, and eventually it won a hearing from many other disciplines, culminating in a major conference of appraisal attended by dozens of scientists and philosophers of science.[50]

The public was first introduced to Lovelock's thinking through a book published in 1979, *Gaia: A New Look at Life on Earth*, followed in 1988 by *The Ages of Gaia*. They explained the scientific issues in clear, simple English, but Lovelock pushed farther into contemporary issues of ethics, religion, and environmental policy. The implications of the hypothesis, he believed, were profound. If true, then the most fundamental principle of life was not individualistic competition but cooperation and symbiosis. Gaia showed that organisms needed each other to survive, and the higher organisms needed the humblest bacterium. A logical flaw in this reasoning came from Lovelock himself: During the first billion years of life, he conjectured, the dominant organisms, cyanobacteria, lived in a methane-rich atmosphere almost devoid of oxygen. They produced more oxygen than reducing compounds in the sea could handle, and consequently free oxygen increased, a deadly pollutant to most existing forms of life. Organisms that could survive in the new atmosphere evolved quickly to become dominant, while the cyanobacteria retreated into oxygen-free refuges, the mud of swamps and bogs, the intestines of animals. Where was Gaia while all this happened? Where was mutualism operating when such a disastrous upheaval occurred, allowing one set of ecosystems to replace another? Lovelock offered the story as evidence of the marvelous adaptiveness of life but did not seem to realize that it undermined his claim that a single life force worked effectively to optimize the conditions for survival.[51]

Passing over such difficulties, some churchmen took Gaia to be one and the same as God, a divine power of harmony extending from the earth to the whole cosmos. Lovelock was astonished by that reading but reacted sympathetically, making clear all the while that he was no Christian but a confirmed agnostic. He confessed to reverential feelings toward Gaia, nonetheless, feelings that he found most alive in country settings where ancient paganism still survived. "The belief that the Earth is alive and to be revered is still held in such remote places as the west of Ireland and the rural parts of some Latin countries," he observed. Sharing such feelings, he had left modern urban civilization to seek a rural home, asking "how can we revere the living world if we can no longer hear the bird song through the noise of traffic, or smell the sweetness of fresh air?" If pagan leanings drove him and family to Wiltshire, they also made him hostile toward the modern "heresy of humanism, that narcissistic devotion to human interests alone." He deplored the overemphasis on human health and welfare he found in the cities, the "gross and excessive domination of nature" emanating from there. Nature was no divine sentient being, he agreed with fellow researchers, but "equally unacceptable to me spiritually is the materialist world of undiluted fact." Gaia was at once a testable hypothesis about biology, though highly speculative, and an object of deep spiritual feelings, though no new theological dogma. Lovelock could not overcome that deep ambivalence in his work.[52]

The ambivalence was very old in English and American culture, as we have seen. Lovelock brought up echoes of his countryman Gilbert White, exploring nature in the groves and meadows of Selborne, not far from Wiltshire. Once again, the modern spirit of science tried to merge, as it had done in the eighteenth century, with arcadian natural piety. Environmentalists found the combination wonderfully appealing, and they made Lovelock one of their most beloved visionaries, a rustified white-haired prophet for the Age of Ecology.

Lovelock, however, for various reasons found postwar environmentalism a flawed sensibility. He perceived it to be too concerned with the health of people, rather than the health of Gaia. Environmentalists were mainly worried about pollution, he observed, from industry, automobiles, pesticides, chlorofluorocarbons (which depleted the upper atmospheric layer of ozone), nuclear bombs, and power plants, none of which he believed was all that serious a threat to the biosphere. Pollution, he pointed out, was natural to Gaia. Carbon monoxide was naturally produced at a rate of billions of tons a year, and the most deadly poisons were manufactured in nature, not in laboratories. Oxygen was one of them—fresh air! Only from the point of view of humans and most other animals was oxygen a desirable gas and the present atmosphere worth protecting; for some species, it was highly toxic, and for all of us, even those who had evolved to need it, oxygen was slowly burning up our cells, destroying the instructions within them about reproduction and repair, eventually bringing death. If early organisms had evolved a way to live with the dangerous gas, so they might learn to live with modern toxic wastes and nuclear radiation too.

I have never regarded nuclear radiation or nuclear power as anything other than a normal and inevitable part of the environment. Our prokaryotic forebears evolved on a planet-sized lump of fall-

out from a star-sized nuclear explosion, a supernova that synthesized the elements that go to make our planet and ourselves.

Lovelock went so far as to argue that the most dreaded
catastrophe imaginable to the age, an all-out nuclear war
between the superpowers, would not be a fatal blow to Gaia,
though for mankind's sake he dreaded it. On a less apocalyptic issue, he pooh-poohed fears that industrial civilization as a whole was a mistake and doomed to fail.
"Industrial regions seldom appear from above to be the denatured deserts which the professional doomsters have led
us to expect," he wrote; even in the most crowded, artificial,
and polluted parts of England, Japan, and the United States,
life bloomed on the edges, waiting its chance to reclaim
lost territory. In the long sweep of time, industrialism appeared to be a small, temporary disturbance. More than that,
Lovelock saw signs that industrial civilization was a self-
correcting entity like Gaia, already noticing its effects and
putting things right again. We must not, therefore, over-
react, overregulate, or otherwise discourage technological
progress in the false hope that a "return to nature" could
or should be attempted.[53]

"All events are interconnected in this best of all possible
worlds," the Enlightenment philosopher Dr. Pangloss told
his pupil Candide. There was a lot of panglossism in James
Lovelock. Harmony was his ruling principle. Harmony between nature and technology was what he sought in his
private life. He was an inventor who loved machines, computers especially, and took a hopeful view of new inventions. Harmony in the political arena was another hope. He
harbored no bitter feelings toward the economic establishment—in fact, he had worked for international oil compa-
nies—nor toward the political structure of the right or the
left. Indeed, he was, on the whole, a happy, gentle man living
in a happy, gentle country that still had much to recommend it. Finally, whatever went wrong, there was always
the view from space, detached and philosophical, that
showed Gaia imperturbably adaptable, harmonizing everything in her reach.

Yet Lovelock was also an environmentalist, a member of
Britain's Ecology (later renamed Green) party, a worried
man. Agriculture, he warned, driven by a growing human

population, was the gravest threat facing the earth. To feed the teeming billions, farmers in country after country were assaulting the very fabric of life—committing "ecocide"—on a scale unmatched by factory owners or bomb makers. The plow was a more destructive tool than the computer or the automobile and the chain saw a more dire threat than the hydrogen bomb, for armed with them and devoted to their use, farmers and ranchers were tearing up the grasslands and clearing away the tropical rain forests on a massive scale, both critical parts of Gaia's body. Elsewhere, the primitive overgrazing of cattle was doing far more damage than any advanced technology, creating dust bowls in Africa, Latin America, and the American West. Rachel Carson had been right about the destructiveness of modern agriculture, the impending danger of a silent spring, Lovelock allowed, but chlorinated pesticides were not the whole, or even the most serious, threat. Aggressive agricultural land expansion was the greater threat, and it was reversing the processes of evolution. If humans ever tried to subdue the continental shelves and harvest their biota, the organisms most needed by Gaia, then a true and mighty calamity would follow. Those were Lovelock's major worries, though they did not seem to bother many urban environmentalists who were unaware of the ecological costs of the food that fed them.

Of course, Lovelock's choice of worries had its own kind of bias. They focused on threats that had touched him personally in ways that radiation poisoning or industrial squalor apparently had not. Shortly after settling into the Wiltshire landscape, Lovelock saw his chosen haven of green peace and birdsong transformed into an agribusiness factory. The fields of diverse grasses and wildflowers he loved were plowed up and reseeded to more productive monocultures, while the hedgerows laid out in olden times were cut down to allow use of larger farm machinery. "Determined to find a place where the environment was not likely to change so drastically again," the Lovelocks moved west to the thatched village of Bowerchalke in north Devon, where they found what they hoped was a more permanent sanctuary. "The recent destruction of the English countryside" was for them "a vandalism almost without parallel in modern history." Scientists had had a role in that damage, as had agronomists, along with politicians of all stripes and capitalistic landowners. They were all the enemies of Gaia, though none was aware of their guilt or especially evil in their motives. Lovelock was aware that his beloved countryside was no wild ecosystem; much of it had been constructed and reconstructed by humans, particularly in the days of Gilbert White, creating a deeply satisfying work of landscape art. That rural heritage appealed to him as an example of how humans might live cooperatively within the whole of nature, helping Gaia manage her affairs. Now that heritage was being lost to modernizing forces.

Thus, from his strong personal feelings for the rural landscape mingled strangely with his enthusiasm for space-age science, Lovelock derived an ecological ethic and preached it to the world. Finally more like Candide than Pangloss, he concluded that we must all cultivate our garden. The whole earth must be our common garden. Nurturing all the forms of life around us ought to become the new work of the species. The Gaian life force did not require that role of humans, and it would go on regardless of what we did, but our own survival did depend on learning how to cooperate with the land and to heal the wounds we had inflicted. We needed to see the world as an organism of which we were a subordinate part.

In his last published work, Lovelock admitted what he had not quite said before, though environmentalists had been saying it since Rachel Carson's day: the earth was seriously ill from human activity and needed the best medical care. Gaia was a little less tough than he had once claimed. "Let us forget human concerns, human rights, and human suffering," he wrote, "and concentrate instead on our planet, which may be sick. We are a part of this Earth and we cannot therefore consider our affairs in isolation. We are so tied to the Earth that its chills or fevers are our chills and fevers also."[54] Pollution, he eventually admitted, was a "great stress" to the global system, along with agriculture. The need, therefore, was for a new planetary medicine utilizing the skills and practical understanding of a doctor—a doctor for the environment, a country doctor.

Lovelock exemplified in his Gaian writings many of the

contradictions motivating the claims and efforts of ecological science in the Age of Ecology: the scientist must be at once an arcadian, a rural physician, and a global technocrat; an authoritative savior of Gaia and yet a self-effacing, minor member of a vast earthly community. That the earth was sick, and the sickness was our doing, was a spreading idea after World War Two. It depended on seeing the earth as a single living organism; otherwise what did the idea of "sickness" or "health" applied to the whole planet really mean? That view of the earth as organism was an old one, going back into prehistoric cultures, but it was reborn in the modern age, and ironically the image of an ailing but ancient organic planet came from the highly polished lens of a mechanical camera carried aloft in a mechanical spaceship.

CHAPTER 17

Disturbing Nature

IF THE OBSERVER always affects the observed, changing it from moment to moment, from glance to glance, then the observed also changes the observer. By the last decades of the twentieth century the biophysical environment had altered considerably from the days of Carolus Linnaeus and Gilbert White, and so had society, the economy, the scientific community, and its dominant ideas about nature. The world seemed more than ever in a tumult of change. By 1985 the human population was approaching five billion, doubling every forty years. All those people affected their surroundings, though to a varying degree. The landscape became a blur of motion. Nearly 500 million automobiles were on the roads, while planes of many nations streaked across the sky like a daily shower of meteors and communication satellites brought the news instantly from the embattled streets of Mogadishu or Los Angeles. What people saw from the vantage of those modes of transportation and communication was nature in upheaval. Each year about eleven million hectares of tropical forests and woodlands were destroyed; the effects could be tracked from space but apparently not prevented on earth. Meanwhile, more and more marriages were falling apart and institutions being discredited. Witness to all the extraordinary transformations going on, science changed its mind about a lot of things. Humans had become a profoundly disturbing element in the natural environment, and, in reaction, ecologists began to find the environment itself a disturbing thing.

On the first Earth Day, it seemed that the great coming struggle would be between what was left of pristine nature, delicately balanced in Eugene Odum's beautifully rational ecosystems, and a human race bent on mindless, greedy destruction. Two decades later, however, ecology had lost any clear notion of what pristine meant. Nature seemed less rational, less stable, and less harmonious. If there was any pattern out there, it was far more difficult to discern than earlier ecologists had supposed. The new views affected ecologists of every sort. Although Robert MacArthur had disagreed with the holistic-thinking Odum brothers about how science ought to be done, he shared with them, and with their common mentor, Evelyn Hutchinson, a belief that nature, at whatever level studied, tended toward equilibrium. The most natural state of nature was balance. That consensus fell apart. Another generation of ecologists began to question all the older ideas, theories, and metaphors, even to assert that nature is inherently unsettled.

Newspaper reporters did not commonly perceive that shift; as they covered oil spills, nuclear plant disasters, and carbon pollution, they continued to speak in terms of "upsetting the balance" and destroying "the ecology." Likewise, many scientists and land managers clung to the language of natural coherence and order. In a 1986 poll taken of its members by the British Ecological Society, 70 percent of the respondents ranked the "ecosystem" as one of the most important concepts their discipline had contributed to understanding the natural world; indeed, it ranked first on the list, outpolling nineteen other concepts. Other broad holistic ideas such as succession, energy flow, and conservation completed the top of the list. Most of the respondents were from the United Kingdom, and they were heavily biased toward "practical holism," including as they did large numbers of zoologists, conservationists, and geographers, and far fewer "theoretical reductionists" of the sort that had come to dominate many American research universities. The concept of predator–prey relations, consequently, was at the bottom of the list, along with population cycles.[1] But did the still popular idea of the ecosystem convey the same meaning it once did of a world of order and stability? Not at all, for many of the leading thinkers in ecology were already pulling away from Odum's influence, from the idea of the ecosystem as an integrated whole in a state of homeostasis, even from the word itself.

The newest Anglo-American textbooks in the field showed those trends unmistakably. Perhaps the most popular text in the United Kingdom was by Michael Begon, John Harper, and Colin Townsend, for whom the study of ecology was divided into three hierarchical levels: the individual organism, the population of a given species, and the ecological community, made up many populations. The ecosystem was conspicuously not one of those levels; out of six hundred pages, they devoted a single paragraph to the ecosystem concept, and then only to reject it as a nonentity. Similarly, the British authors R. J. Putnam and S. D. Wratten mentioned the ecosystem in passing but preferred to focus on competition among species as the conceptual heart of ecology. The same could be said for the big-selling American textbook author Paul Colinvaux and for newcomer Peter Stiling, whose introductory text of 1992 gave the ecosystem less than forty pages out of six hundred, with most of the emphasis going instead to such topics as natural selection, foraging for resources, food webs, and community change over time. More true to Odum's legacy was the Stanford team of Paul Ehrlich and Jonathan Roughgarden, who organized their text into the older four-tiered hierarchy, rising from the individual organism through populations and communities to the ecosystem (though Odum had reversed the order, starting from the top down as it were). And there was still Robert Ricklefs, turning out the several editions of his best-selling text, keeping the traditions alive by arguing for the essential orderliness of nature. Different authors, different emphases. Still, the field was perceptibly moving away from that unified theory that had sought to bring the living and the nonliving together into a single, coherent, balanced, and orderly system.[2]

A telling question that separated the generations was whether the outcome of ecological succession was a state of stability or not. When a new assortment of species entered a landscape and replaced the one that was there, ecologists said succession had occurred. A pine grove replaced an aspen one, or oaks and hickories replaced a tallgrass prairie. If the sequence began on bare rock, the pattern of succession was called "primary"; when vegetation had been disturbed but the soil not destroyed, as when a fire swept across a prairie or a hurricane leveled a wood, ecologists spoke of "secondary" succession.[3] Either variety was supposed to reach a final resting point. Succession marched down a straight and narrow road to equilibrium, also called the climax or homeostatic stage. Burning down the climax forest, therefore, meant throwing succession into an earlier, more backward, and unstable state.

So had gone the conventional view. Then in 1973, the *Journal of the Arnold Arboretum* published an article by two scientists associated with the Massachusetts Audubon Society, William Drury and Ian Nisbet, challenging that view fundamentally. Their observations, drawn from southern New England's temperate forests, led them to assert that the process of ecological succession did not lead anywhere. Change went on in the composition of the landscape without any determinable direction, and it went on forever, never reaching any state of stability. They found no evidence of a progressive development over time: no trend toward biomass constancy, diversification of species, cohesiveness of plant and animal communities, or biotic control over the inorganic environment. Indeed, they found none of the criteria Eugene Odum had posited for mature ecosystems. The forest, they insisted, no matter what its age, was nothing but an erratic, shifting mosaic of trees and other plants. "Most of the phenomena of succession," they argued, "should be understood as resulting from the differential growth, differential survival, and perhaps differential dispersal of species adapted to grow at different points on stress gradients." In other words, they could see lots of individual species doing their own thing, but they could discover no emergent order among the species, nor any "strategy" to achieve one.[4]

Prominent among the authorities they cited in support of their view was the nearly forgotten Henry Gleason, who in 1926 had challenged Frederic Clements and his theory of the climax in an article provocatively entitled, "The Individualistic Concept of the Plant Association." Gleason had argued that we live in a world of constant flux and impermanence, not one tending toward stability. There was no such thing, he argued, as a balance of nature or an equilibrium or steady state. Each and every plant association was nothing but a temporary mingling of species along the road, here for a brief moment today and on their way to somewhere else tomorrow. The mingling was pure anarchy. "Each... species of plant," he wrote, "is a law unto itself," struggling against other species for resources. We look for cooperation in nature and we find only competition. We look for organized wholes, and we discover only loose atoms and fragments. We hope for order, but all we see is a wild jostling of species, each seeking its own advantage in utter disregard of the welfare of others.[5]

Gleason drew those conclusions from traveling along the Mississippi River, observing the alluvial forests, one of the most shifting environments in North America. Undoubtedly, he was right that such a flood-prone place never achieved any climax stage, and that discrete communities were hard to isolate and identify, but whether he was right to generalize that peculiar environment to the whole of nature was questionable. And that he chose to describe all of nature by the highly political term "individualistic" made him at least as guilty of metaphoric excess as any of the holistic ecologists. Despite those weaknesses, which had led earlier ecologists to dismiss his conclusions, Drury and Nisbet revived his lost reputation and theory. Eventually, their challenge to the climax theory became the core idea of what some scientists hailed as a new, revolutionary paradigm in ecology.

In 1977 two other biologists, Joseph Connell and Ralph Slatyer, continued the attack on climax or steady-state thinking by denying the old claim that an invading community of pioneering species, constituting the first stage in succession, worked to prepare the ground for its successors, like a group of Daniel Boones blazing the trail for civilization. The first comers, according to Connell and Slatyer, managed in most cases to stake out their claims and defend them successfully. They did not give way before a later group of long-term settlers. Only when the pioneers died or were damaged by natural disturbances, thus freeing the resources they had monopolized, did latecomers find a foothold and get established.[6]

As this assault on established notions gathered momentum, the word "disturbance" began to appear more and more frequently in the scientific literature and be taken far more seriously. "Disturbance," connoting extreme exogeneous change, was not a common subject in Odum's heyday, let alone that of Clements or other founding figures, and it almost never appeared in combination with the adjective "natural." Now, however, it was as though scientists were out looking strenuously for signs of disturbance—especially signs of disturbance that were not caused by humans—and they were finding them everywhere, leaving little tranquility in primitive nature. Fire became a commonly mentioned disturber, so commonly in fact that nature seemed to be constantly ablaze. So was wind in the form of violent hurricanes and tornadoes, ripping through the trees and knocking them down. So were invading populations of microbes, pests, and predators. And then there were volcanic eruptions to be factored in. Grinding ice sheets. Devastating droughts. Above all, it was those last sorts of disturbances, caused by the restlessness of climate, on which the newest generation of ecologists fastened.

One of the most important expressions of the new post–Odum ecology was a book of essays edited by S. T. A. Pickett and P. S. White in 1985. Though some of the authors in the final section of the book dealt with ecosystems, the word had lost much of its original substance. Two authors in fact began by complaining that too many scientists assumed that "homogeneous ecosystems are a reality," when in truth "virtually all naturally occurring and man-disturbed ecosystems are mosaics of environmental conditions." "Historically," they wrote, "ecologists have been slow to recognize the importance of disturbances and the heterogeneity they generate." The reason for that reluctance was clear: "The majority of both theoretical and empirical work has been dominated by an equilibrium perspective." Repudiating that perspective, the authors took the reader off to the tropical forests of South and Central America and to the Everglades of Florida, demonstrating instability on every hand—a wet, green world undergoing continual disturbance, or, as they preferred to say, a world "of perturbations," big and small. Another essay described even the grasslands of North America as a regularly perturbed environment, a "dynamic, fine-textured mosaic" that was kept in a state of upheaval by the workings of badgers, pocket gophers, and mound-building ants, along with fire, drought, and eroding wind and water. The persistent message in the various essays was that the climax notion was dead, the ecosystem concept had receded into vagueness, and in their place stood the idea of the lowly "patch." Nature should be regarded as a shifting landscape of vegetative patches of all textures and colors, a veritable patchwork quilt of living things, changing continually through time and space, responding to an unceasing barrage of perturbations. The stitches in that quilt never held for long.[7]

This new picture was derived, as Gleason's had been, from observations made over rather short periods of time, and to be more fully credible the picture needed longer-term data. Those data lay buried in the sediments of lakes left behind by retreating ice sheets. Northern European scholars had been the first to go digging in such sediments. They had developed a technique known as palynology, the study of fossil pollen, which like old bones could be used to reveal nature's past. The leading American practitioner of the technique was Margaret Davis of the University of Minnesota, who undertook to rewrite the history of the North American forest from sedimentary archives. Standard plant distribution maps had long showed great sturdy kingdoms of deciduous forests lying across what is now the eastern United States, mixed forests surrounding the Great Lakes, boreal forests across the Canadian north, and to the far north the cold kingdom of tundra. But studied historically, those regimes proved to be as impermanent as any human ones. Davis took the Quaternary period, the last 2 million years during which ice sheets advanced and retreated in the northern latitudes, as her time frame. Had anyone taken time-lapse photographs of Minnesota or Massachusetts during that period, he would have had a dramatic story to show. During the last glacial maximum, 18,000 years ago, the ice sheets covered a third of the continents, and the continental shelves lay exposed as the sea level fell. Even the tropics were affected by the glacial cycles, though far less violently. Vegetation everywhere had to shift out of the way of the ice or of colder, wetter air. Animals could fly or walk to more favorable climes, but the trees were much slower to migrate, and some species were much slower than others. Holistic ecologists had long assumed that species living together, needing each other, must have migrated en masse, and then, when the ice retreated, returned en masse. But Davis found no evidence for that communitarianism. They left in a ragged rout. Trees, to be sure, are by nature less dependent on each other than animals are; they seem to do little more than struggle for space against their competitors. In the great cooling they had shown themselves to be classic individualists.

As the climate began to alter again, warming rapidly and melting the last ice sheet, southern New England once again furnished a revealing window on that ragged scene. First, ponds and lakes dotted a tundra landscape, then spruce trees invaded for a while, then pines and birches came along about 8,000 to 9,500 years ago, making the area resemble modern-day Ontario. Then came the deciduous trees straggling back from their refuges in northern Florida and the lower Mississippi valley, each species following a different migration route and a different schedule. The hickories arrived some 4,000 years ago, the chestnuts 1,000 years later.[8]

Climate was the dominant reason for all that profound instability in organic nature. Clements had believed in long-term climatic regularities, allowing his grassland climaxes to persist, but according to Davis and other palynologists, he had been wrong. Davis, however, did not consider the time scale used by scientists like James Lovelock, which showed that the earth's climate, examined over eons not millennia, had been remarkably steady and the ice sheets were, from the perspective of outer space, only small blips on a large monotonous graph. Her sedimentary archives did not encourage that perspective; her time frame was shorter and the blips looked awfully big and irregular. "For the last 50 years or 500 or 1,000," she wrote, "as long as anyone would claim for 'ecological time'—there has never been an interval when temperature was in a steady state with symmetrical fluctuations about a mean.... Only on the longest time scale, 100,000 years, is there a tendency toward cyclical variation, and the cycles are asymmetrical, with a mean much different from today."[9] The evidence for that conclusion was ample; only its interpretation was open to dispute. Determining whether nature is "stable" or "unstable" depends entirely on where the observer stands, on what time scale is chosen, and on how the terms are used. Does stability mean a constancy of species in a given area, and is that constancy to be measured over months or decades or centuries or millennia or eons? Or does it mean a quality of resilience, a capacity for ecological communities to recover and reassemble after catastrophic disturbance, however frequently it occurs? Is the fact that there have been deciduous forests thriving someplace in North America over a span of tens of millions of years evidence of stability or instability?[10]

Standing in the same landscapes of North America but looking at other factors than climate, scientists could come to different conclusions than Davis drew. In the mid-1960s two forest ecosystem specialists, Herbert Bormann and Gene Likens, organized an experimental project in the Hubbard Brook section of New Hampshire's White Mountains National Forest, an area settled by white colonists two hundred years earlier and cut over repeatedly, now grown back to sugar maples, yellow birch, red spruce, and balsam fir. Inspired by Eugene Odum, they identified a half-dozen small "watershed-ecosystems" and began to study their species composition, nutrient cycling, biomass production, soil erosion, and the like. One unit they "devegetated" to observe the effects of bare slopes on stream runoff; other ecosystems they left intact. Over the next several decades the Hubbard Brook studies became the most famous in the United States for precision of data, number of publications, and comprehensiveness of approach. They also lent rather more support to Odum's theory of a steady state than to the Gleason–Davis picture of utter anarchy. Examined over hundreds, not thousands, of years, the forest showed little sign of catastrophic disturbance apart from the European axe. Fires set by lightning or Indians were uncommon, and hurricanes seldom reached the area. Even when clear-cut by the colonists (removing almost every tree), the forests eventually recovered, showing in a few centuries the qualities of a mature ecosystem. Within that overall stability the experimenters admittedly found irregular patches where some of the trees were younger than the norm, leading them to describe the scene as a "shifting-mosaic steady state." The phrase nicely borrowed from the critics of Odum and Clements while reaffirming traditional thinking about the balance of nature.[11]

The protean text of nature was becoming a bible in the hands of many conflicting interpreters who could find a verse somewhere in its pages, often within the same chapter, for any creed or dogma they professed. Nonetheless, despite all the disputing over different texts, different places, and different scales, a gradual consensus began to emerge and it stressed the naturalness of disturbance. A major voice in forest ecology, Daniel Botkin, who had designed the computer program employed at Hubbard Brook, summed up the new opinion with an assured voice:

Until the past few years, the predominant theories in ecology either presumed or had as a necessary consequence a very strict concept of a highly structured, ordered, and regulated, steady-state ecological system. Scientists know now that this view is wrong at local and regional levels ... that is, at the levels of population and ecosystems. Change now appears to be intrinsic and natural at many scales of time and space in the biosphere.

"Wherever we seek to find constancy" in nature, Botkin wrote, "we discover change.... We see a landscape that is always in flux, changing over many scales of time and space, changing with individual births and deaths, local disruptions and recoveries, larger scale responses to climate from one glacial age to another, and to the slower alterations of soils, and yet larger variations between glacial ages."[12]

Now, of course, scientists had known about the Ice Age and droughts, individual births and deaths, raging fires and winds for a considerable time, though much of the sedimentary evidence was new. Yet until very recently they had not let any of those disruptions spoil their theories about balanced plant and animal associations. They saw and yet they dismissed such forces as relatively insignificant—not decisive threats to the prevailing order of nature. Why then did the post-Odum generation give so much weight to those same changes, often to the point of seeing nothing but instability in the landscape? Was it a matter only of recognizing new scientific evidence, or was it due to a deeper cultural shift going on?

Evidence supporting the former explanation came heavily from the growing subfield of population biology, that is, from ecologists who were not trained in ecosystem analysis. When they looked at a forest, the population ecologists saw only the various species of trees, and counted them—so many white pines, so many hemlocks, so many maples and birches. They insisted that if they could know all there was to know about the species that constituted a forest, and could measure their abundance in precise, quantitative terms, they would know all there was to know about that forest. It had no "emergent" or organismic properties, creating some whole greater than the sum of its parts, requiring holistic understanding. If ecosystems or communities existed, they did so as mere epiphenomena generated by the activities of individual species. Outfitted with computers that could track the rise and fall of those populations, and with a new array of theoretical models, logistic curves, and equations to describe the data, they brought a degree of mathematical precision to ecology that was awesome to contemplate.

On the other hand, more was going on in ecological theory than the rising influence of population studies. The long-time dean of populationists, Robert MacArthur, had used some of the same tools but come to very different conclusions than his successors. For him, as for later populationists, competition among species had been the foundation principle of ecology, as it was of life in general, and the structure of any ecological community was determined primarily by that competition. But MacArthur had believed that competition always produced a finely tuned balance in nature's machinery. Species swung back and forth as on a fixed pendulum, and the motion of their competitive interaction was exactly predictable. The newer populationists disagreed with that way of thinking. They insisted that any structure found in ecological communities was nothing but the product of interactive populations, and then they insisted that they could find little if any balance. When they looked at population histories for any patch of land, they saw wildly swinging oscillations, not the rhythmic movements of a pendulum. Populations rose and fell erratically, like stock market prices, automobile sales, and dressmakers' hemlines. Nor did communities reliably exhibit the same structure under similar environmental conditions. We live, they began to insist, in a nonequilibrium world of many billion organisms bumping madly against one another.

One of the leaders of the new generation of populationists, John Wiens, explained how he had begun his studies "fervently embracing the existing views of competitively structured, equilibrium communities. But I have become skeptical of much of this dogma, and believe now that we know far less about the patterns and processes of communities than we think we do." Populations might even be so independent of one another that they might not compete at all. Their numbers might be determined not by the pressures of fighting over a limited amount of food, like rival bacteria in the constrained and controlled habitat of a Petri dish, but by completely unpredictable variations in the abiotic environment. According to another dissident, Robert Colwell, the landscape looked like "a sometimes turbulent and bewildering place where disturbance, natural enemies, biochemistry, life histories, and behavior play leading roles, along with the original cast of competitors." That was the way the world looked to the new populationists because, in large part, they looked at the old data with changed eyes.[13]

The most outspoken critic of the competition-leading-to-balance model in ecology was Daniel Simberloff, the defaunation expert of the Florida Keys. For him, the underlying issue raised by the revisionists was much larger than anyone had suspected; it was nothing less than whether ecology was to be placed on a true material basis or not. Science, he argued as had many others before him, depended on a material view of the universe. That meant purging it of all immaterialism, of "Platonic idealism and Aristotelian essentialism," which had viewed biophysical nature as the imperfect embodiment of fundamental, unchanging essences, like ideas in the mind of God, or like the ecosystem in the mind of Odum. Every super-organismic, holistic notion had to be weeded out of ecology, for there was no material substance to any of them. Precisely that, Simberloff said, was what Henry Gleason had tried to do back in the twenties—fight against the old metaphysics still lurking in ecology—and his plea for "individualism" had been a broom to sweep away the idealist cobwebs. But then Simberloff went on to assert that the biology of MacArthur had plenty of cobwebs of its own. Although indubitably materialist and reductionist, his work had been flawed by a faith in mechanistic determinism. Any rigid cause-and-effect theory, whatever its controlling metaphor, organicism or mechanism, was a lingering remnant of nonscientific thinking—shades of archaic idealism. MacArthur, like Odum or Clements, had tried to make nature into a single, coherent picture where all the pieces fitted firmly together. So for that matter had Sir Isaac Newton. So had anyone who talked confidently about specific causes always producing specific, exact effects. A genuine scientific materialism, in contrast, rejected determinism, because matter was fundamentally indeterminate and could not be wholly captured by any precise calculus. Nature was neither a simple machine nor a wispy ghost dwelling in the machine. The long war between the rival metaphors was over, both were exhausted and defeated. Nature, it was now claimed, followed the rules of chance, not necessity.[14]

What Simberloff came very close to saying was that all theories, all abstractions, all metaphors, in ecology were suspect, for all smacked of metaphysics. All of them tried to reduce the disorderliness of nature to a single all-encompassing idea, when it was "the individuality of populations and communities" that was "their most striking, intrinsic, and inspiring characteristic." The living world of nature was inherently a world of unique and unpredictable individual events, setting biology off from the physical sciences and making it difficult for physical scientists to understand biological phenomena. "We will not, in the future," he wrote, "have sufficient information or insight to produce equations as predictive as those of most physicists or engineers."[15]

The strenuous effort that had gone into making the field of ecology over into a branch of physics, into emulating the big-money operations of the physical sciences, or into launching space-age projects like the International Biological Program had been misguided in Simberloff's view. In reacting hostilely to those efforts, he was clearly thinking about more than nature. When he admitted to being "inspired" by a nature that defied all firm predictions, he gave himself away. A world of chance implied a world of freedom, social as well as natural. The dominant traditions in ecology repelled him in large part because they reflected a kind of society, and a kind of science, he did not want to join: rigid, law-making, ordered, grandiose, bureaucratic.

Of course, Simberloff had his own comprehensive picture of the whole, his own set of abstractions, to push. He called his ecology a science of "probabilism." "The most complete statement which can be made about the world," he declared, "is a probabilistic one: a distribution of probabilities of states of the physical universe (or some part of it), or a specified statistical distribution of possible outcomes of some event." Probabilists believed in relative, not absolute, truth. Certainty in knowledge was unattainable, and thus all we could hope to establish was a likelihood that nature would act in this way or that. Probabilism spoke the language of the gambler: there was, it might say, a two-in-three chance that the next decade would become warmer than this one, there was a four-in-five chance that all the hemlocks in an area would disappear if it did. Organisms, it might be claimed, *generally* behaved in such and such a way, but in any given case the scientist could not be altogether sure they would. He could only offer an approximation.[16]

Simberloff admitted that there was something "profoundly disturbing" about a nature in which so much was unpredictable, so much had to be assigned to chance, so much freedom and randomness were at play. The idea of living in an unbalanced, unpredictable world raised people's fears, upset deeply seated views, threatened the secure. But that was the picture of nature many younger ecologists like himself began to embrace. Their hero in a struggle for acceptance was Charles Darwin, the great revolutionary of the previous century, the most important figure in the history of ecology, and a materialist through and through. Darwin had raised people's fears by unsettling their ideas about nature. He had had to fight against entrenched views with the authority of organized religion behind them. Nonetheless, he had succeeded in putting biology on a new, more modern basis. His theory of evolution through natural selection rejected the idea of species as fixed entities, or ideal types, created by God in the beginning of time, but also rejected the archaic image of organic nature as a precisely balanced machine resembling the planets moving in their spheres. Evolution, he showed, was a more ragged and opportunistic process than traditional thinking or common metaphors had allowed. No one could predict what new creatures might evolve next. The world was open-ended.

Such a reading of Darwin as the father of ecological probabilism was not completely plausible. He had indeed overthrown the notion of species as ideal types arrayed in a divine plan and insisted on explaining things in pure, material terms, with no recourse to mysterious indwelling forces or an anima mundi or a directing spiritual power. But for all that, Darwin was not really a probabilist. He did not, that is, think of nature as fundamentally stochastic, changing in random ways that did not observe strict, simple laws of cause and effect. Indeed, his views more closely anticipated those of Robert MacArthur a century later in that he understood competition to be the dominant process in nature and was sure that competition always produced a tightly interwoven structure of balance and order.

Darwin, however, had become almost everybody's hero in ecology, an authority that many rival ecologists wanted on their side. His name had earlier been recruited by the critics of Odum's ecosystems ecology. That paradigm had come to seem, in its rather static functionalism, to be very un-Darwinian, and a shift had begun toward an "evolutionary ecology," as G. H. Orians first proclaimed in 1962. Instead of merely describing the interrelationships of living organisms with their environment, or explaining how things functioned, ecology must show how they had come to be what they were—the why of relationships as well as the how. By that point in the history of science the whole study of evolution was enjoying a powerful renaissance, a "new synthesis" it was called, in which Darwin's natural selection and Gregor Mendel's genetics were joined together into a single program of research. Biologists now believed they had the full set of theories needed to understand the lives of organisms. They could give a reason, better than any that Darwin could give, as to why variations among plants and animals appeared in the first place—namely, the recombination of genes through sexual reproduction; and they also had refined Darwin's explanation for why some variations survived and others did not—the selective pressures of the environment. Although the latter theme was through-and-through ecological, the ecologists had been slow to take part in the new synthesis, allowing the geneticists to dominate. They were too interested in functional analysis of ecosystems. Now, that lag was much regretted. As John Harper declared, "The theory of evolution by natural selection is an ecological theory—founded on ecological observation by perhaps the greatest of all ecologists. It has been adopted by and brought up by the science of genetics, and ecologists, being modest people, are apt to forget their distinguished parenthood." But not for long, as suddenly Darwin came looming out of the shadows, his face before every ecologist. The title of Evelyn Hutchinson's book of essays, *The Ecological Theater and the Evolutionary Play*, published in 1965, captured the newly awakened interest in Darwinism perfectly: ecologists must take as their proper province the study of the theater in which the drama of evolution was unfolding.

The rediscovery of Darwin was also a rediscovery of competitive struggle as the leading theme in biology, and it forced ecologists to look for competition where many had been firmly convinced nature showed mainly a spirit of altruism and cooperation. Science must get back to the bloody warfare of tooth and claw. Then came a question of profoundly disturbing implications: If competition was indeed so important in making the ecological theater what it was, then on what level of biological organization should they be looking? Which entities were actually doing the competing, which were the real actors in the play? Was it ecosystems that were competing against one another? Was it communities? Or was it really only the individual organisms? If the ecosystem was supposed to be the key entity in ecology, then what was the ecosystem competing against—other ecosystems? How, unless there were two or more ecosystems fighting to possess a plot of land, could the ecosystem be a real entity after all, shaped by the forces of evolution? How, for that matter, could an entity as big as Gaia, the total system of life on the planet, be considered real, a product of natural selection? Gaia, argued some critics, had no competitors on this earth, and logically could have none. If there was no competition, if there could be none at the level of the whole planet, there could be no selection going on. And if there was no selection, then there was no evolution, no existence, no entity. Earlier ecologists had tried to escape that rigorously reductive Darwinian logic by suggesting that supra-individual entities had emerged through "adaptation" to their environment, not through competition; that is, they had evolved through trying to fit themselves to their surroundings without taking it away from rivals. But in 1966 the staunchly neo-Darwinian biologist George Williams exploded such thinking by showing that even adapting to the environment could be achieved only by individual organisms, not groups. There was no such thing, he argued, as "group selection." If he was right, and most ecologists believed he was, then that was a devastating blow against all holistic ecosystems thinking.

The turn toward Darwinistic evolutionism characterizes the past two or three decades in ecology, though "turn" hardly conveys the turbulent heterogeneity of the science in that period, the heated controversies over cooperation versus competition, wholes versus parts, populations versus ecosystems that have touched scientists' beliefs in the deepest way. Neo-Darwinism was itself premised on the primacy of conflict. Its proponents dismissed cooperation-centered ecology as bad science that had tried to find in nature some support for their ethical point of view—their "love thy neighbor" views, as George Williams snorted. But then, as we have seen, the battles did not end there with a resounding triumph over benign holism, for those who had carried the Darwinian banner of competition were soon overtaken from the rear by a boisterous group claiming to be themselves the true heirs of Darwin. They wanted to paint on the banner the words "random" and "stochastic," even if doing so meant painting over the words "competition," "balance," and "stability." The logic of Darwinism for them led finally to the conclusion that the world was always in the making, always impossible to predict. If the individual organism was indeed the key player, and there was less and less disputing that view, then we could not say exactly what the individual would do. Freedom would rule.

Behind the neo-neo-Darwinism of Simberloff, Wiens, and others was more than a wrangle going on within the ranks of ecology over who should carry the banner of Darwin. Similar ideas about stochaticism and instability were appearing throughout the mathematical, natural, and social sciences, as well as within the humanities, indicating a change occurring within the worldview of all advanced technological societies. It was nothing less than the discovery, and even in some circles the celebration, of disorder. All nature, all human life, many began to claim, is *fundamentally* erratic, discontinuous, and unpredictable. The world is full of surprising events, and they keep hitting us in the face. Dark clouds collect overhead, with rain appearing imminent, and then abruptly they disperse and the rain doesn't fall, leaving the weather forecasters looking sheepish. Cars suddenly bunch up on the freeway, and the traffic controllers fly into a frenzy, all their plans gone awry. A man's heart beats regularly year after year, then suddenly begins to skip a beat now and then, and the physicians are uncertain why. A Ping-Pong ball bounces off the table in an unexpected direction. Each and every little snowflake falling out of the sky turns out to be completely unlike any other, due to minute differences in their conditions. All those were ways in which nature seemed to be imponderable and inconsistent. If the ultimate test of any body of scientific knowledge was its ability to predict events, then the sciences, despite so many grand successes, were frequently failing the test.

Making sense of that failure was the mission of an altogether new kind of inquiry calling itself the science of chaos. Some said it portended a revolution in thinking that was equivalent to quantum mechanics or relativity. Like those other theories, the theory of chaos rejected tenets going back as far as the days of the founders of modern science. In fact, what was occurring was not two or three separate theories popping up in different disciplines but a single revolution rising up against all the principles, laws, models, and applications of classical science, the science ushered in by the great Scientific Revolution of the seventeenth and eighteenth centuries.[17]

Throughout the modern era the scientific community had assumed that nature, despite a few appearances to the contrary, was a perfectly manageable system of simple, linear, rational order. The metaphor for that system had been the clock, arguably the dominant machine of the modern age. Nature ticked on and on with clocklike precision. Sir Isaac Newton had believed that image and had tried to write the mathematical equations that would describe all the gears and wheels whirling inside the apparatus. The French mathematician Pierre Simon de Laplace had agreed: Give him all the facts, he promised, and he would describe that clockwork order in complete detail. Standing outside and above nature, he would plot all the lines along which everything must move, the speed of movement, and the collisions that must occur. He would, that is, become like God, who already had all the facts. For some scientists and philosophers in the twentieth century, the invention of the computer seemed to bring that godlike knowledge closer to human grasp, but then the computers started to reveal a surprising degree of disorder, unperceived by pencil-and-paper calculators. Even the simplest equations could generate on the screen a motion that was so complex it appeared random. For whatever reason, whether because the empirical data suggested it or because extrascientific cultural trends did— the experience of so much rapid, unpredictable, disturbing change in the world around them—scientists were beginning to pay attention to what they had long managed to avoid seeing. Nature was far more complex than they had ever realized, or indeed, some were beginning to hint, than science ever could realize.[18]

Chaos was, like Gaia, a word that came welling up from

the lost pagan cosmology of ancient Greece to seize the imagination of avant-garde scientists. If the earth goddess had long ago brought life and order into existence, then chaos had been her opposite: the realm where disorder still ruled, a dark underworld that had existed before creation did and where the dead were still condemned to dwell. Chaos was evil, Gaia was good. Without ever quite acknowledging its parentage, modern science had been in a sense the offspring of Gaia, growing up with a strong, unquestioned faith in the benevolent rule of law and order in the universe. Acting on that faith, scientists had seen themselves as discoverers of the "laws of nature." Now, however, they began to wonder whether they had been wrong. Perhaps nature was ruled by that primordial lawless force after all, and order was only the dream of man. Instead of order happily emerging out of chaos, it was chaos that kept boiling up from the darkness, breaking down order.

The scientific study of chaos began (if one could talk thus about so pervasive a set of ideas) in 1961 with efforts to simulate weather and climate patterns on a computer at the Massachusetts Institute of Technology. There, meteorologist Edward Lorenz came up with his now famous "butterfly effect," the notion that a butterfly stirring the air today in a Chinese park can transform the storm systems appearing next month over a North American city. Scientists called that phenomenon a "sensitive dependence on initial conditions." What it meant was that tiny differences in input might quickly become substantial differences in output. A corollary was that we could not know, even with all our artificial-intelligence apparatus, every one of the tiny differences that were occurring at any place or any point in time; and even if we could, we still could not know which tiny differences would produce which particular substantial differences in output. Which butterfly in which park and which particular flap of its wings should we pay attention to? Which storm, which flood, going on thousands of miles away? There were simply too many variables to plot all the lines of influence, of cause and effect. As a consequence, scientists must acknowledge that nature is essentially non-linear in its processes. Weather was the classic example of that fact: Weather was emphatically nonlinear. Beyond a short range of, say, two or three days, weather predictions were not worth the paper they were written on.

The implications of the "butterfly effect" for the field of ecology were profound. If a single flap of an insect's wings on another continent could lead to a torrential downpour in New York City, then what might it do to the Greater Yellowstone Ecosystem? What could ecologists possibly know about all the forces impinging on, or about to impinge on, any piece of land, any community of organisms? What could they safely ignore in the way of exogenous forces and what must they give strict attention to? What distant, invisible, minuscule events might even now be happening that would change the very structure of the plant and animal life in our backyards? That was the challenge presented by the science of chaos, and it altered the imagination of many scientists dramatically.

Despite the growing popularity of the new ideas, however, ecologists were among the last to become interested in them and only a few ever made a full conversion to the science of chaos. But a discernible move toward the new way of thinking came in 1974 when Robert May, a physicist from Australia who moved to the biology department at Princeton and eventually took over Robert MacArthur's chair in the department, published an essay on ecology with the word "chaos" in its title.[19] He admitted that the mathematical models he and others had been trying to construct for various populations were inadequate approximations of the ragged life histories of organisms. They did not fully explain, for example, the aperiodic outbreaks of gypsy moths in eastern hardwood forests or the Canadian lynx cycles in the subarctic. Wildlife populations often did not follow some simple pattern of increase, saturation, competition, struggle, and balance. One could find, to be sure, many stable points and cycles, but one could also find everywhere the hand of chaos.

In the previous year May had published a book that overturned one of the oldest and most widely accepted arguments in ecology, that the more diversified the species are living in an area, the more complex their linkages are, and the stabler the system is. Charles Elton had been among the earliest to support that idea with scientific evidence showing that northern tundra landscapes, which had very few species, were far less stable than tropical ones, where much of the planet's biological diversity dwelled. Conservationists had found that idea intuitively right, and they had called for preserving species diversity as the key to preserving a stable environment. In contrast, May, working with theoretical models on a computer, found that the more species there were, the more fragile was the system. "Confronted with disturbances beyond their normal experience," he noted, such communities tended to crumple. Above all, the tropical rainforests seemed the epitome of permanence, but in fact they were so fragile that some had begun to term them "nonrenewable resources," for once cut down, they did not regenerate. In contrast, much simpler communities were often able to spring back, following a disturbance, and restore themselves. In the United States, for example, the east coast marsh grass, *Spartina alterniflora*, grew in vast homogenous stands that resembled agriculture's monocultures, and therefore ought to have been vulnerable to instability; but actually it proved to be remarkably stable through all the vicissitudes of weather. May cautioned that he was not advocating the turning of diverse nature into industrialized corn or wheat fields, for the latter did not have the "evolutionary pedigree" of nature's monocultures.

Until such time as we better understand the principles which govern natural associations of plants and animals, we would do well to preserve large chunks of pristine ecosystems. They are unique laboratories. Quite apart from valid ethical and aesthetic considerations, there are pragmatic reasons why we should query the increasingly universal replacement of natural ecosystems, with their long evolutionary history, by agroecosystems, which are usually intrinsically unstable.

Although at that time May was still using the ecosystem concept, his subsequent research into chaotic behavior focused increasingly on stability and instability within the populations of discrete species.

In his 1985 Croonian lecture for the Royal Society of London, May took up a problem straight out of Gilbert White's ramblings around Selborne. White had made an annual count of the number of swifts in the village and consistently found eight pairs. Two centuries later there were still six pairs regularly found in residence, a remarkable example of nature's constancy. On the other hand, White had found no wasps on his fruit trees in 1781, then two years later he found "myriads" of them, an example of nature's irregularities that had continued right down to the present. The point was that species did not all exhibit the same demographic patterns. Some remained numerically constant over long periods of time, others oscillated greatly from generation to generation but always around a stable long-term norm, while still others fluctuated radically each year, with no apparent norm, even when weather conditions were steady, suggesting there was something chaotic in their genetic makeup or response to environment. All those species differences had an impact on the structure of nature. May remained confident that every individual species pattern was "deterministic," that is, had identifiable causes, and that even the nonlinear irregularities would one day be found to have discernible boundaries so that science could build mathematical models of them. Yet the variability found among species made the science of ecology far more complicated than had long been supposed.[20]

Subsequently, May, who moved on from America to Britain, became the most widely cited figure in the standard college textbooks of ecology. His followers in research tried to track down and capture those nonlinearities in species abundance, whether among Canadian predators or human viruses, trying to bring their subject into line with chaotic theory. Among them was William Schaffer, who though originally a student of MacArthur's, was struck like May by the anomaly of unpredictable population fluctuations. Though taught to believe in "the so-called 'Balance of Nature,' " he wrote, "the idea that populations are at or close to equilibrium," ecological patterns began to look very different than that. He described himself as having to reach boldly across the disciplines in order to make connections with the theory of chaos developing in the other natural sciences in order to free himself from his field's restrictive past. Ecologists, he began admitting to himself, could never specify a system's state at any given time with infinite precision; therefore, they could never make long-term predictions about what would happen to its various species, whether in response to external perturbations or to the species' own behavioral dynamics. But with others they could make a science out of those conditions.[21]

Thus, the new ecology of chaos was not a total surrender to the idea of disorder, or to a philosophy of complete indeterminism, or to some obscurantist repudiation of science itself. Rather, ecologists were saying that if there was any order out there, it was going to be much more difficult to locate and describe than they had thought, and that it would always have an unruly element of indeterminancy in it. Perhaps some of them were beginning to sense that, as observers, they were always themselves standing in the picture they were observing, influencing it by their presence. Science can never get on the outside of nature, like the Judeo-Christian God, disinterested, remote, and detached, but must be carried on from within the whole—never seeing that whole completely but only its parts impinging on the observer, reacting to the observer. Yet the pursuit of science would not be abandoned because of this difficulty. May and others would not give up altogether their dream of finding rational order; it was too entrenched a faith, too vital to the mission of their lives, to toss aside abruptly. So, chastened but not discouraged, they looked for the limits or boundaries of chaos, the regularities of irregularity. As Ian Stewart explained, the mathematics on which chaos theory depended began to treat order and chaos as two distinct manifestations of an underlying determinism.[22] Nature could exist in a variety of states, some ordered, some chaotic, all connected in a continuous spectrum. If harmony and discord could be combined into beautiful music, then order and chaos might be combined into beautiful math and beautiful ecology.

Modern science lurches on from theory to theory, fad to fad, intellectual breakthrough to breakthrough, with breathless new claimants to a Nobel Prize appearing each and every season. The latest fashionable set of ideas, following chaos, was complexity. It promised still another grand, comprehensive, interdisciplinary theory about the nature of matter and energy, time and space, one linking physics, biology, and even history, anthropology, and economics into a single inquiry; and once more there were a number of ecologists joining in the search for the underlying commonalities. Complexity, according to one interpretation, was "the emerging science at the edge of order and chaos." If nature showed a fundamental capacity to be disorderly, it was pointed out, then order also had to be acknowledged and studied. There might not be any large overarching order inherent in nature, but there was plenty of evidence of conditions of change giving way to those of order, of order dissolving into change. The elements might stay the same but continually they rearranged themselves into new patterns, like a kaleidoscope turning round and round from one glittering starburst to another. We must conceive of ecosystems then, not as permanent entities engraved on the face of the earth but as shifting patterns in the endless flux, always new, always different. Ecosystems emerged out of the evolutionary turmoil in the grasslands or coral seas just as human kingdoms, empires, and civilizations arose out of the constant turmoil in people's lives, and then they fell apart. Like eddies appearing in a turbulent stream, such complex systems did not last forever, but while they lasted they showed an astonishing capacity for dynamic cohesion, stability, and order. Why was that? What organizing principles did all such complex systems have in common? What explained the sudden appearance of that order, structure, and organization from time to time, and how and why did that order often persist in the face of so much disorderliness all around?

With the arrival of complexity theory the questions agitating theoretical science had come full circle. First, the idea of a fundamental tendency toward equilibrium in nature had been challenged and thrown out by scientists, disequilibrium appearing to be a truer state of being. Then equilibrium began to reappear as a widespread potentiality within nature that required explaining. The most recent theories brought science back to ancient insights, long neglected, particularly the view that unresolvable contradictions exist in nature and yet somehow they merge into one unified flow. As the economist Brian Arthur put it, the discovery of complexity recovered the wisdom in such old philosophies as Taoism, which holds that "the world started with one, and the one became two, and the two became many, and the many led to myriad things."[23]

The utilitarian and moral implications in those cascading waves of thinking in the scientific community were at least as difficult to sort out as the ideas themselves. Did chaos theory, for example, promote, in Ilya Prigogine and Isabelle Stenger's words, "a renewal of nature," a less hierarchical view of life, and a set of "new relations between man and nature and between man and man"?[24] Or did it increase modern man's alienation from nature, his withdrawal into doubt and self-absorption, driven by fear that nature was becoming impossible to understand? What was there to admire or respect in a nature characterized by so much stochastic irregularity? How were people supposed to behave if that characterization of nature were true? If there was so much natural disturbance going on anyway, why should humans be worried about introducing a little more of it—adding a bit of rearranging of their own? Why not go ahead and flap their wings in the park, along with the butterflies, free of guilt that they might be doing any special damage? What, after all, did the phrase "environmental damage" mean when there was so much natural upheaval and unpredictability all around? Did the postwar environmental movement to which Paul Sears, Eugene Odum, and Rachel Carson belonged, or the conservation tradition that preceded them, make sense any longer or offer direction?

Ecologists seemed divided among themselves on the advice they gave to society on how to act on the earth. One group, reflecting some of the new disequilibrium thinking, began to challenge the public perception that ecology and environmentalism were one and the same thing. Some ecologists were bored with trying to preserve the planet in a state of health. Thomas Söderqvist, in a study of ecology in Sweden, which followed fashions similar to those in Britain and the United States, concluded that members of the most recent generation in the field

seem to do ecology for fun only, indifferent to practical problems, including the salvation of the nation. They are mathematically and theoretically sophisticated, sitting indoors calculating on computers, rather than traveling out in the wilds. They are individualists, abhorring the idea of large-scale ecosystem projects.

Indeed, the transition from ecosystem ecology to evolutionary ecology seems to reflect the generational transition from the politically conscious generation of the 1960s to the "yuppie" generation of the 1980s.[25]

That characterization should not be applied to every scientist who published on patch dynamics or disturbed regimes or chaotic predator–prey cycles, but it did draw attention to an unmistakable tendency among many of the post-Odum generation to disassociate themselves from environmental reform as much as from his unified ecosystem theory. For some scientists, a nature characterized by highly individualistic associations, constant disturbance, and incessant change was clearly more ideologically satisfying than Odum's ecosystems, with their connotations of cooperation, collective action, and environmentalism.

An American case in point was Paul Colinvaux, author of the popular introduction to neo-Darwinian ecology, *Why Big Fierce Animals Are Rare* (1978). His chapter on ecological succession began with these highly political lines: "If the planners really get hold of us so that they can stamp out all individual liberty and do what they like with our land, they might decide that whole counties full of inferior farms should be put back into forest." Clearly, he was not enthusiastic about land-use planning or forest restoration, or indeed about environmentalism as a whole. Colinvaux was very clear about the need to get some distance between himself and groups like the Sierra Club. Then he ended that same chapter with revealing and self-assured words:

We can now ... explain all the intriguing, predictable events of plant successions in simple, matter of fact, Darwinian ways. Everything that happens in successions comes about because all the different species go about earning their livings as best they may, each in its own individual manner. What look like community properties are in fact the summed results of all these bits of private enterprise.[26]

Apparently, if this writer was any indication, the old *social* Darwinism was back on the scene, walking the halls of science, and at least some of the turn away from Odum's generation might have owed something to a revulsion among scientists toward what they perceived as a threat to capitalistic and libertarian values.

Others, however, drew somewhat different conclusions from the recent disequilibrium trends in ecology. Daniel Botkin was one of the most articulate advocates of a new, chastened set of environmentalist policies. Arguing for a "new ecology for the twenty-first century," he recommended an environmentalism that was more friendly toward manipulating and dominating nature. The world of nature he compared to a symphony hall where several compositions were being played at once, "each with its own pace and rhythm." Humans, he advocated, should put themselves in the position of nature's conductor. "We are forced to choose among these [compositions], which we have barely begun to hear and understand." If there was any order to be heard in nature, it must be our achievement. "Nature in the 21st century," he argued, "will be a nature that we make." Enlightened by the recent trends in ecological theory, humans had arrived at a new view of earth "in which we are a part of a living and changing system whose changes we can accept, use, and control, to make the Earth a comfortable home, for each of us individually and for all of us collectively in our civilizations."

Botkin, like Colinvaux, criticized the early phases of the environmental movement for its radical, sometimes hostile, rejection of modern technology and progress. We need a science of ecology, he believed, that approaches economic development in a more "constructive and positive manner." The environmentalism of the postwar years had been "essentially a disapproving, and in this sense, negative movement, exposing the bad aspects of our civilization for our environment." Now, science showed that such gloomy negativism was unwarranted and should be replaced by a stance "that combine[s] technology with our concern about our environment in a constructive and positive manner."[27]

Those recommendations constituted a new permissiveness in ecology—a new tolerance toward accommodating human desires for greater wealth and power than early environmentalism had allowed, a more tolerant science than the ecology of Sears, Commoner, Carson, or Odum, with its emphasis on the preservation of a balanced nature, had been. The disturbance-impressed ecology of Botkin and others accepted human demands as the primary test of what should be done with the earth, and their list of acceptable demands was expansive. They denied that there was any firm guide to behavior to be found in nature, past or present, or even much reason for limiting human wants or rejecting progress. But their "ecology for a new century" was often very vague on what kind of conservation specifically should be practiced. The only guidance Botkin offered on which human disturbances were okay and which were not was an observation that slow rates of change were "more natural" than rapid ones and therefore more desirable. "We must be wary," he warned, "when we engineer nature at an unnatural rate and in novel ways."[28] But what did that formula really mean? What was unnaturally rapid or novel under so restless a sky?

Earlier, the equilibrium theorists had confidently claimed that they could determine what was safe for humans to do and what was not. Their standard advice had been to take from nature only a sustainable yield from healthy ecosystems, without harming the resilience or stability of the whole. Scientists thought they could determine with relative ease what that yield should be. They had only to determine the steady-state population levels in the ecosystem and then calculate how many fish could be caught each year or how many trees could be harvested or how much pollution could be absorbed without affecting the wonderful balance. Humans must learn how to take off the interest in nature's economy without touching the fixed capital. Now, however, the very concept of what was a normal yield or output had become far more ambiguous. Botkin showed that it was just such misguided assurances of stability in natural populations that had led to overfishing the California sardine industry—and to the total collapse of that industry in the 1950s.[29]

If the natural populations of fish and other organisms were in such chaotic flux that scientists could not confidently set maximum sustained yield targets, could they instead discover a more flexible standard of "optimum yield," one that would allow a more generous margin for error and fluctuations? That was where most expert advice came to rest in response to the new trends in thinking: Harvest freely all the commodities you need from nature, but do so at a slower rate to avoid overstressing a system in stochastic change. But then the experts still had to discover what that safe optimum rate was, and it could not be discovered without addressing the more basic challenges raised by recent ecological thinking about what was optimal in a natural world subject to so much disturbance, so much unpredictable turbulence.

Precisely at that point applied ecology found itself getting incoherent as it turned away from a unified systems theory or theory of competitive balance. It was in danger of losing any sense, intuitive or empirical, of what a healthy environment looks like. Had that been the final upshot of the disequilibrium and chaotic paradigm in ecology, then popular environmentalism must eventually find itself wandering confused and uncertain, without its scientific tutor. But then by the late 1980s and early 1990s scientists of the post-Odum and post-MacArthur generation began to find their way toward a revived environmentalism. A new cause emerged for many of them—the conservation of biological diversity, or "biodiversity." Ecologists began to argue that, whatever the uncertainties of theory, we must prevent the extinction of any and all species of plants or animals at the hand of man, and that the accumulated knowlege of biotic populations, so erratically rising and falling, could help us do just that. Even if we could not determine rigidly what a healthy ecosystem was, or a healthy state of homeostasis for the earth, or even identify a clear point of stable balance between competing species, we could at least use the new insights of ecology to save declining species, populations, communities, and ecosystems from extinction. Ecology, which had become the immensely complicated study of the fluctuating abundance of species, must now become an instrument to stop an alarming trend toward plant and animal losses.

Despite centuries of scientific exploration, no one really knew just how many species were out there in the world. Three million seemed a sure minimum, but the maximum number might be as many 30, or even 100, million. The canopies of the tropical rain forests alone might be the home of tens of millions of insect species, living out their lives high above the ground far from human eyes. Each year 1 percent of the planet's rain forests was cleared for agricultural purposes, mainly cattle grazing. Consequently, many irreplaceable species must be disappearing each year without any scientist ever discovering them. The recent rate of extinction was perhaps the greatest experienced by that particular biome over the last 150 million years, mounting to as high as 10,000 species a year in the last decade of the twentieth century. The public joined in the growing scientific concern about extinction, though generally it worried more about losing the charismatic species like mountain gorillas, Indian tigers, or Oregon's spotted owls than the less appealing phyla, where the loss was actually greatest. Almost anywhere one looked in the plant and animal kingdoms, the picture was getting very grim: an acceleration of extinction so great that it amounted to a reversal of the processes of biological evolution. Millions of years, even hundreds of millions of years, of natural selection were suddenly being undone by the explosively increasing numbers of Homo sapiens.

One man who found the uncharismatic insects an especially appealing, lovable lot was the Harvard ecologist Edward Wilson, who, as we have seen, had been a friend and colleague of Robert MacArthur's. Wilson became one of the most active leaders in the cause of conserving biodiversity on earth. He had worked in the South American tropics repeatedly, as well as the Florida mangrove islets, and had a passionate feeling for their beauty and liveliness. Now, under the threat of losing that treasure, he began to preach the need for a new conservation ethic, one inspired by the land ethic of Aldo Leopold but focused on preserving individual species more than community integrity. "Every species allowed to go extinct," he wrote,

is a slide down the rachet, an irreversible loss for all. It is time to invent moral reasoning of a new and more powerful kind, to look to the very roots of motivation and understand why, in what circumstances and on which occasions, we cherish and protect life. The elements from which a deep conservation ethic might be constructed include the impulses and biased forms of learning loosely classified as biophilia.

Biophilia was supposed to be an innate human tendency to love other living things and care about their survival; it was a plausible but highly speculative notion. That such a tendency might evolve culturally into a new preservationist ethic toward other forms of life was decidedly hopeful thinking. Nonetheless, to rally scientists as well as the public behind that ethic became Wilson's great personal mission. In 1986 he organized and chaired a National Forum on BioDiversity in Washington, and in that same year the Society for Conservation Biology was founded.[30]

The growing sense of urgency for preserving species diversity caught up many population biologists, along with ecosystem ecologists, and indeed scientists of every sort. One of the most prominent leaders, Michael Soulé, explained that many of the scientists were trying to get out of the small academic box they had made for themselves and rejoin a broader intellectual and moral community. Conservation biology offered a broader engagement, an escape from intellectual isolation and elitism. Self-interest also motivated many, for their research sites were being spoiled in many places by rapid development.[31] Whatever their motivation, scientists tried to forge a new consensus among themselves: Whatever disagreements they may have had about progress, technology, the balance of nature, the predominance of cooperation or competition in nature, or of chaos or order, preserving biological diversity became a unifying imperative. All the other social and environmental threats, including pollution and resource depletion, paled beside this one and demanded a strong scientific response. "This is the folly," Wilson warned, "our descendents are least likely to forgive us."[32]

By the last decade of the century the science of ecology, after so many intense, complicated theoretical debates, found itself in a more uncertain state of mind about its implications for modern technological civilization than it had been in the two or three decades following World War Two. Yet, surprisingly, it also found itself regrouping around a new conservation ideal that was, if not exactly required by new theories, at least was not contradicted by them. Apparently, moral ideals have a way of unexpectedly precipitating themselves out of the flux of events, the uncertainities of theory. As one set of environmental perceptions and values faded away, another began to take its place. Nature, ecologists began to argue, is wild and unpredictable. Nature is in deep, important ways quite disorderly. Nature is a seething, teeming spectacle of diversity. Nature, for all its strange and disturbing ways, its continuing capacity to elude our understanding, still needs our love, our respect, and our help.

The Disorder of History

Science, I have been suggesting in these pages, is not a single-minded, monolithic force marching through time. It is not the pure, disinterested search for knowledge many of its supporters make it out to be, nor is it an undeviating advance along an "edge of objectivity," as others have claimed, nor is it what some critics have called a purely "alienated vision." None of those notions adequately reflects the ever-changing reality of the scientific enterprise. Science has had as many schisms, conflicts, dissensions, and personality contrasts as any human activity. A less protean enterprise could never have accommodated so many minds or described so many of nature's patterns. Precisely because of that internal diversity of outlook, science has contributed vastly to expanding our vision of the natural world and of our place within it. Science has been a house with many doors, some leading to one view of nature, some to another. But as the philosopher William James wrote of his summer cottage in New Hampshire, those doors have generally opened outward.[33]

Ecology has been one of the more interesting dimensions of this eclectic scientific inquiry. Over more than two centuries of growth, it has given us a wide array of perspectives on nature, all of which can claim some degree of truth. Many of ecology's past ideas linger in the air today. One can still hear now and then the ideas of Carolus Linnaeus or Gilbert White, of early imperialists or arcadians, of the finely contrived balance-of-nature idea. Then at other times one can hear the echoes of Romantic biology, of holistic organicism, and of Thoreau's subversive encounter with nature. There is no escaping the persistence of the past. Ecology in the late twentieth century is inevitably the product of its long and complex intellectual tradition regardless of how

strongly it believes in its own novelty or validity. Failing
to accept that indebtedness to the past, or to realize how
diverse and contradictory that past has been, we will not
make much headway toward a deep understanding of our
current ideas about nature.

Despite many floating echoes from the past, however, a
strong trend in ecology has been apparent over time: its
picture of nature has been thoroughly historicized, beginning in the nineteenth century, but especially accelerating
during the past two decades, until ecology has become a
branch of history. I do not mean by history a mere department or discipline in the university, or history as a record
merely of human achievement. Rather, I mean history as a
more general sense of the past, nature's past as well as
humankind's past, and a sense of how that past was different
from the present. I mean, in other words, history as a concern with change over time, with development and evolution and becoming. How that historicization altered science
is the theme of a book by Stephen Toulmin and June Goodfield, entitled *The Discovery of Time.* "The picture of the
natural world we all take for granted today," they point out,
"has one remarkable feature, which cannot be ignored in
any study of the ancestry of science: it is a *historical* picture."[34] The new picture began to emerge during the period
1810 to 1830 as scientists began to realize how much time
had transpired on the earth and how much had changed
over that span of time. A static world of fixed, hierarchical
relations began to give way to another nature, evolving,
contingent, revolutionary, conflicted, catastrophic at times,
always in a state of flux. Geology was the first science to
discover time; the first great geologists, James Hutton, William Playfair, and Charles Lyell, were all historians of deep
time, finding the annals of former worlds written in beds
of chalk and old red sandstone.

It is no coincidence that the modern academic discipline
of history had its roots in that same era when scientists
began to discover deep time. Like the newly discovered
fossils lying embedded in the dust, waiting to be exhumed
and analyzed, great political empires of the past had to be
dug up and explained. A generation that had been through
many profoundly interrelated revolutions could not help

wondering how long it would be before the next upheaval came along. Thomas Jefferson, one of the most ardent students of ancient empires, called for making a revolution in every generation. The future promised to be unlike anything ever seen before, and the past became its mirror, full of strange, exotic ruins demanding explanation. Historians like Gibbon, Macauley, Michelet, von Ranke, Bancroft, and Parkman began to write long, eloquent meditations on the meaning of the past.

Nor is it a mere coincidence that the same century that created the modern study of history, that became fascinated by a very long human chronology, that discovered in the fossil record the traces of countless extinct species, saw the appearance of the theory of evolution through natural selection. Charles Darwin turned biology into history—the history of flora and fauna jostling for space, branching out to new territory, overthrowing established regimes. According to Toulmin and Goodfield, Darwin's book *On the Origin of Species* "broke down the artificial barrier between Science—which had hitherto been concerned with the static Order of Nature—and History, which studied the development of humanity. So the two most powerful intellectual currents in the nineteenth century were united. Whether we consider geology, zoology, political philosophy or the study of ancient civilizations, the nineteenth century was in every case the Century of History—a period marked by the growth of a new, dynamic world-picture."[35]

But with Darwin, as with other thinkers of the nineteenth century, change was never all there was. Change led somewhere; it had a positive direction, conventionally called Progress. Darwin described evolution as a blooming tree of life, suggesting that change was coherent and contained, like the growth of an organism, whose parts increase or even replace one another but the whole remaining one entity. Once taken root, that tree of life goes on growing forever, until it covers the earth. Nature, like human society, told a story of constant upheaval, but the observer could still find a benevolent order and pattern in the story.

Out of that new historicized biology came the field of ecology, though it was not until the 1890s that ecology could be said to have achieved a disciplinary status. How could the new science be anything but historical, born as it was at the end of the great century of historical and developmental consciousness? Its founders, including Ernest Haeckel, Eugenius Warming, and, early in the twentieth century, Henry Cowles and Frederic Clements, were all intensely aware of the biological and geological past, of time's arrow flying unstoppably over the land. Like Darwin, however, they believed that change is not at all disorderly or directionless. Change unmakes order but also makes it anew. Despite a thousand mishaps, nature has its regularities, its great coherences that persist over time, giving the landscape a standard of normality.

Toulmin and Goodfield to the contrary notwithstanding, the growing fascination with the past remained, until very recently, compartmentalized into two distinct and separate spheres, one for people and another for the rest of the natural world. The former sphere, the human story, was the first to lose a sense of order and break down into narrative chaos. Following such traumas as the Holocaust and the atomic bomb, or more benign upheavals such as the sexual revolution and global trade, human history became tumultuous, unpredictable, and at times profoundly destructive. Meanwhile, the second sphere of historical consciousness, the history of nature, still seemed to the scientific as well as the popular mind to be an orderly, predictable, and conservative sphere. The great challenge facing humankind, proclaimed the popular ecological literature of the 1960s, was to rescue human history from its self-destructive energies and bring it into conformity with the stabler history of nature.

I grew up with that sort of thinking, as did so many other historians and ecologists, and still find plenty of good evidence and solid reason to support it. The history we are writing on the planet has become more destructive than ever, destructive of species, of biological communities, of ecosystems, and of our own security and happiness; clearly we need a different way of living than the one we have been pursuing. But can nature unequivocally and unambiguously furnish that way? Does nature provide us with a set of overarching norms for redirecting the history of humankind?

If I had written a history of the United States in the 1960s, the era of Odum's prominence, that described the nation as moving through a series of predictable "developmental stages" to a condition of maturity characterized by lower net production but higher stability (i.e., resistance to external perturbations), higher diversity, closed mineral cycles, good nutrient conservation, and low entropy, my colleagues would have wondered what substance I was abusing. Unlike nature, the nations of the world, it was commonly understood, may "develop," but they never reach a steady state. In that decade the United States was certainly a highly developed country, at least in industrial terms, but its population was growing, not stabilizing, its resources were depleting, its cities were burning, its streets were filled with antiwar protesters, many of its leaders were getting shot. An observer of those changes might well have asked why the history of American society should be so much more chaotic than the history of an oak-hickory forest. Why should the past thousand years of human activity look so much more unsettled than the past hundred million years of other species?

But now, as we have seen, scientists have abandoned that equilibrium view of nature and invented a new one that looks remarkably like the human sphere in which we live. We can no longer maintain that either nature or society is a stable entity. All history has become a record of disturbance and that disturbance comes from both cultural *and* natural agents, including droughts, earthquakes, pests, viruses, corporate takeovers, loss of markets, new technologies, increasing crime, new federal laws, and even the invasion of America by French literary theory.

One of the most important insights of the modern discovery of time is that all ideas, past, present, and future, are grounded in particular historical contexts. That discovery includes the ideas of politicians, businessmen, scientists, and even historians—it covers *all* ideas. We call this insight the principle of historicism, or historical relativism. Supposedly, it gives us greater objectivity toward and sympathy for the people of the past who could not share our blessings of enlightenment; at the same time, it is supposed to free us from any blind allegiance to present-day opinions.

If we must explain the past in its own terms, as historicism argues, then we must also be wary of uncritically accepting the conditions that govern our own way of thinking.

The intent of these chapters has been to include the science of ecology within the purview of historicism, to argue that ecological ideas are only valid relatively, that they are suited to and rooted in their times.[36] Science must not be exempted, as it often is, from this kind of analysis; nor can the scientist, by any act of will or training, isolate his or her perception of nature from the rest of mental life. In all intellectual endeavors there may be certain timeless tests of logic and empirical validation to be met, but there are also biases of selectivity and emphasis derived from the environing culture and from deeply felt personal experience. This history of ecological ideas has shown how impossible it has been to screen out such biases. Any attempt to do so, to divorce nature from the rest of the human condition, leads to a doctrine of intellectual and moral alienation, in which scientific consciousness tries to deal coolly, abstractly, with a nature distanced from the needs and concerns of humanity. In truth, science has no more claim to absolute truth, permanence, infallibility, or comprehensiveness than any other field of thought. As Arthur Lovejoy once noted, the history of all ideas leads to an understanding of how "every age tends to exaggerate the scope and finality of its own discoveries, or re-discoveries, to be so dazzled by them that it fails to discern clearly their limitations and forgets aspects of truth of prior exaggerations against which it has revolted."[37] Undoubtedly, this tendency to denigrate the past and exalt the present is a useful trait when one needs to believe in the truthfulness of one's own ideas, and scientists have been perhaps no more guilty than any others in this regard.

Carried far enough, the philosophy of historicism teaches us that we must also try to write the history of our obsession with history. We must try to understand, that is, the fixation on radical change that has characterized our recent outlook. Where is it coming from? The obvious answer is that it is coming from the experience of rapid social transformation that has been gaining momentum. Earlier generations, going back hundreds of thousands of years, experienced change too, but in a very different context. According to Claude Lévi-Strauss, "the characteristic feature of the savage mind is its timelessness; its object is to grasp the world as both a synchronic and a diachronic totality."[38] Later, in post-hunting and gathering societies where agriculture dominated daily life, the idea of change still remained more cyclical than linear; the recurrent cycle of annual crops was more immediately real to people than the long-term evolution of human life. Nature appeared as a permanent order, created in the beginning of time by decree or coming spontaneously into being but never altering in its essential properties or relations. That, however, is not the way modern people understand the world or time, and the reason must lie in our changed material and cultural circumstances.

We live on the other side of a revolution in consciousness brought about by the forces of modern capital, technology, and economic materialism. The description of those forces is too complicated to go into here, but despite a bit of hyperbole and oversimplification, Karl Marx and Friedrich Engels were largely right when they credited modern capitalism with creating a new passion for change and a new attitude toward time.

Constant revolutionizing of production, uninterrupted disturbance of all social conditions, everlasting uncertainty and agitation distinguish [this] epoch from all earlier ones. All fixed, fast-frozen relations, with their train of ancient and venerable prejudices and opinions, are swept away. All new-formed ones become antiquated before they can ossify. All that is solid melts into air, all that is holy is profaned.[39]

Marx and Engels were thinking primarily about the effects of capitalism on ideas of social community in the transition from an ancient rural to a modern urban setting, but we can see how readily their words also apply to our understanding of the natural order. The sense of the ecological whole that once seemed so solid and unshakable has tended, along with all other ideas, to melt into air.

Marx and Engels welcomed that new sense of flux, indeed built their theory of dialectical materialism on it, following the great philosopher of history, Georg Wilhelm Friedrich Hegel. Marx and Engels believed that the undermining of traditional ideas about time and order was necessary to free

people from the prejudices of the past. You cannot, therefore, find in them much concern about preserving any
ancient feeling for nature or even any concern for environmental preservation. But they did predict that one day
history would come to an end in a timeless utopia of the
classless society. The disorder of constant economic upheaval would cease and society would finally reach a steady
state of established relations, an equilibrium of justice,
when nature too would exist in some state of equilibrium,
though one firmly under technological control. That prediction seems to have been proved wrong in recent decades.
After World War Two the pace of change has, in fact, not
slowed down but on the contrary has accelerated remarkably. Moreover, we have seen not the achievement of justice
for all but rather an exacerbation of global inequalities. Today, for many, the socialist dream of a glorious end to capitalist turmoil has collapsed and lies in shambles.[40]

Industrial capitalism, blaring its triumph over all rivals,
promising a "new world order" in which there is to be an
endless pursuit of wealth, offers no promise whatever of
ever achieving a steady state in either social, economic, or
ecological terms. Its ruling vision is one of ceaseless change,
infinite possibilities, and boundless creativity. In light of
its past record we can expect that global capitalism will
continue to promote unchecked economic and population
growth, will continue to stoke the rising aspirations of the
poor without really satisfying them, and will intensify its
currently intense demands on nature. The effect of that
economic culture will be to dissolve whatever fragmentary
notions of stability, order, or normality are left to us, and
we will be left more than ever dwelling in a world where
change has become the dominant principle of life.

So, in this manner, we historians can explain the modern
tendency to turn nature into a mirror image of our society,
reflecting back the chaotic energies of capital and technology. And by offering that kind of explanation we can free
ourselves from a mindless, uncritical allegiance to the new
orthodoxy, as historical analysis has liberated us from previous orthodoxies and promoted critical thinking. Fortified
by the principle of historicism, we can approach recent ecological models that dramatize disturbance with a sense of

skepticism and independence. If they are not the mere reflection of global capitalism and its ideology, they are nonetheless highly compatible with that force rearranging the earth. The newest ecology, with its emphasis on competition and disturbance, is congruent with what Frederic Jameson has called the "logic of late capitalism."[41]

But having glimpsed that connection between the science of ecology and its cultural and economic conditions, are we then free to believe something else? The answer must be yes, and yet also no. The philosophy of historical relativism grants us freedom from dogmatic thinking but no firm guidance to belief. It cannot really invalidate the intellectual tendencies of our time, or any other time, or offer new ideas of order to believe in. On the contrary, historicism can eventually lead either to a complete cynicism or to the acceptance of any set of ideas or any environment that humans have created as thoroughly legitimate. By the logic of historicism Disneyland must be as legitimate an environment as Yellowstone National Park, a wheat field as legitimate as a prairie, a megalopolis of thirty million people as legitimate as a village. Each has been the product of history and therefore each must stand equal to any other. Each offers unique dynamics to be probed and understood, but any set of historical dynamics, like any set of beliefs or institutions, must appear to the consistent historicist to be as good as any other.

If the study of human or natural history required us to adopt such a rigid historicist position, then I would be ready to join those who call for the wholesale rejection of modern historical consciousness as a corrupting worldview. I would accept the arguments of that trenchant critic of modernism, Edward Goldsmith, who has called for a rejection of recent ecology and a harkening back to a prehistorical and premodern consciousness, to a chthonic or folk worldview that antedates modern historical thinking.[42] But such a wholesale rejection is neither possible at this point in time nor is it required of us; accepting modernity or its historical worldview does not oblige us to embrace all of modernity uncritically or to adopt an extreme version of historicism. We can acknowledge the flow of history, going back at least two million years for humans, billions for the rest of nature, without getting completely lost in the labyrinths of time. I want to suggest now several conclusions that it seems to me our knowledge of the ecological past, both humankind's and nature's, allows us to draw. They are conclusions that transcend our present-day circumstances. They seem to me to be as objectively true as we can make them, supported by substantial evidence and reason. And they are conclusions that cover *both* nature and human society, acknowledging that we cannot set up any impermeable barrier between the two spheres.

In the first place, informed reason allows us to say that living nature, for all its private, individualistic strivings, works by the principle of interdependency. Indeed, it can only work by that principle. No organism or species of organism has any chance of surviving without the aid of others. John Muir once declared, "When we try to pick out anything by itself, we find it hitched to everything else in the universe."[43] New proof of that interdependency principle has come to light in the postwar era. Send any individual organism or any population of organisms into outer space alone, without any of the services provided by other kinds of organisms, from soil fertility to oxygen generation, and it will not survive. It needs its evolutionary companions.

For a while to be sure, many human beings lost sight of that truth, even began to imagine that they could live by their technological prowess alone. But the past few decades have demolished that illusion. All the changes we find going on in civilization, it is now clear, are only changes in the patterns of that interdependency, not in the reality or extent of the interdependency itself. What we call the environmental movement of the post–World War Two era has been essentially a reawakening to the realization that we must depend on other forms of life to survive; we have no other options. Progress has not made our condition different in this respect from that of our remotest ancestors. Being clever and adaptable, we have learned how to make substitutions in our dependencies and to alter the geography of our dependency—for example, North American Indians have learned to buy and eat Central American beef instead of Canadian moose—but we have not learned how to live on a planet that is dead.

The full implications of our ecological dependency are still working their way into the heads of economic and political leaders, but already they are eroding any grandiose claims of conquest over the earth and of our invulnerability before the forces of nature. Consequently, the extinction of obscure species has become a global concern, expressed in international treaties. Communities, states, and nations are no longer so sure they can manage without those species, even if many of them play only a remote, distant, or obscure role in human welfare. At the same time an awareness of our dependency on the whole fabric of life is stimulating a sense of dependence on other people, most of them strangers to us but locked with us in a common predicament. Again, the forms of dependency may change. The solidarity of the face-to-face group, working together for survival, may become transformed into something larger, perhaps something less effective, into a single global audience instantly tuned into the fate of victims of disease, tyranny, poverty, or forest destruction wherever they live. Thus, the fact of interdependence binding all living things into a kind of community has not been invalidated by the rapid pace of recent change or the many uncertainties that change has produced.

In the second place, our study of the past has uncovered models of successful adaptation that we can learn from today. They are not values in themselves but rather are lessons drawn from nature, applicable to the values we have chosen. The natural world may not provide any overall, sufficient norm for us to follow, or any single transcendent good that we can discover, but it does provide a wealth of models, depending on what it is we want to achieve. If we want to fly, for example, we can find models in the wings of birds, models that took tens of millions of year to perfect. If we want to stop soil erosion or survive drought, we have a model in the tallgrass prairie, which retains far more of the rain that falls than a wheat monoculture does and can bound back from a severe dry spell that would completely kill a planted domestic crop. We may not think about such models as lessons derived from history, but they are all the products of past experience, and it is the biologist, thinking historically, who reveals how they came into being, by a process of evolution that we can call the unfolding wisdom of life.

Similarly, environmental history sets before us models of human communities that have been more successful in using resources than we in some respects. For example, if social longevity is high in our hierarchy of values, if we want to survive as a people and as a species for the longest possible time, then we can find in the past a wealth of examples that have something useful to teach. We cannot find in the past or present any societies that are perfect in every aspect, or examples that we can simply revive lock, stock, and barrel from extinction; but we can find models to study and learn from. They exist within the borders of the United States and in every part of the earth—communities that have managed to fit themselves to their places for impressively long periods of time, that are less destructive of the biota around them, that may have acquired some vital knowledge of place that we lack. They may have not escaped the hand of time, but they have come closer than we to withstanding it. My own research as a historian suggests that such enduring communities, whether based on hunting-and-gathering techniques or on agriculture, have had one dominant characteristic: they have created rules, and many of them, sometimes highly intentional rules and at other times rules embedded in folk tradition, but always rules based on intimate local experience, to govern their behavior. They have not tried to "live free" of nature or of the group, nor have they resented restraints on individual initiative, or left it to each individual to decide completely how to behave. On the contrary, they have accepted many kinds of limits on themselves and enforced them on one another. Their methods of enforcement may not meet our modern American standards of privacy or of justice, or be compatible with our modern sense of strong personal rights, and certainly they can stifle creativity or originality. But throughout history, having those rules and enforcing them vigorously seems to be a requirement for long-term ecological survival.

How we use such models from other eras and places to

inform the values or norms chosen for our own lives is a very difficult question. Clearly, we cannot merely turn all our wheat fields, no matter how inadequate ecologically they may be, back into bluestem prairies, nor can we turn industrial capitalism back into a medieval alpine village or an Australian aborigine's camp. We simply cannot go back in time and undo all that has happened. We are, in that sense, prisoners of time. But we can approach the record of the past with much more respect, admitting that most of the innovations we have recently made are not likely to survive, that what is old among us may by that very fact be worthy of respect and mimicry, that what is *very* old may be wise.

In the third place, history reveals not merely that change is real but also that change is various. All change is not the same, nor are all changes equal. Some changes are cyclical, some are not. Some changes are linear, others are not. Some changes take an afternoon to accomplish, some a millennium. We can no more take any particular kind of change as absolutely normative than we can take any particular state of equilibrium as normative. The fact that ice sheets once scraped their way across Illinois does not provide any kind of justification for a corporation that wants to strip coal from the state. We know this, but sometimes we get confused by talk about all change being "natural." In a loose sense, the statement is true, but it is also meaningless. No one really maintains that whatever is is right, or that whatever happens is good. We understand that there are changes in nature that work against us as well as for us, changes that we have to defend ourselves against, even if we cannot prevent them. The challenge is to determine which changes are in our enlightened self-interest and are consistent with our most rigorous ethical reasoning, always remembering our inescapable dependency on other forms of life.

Environmental conservation becomes, in the light of this historical awareness, an effort to protect certain rates of change going within the biological world from incompatible changes going on within our economy and technology. It is not a program of locking nature up within a museum case, freezing it for all time. Rather, it is a pattern of behavior based on the idea that preserving a diversity of change ought to stand high in our system of values, that promoting the coexistence of many beings and many kinds of change is a rational thing to do. The pace of innovation in computer chips may be appropriate to a competitive business community, but it is not appropriate to or always compatible with the evolution of a redwood forest. Some things take longer to grow or improve. Some things cannot adapt as fast as others. These are differences revealed by the history of nature and society. Today, historians of every sort can no longer can claim that there is a single universal narrative of change that all species, all communities, all places must conform to. "History" has given way to "histories." Each of those histories needs space in which to play itself out, to unwind its narrative. That is precisely what the modern idea of conservation must aim to do: provide the space, either set aside in large discrete blocks or protected within the interstices of the landscape, so that all the many earthly histories can coexist—the history of a coral reef alongside the history of a coastal city, the history of a tropical rain forest alongside the history of a political struggle. Such a strategy of trying to conserve a diversity of changes may seem paradoxical, but it is founded on a crucial and reasonable insight. We may have to live with change, may even be the products of change, but we do not always know— indeed, we *cannot* always know—which changes are vital and which are deadly.

These are conclusions about the real world, I believe, that the intertwined study of nature and society leads us to make today, conclusions that stand up well because they are based on knowledge and reason, not merely on private fantasies. Whether we choose to learn from the past or not, the past is our most reliable instructor in reality. We no longer can locate nature in some timeless state of perfection, accessible through perfectly detached science, nor do we have revelation or authority to depend upon. Only by understanding that constantly changing past, a past in which humankind and nature were always one integrated whole, can we discover with the aid of imperfect human reason, all that we value and all that we defend.

NOTES

Facts of publication are given only for those sources not listed in the Bibliography.

PART ONE

Chapter 1

1. Washington Irving, "Rural Life in England," *The Sketch Book* (New York, 1961 ed.), p. 70.

2. Cecil S. Emden, *Gilbert White in His Village*. Walter Johnson (ed.), "Introduction" to *Gilbert White's Journals*. Edwin Way Teale, "The Selborne Nightingale." "The Deserted Village," in *The Poetical Works of Oliver Goldsmith*, ed. Austin Dobson (London, 1927), p. 28.

3. Gilbert White, *The Natural History of Selborne*, pp. 134, 208–9, 217, 328. Charles F. Mullett, "*Multum in Parvo*: Gilbert White of Selborne."

4. White, *Natural History*, p. 49.

5. *Ibid.*, pp. 22, 57, 174–75, 350.

6. *Ibid.*, pp. 43, 77, 128.

7. *Ibid.*, pp. 186–87, 226.

8. *Ibid.*, pp. 57–60. On pastoralism generally, see Bruno Snell, "Arcadia: The Discovery of a Spiritual Landscape"; J. E. Congleton, *Theories of Pastoral Poetry in England, 1684–1798* (Gainesville, Fla., 1952); Elizabeth Nitchie, *Vergil and the English Poets* (New York, 1919); and Leo Marx, *The Machine in the Garden: Technology and the Pastoral Ideal in America* (New York, 1964), pp. 88–107.

9. White, "Selborne Hanger: A Winter Piece" (1763), in R. M. Lockley, *Gilbert White*, pp. 126–27.

10. Paul Mantoux, *The Industrial Revolution in the Eighteenth Century*. E. J. Hobsbawm, *The Age of Revolution: 1789–1848*, esp. chs. 2 and 9. George Trevelyan, *History of England*, p. 601.

11. Arthur Young's most famous work was *Rural Oeconomy: or, Essays on the Practical Parts of Husbandry* (1770), which was a sequel to his *Farmer's Letters to the People of England* (1767). See

also Kenneth MacLean, *Agrarian Age: A Background for Wordsworth* (New Haven, Conn., 1950), and W. G. Hoskins, *The Making of the English Landscape* (London, 1955), ch. 6.

12. *The Life and Letters of Gilbert White*, II, pp. 275–86. *The Life and Letters of Charles Darwin*, ed. Francis Darwin (New York, 1898), I, p. 426. James Russell Lowell, "My Garden Acquaintance," in *My Study Windows* (Boston, 1871), pp. 1–23.

13. John Burroughs, "Gilbert White's Book," in *Indoor Studies*, Vol. 7 of *The Writings of John Burroughs*, pp. 178–79. "Introduction" (1895), *The Natural History of Selborne* (New York, 1907 ed.), p. viii. Lockley, p. 125.

14. W. W. Fowler, "Gilbert White of Selborne," pp. 182–83.

15. "Back to Nature." Francis Halsey, "The Rise of Nature Writers," *American Monthly Review of the Reviews* 26 (November 1902): 567–571. Peter J. Schmitt, *Back to Nature: The Arcadian Myth in Urban America*. Philip Hicks, *The Development of the Natural History Essay in American Literature*.

16. "Back to Nature," p. 306. Burroughs, "An Open Door," in *Indoor Studies*, pp. 242–43. See also "Science and Literature," *ibid.*, pp. 49–74.

17. Burroughs, "The Noon of Science," in *The Summit of the Years*, vol. 17 of *Writings*, pp. 64–67, 73–75. On Hudson, see Richard Haymaker, *From Pampas to Hedgerows and Downs: A Study of W. H. Hudson*, and Robert Hamilton, *W. H. Hudson: The Vision of the Earth*. Muir is quoted in Douglas Strong, *The Conservationists* (Reading, Mass., 1971), p. 97.

18. Grant Allen, "Introduction," *Natural History of Selborne* (London, 1900 ed.), pp. xxxiii–xl.

19. Emden, esp. ch. 1.

20. H. J. Massingham, "Introduction" to *The Writings of Gilbert White* (London, 1938), I, pp. xiii–xxvi. A similar interpretation appears in Charles Raven's description of White's books: "It recaptures that sense of the worth and cohesion and wholeness of the natural order which the men of the seventeenth century had revealed." (*Natural Religion and Christian Theology*, p. 161.)

21. Ludwig von Bertalanffy, *Modern Theories of Development*, p. 190.

22. Barry Commoner, *Science and Survival*, esp. ch. 3. See also his more recent work, *The Closing Circle: Nature, Man and Technology*.

23. William Murdoch and James Connell, "All About Ecology."

24. Paul Sears, "Ecology—A Subversive Subject." Also see Paul Shepard, "Ecology and Man—A Viewpoint," in *The Subversive Science: Essays Toward an Ecology of Man*, Paul Shepard and

Daniel McKinley, eds. (Boston, 1969), p. 9; and Bernard James, *The Death of Progress* (New York, 1973), pp. 82–88.

25. Rachel Carson, quoted in Paul Brooks, *The House of Life: Rachel Carson at Work* (Boston, 1972), p. 319. Her chief works include *Under the Sea Wind* (1941), *The Sea Around Us* (1951, rev. ed. 1961), *The Edge of the Sea* (1955), and *Silent Spring* (1962).

Chapter 2

1. Lynn White, Jr., "The Historical Roots of Our Ecologic Crisis" (1967). Ian Barbour (ed.), *Western Man and Environmental Ethics*. David and Eileen Spring (eds.), *Ecology and Religion in History*. John Black, *The Dominion of Man*. Edvard Westermarck, *Christianity and Morals*, ch. 19. George Williams, *Wilderness and Paradise in Christian Thought*. C. D. F. Moule, *Man and Nature in the New Testament*.

2. For the impact of science on eighteenth-century poetry, see William Jones, *The Rhetoric of Science* (London, 1966), Nicholas Berdyaev, *The Meaning of History* (Cleveland, Ohio, 1962), p. 106. John Dillenberger, *Protestant Thought and Natural Science* (Garden City, N.Y., 1960).

3. Francis Bacon, "The Great Instauration," in *The Works of Francis Bacon*, I, p. 39; "The New Atlantis," *ibid.*, p. 398; "The New Organon," *ibid.*, pp. 47–48.

4. Linnaeus is quoted by Theodor Fries, *Linnaeus*, p. 9. Also see Wilfred Blunt, *The Compleat Naturalist: A Life of Linnaeus*; Heinz Goerke, *Linnaeus*; and Knut Hagberg, *Carl Linnaeus*.

5. Linnaeus extended his system to animals in the tenth edition of the *Systema Naturae* (1758). Earlier, in the *Philosophica Botanica* (1751), he outlined the rudiments of a "natural" system, based on the whole organism rather than the reproductive organs alone; this task was later completed by Antoine de Jussieu and Alphonse de Candolle. See Abraham Wolf, *A History of Science, Technology, and Philosophy in the Eighteenth Century*, pp. 426–59; and James Larson, *Reason and Experience: The Representation of Natural Order in the Works of Carl von Linné*.

6. Arthur O. Lovejoy, in "The Place of Linnaeus in the History of Science," is rather harsh in his judgment of Linnaeus' scientific contributions. A more positive evaluation is given by Erik Nordenskiöld in *The History of Biology*, pp. 203–18.

7. Fries, p. 309. Sir William Jardine, "Memoir of Linnaeus," *The Naturalist's Library* (Edinburgh, 1843), vol. 14, p. 59. On Linnaeus' popularity in England, see W. P. Jones, "The Vogue of Natural History in England, 1750–1770," and Hagberg, pp. 159–61. Hagberg argues that "the Linnaean observance of nature won a greater following in England than in Sweden."

8. Linnaeus, "Specimen academicum de Oeconomia Naturae" (Isaac J. Biberg, respondent). Translated into English by Benjamin Stil-

lingfleet in *Miscellaneous Tracts Relating to Natural History, Husbandry, and Physick* (1759); quotations which follow are taken from the second edition (London, 1762), pp. 37–129. A recent compilation of Linnaeus' ecological writings is Camille Limoges (ed.), *L'Equilibre de la nature*.

9. Digby used the phrase in his essay *A Late Discourse . . . Touching the Cure of Wounds by the Powder of Sympathy*. "Economy" also referred to the anatomy and physiology of the organism. See, for instance, John Hunter's *Observations on Certain Parts of the Animal Economy* (1786) and Erasmus Darwin's *The Botanic Garden: The Economy of Vegetation* (1791). The *Oxford English Dictionary* gives the other meanings and their history.

10. On natural theology, see Charles Raven, *Natural Religion and Christian Theology*; Richard Westfall, *Science and Religion in Seventeenth-Century England* (New Haven, Conn., 1958); Basil Willey, *The Eighteenth-Century Background*, ch. 2; and Clarence Glacken, *Traces on the Rhodian Shore*, pp. 375–428.

11. For the scientific revolution and its philosophy of nature, see, among other works: R. G. Collingwood, *The Idea of Nature*, part 2; Herbert Butterfield, *The Origins of Modern Science*; Alfred North Whitehead, *Science and the Modern World* (New York, 1925), chs. 2–4; Karl Heim, *The Transformation of the Scientific World View*; E. A. Burtt, *The Metaphysical Foundations of Modern Science*; and Marie Boas, "The Establishment of the Mechanical Philosophy." On the relation of early scientists to technology, see Robert Merton, *Science, Technology, and Society in Seventeenth-Century England*; Harcourt Brown, "The Utilitarian Motive in the Age of Descartes"; and Walter Houghton, Jr., "The History of Trades: Its Relation to Seventeenth-Century Thought."

12. Stillingfleet, *Miscellaneous Tracts*, pp. 127–28. George Cheyne, *Philosophical Principles of Religion, Natural and Revealed*, 4th ed., (London, 1734), pp. 146–47. Herbert Drennon, "Newtonianism: Its Methods, Theology and Metaphysics." F. E. L. Priestley, "Newton and the Romantic Concept of Nature." Leslie Stephen, *History of English Thought in the Eighteenth Century*, vol. 1. Alexander Koyré, *From the Closed World to the Infinite Universe*.

13. *The Philosophical Writings of Henry More*, pp. 169, 270. Glacken, p. 395. On the revival of animism, see Hiram C. Hayden, *The Counter-Renaissance* (New York, 1950).

14. John Ray, *The Widsom of God Manifested in the Works of Creation*, pp. 11–12, 25–26. See also Charles Raven, *John Ray, Naturalist*, esp. pp. 37, 455, 458.

15. Ray, pp. 35–36, 76.

16. William Derham, *Physico-Theology*, p. 179. Basil Willey calls this optimistic view "cosmic toryism": the notion that this is the best of all possible worlds; that "whatever is, is right," as Alexander Pope claimed. (Willey, ch. 3.)

17. *Leviathan* (1651), in *The Works of Thomas Hobbes* (London, 1839), chs. 13–14.

18. Soame Jenyns, "On the Chain of Universal Being," in *Disquisitions on Several Subjects* (London, 1782), pp. 7–8. *Spectator*, no. 404 (June 13, 1712). Richard Pulteney, *A General View of the Writings of Linnaeus*, pp. 318–19. Arthur O. Lovejoy, *The Great Chain of Being*, esp. chs. 6–8.

19. William Smellie, *The Philosophy of Natural History*, pp. 345–58. Linnaeus, quoted in Hagberg, p. 193. William Kirby, *On the Power, Wisdom, and Goodness of God Manifested in the Creation of Animals and in Their History, Habits, and Instincts* (London, 1835), II, p. 526.

20. John Bruckner, *A Philosophical Survey of the Animal Creation*, part 1, section 1; also pp. 34, 50, 76–77, 133. Bruckner (1726–1804) immigrated to England from Belgium to become pastor of the Norwich church of the Walloons.

21. *Ibid.*, part 2, sections 1 and 5; also pp. 9, 40, 150.

22. *Ibid.*, part 1, section 4; also p. 160.

23. *Ibid.*, part 2, section 5; also pp. 9–10, 18–19, 138.

24. *Ibid.*, pp. 95, 101–4, 121, 134–35.

25. W. S. W. Ruschenberger, "A Notice of the Origin, Progress, and Present Condition of the Academy of Natural Sciences of Philadelphia" (Philadelphia, 1852), p. 12. Smellie, p. 353. Derham, pp. 224–25.

26. See George Lewis Buffon, *Natural History, General and Particular*, I, p. 282; III, pp. 300–305; VI, p. 260. Also John B. Bury, *The Idea of Progress*; Lilo Luxembourg, *Francis Bacon and Denis Diderot*; J. Félix Mourisson, *Philosophies de la nature: Bacon, Boyle, Toland, Buffon*; and Daniel Mornet, *Les sciences de la nature en France au XVIIIᵉ siècle*.

27. Ray, pp. 113–18, 128–29.

28. Rev. Nicholas Collin, "An Essay on Those Inquiries in Natural Philosophy, which at present are Most Beneficial," *Transactions of the American Philosophical Society* 3 (1793): xxiv. On utilitarianism in the eighteenth century, see Paul Hazard, *European Thought in the Eighteenth Century*, esp. pp. 22–23; and Daniel Boorstin, *The Lost World of Thomas Jefferson* (Boston, 1958).

29. Grew's paper, probably written in 1707, is discussed in E. A. J. Johnson, *Predecessors of Adam Smith: The Growth of British Economic Thought* (New York, 1937), ch. 7. Adam Smith, whose *Wealth of Nations* appeared in 1776, also wrote natural science essays, several of which can be found in *The Early Writings of Adam Smith*. Unfortunately, there is no study of attitudes toward nature among these early economists. A good illustration of agrarian influence on early ecological study is Frank Egerton, "Richard

Bradley's Understanding of Biological Productivity: A Study of Eighteenth-Century Ecological Ideas," *Journal of the History of Biology* 2 (Fall 1969): 391–411.

30. Thomas Ewbank, *The World a Workshop; or, The Physical Relationship of Man to the Earth*, pp. 22–23, 93, 118–19, 162, 171–73.

31. Mircea Eliade, *The Sacred and the Profane: The Nature of Religion*, pp. 116–17.

PART TWO

Chapter 3

1. *Journal*, in *The Works of Henry Thoreau*, III, ch. 7; IV, p. 174. This standard Walden Edition has been used throughout for most references. Its first six volumes, comprising the works prepared by Thoreau for publication, are referred to in the following notes as W., I through VI. The remaining fourteen volumes, Thoreau's daily journal, are herein cited as *J.*, I through XIV. The journal for the years 1840–41 is reprinted in *Consciousness in Concord*, ed. Perry Miller. In the case of *Walden* and *The Maine Woods*, I have used the most recent scholarly editions.

2. *J.*, II, pp. 13–15; IX, pp. 156–58; XI, p. 137.

3. Good accounts of Thoreau's life are given in Walter Harding, *The Days of Henry Thoreau*; Henry Seidel Canby, *Thoreau*; and Henry S. Salt, *The Life of Henry David Thoreau*. For general studies of his ideas during this period, I have profited from Joseph Wood Krutch, *Henry David Thoreau*, and Leo Stoller, *After Walden: Thoreau's Changing Views on Economic Man*.

4. *J.*, V, pp. 46, 65, 83; VII, p. 449; XII, pp. 156–57. Thoreau's Fact Book, I, pp. 18–28, 107–8; II, pp. 277–83.

5. For the history of Concord, see Ruth Wheeler, *Concord: Climate for Freedom*, and Townsend Scudder, *Concord: American Town*.

6. *J.*, III, pp. 251–53, 270–71, 286–88, 308–9, 346–48.

7. *J.*, I, p. 360; XII, p. 96; XIV, pp. 146–47. See also John B. Wilson, "Darwin and the Transcendentalists," *Journal of the History of Ideas* 26 (April–June 1965): 286–290.

8. *J.*, II, p. 426; VIII, pp. 109–10; XIV, p. 149.

9. *J.*, V, p. 120; IX, pp. 18–21; X, pp. 271–72, 462–64; XI, pp. 59–62; XII, pp. 133, 154–55. *The Correspondence of Henry David Thoreau*, p. 310. On Thoreau's scientific studies, see the following: Alec Lucas, "Thoreau, Field Naturalist"; Henry Weller, *Birds and Men*, ch. 7; Leo Stoller, "A Note on Thoreau's Place in the History of Phenology"; Reginald Cook, *Passage to Walden*, pp. 173–204; Raymond Adams, "Thoreau's Science." For background, see William Martin Smallwood, *Natural History and the American Mind* (New York, 1941).

10. *J.*, VIII, pp. 150, 220–22.

11. *J.*, VII, pp. 132–37. Timothy Dwight, *Travels in New England and New York*, I, p. 21. Charles E. Carroll, *The Timber Economy of Puritan New England*, ch. 2. Betty Thomson, *The Changing Face of New England*, esp. chs. 8 and 9. Neil Jorgensen, *A Guide to New England Landscape*, part 3. A. F. Hawes, "The New England Forest in Retrospect." Richard Eaton, *A Flora of Concord*.

12. Prefatory advertisement, *Annals of the Lyceum of Natural History of New-York* 1 (1824). George B. Emerson's book was published in Boston in 1846. For a review of other works in the survey, see Thoreau's "Natural History of Massachusetts" (1842), in *Excursions, W.*, V.

13. G. B. Emerson, pp. 1–22.

14. *Ibid.*, pp. 23–36.

15. *J.*, VIII, p. 335; X, pp. 39–40; XIV, pp. 166, 200.

16. "The Succession of Forest Trees" (1860), *Excursions, W.*, V, pp. 184–204. *J.*, XIII, pp. 50–51; XIV, chs. 2–4. See also Kathryn Whitford, "Thoreau and the Woodlots of Concord" and "Thoreau: Pioneer Ecologist and Conservationist." Harding, pp. 435, 440. Thoreau, "The Dispersion of Seed."

17. *J.*, XIV, pp. 133–35, 141, 150, 162, 243.

18. *J.*, XIV, pp. 152–61, 213, 224–30, 243–47.

19. *J.*, II, pp. 461–62; X, p. 51; XIV, pp. 161, 306–7.

20. *J.*, V, p. 293; XIV, pp. 262–63, 268. On Thoreau's attitude toward the wild, see Roderick Nash, *Wilderness and the American Mind*, ch. 5.

21. *J.*, XII, p. 387. Thoreau, *Huckleberries*, pp. 31–35.

22. *J.*, VIII, p. 330. In the spring of 1852 Thoreau wrote: "As [Abraham] Cowley loved a garden, so I a forest." (*J.*, III, p.438.)

Chapter 4

1. *J.*, IV, p. 410; VIII, p. 44.

2. *Correspondence*, pp. 45, 491. *J.*, IV, p. 472; IX, p. 200.

3. *J.*, VI, pp. 478–79; X, pp. 262–63.

4. *J.*, I, p. 237; III, pp. 56–57; VIII, p. 384; XII, pp. 67, 113–14.

5. *J.*, I, p. 71; III, p. 165; VII, pp. 112–13. *Walden*, p. 309.

6. *J.*, IX, pp. 246–47, 354. *The Maine Woods*, pp. 63–64, 69–71.

7. *The Works of George Berkeley*, III, p. 257.

8. For an overly mechanical breakdown of the various "unit-ideas" of this movement, see Arthur O. Lovejoy, "On the Discrimination of Romanticisms." A fuller and better account is H. G. Schenk, *The Mind of the European Romantics*.

9. Newton Stallknecht, *Strange Seas of Thought: Studies in William Wordsworth's Philosophy of Man and Nature*, chs. 1 and 3, esp. pp. 91–92. Eric Heller, "Goethe and the Idea of Scientific Truth," in *The Disinherited Mind*, p. 6. "Epirrhenia," in *Goethe's Botanical Writings*, p. 214. Also Joseph Warren Beach, *The Concept of Nature in Nineteenth-Century Poetry*, esp. ch. 3.

10. E. D. Hirsch, *Wordsworth and Schelling: A Typological Study of Romanticism*, p. 18.

11. *J.,* I, pp. 115, 364; IV, p. 492; XI, p. 275; XII, p. 44.

12. *J.,* I, pp. 89–90, 339; II, p. 111; VIII, p. 139; IX, p. 210; XI, pp. 450–51. See also Alexander Gode-von Aesch, *Natural Science in German Romanticism*, p. 13.

13. *J.,* I, p. 462; II, p. 97; III, pp. 381–82; IV, pp. 422, 445–46. Humanism may be defined as the philosophy that gives primary importance to human interests rather than to God or to Nature. It may emphasize either an ethic of human welfare and social service, as in Baconian science, or an aesthetic concern for self-culture ad creativity. See, among other works on this subject, Willson Coates, Hayden White, and J. Salwyn Schapiro, *The Emergence of Liberal Humanism* (New York, 1966), vol. 1.

14. *J.,* I, p. 375; IX, p. 331; XI, pp. 324–28, 338. *Huckleberries*, pp. 23, 26. *Correspondence*, p. 52.

15. *J.,* IX, pp. 45–46; VI, p. 4; X, p. 473. *Correspondence*, p. 257. *A Week on the Concord and Merrimack Rivers* (1849), *W.,* I, p. 182. In this work he also declared that he preferred Pan and the gods of Greece to New England's Jehovah (p. 66).

16. *J.,* I, p. 298; IV, pp. 84–85; IX, p. 344.

17. Edward Deevey, Jr., "A Re-Examination of Thoreau's *Walden.*" See also Nina Baym, "Thoreau's View of Science"; and Charles Metzger, "Thoreau on Science." On Goethe, the following are useful: Victor Lange, "Goethe: Science and Poetry"; Rudolf Magnus, *Goethe as a Scientist*; Karl Vietor, *Goethe the Thinker*, pp. 11–54; and Heller, "Scientific Truth."

18. Heller, p. 30. Also see Theodore Roszak, *Where the Wasteland Ends* (Garden City, N.Y., 1973), pp. 302–17.

19. Charles Gillispie, *The Edge of Objectivity*, pp. 156, 351.

20. *J.,* VI, pp. 236–38; X, pp. 164–65; XIII, p. 169.

21. *J.,* XI, pp. 359–60; XII, pp. 371–72.

22. *J.,* XI, p. 360; XII, pp. 23–24; XIII, pp. 141, 154–56. *Week, W.,* I, pp. 388–89.

23. *Maine Woods*, pp. 181–82.

24. *Ibid.,* p. 121. *J.,* XII, pp. 123–25, 170–71.

25. *Correspondence*, pp. 175–76. *J.,* VI, pp. 310–11, 452; IX, p. 343.

26. *J.*, I, p. 253; III, pp. 123–24; IV, pp. 136–37; X, pp. 294–95, 298; XIV, p. 295. "Natural History of Massachusetts," *W.*, V, p. 131.

27. *Correspondence*, p. 283. *J.*, II, p. 406; III, p. 378; IV, p. 239; XIV, p. 117.

Chapter 5

1. *J.*, V., p. 45. The ambivalence in his thinking is well illustrated in James McIntosh's *Thoreau as Romantic Naturalist: His Shifting Stance Toward Nature.*

2. *J.*, II, p. 46; VI, p. 293; IX, pp. 150–51.

3. *J.*, XI, p. 282. This side of Thoreau is the major theme of Sherman Paul, *The Shores of America: Thoreau's Inward Exploration.*

4. *J.*, I, p. 265; II, p. 30; IV, p. 128. *W.*, V, p. 40. *Consciousness in Concord*, p. 182.

5. *Walden*, pp. 215–17. See also Lawrence Willson, "Thoreau and the Natural Diet," *South Atlantic Quarterly* 57 (1958): 86–103. The Fruitlands experiment is discussed in Alice Felt Tyler, *Freedom's Ferment* (New York, 1962), pp. 172–75.

6. *Walden*, pp. 219–20. *J.*, IX, pp. 116–17.

7. *Walden*, pp. 220–21.

8. "Nature," in *Selections from Ralph Waldo Emerson*, pp. 21–56. See also Sherman Paul, *Emerson's Angle of Vision: Man and Nature in American Experience*; Octavius Frothingham, *Transcendentalism in New England*, esp. ch. 9; and Stephen Whicher, *Freedom and Fate: An Inner Life of Ralph Waldo Emerson.*

9. Emerson, "Nature," pp. 54, 56.

10. Emerson, "The Uses of Natural History" (1833), *The Early Lectures of Ralph Waldo Emerson*, vol. 1, pp. 11, 23–24. "On the Relation of Man to the Globe" (1834), *ibid.*, pp. 35, 42, 48. "Nature," p. 38. On Bacon's contribution to Romanticism, and for the millennial and perfectionist side of this movement generally, see M. H. Abrams, *Natural Supernaturalism: Tradition and Revolution in Romantic Literature* (New York, 1971), esp. pp. 59–65. For Thoreau's reaction to the drive for power, see *J.*, II, p. 150.

11. *J.*, VI, p. 85; IX, p. 121. Further important distinctions, especially on their respective relations to nature, have been made by Joel Porte, *Emerson and Thoreau: Transcendentalists in Conflict.*

12. *J.*, I, p. 384; IV, p. 313; IX, p. 37; XI, p. 441. *Walden*, p. 210.

13. *J.*, I, p. 326; II, pp. 201–5. In the *Week*, Thoreau feared that he had been living "with no root in the land/To keep my branches green." *W.*, I, p. 410.

14. *J.*, II, p. 470; V, p. 446; VIII, pp. 7–8, 31; X, pp. 131, 146; XII, p. 297.

15. *J.*, I, pp. 215, 315.

PART THREE

Chapter 6

1. For descriptions of the archipelago, see William Beebe, *Galápagos: World's End* (New York, 1924); Irenaus Eibl-Eibesfeldt, *The Galápagos: Noah's Ark of the Pacific* (Garden City, N.Y., 1961); and N. J. and Michael Berrill, *The Life of Sea Islands* (New York, 1969), pp. 66–99.

2. Charles Darwin, *The Voyage of the Beagle*, ed. Leonard Engel, pp. 375, 379. This is a new, retitled edition of Darwin's *Journal of Researches into the Natural History and Geology of the Countries Visited During the Voyage of H. M. S. Beagle Round the World . . .* (1845). It will be cited herein as *Journal/Beagle*. In its first published form (1839), where it bore an even longer title, this work was the third volume in the full narrative report of the *Beagle* expedition.

3. *Journal/Beagle*, pp. 379–82, 398. See also David Lack, *Darwin's Finches* (New York, 1947); and Nora Barlow, "Charles Darwin and the Galápagos Islands," *Nature* 136 (1935): 391; and *Charles Darwin and the Voyage of the "Beagle,"* p. 246.

4. *Journal/Beagle*, p. 375.

5. "The Encantadas, or 'Enchanted Isles'," in *Herman Melville*, ed. R. W. B. Lewis, p. 126. See also Charles Anderson, *Melville in the South Seas*, pp. 48–51, 326–27.

6. "The Encantadas," pp. 123, 130–34.

7. *Ibid.*, p. 127.

8. For an excellent discussion of Melville's "disillusioned" mind, see Harry Levin, *The Power of Blackness* (New York, 1958), esp. chs. 6 and 7. *Journal/Beagle*, pp. 24, 27, 42–45, 101–4, 129.

9. *Journal/Beagle*, pp. 32, 119–20, 487, 488n. See also Alan Moorehead, *Darwin and the Beagle* (New York, 1969); and Robert Hopkins, *Darwin's South America* (New York, 1969).

10. *Journal/Beagle*, pp. 131–32, 173–77.

11. *Ibid.*, pp. 2, 32, 172, 210, 303–14, 501–2.

12. On Romanticism and the pursuit of fear, see Marjorie Nicholson, *Mountain Gloom and Mountain Glory* (Ithaca, N.Y., 1959); Mario Praz, *The Romantic Agony* (London, 1933); and Kenneth Clark, *The Romantic Rebellion* (London, 1974).

13. Francis Parkman, *The Oregon Trail*, p. 233.

14. *Journal/Beagle*, pp. 413, 423–25, 430–31, 500, 502.

15. "Darwin's Notebooks on the Transmutation of Species," part 4, p. 113.

Chapter 7

1. William Whewell, *The Philosophy of the Inductive Sciences*, I, p. 113.

2. *The Life and Letters of Charles Darwin*, I, p. 30. For Darwin's early life, see Gertrude Himmelfarb, *Darwin and the Darwinian Revolution*, chs. 1 and 2; "Autobiography," in *Darwin for Today*, ed. Stanley Edgar Hyman, pp. 323–404; Ruth Moore, *Charles Darwin*; and Geoffrey West, *Charles Darwin: A Portrait*.

3. "Autobiography," p. 354.

4. *Ibid.*, p. 361.

5. Quoted in Helmut De Terra, *Humboldt*, p. 87 (underscored in text); see also pp. 74–75, 270, on Humboldt and Goethe. For more biographical data, see the following: Douglas Botting, *Humboldt and Cosmos* (New York, 1973); Edward Dolan, *Green Universe: The Story of Alexander von Humboldt* (New York, 1959); Victor von Hagen, *South America Called Them* (New York, 1945); Eric Nordenskiöld, *History of Biology*, trans. Leonard Eyre (New York, 1928), pp. 314–16; Karl Bruhns, *Life of Alexander von Humboldt*.

6. Alexander von Humboldt, *Essai sur la Géographie des Plantes*, pp. v, 13–14, 30, 32–35.

7. Quoted in Charlotte Kellner, *Alexander von Humboldt*, p. 233.

8. Humboldt, *Cosmos: A Sketch of a Physical Description of the Universe*, I, pp. vii, 24, 42; III, pp. 24–25.

9. Humboldt, *Personal Narrative of Travels to the Equinoctial Regions of the New Continent, During the Years 1799–1804*, pp. viii, 35. "Preface" by Helen Williams (trans. and ed.), *ibid.*, p. iv. Erwin Ackerknecht, "George Forster, Alexander von Humboldt, and Ethnology," pp. 92–93. See also Louis Agassiz, "Address Delivered on the Centennial Anniversary of the Birth of Alexander von Humboldt," Boston Society of Natural History, 1869. Other speakers on that gala occasion included Ralph Waldo Emerson, Noah Porter, and John Greenleaf Whittier; the oratory was served up with a sprinkling of prayers, ceremonial verses, Bach's *Toccata in F*, and an oyster stew.

10. *Journal/Beagle*, pp. 12, 500. *Life and Letters*, I, p. 66. *Charles Darwin's Diary of the Voyage of H. M. S. "Beagle,"* p. 39. For other aspects of Humboldt's contribution, see Frank Egerton, "Humboldt, Darwin, and Population."

11. Humboldt, *Aspects of Nature*, pp. 40–42, 211.

12. On the revolution in geology, see Leonard Wilson, *Charles Lyell: The Years to 1841*; Charles Gillispie, *Genesis and Geology*; and Loren Eiseley, *Darwin's Century*, chs. 3 and 4.

13. John C. Greene, *The Death of Adam*, chs. 3 and 4.

14. Charles Lyell, *The Principles of Geology*, II, pp. 66–68, 70–72, 88.

15. *Ibid.*, pp. 88*ff.*, 143–44.

16. *Ibid.*, pp. 121–22, 146–54.

17. *Ibid.*, pp. 84, 145, 156, 207.

18. *Ibid.*, pp. 130–32, 140. A similar analysis of Lyell's inconsistency may be found in Frank Egerton, "Studies of Animal Population from Lamarck to Darwin," pp. 236–40.

19. See *Sir Charles Lyell's Scientific Journals on the Species Question;* also Eiseley, pp. 108–15.

20. Lyell, *Principles,* II, pp. 68, 71, 82. Augustin de Candolle, "Géographie Botanique." A. Hunter Dupree, *Asa Gray,* pp. 235–36.

Chapter 8

1. Adam Sedgwick to Dr. Samuel Butler, quoted in Himmelfarb, *Darwin and the Darwinian Revolution,* pp. 79–80.

2. Charles to Emma Darwin, in *A Century of Family Letters, 1792–1896,* I, p. 277. Gavin De Beer, *Charles Darwin: A Scientific Biography,* p. 110.

3. *Life and Letters,* I, p. 243, 245, 253, 260, 288.

4. Friedrich Engels, *The Condition of the Working Class in England* (Rev. ed., New York, 1958), pp. 30–32.

5. "Autobiography," in *Darwin for Today,* p. 388. See also Peter Vorzimmer, "Darwin, Malthus, and the Theory of Natural Selection," pp. 527–42.

6. Thomas Malthus, *Essay on Population, 1798,* pp. 15–16, 26, 204, 361. See also Himmelfarb, pp. 132–38; Kenneth Smith, *The Malthusian Controversy;* George McCleary, *The Malthusian Population Theory;* David Glass, *Introduction to Malthus;* and Grosvenor Griffith, *Population Problems in the Age of Malthus.*

7. Malthus, *Essay,* pp. 181–82.

8. *Ibid.*, pp. 361, 364, 395. McCleary, p. 74.

9. For further background on Malthus and Darwin, see Robert Young, "Malthus and the New Evolutionists." Also see Herbert Spencer's "Theory of Population Deduced from the General Law of Animal Fertility," *Westminster Review* n.s. 1 (1852): 468–501.

10. Eiseley, chs. 2 and 5. Bentley Glass et al. (eds.), *Forerunners of Darwin, 1745–1859.* Milton Millhauser, *Just Before Darwin: Robert Chambers and the Vestiges.* A. S. Packard, *Lamarck: The Founder of Evolution.*

11. Maurice Mandelbaum, "The Scientific Background of Evolutionary Theory in Biology." Peter Vorzimmer, "Darwin's Ecology and Its Influence Upon His Theory." W. Frank Blair, "Ecology and Evolution." Herbert Marsh and Jean Langenheim, "Natural Selection as an Ecological Concept."

12. *On the Origin of Species*, pp. 3–4, 60, 71–74, 80. W. L. McAtee, "The Cats to Clover Chain." Darwin's sense of the interdependent "web of life" is especially well discussed in Paul Sears, *Charles Darwin: The Naturalist as a Cultural Force*, pp. 84–95.

13. *Origin*, p. 102. "Darwin's Notebooks," part 1, 2:2, pp. 25, 65. *Journal/Beagle*, pp. 176, 397. Darwin's idea of "place" owes much to the influence of Linnaeus. See Robert Stauffer, "Ecology in the Long Manuscript Version of Darwin's *Origin of Species* and Linnaeus' *Oeconomy of Nature*." See also *Charles Darwin's Natural Selection*.

14. *Origin*, pp. 75–76, 102, 172, 315.

15. *Ibid.*, pp. 109–10. "Darwin's Notebooks," part 4, pp. 162–63, 173. Also "Essay of 1844," pp. 103–5.

16. Darwin, "Essay of 1844," pp. 84–85, 98–103. *Origin*, p. 73.

17. "Darwin's Notebooks," part 1, p. 53. Himmelfarb, pp. 149, 151. *Origin*, pp. 81, 102–3, 108. For a more recent account of isolation and speciation, see Ernst Mayr, *Population, Species, and Evolution* (Cambridge, Mass., 1970), ch. 18.

18. "Autobiography," in *Darwin for Today*, p. 388. "Darwin's Notebooks," part 4, pp. 169–70.

19. *Life and Letters*, II, pp. 6–9; see also I, p. 531. *More Letters of Charles Darwin*, I, p. 151.

20. "Darwin's Notebooks," part 2, 2:3, p. 99.

21. *Life and Letters*, I, p. 481.

22. Darwin to Graham, in *Life and Letters*, I, p. 286. "Darwin's Notebooks," part 4, p. 166. *Origin*, pp. 62, 472.

23. On Wallace's ideas, the famous Linnaean Society meeting of 1858, and Darwin's reaction to rivalry, see Himmelfarb, pp. 242–50; and Barbara Beddall, "Wallace, Darwin, and the Theory of Natural Selection."

24. *More Letters*, I, pp. 40–41. For good background on Darwin's challenge to orthodox biologists, see Thomas Kuhn, *The Structure of Scientific Revolutions*; and John C. Greene, "The Kuhnian Paradigm and the Darwinian Revolution."

25. *Life and Letters*, II, pp. 26, 76, 87, 101, 103, 109.

26. This point is especially well argued by Michael Ghiselin in *The Triumph of the Darwinian Method*, against such recent critics of Darwin's methodology as Himmelfarb and Eiseley. See, too, David Hull, *Darwin and His Critics*, pp. 3–77.

Chapter 9

1. *Journal/Beagle*, pp. 205, 213.

2. *Ibid.*, ch. 18. Although it is not directly relevant to the late Victo-

rians, Roy Harvey Pearce's *Savagism and Civilization: A Study of the Indian and the American Mind* (Baltimore, 1965) is useful for understanding the historical roots of this mood.

3. "Author's Introduction" (Sept. 1900), in James G. Frazer, *The New Golden Bough*, p. xxv. See also J. W. Burrow, *Evolution and Society: A Study in Victorian Social Theory*; and John B. Bury, *The Idea of Progress* (London, 1924), pp. 330–49.

4. George Perkins Marsh, "The Study of Nature," p. 36. See also John Wesley Powell, "Relation of Primitive Peoples to Environment, Illustrated by American Examples," and "From Barbarism to Civilization," p. 123.

5. Richard Hofstadter, *Social Darwinism in American Thought*, esp. ch. 2 on Herbert Spencer's appeal. Donald Fleming, "Social Darwinism." James Allen Rogers, "Darwinism and Social Darwinism."

6. On Ward, see Hofstadter, ch. 4. Henry Steele Commager (ed.), "Introduction" to *Lester Ward and the General Welfare State*, pp. xi–xxxviii. Ralph Henry Gabriel makes Ward one of the key spokesmen for the "new humanism" or "religion of humanity" in *The Course of American Democratic Thought* (New York, 1956), pp. 215–20, 226.

7. Lester Ward, *The Psychic Factors of Civilization*, pp. 244–61.

8. *Ibid.*, p. 262.

9. Thomas Huxley, *Man's Place in Nature*, pp. 129–30. The best study of Huxley's career and ideas is William Irvine's *Apes, Angels, and Victorians* (London, 1955).

10. Thomas and Julian Huxley, *Evolution and Ethics, 1893–1943*, pp. 79, 81. See also John Stuart Mill, "Nature," which anticipated most of Huxley's argument. For a response to Huxley's stance, see Prince Peter Kropotkin's *Mutual Aid* (London, 1902), which argued that cooperation is more "natural" than the law of tooth and fang, among members of the same species.

11. William James, "A Moral Equivalent to War."

12. Thomas Huxley, "Prolegomena" (1894), in *Evolution and Ethics*, pp. 38–44.

13. Hood is quoted in Walter Houghton, *The Victorian Frame of Mind*, p. 196.

14. "Darwin's Notebooks," I, p. 69. In the *Life and Letters* (I, p. 368) version, the phrase "all netted together" is given as "all melted together."

15. *Life and Letters*, I, p. 310–12; II, pp. 166, 354, 377. For another view of this aspect of Darwin's character, see Donald Fleming, "Charles Darwin, The Anaesthetic Man." See also *The Animal World of Albert Schweitzer* (Boston, 1950); and William Ritter, *Charles Darwin and the Golden Rule*, pp. 32, 56, 68–69, 372–73.

16. *The Descent of Man*, pp. 471–511, esp. p. 492, on "sympathy beyond the confines of man." See also Stanley Edgar Hyman, *The Tangled Bank*, pp. 42, 50, on Darwin's "totemic brotherhood" with other creatures.

17. Sedgwick to Darwin, in *Life and Letters*, II, p. 45. See also Sedgwick's review of William Chambers' *Vestiges of Creation* in the *Edinburgh Review* 82 (1845): 1–85. *Descent of Man*, pp. 411–12. Himmelfarb, p. 153. *More Letters*, I, p. 237.

18. *More Letters*, I, pp. 31–36. De Beer, pp. 93, 251. See *Life and Letters*, I, p. 426, for Darwin's "pilgrimage" to Selborne in the 1850s.

19. William H. Hudson, *Birds and Man*, p. 253. John Muir, *A Thousand-Mile Walk to the Gulf*, p. 139. E. P. Evans, "Ethical Relations Between Man and Beast," p. 634. Liberty Hyde Bailey, *The Holy Earth*, pp. 30–31. Thomas Hardy is quoted in Henry S. Salt, *Seventy Years Among Savages*, pp. 203–4. See also E. S. Turner, *All Heaven in a Rage* (London, 1964), esp. pp. 229–37.

20. Henry S. Salt, *The Creed of Kinship*, and *Seventy Years Among Savages*, pp. 74, 122, 131–32. See also Bertram Lloyd (ed.), *The Great Kinship* (London, 1921); John Howard Moore, *The Universal Kinship* (Chicago, 1906); and Stephen Winsten, *Salt and His Circle* (London, 1951).

PART FOUR

Chapter 10

1. Ernst Haeckel, *Generelle Morphologie der Organismen*, I, p. 8; II, pp. 253–56, 286–87. Haeckel, *The Wonders of Life*, p. 80. See also Robert Stauffer, "Haeckel, Darwin, and Ecology," pp. 138–44; and Emanuel Rádl, *History of Biological Theories*, pp. 122–46.

2. Haeckel, translated and quoted in "Preface" by Warder Allee et al. (AEPPS), *Principles of Animal Ecology* (Philadelphia, 1949). Charles Bessey, *Science* 15 (April 11, 1902): 573–574.

3. August Grisebach's ideas are summarized in his major work, *Der Vegetation der Erde*. S. Charles Kendeigh, "History and Evaluation of Various Concepts of Plant and Animal Communities in North America," pp. 152–71. R. H. Whittaker, "Classification of Natural Communities," *Botanical Reviews* 28 (1962): 1–239. Erik Nordenskiöld, *The History of Biology* (New York, 1928), pp. 558–61.

4. C. Hart Merriam, "Results of a Biological Survey of the San Francisco Mountain Region and Desert of the Little Colorado, Arizona." *Selected Works of Clinton Hart Merriam*. See also Keir Sterling, *Last of the Naturalists: The Career of C. Hart Merriam* (New York, 1974); Kendeigh, pp. 160–61; and A. Hunter Dupree, *Science in the Federal Government* (Cambridge, Mass., 1957), pp. 238–39.

5. Victor Shelford, "Life Zones, Modern Ecology, and the Failure of Temperature Summing," and "The Relative Merits of the Life Zone and Biome Concepts." Roger Tory Peterson, "Life Zones, Biomes, or Life Forms?" Rexford Daubenmire, "Merriam's Life Zones of North America."

6. Oscar Drude, *Manuel de géographie botanique*. Andreas Schimper, *Plant Geography upon a Physiological Basis*; see also Richard Brewer, *A Brief History of Ecology. Part I: Pre-Nineteenth Century to 1910*. Hugh Raup, "Trends in the Development of Geographic Botany."

7. Eugenius Warming, *The Oecology of Plants*, pp. 5, 369–70, 373. Frederic E. Clements, "Darwin's Influence upon Plant Geography and Ecology."

8. Warming, pp. 83, 91, 94, 140, 366.

9. Warming, chs. 3, 22–26. Anton de Bary, *Die Erscheinung der Symbiose*. See also these early works: Pierre van Beneden, *Animal Parasites and Messmates* (New York, 1876); Oskar Hertwig, *Die Symbiose oder das Genossenschaftsleben in Tierreich* (Jena, Germany, 1883); Roscoe Pound, "Symbiosis and Mutualism"; Frederick Keeble, *Plant-Animals: A Study in Symbiosis* (Cambridge, England, 1910).

10. Warming, chs. 94–95.

11. Warming, chs. 94–95, esp. p. 356. Brewer, *Brief History*, pp. 2–3; Bodenheimer, pp. 134–35; Rupert Furneaux, *Krakatoa*.

12. *Science* 15 (March 28, 1902): 511; (April 11, 1902): 573–574; (May 9, 1902): 747–749. Oscar Drude, "The Position of Ecology in Modern Science"; see also Benjamin Robinson, in same publication, pp. 191–203.

13. Paul Sears, "Some Notes on the Ecology of Ecologists," *Scientific Monthly* 83 (July 1956): 23. Barrington Moore, "The Scope of Ecology." Charles C. Adams, "The New Natural History— Ecology," and *Guide to the Study of Animal Ecology*, ch. 3.

14. Allee et al. (AEPPS), ch. 1. W. F. Ganong, "The Cardinal Principles of Ecology." Edward Kormondy (ed.), *Readings in Ecology*, Introduction and part 1. Victor E. Shelford, *Laboratory and Field Ecology*, p. 2; see also his *Animal Communities in Temperate America*, pp. 1, 302–3.

Chapter 11

1. Arthur G. Tansley, "The Early History of Modern Plant Ecology in Britain." Also Charles C. Adams, "Patrick Geddes, Botanist and Human Ecologist"; and Paul Sears, "Ecology of Ecologists," p. 26. On the French–Swiss influence and its ideas, see Rudy Becking, "The Zurich–Montpellier School of Phytosociology," *Botanical Reviews* 23 (July 1957): 411–488; and Charles Flauhault, "Le Progrès de la géographie botanique depuis 1884."

2. Drude, "Position of Ecology," p. 179. Tansley, "The Use and Abuse of Vegetational Concepts and Terms," p. 285. Victor E. Shelford, "The Organization of the Ecological Society of America, 1914–1919." Donald Fleming, "American Science and the World Scientific Community."

3. Henry C. Cowles, "The Ecological Relations of the Vegetation on the Sand Dunes of Lake Michigan," and "The Physiographic Ecology of Chicago and Vicinity." See also the even earlier work of Conway Macmillan, "Observations on the Distribution of Plants Along the Shore at Lake of the Woods."

4. William Cooper, "Henry Chandler Cowles." Tansley, "Use and Abuse," p. 284; Sears, "Ecology of Ecologists," pp. 24–25.

5. Andrew Denny Rodgers, *American Botany, 1873–1892: Decades of Transition.* Sears, "Ecology of Ecologists," p. 24.

6. H. L. Shantz, "Frederic Edward Clements (1874–1945)." Tansley, "Frederic Edward Clements." John Phillips, "A Tribute to Frederic E. Clements and His Concepts in Ecology." Roscoe Pound, "Frederic E. Clements as I Knew Him." Pound and Clements, *The Phytogeography of Nebraska.*

7. Clements, *The Development and Structure of Vegetation,* pp. 5–7, 91–149; *Plant Succession,* esp. pp. 1–6; "Plant Succession and Human Problems" (1935), in *The Dynamics of Vegetation: Selections from the Writings of F. E. Clements,* p. 8; "The Nature and Structure of the Climax" (1936), *ibid.,* pp. 119–60.

8. Clements, *Research Methods in Ecology,* pp. 5, 199; "Succession and Human Problems," pp. 1–2; "Social Origins and Processes Among Plants," in *A Handbook of Social Psychology,* ed. Carl Murchison (Worcester, Mass., 1935), p. 35; *Plant Succession,* pp. 124–25. See also John Phillips, "Succession, Development, the Climax, and the Complex Organism: An Analysis of Concepts."

9. Pound, "Clements as I Knew Him," p. 113. Clements, John Weaver, and Herbert Hanson, *Plant Competition,* p. 314. Phillips, "Succession," part 1, p. 570.

10. Herbert Spencer, "The Social Organism." C. Lloyd Morgan, *Spencer's Philosophy of Science* (Oxford, 1913), pp. 6–7.

11. For Spencer's social theory and its influence, see his *Principles of Sociology;* J. W. Burrow, *Evolution and Society* (Cambridge, 1966), ch. 6; Richard Hofstadter, *Social Darwinism in America* (Boston, 1959, rev. ed.); and Cynthia Russett, *The Concept of Equilibrium in American Social Thought* (New Haven, Conn., 1966), ch. 3.

12. Herbert Spencer, *The Principles of Biology,* II, pp. 396–408, 537.

13. Spencer, "Evolutionary Ethics." Clements, Weaver, and Hanson, *Plant Competition,* esp. pp. 314–27.

14. Clements and Shelford, *Bio-Ecology,* pp. 2–20; also see John Phillips, "The Biotic Community."

15. Clements and Shelford, ch. 8. John Weaver, *North American Prairie* (Lincoln, Nebr., 1954), and, with F. W. Albertson, *Grasslands of the Great Plains* (Lincoln, Nebr., 1956). David Costello, *The Prairie World* (New York, 1969). H. L. Shantz, "The Natural Vegetation of the Great Plains Region." Frank Gates, *Grasses in Kansas* (Topeka, Kans., 1937).

16. Clements, "Nature and Structure of the Climax," in *Climax*, p. 256. Peter Farb, *The Living Earth*, p. 99. Durward Allen, *The Life of Prairies and Plains*. David Dary, *The Buffalo Book* (New York, 1974), pp. 28–29. Waldo Wedel, *Prehistoric Man on the Great Plains* (Norman, Okla., 1961).

17. Walter P. Webb, *The Great Plains*, chs. 2–3. Arthur Vestal, "Internal Relations of Terrestrial Associations," *American Naturalist* 18 (1914): 413–445.

18. See, for example, Charles C. Adams, *Guide to the Study of Animal Ecology*, pp. 11, 25–28; and Clements and Ralph Chaney, *Environment and Life in the Great Plains*.

19. Henry Nash Smith, "Introduction" to James Fenimore Cooper's *The Prairie* (New York, 1950 ed.), pp. xii–xx, and *Virgin Land: The American West as Symbol and Myth*, ch. 22. Ray Billington, *America's Frontier Heritage*. George R. Pierson, "The Frontier and American Institutions," *New England Quarterly* 15 (1942): 224–255. An offshoot of the ecological succession idea is the geographer's sequent–occupance model. See Marvin Mikesell, "The Rise and Decline of 'Sequent Occupance,' " pp. 149–69.

Chapter 12

1. Vance Johnson, *Heaven's Tableland: The Dust Bowl Story*, pp. 153–60. Also see Fred Floyd, "A History of the Dust Bowl."

2. Soil Conservation Service, USDA, "Some Information about Dust Storms and Wind Erosion on the Great Plains." Robert Silverberg, *The Challenge of Climate*, pp. 274–79.

3. Ivan Tannehill, *Drought: Its Causes and Effects*, chs. 4 and 10. John Weaver, *Prairie Plants and Their Environment* (Lincoln, Nebr., 1968), chs. 8–9. Edward Higbee, *The American Oasis*, pp. 128–30. Stanley Vestal, *Short Grass Country* (New York, 1941), ch. 11.

4. Dorothea Lange and Paul Taylor, *An American Exodus*. Carey McWilliams, *Ill Fares the Land*, ch. 10.

5. Walter Stein, *California and the Dust Bowl Migration*, p. 15. McWilliams, p. 191.

6. Writers' Program, Works Progress Administration, *Oklahoma: A Guide to the Sooner State* (Norman, Okla., 1941). Carl Kraenzel, *The Great Plains in Transition*, pp. 137–64. Edwin McReynolds, *Oklahoma: A History of the Sooner State*, ch. 12. Alice Marriott and Carol Rachlin, *Oklahoma: The Forty-sixth Star*, chs. 5–7.

7. Stein, ch. 1; McWilliams, chs. 10 and 15.

8. Vance Johnson, *Heaven's Tableland*, pp. 166–70. John Bennett et al., "The Problem: Subhumid Areas," in United States Department of Agriculture, *Soils and Men*, p. 68. Lange and Taylor, p. 82. Soil Conservation Service, "Dust Storms and Wind Erosion."

9. Archibald MacLeish, "The Grasslands," p. 59. See also Weaver and Albertson, *Grasslands of the Great Plains*, pp. 92, 118–19. Tom Dale and Vernon Carter, *Topsoil and Civilization*, pp. 229–30. Lawrence Svobida, *An Empire of Dust*.

10. Webb, *Great Plains*, chs. 7–8. Allan Bogue, *From Prairie to Cornbelt*, ch. 1. Martyn Bowden, "The Great American Desert and the American Frontier, 1880–1882: Popular Images of the Plains." Henry Nash Smith, "Rain Follows the Plow: The Notion of Increased Rainfall for the Great Plains, 1844–1880," and *Virgin Land*, ch. 16. David Emmons, *Garden in the Grasslands*. Vance Johnson, pp. 56–57.

11. Gilbert Fite, "Daydreams and Nightmares: The Late Nineteenth-Century Agricultural Frontier." David Shannon, *The Farmer's Last Frontier*. W. D. Johnson, "The High Plains and Their Utilization." Henry Nash Smith, *Virgin Land*, ch. 19. Wallace Stegner, *Beyond the Hundredth Meridian*, ch. 3.

12. Vance Johnson, chs. 11 and 12. Russell McKee, *The Last West: A History of the Great Plains in North America*, pp. 261–73. Mary Hargreaves, *Dry Farming in the Northern Great Plains, 1900–1925*. Webb, *Great Plains*, pp. 366–74. "Dry Farming—The Hope of the West," *Century Magazine* 72 (1906). James Bennett, "Oasis Civilization in the Great Plains."

13. Vance Johnson, pp. 146, 153. Leslie Hewes, *The Suitcase Farming Frontier*. Great Plains Committee report, "The Future of the Great Plains," pp. 4–5, 42.

14. Soil Conservation Service, "Dust Storms and Wind Erosion." MacLeish, "The Grasslands," part 3: "Men Against Dust." Arthur Schlesinger, Jr., *The Coming of the New Deal*, chs. 5 and 20. Stewart Udall, *The Quiet Crisis*, ch. 10. Thomas Wessel, "Roosevelt and the Great Plains Shelterbelt," *Great Plains Journal* 8 (1969): 57–74.

15. "Future of the Great Plains," pp. 2–5.

16. *Ibid.*, pp. 63–67. A principal influence on the committee's thinking was Aldo Leopold's essay, "The Conservation Ethic."

17. See, for instance, "Future of the Great Plains," p. 11; David Lilienthal, *TVA: Democracy on the March* (New York, 1953), ch. 6; Arthur Ekirch, Jr., *Man and Nature in America* (New York, 1963), ch. 9; Anna Lou Riesch, "Conservation under Franklin D. Roosevelt," Ph.D. thesis, University of Washington (1952). For the earlier conservation philosophy, the standard account is Samuel Hays, *Conservation and the Gospel of Efficiency: The Progressive Conservation Movement, 1890–1920* (Cambridge, Mass., 1959).

18. Roger C. Smith, "Upsetting the Balance of Nature, with Special Reference to Kansas and the Great Plains." Paul Sears, *Deserts on the March*, esp. chs. 13 and 17; see, too, Sears' "Floods and Dust Storms." Edward Graham, "Soil Erosion as an Ecological Process."

19. John Weaver and Evan Flory, "Stability of Climax Prairie and Some Environmental Changes Resulting from Breaking," *Ecology* 15 (October 1934): 333–347. Weaver, *North American Prairie*, pp. 271, 325.

20. Clements and Chaney, *Environment and Life in the Great Plains*, pp. 37–51. Also see Clements' "Succession and Human Problems" (1935), "Climaxes, Succession, and Conservation" (1937–39), and "Ecology in the Public Service" (1935)—all reprinted in *Dynamics of Vegetation*.

21. Clements, "Climatic Cycles and Human Populations in the Great Plains" (1938), in *Dynamics of Vegetation*. Clements and Chaney, p. 3.

22. Clements and Chaney, p. 49. "Ecology in the Public Service," pp. 249–54.

23. MacLeish, "The Grasslands," pp. 186–88.

24. Herbert Gleason, "The Structure and Development of the Plant Association," "The Individualistic Concept of the Plant Association," and "Further Views on the Succession Concept."

25. Tansley, "Use and Abuse."

26. James Malin, *The Grassland of North America: Prolegomena to Its History*; see in particular chs. 1–7 for his use of ecological science. For comments on Webb, see *ibid.*, ch. 15, and Malin, "The Grassland of North America: Its Occupance and the Challenge of Continuous Reappraisals."

27. Special Presidential Committee, "A Report on Drought in the Great Plains and Southwest." H. H. Finnell, "The Dust Storms of 1954." Malin, *Grassland: Prolegomena*, pp. 136–37, and "Grassland: Occupance," p. 365.

28. Malin, "Soil, Animal, and Plant Relations of the Grassland, Historically Reconsidered," pp. 210, 219. See also "Man, the State of Nature, and the Climax" (1950), ch. 24 in *Grassland: Prolegomena*, and *ibid.*, pp. 119, 130–31, 406, 426.

29. Malin, "Dust Storms." *Grassland: Prolegomena*, pp. 137, 405. "Soil, Animal, and Plant Relations," pp. 211–13.

30. Malin, *Grassland: Prolegomena*, pp. 426–27; "Grassland: Occupance," pp. 353–55. Carl Sauer, "Grassland Climax, Fire, and Man," and *Agricultural Origins and Dispersals*, pp. 15–18. Philip Wells, "Scarp Woodlands, Transported Grassland Soils, and the Concept of Grassland Climate in the Great Plains Region," *Sci-*

ence 148 (April 9, 1965): 246–249. Omer Stewart, "Why the Great Plains Are Treeless," *Colorado Quarterly* 2 (1955): 40–50. Victor Shelford, "Deciduous Forest, Man, and the Grassland Fauna." Edwin Komarek, Sr., "Fire Ecology—Grasslands and Man." On the relation of fire to the forest climax, see the other annual volumes in this series, as well as Ashley Shiff, *Fire and Water: Scientific Heresy in the Forest Service* (Cambridge, Mass., 1962).

31. Malin, "Grassland: Occupance," pp. 358–59. Webb, *Great Plains*, pp. 205–7, 226–28. For another critique of Webb's "determinism," see David Shannon, *An Appraisal of Walter Prescott Webb's "The Great Plains"* (New York, 1940).

32. Malin, "Soil, Animal, and Plant Relations," pp. 207, 220; "Grassland: Occupance," pp. 360–62; *Grassland: Prolegomena*, ch. 21.

33. Malin, *Grassland: Prolegomena*, pp. 154–55.

34. Hugh Raup, "Some Problems in Ecological Theory and Their Relation to Conservation." See also Frank Egler, "A Commentary on American Plant Ecology," *Ecology* 32 (1951): 677–695, and "Vegetation as an Object of Study," *Philosophy of Science* 9 (1942): 245–260. Ramon Margalef, *Perspectives on Ecological Theory*, p. 32.

35. R. H. Whittaker, "A Consideration of Climax Theory," *Ecological Monographs* 23 (1953): 41–78. See also Stanley Cain, "The Climax and Its Complexities."

36. H. L. Shantz, "The Ecological Approach to Land Management." For further evidence of the impact of climax ecology on conservation, see E. J. Kotok, "The Ecological Approach to Conservation Programs," and Walter Cottam, "The Role of Ecology in the Conservation of Renewable Resources." Edward Graham, Seymour Harris, and Edward Ackerman, "A Symposium—The Ecological Approach to Land Use."

37. For example, see the following: Howard Odum and Harry Morse, *American Regionalism*, ch. 14, esp. pp. 326–27; George Carter, *Plant Geography and Culture History in the American Southwest* (New York, 1945); and Robert Dickinson, *Regional Ecology* (New York, 1970).

38. Herbert Hanson, "Ecology in Agriculture."

PART FIVE

Chapter 13

1. George Laycock, "Travels and Travails of the Song-Dog." Joe Van Wormer, *The World of the Coyote*. Heavily polemical but well supported by evidence is Jack Olson, *Slaughter the Animals, Poison the Earth* (New York, 1971). On the wolf, see L. David Mech, *The Wolf*; Paul Errington, "Of Wilderness and Wolves"; and Douglas Pimlott, "Wolves and Men in North America."

2. J. Frank Dobie, *The Voice of the Coyote*, p. x. Theodore Roosevelt, "A Cougar Hunt on the Rim of the Grand Canyon," *The Outlook* 105 (May 1913): 260. See also Frank Graham, Jr., *Man's Dominion: The Story of Conservation in America*, pp. 272–78.

3. The standard interpretation of Progressive conservation remains Samuel Hays, *Conservation and the Gospel of Efficiency*. See also J. Leonard Bates, "Fulfilling American Democracy: The Conservation Movement, 1907 to 1921."

4. Jenks Cameron, *The Bureau of the Biological Survey*, ch. 1. Victor Shelford, "Biological Control of Rodents and Predators," pp. 331–32. Robert Connery, *Governmental Problems in Wild Life Conservation*. Advisory Committee on Predator Control (Stanley A. Cain, chairman), "Predator Control—1971" (report to the Council on Environmental Quality and Department of the Interior), pp. 1–2. This is the famous Cain Report that led to the curtailment of poison distribution on public lands in 1972.

5. Sigurd Olson, "A Study in Predatory Relationships, with Particular Reference to the Wolf." Cameron, pp. 51–52. W. C. Henderson, "The Control of the Coyote."

6. The continuing influence of the sheep industry on government wildlife programs was still being noted in the Leopold Report of 1964, "Predator and Rodent Control in the United States," by the Advisory Board in Wildlife Management (A. Starker Leopold, chairman).

7. Cameron, *The Bureau*, p. 40. Vernon Bailey, "Destruction of Wolves and Coyotes: Results Obtained during 1907." The official attitude toward predatory birds, however, was much more positive, as represented by A. K. Fisher's pamphlet, "Cause of the Prejudice Against Birds of Prey," BBS Circular no. 61 (1907).

8. Gifford Pinchot, *Breaking New Ground*, pp. 120, 342–43. Consult also Nelson McGeary, *Gifford Pinchot, Forester-Politican* (Princeton, N.J., 1960); and Elmo Richardson, *The Politics of Conservation: Crusades and Controversies, 1897–1913*.

9. Pinchot, p. 31.

10. John Lorain, *Nature and Reason Harmonized in the Practice of Husbandry*, esp. pp. 24–27; see also Clarence Glacken, *Traces on the Rhodian Shore* (Berkeley, Calif., 1967), pp. 693–98. George Perkins Marsh, *Man and Nature: Or, Physical Geography as Modified by Human Action*, pp. 91–92. Also see David Lowenthal, *George Perkins Marsh, Versatile Vermonter* (New York, 1958). For Pinchot's reaction to Marsh, see Pinchot, pp. xvi–xvii.

11. On the development of game conservation, consult James Trefethen, *Crusade for Wildlife* (Harrisburg, Pa., 1961), and *Wildlife Management and Conservation* (Boston, 1964).

12. Emerson Hough, "The President's Forest." John Russo, "The Kaibab North Deer Herd—Its History, Problems, and Manage-

ment." D. Irwin Rasmussen, "Biotic Communities of Kaibab Plateau, Arizona."

13. Rasmussen, pp. 236–38. Refer also to Walter P. Taylor (ed.), *The Deer of North America* (Harrisburg, Pa., 1956).

14. Aldo Leopold, *Game Management*, p. 21. The only full-scale study of Leopold's career is Susan Flader's *Thinking Like a Mountain: Aldo Leopold and the Evolution of an Ecological Attitude Toward Deer, Wolves, and Forests.* For shorter accounts, note Roderick Nash, *Wilderness and the American Mind*, ch. 11; and Donald Fleming, "Roots of the New Conservation Movement."

15. Leopold, *Game Management*, pp. viii, 3, 20, 396.

16. Flader, pp. 59–61, 93–94.

17. John Muir, the most prominent defender of the western wilderness, apparently had little interest in predators. Other conservationists, including the founders of the National Audubon Society, actually supported the idea of predator reduction. Among wildlife they favored the birds and small mammals, and their notion of "refuges" for these creatures was sometimes meant to protect them from predators as well as human exploiters. This official stance of the Audubon Society came under blistering attack by Rosalie Edge in the 1930s; see her papers in the Denver, Colo., Public Library's Conservation Center.

18. Charles C. Adams, "The Conservation of Predatory Mammals." "Symposium." The Yellowstone resolutions are reprinted in *The Living Wilderness* (Summer 1950): 29.

19. Lee Dice, "The Scientific Value of Predatory Mammals." Adams, "Conservation of Predatory Mammals," pp. 90, 94, and "Rational Predatory Animal Control," *Journal of Mammalogy* 11 (August 1930): 357.

20. Stanley Young to Arthur Carhart, Nov. 24, 1930, in the Stanley P. Young Papers. See, too, Young's monograph, "The Saga of Predatory Animal Control," typescript, 1956 (?) in the same archives. Also his book, with E. A. Goldman, *The Wolves of North America.*

21. A corollary of this pragmatic stance was to oppose predator reduction programs on the grounds of their frequent accidental killing of non-target species, especially the valuable fur-bearing carnivores like mink, badgers, and ermine. For an example of this common argument, see Joseph Dixon, "Fur-bearers Caught in Traps Set for Predatory Animals," *Journal of Mammalogy* 11 (August 1930): 373–376.

22. Olaus Murie, "Memorandum to Mr. Redington," Aug. 30, 1929 (carbon copy in Olaus Murie Papers). Henderson, "Control of the Coyote," p. 347.

23. The most thorough studies on the subject have been Paul Errington's; see his "What Is the Meaning of Predation?," "A Ques-

tion of Values," and *Of Predation and Life*, esp. pp. 204–5. Also useful is Durward Allen, *Our Wildlife Legacy*, chs. 14 and 15.

24. E. A. Goldman, "The Predatory Mammal Problem and the Balance of Nature," and "The Coyote—Archpredator." *New Mexico Conservationist* (April 1930): 14–15.

25. Walter Howard, "Means of Improving the Status of Vertebrate Pest Control." Goldman, "The Predatory Mammal Problem," p. 31. Ira Gabrielson, *Wildlife Conservation*, p. 208.

26. Olaus Murie's career and outlook on nature are best reflected in his and his wife's book of recollections, *Wapiti Wilderness*. The summary given here is also based on extensive reading in his letters and other papers.

27. "Memorandum to Redington," p. 4. O. M. to Redington, Oct. 11, 1930. To A. Brazier Howell, May 7, 1931. To Hildebrand, Aug. 28, 1950. To Cottam, Dec. 7, 1949. See also O. M. to Cottam, Dec. 31, 1947, and to Clifford Presnall, Dec. 7, 1952, on the subservience of the Fish and Wildlife Service to economic rather than ecological values. All in the Olaus Murie Papers.

28. Leopold, *Game Management*, pp. 422–23.

29. Leopold, "The Conservation Ethic."

30. Flader, *Thinking Like a Mountain*, pp. 28–30.

31. Leopold, *A Sand County Almanac*, pp. xix, 124–27, 162–63, 190, 202–10.

32. *Ibid.*, pp. xviii, 237–64.

33. *Ibid.*, pp. 189–90, 247.

34. *Ibid.*, pp. 190, 210, 251.

Chapter 14

1. Hermann Reinheimer, *Evolution by Cooperation: A Study in Bio-Economics*, pp. ix–x, 19, 41, 46, 194.

2. Robert Usinger, *The Life of Rivers and Streams*, pp. 110*ff*.

3. John Maynard Keynes, *The General Theory of Employment, Interest, and Money* (London, 1936), p. 383.

4. H. G. Wells, Julian Huxley, and G. P. Wells, *The Science of Life*, p. 961.

5. Charles Elton, *Animal Ecology*, pp. vii–viii, xiv. Elton's other works include *Animal Ecology and Evolution* (1930), *Voles, Mice and Lemmings* (1942), and *The Ecology of Invasions by Animals and Plants* (1958).

6. See *Animal Ecology*, ch. 5. An anticipation of these ideas was Stephen Forbes, "The Lake as a Microcosm," and "On Some Interactions of Organisms." Forbes was the first director of the Illinois State Laboratory, which carried out practical and theoreti-

cal researches in economic biology; later he became professor of zoology at the University of Illinois.

7. A. Thienemann, *Limnologie*. Note also his "Der Produktions-begriff in der Biologie," and "Grundzüge einen allgemeinen Oekologie."

8. Again, Elton's concepts of pyramid of numbers and biomass were not wholly original. Karl Semper, professor at the University of Wurzburg, Germany, was very close to these same ideas in his *Animal Life as Affected by the Natural Conditions of Existence* (New York, 1881), p. 52. The key work on territoriality was Henry E. Howard's *Territory and Bird Life* (London, 1920).

9. On niches, see Joseph Grinnell, "The Niche-Relationships of the California Thrasher," *Auk* 34 (1917): 427–433.

10. G. F. Gause, *The Struggle for Existence*. O. Gilbert, T. B. Reynoldson, and J. Hobart, "Gause's Hypothesis: An Examination." Garrett Hardin, *Nature and Man's Fate*, pp. 80–85. Jay M. Savage, "The Concept of Ecologic Niche." Miklos Udvardy, "Notes on the Ecological Concepts of Habitat, Biotope, and Niche." A. C. Crombie, "Interspecific Competition."

11. Charles Elton, *The Pattern of Animal Communities*, pp. 382–83.

12. Arthur G. Tansley, "The Use and Abuse of Vegetational Concepts and Terms." Herbert Gleason, "The Individualistic Concept of the Plant Association," *Bulletin of Torrey Botanical Club* 53 (January 1926): 7–26. C. H. Muller, "Science and Philosophy of the Community." J. Roger Bray, "Notes Toward an Ecologic Theory."

13. Tansley, pp. 299–303. David Gates, "Toward Understanding Ecosystems," pp. 4–6. For a professedly non-mechanistic application of the system model to biology, see Ludwig von Bertalanffy, "An Outline of General System Theory," "The Theory of Open Systems in Physics and Biology," and *Problems of Life: An Evaluation of Modern Biological Thought*.

14. On biology and thermodynamics, see Eugene Odum, "Energy Flow in Ecosystems: A Historical Review." A. J. Lotka, *Elements of Physical Biology*. Harold Blum, *Time's Arrow and Evolution*. Cynthia Russett, *The Concept of Equilibrium in American Social Thought*, ch. 2. L. Brillouin, "Life, Thermodynamics, and Cybernetics."

15. Edgar Transeau, "The Accumulation of Energy by Plants."

16. Chancey Juday, "The Annual Energy Budget in an Inland Lake." The "budget" concept evidently came from Juday's longtime associate E. A. Birge; see his work, "The Heat Budgets of American and European Lakes."

17. Raymond Lindeman, "The Trophic–Dynamic Aspect of Ecology." G. Evelyn Hutchinson, in same publication, pp. 417–18. The word "biocoenosis," commonly used for over a half-century

in ecology, derives from Karl Möbius' important study of "The Oyster and Oyster-Culture." Möbius was professor of zoology at Kiel and a major figure in the Continental development of ecological science. Lindeman was influenced not only by him and by others mentioned in the text, but also by the several limnological studies carried out by Professors Hutchinson and Edward Deevey of Yale.

18. Lawrence Slobodkin, "Energy in Animal Ecology." Manfred Engelmann, "Energetics, Terrestrial Field Studies, and Animal Productivity." D. G. Kozlovsky, "A Critical Evaluation of the Trophic Level Concept: I. Ecological Efficiencies." W. Ohle, "Bioactivity, Production, and Energy Utilization of Lakes." A. MacFayden, "The Meaning of Productivity in Biological Systems."

19. D. F. Westlake, "Comparisons of Plant Productivity." C. R. Goldman (ed.), *Primary Productivity in Aquatic Environments.* Edward Kormondy, *Concepts of Ecology,* pp. 18–21. Lamont Cole, "The Ecosphere." George Woodwell, "The Energy Cycle of the Biosphere," *Scientific American* 223 (Sept. 1970): 67–74.

20. Three key syntheses in the New Ecology are Eugene Odum, *Fundamentals of Ecology;* John Phillipson, *Ecological Energetics;* and David Gates, *Energy Exchange in the Biosphere.* See, too, Eugene Odum et al., "The New Ecology."

21. Richard Ely, "Conservation and Economic Theory," p. 6.

22. N. P. Naumov, *The Ecology of Animals,* p. 558. Stephen Spurr, "The Natural Resource Ecosystem," p. 3. Kenneth Watt, *Ecology and Resource Management: A Quantitative Approach,* ch. 4, esp. pp. 54–56.

23. Wells, Huxley, and Wells, *The Science of Life,* p. 1029. A good recent example of the managerial ethos is Earl Murphy's *Governing Nature* (Chicago, 1967). Murphy predicts (p. 13) that "the living community in nature is at the beginning of a course of treatment quite analogous to that laid out for the modern urban bourgeois.... Under such conditions, the life of man is artificial, but it flourishes materially. A similar artificiality, when it can be established, produces a like flourishing in nature."

Chapter 15

1. Alfred North Whitehead, *Science and the Modern World,* pp. 58–59.

2. *Ibid.,* pp. 39, 71, 76, 138. See, too, his lecture, "Immortality," in *The Philosophy of Alfred North Whitehead.* Here he declared (p. 687): "Every entity is only to be understood in terms of the way in which it is interwoven with the rest of the Universe." Also note his book *The Concept of Nature.*

3. Relevant here is B. J. Blin-Stoyle, "The End of Mechanistic Philosophy and the Rise of Field Physics." See also Edward Mad-

den, "The Philosophy of Science in Gestalt Theory." Eduard Lindeman, "Ecology: An Instrument for the Integration of Science and Philosophy." J. H. Woodger, *Biological Principles* (London, 1929). For critiques of this emphasis on context and organic wholeness, see the following: D. C. Phillips, "Organicism in the Late Nineteenth and Early Twentieth Centuries" *Journal of the History of Ideas* 31 (July–Sept. 1970): 413–432. Morton Beckner, *The Biological Way of Thought* (Berkeley, Calif., 1968), pp. 3–12; and Ernest Nagel, *The Structure of Science* (New York, 1961), pp. 398–446.

4. Whitehead, *Science and the Modern World*, pp. 55, 74.

5. *Ibid.*, pp. 79–80, 86–90.

6. *Ibid.*, pp. 157, 173.

7. *Ibid.*, pp. 184–85.

8. For Lewis Mumford's organicism, note among other works his *Technics and Civilization*, pp. 368–73, where his "organic ideology" is explicitly derived from the ecological concept of "interrelationship and integration." Robert Park, *Human Communities: The City and Human Ecology*. Charles C. Adams, "The Relation of General Ecology to Human Ecology"; "A Note for Social-Minded Ecologists and Geographers"; "Patrick Geddes, Botanist and Human Ecologist," *Ecology* 26 (January 1945): 103–104; and "Relation of Ecology to Human Welfare—The Human Situation." Walter P. Taylor, "Significance of the Biotic Community in Ecological Studies," and "What Is Ecology and What Good Is It?"

9. William Morton Wheeler, "The Ant Colony as an Organism," reprinted in *Foibles of Insects and Men*. A good account of his ideas and life is Mary Alice and Howard Ensign Evans, *William Morton Wheeler, Biologist* (Cambridge, Mass., 1970); note esp. pp. 263–65 on his organismic thinking.

10. C. Lloyd Morgan, *Emergent Evolution*. Arthur O. Lovejoy, "The Meaning of 'Emergence' and Its Modes." Stephen Pepper, "Emergence." George Conger, "The Doctrine of Levels." Sewall Wright, "The Emergence of Novelty," *Journal of Heredity* 26 (1935): 369–373. Alex Novikoff, "The Concept of Integrative Levels and Biology." J. S. Rowe, "The Levels of Integration Concept and Ecology." Paul Sears, "Integration at the Community Level."

11. Jan Smuts, *Holism and Evolution*, p. 99. Also Frank Egler, "A Commentary on American Plant Ecology," *Ecology* 32 (October 1951): 673–695.

12. William Morton Wheeler, "Emergent Evolution of the Social"; also "Emergent Evolution and the Development of Societies" (1928), reprinted in his *Essays in Philosophical Biology*.

13. Whitehead, *Science and the Modern World*, pp. 171–72.

14. Wheeler, "Ant Colony" and "Hopes in the Biological Sciences," in *Essays in Philosophical Biology*.

15. Wheeler, quoted by Evans and Evans, pp. 308–9.

16. Karl Schmidt, "Warder Clyde Allee." Allee et al. (AEPPS), *Principles of Animal Ecology*, p. 436. Alfred Emerson, "The Biological Basis of Social Cooperation," p. 15.

17. Allee, "Cooperation Among Animals," and *Animal Aggregations: A Study in General Sociology*, chs. 9–16 and pp. 355–57.

18. Robert Redfield (ed.), Introduction to "Levels of Integration in Biological and Social Systems," p. 4. Alfred Emerson, "Ecology, Evolution, and Society," p. 118; this essay was Emerson's presidential address before the Ecological Society of America. The group's debt to Herbert Spencer was made clear in Ralph W. Gerard and Alfred Emerson, "Extrapolation from the Biological to the Social," *Science* n.s. 101 (June 8, 1945): 582–85.

19. Ralph W. Gerard, "Higher Levels of Integration," in Redfield, "Levels," pp. 83, 85.

20. Emerson, "Biological Basis of Social Cooperation," p. 17. Gerard, "Biological Basis for Ethics," p. 115. Another explicit reaction to World War Two was Allee's "Where Angels Fear to Tread: A Contribution from General Sociology to Human Ethics." It was one more plea for world peace and cooperation as taught by nature.

21. Wheeler, "The Organization of Research" (1920), and "The Termitodoxa, or Biology and Society" (1919), in *Foibles of Insects and Men*; and "Emergent Evolution of the Social," pp. 42–45.

22. Emerson, "Biological Basis of Social Cooperation," pp. 16–17. Gerard, "Higher Levels of Integration," p. 82.

23. Joseph Wood Krutch, *The Modern Temper*, esp. ch. 2, "The Paradox of Humanism"; *The Twelve Seasons*, p. 13; *If You Don't Mind My Saying So*, p. 357; "Conservation Is Not Enough," in *The Voice of the Desert*, pp. 194–95; *The Great Chain of Life*, pp. 161–62. See also Krutch's autobiography, *More Lives Than One*, esp. pp. 290–334 on his "conversion."

PART SIX

Chapter 16

1. Robert Jungk, *Brighter Than a Thousand Suns*, pp. 196–202. Alice Kimball Smith, *A Peril and a Hope: The Scientists' Movement in America, 1945–47* (Chicago, 1965).

2. Neal Hines, "Bikini Report," *Scientific Monthly* 72 (February 1951): 102–13; Richard Miller, *Under the Cloud: The Decades of Nuclear Testing* (New York, 1986), pp. 75–79. The first shot, called Able, occurred on July 1, and the second, Baker, on July 25.

3. Philip L. Fradkin, *Fallout*, chaps. 6–7.

4. *Science* 123 (22 June 1956): 1110–11. Representative of the popular press coverage of the issues are *Newsweek* 47 (June 25, 1956): 70; and *Time* 67 (June 25, 1956): 64–65.

5. According to Donald Fleming, the catalyzing factor in Commoner's political involvement was a request by presidential candidate Adlai Stevenson in 1956 for information on fallout from atmospheric testing—"the first time a scientific issue had been introduced into a presidential campaign." See Fleming, "Roots of the New Conservation Movement," p. 42.

6. Rachel Carson, *The Sea Around Us*, p. xi.

7. Rachel Carson, *Silent Spring*, pp. 8, 297.

8. For excellent discussions of Carson as a feminist, consult Vera Norwood, *Made from This Earth: American Women and Nature* (Chapel Hill, N.C., 1993), pp. 143–71; and H. Patricia Hynes, *The Recurring Silent Spring* (New York, 1989), pp. 180–215. For a general account of Carson's life and work, see Paul Brooks, *The House of Life: Rachel Carson at Work* (Boston, 1972).

9. In 1967, a group of American scientists founded the Environmental Defense Fund, which, inspired by Carson, succeeded in getting DDT banned in 1972 as a threat to both human life and natural ecosystems. See Thomas R. Dunlap, *DDT: Scientists, Citizens, and Public Policy* (Princeton, N.J., 1981); and John Perkins, *Insects, Experts, and the Insecticide Crisis: The Quest for New Pest Management Strategies* (New York, 1982), pp. 86–87.

10. "Environmentalism," *Encyclopaedia of the Social Sciences*, vol. 5 (New York, 1931), p. 561.

11. Samuel Hays (in *Beauty, Health, and Permanence*, p. 55) identifies the period after 1965 as a new phase in American environmental politics when pollution took its place alongside the older conservation concerns.

12. The Russian scientist Vladimir Vernadsky, a student of the relation of living organisms to geochemical cycles, was the first to develop the biosphere concept scientifically. He defined it as "that part of the atmosphere and surface of the earth where life exists." Kendall E. Bailes, *Science and Russian Culture in an Age of Revolutions: V. I. Vernadsky and His Scientific School, 1863–1945* (Bloomington, Ind., 1990), pp. 123–24.

13. Betty J. Meggers, "Environmental Limitation on the Development of Culture," *American Anthropologist* 56 (October 1954): 801–24; Julian H. Steward, *The Theory of Cultural Change* (Urbana, Ill., 1955); Carl Ortwin Sauer, *Land and Life*, ed. John Leighly (Berkeley, Calif., 1963); Fairfield Osborn, *Our Plundered Planet* (Boston, 1948); William Vogt, *Road to Survival* (New York, 1948). The proceedings of the Princeton symposium were published in *Man's Role in Changing the Face of the Earth*, ed. William L. Thomas, Jr.

14. Paul B. Sears, "The Processes of Environmental Change by Man," in Thomas, *Changing the Face of the Earth*, p. 471.

15. Frank Fraser Darling, *Wilderness and Plenty*, p. 54.

16. Paul R. Ehrlich, *The Population Bomb;* Donella H. Meadows, Dennis L. Meadows, Jørgen Randers, and William W. Behrens III, *The Limits to Growth* (New York, 1972); Edward Goldsmith, *Blueprint for Survival;* and E. F. Schumacher, *Small Is Beautiful* (London, 1973).

17. Barry Commoner, *The Closing Circle*, pp. 94, 200, 268. Commoner identified four basic laws of ecology, which became widely cited as the popular essence of the science: (1) Everything is connected to everything else; (2) everything must go somewhere; (3) nature knows best; and (4) there is no such thing as a free lunch (pp. 33–46).

18. U.S. public expenditures for pollution control rose from about $800 million in 1969 to $4.2 billion in 1975. *Environmental Quality: The Sixth Annual Report of the Council on Environmental Quality* (Washington, D.C., 1975), p. 527. Great Britain likewise increased its expenditures, and the results were notable: Output of smoke fell from over 2 million metric tons in 1953 to 0.5 million in 1976. The mileage of unpolluted rivers went up from 14,603 in 1958 to 17,279 in 1972, an increase of 18 percent. See Eric Ashby, *Reconciling Man with the Environment* (Stanford, Calif., 1978), pp. 6–7.

19. Michael McCloskey, *Ecotactics*, ed. John Mitchell and Constance Stallings, p. 11. William Ophuls, *Ecology and the Politics of Scarcity Revisited*, p. 3.

20. *Newsweek* 75 (May 4, 1970): 26–28. For other coverage see *Time* 94 (April 27, 1970): 46.

21. Arne Naess, "The Shallow and the Deep, Long-Range Ecology Movements"; and Bill Devall and George Sessions, *Deep Ecology*, pp. 65–76.

22. Paul Sears, *Deserts on the March*, p. 162.

23. *Ibid.*, p. 177.

24. *Ibid.*, p. 142.

25. A painting of Commoner appeared on the cover of the February 2, 1970, issue of *Time* (vol. 95), against a background divided between environmental darkness (a landscape of industrial pollution) and light (a green, pleasant countryside). In the issue publisher Henry Luce described Commoner as the "leader of a tiny band of once sheltered scientists who have suddenly risen to prominence and sometimes sound like new Jeremiahs." See also the accompanying article, "Fighting to Save the Earth from Man," pp. 56–63.

26. LaMont Cole, "The Impending Emergence of Ecological

Thought," p. 30; G. Clifford Evans, "A Sack of Uncut Diamonds," p. 37; H. N. Southern, "Ecology at the Crossroads," p. 1.

27. Robert L. Burgess, "United States," in *Handbook of Contemporary Developments in World Ecology*, ed. Edward J. Kormondy and J. Frank McCormick, pp. 69–70.

28. This insistence on the reality of holism, mutualism, and the common good in nature appears strikingly throughout Eugene P. Odum's introductory essay for *Ecosystem Theory and Application*, ed. Nicholas Polunin, pp. 1–11.

29. Shelford wanted the society to acquire and protect undisturbed natural communities, but, blocked by hostile eastern members, he was forced to go outside the society to establish the Ecologists' Union, which later evolved into the Nature Conservancy, a private land-acquisition organization that would become phenomenally successful. Interestingly, the name chosen was the same as Britain's Nature Conservancy, a government agency established by the Labor administration in 1947, "the most significant milestone in British ecology," according to Andrew Duff and Philip Lowe ("Great Britain," in Kormondy and McCormick, *Handbook*, p. 145). In Britain, it became the government's responsibility to preserve natural areas; while in the United States, it became a program privately run by ecologists and philanthropists.

30. Eugene P. Odum, "The Emergence of Ecology as a New Integrative Discipline," p. 1290.

31. On the relations of the Odums to atomic research, see Joel B. Hagen, *An Entangled Bank*, chap. 6.

32. Eugene P. Odum, *Fundamentals of Ecology*, p. 8.

33. See, for example, the classic anticipation of modern ecology, Stephen Forbes' "The Lake as a Microcosm," first published in the *Bulletin of the Peoria [Illinois] Scientific Association* (1887).

34. Eugene P. Odum, "The Strategy of Ecosystem Development," p. 266.

35. The term "homeostasis" came from Walter Cannon, *The Wisdom of the Body*, rev. ed. (New York, 1939). The term did "not imply something set and immobile. It means a condition which may vary, but which is relatively constant" (p. 24). Odum's adoption of it indicates that he tended to see the ecosystem as a superorganism, comparable with the human body.

36. The terms "K-selection" and "r-selection" came from Robert MacArthur and Edward O. Wilson, *The Theory of Island Biogeography*.

37. Odum, *Fundamentals of Ecology*, pp. 271–72.

38. Odum, "Strategy of Ecosystem Development," p. 266.

39. Eugene P. Odum, *Ecology and Our Endangered Life-Support System*, prologue.

40. Peter J. Taylor, "Technocratic Optimism, H. T. Odum, and the Partial Transformation of Ecological Metaphor after World War II."

41. Howard T. Odum, *Environment, Power, and Society*, pp. 274–84.

42. W. Frank Blair, *Big Biology*, p. 163. For British participation, see E. Barton Worthington, *The Ecological Century*, pp. 160–77. See also Robert P. McIntosh, *The Background of Ecology*, pp. 213–21.

43. A thorough account of MacArthur's work and his influences is Sharon E. Kingsland, *Modeling Nature*. Kingsland sees MacArthur as rejecting the historical thinking common in traditional biology since Darwin, with its emphasis on the evolution of the unique individual or event. "The very act of imposing mathematics (or any model) on nature often involved a rejection of history in favor of a harmonious, unifying concept" (p. 8).

44. MacArthur wrote that "the ecologist and the physical scientist tend to be machinery oriented, whereas the paleontologist and most biogeographers tend to be history oriented" (*Geographical Ecology*, p. 1).

45. MacArthur and Wilson, *The Theory of Island Biogeography*, p. 181.

46. Edward O. Wilson and Daniel S. Simberloff, "Experimental Zoogeography of Islands."

47. Stephen D. Fretwell, "The Impact of Robert MacArthur on Ecology," pp. 9–10.

48. Yrjö Haila, "On the Semiotic Dimension of Ecological Theory," pp. 378, 382–83. See also David Abram, "The Mechanical and the Organic: On the Impact of Metaphor in Science," in *Scientists on Gaia*, ed. Stephen H. Schneider and Penelope J. Boston, pp. 66–74.

49. Lawrence J. Henderson, *The Fitness of the Environment: An Inquiry into the Biological Significance of the Properties of Matter* (New York, 1913).

50. Lynn Margulis and James Lovelock, "Gaia and Geognosy," in *Global Ecology*, ed. Mitchell B. Rambler, Lynn Margulis, and Rene Fester, p. 6; Odum, *Ecology and Our Endangered Life-Support Systems*, pp. 59–64. The conference on Lovelock's ideas was held in 1988 in San Diego, California, and published as *Scientists on Gaia*. The most hostile paper was given by James W. Kirchner, of the Department of Geology and Geophysics at the University of California at Berkeley, who argued that the hypothesis offered, in its weaker form, nothing new, and in its stronger form, was un-

testable; he objected mainly to the implication that Gaia was a purposeful entity (pp. 38–46).

51. James Lovelock, *The Ages of Gaia*, pp. 94–96. Lovelock referred to the appearance of free oxygen in the air as the first and greatest pollution catastrophe in earth's history, for it devastated the anaerobic bacteria.

52. *Ibid.*, pp. 203–23.

53. *Ibid.*, pp. 174–75; James Lovelock, *Gaia*, pp. 107–22.

54. James Lovelock, *Healing Gaia*, p. 18.

Chapter 17

1. J. M. Cherrett, "Key Concepts: The Results of a Survey of Our Members' Opinion," in Cherrett, *Ecological Concepts*, pp. 1–16.

2. See Michael Begon, John L. Harper, and Colin R. Townsend, *Ecology*, pp. 591–92. R. J. Putnam and S. D. Wratten, *Principles of Ecology*, p. 43. Peter Stiling, *Introductory Ecology*, pp. 358–96. Robert E. Ricklefs, *Ecology*, esp. chap. 2. See also Robert Leo Smith, *Elements of Ecology*, 2nd ed. (New York, 1986), which admits that the author has shifted from an "ecosystem approach" to more of an "evolutionary approach" (p. xiii).

3. A clear discussion of both types of succession can be found in Paul Ehrlich's *The Machinery of Nature*, pp. 268–71.

4. William H. Drury and Ian C. T. Nisbet, "Succession," *Journal of the Arnold Arboretum* 54 (July 1973): 360.

5. Henry A. Gleason, "The Individualistic Concept of the Plant Association."

6. Joseph H. Connell and Ralph O. Slatyer, "Mechanisms of Succession in Natural Communities and Their Role in Community Stability and Organization," p. 1140.

7. Orie L. Loucks, Mary L. Plumb-Mentjes, and Deborah Rogers, "Gap Processes and Large-Scale Disturbances in Sand Prairies," pp. 72–85, and James R. Karr and Kathryn E. Freemark, "Disturbance and Vertebrates: An Integrative Perspective," in S. T. A. Pickett and P. S. White, *Ecology of Natural Disturbance*, pp. 154–55.

8. Margaret B. Davis, "Palynology and Environmental History During the Quaternary Period."

9. Margaret Bryan Davis, "Climatic Instability, Time Lags, and Community Disequilibrium," p. 269.

10. This argument is made by Mark Williamson, "Are Communities Ever Stable?" in *Colonization, Succession and Stability*, ed. A. J. Gray, M. J. Crawley, and P. J. Edwards (Oxford, 1987), pp. 353–70.

11. F. Herbert Bormann and Gene E. Likens, "Catastrophic Disturbance and the Steady State in Northern Hardwood Forests."

12. Daniel Botkin, *Discordant Harmonies*, pp. 10, 62.

13. John A. Wiens, "On Understanding a Non-Equilibrium World: Myth and Reality in Community Patterns and Processes," in Donald R. Strong, Jr., Daniel Simberloff, Lawrence G. Abele, and Ann B. Thistle, *Ecological Communities*, p. 440. Cowell quoted in Roger Lewin, "Predators and Hurricanes Change Ecology," p. 738.

14. Daniel Simberloff, "A Succession of Paradigms in Ecology," pp. 13–22.

15. *Ibid.*, pp. 25–26.

16. *Ibid.*, p. 11.

17. This argument is made by Ilya Prigogine and Isabelle Stengers in their book *Order Out of Chaos*. Prigogine won the Nobel Prize in 1977 for his work on the thermodynamics of nonequilibrium systems.

18. An excellent account of the change in thinking is James Gleick, *Chaos: The Making of a New Science*. What Gleick does not explore are the striking intellectual parallels between chaotic theory in science and postmodern discourse in literature and philosophy. Postmodernism is a sensibility that has abandoned the historic search for unity and order in nature, taking an ironic view of existence and debunking all established faiths. According to Todd Gitlin, "Post-Modernism reflects the fact that a new moral structure has not yet been built and our culture has not yet found a language for articulating the new understandings we are trying, haltingly, to live with. It objects to all principles, all commitments, all crusades—in the name of an unconscientious evasion." On the other hand, and put more positively, the new sensibility leads to a new emphasis on democratic coexistence: "a new 'moral ecology'—that in the preservation of the other is a condition for the preservation of the self." See Gitlin, "Post-Modernism: The Stenography of Surfaces," *New Perspectives Quarterly* 6 (Spring 1989): 57, 59. See also N. Catherine Hayles, *Chaos Bound: Orderly Disorder in Contemporary Literature and Science* (Ithaca, N.Y., 1990), esp. chap. 7.

19. Robert M. May, "Biological Populations with Nonoverlapping Generations: Stable Points, Stable Cycles, and Chaos."

20. Robert M. May, "When Two and Two Do Not Make Four," pp. 242–43.

21. William M. Schaffer, "Chaos in Ecology and Epidemiology," p. 233.

22. Ian Stewart, *Does God Play Dice?*, p. 22.

23. Brian Arthur quoted by M. Mitchell Waldrop, *Complexity*, p. 320.

24. Prigogine and Stengers, *Order Out of Chaos*, pp. 312–13.

25. Thomas Söderqvist, *The Ecologists*, p. 281.

26. Paul Colinvaux, *Why Big Fierce Animals Are Rare*, pp. 117, 135.

27. Botkin, *Discordant Harmonies*, pp. 6.

28. Ibid., p. 190.

29. See also Arthur F. McEvoy, *The Fisherman's Problem: Ecology and Law in California Fisheries, 1850–1980* (New York, 1986), pp. 6–7, 10, 150–51.

30. Edward O. Wilson, *Biophilia*, pp. 138–39.

31. Michael Soulé, "Conservation Biology and the 'Real World,' " pp. 3–5.

32. Wilson, *Biophilia*, p. 121.

33. Ralph Barton Perry, *The Thought and Character of William James* (New York, 1948), p. 175.

34. Stephen Toulmin and June Goodfield, *The Discovery of Time*, p. 17.

35. *Ibid.*, p. 232.

36. A contrary view of science and historicism is expressed in Werner Stark, *The Sociology of Knowledge* (London, 1958), pp. 164–67. Other useful treatments of the subject are Karl Mannheim's *Ideology and Utopia* (London, 1936); Robert Merton, "The Sociology of Knowledge," in *Social Theory and Social Structure* (Glencoe, Ill., 1949); and Peter L. Berger and Thomas Luckmann, *The Social Construction of Reality* (Garden City, N.Y., 1966), esp. pp. 1–18.

37. Arthur O. Lovejoy, "Reflections on the History of Ideas," p. 17.

38. Claude Levi-Strauss, *The Savage Mind* (Chicago, 1966), p. 263.

39. Karl Marx and Friedrich Engels, "Manifesto of the Communist Party," in *Basic Writings on Politics and Philosophy: Karl Marx and Friedrich Engels*, ed. Lewis S. Feuer (Garden City, N. Y., 1959), p. 10.

40. A new, "green" socialism has emerged in recent years, seeking to recover the neglected insights of Karl Marx and Friedrich Engels into the human–nature relation and to link the cause of protecting the earth with that of achieving a more equitable distribution of resources. The American journal *Capitalism, Nature Socialism*, edited by James O'Connor, is the best guide to this movement.

41. See Frederic Jameson, *Postmodernism: The Cultural Logic of Late Capitalism* (Durham, N.C., 1991), pp. 1–54. By "late capitalism" Jameson means a capitalism that is multinational in form, postindustrial in its sources of wealth, and dependent on modern communications and artificial intelligence for its operations. For another view of postmodernism and its relation to capital, see

David Harvey, *The Condition of Postmodernity: An Enquiry into the Origins of Cultural Change* (Oxford, 1989). Harvey believes that we are freeing ourselves not only from the logic of capital but also from the authority of objective science that has so long dominated our consciousness.

42. Edward Goldsmith, *The Way*, pp. 63–69. Goldsmith argues that, since all science is subjective and culturally bound, we are free to reject it and restore a more religious interpretation of nature. However, it is not clear why that restoration would be more valid or more immune to doubt than science.

43. John Muir, *My First Summer in the Sierra* (1911; repr. Boston, 1944), p. 157.

GLOSSARY OF TERMS

ANIMISM: The notion, found especially in pagan, polytheistic cultures, that everything in nature—animals, plants, even rocks—has an indwelling spirit or consciousness. This spirit is distinct from and superior to matter; it is an organizing power that eludes scientific investigation. And, like the individual entity, nature as a whole is governed by a vital principle, the *Anima Mundi*, a mysterious force animating the universe. Animism has commonly been an unacceptable, even heretical, concept in Judeo-Christian religion. A similar idea, *vitalism*, also endows nature with an immaterial, innate force and is also of pagan origin, in the writings of Aristotle.

ARCADIANISM: The ideal of a simple rural life in close harmony with nature. The word derives from a mountainous region in ancient Greece called Arcady, whose inhabitants supposedly dwelt in an Eden-like state of innocence, at peace with the earth and its creatures. As an environmental vision in modern times, arcadianism has often been a naive surrender to nostalgia, but it has nonetheless contributed to the growth of an ecological ethic of coexistence rather than domination; humility rather than self-assertion; man as a part of, rather than superior to, nature.

ECOLOGY: The branch of biology that deals with interrelationships. The name was coined in 1866 by Ernst Haeckel, for his study of the patterns of relations between organisms and their environment. But the study of ecology is much older than the name; its roots lie in earlier investigations of the "economy of nature." The major theme throughout the history of this science and the ideas that underlie it has been the interdependence of living things. An awareness, more philosophical than purely scientific, of this quality is what has generally been meant by the "ecological point of view." Thus, the question of whether ecology is primarily a science or a philosophy of interrelatedness has been a persistent identity problem. And the nature of this interdependence is a parallel issue: Is it a system of economic organization or a moral community of mutual tolerance and aid?

ECOSYSTEM: A term coined in 1935 by Arthur Tansley to replace the more anthropomorphic "community." It has since become the central organizing idea in ecology. As a model of interrelatedness in nature, it presents both the biological and non-biological aspects of the environment as one entity, with strong emphasis on measuring the cycling of nutrients and the flow of energy in the system—whether it be a pond, a forest, or the earth as a whole.

EMERGENT EVOLUTION: A theory in science and philosophy proposed in the early twentieth century as a way out of the vitalist–mechanist debate. C. Lloyd Morgan and others claimed that, through evolution, new entities may "emerge," exhibiting unprecedented qualities that are not analyzable in terms of their antecedents, and requiring new modes of study. Life emerging out of brute matter is one example. The ecologists William Morton Wheeler and Warder Allee later defined new "emergents" in social terms: the spontaneous appearance of progressively higher levels of cooperative social patterns in nature. The idea of emergence has contributed to the ethical vision of interdependence, or the "ecological point of view"; it has also been closely associated with organicist and holistic approaches in science.

IMPERIALISM: The view that man's proper role on earth is to extend his power over nature as far as possible. The implicit analogy is with the establishment of one nation's rule over others outside its borders—that is, with the founding of political empires. Francis Bacon was among the first to suggest that a similar dominion should be achieved by the human species over the natural world, through the aid of a science-based technology. That science can so serve as an imperialistic force has been a recurrent theme in the modern era. It is, in fact, an ethic that has often justified and even directed the pursuit of knowledge.

MECHANISM: A philosophy of nature that has been highly influential in the development of modern science. In its earliest and most simplistic phase, this theory made nature strictly analogous to a machine—even to so basic an apparatus as gears and pulleys. Although this did in one sense encourage people to perceive the world as an interconnected whole, it proved inadequate to explain living organisms and their relations. A more sophisticated and enduring form of mechanism is that which explains all nature as a system of matter in motion, entirely subject to the laws of physics and chemistry. Many biologists and philosophers have considered this kind of analysis overly "reductive"—though what has been left out is often hard to specify.

NEOPLATONISM: A philosophical tradition based on some of the ideas of Plato—particularly the concept of an unchanging, perfect "One" above and beyond the transient, inferior world of nature. The One stands for an immaterial order not accessible to the senses, but that exerts a powerful unifying force over the diverse and disharmonious physical world. The founder of this tradition was Plotinus (A.D. 205–270); among its later exponents were the Cambridge

Platonists of the seventeenth century and many of the Romantics of the nineteenth. In all its forms of expression, Neoplatonism has taken a holistic view of nature—unity in multiplicity, a world of sympathy and interdependence—and has been an important influence on ecological thought.

NEW ECOLOGY: The most recent phase in the history of this science. Beginning in the 1930s and gaining widespread acceptance by the 1960s, the New Ecology has emphasized the quantitative study of energy flow and "ecological efficiency" in nature, using the ecosystem idea. Other terms, such as "producers" and "consumers," give the New Ecology a distinctly economic cast. Major figures in the development of this model include Raymond Lindeman, G. Evelyn Hutchinson, Eugene Odum, and David Gates.

ORGANICISM: A philosophy that takes the living organism as model and metaphor for all nature. It assumes that the organism possesses qualities that elude physico-chemical analysis, and that these result from the integrated functioning of the whole; in other words, the whole is more than the sum of its parts. Applying this principle to ecology, the order of nature is viewed as a "complex organism," not unlike the human body. Thus each component of nature—each plant or animal—can only be fully understood as it participates in and depends upon the whole. The quality of interdependence is most important here, and it may be a metaphysical and moral vision more than a scientific argument. In ethical terms, this philosophy often implies a repudiation of individualism in favor of community and cooperation. It is a key concept in the "ecological point of view."

TRANSCENDENTALISM: A major school of idealist or Neoplatonist philosophy among American Romantics of the nineteenth century. Its chief exponent was Ralph Waldo Emerson, who taught his followers to celebrate nature as an inspiring reflection of the divine "One" or "Oversoul," while at the same time regarding it as an imperfect, even degraded, sphere to be "transcended"—that is, dominated and left behind in man's search for perfect order. This dualistic stance was shared by Henry David Thoreau, although he managed to reconcile the two views more fully than other Transcendentalists.

SELECTED BIBLIOGRAPHY

Part One

"Back to Nature." *Outlook* 74 (June 6, 1903): 305–307.
Bacon, Francis. *The Works of Francis Bacon.* Edited by James Spedding et al. 2 vols. New York, 1872–78.
Barbour, Ian, ed. *Western Man and Environmental Ethics.* Reading, Mass., 1973.
Bertalanffy, Ludwig von. *Modern Theories of Development.* Translated by J. H. Woodger. Oxford, 1933.
Black, John. *The Dominion of Man.* Edinburgh, 1970.
Blunt, Wilfred. *The Compleat Naturalist: A Life of Linnaeus.* New York, 1971.
Boas, Marie. "The Establishment of the Mechanical Philosophy." *Osiris* 10 (1952): 412–541.
Brown, Harcourt. "The Utilitarian Motive in the Age of Descartes." *Annals of Science* 1 (1936): 189–192.
Bruckner, John. *A Philosophical Survey of the Animal Creation.* London, 1768.
Buffon, George Louis Leclerc, Comte de. *Natural History, General and Particular.* Translated by William Smellie. 10 vols. London, 1785.
Burroughs, John. *The Writings of John Burroughs.* Riverby ed. 17 vols. Boston, 1904–13.
Burtt, E. A. *The Metaphysical Foundations of Modern Science* (1925). Rev. ed. Garden City, N.Y., 1932.
Bury, John B. *The Idea of Progress.* London, 1924.
Butterfield, Herbert. *The Origins of Modern Science* (1949). Rev. ed. New York, 1951.
Collingwood, R. G. *The Idea of Nature.* Oxford, 1945.
Commoner, Barry. *The Closing Circle: Nature, Man and Technology.* New York, 1971. *Science and Survival.* New York, 1966.
Derham, William. *Physico-Theology* (1713). Edinburgh, 1773.
Drennon, Herbert. "Newtonianism: Its Methods, Theology, and Metaphysics." *Englische Studien* 68 (1933–34): 397–409.
Eliade, Mircea. *The Sacred and the Profane: The Nature of Religion.* New York, 1959.
Emden, Cecil S. *Gilbert White in His Village.* London, 1956.
Ewbank, Thomas. *The World a Workshop: or, The Physical Relationship of Man to the Earth.* New York, 1855.

Fowler, W. W. "Gilbert White of Selborne." *Macmillan's* 68 (July 1893): 182–189.

Fries, Theodor. *Linnaeus*. Translated by Benjamin Jackson. London, 1923.

Glacken, Clarence. *Traces on the Rhodian Shore: Nature and Culture in Western Thought from Ancient Times to the End of the Eighteenth Century*. Berkeley, Calif., 1967.

Goerke, Heinz. *Linnaeus*. Translated by Denver Lindley. New York, 1973.

Hagberg, Knut. *Carl Linnaeus*. Translated by Alan Blair. London, 1952.

Hamilton, Robert. *W. H. Hudson: The Vision of the Earth*. London, 1946.

Haymaker, Richard. *From Pampas to Hedgerows and Downs: A Study of W. H. Hudson*. New York, 1954.

Hazard, Paul. *European Thought in the Eighteenth Century*. Translated by J. L. May. New Haven, Conn., 1954.

Heim, Karl. *The Transformation of the Scientific World View*. New York, 1953.

Hicks, Philip. *The Development of the Natural History Essay in American Literature*. Philadelphia, 1924.

Hobbes, Thomas. *The English Works of Thomas Hobbes*. Edited by W. Molesworth. 11 vols. London, 1839–45.

Hobsbawm, E. J. *The Age of Revolution: 1789–1848*. London, 1962.

Houghton, Walter, Jr. "The History of Trades: Its Relation to Seventeenth-Century Thought." *Journal of the History of Ideas* 2 (1941): 33–60.

Jones, W. P. "The Vogue of Natural History in England, 1750–1770." *Annals of Science* 2 (1937): 348–352.

Koyré, Alexander. *From the Closed World to the Infinite Universe*. Baltimore, 1957.

Larson, James. *Reason and Experience: The Representation of Natural Order in the Works of Carl von Linné*. Berkeley, Calif., 1971.

Limoges, Camille, ed. *L'Equilibre de la nature*. Paris, 1972.

Linnaeus, Carolus. "Specimen academicum de Oeconomia Naturae." *Amoenitates Academicae* II (1751): 1–58.

Lockley, R. M. *Gilbert White*. London, 1954.

Lovejoy, Arthur O. *The Great Chain of Being*. Cambridge, Mass., 1936. "The Place of Linnaeus in the History of Science." *Popular Science Monthly* 71 (December 1907): 498–508.

Luxembourg, Lilo. *Francis Bacon and Denis Diderot*. Copenhagen, 1967.

Mantoux, Paul. *The Industrial Revolution in the Eighteenth Century*. Translated by Marjorie Vernon. Rev. ed. London, 1928.

Merton, Robert. *Science, Technology, and Society in Seventeenth-Century England*. New York, 1938.

More, Henry. *The Philosophical Writings of Henry More*. Edited by Flora MacKinnon. New York, 1925.

Mornet, Daniel. *Les Sciences de la nature en France au XVIIIe siècle*. Paris, 1911.

Moule, C. D. F. *Man and Nature in the New Testament.* Philadelphia, 1967.

Mourisson, J. Felix. *Philosophies de la nature: Bacon, Boyle, Toland, Buffon.* Paris, 1887.

Mullett, Charles F. "*Multum in Parvo:* Gilbert White of Selborne." *Journal of the History of Biology* 2 (Fall 1969): 363–390.

Murdoch, William, and James Connell. "All About Ecology." In *Economic Growth vs. the Environment,* edited by Warren Johnson and John Hardesty. Belmont, Calif., 1971.

Nordenskiöld, Erik. *The History of Biology.* Translated by Leonard Eyre. New York, 1928.

Priestley, F. E. L. "Newton and the Romantic Concept of Nature." *University of Toronto Quarterly* 17 (1948): 323–336.

Pulteney, Richard. *A General View of the Writings of Linnaeus.* London, 1781.

Raven, Charles. *John Ray, Naturalist.* Cambridge, England, 1942. *Natural Religion and Christian Theology.* Cambridge, England, 1953.

Ray, John. *The Wisdom of God Manifested in the Works of Creation.* London, 1691.

Schmitt, Peter J. *Back to Nature: The Arcadian Myth in Urban America.* New York, 1969.

Sears, Paul. "Ecology—A Subversive Subject." *BioScience* 14 (July 1964): 11–13.

Smellie, William. *The Philosophy of Natural History.* Philadelphia, 1791.

Smith, Adam. *The Early Writings of Adam Smith.* Edited by J. Ralph Lindgren. New York, 1967.

Snell, Bruno. "Arcadia: The Discovery of a Spiritual Landscape." In *The Discovery of the Mind: The Greek Origins of European Thought.* Translated by T. G. Rosenmeyer. Cambridge, Mass., 1953.

Spring, David and Eileen Spring, eds. *Ecology and Religion in History.* New York, 1974.

Stephen, Leslie. *History of English Thought in the Eighteenth Century.* 2 vols. New York, 1876.

Stillingfleet, Benjamin, ed. *Miscellaneous Tracts Relating to Natural History, Husbandry, and Physick* (1759). London, 1762.

Teale, Edwin Way. "The Selborne Nightingale." *Audubon* 72 (September 1970): 58–67.

Trevelyan, George. *History of England.* London, 1945.

Westermarck, Edvard. *Christianity and Morals.* New York, 1939.

White, Gilbert. *Gilbert White's Journals.* Edited by Walter Johnson. New York, 1970. *The Life and Letters of Gilbert White.* Edited by Rashleigh Holt-White. 2 vols. London, 1901. *The Natural History of Selborne* (1788). New York, 1899.

White, Lynn, Jr. "The Historical Roots of Our Ecologic Crisis." In *Machina ex Deo: Essays in the Dynamism of Western Culture.* Cambridge, Mass., 1968.

Willey, Basil. *The Eighteenth-Century Background.* London, 1940.

Williams, George. *Wilderness and Paradise in Christian Thought.* New York, 1962.

Wolf, Abraham. *A History of Science, Technology, and Philosophy in the Eighteenth Century.* New York, 1939.

Young, Arthur. *Rural Oeconomy: or, Essays on the Practical Parts of Husbandry.* London, 1770.

Part Two

Adams, Raymond. "Thoreau's Science." *Scientific Monthly* 60 (May 1945): 379–382.

Baym, Nina. "Thoreau's View of Science." *Journal of the History of Ideas* 26 (April–June 1965): 221–234.

Beach, Joseph Warren. *The Concept of Nature in Nineteenth-Century Poetry.* New York, 1936.

Berkeley, George. *The Works of George Berkeley.* Edited by Alexander Fraser. Oxford, 1891.

Canby, Henry Seidel. *Thoreau.* Boston, 1939.

Carell, Stanley. *The Senses of Walden.* New York, 1972.

Carroll, Charles E. *The Timber Economy of Puritan New England.* Providence, R.I., 1973.

Cook, Reginald. *Passage to Walden.* Boston, 1949.

Deevey, Edward, Jr. "A Re-Examination of Thoreau's *Walden.*" *Quarterly Review of Biology* 17 (March 1942): 1–10.

Dwight, Timothy. *Travels in New England and New York.* Edited by Barbara Solomon. Cambridge, Mass., 1969.

Eaton, Richard. *A Flora of Concord.* Cambridge, Mass., 1974.

Emerson, George B. *A Report on the Trees and Shrubs Growing Naturally in the Forests of Massachusetts.* Boston, 1846.

Emerson, Ralph Waldo. *The Early Lectures of Ralph Waldo Emerson.* Edited by Stephen Whicher and Robert Spiller. Cambridge, Mass., 1959. *Selections from Ralph Waldo Emerson.* Edited by Stephen Whicher. Boston, 1957.

Frothingham, Octavius. *Transcendentalism in New England* (1876). Edited by Sydney Ahlstrom. Philadelphia, 1959.

Gillispie, Charles. *The Edge of Objectivity.* Princeton, N.J., 1960.

Harding, Walter. *The Days of Henry Thoreau.* New York, 1966.

Hawes, A. F. "The New England Forest in Retrospect." *Journal of Forestry* 21 (1923): 209–224.

Heller, Eric. *The Disinherited Mind.* New York, 1957.

Hirsch, E. E. *Wordsworth and Schelling: A Typological Study of Romanticism.* New Haven, Conn., 1960.

Jorgensen, Neil. *A Guide to New England Landscape.* Barre, Vt., 1971.

Krutch, Joseph Wood. *Henry David Thoreau.* New York, 1948.

Lange, Victor. "Goethe: Science and Poetry." *Yale Review*, n.s. 38 (Summer 1949): 623–639.

Lovejoy, Arthur O. "On the Discrimination of Romanticisms." Chapter 12 in *Essays in the History of Ideas.* Baltimore, 1948.

Lucas, Alec. "Thoreau, Field Naturalist." *University of Toronto Quarterly* 23 (April 1954): 227–232.

Magnus, Rudolf. *Goethe as a Scientist.* Translated by Heinz Norden. New York, 1949.

McIntosh, James. *Thoreau as Romantic Naturalist: His Shifting Stance Toward Nature.* Ithaca, N.Y., 1974.

Metzger, Charles. "Thoreau on Science." *Annals of Science* 12 (September 1956): 206–211.

Nash, Roderick. *Wilderness and the American Mind.* Rev. ed. New Haven, Conn., 1973.

Paul, Sherman. *Emerson's Angle of Vision: Man and Nature in American Experience.* Cambridge, Mass., 1952. *The Shores of America: Thoreau's Inward Exploration.* Urbana, Ill., 1958.

Porte, Joel. *Emerson and Thoreau: Transcendentalists in Conflict.* Middletown, Conn., 1966.

Salt, Henry S. *The Life of Henry David Thoreau.* London, 1890.

Schenk, H. G. *The Mind of the European Romantics.* London, 1966.

Scudder, Townsend. *Concord, American Town.* Boston, 1947.

Stallknecht, Newton. *Strange Seas of Thought: Studies in William Wordsworth's Philosophy of Man and Nature.* Bloomington, Ind., 1958.

Stoller, Leo. *After Walden: Thoreau's Changing Views on Economic Man.* Stanford, Calif., 1957. "A Note on Thoreau's Place in the History of Phenology." *Isis* 47 (June 1956): 172–181.

Thomson, Betty. *The Changing Face of New England.* New York, 1958.

Thoreau, Henry David. *Consciousness in Concord.* Edited by Perry Miller. Boston, 1958. *The Correspondence of Henry David Thoreau.* Edited by Walter Harding and Carl Bode. New York, 1958. "The Dispersion of Seed." Ms., Berg Collection, New York Public Library. *Huckleberries.* Edited by Leo Stoller. Iowa City, Iowa, 1970. *The Maine Woods.* Edited by Joseph J. Moldenhauer. Princeton, N.J., 1972. *Thoreau's Fact Book.* Edited by Kenneth Cameron. 2 vols. Hartford, Conn., 1966. *Walden* (1854). Edited by J. Lyndon Shanley. Princeton, N.J., 1971. *The Works of Henry Thoreau.* Walden edition. 20 vols. Boston, 1906.

Vietor, Karl. *Goethe the Thinker.* Translated by Bayard Morgan. Cambridge, Mass., 1950.

Weller, Henry. *Birds and Men.* Cambridge, Mass., 1955.

Wheeler, Ruth. *Concord: Climate for Freedom.* Concord, Mass., 1967.

Whicher, Stephen. *Freedom and Fate: An Inner Life of Ralph Waldo Emerson.* Philadelphia, 1953.

Whitford, Kathryn. "Thoreau and the Woodlots of Concord." *New England Quarterly* 23 (September 1950): 291–306. "Thoreau: Pioneer Ecologist and Conservationist." *Scientific Monthly* 73 (1951): 291–296.

Wilson, John B. "Darwin and the Transcendentalists." *Journal of the History of Ideas* 26 (April–June 1965): 286–290.

Part Three

Ackerkneckt, Erwin. "George Forster, Alexander von Humboldt, and Ethnology." *Isis* 46 (June 1955): 83–95.

Anderson, Charles. *Melville in the South Seas.* New York, 1939.

Bailey, Liberty Hyde. *The Holy Earth.* New York, 1915.

Barlow, Nora. *Charles Darwin and the Voyage of the "Beagle."* New York, 1945.

Beddall, Barbara. "Wallace, Darwin, and the Theory of Natural Selection." *Journal of the History of Biology* 1 (Fall 1968): 261–321.

Blair, W. Frank. "Ecology and Evolution." *Antioch Review* 19 (1959): 47–55.

Bruhns, Karl. *Life of Alexander von Humboldt.* Translated by J. and C. Lassell. 3 vols. London, 1873.

Burrow, J. W. *Evolution and Society: A Study in Victorian Social Theory.* Cambridge, England, 1966.

Candolle, Augustin de. "Géographie botanique." *Dictionnaire des Sciences Naturelles*, vol. 18, p. 384. Paris, 1820.

Cannon, Walter. "The Basis of Darwin's Achievement." *Victorian Studies* 5 (December 1961): 107–134.

Darwin, Charles. *A Century of Family Letters, 1792–1896.* Edited by Henrietta Litchfield. 2 vols. London, 1915. *Charles Darwin's Diary of the Voyage of H.M.S. "Beagle."* Edited by Nora Barlow. Cambridge, England, 1933. *Charles Darwin's Natural Selection: Being the Second Part to His Big Species Book Written from 1856 to 1858.* Edited by Robert Stauffer. Cambridge, England, 1975. *Darwin for Today.* Edited by Stanley Edgar Hyman. New York, 1963. "Darwin's Notebooks on the Transmutation of Species." Edited by Gavin De Beer. *Bulletin of British Museum (Natural History)*, Historical series, 2:3–5 (1960). *The Life and Letters of Charles Darwin.* Edited by Francis Darwin. 2 vols. New York, 1898. *More Letters of Charles Darwin.* Edited by Francis Darwin and A. C. Seward. 2 vols. London, 1903. *On the Origin of Species* (1859). Facsimile edition. Cambridge, Mass., 1964. *The Origin of Species* (1859) and *The Descent of Man* (1871). Modern Library edition. New York, n.d. *The Voyage of the Beagle* (1839). Edited by Leonard Engel. Garden City, N.Y., 1962.

De Beer, Gavin. *Charles Darwin: A Scientific Biography.* Garden City, N.Y., 1963.

De Terra, Helmut. *Humboldt.* New York, 1955.

Dupree, A. Hunter. *Asa Gray.* New York, 1968.

Egerton, Frank. "Humboldt, Darwin, and Population." *Journal of the History of Biology* 3 (Fall 1970): 326–360. "Studies of Animal Population from Lamarck to Darwin." *Journal of the History of Biology* 1 (Fall 1968): 225–259.

Eiseley, Loren. *Darwin's Century: Evolution and the Men Who Discovered It.* Garden City, N.Y., 1958.

Ellegard, Alvar. "The Darwinian Revolution and Nineteenth-Century Philosophies of Science." *Journal of the History of Ideas* 18 (June 1957): 362–393.

Evans, E. P. "Ethical Relations Between Man and Beast." *Popular Science Monthly* (September 1894): 634–646.

Fleming, Donald. "Charles Darwin: The Anaesthetic Man." *Victorian Studies* 4 (1961): 219–236. "Social Darwinism." In *Paths of*

American Thought, edited by Arthur Schlesinger, Jr., and Morton White. Boston, 1963.

Frazer, James G. *The New Golden Bough* (1900). Edited by Theodor Gaster. New York, 1959.

Ghiselin, Michael. *The Triumph of the Darwinian Method*. Berkeley, Calif., 1969.

Gillispie, Charles. *Genesis and Geology*. Cambridge, Mass., 1951.

Glass, Bentley, et al., eds. *Forerunners of Darwin, 1745–1859*. Baltimore, 1959.

Glass, David. *Introduction to Malthus*. New York, 1953.

Greene, John C. *The Death of Adam*. Ames, Iowa, 1959. "The Kuhnian Paradigm and the Darwinian Revolution." In *Perspectives in the History of Science and Technology*, edited by Duane Roller. Norman, Okla., 1971.

Griffith, Grosvenor. *Population Problems in the Age of Malthus*. Cambridge, England, 1926.

Himmelfarb, Gertrude. *Darwin and the Darwinian Revolution*. New York, 1962.

Hofstadter, Richard. *Social Darwinism in American Thought*. Rev. ed. Boston, 1955.

Houghton, Walter. *The Victorian Frame of Mind*. New Haven, Conn., 1957.

Hudson, William H. *Birds and Man*. New York, 1923.

Hull, David. *Darwin and His Critics: The Reception of Darwin's Theory of Evolution by the Scientific Community*. Cambridge, Mass., 1973.

Humboldt, Alexander von. *Aspects of Nature*. Translated by Mrs. Sabine. Philadelphia, 1850. *Cosmos: A Sketch of a Physical Description of the Universe*. Translated by E. C. Otté. 3 vols. New York, 1860. *Essai sur la Géographie des Plantes* (1805). Mexico City, 1955. *Personal Narrative of Travels to the Equinoctial Regions of the New Continent, during the Years 1799–1804*. Translated and abridged by Helen Williams. Philadelphia, 1815.

Huxley, Thomas. *Evolution and Ethics, 1893–1943*, with Julian Huxley. London, 1947. *Man's Place in Nature* (1863). Ann Arbor, Mich., 1959. "The Struggle for Existence: A Programme." *The Nineteenth Century* 23 (February 1888): 161–180.

James, William. "A Moral Equivalent to War." Association for International Conciliation, Leaflet no. 27 (1910).

Kellner, Charlotte. *Alexander von Humboldt*. London, 1963.

Kuhn, Thomas. *The Structure of Scientific Revolutions* (1962). Rev. ed. Chicago, 1970.

Lyell, Charles. *The Principles of Geology*. 3 vols. London, 1830–33. *Sir Charles Lyell's Scientific Journals on the Species Question*. Edited by Leonard Wilson. New Haven, Conn., 1970.

Malthus, Thomas. *Essay on Population, 1798*. Edited by James Bonar. London, 1926.

Mandelbaum, Maurice. "The Scientific Background of Evolutionary Theory in Biology." *Journal of the History of Biology* 18 (June 1957): 342–361.

Marsh, George Perkins. "The Study of Nature." *Christian Examiner* (January 1860): 33–61.

Marsh, Herbert and Jean Langenheim. "Natural Selection as an Ecological Concept." *Ecology* 42 (January 1961): 158–165.

McAtee, W. L. "The Cats to Clover Chain." *Scientific Monthly* 65 (1947): 241–242.

McCleary, George. *The Malthusian Population Theory*. London, 1953.

McKinney, Henry Lewis. *Wallace and Natural Selection*. New Haven, Conn., 1972.

Melville, Herman. *Herman Melville*. Edited by R. W. B. Lewis. New York, 1962.

Mill, John Stuart. "Nature." In *Three Essays on Religion*. New York, 1874.

Millhauser, Milton. *Just Before Darwin: Robert Chambers and the Vestiges*. Middletown, Conn., 1959.

Moore, Ruth. *Charles Darwin*. New York, 1955.

Muir, John. *A Thousand-Mile Walk to the Gulf*. Edited by William Badé. Boston, 1916.

Packard, A. S. *Lamarck: The Founder of Evolution*. London, 1901.

Parkman, Francis. *The Oregon Trail* (1849). Garden City, N.Y., 1945.

Powell, John Wesley. "From Barbarism to Civilization." *American Anthropologist* 1 (April 1888): 97–123. "Relation of Primitive Peoples to Environment, Illustrated by American Examples." In *Annual Report, Smithsonian Institution, 1895*. Washington, 1896.

Ritter, William. *Charles Darwin and the Golden Rule*. Edited by Edna Bailey. Washington, 1954.

Rogers, James Allen. "Darwinism and Social Darwinism." *Journal of the History of Ideas* 33 (April–June 1972): 265–280.

Salt, Henry S. *The Creed of Kinship*. London, 1935. *Seventy Years Among Savages*. London, 1921.

Sears, Paul. *Charles Darwin: The Naturalist as a Cultural Force*. New York, 1950.

Smith, Kenneth. *The Malthusian Controversy*. London, 1951.

Stanley, Oma. "T. H. Huxley's Treatment of 'Nature.'" *Journal of the History of Ideas* 18 (January 1957): 120–127.

Stauffer, Robert. "Ecology in the Long Manuscript Version of Darwin's *Origin of Species* and Linnaeus' *Oeconomy of Nature*." *Proceedings of American Philosophical Society* 104 (1960): 235–241.

Thomson, J. Arthur. *Concerning Evolution*. New Haven, Conn., 1925. *The Science of Life*. London, 1910.

Vorzimmer, Peter. *Charles Darwin: The Years of Controversy: The Origin of Species and Its Critics, 1859–1882*. Philadelphia, 1970. "Darwin, Malthus, and the Theory of Natural Selection." *Journal of the History of Ideas* 30 (October–December 1969): 527–542. "Darwin's Ecology and Its Influence Upon His Theory." *Isis* 56 (1965): 148–155.

Ward, Lester. *Lester Ward and the General Welfare State*. Edited by Henry Steele Commager. Indianapolis, 1967. *The Psychic Factors of Civilization*. Boston, 1893.

West, Geoffrey. *Charles Darwin: A Portrait.* New Haven, Conn., 1938.

Whewell, William. *The Philosophy of the Inductive Sciences.* 2 vols. London, 1840.

Wilson, Leonard. *Charles Lyell: The Years to 1841.* New Haven, Conn., 1972.

Young, Robert. "Malthus and the New Evolutionists: The Common Context of Biological and Social Theory." *Past and Present* 43 (May 1969): 109–145.

Part Four

Adams, Charles C. *Guide to the Study of Animal Ecology.* New York, 1913. "The New Natural History—Ecology." *American Museum Journal* 17 (April 27, 1917): 491–494. "Patrick Geddes, Botanist and Human Ecologist." *Ecology* 26 (January 1945): 103–104.

Allen, Durward. *The Life of Prairies and Plains.* New York, 1967.

Bary, Anton de. *Die Erscheinung der Symbiose.* Strasbourg, 1879.

Bennett, James. "Oasis Civilization in the Great Plains." *Great Plains Journal* 7 (1967): 26–32.

Billington, Ray. *America's Frontier Heritage.* New York, 1966.

Bogue, Allan. *From Prairie to Cornbelt.* Chicago, 1963.

Bowden, Martyn. "The Great American Desert and the American Frontier, 1880–1882: Popular Images of the Plains." In *Anonymous Americans,* edited by Tamara Hareven. Englewood Cliffs, N.J., 1971.

Brewer, Richard. *A Brief History of Ecology. Part I: Pre-Nineteenth Century to 1910.* Occasional Paper no. 1, C. C. Adams Center for Ecological Studies. Kalamazoo, Mich., 1960.

Cain, Stanley. "The Climax and Its Complexities." *American Midland Naturalist* 21 (1939): 146–181.

Cittadino, Eugene. *Nature as the Laboratory: Darwinian Plant Ecology in the German Empire, 1880–1900.* Cambridge, 1990.

Clements, Frederic E. "Darwin's Influence upon Plant Geography and Ecology." *American Naturalist* 43 (1909): 143–151. *The Development and Structure of Vegetation.* Lincoln, Nebr., 1904. *The Dynamics of Vegetation: Selections from the Writings of F. E. Clements.* Edited by B. W. Allred and E. S. Clements. New York, 1949. *Plant Succession.* Washington, 1916. *Research Methods in Ecology.* Lincoln, Nebr., 1905. "Social Origins and Processes Among Plants." In *A Handbook of Social Psychology,* edited by Carl Murchison. Worcester, Mass., 1935. *Bio-Ecology,* with Victor Shelford. New York, 1939. *Environment and Life in the Great Plains,* with Ralph Chaney. Washington, 1937. *Plant Competition,* with John Weaver and Herbert Hanson. Washington, 1929.

Coleman, William. "Evolution into Ecology? The Strategy of Warming's Ecological Plant Geography." *Journal of the History of Biology* 19 (Summer 1986): 181–196.

Cooper, William. "Henry Chandler Cowles." *Ecology* 16 (July 1935): 281–283.

Cottam, Walter. "The Role of Ecology in the Conservation of Renewable Resources." In *Proceedings, InterAmerican Conference on Conservation of Renewable Natural Resources.* Washington, 1948.

Cowles, Henry C. "The Ecological Relations of the Vegetation on the Sand Dunes of Lake Michigan." *Botanical Gazette* 27 (1899): 95. "The Physiographic Ecology of Chicago and Vicinity." *Botanical Gazette* 31 (1901): 73–108.

Dale, Tom, and Vernon Carter. *Topsoil and Civilization.* Norman, Okla., 1955.

Daubenmire, Rexford. "Merriam's Life Zones of North America." *Quarterly Review of Biology* 13 (1938): 327–332.

Drude, Oscar. *Manuel de géographie botanique.* Paris, 1897. "The Position of Ecology in Modern Science." In *International Congress of Arts and Science, St. Louis, 1904,* vol. 5. Boston, 1906.

Emmons, David. *Garden in the Grasslands.* Lincoln, Nebr., 1971.

Farb, Peter. *The Living Earth.* New York, 1959.

Finnell, H. H. "The Dust Storms of 1954." *Scientific American* 191 (July 1954): 25–29.

Fite, Gilbert. "Daydreams and Nightmares: The Late Nineteenth-Century Agricultural Frontier." *Agricultural History* 40 (1966): 285–293.

Flauhault, Charles. "Le Progrès de la géographie botanique depuis 1884." *Progressus rei botanical* 1 (1907): 243–317.

Floyd, Fred. "A History of the Dust Bowl." Ph.D. thesis, University of Oklahoma, 1950.

Furneaux, Rupert. *Krakatoa.* Englewood Cliffs, N.J., 1964.

Ganong, W. F. "The Cardinal Principles of Ecology." *Science* 19 (March 25, 1904): 493–498.

Gleason, Henry A. "Further Views on the Succession Concept." *Ecology* 8 (1927): 299–326. "The Individualistic Concept of the Plant Association." *Bulletin of Torrey Botanical Club* 53 (1926): 7–26. "The Structure and Development of the Plant Association." *Bulletin of Torrey Botanical Club* 44 (1917): 463–481.

Graham, Edward. "Soil Erosion as an Ecological Process." *Scientific Monthly* 55 (July 1942): 42–51. "A Symposium—The Ecological Approach to Land Use," with Seymour Harris and Edward Ackerman. *Journal of Soil and Water Conservation* 1 (October 1946): 55.

Great Plains Committee. "The Future of the Great Plains." Washington, 1936.

Grisebach, August. *Der Vegetation der Erde.* Leipzig, Germany, 1872.

Haeckel, Ernst. *Generelle Morphologie der Organismen.* 2 vols. Berlin, 1866. *The Wonders of Life.* London, 1904.

Hanson, Herbert. "Ecology in Agriculture." *Ecology* 20 (April 1939): 111–117.

Higbee, Edward. *The American Oasis.* New York, 1957.

Johnson, Vance. *Heaven's Tableland: The Dust Bowl Story.* New York, 1947.

Johnson, W. D. "The High Plains and Their Utilization. Part I." In

United States Geological Survey, *Twenty-first Annual Report.* "Part II." In *Twenty-second Annual Report.* Washington, 1901 and 1902.

Keeble, Frederick. *Plant-Animals: A Study in Symbiosis.* Cambridge, England, 1910.

Kendeigh, S. Charles. "History and Evaluation of Various Concepts of Plant and Animal Communities in North America." *Ecology 35* (April 1954): 152–171.

Komarek, Edwin, Sr. "Fire Ecology—Grasslands and Man." In *Proceedings,* Fourth Annual Tall Timbers Fire Ecology Conference, March 18–19, 1965.

Kormody, Edward, ed. *Readings in Ecology.* Englewood Cliffs, N.J., 1965.

Kotok, E. J. "The Ecological Approach to Conservation Programs." In *Proceedings,* InterAmerican Conference on Conservation of Renewable Natural Resources. Washington, 1948.

Kraenzel, Carl. *The Great Plains in Transition.* Norman, Okla., 1955.

Lange, Dorothea, and Paul Taylor. *An American Exodus* (1939). New Haven, Conn., 1969.

MacLeish, Archibald. "The Grasslands." *Ffortune* 12 (November 1935): 59.

MacMillan, Conway. "Observations on the Distribution of Plants Along the Shore at Lake of the Woods." *Minnesota Botanical Studies* 1 (1897): 949–1023.

Malin, James. "Dust Storms." *Kansas Historical Quarterly* 14 (May, August, November 1946). "The Grassland of North America: Its Occupance and the Challenge of Continuous Reappraisals." In *Man's Role in Changing the Face of the Earth,* edited by William Thomas. Chicago, 1956. *The Grassland of North America: Prolegomena to Its History with Addenda.* Lawrence Kans., 1956. "Soil, Animal, and Plant Relations of the Grassland, Historically Reconsidered." *Scientific Monthly* 76 (April 1953): 207–220.

Margalef, Ramon. *Perspectives on Ecological Theory.* Chicago, 1968.

Marriott, Alice and Carol Rachlin. *Oklahoma: The Forty-sixth Star.* Garden City, N.Y., 1973.

McKee, Russell. *The Last West: A History of the Great Plains in North Amerca.* New York, 1974.

McReynolds, Edwin. *Oklahoma: A History of the Sooner State.* Norman, Okla., 1954.

McWilliams, Carey. *Ill Fares the Land.* New York, 1942.

Merriam, C. Hart. "Results of a Biological Survey of the San Francisco Mountain Region and the Desert of the Little Colorado, Arizona." *North American Fauna,* no. 3. Washington, 1890. *Selected Works of Clinton Hart Merriam.* Edited by Keir Sterling. New York, 1974.

Mikesell, Marvin. "The Rise and Decline of 'Sequent Occupance': A Chapter in the History of American Geography." In *Geographies of the Mind,* edited by David Lowenthal and Martyn Bowden. New York, 1976.

Moore, Barrington. "The Scope of Ecology." *Ecology* 1 (January 1920): 3–5.

Peterson, Roger Tory. "Life Zones, Biomes, or Life Forms?" *Audubon* 44 (1942): 21–30.

Phillips, John. "The Biotic Community." *Journal of Ecology* 19 (1931): 1–24. "Succession, Development, the Climax, and the Complex Organism: An Analysis of Concepts." *Journal of Ecology* 22 (1934): 554–571; 23 (1935): 210–246, 488–508. "A Tribute to Frederic E. Clements and His Concepts in Ecology." *Ecology* 35 (April 1954): 114–115.

Pound, Roscoe. "Frederic E. Clements As I Knew Him." *Ecology* 35 (April 1954): 112–113. "Symbiosis and Mutualism." *American Naturalist* 27 (1892): 509–520. *The Phytogeography of Nebraska*, with Frederic E. Clements. Lincoln, Nebr., 1898.

Rádl, Emanuel. *History of Biological Theories*. Oxford, 1930.

Raup, Hugh. "Some Problems in Ecological Theory and Their Relation to Conservation." *Journal of Ecology* 52, suppl. (1964): 19–28. "Trends in the Development of Geographic Botany." *Annals of Association of American geographers* 32 (1942): 319–354.

Rodgers, Andrew Denny. *American Botany, 1873–1892: Decades of Transition*. Princeton, N.J., 1944.

Sauer, Carl. A *Agricultural Origins and Dispersals*. 2nd ed. Cambridge, Mass., 1969. "Grassland Climax, Fire and Man." *Journal of Range Management* 3 (January 1950): 16–21.

Schimper, A. F. W. *Plant Geography upon a Physiological Basis* (1898). Revised and edited by Percy Groom and Isaac Balfour. Oxford, 1903.

Schlesinger, Arthur, Jr. *The Coming of the New Deal*. Boston, 1958.

Sears, Paul "Black Blizzards." In *America in Crisis*, edited by Daniel Aaron. New York, 1952. "Botanists and the Conservation of Natural Resources." In *Fifty Years of Botany*, edited by William C. Steere. New York, 1958. *Deserts on the March*. Norman, Okla., 1935. "Floods and Dust Storms." *Science* 83 (March 27, 1936) suppl. 9. "O, Bury Me Not: Or, The Bison Avenged." *New Republic* 91 (May 12, 1937): 7–10.

Shannon, David. *The Farmer's Last Frontier*. New York, 1945.

Shantz, H. L. "The Ecological Approach to Land Management." *Journal of Forestry* 48 (October 1950): 673–675. "Frederic Edward Clements (1874–1945)." *Ecology* 26 (October 1945): 317–319. "The Natural Vegetation of the Great Plains Region." *Annals of Association of American Geographers* 13 (1923): 81–107.

Shelford, Victor E. *Animal Communities in Temperate America*. Chicago, 1913. "Deciduous Forest, Man, and the Grassland Fauna." *Science* 100 (1944): 135–140. *Laboratory and Field Ecology*. Baltimore, 1929. "Life Zones, Modern Ecology, and the Failure of Temperature Summing." *Wilson Bulletin* rr (1932): 144–1957. "The Organization of the Ecological Society of America, 1914–1919." *Ecology* 19 (1938): 164–166. "The Relative Merits of the Life Zone and Biome Concepts." *Wilson Bulletin* 57 (1945): 248–252.

Silverberg, Robert. *The Challenge of Climate*. New York, 1969.
Smith, Henry Nash. "Rain Follows the Plow: The Notion of Increased Rainfall for the Great Plains, 1944–1980." *Huntington Library Quarterly* 10 (1947): 169–193. *Virgin Land: The American West as Symbol and Myth*. Cambridge, Mass., 1950.
Smith, Roger C. "Upsetting the Balance of Nature, with Special Reference to Kansas and the Great Plains." *Science* 75 (June 24, 1932): 649–654.
Soil Conservation Service, United States Department of Agriculture. "Some Information about Dust Storms and Wind Erosion on the Great Plains." March 30, 1953.
Special Presidential Committee. "A Report on Drought in the Great Plains and Southwest." October 1958.
Spencer, Herbert. "Evolutionary Ethics." In *Various Fragments*. New York, 1898. *The Principles of Biology* (1864–67) Rev. ed. 2 vols. London, 1899. *The Principles of Sociology*. 3 vols. London, 1876–96. "The Social Organism." *Westminster Review* 73 January 1860): 90–121.
Stauffer, Robert. "Haeckel, Darwin, and Ecology." *Quarterly Review of Biology* 32 (June 1957): 138–144.
Stegner, Wallace. *Beyond the Hundredth Meridian*. Boston, 1954.
Stein, Walter. *California and the Dust Bowl Migration*. Westport, Conn., 1973.
Steinbeck, John. *The Grapes of Wrath*. New York, 1939.
Svobida, Lawrence. *An Empire of Dust*. Caldwell, Idaho, 1940.
Tannehill, Ivan. *Drought: Its Causes and Effects*. Princeton, N.J., 1947.
Tansley, Arthur G. "The Early History of Modern Plant Ecology in Britain." *Journal of Ecology* 35 (1947): 130–137. "Frederic Edward Clements." *Journal of Ecology* 34 (1946): 194–196. "The Use and Abuse of Vegetational Concepts and Terms." *Ecology* 16 (July 1935): 292.
Tobey, Ronald C. *Saving the Prairies: The Life Cycle of the Founding School of American Plant Ecology, 1895–1955*. Berkeley, Calif., 1981.
Udall, Stewart. *The Quiet Crisis*. New York, 1963.
United States Department of Agriculture. *Soils and Men*. Washington, 1938.
Warming, Eugenius. *The Oecology of Plants* (1895). Rev. ed. Oxford, 1909.
Webb, Walter P. *The Great Plains*. Boston, 1931.

Part Five

Adams, Charles C. "The Conservation of Predatory Mammals." *Journal of Mammalogy* 6 (May 1925): 83–96. "A Note for Social-Minded Ecologists and Geographers." *Ecology* 19 (July 1938): 500–502. "The Relation of General Ecology to Human Ecology." *Ecology* 16 (July 1935): 316–325.
Advisory Board in Wildlife Management for the Secretary of Interior

(A. Starker Leopold, chairman). "Predator and Rodent Control in the United States." *Transactions of North American Wildlife Conference* 29 (March 1964): 27–49.

Advisory Committee on Predator Control (Stanley A. Cain, chairman). "Predator Control—1971." Report to Council on Environmental Quality and Department of Interior. January 1972.

Allee, Warder C. *Animal Aggregations: A Study in General Sociology.* Chicago, 1931. "Cooperation Among Animals." *American Journal of Sociology* 37 (November 1931): 386–398. "Where Angels Fear to Tread: A Contribution from General Sociology to Human Ethics." *Science,* n.s. 97 (June 11, 1943): 517–525. *Principles of Animal Ecology,* with Alfred Emerson, Thomas Park, Orlando Park, and Karl Schmidt. Philadelphia, 1949.

Allen, Durward. *Our Wildlife Legacy.* New York, 1954.

Bailey, Vernon. "Destruction of Wolves and Coyotes: Results Obtained during 1907." United States Department of Agriculture, Bureau of Biological Survey, Circular no. 63, 1908.

Bates, J. Leonard. "Fulfilling American Democracy: The Conservation Movement, 1907 to 1921." *Mississippi Valley Historical Review* 44 (June 1957): 29–57.

Bates, Marston. *The Forest and the Sea.* New York, 1960.

Bertalanffy, Ludwig von. "An Outline of General System Theory." *British Journal for the Philosophy of Science* 1 (1950): 134–165. *Problems of Life: An Evaluation of Modern Biological Thought.* New York, 1952. "The Theory of Open Systems in Physics and Biology." *Science* 11 (1950): 23–29.

Birge, E. A. "The Heat Budget of American and European Lakes." *Transactions of the Wisconsin Academy of Science, Arts, and Letters* 18 (1915): 166–213.

Blin-Stoyle, B. J. "The End of Mechanistic Philosophy and the Rise of Field Physics." In *The Turning Point in Physics.* Amsterdam, 1959.

Blum, Harold. *Time's Arrow and Evolution* (1951). Rev. ed. New York, 1962.

Bray, J. Roger. "Notes Toward an Ecologic Theory." *Ecology* 39 (October 1958): 770–776.

Brillouin, L. "Life, Thermodynamics and Cybernetics." *American Scientist* 37 (1949): 554–568.

Cameron, Jenks. *The Bureau of the Biological Survey.* Washington, 1929.

Chisholm, Anne. *Philosophers of the Earth: Conversations with Ecologists.* New York, 1972.

Cole, Lamont. "The Ecosphere." *Scientific American* 198 (April 1958): 83–92.

Conger, George. "The Doctrine of Levels." *Journal of Philosophy* 22 (1925): 309–321.

Connery, Robert. *Governmental Problems in Wild Life Conservation.* New York, 1935.

Crombie, A. C. "Interspecific Competition." *Journal of Animal Ecology* 16 (1947): 47–73.

Dice, Lee. "The Scientific Value of Predatory Mammals." *Journal of Mammalogy* 6 (February 1925): 25–27.

Dobie, J. Frank. *The Voice of the Coyote* (1949). Lincoln, Nebr., 1961.

Elton, Charles. *Animal Ecology* (1927). Rev. ed. New York, 1966. *Animal Ecology and Evolution.* London, 1930. *The Ecology of Invasions by Animals and Plants.* London, 1958. *The Pattern of Animal Communities.* London, 1966. *Voles, Mice and Lemmings.* Oxford, 1942.

Ely, Richard. "Conservation and Economic Theory." In *The Foundations of National Prosperity.* New York, 1917.

Emerson, Alfred. "The Biological Basis of Social Cooperation." *Transactions of the Illinois State Academy of Science* 39 (May 1946): 9–18. "Ecology, Evolution, and Society." *American Naturalist* 77 (March–April 1943): 97–118.

Engelmann, Manfred. "Energetics, Terrestrial Field Studies, and Animal Productivity." *Advances in Ecological Research* 3 (1966): 73–116.

Errington, Paul. *Of Predation and Life.* Ames, Iowa, 1967. "Of Wilderness and Wolves." *Journal of Wildlife Management* 33 (Autumn 1969): 3–7. "A Question of Values." *Journal of Wildlife Management* 11 (July 1947): 267–272. "What Is the Meaning of Predation?" *Annual Report of the Smithsonian Institution, 1936.* Washington, 1937.

Flader, Susan. *Thinking Like a Mountain: Aldo Leopold and the Evolution of an Ecological Attitude Toward Deer, Wolves, and Forests.* Columbia, Mo., 1974.

Forbes, Stephen. "The Lake as a Microcosm." *Bulletin of the Scientific Association of Peoria, Illinois* (1887): 77–87. "On Some Interactions of Organisms." *Bulletin of the Illinois State Laboratory of Natural History* 1 (1903): 3–18.

Gabrielson, Ira. *Wildlife Conservation.* New York, 1948.

Gates, David. *Energy Exchange in the Biosphere.* New York, 1962. "Toward Understanding Ecosystems." *Advances in Ecological Research* 5 (1968): 1–35.

Gause, G. F. *The Struggle for Existence.* Baltimore, 1934.

Gerard, Ralph W. "Biological Basis for Ethics." *Philosophy of Science* 9 (January 1942): 92–120.

Gilbert, O., with T. B. Reynoldson and J. Hobart. "Gause's Hypothesis: An Examination." *Journal of Animal Ecology* 21 (1952): 310–312.

Goldman, C. R., ed. *Primary Productivity in Aquatic Environments.* Berkeley, Calif., 1966.

Goldman, E. A. "The Coyote—Archpredator." *Journal of Mammalogy* 11 (August 1930): 330–331. "The Predatory Mammal Problem and the Balance of Nature." *Journal of Mammalogy* 6 (February 1925): 28–33.

Graham, Frank, Jr. *Man's Dominion: The Story of Conservation in America.* New York, 1971.

Hardin, Garrett. *Nature and Man's Fate.* New York, 1959.

Hays, Samuel. *Conservation and the Gospel of Efficiency: The Pro-*

gressive Conservation Movement, 1890–1920. Cambridge, Mass., 1959.

Henderson, W. C. "The Control of the Coyote." *Journal of Mammalogy* 11 (August 1930): 336–350.

Hough Emerson. "The President's Forest." *Saturday Evening Post* 194 (January 14, 1922): 6–7; (January 21, 1922): 23.

Howard, Walter. "Means of Improving the Status of Vertebrate Pest Control." *Transactions of the 27th North American Wildlife and Natural Resource Conference*. Washington, 1962.

Juday, C. "The Annual Energy Budget in an Inland Lake." *Ecology* 21 (1940): 438–450.

Jungk, Robert. *Brighter Than a Thousand Suns*. New York, 1958.

Kormondy, Edward. *Concepts of Ecology*. Englewood Cliffs, N.J., 1969.

Kozlovsky, D. G. "A Critical Evaluation of the Trophic Level Concept: I. Ecological Efficiencies." *Ecology* 49 (1968): 48–60.

Krutch, Joseph Wood. *The Great Chain of Life*. Boston, 1956. *If You Don't Mind My Saying So*. New York, 1964. *The Modern Temper*. New York, 1949. *More Lives Than One*. New York, 1962. *The Twelve Seasons*. New York, 1949. *The Voice of the Desert*. New York, 1955.

Laycock, George. "Travels and Travails of the Song-Dog." *Audubon* 76 (September 1974): 16–31.

Leopold, Aldo. "The Conservation Ethic." *Journal of Forestry* 31 (October 1933): 634–643. *Game Management*. New York, 1933. *A Sand County Almanac, with Essays on Conservation from Round River*. New York, 1970.

Lindeman, Eduard. "Ecology: An Instrument for the Integration of Science and Philosophy." *Ecological Monographs* 10 (July 1940): 367–372.

Lindeman, Raymond. "The Trophic–Dynamic Aspect of Ecology." *Ecology* 23 (October 1942): 399–417.

Lorain, John. *Nature and Reason Harmonized in the Practice of Husbandry*. Philadelphia, 1825.

Lotka, A. J. *Elements of Physical Biology*. New York, 1925.

Lovejoy, Arthur O. "The Meaning of 'Emergence' and Its Modes." *Proceedings of the Sixth International Congress of Philosophy, 1926*. New York, 1927.

MacFayden, A. "The Meaning of Productivity in Biological Systems." *Journal of Animal Ecology* 17 (1948): 75–80.

Madden, Edward. "The Philosophy of Science in Gestalt Theory." In *Readings in the Philosophy of Science*, edited by Herbert Feigl and May Brodbeck. New York, 1953.

Marsh, George Perkins. *Man and Nature: Or, Physical Geography as Modified by Human Action* (1864). Cambridge, Mass., 1965.

Mech, L. David. *The Wolf*. Garden City, N.Y., 1970.

Mitchell, John G., and Constance Stallings, eds. *Ecotactics: The Sierra Club Handbook for Environmental Activists*. New York, 1970.

Mitman, Gregg. "From the Population to Society: The Cooperative

Metaphors of W. C. Allee and A. E. Emerson." *Journal of the History of Biology* 21 (Summer 1988): 173–194. *The State of Nature: Ecology, Community, and American Social Thought, 1900–1950.* Chicago, 1992.

Möbius, Karl. "The Oyster and Oyster-Culture (1877)." Translated by H. J. Rice. *Report of the U.S. Commission of Fish and Fisheries, 1880.* Washington, 1883.

Morgan, C. Lloyd. *Emergent Evolution.* London, 1923.

Muller, C. H. "Science and Philosophy of the Community." *American Scientist* 46 (1958): 294–308.

Mumford, Lewis. *Technics and Civilization.* New York, 1934.

Murie, Adolf. *The Wolves of Mount McKinley.* Fauna of National Parks of U.S., Department of Interior. Fauna Series no. 5, 1944.

Murie, Olaus. The Papers of Olaus Murie. Denver, Colo., Public Library, Conservation Center. *Wapiti Wilderness,* with Margaret Murie. New York, 1966.

Nash, Roderick. *Wilderness and the American Mind.* Rev. ed. New Haven, Conn., 1973.

Naumov, N. P. *The Ecology of Animals.* Translated by Frederick Plous, Jr. Urbana, Ill., 1972.

Novikoff, Alex. "The Concept of Integrative Levels and Biology." *Science,* n.s. 101 (March 2, 1945): 209–215.

Odum, Eugene, et al. "The New Ecology." *BioScience* 14 (July 1964): 7–41.

Ohle, W. "Bioactivity, Production, and Energy Utilization of Lakes." *Limnology and Oceanography* 1 (1956): 139–149.

Olson, Sigurd. "A Study in Predatory Relationships with Particular Reference to the Wolf." *Scientific Monthly* 46 (April 1938): 323–336.

Park, Robert. *Human Communities: The City and Human Ecology.* Glencoe, Ill., 1952.

Pepper, Stephen. "Emergence." *Journal of Philosophy* 23 (1926): 241–245.

Phillipson, John. *Ecological Energetics.* London, 1966.

Pimlott, Douglas. "Wolves and Men in North America." *Defenders of Wildlife News* 42 (Spring 1967): 36.

Pinchot, Gifford. *Breaking New Ground.* New York, 1947.

Rasmussen, D. Irwin. "Biotic Communities of Kaibab Plateau, Arizona." *Ecological Monographs* 11 (July 1941): 229–275.

Redfield, Robert, ed. "Levels of Integration in Biological and Social Systems." *Biological Symposia,* vol. 8. Lancaster, Pa., 1942.

Reinheimer, Hermann. *Evolution and Cooperation: A Study in Bio-Economics.* New York, 1913.

Richardson, Elmo. *The Politics of Conservation: Crusades and Controversies, 1897–1913.* Berkeley, Calif., 1962.

Rowe, J. S. "The Levels of Integration Concept and Ecology." *Ecology* 42 (April 1961): 420–427.

Russett, Cynthia. *The Concept of Equilibrium in American Social Thought.* New Haven, Conn., 1966.

Russo, John. "The Kaibab North Deer Herd—Its History, Problems

490 • *Bibliography*

and Management." State of Arizona Fish and Game Department, *Wildlife Bulletin* 7 (July 1964).

Savage, Jay M. "The Concept of Ecologic Niche, with Reference to the Theory of Natural Coexistence." *Evolution* 12 (1958): 111–112.

Schmidt, Karl. "Warder of Clyde Allee." *Biographical Memoirs*, vol. 30. New York, 1957.

Sears, Paul B. "Integration at the Community Level." *American Scientist* 37 (April 1949): 235–242.

Semper, Karl. *Animal Life as Affected by the Natural Conditions of Existence*. New York, 1881.

Shelford, Victor E. "Biological Control of Rodents and Predators." *Scientific Monthly* 55 (October 1942): 331–341.

Slobodkin, Lawrence. "Energy in Animal Ecology." *Advances in Ecological Research* 1 (1962): 69–102.

Smuts, Jan. *Holis and Evolution*. New York, 1926.

Spurr, Stephen. "The Natural Resource Ecosystem." In *The Ecosystem Concept in Natural Resource Management*, edited by George Van Dyne. New York, 1969.

"Symposium." *Journal of Mammalogy* 11 (August 1930): 325–389.

Tansley, Arthur G. "The Use and Abuse of Vegetational Concepts and Terms." *Ecology* 16 (July 1935): 284–307.

Taylor, Walter P. "Significance of the Biotic Community in Ecological Studies." *Quarterly Review of Biology* 10 (September 1935): 296. "What Is Ecology and What Good Is It?" *Ecology* 17 (July 1936): 335–336.

Thienemann, A. "Grundzüge einen allgemeinen Oekologie." *Archiv für Hydrobiologie* 35 (1939): 267–285. *Limnologie*. Breslau, 1926. "Der Produktionsbegriff in der Biologie." *Archiv für Hydrobiologie*, suppl. 22 (1931): 616–622.

Transeau, Edgar. "The Accumulation of Energy by Plants." *Ohio Journal of Science* 26 (1926): 1–10.

Udvardy, Miklos. "Notes on the Ecological Concepts of Habitat, Biotope, and Niche." *Ecology* 40 (1959): 725–728.

Usinger, Robert. *The Life of Rivers and Streams*. New York, 1967.

Van Wormer, Joe. *The World of the Coyote*. Philadelphia, 1964.

Watt, Kenneth. *Ecology and Resource Management: A Quantitative Approach*. New York, 1968.

Wells, H. G., with Julian Huxley and G. P. Wells. *The Science of Life*. New York, 1939.

Westlake, D. F. "Comparisons of Plant Productivity." *Biological Reviews* 38 (1963): 385–425.

Wheeler, William Morton. "Emergent Evolution of the Social." *Proceedings of the Sixth International Congress of Philosophy, 1926*. New York, 1927. *Essays in Philosophical Biology*. Cambridge, Mass., 1939. *Foibles of Insects and Men*. New York, 1928.

Whitehead, Alfred North. *The Concept of Nature*. Cambridge, England, 1920. *The Philosophy of Alfred North Whitehead*. Edited by Paul Schilpp. Evanston, Ill., 1941. *Science and the Modern World*. New York, 1925.

Young, Stanley P. The Papers of Stanley P. Young. Denver, Colo., Public Library, Conservation Center. *The Wolves of North America*, with E. A. Goldman. Washington, 1944.

Part Six

Acot, Pascal. *Histoire de l'écologie*. Paris, 1988.

Allen, T. F. H., and Thomas B. Starr. *Hierarchy: Perspectives for Ecological Complexity*. Chicago, 1982.

Barash, David P. "The Ecologist as Zen Master." *American Midland Naturalist* 89 (January 1973): 214–217.

Beatty, John. "Ecology and Evolutionary Biology in the War and Postwar Years: Questions and Comments." *Journal of the History of Biology* 21 (Summer 1988): 245–263.

Begon, Michael, John L. Harper, and Colin R. Townsend. *Ecology: Individuals, Populations, and Communities*. Sunderland, Mass., 1986.

Blair, W. Frank. *Big Biology: The US/IBP*. Stroudsburg, Pa., 1977.

Bormann, F. Herbert and Gene E. Likens. "Catastrophic Disturbance and the Steady State in Northern Hardwood Forests." *American Scientist* 67 (November–December 1979): 660–669. *Pattern and Process in a Forested Ecosystem: Disturbance, Development and the Steady State Based on the Hubbard Brook Ecosystem Study*. New York, 1979.

Botkin, Daniel B. "A Grandfather Clock down the Staircase: Stability and Disturbance in Natural Ecosystems." In *Forests: Fresh Perspectives from Ecosystem Analysis*, edited by Richard H. Waring. Corvallis, Ore., 1980. *Discordant Harmonies: A New Ecology for the Twenty-first Century*. New York, 1990.

Bramwell, Anna. *Ecology in the 20th Century: A History*. New Haven, Conn., 1989.

Carson, Rachel. *The Sea Around Us*. New York, 1961; reprint ed., 1989. *Silent Spring*. Boston, 1962.

Cherrett, J. M., ed. *Ecological Concepts: The Contribution of Ecology to an Understanding of the Natural World*. Oxford, 1989.

Cole, LaMont C. "The Impending Emergence of Ecological Thought." *BioScience* 14 (July 1964): 30–32.

Colinvaux, Paul A. *Introduction to Ecology*. New York, 1973. *Why Big Fierce Animals Are Rare: An Ecologist's Perspective*. Princeton, N.J., 1978.

Collins, James P. "*Evolutionary Ecology* and the Use of Natural Selection in Ecological Theory." *Journal of the History of Biology* 19 (Summer 1986): 257–288.

Commoner, Barry. *The Closing Circle: Nature, Man, and Technology*. New York, 1971. *Science and Survival*. New York, 1966.

Connell, Joseph H., and Ralph O. Slatyer. "Mechanisms of Succession in Natural Communities and Their Role in Community Stability and Organization." *The American Naturalist* 111 (November–December 1977): 1119–1144.

Cotgrove, Stephen. *Catastrophe or Cornucopia: The Environment, Politics and the Future*. New York, 1982.

Cowell, Robert A. "The Evolution of Ecology." *American Zoologist* 25 (1985: 771–777.

Darling, Frank Fraser. *Wilderness and Plenty*. Boston, 1970.

Davis, Margaret B. "Climatic Instability, Time Lags, and Community Disequilibrium." In *Community Ecology*, edited by Jared Diamond and Ted J. Case. New York, 1986. "Palynology and Environmental History During the Quaternary Period." *American Scientist* 57 (Autumn 1969): 317–332. "Quaternary History and the Stability of Forest Communities." In *Forest Succession: Concepts and Applications*, edited by Darrel C. West, Herman H. Shugart, and Daniel B. Botkin. New York, 1981.

Deléage, Jean-Paul. *Histoire de l'écologie: Une science de l'homme et de la nature*. Paris, 1992.

Devall, Bill, and George Sessions. *Deep Ecology: Living As If Nature Mattered*. Salt Lake City, Utah, 1985.

Drouin, Jean-Marc. *Réinventer la nature: L'écologie et son histoire*. Paris, 1991.

Drury, William H., and Ian C. T. Nisbet. "Succession." *Journal of the Arnold Arboretum* 54 (July 1973): 331–368.

Dupré, John. *The Disorder of Things: Metaphysical Foundations of the Disunity of Science*. Cambridge, Mass., 1993.

Ehrlich, Paul R. *The Machinery of Nature*. New York, 1986. *The Population Bomb*. New York, 1968.

Ehrlich, Paul R., and Jonathan Roughgarden. *The Science of Ecology*. New York, 1987.

Evans, G. Clifford. "A Sack of Uncut Diamonds: The Study of Ecosystems and the Future Resources of Mankind." *Journal of Ecology* 64 (March 1976): 1–38.

Finegan, Bryan. "Forest Succession." *Nature* 312 (November 8, 1984): 109–114.

Fleming, Donald. "Roots of the New Conservation Movement." *Perspectives in American History* 6 (1972): 7–91.

Fradkin, Philip L. *Fallout: An American Tragedy*. Tucson, Ariz., 1989.

Fretwell, Stephen D. "The Impact of Robert MacArthur on Ecology." *Annual Review of Ecology and Systematics* 6 (1975): 1–13.

Futuyama, Douglas J. "Reflections on Reflections: Ecology and Evolutionary Biology." *Journal of the History of Biology* 19 (Summer 1986): 303–312.

Gleason, Henry A. "The Individualistic Concept of the Plant Association." *Bulletin of the Torrey Botanical Club* 53 (January 1926): 7–26. "The Individualistic Concept of the Plant Association." *American Midland Naturalist* 21 (January 1939): 92–110.

Gleick, James. *Chaos: The Making of a New Science*. New York, 1987.

Goldsmith, Edward. *The Way: An Ecological World-View*. Boston, 1993. *Blueprint for Survival*. London, 1972.

Goodman, Daniel. "The Theory of Diversity–Stability Relationships in Ecology." *Quarterly Review of Biology* 50 (September 1975): 237–266.

Hagen, Joel B. "Ecologists and Taxonomists: Divergent Traditions in Twentieth-Century Plant Geography." *Journal of the History of Biology* 19 (Summer 1986): 197–214. *An Entangled Bank: The Origins of Ecosystem Ecology*. New Brunswick, N.J., 1992.

Haila, Yrjö. "Ecology Finding Evolution Finding Ecology." *Biology and Philosophy* 4 (April 1989): 235–244. "On the Semiotic Dimension of Ecological Theory: The Case of Island Biogeography," *Biology and Philosophy* 1 (1986): 377–387.

Haila, Yrjö, and Richard Levins. *Humanity and Nature: Ecology, Science, and Society*. London, 1992.

Hairston, Nelson G., Frederick E. Smith, and Lawrence B. Slobodkin. "Community Structure, Population Control, and Competition." *American Naturalist* 94 (November–December 1960): 421–425.

Harper, J. L. "A Darwinian Approach to Plant Ecology." *Journal of Ecology* 55 (July 1967): 247–270.

Hays, Samuel P. *Beauty, Health, and Permanence: Environmental Politics in the United States, 1955–1985*. New York, 1987.

Hutchinson, G. Evelyn. *The Ecological Theater and the Evolutionary Play*. New Haven, Conn., 1965. *An Introduction to Population Biology*. New Haven, Conn., 1978.

Jordan, Carl F. "Do Ecosystems Exist?" *American Naturalist* 118 (August 1981): 284–287.

Joseph, Lawrence E. *Gaia: The Growth of an Idea*. New York, 1990.

Jungk, Robert. *Brighter Than a Thousand Suns: A Personal History of the Atomic Scientists*. New York, 1958.

Keller Evelyn Fox. "Demarcating Public from Private Values in Evolutionary Discourse." *Journal of the History of Biology* 21 (Summer 1988): 195–211.

Kimmler, William C. "Advantage, Adaptiveness, and Evolutionary Ecology." *Journal of the History of Biology* 19 (Summer 1986): 215–233.

Kingsland, Sharon E. "Mathematical Figments, Biological Facts: Population Ecology in the Thirties." *Journal of the History of Biology* 19 (Summer 1986): 235–256. *Modeling Nature: Episodes in the History of Population Ecology*. Chicago, 1985.

Kormondy, Edward J., and J. Frank McCormick, eds. *Handbook of Contemporary Developments in World Ecology*. Westport, Conn., 1981.

Levins, Richard, and Richard Lewontin. *The Dialectical Biologist*. Cambridge, Mass., 1985.

Lewin, Roger. *Complexity: Life at the Edge of Chaos*. New York, 1992. "Predators and Hurricanes Change Ecology." *Science* 221 (August 19, 1983): 737–740. "Santa Rosalia Was a Goat." *Science* 221 (August 12, 1983): 636–639.

Lovejoy, Arthur O. "Reflections on the History of Ideas." *Journal of the History of Ideas* 1 (January 1940): 3–23.

Lovelock, James. *The Ages of Gaia: A Biography of Our Living Earth*. Oxford, 1988. *Gaia: A New Look at Life on Earth*. Oxford, 1979; reprint 1987. *Healing Gaia: Practical Medicine for the Planet*. New York, 1991.

MacArthur, Robert H. *Geographical Ecology*. New York, 1972.

MacArthur, Robert H., and Edward O. Wilson. *The Theory of Island Biogeography*. Princeton, N.J., 1967.

McIntosh, Robert P. *The Background of Ecology: Concept and Theory*. Cambridge, 1985.

May, Robert M. "Biological Populations with Nonoverlapping Generations: Stable Points, Stable Cycles, and Chaos." *Science* 186 (November 15, 1974): 645–647. "Simple Mathematical Models with Very Complicated Dynamics." *Nature* 261 (June 10, 1976): 459–467. *Stability and Complexity in Model Ecosystems*. Princeton, N.J., 1973. "Stability in Ecosystems: Some Comments." In *Unifying Concepts in Ecology*, edited by W. H. van Dobben and R. H. Loew-McConnell. The Hague, 1975. "When Two and Two Do Not Make Four: Nonlinear Phenomena in Ecology." *Proceedings of the Royal Society of London, Series B* (August 22, 1986): 241–266.

Michod, Richard E. "On Fitness and Adaptedness and Their Role in Evolutionary Explanation." *Journal of the History of Biology* 19 (Summer 1986): 289–302.

Mitchell, John, and Constance Stallings, eds. *Ecotactics: The Sierra Club Handbook for Environmental Activists*. New York, 1970.

Naess, Arne. "The Shallow and the Deep, Long-Range Ecology Movements: A Summary." *Inquiry* 16 (Spring 1973): 95–100.

Nicholson, Max. *The Environmental Revolution: A Guide for the New Masters of the World*. London, 1970.

Oates, David. *Earth Rising: Ecological Belief in an Age of Science*. Corvallis, Ore., 1989.

Odum, Eugene P. *Ecology and Our Endangered Life-Support Systems*. Sunderland, Mass., 1989. "The Emergence of Ecology as a New Integrative Discipline." *Science* 195 (March 25, 1977): 1289–1293. "Energy Flow in Ecosystems: A Historical Review." *American Zoologist* 8 (February 1968): 11–18. *Fundamentals of Ecology*. 3rd ed. Philadelphia, 1971. "The Strategy of Ecosystem Development." *Science* 164 (April 18, 1969): 262–270. "Trends Expected in Stressed Ecosystems." *BioScience* 35 (July–August 1985): 419–422.

Odum, Howard T. *Environment, Power, and Society*. New York, 1971.

Ophuls, William. *Ecology and the Politics of Scarcity Revisited. The Unravelling of the American Dream*. New York, 1977; 1992

Pepper, David. *The Roots of Modern Environmentalism*. London, 1984.

Peters, Robert Henry. *A Critique for Ecology*. Cambridge, 1991.

Pickett, S. T. A. "Succession: An Evolutionary Interpretation." *American Naturalist* 110 (January–February 1976): 107–119.

Pickett, S. T. A., and P. S. White, eds. *The Ecology of Natural Disturbance and Patch Dynamics*. Orlando, Fla., 1985.

Pimm, Stuart L. *The Balance of Nature? Ecological Issues in the Conservation of Species and Communities*. Chicago, 1991.

Polunin, Nicholas, ed. *Ecosystem Theory and Application*. Chichester, 1986.

Pomeroy, L. R., and J. J. Alberts, eds. *Concepts of Ecosystem Ecology: A Comparative View*. New York, 1988.

Prigogine, Ilya, and Isabelle Stengers. *Order Out of Chaos: Man's New Dialogue with Nature*. Boulder, Colo., 1984.

Putnam, R. J., and S. D. Wratten. *Principles of Ecology*. London, 1984.

Rambler, Mitchell B., Lynn Margulis, and Rene Fester, eds. *Global Ecology: Towards a Science of the Biosphere*. San Diego, Calif., 1989.

Richardson, Jonathan L. "The Organismic Community: Resilience of an Embattled Ecological Concept." *BioScience* 30 (July 1980): 465–471.

Ricklefs, Robert E. *Ecology*. 3rd ed. New York, 1990.

Schaffer, William M. "Chaos in Ecology and Epidemiology." In *Chaos in Biological Systems*, edited by H. Degan, A. V. Holden, and L. F. Olsen. New York, 1987. "Order and Chaos in Ecological Systems." *Ecology* 66 (February 1985): 93–106.

Schneider, Stephen H., and Penelope J. Boston, eds. *Scientists on Gaia*. Cambridge, Mass., 1991.

Sears, Paul. *Deserts on the March*. 3rd ed. Norman, Okla., 1959.

Simberloff, Daniel. "A Succession of Paradigms in Ecology: Essentialism to Materialism and Probabilism." *Synthese* 43 (1980): 3–39.

Söderqvist, Thomas. *The Ecologists: From Merry Naturalists to Saviours of the Nation. A Sociologically Informed Narrative Survey of the Ecologization of Sweden, 1895–1975*. Stockholm, 1986.

Soulé, Michael E. "Conservation Biology and the 'Real World.'" In *Conservation Biology: The Science of Scarcity and Diversity*, edited by Michael Soulé. Sunderland, Mass., 1986.

Southern, H. N. "Ecology at the Crossroads." *Journal of Ecology* 58 (March 1970): 1–11.

Stewart, Ian. *Does God Play Dice? The Mathematics of Chaos*. Oxford, 1989.

Stiling, Peter. *Introductory Ecology*. Englewood Cliffs, N.J., 1992.

Strong, Donald R., Jr., Daniel Simberloff, Lawrence G. Abele, and Anne B. Thistle, eds. *Ecological Communities: Conceptual Issues and the Evidence*. Princeton, N.J., 1984.

Taylor, Peter J. "Technocratic Optimism, H. T. Odum, and the Partial Transformation of Ecological Metaphor after World War II." *Journal of the History of Biology* 21 (Summer 1988): 213–244.

Thomas, William L., Jr., ed. *Man's Role in Changing the Face of the Earth*. Chicago, 1956.

Toulmin, Stephen, and June Goodfield. *The Discovery of Time*. Chicago, 1977.

Waldrop, M. Mitchell. *Complexity: The Emerging Science at the Edge of Order and Chaos*. New York, 1992.

Williamson, Mark. "Are Communities Ever Stable?" In *Colonization, Succession, and Stability*, edited by A. J. Gray, M. J. Crawley, and P. J. Edwards. Oxford, 1987.

Wilson, David Sloan. "Evolution on the Level of Communities." *Science* 192 (June 25, 1976): 1358–1360. "The Group Selection Controversy: History and Current Status." *Annual Review of Ecology and Systematics* 14 (1983): 159–187. "Holism and Reductionism in Evolutionary Ecology." *Oikos* 53 (September 1988): 269–273.

Wilson, Edward O., ed. *Biodiversity*. Washington, D.C., 1988. "Biodiversity, Prosperity, and Value." In *Ecology, Economics, Ethics: The Broken Circle*, edited by F. Herbert Bormann and Stephen R. Kellert. *Biophilia*. Cambridge, Mass., 1984. *The Diversity of Life*. Cambridge, Mass., 1992.

Wilson, Edward O., and Daniel S. Simberloff. "Experimental Zoogeography of Islands: Defaunation and Monitoring Techniques," and "Experimental Zoogeography of Islands: The Colonization of Empty Islands." *Ecology* 50 (Early Spring 1969): 267–289.

Worthington, E. Barton. *The Ecological Century: A Personal Appraisal*. Oxford, 1983.

INDEX

biocentric attitude of, 180–184; on climate, 195; and Humboldt, 137–138; Lyell's influence on, 144; and Malthus, 149, 153–154; as product of his culture, 169; successors of, 203; mentioned, xii, 14, 39, 42, 55, 63, 66, 136, 194, 313, 375. *See also* Darwinian ecology; Social Darwinists

Darwin, Erasmus, 155

Darwin, Francis, 183

Darwinian ecology, 114–187; neo, 402–405, 414; outmoded, 292–293, 300, 313. *See also* Darwin, Charles

Davis, Margaret, 394–395

DDT (dicholoro-diphenyl-trichloroethane), 349

De Beer, Gavin, 184

Deciduous forest project, 373

Deevey, Edward, 311

Derham, William, 38, 44, 51

Descartes, René, 39–42 passim

Descent of Man, The, 164–165, 181

Deserts on the March, 233

Development and Structure of Vegetation, The, 209

Development succession, 202, 206

Dice, Lee, 276

Digby, Sir Kenelm, 37

Discovery of Time, The (Toulmin and Goodfield), 421

Divergence, principle of, 160–163

Division of Economic Ornithology and Mammalogy, 196, 262

Division of Entomology, 262

Dobie, J. Frank, 260

Down, Kent, Eng., 147, 181, 183

Driesch, Hans, 321

Drought, Clements on, 236

Drude, Oscar, 198, 203, 206

Druids, 87, 88, 103

Drury, William, 391, 392

Dubos, René, 357

Dust Bowl, 219–220, 221–253; mentioned, xii, 190

Dust storms, 221–222, 233, 244

Dynamic ecology, 206

Earth Day, 340, 356–358, 369

Ecological community, 390

Ecological pragmatism, 278

Ecological Society of America, 206, 251, 320, 326, 363

Ecological Theater and the Evolutionary Play, The (Hutchinson), 403

"Ecological Theory and Conservation," 248–249

Ecology: aim of historical study of, ix–x; chaos theory of, 405–412, 413; and chemical contamination, 349, 354–355; as a comparative science, 135; and conservation of biodiversity, 417–420; cultural, 352; Darwinian, 113–187; disequilibrium trends in, 388–417, 427–428; early twentieth-century, 189–253, 351; eighteenth-century, 1–55; etymology of, 191–193; and evolution, 155–156; and geography, 193–202, historicization of, 421–433; intellectual tradition of, 420–421; modern definitions of, 204, 378; in nuclear age, 342–347, 354, 364, 383–384; organismic theory of, 41; Romantic, 57–111; and scientific theory, 359–387; of sea, 347–349; subfields of, 340–341; and women's culture, 349–350, 358; See also *Oecologie*

Ecology, Age of, ix, 284, 306, 322–335, 340, 358, 359

Ecology and Resource Management, 314

"Ecology group," 326, 331

Ecology journal, 203

Ecology movement, 21–25, 350–359, 415, 429

Economics and ecology, 37, 150–151, 291–315, 426–427

"Economy of mind," 174–175

"Economy of nature" concept, x, 156, 192. *See also* Nature's economy

Ecosystem, 302, 307–311, 389, 390, 393, 394, 398; research, 371–373; as shifting, 412; unified theory of, 364–371, 373

Eden, Huxley's Garden of, 178

Edentates, 124, 164

Edge of the Sea (Carson), 348

Ehrlich, Paul, vii, 353–354, 357, 390

Einstein, Albert, 342

Élan vital, 43, 321

Eliade, Mircea, 55

Elton, Charles, 203, 294–301, 306, 309, 352, 408–409

Ely, Richard, 312

Emden, Cecil, 19

Emergent evolution, 321–323

Emerson, Alfred, 326, 329, 331

Emerson, George B., 68–70, 107

Emerson, Ralph Waldo, 71, 99, 103–107; mentioned, 100, 136, 327

506 • *Index*

CPSIA information can be obtained
at www.ICGtesting.com
Printed in the USA
LVHW010442120121
676227LV00009B/131

9 780521 468343